Antitrust

EXAMPLES & EXPLANATIONS

EXAMPLES & EXPLANATIONS

Antitrust

Fourth Edition

Christopher L. Sagers
Charles R. Emrick Jr.—Calfee Halter & Griswold Prof. of Law
CSU College of Law
Cleveland State University

ASPEN
PUBLISHING

To contact Customer Service, e-mail customer.service@aspenpublishing.com, call 1-800-950-5259, or mail correspondence to:

Aspen Publishing
Attn: Order Department
1 Wall Street
Burlington, MA 01803

1 2 3 4 5 6 7 8 9 0

ISBN 979-8-8890-6809-9

Library of Congress Cataloging-in-Publication Data

Names: Sagers, Christopher L., 1970- author
Title: Antitrust / Christopher L Sagers.
Description: Fourth edition. | Burlington, MA : Aspen Publishing, 2026. | Series: Examples & explanations | Includes bibliographical references and index. | Contents: Part I. An introduction to antitrust law—Chapter 1. The history, nature, and theory of federal competition policy—Part II. The economic foundations of contemporary antitrust—Chapter 2. Part one of a two-part strategy for understanding antitrust economics—Chapter 3. Part two of the two-part strategy: economic generalizations that pervade modern antitrust—Chapter 4. The all-important concept of market power—Part III. Conspiracies in restraint of trade—Chapter 5. An introduction to the Sherman Act—Chapter 6. Per se offenses—Chapter 7. The rule of reason and the doctrine of ancillary restraints—Chapter 8. Section 1 – the long struggle to define an intermediate rule of reason and the law of the sliding scale—Chapter 9. One further problem in horizontal cooperation: exchanges of information—Chapter 10. Antitrust and the distribution of goods—Chapter 11. Tying and exclusive contracting—Part V. Proof of conspiracy—Chapter 12. Proof of conspiracy under the Sherman Act—Part VI. Confronting Mr. Big: the law of monopoly—Chapter 13. The offense of monopolization—Chapter 14. Attempted monopolization and conspiracy to monopolize—Part VII. Antitrust, innovation, and intellectual property—Chapter 15. Antitrust, innovation, and intellectual property—Part VIII. Price discrimination—Chapter 16. Price discrimination and the Robinson-Patman Act—Part IX. Antitrust aspects of mergers and acquisitions—Chapter 17. Antitrust aspects of mergers and acquisitions—Chapter 18. Merger review under Hart-Scott-Rodino—Part X. Institutions and procedures in antitrust—Chapter 19. Institutions and procedures in antitrust—Part XI. The scope of antitrust—Chapter 20. The scope of antitrust generally—Chapter 21. Antitrust and politics—Chapter 22. Antitrust and the regulated industries—Chapter 23. The labor exemption—Appendix Further Topics in Antitrust Economics: The Problem of Industrial Organization—Glossary—Table of Cases—Index . | Summary: "What is "antitrust"? To put it simply, under federal antitrust law, it is the policy of the United States that private persons may not take actions to interfere improperly in the functioning of competitive markets"—Provided by publisher.
Identifiers: LCCN 2025051654 (print) | LCCN 2025051655 (ebook) | ISBN 9798889068099 paperback | ISBN 9798889068112 epub | ISBN 9798889068105ebook
Subjects: LCSH: Antitrust law—United States
Classification: LCC KF1649 .S35 2026 (print) | LCC KF1649 (ebook)
LC record available at https://lccn.loc.gov/2025051654
LC ebook record available at https://lccn.loc.gov/2025051655

ABOUT ASPEN PUBLISHING

Aspen Publishing is a leading provider of legal education content and digital learning solutions in the United States and globally. Our innovative products and platforms—designed based on best practices in learning science—engage students and enhance outcomes. From textbooks and audiobooks authored by renowned experts to digital platforms and products like LEAF, Connected eBooks, Connected Quizzing, PracticePerfect, and JD-Next, we empower the next generation of legal professionals with innovative, trusted, and accessible resources.

The Aspen Casebook Series, affectionately known as the "red and black" casebooks among law faculty and students, includes hundreds of highly regarded textbooks across more than 80 disciplines. These range from foundational courses like Torts and Contracts to emerging electives such as Sustainability and the Law of Policing. Our study aids, including the popular *Examples & Explanations* series, help law students master complex topics with clarity and confidence.

Aspen's expertise extends to undergraduate education with our Paralegal, Criminal Justice, and Business Law series, offering the same hallmark quality to a broader audience. JD-Next, our groundbreaking online law school prep course and admissions test, provides a realistic preview of law school, equips students with essential skills for academic success, and evaluates their readiness for legal studies.

Aspen Publishing Is Proud to Be a UWorld Company

Since 2003, UWorld has been a global leader in developing high-quality learning tools for students preparing for high-stakes exams. With a commitment to excellence, UWorld has helped millions of students in undergraduate, graduate, and professional programs in fields such as medicine, nursing, finance, and law achieve their academic and career goals.

Founded by Chandra S. Pemmasani, M.D., during his medical residency, UWorld began focusing on medical education and has since expanded into various academic fields, including law. In 2020, UWorld launched its Legal vertical, starting with its comprehensive Multistate Bar Exam (MBE®) Question Bank, followed by the acquisition of Themis Bar Review, which integrated resources to provide a complete bar exam preparation experience. In 2024, UWorld expanded its offerings by acquiring Aspen Publishing, enhancing its suite of legal education products.

Today, UWorld offers an unparalleled range of study materials that blend active learning methods with expert content, ensuring students and educators can access the most effective resources. From bar preparation to law school success, UWorld is committed to supporting the next generation of legal professionals. Learn more at uworld.com.

This fourth edition is dedicated to my mother,
for her sainted perseverance.

Summary of Contents

PART IV. VERTICAL RESTRAINTS

PART V. PROOF OF CONSPIRACY

PART VI. CONFRONTING MR. BIG: THE LAW OF MONOPOLY

PART VII. ANTITRUST, INNOVATION, AND INTELLECTUAL PROPERTY

PART VIII. PRICE DISCRIMINATION

PART IX. ANTITRUST ASPECTS OF MERGERS AND ACQUISITIONS

PART X. INSTITUTIONS AND PROCEDURES IN ANTITRUST

PART XI. THE SCOPE OF ANTITRUST

Contents

PART V. PROOF OF CONSPIRACY

PART VI. CONFRONTING MR. BIG: THE LAW OF MONOPOLY

PART VII. ANTITRUST, INNOVATION, AND INTELLECTUAL PROPERTY

PART VIII. PRICE DISCRIMINATION

Chapter 16 Price Discrimination and the Robinson-Patman Act 275

PART IX. ANTITRUST ASPECTS OF MERGERS AND ACQUISITIONS

Preface to the First Edition

The conviction driving this book is that two challenges usually cause antitrust students the most difficulty, but that neither actually has to be that challenging at all. They are (1) the learning of economic theory and (2) the interrelatedness of antitrust issues. This book approaches both problems strategically, and it combines its strategy with the tried and proved question-and-answer pedagogy of the *Examples & Explanations* series.

As for economics, the good news is that the bare minimum economic theory one needs to understand the antitrust case law is not really that hard at all, even for students without prior economics training. There may be plenty more to say about the economics of antitrust issues in policy debates and academic seminars, and antitrust practitioners tend to be economically sophisticated. But none of that advanced material is needed to learn the basic law as the courts apply it. This book approaches the teaching of the minimum core of economics with a two-part strategy, set out in Chapters 2 and 3. As the first part, §2.2 introduces all the economic theory a student really needs to understand the cases and presents it in a purely intuitive way, without any mathematics. (For those students who want or need to learn this material with more rigor, §2.3 supplements the introduction by re-explaining the same material in the more traditional, quantitative manner. My hope is that §2.3 presents it in a way that is still accessible to any student who wants to learn it.) As the second part of the two-part strategy, Chapter 3 takes the economic basics a step further by introducing a set of economic generalizations that run throughout antitrust and help explain much of the law as it now stands. The book also includes more economic material for students who want it and for students whose teachers take a more in-depth approach.

As for interrelatedness, the problem is that, in antitrust, everything seems to relate to everything else, and so it can be hard to know where to start. Especially early in the semester of an antirust course, it can be difficult for an instructor to explain anything because learning any one thing seems to call for an understanding of so many other things. Often this leaves the student at sea for much of the semester. But this doesn't have to be the case, because there are some very general concepts in antitrust that can be explained first, without reference to anything else, and so it is possible to teach antitrust concepts by moving from the most general to the more specific.

We can begin with a basic generalization about what antitrust *is*. To borrow from Chapter 1:

> *Under federal antitrust law, it is the policy of the United States that private persons may not take actions to interfere improperly in the functioning of competitive markets.*

Furthermore, almost all of the law that now gives life to this most general policy can be boiled down to the law surrounding three causes of action—challenges to conspiracies under §1 of the Sherman Act, challenges to monopolies under §2 of the Sherman Act, and challenges to mergers and acquisitions under §7 of the Clayton Act. What's more, these three causes of action turn out to have a great deal in common. Because they share so much, we can identify what is most general about them and move from that most general basis to the more specific details. What they share most generally is that each of them is meant to prohibit only those interferences with competition that are *unreasonable*. Antitrust has come to define unreasonable interference as private conduct that causes more harm to a market than benefit for it. And as it now exists, antitrust looks for both harm and benefit by using the tools of economic theory. In other words, the single most basic idea in current antitrust law is the simple economic theory that will be laid out using the two-part strategy in Chapters 2 and 3.

Next, a basic insight of this economic theory is that private interferences in markets are likely to be net harmful—that is, they are likely to be unreasonable—where some feature or weakness in the market prevents that market from correcting itself. Most economists believe that when a firm tries to raise its prices or otherwise abuse consumers, the market will usually self-correct by causing that firm to lose sales. But sometimes markets do not do that, and where a market's self-corrective power is hindered, a firm within it might have some power to raise prices or otherwise misbehave. Such a firm is said to have *market power*, and the concept of market power has come to have truly fundamental significance in antitrust. Each of the three causes of action that make up antitrust will in most cases require a plaintiff to prove that a defendant holds market power, because without it, a defendant that tries to engage in abuses of a market should just suffer lost sales. Because plaintiffs must prove market power according to the same doctrinal test no matter what cause of action at issue, proof of market power is the next most general concept in antitrust law. It is explained in Chapter 4.

With economic theory and market power under our belt, we can move on to more specific details of the three major causes of action, and that study will take up the next several chapters of the book. Finally, the remaining chapters cover more peripheral matters, such as the intersection of antitrust and intellectual property (Chapter 15), the problem of price discrimination (Chapter 16), antitrust procedural issues (Chapter 19), and the scope of antitrust (Chapters 20-23).

I thank Lynn Churchill of Wolters Kluwer for the opportunity to write this book. She was an awfully nice person to work with. As for Peter Skagestad, the editor who shepherded the book and who manages the entire Examples and Explanations series, what can one say? As if it were not enough to oversee a series that set a standard in legal education (in a second language no less), he is a polyglot philosopher economist who has interesting things to say about matters from regulatory policy to Charles Sanders Peirce. More important to me, in any event, were his patience and forbearance. I am thankful for feedback from Peter Carstensen and from several anonymous reviewers, who undertook a large and thankless task and gave very effective advice. This book also benefited from the financial support of the Cleveland-Marshall summer scholarship fund and my sabbatical leave from the Cleveland-Marshall College of Law.

The four-year-old boy to whom this book is dedicated wrote the heck out of a book of his own while I was writing this one, and it was darn nice for a dad to have him as a working companion. His book, he tells me, is written entirely in Ant-Chinese, a language that only ants understand, and is called *My Son Is a Peanut*. He is a good egg. My wife, Annie, is beyond the reach of my thanks for her support and the sacrifices she has made for me.

Christopher L. Sagers

May 2011

Preface to the Fourth Edition

Over this book's fifteen-year lifetime, many things have *happened* in antitrust, but it is a different question to know which of them *mattered*.

Since the last edition in particular, there got to be a lot of talk about antitrust. Popular interest in the policy surged, for various reasons it seems, and sometimes it seemed to be everywhere in popular media and retail politics. That was remarkable, because for decades on end it had been basically absent from Americans' daily awareness. There was also some real-world enforcement activity, though less than one might guess from reading the papers. While it all mattered in some sense, reasonable minds differ on what if any of it changed substantive policy or its effect on the world. That must in some part reflect the times, as the daily news-informational tumult in our divided age can be a challenge to interpret. But it also reveals something significant about the real nature of the policy and its relationship to the debate that surrounds it. The two things are not the same.

There was plenty of reason to care about antitrust and, for some, to long for its return. Popular concern was especially driven by the revolution in high technology. The power of a small number of rapidly growing firms raised traditional antitrust concern for many, as for the impacts of e-commerce on small retailers and suppliers. There was a sense that e-tailers had wrecked Main Street, and posed plenty of other epochal, destructive social changes. Big Tech firms stoked broader political fears as well. Some thought that they fostered misinformation that might have thrown a presidential election, while others thought they censored political opinions and impaired free speech.

Meanwhile, a body of empirical evidence began to suggest increasing industrial concentration and market power throughout the economy. The trend arguably began at the time of the conservative antitrust revolution, around 1980. The evidence is very complex and interpreting it remains very controversial, but economists from varying points of view have guardedly begun to acknowledge that systematic harm may have occurred in the economy, and it may have had something to do with relaxed antitrust enforcement.

And so antitrust became ordinary politics again. Among other things it became an issue in presidential election politics for the first time in perhaps seventy years,[1] and its reform was a priority in the messaging and initiatives

1. George Slover, Am. Antitr. Inst., Obama Inauguration Speech Mentions Antitrust: References to the Antitrust Laws in Presidential Inaugural Addresses—Now and Then (Jan. 20, 2013).

of the Biden administration.[2] So far it appears to remain salient and just as political during the second Trump administration, which has announced a number of eye-catching initiatives and made a strongly-worded point of rescinding much of the Biden administration's approach.

But for all the parties' rhetoric and denunciation of their purported difrerences,[3] and for all the promises and fears of change, a surprising fact remains: there is not that much evidence of difference between them. Rhetoric aside, their management of the substantive policy is basically the same, or at least it has been for past few decades.

Surely the most eye-catching action was government lawsuits against Big Tech firms. Those cases have gone rather well for the government, and if they survive appeal, they could generate significant change in the sector.[4] They were litigated during the Biden administration, and superficially they match the political arguments on which that administration made priorities of antitrust and tech. So one might think they distinguish the Biden administration from its predecessor. But two of the most important of them were initially filed in the first Trump administration, and they will all likely conclude during the second. And indeed, despite promises by reform advocates that antitrust would be reinvigorated with iconoclastic new thinking, the cases involve no theoretical innovation. They are thoroughly traditional,[5] and some administration of either party would have brought them sooner or later. The Big Tech revolution was one of a handful

2. *See, e.g.*, Exec. Order No. 14036 on Promoting Competition in the American Economy, 86 Fed. Reg. 36,987 (July 9, 2021) (establishing a "whole of government" program to encourage more antitrust enforcement and re-prioritize competition values across regulatory programs).

3. *Compare* Jonathan Kanter, Ass't Att'y Gen., U.S. Dep't of Justice, Speech, *Farewell Address* (Dec. 17, 2024) (attacking prior administrations' "deliberate and decades-long effort to dismantle ... antitrust enforcement"), *with* FTC, Press Release, *FTC Chairman Applauds Revocation of Biden-Harris Executive Order on Competition* (Aug. 14, 2025) ("applaud[ing]" revocation of "failed policies [and] undue hostility"); U.S. Dep't of Justice, Press Release, Statement on Revocation of Biden-Harris Executive Order on Competition (Aug. 13, 2025) ("salut[ing]" revocation of Biden order's "overly prescriptive and burdensome approach" in order to "unleash[] the new American Golden Age").

4. To date the most significant developments have been the government's success in two separate actions against Google, finding it to have monopolized the markets for internet search and online advertising technology. *United States v. Google LLC*, 778 F. Supp. 3d 797 (2025); *United States v. Google LLC*, 747 F. Supp. 3d 1 (D.D.C. 2024). As of this writing, the courts have yet to enter remedy orders in those cases, but the government has sought structural relief—some breaking up of the Google organization—in both. The other major Big Tech cases are 581 *FTC v. Facebook, Inc.*, 581 F. Supp. 3d 34 (D.D.C. 2022), and *FTC v. Amazon.com, Inc.*, 2:23-cv-01495-JHC (W.D. Wa. Oct. 31, 2024) (second amended complaint), both of which remain in earlier stages of litigation. The cases initially brought in the Trump administration are *Facebook* and the Google internet search case.

5. Their theories of liability depend heavily on the seminal decision in *United States v. Microsoft Corp.*, 254 F.3d 34 (D.C. Cir. 2001), which was itself a symbol of bipartisan consensus. *Microsoft* was decided unanimously by the D.C. Circuit en banc, and happened to be written by a judge who'd been a Republican antitrust enforcement official.

of major technological disruptions in our history, and like several prior episodes it resulted in changes and conduct that would more or less inevitably invite antitrust response.

Likewise, despite criticism of the Biden administration's alleged crack down on mergers—criticism that from some conservatives and business leaders bordered on the apocalyptic—merger enforcement actually fell during the Biden administration, even while merger activity increased. That is thoroughly unsurprising. Solid evidence suggests that real rates of merger enforcement have been quite stable across different administrations for a long time.[6]

So did things happen in the recent years of antitrust enthusiasm, that actually mattered? Certainly. The government overhauled its *Merger Guidelines* in 2023 and adopted a new vertical merger policy for the first time in decades. The courts of appeals decided plenty of cases with important consequences, possibly most important being monopolization decisions that could revive theories of liability thought to have been killed off by the Supreme Court.[7] Any number of similar events will be recounted in this revised edition and their consequences explained.

None of this is meant as a criticism of any administration or either party, except for those activists and political entrepreneurs who've exaggerated facts or stoked popular frustrations for their own gain. It also is no argument that the enforcement status quo or its stability is a good thing. Very much to the contrary. While the entire remainder of this book will remain as neutral as I am able to make it, I'll continue to make an exception here that I first made in the last edition. The state of the law has come to be a serious problem, and the judiciary has caused it for reasons that were always controversial and no longer have even the support they once had. There do now appear to be concrete economic harms associated with concentration and market power, and they may have been caused in part by

6. Jeffrey T. Macher & John W. Mayo, *The Evolution of Merger Enforcement Intensity: What Do the Data Show?*, 17 J. Comp. L. & Enf. 708 (2021) (econometric measure of real enforcement rates for 1979-2017).

7. No plaintiff has won meaningful success in any price predation case in the thirty years since *Brooke Group Ltd. v. Brown & Williamson Tobacco Corp.*, 509 U.S. 209 (1993), and until very recently none had done better in any unilateral refusal to deal case since *Verizon Commcns., Inc. v. Law Offs. of Curtis V. Trinko, LLP*, 540 U.S. 398 (2004). Recent action in the Courts of Appeals may change that. Several courts continued narrowing the death-knell of *Brooke Group* by limiting it to circumstances in which the only challenged conduct is the defendant's pricing. *See, e.g., McWane, Inc. v. FTC*, 783 F.3d 814, 833-835 (11th Cir. 2015). Likewise, in refusal to deal law, the Fourth Circuit's decision in *Duke Energy Carolinas, LLC v. NTE Carolinas II, LLC*, 111 F.4th 337 (4th Cir. 2025) suggested that *Trinko* might be limited to regulated industries. Other courts found illegal exclusion even under *Trinko*'s purportedly impenetrable armor, *see, e.g., Steward Health Care System, LLC v. Blue Cross & Blue Shield of R.I.*, 311 F. Supp. 3d 468 (D.R.I. 2018), and several courts continued to emphasize that it has no relevance to refusals to deal with non-competitors, *Chase Mfg. Co. v. Johns Manville Corp.*, 84 F.4th 1157, 1173 (10th Cir. 2023); *United States v. Google LLC*, 778 F. Supp. 3d 797, 865-867 (E.D. Va. 2025).

judicial antitrust reforms since the 1970s. Reviving a more active antitrust could be of value.

I will end with a story that seems emblematic. In one of the government's two actions against Google, it was discovered that Google and the Apple computer corporation kept up a long-term arrangement concerning internet search. After Google's initial successes in the early 2000s, the companies agreed that Google would pay Apple a share of its search advertising revenues. In exchange Apple would install Google's search engine as standard software on its devices, including on its then-new iPhone. Described that way, the deal may seem pretty harmless—just a garden-variety marketing and distribution arrangement, and frankly kind of a win-win for all involved. But it's come to light that over time Apple also agreed to a number of restrictions on its own products, including what software of its own that it could pre-install on Apple devices. In effect, Apple agreed that it would not include its own search software or products that would compete with the pre-installed Google search engine. In other words, Apple seems to have agreed that it would keep out of the business of search. Meanwhile, the payments that Google would make to Apple grew to be impossibly large—by the end, Google was giving Apple upwards of twenty *billion* dollars per year, amounting in some years to well over 10 percent of Google's entire, company-wide profits. But strikingly, during the years of the agreement Apple did in fact build search capacity, though it never directly sold it to the public. Apple built a general search "index" containing billions of web pages, making it one of the few companies in existence to own such a resource. Creating it likely consumed billions of dollars, but it really could serve no purpose except for Apple to enter as a competing search provider—or perhaps to be a reminder to Google that, if the payments ever stopped, Apple would do so.

This is all quite extraordinary. It should be said that the real facts are surely more complex than can be known from the publicly available record, and we can only infer what may have been the purpose and details of this arrangement. But from what publicly appears, this may have been an agreement that Apple would keep out of search in exchange for a cut of Google's monopoly profits. If so it was the grossest and most obviously illegal of antitrust violations. It is the sort of thing that every sophisticated business leader knows to be illegal, because it is the kind of thing for which people routinely go to prison. And yet these extremely sophisticated businesspeople and their lawyers apparently thought it was permissible, or at least that they would be able to defend it in court. That is quite something, and if antitrust really is so fallow, it may be time for reform.

Chris Sagers

August 2025

PART I

An Introduction to Antitrust Law

CHAPTER 1

The History, Nature, and Theory of Federal Competition Policy

§1.1 WHAT IS "ANTITRUST"?

What is "antitrust"? To put it simply, *under federal antitrust law, it is the policy of the United States that private persons may not take actions to interfere improperly in the functioning of competitive markets.*

Antitrust, as it is ordinarily studied in law schools, is mainly the law that arises under three short provisions of two federal statutes: Sections 1 and 2 of the Sherman Antitrust Act, 15 U.S.C. §§1-2, and §7 of the Clayton Act, 15 U.S.C. §18. The way that these three provisions serve the policy—the way that they prevent actions that interfere with healthy competition—is that they prohibit three broad classes of conduct in which business persons might engage. Sherman Act §1 prohibits "contract[s], combination[s] . . . or conspirac[ies]" by which business people might seek to "restrain[] . . . trade." This means roughly that persons engaged in business cannot agree among themselves to do things to injure their markets. The ways they might do such a thing would include agreements among themselves about the minimum price at which they will sell some good, or a division of geographical markets in which they will not compete with one another, or any of a range of similar kinds of agreements. Sherman Act §2 prohibits "monopolization." That is, it makes it illegal for very large businesses to exclude their competitors from the marketplace. Finally, Clayton Act §7 prohibits "acquisitions" by one firm of the assets or control of another, where the acquisition would "substantially . . . lessen competition, or . . . tend to create a monopoly." Each of these statutory provisions sets out a cause of action, and they are enforced through government and private lawsuits. In other words, it is not really simplifying too much to say that *most of federal antitrust law boils down to three causes of action*—for conspiracies under §1, monopolization under §2, and trade-restraining acquisitions under §7.

A very important first observation, though, is that none of these rules flatly prohibits *all* "conspiracies in restraint of trade," or *all* "monopolies," or *all* acquisitions. They prohibit only those that are *unreasonable*. A fact to which much of your antitrust course will be devoted is that the whole history of antitrust policy can be understood as the effort to work out the content of that term "reasonable." That question, at the very heart of antitrust, remains controversial.

Antitrust for our purposes will be an exclusively federal body of law and it is litigated exclusively in the federal courts.[1] Most states also have their own antitrust laws, but they largely track federal law and tend not to be given much attention in antitrust courses. The Sherman and Clayton Acts are not the only federal statutes that make up this law, though most antitrust courses focus predominantly on Sherman Act §§1 and 2 and Clayton Act §7. Two other statutes were adopted early on to supplement the more fundamental antitrust rules—the Federal Trade Commission Act of 1914, which created an independent competition agency known as the Federal Trade Commission, and the Robinson-Patman Act of 1936, which limits the freedom of sellers to "discriminate" against buyers (i.e., to charge different prices to different buyers of the same product).

Some notion of a policy of free competition is very old in our law. Now 135 years old, the Sherman Act is among the oldest federal statutes still in force. But it explicitly built upon a much older tradition in English and American law. As early as 1624 the English parliament constrained royally granted monopolies,[2] and the English courts as early as 1414 began adopting common law rules to promote the policy of free competition.[3] Antipathy to monopoly also found expression in early American law.[4] Of particular significance for our purposes are certain common law rules of the

1. *Marrese v. Am. Acad. of Orthopaedic Surgeons*, 470 U.S. 373, 379-380 (1985); *Gen. Inv. Co. v. Lake Shore & Michigan Southern Ry. Co.*, 260 U.S. 261, 287 (1922).

2. *See The Statute of Monopolies*, 1624, 21 Jac. c. 3 (1624), reprinted in vol. 4 pt. 2 *Statutes of the Realm* at 1212 (William S. Hein & Co., 1993) (invalidating, with certain exceptions, all monopolies "of or for the sole buying, selling, making, working, or using of any thing within this Realm"); cf. 3 Edward Coke, *Institutes of the Laws of England* 181 (facsimile ed., 1985) (1797) ("[A]ll grants of monopolies are again[s]t the ancient and fundamental laws of this kingdom.").

3. *See, e.g.*, Harlan M. Blake, *Employee Agreements Not to Compete*, 73 Harv. L. Rev. 625, 631-637 (1960) (discussing the celebrated 1414 decision in *Dyer's Case*, Y.B. Mich. 2 Hen. 5, f. 5, pl. 26 (C.P. 1414), which refused to enforce a covenant not to compete, and the complex system of European craft guilds from which it arose).

4. *See, e.g.*, Md. Const. art. XXXIX (1776) ("[M]onopolies are odious, contrary to the spirit of a free government, and the principles of commerce, and ought not to be suffered."). It should be remembered that the term "monopoly" in the late eighteenth century normally

eighteenth and nineteenth centuries that would later have direct importance for interpretation of the Sherman Act. On the one hand, the Anglo-American common law has long professed to value the freedom of individuals to enter into contracts as they see fit, and the freedom of property owners to use their property as they choose. The courts often explained these policies as meant to foster healthy trade. But the courts have also long worried that some contracts could actually impede healthy trade in certain ways. Courts were particularly concerned about contracts that would prohibit a person from competing in a particular market, such as a covenant not to compete between a master craftsman and an apprentice, which lasted for too long or prohibited competition over too broad a territory. From these concerns arose a body of common law rules to govern what the courts came to describe as contracts "in restraint of trade" and "monopoly." This case law was voluminous and familiar to American lawyers when the Sherman Act was adopted in 1890. Indeed, the Sherman Act explicitly incorporates these two common law terms—it prohibits both "contracts . . . in restraint of trade" and "monopoliz[ation]." The legislative history suggests that this choice was deliberate, and it has not been lost on the courts. They have made reference to common law in interpretation of the Act throughout its history.[5]

The Sherman Act was adopted at a pivotal time in American history.[6] Prior to about the 1850s, the United States had remained a predominantly agrarian economy whose commercial sectors were mainly populated by small businesses. But the nineteenth century was a time of change. Changes toward the end of that century were so dramatic that it has become common to refer to the period of the Civil War (1861-1865) and the next few decades as the "American Industrial Revolution." As one antitrust historian put it, the changes during that time were so significant that it was the "formative birth-time of [America's] basic institutions."[7] Transcontinental transportation, mass communications, and large-scale industrial production all began at about mid-century, and from then grew very rapidly. One interesting aspect of this development was that for economic reasons businesses felt compelled to produce their products in larger volumes. First, new

---

connoted *government-granted* monopolies, not those acquired merely through success in business. The latter were still rare.

5. *See, e.g., Associated Gen. Contractors of California, Inc. v. Carpenters*, 459 U.S. 519, 531-532 (1983); *Natl. Socy. of Profl. Engrs. v. United States*, 435 U.S. 679, 687-688 (1978); *Standard Oil Co. of New Jersey v. United States*, 221 U.S. 1, 58-59 (1911); *see also Copperweld Corp. v. Independence Tube Corp.*, 467 U.S. 752, 786 (1984) (Stevens, J., dissenting).

6. For background on the following historical summary, *see* Louis Hartz, *The Liberal Tradition in America* (1963); James Willard Hurst, *Law and the Conditions of Freedom in the Nineteenth Century United States* (1964); Martin J. Sklar, *The Corporate Reorganization of American Capitalism, 1890-1916:The Market, The Law, and Politics* (1988); Gary Gerstle, *The Protean Character of American Liberalism*, 99 Am. Hist. Rev. 1043 (1994).

7. Sklar, *supra* note 6, at 2.

technological innovations in manufacturing processes led to better products and more efficient manufacturing, but they also typically required expensive investments in new plants and equipment. Large fixed investments have to be recouped somehow, and the larger they are the more pressure the manufacturer will feel to spread them over lots of sales. (This implies the concept of "economies of scale," which is discussed in the glossary at the end of this book.) Second, a consequence of the expanding range and capacity of American transportation—most obviously, on the new national rail system—was that the markets that one seller could serve had become much larger. Accordingly, businesses in many industries were able to begin producing on a scale that would have been unworkable before, because there would not have been enough customers in their local markets to buy all their products. In any case, producing goods on a large scale implies certain economic consequences. Most importantly for our purposes, it implies a concentration of production in the hands of a comparatively small number of large-scale producers and, usually, the elimination of some or all of their smaller competitors. Where significant scale economies are present, larger producers will typically have cost advantages over their smaller competitors, and in a competitive market those advantages normally will be fatally effective against the smaller rivals. At least in part for this reason, this period saw a wave of consolidations in industry larger than any that had come before it. Competing businesses either merged with one another or acquired the assets of their defeated rivals, such that fewer and fewer businesses came to control many industries. Indeed, there was so much consolidation during the period from about 1895 to 1905 that it is now remembered as the "Great Merger Wave."[8]

These and other events also appear to have led to a growing alienation and political anxiety among the middle and working classes, and this fact had direct relevance to the coming of antitrust law. Some urban intellectuals and the gentry of earlier decades, who would form the backbone of

---

8. Described and extensively analyzed in Alfred D. Chandler, Jr., *The Visible Hand: The Managerial Revolution in American Business* (1977) and Naomi Lamoreaux, *The Great Merger Movement in American Business, 1895-1904* (1985). It has not escaped notice among the critics of antitrust that the merger wave began in the mid-1890s—*after* the adoption of the Sherman Act. That is arguably pretty ironic, if it is true, because many people assume that the Sherman Act was adopted to prevent large consolidations. Critics have suggested that the Sherman Act, far from preventing monopoly and accretions of market power, actually *caused* the Great Merger Wave. *See, e.g.*, George Bittlingmayer, *Did Antitrust Policy Cause the Great Merger Wave?* 28 J.L. & Econ. 77 (1985). However, there is substantial reason to believe that there was no causal connection at all between antitrust and merger activity at the turn of the century, and that the merger wave would have come regardless of whether there were a federal antitrust statute. If anything, the merger wave and the adoption of the Sherman Act were two events that both were caused by the larger social and economic changes of the nineteenth century. *See generally* Chris Sagers, *#LOLNothingMatters*, 63 Antitrust Bulletin 7, 27 n.112 (2018); Donald J. Smythe, *The Supreme Court and the Trusts: Antitrust and the Foundations of Modern American Business Regulation from* Knight *to* Swift, 39 U.C. Davis L. Rev. 85 (2005).

Progressive politics, came to share an animosity toward big business. At the same time, manufacturing on a mass scale required large work forces and employed large numbers of immigrant and formerly rural laborers at low wages, leading to the growth of a poor and landless class of urban workers. This group, which increasingly sought to organize through labor unions, and small rural farmers alike felt oppressed and deprived of normal economic opportunity.

Thus, by the time of adoption of the Sherman Act the American Industrial Revolution had led to alarming social unease. While numerous, often conflicting theories have sought to explain the original congressional intent of the Sherman Act, there is no doubt that its backdrop was the public alarm over the perceived *political* power of concentrated capital. To some large extent, the statute was a congressional attempt to quell popular unrest.[9]

It is worth pointing out in these introductory materials that antitrust bears certain institutional peculiarities. First, the vague, sparse language of the Sherman Act is in noticeable contrast to most statutes still in force, which either go into much more detail or appoint some federal administrative agency to provide detail through regulations. Because they are so broad and vague, the antitrust statutes are commonly thought to grant common law lawmaking authority under which the federal courts have been tasked with the creation of a federal policy of free competition. The courts themselves have stoked much of the controversy that has always surrounded antitrust in their use of this lawmaking power and by their varying allegiances to economic theory.

In any case, in fulfilling their lawmaking function the federal courts have evolved what might be called a "category approach" to antitrust. Over the years they have developed a handful of categories into which they place particular examples of challenged conduct, and then they treat that conduct like all other cases in the given category. For example, as we will learn, some conduct is described as "horizontal price fixing"—it involves some agreement among direct, head-to-head competitors that will stabilize the prices at which they sell competing goods or services. All such cases are then subjected to the same legal treatment. As it happens, this particular category is reserved for the most obviously illegal and most harshly punished antitrust violations.

In employing the category approach, maybe the most fundamental category for the courts is to decide whether the conduct challenged in any particular antitrust lawsuit is unilateral or multilateral. Recall that Sherman

9. *See generally* David Millon, *The Sherman Act and the Balance of Power*, 61 S. Cal. L. Rev. 1219, 1219-1220 (1988) ("The statute's two succinct, unequivocal sections were the dying words of a tradition that aimed to control political power through decentralization of economic power, which in turn was to be achieved through protection of competitive opportunity.").

Act §1 covers only multilateral conduct—it applies only to "contract[s], combination[s], . . . or conspirac[ies], in restraint of trade." Therefore, one person acting alone cannot violate §1. Section 2, on the other hand, applies for the most part only to unilateral conduct. That section makes it illegal to "monopolize, or attempt to monopolize" any particular market.[10] Courts are now of the view that division of the statute into these two sections implies a subtle but significant commitment of public policy. It is usually more difficult to prove a cause of action under §2 than under §1, because §2 requires the plaintiff to prove "monopoly power." Therefore, the Sherman Act implies a view that unilateral business conduct poses less danger to the economy than multifirm agreements among competitors do. As the Supreme Court has said:

> Concerted activity subject to §1 is judged more sternly than unilateral activity under §2. . . . The reason Congress treated concerted behavior more strictly than unilateral behavior is readily appreciated. Concerted activity inherently is fraught with anticompetitive risk. It deprives the marketplace of the independent centers of decisionmaking that competition assumes and demands. . . . This not only reduces the diverse directions in which economic power is aimed but suddenly increases the economic power moving in one particular direction.

Copperweld Corp. v. Independence Tube Corp., 467 U.S. 752, 768 (1984). *Accord American Needle, Inc. v. NFL*, 560 U.S. 183, 190-191 (2010).

In any event, as we shall see, the category approach has its own problems. Sometimes the courts have lumped together in one category different kinds of conduct that turn out to have different consequences for the health of markets, even if they might seem superficially similar. Subjecting them both to the same legal treatment might be inappropriate. A separate problem is that it can actually be quite difficult to decide into which category a particular kind of conduct belongs, even when the definition of the category seems simple. Indeed, as we shall see, one of the hardest labels to apply can be the seemingly simple one of horizontal price fixing.

A second institutional peculiarity in antitrust is that it is enforced in a broad range of ways, and this fact has sparked a fair bit of controversy. Two separate federal agencies enforce it, and they have largely overlapping jurisdiction to do so. First, the Justice Department can prosecute criminal violations of the antitrust statutes, it can seek injunction of any violation of antitrust, and it oversees a process of "premerger review" of which we will learn more later. Second, the Federal Trade Commission has essentially identical jurisdiction to enforce antitrust and oversee premerger review,

---

10. Actually, §2 also makes it illegal to "combine or conspire with any other person or persons, to monopolize" any market. However, this part of §2 is rarely enforced.

the only major difference being that FTC has no role in criminal enforcement. (Federal criminal prosecutions of any sort can be brought only by the Department of Justice.) But the same body of antitrust law is also enforced through a private, money-damages cause of action, and therein lies one of the most dramatic aspects of antitrust enforcement. Private plaintiffs who succeed in showing an antitrust violation can recover not only the damages it caused them personally, but *three times that amount*, under the so-called "treble" damages rule. Finally, state governments also have a role in enforcing antitrust. They can sue antitrust defendants for injuries that may have been caused to the states themselves (as, for example, when bidders for public construction contracts conspire to fix the prices at which they will bid), and they can also sue in a representative capacity to redress injuries caused to their own citizens.

§1.2 CONTEMPORARY ANTITRUST IN THE BIGGER PICTURE

By most accounts, antitrust is a doctrine in significant flux and it has been for a long time. Antitrust by its nature is inescapably political and involves some of the most controversial issues of modern times. Opinions vary on whether the controversy that has always seemed such a part of it really reflects fundamental differences of opinion. According to one traditional view, antitrust jurisprudence has throughout its 135 years swung between plaintiff-friendly and defendant-friendly interpretations. A different perspective is that, in fact, there hasn't been a swinging pendulum, at least in modern thought and as measured by actual enforcement in the agencies and the courts, and that policy has been comparatively stable for several decades.[11] But however that may be, there certainly has been lots of sound and fury, and so it seems useful for the student of antitrust to spend some time putting it in its political context.

Antitrust began in theoretical dispute and has more or less stayed there. At the time of the Sherman Act's adoption, professional economists in America were in serious doubt about the best way to deal with the problems of industrial revolution. Many economists of the day believed that industrial changes had altered the basic rules of economics, and that in many industries open competition would simply no longer be possible. Accordingly, there could be no virtue for them in a statute like the Sherman Act, which in effect required businesses to compete with one another. Indeed, a significant

11. *See, e.g.*, William E. Kovacic, *The Modern Evolution of U.S. Competition Policy Enforcement Norms*, 71 Antitrust L.J. 377 (2003); Thomas B. Leary, *The Essential Stability of Merger Policy in the United States*, 70 Antitrust L.J. 105 (2002).

portion of economic opinion had it that industrial concentration was not only inevitable but was natural and healthy. Persons of that opinion would hardly think it wise to adopt a policy under which businesses were not allowed to coordinate their affairs through combinations and conspiracies.

Even though those views are no longer taken very seriously, contentious debate has never ended over the best way to understand the economy and the best policy by which to govern it. For the contemporary antitrust practitioner, probably the most important aspect of this long history of disagreement has been that we are still in the midst of a doctrinal revolution, driven by the thinking of economists, underway for about the past 50 years. The Warren Court, so known for its Chief Justice Earl Warren, come under much criticism for a series of antitrust decisions from the mid-1950s through the late-1960s. The Court held a variety of different classes of conduct to be automatically illegal. As we shall see, ever since the Sherman Act was adopted the courts have held at least some kinds of conduct to be "per se" illegal in this way, and even now a few classes of conduct remain subject to per se rules. What was striking about the Warren years was the range of what the Court made per se illegal.

One famous emblem of frustration with this trend came in a merger case under Clayton Act §7. Toward the end of a long and vigorous dissent, decrying the Court's finding of liability under this section for a takeover by one small grocery chain of another, Justice Stewart said, "The sole consistency that I can find [in our case law] is that in litigation under §7, the Government always wins." *United States v. Von's Grocery Co.*, 384 U.S. 270, 301 (1966) (Stewart, J., dissenting).

Whether he was right or wrong, Justice Stewart was not alone. Starting in the mid-1970s the Supreme Court and the lower federal courts began very seriously to reconsider the Warren Court's strict rules and to ask whether they could be squared with prevailing economic theory. The answer, for many observers since then, has been that most of those rules could not be. It was an age of a conservative revolution in economic thought colloquially known as the "Chicago School" period, since many of its proponents were affiliated with the University of Chicago, and its rise influenced opinions and impacted American politics. It bears noting, however, that changing judicial views on the most important of antitrust courts—the Supreme Court—also coincided with a period of significant changes in its personnel, which brought with them changing priorities and sympathies.[12] Debate

12. Generalizations of this kind court controversy, but for what it may be worth: In the short period between 1969 and 1975, Presidents Nixon and Ford appointed five Justices—Burger (appointed as Chief, to replace Warren), Blackmun, Powell, Rehnquist, and Stevens. They replaced Chief Justice Warren and Justices Fortas, Harlan, Black, and Douglas. Along with Justice Stewart, an Eisenhower appointee, a bloc of the most conservative of these new Justices—Chief Justice Burger and Justices Powell and Rehnquist—were often able to form majorities with one or more of their five remaining colleagues. It is commonly presumed that this new bloc was able to reach positions that were at least superficially more

continues whether the conservative antitrust revolution occurred because changing economic theory persuaded judges to change their minds, or just because changing politics replaced the judges themselves. In fairness, it may be that neither explanation fully satisfies. Prior to the appointment of Chief Justice Roberts in 2005, the sitting Justices had served together longer than any other panel of Justices in U.S. history, and were reasonably balanced between Democratic and Republican appointees, and it was during that time that the Court decided many of the long series of significantly restrictive cases that date at least to 1992.

But whatever may be the explanation, results before the Supreme Court for decades have strikingly, lopsidedly favored defendants and retrenched substantive antitrust. Plaintiffs won only two cases before the Court on the merits in more than 30 years, and one of those was sharply divided and controversial.[13] Some of the many defense decisions that have proven epochal include *Bell Atl. Corp. v. Twombly*, 550 U.S. 544 (2007), which increased the minimum allegations necessary to plead antitrust conspiracy and appears significantly to have impacted new case filings;[14] *Leegin Creative Leather Prods., Inc. v. PSKS, Inc.*, 551 U.S. 877 (2007), which completed the Court's program of repealing Warren-Court per se rules, and has largely rendered vertical restraints impossible to challenge, overruling the century-old ban on vertical price-fixing of *Dr. Miles Med. Co. v. John D. Park & Sons Co.*, 220 U.S. 373 (1911);[15] *Brooke Group Ltd. v. Brown & Williamson Tobacco Corp.*, 509 U.S. 209 (1993), which made price predation effectively impossible to challenge, and *Pac. Bell Tel. Co. v. linkLine Commcns., Inc.*, 555 U.S. 438 (2009), and *Verizon Commcns., Inc. v. L. Offices of Curtis V. Trinko, LLP*, 540 U.S. 398 (2004), which did the same for unilateral refusals to deal; and *Ohio v. American Express Co.*, 585 U.S. 529 (2018), the consequences of which remain uncertain but are potentially significant.[16] Admittedly, plaintiffs won some cases before the Court

---

conservative than those that had been possible in the Warren Court. *See* Sagers, *supra* note 8, at 20-21. *See generally* Howard R. Lurie, *Mergers Under the Burger Court: An Anti-Antitrust Bias and Its Implications*, 23 Vill. L. Rev. 213 (1978). On political developments in this period generally, see Laura Kalman, *Right Star Rising: A New Politics, 1974-1980* (2010); Sean Willentz, *The Age of Reagan: A History, 1974-2008* (2008).

13. Those two cases were *NCAA v. Alston*, 594 U.S. 69 (2021) and *FTC v. Actavis*, 570 U.S. 136 (2013).

14. *Twombly* and other pretrial matters are discussed in Chapter 12.

15. *Leegin*, *Dr. Miles*, and the body of law they govern, known as "resale price maintenance," are discussed in Chapter 10. There were other changes in rules governing vertical relationships, like the limitation on the so-called "tying" cause of action in *Illinois Tool Works, Inc. v. Independent Ink, Inc.*, 547 U.S. 28 (2006) (*Independent Ink* and the law of tying are discussed in Chapter 11), and a new rule to govern a certain kind of vertical abuse by dominant firms, in *Weyerhaeuser Co. v. Ross-Simmons Hardwood Lumber Co.*, 549 U.S. 312 (2007) (*Weyerhaeuser* involved the problem of "predatory buying"; this and other kinds of dominant-firm unilateral conduct are discussed in Chapter 13).

16. *American Express* is discussed at various points in the book, especially Chapter 4. Other developments during this period may prove important as well, like the possibly significant

over this long period, but in almost every such case they won only on the question of whether or not antitrust should *apply*, not who should win.[17] The only cases in over 30 years in which the Court ruled for a plaintiff on the merits were *FTC v. Actavis*, 570 U.S. 136 (2013) and *NCAA v. Alston*, 594 U.S. 69 (2021). In *Activis* the Court split 5-4 and the case drew a strong dissent; *Alston* much more unequivocally and unanimously supported plaintiffs, but it also involved the fairly extraordinary circumstance that the defendant conceded 100% market share and monopsony power, and the case was tried fully to the merits on the facts.

Predictions of the future remain hazardous. As matters already stand, only a narrow range of conduct remains per se illegal—effectively only naked horizontal price fixing and market allocation. Merger law has been restricted so radically that only the largest horizontal mergers can be challenged. Unilateral exclusion is rarely challenged, and vertical restraints cases are so rare that vertical restraints are effectively per se legal. A range of other conduct is effectively no longer challenged at all. But most of that result was actually accomplished before the Supreme Court's most recent personnel changes. One imagines that if there is any further substantive change in the law, it will be in yet more conservative directions. Since the appointment of Chief Justice Roberts in 2005 the Court has added four conservatives (Alito, Gorsuch, Kavanaugh, and Coney Barrett) and now has only three liberals (Sotomayor, Kagan, and Jackson). The conservative appointees have shown themselves to be strong antitrust skeptics in various ways, sometimes radically so. What impact their views may have is not easy to predict, but the Court's recent work in *Ohio v. American Express Co.*, 585 U.S. 529 (2018), suggests that evolution in the law is not over and may yet prove very significant. That said, *Alston* unanimously affirmed a plaintiff verdict in a major §1 case. And after all, the law being as difficult to enforce as it is, it has hard to imagine changes that really could make it even more favorable to defendants. But time will tell.

---

restrictions on the monopolization cause of action in *Verizon Commcns., Inc. v. Law Offices of Curtis V. Trinko*, 540 U.S. 398 (2004) and *Pac. Bell Tel. Co. v. Linkline Commcns., Inc.*, 555 U.S. 438 (2009) (both cases discussed in Chapter 13), and what might be a significant expansion of immunity from antitrust for regulated firms, in *Credit Suisse First Boston Ltd. v. Billing*, 551 U.S. 264 (2007) (discussed in Chapters 20-23).

17. *American Needle, Inc. v. NFL*, 560 U.S. 183 (2010), and *FTC v. Phoebe Putney Health System, Inc.*, 568 U.S. 216 (2013), both ruled unanimously for plaintiffs and included language about which some pro-enforcement observers were cautiously optimistic. Plaintiffs also won in *Apple, Inc. v. Pepper*, 587 U.S. 273 (2019). Each of those cases, however, actually went only to the scope of antitrust, and not to its substance. That is, they merely held that antitrust should apply to the facts alleged, and did not reach the merits.

§1.3 USING THIS BOOK

This book is organized around one central problem, which is a basic problem for teachers of antitrust—that it is hard to know where to start, because everything relates to everything else. This book takes the view that that is actually not such a problem. The issue is just that there are some issues in antitrust that are of *very* general relevance. So the book is built to move from the general to the specific.

The book begins with what is now probably the most general subject of all in antitrust—economic theory. Contemporary antitrust is to some large extent an application of microeconomic theory as the policy of the United States, and understanding antitrust cases takes a bit of economic sophistication. We will begin the book with an introduction to the subject. One nice lesson is that in order to understand the antitrust case law as it now exists, one actually needs only a few basic tools in one's economic toolkit. It is worth remembering that antitrust policy ultimately is in the hands of a federal judiciary who mainly are trained only as generalist attorneys, and not as economists. (Admittedly, some federal judges have very sophisticated expertise with economic theory,[18] and much of the rest of the federal judiciary can be quite sophisticated in these matters as well. However, few federal judges have any very substantial formal training in economics and, as of the date of this writing, no currently sitting federal judge or Justice holds any graduate degree in economics.) Accordingly, we will boil the economic theory we need to know down to a handful of what we will call "Ground Rules of Antitrust Economics," to which we will make reference throughout the book.

We will then move on to two other very abstract subjects that will be with us for the rest of the book. First, we will begin with a very abstract idea, one that will play a role in virtually all of the case law we study. That theme is "market power." As we shall see, in most cases a defendant can be found to have violated antitrust only if it holds "power" within some properly defined "market." A firm is said to have this power when it is able to raise its prices or take other action detrimental to customers without losing its business. Determining when this is the case has proven to be something of a challenge for economists and the courts, and has been a matter of much controversy.

18. Famously, Judges Posner and Easterbrook of the Seventh Circuit Court of Appeals were both faculty of the University of Chicago Law School, where they were influential figures of the so-called "law and economics" movement. Likewise, Judge Douglas Ginsburg of the D.C. Circuit and former Justice Breyer of the U.S. Supreme Court were both professors at Harvard Law School, where they both taught antitrust, and both were frequently noted for their economic sophistication. The former Justice John Paul Stevens, too, was noted over his long career for the economic sophistication of his antitrust decisions.

The book then begins systematic study of the specific rules of substantive antitrust law, and again one way to think about those rules is that they basically boil down to three causes of action: challenge to conspiracies under Sherman Act §1, monopolies under Sherman Act §2, and acquisitions under Clayton Act §7. Of course, that probably makes it sound easier than it really is. For one thing, learning what is useful to know about these three theories of liability takes up most of the following several hundred pages. But also, we should perhaps remember that not *all* of antitrust boils down to these three causes of action. We will also cover topics such as price discrimination (regulated under the Robinson-Patman Act, which appears as Clayton Act §2), the interface of antitrust and intellectual property, the fairly complex Hart-Scott-Rodino premerger approval process (which technically is just a tool for enforcing Clayton Act §7, but has become a complex area of law in its own right), and the complicated problem of the scope of antitrust.

In any case, we begin study of the specific doctrinal rules of antitrust with the rules governing multilateral conduct—that is, the several kinds of conduct that can violate Sherman Act §1. These include price fixing, market divisions, boycotts (also known as "concerted refusals to deal"), and vertical restraints (including price and non-price restraints), information sharing, and a peculiar kind of violation, which can also be dealt with under a few other statutory provisions, known as "tying." We then move on to our study of Sherman Act §2 and the law of unilateral conduct, focusing mainly on the law of "monopolization." That will be followed by a study of mergers and acquisitions, the realm of Clayton Act §7. Mergers is an important segment of antitrust practice that also happens to be quite peculiar, in that it has become highly bureaucratized and removed from the litigation-oriented practice that characterizes the rest of antitrust. Then a few more miscellaneous topics follow: price discrimination under the Robinson-Patman Act and the interface of antitrust and intellectual property. There follows a consideration of the set of institutions and procedures that are peculiar to antitrust: its range of enforcement mechanisms, the several special rules that govern private enforcement, and remedies issues. Finally, we will consider one other important but nonsubstantive branch of the law, the scope of antitrust. The body of law making up its scope is uncommonly extensive and complex, and consists mainly of a series of statutory and case law exemptions for various businesses and conduct. Specifically, we will consider a set of case law rules exempting conduct that takes place within the political system, even when it may in some sense be anticompetitive. We will also consider rules stating the general scope of antitrust, rules governing its reach overseas, the conduct of otherwise regulated businesses, and the conduct of labor unions.

§1.4 A ONE-PAGE CRIB SHEET TO THE ENTIRE LAW OF ANTITRUST

So in the end, remember this:

1. Learning antitrust is predominantly about learning the law of three causes of action:
   a. Challenges to *conspiracy*, or multilateral conduct, under Sherman Act §1;
   b. Challenges to *monopolization*, or unilateral conduct, under Sherman Act §2; and
   c. Challenges to *acquisitions* under Clayton Act §7.
2. On a very general level, each of these causes of action has the same basic form. The plaintiff must:
   a. point to some specific conduct—whether the conduct is conspiracy, the acquisition or maintenance of a monopoly, or a merger or other acquisition; and
   b. show that the conduct was *unreasonable*.
3. Proof that conduct is unreasonable ordinarily involves the application of two separate concepts, which apply in the same way throughout antitrust:
   a. Rules for proving *market power*, which ordinarily the plaintiff must show the defendant to hold; and
   b. A comparatively simple set of economic principles used by courts to determine whether the challenged conduct, if undertaken by a firm with market power, would be harmful to competition. In most cases, asking whether such conduct would be harmful to competition usually means asking whether it could:
      i. cause prices to go up or
      ii. cause output to go down.
4. Finally, there is just a *little* bit more that a student might expect to face in most antitrust courses, which include the following:
   a. Price discrimination under the Robinson-Patman Act;
   b. The interface of antitrust and intellectual property;
   c. The special institutional arrangements and procedural rules of the law, and
   d. The scope of antitrust, including international antitrust, statutory exemptions, and the case law immunity doctrines.

PART II

The Economic Foundations of Contemporary Antitrust

CHAPTER 2

Part One of a Two-Part Strategy for Understanding Antitrust Economics

> Every individual necessarily labours to render the annual revenue of the society as great as he can. He generally, indeed, neither intends to promote the publick interest, nor knows how much he is promoting it. . . . He intends only his own gain, and he is in this, as in many other cases, led by an invisible hand to promote an end which was no part of his intention.
>
> —*Adam Smith*[1]

> [T]he ideas of economists and political philosophers, both when they are right and when they are wrong, are more powerful than is commonly understood. Indeed the world is ruled by little else. Practical men, who believe themselves to be quite exempt from any intellectual influences, are usually the slaves of some defunct economist. . . . I am sure that the power of vested interests is vastly exaggerated compared with the gradual encroachment of ideas.
>
> —*John Maynard Keynes*[2]

§2.1 THE ROLE OF ECONOMICS IN ANTITRUST

Antitrust as it now exists is essentially an application of economic theory. So, to understand the case law, we will need to learn some of that theory, and that will be this chapter's purpose.

1. Adam Smith, *An Inquiry into the Nature and Causes of the Wealth of Nations*, vol. 1, bk. iv, ch. ii (1776).
2. John Maynard Keynes, *The General Theory of Employment, Interest, and Money* 383 (1936).

Now, as we observed in the introduction, the current core of antitrust policy can be boiled down in its simplest form to a definition something like this: *Under federal antitrust law, it is the policy of the United States that private persons may not take actions to interfere improperly in the functioning of competitive markets*. In fact, this probably captures pretty well the nub of antitrust policy as it has always existed, throughout its 135-year history. The problem is that this simple formulation conceals a few challenging and unelaborated ideas: What exactly does it mean to interfere "improperly" in the functioning of a "market" that is otherwise "competitive"? The courts have given varying answers over time. They have almost always held that, in order to be illegal, "interferences" with markets must somehow impair those markets *unreasonably*. But that still leaves a pretty big undefined term at the heart of antitrust: What does it mean to impair a market unreasonably? For better or worse, in recent decades courts have come to give that idea content pretty much exclusively by relying on economic theory.[3] To put it simply, that critical, central concept within antitrust law—"reasonableness"—now boils down to the following question: *Did some conduct challenged by a plaintiff injure a market in some way that, according to economic theory, causes a net harm to consumers?*

As the case law now stands, we can come up with plausible, rough answers to that question in most antitrust cases—and therefore we can understand pretty well how the courts ordinarily handle them—without that much economic theory. In fact, the minimum necessary collection of ideas can be distilled to a set of simple rules, and in this book we will call them the "Ground Rules of Antitrust Economics." They can be explained intuitively and in this book we shall do so. They will be set out in §2.2.

But, obviously enough, it would be misleading to imply that economic theory is really all that simple or that there is nothing to be gained by antitrust students having a deeper understanding of more advanced topics. This book uses a two-part strategy to introduce all the economics you are likely to need in your antitrust course. First, in addition to laying out the Ground Rules, this chapter aims to support study in a fair bit more depth. Section 2.2 begins by explaining the Ground Rules purely intuitively—and that, again, is probably enough in itself for an adequate basic understanding of the case law—and §2.3 then reexplains the same material and expands on it, according to the more traditional approach.

You might choose to use this material in different ways, depending on how much your antitrust course focuses on explicit economic theory,

3. This is not to say that sympathy with economic theory is all that new. As we shall see, some very old, important antitrust cases draw on economic principles like the ones discussed in this chapter. But two things about it are fairly new. First, economic theory itself has changed during the lifetime of antitrust, and so the principles on which the courts rely are themselves new. Second, the role economic theory has come to play in defining antitrust rules has become pretty much exclusive.

and how much depth you want to give yourself in preparing for it. If you are new to economics and if your professor has not emphasized economic theory as such, you might content yourself only with working through the Ground Rules in §2.2. If your course focuses more explicitly on concepts from economic theory, you might work through the Ground Rules but also give some real thought to the material in §2.3 even if it's new to you and it feels like a bit of a challenge. If your economics background is solid, you might skip the Ground Rules and just use §2.3 as a refresher.

It is probably a good idea to reemphasize something: Including both the Ground Rules and the traditional explanation in §2.3 is not meant to imply that you *must* master the material in §2.3. That material is challenging to students new to economics—which characterizes probably most law students at most schools—and many antitrust professors do not demand that students master economics in that level of detail. The goal in this chapter is only to make sure you've got as much material as you *might* need, depending on how much emphasis your professor puts on economic theory for its own sake.

The second part of the strategy is in Chapter 3, which does something quite different. That chapter sets out a series of essentially economic generalizations that courts have employed throughout the antitrust case law. These are all relatively simple ideas that supplement the basic economics set out in the Ground Rules, but they are also fundamental to an understanding of antitrust. They include (1) the rough, current consensus that antitrust fundamentally protects *consumers*, as opposed to the other basic economic goals that it might take as its central purpose, any one of which might change some of its rules; (2) the idea that antitrust protects *competition*, not *competitors*; (3) the idea that in antitrust litigation, social values other than competition can never trump the value of competition; (4) the idea that antitrust is (almost) always agnostic about the actual prices charged in markets in question; and (5) the distinction between "horizontal" and "vertical" relationships and its economic importance.

Finally, there is one last and somewhat less central component in this book's treatment of economics. There are a handful of other topics that are a bit more advanced, and that come up in various places throughout the antitrust case law, all of which are ordinarily thought of as part of a branch of economics known as "industrial organization" theory. So, for example, the "theory of oligopoly" is relevant to proof of conspiracy (discussed in Chapter 12), to the law of information sharing (Chapter 9), and to the law of horizontal merger (Chapter 17). But it seemed awkward to try to include any detailed explanation of such topics in these already lengthy introductory economics chapters, and also awkward to restate them each time they were relevant throughout the book. So, they are covered in an appendix at the end. When topics in the appendix are relevant at any given point, appropriate cross references are given.

§2.2 ECONOMIC THEORY EXPLAINED INTUITIVELY: THE GROUND RULES OF ANTITRUST ECONOMICS

Contrary to what a person might think, the economics with which we are concerned is not so much about dollars and cents. It is a model that attempts to explain how individual human beings make decisions, and from that model it attempts to explain how larger institutions in society operate. In other words, at its core, economics is actually a *theory of human behavior*.[4] The basic psychological claim made by this psychological theory is that individual humans will tend to make those choices in life that maximize their own "welfare"; that is, given two choices, and if all other things are equal, a person will tend to make the choice that gives them the most of what he or she wants. Working only from this most basic claim, economists have built up a complex theory about how markets and indeed whole societies operate.

Though the larger theory can be complicated, the basic economic insight that runs throughout antitrust law is painfully simple.[5] The idea is that when a given market functions in a healthy, competitive manner, the pressure that competing sellers of some product put on one another, in their efforts to steal away business, will force them all to sell at the lowest possible price. If the market is healthy, consumers should have no trouble knowing how one seller's price compares to others, and, in principle, particular sellers should have no real trouble matching whatever technological or other advantages are devised by their competitors. So, if the market is healthy, attempts to raise prices should encourage the swift discipline of lost business. An attempt by a seller to squeeze more profit out of its product will simply drive customers to other sellers of the same product. All of this is so because of that most basic psychological insight mentioned above: Individuals will make that choice that gives them the most of what they want. The appropriate choice as to the purchase of any product, assuming the products to choose from are identical, is the one that is cheapest.

This phenomenon by which sellers force one another to sell as cheaply as possible is known as "price competition." It will remain the central

---

4. This statement is actually a little incautious. Strictly speaking, most economists are not concerned with the behavior of *individuals*. The model is used to explain how individuals behave *on average*, and that model of average behavior is used to explain the functioning of markets.

5. Though, with apologies to William of Ockham, that does not actually prove that it is correct. Cf. *William of Ockham*, in *Stanford Encyclopedia of Philosophy*, available at http://plato.stanford.edu/entries/ockham/ (noting the famous principle of "Ockham's Razor," attributed to William, under which that theory is to be preferred that explains a phenomenon most simply). While surely there are those to whom economic theory's very simplicity is its best virtue, there are also many who do not see it that way at all. As we shall see, a persistent theme among critics of traditional economics is that by assuming away so much of the complexity of real-world affairs, it cannot explain them adequately.

concept throughout your antitrust course for one simple reason. As they now understand antitrust law, the courts take it for granted that the only way a defendant could cause any harm that is in any way prohibited by antitrust is if the defendant is able to raise its prices to consumers. We will come to see more clearly why the courts think that, as we work through the Ground Rules and the rest of this book.

§2.2.1 The Ground Rules

The Ground Rules are as follows. (Throughout the rest of this chapter, words in **bold** are defined in the glossary at the end of the book.)

1. Our antitrust laws have come over time to embody a policy that **markets** should be allowed to regulate themselves. The policy is based on the theoretical commitment that, when left alone, **markets** can not only regulate themselves, but can ordinarily do so in a way superior to either private or government interference.
2. Economists believe that this automatic system works best when certain conditions apply, and the policy underlying antitrust is the effort to make the American marketplace resemble those ideal market conditions as much as possible.
3. Though these conditions are never fully attainable in reality, it is useful for theoretical purposes to hypothesize a world in which they are perfectly realized. In their perfect form, the conditions are:
   a. The absence of **entry barriers**,
   b. Perfect information for all buyers and sellers (including information as to cost, price, and all alternative products or services),
   c. Fungibility of products or services in the market, and
   d. Zero **transaction costs**.[6]
4. Markets under the ideal conditions are thought to do the best possible job of the regulation of production because they **optimize resource allocation**. They do this because **perfect competition** demands the lowest possible prices for products. As soon as a seller raises its price above the bare minimum needed to cover costs, other competitors will be able to steal that seller's business.

6. For a more detailed treatment of the features of perfectly competitive markets, see Dennis W. Carlton & Jeffrey M. Perloff, *Modern Industrial Organization* ch. 3 (3d ed. 2000). For interesting discussions of the theory's origins, see George J. Stigler, *Perfect Competition, Historically Contemplated*, 65 J. Pol. Econ. 1 (1957), and Paul McNulty, *A Note on the History of Perfect Competition*, 75 J. Pol. Econ. 395 (1967). If you *really* want to know about its history, see Joseph A. Schumpeter, *History of Economic Analysis* (Mark Perlman, trans., rev. ed. 1996).

   a. Because new **entry** will continue until the good or service is sold at the lowest possible price, the **long-run equilibrium** price in **perfect competition** is exactly equal to the cost of production (a part of which is a competitive **return on investment** for those who invested in the business). This means that all producers in a **perfectly competitive market** will earn zero **economic profit**.
   b. Moreover, **competition** over time will tend continually to push down the **cost** of production to the cheapest possible means that is technologically feasible at a given time, because every producer has an incentive to improve its own **productive efficiency**.
   c. Producers have that incentive because if they can lower their costs in ways that other sellers can't match, then they can either earn some **economic profit** at the prevailing price or steal competitors' business by charging lower prices.
   d. This competitive process therefore tends to reduce price and cost to the lowest possible level, and devotes the least possible amount of society's wealth to any particular productive endeavor, leaving more for all other endeavors.
   e. It can be shown mathematically (and in simplified form it will be in §2.3) that this state of affairs allows the most people to have the most of what they want, and that no rearrangement of affairs could make anyone better off. It is therefore said that competition **optimizes resource allocation**.

5. In reality the ideal conditions are not only not perfectly attainable, but even to the extent that they are attained in a particular case, they are not always self-preserving. They can be impaired in several ways, either by naturally occurring failures in particular **markets** or by the intentional acts of persons or governments. A nonexclusive list of possible impairments would include:
   a. **Entry barriers**, which could include any number of special costs or difficulties, examples of which might be:
      i. high start-up **costs** (especially if they are **sunk**),
      ii. regulatory barriers, like license requirements, and
      iii. control by one seller of facilities essential to effective **competition**.
   b. Informational dysfunctions, which could include:
      i. information costs,
      ii. fraud, and
      iii. asymmetries—which are likely to exist, for example, between manufacturers and retail consumers or between trained professionals and their clients.
   c. Product **differentiation** and imperfect **substitutes** that frustrate fungibility.

6. A basic fact is that competitors are hostile to free **competition**. It drives their prices, and therefore their **profits**, down. They therefore have strong incentives to abuse **markets** and will take steps to create market impediments like those identified in item 5 wherever it is profitable for them to do so.
7. A second basic fact is that since the ideal conditions are neither fully attainable nor always self-preserving, it is possible that in a particular **market** healthy **competition** may not prevail, and therefore some one or a group of producers will acquire some **market power**. **Market power** is the ability of a seller to raise its prices without simply losing its business, which, under the arguments above, a seller without **market power** should be unable to do.
8. A third basic fact is that for a seller with **market power** it is almost always more profitable to raise price above the **competitive price**, even though that seller will then sell fewer units. This is true only up to that point called the **monopoly price**; an increase in price above that point will begin to reduce the **monopoly** seller's **profits**. This third basic fact is true because of the relationship between demand and the **cost** of production at different levels of total output. This third basic fact provides the motive for item number 6.
9. A fourth basic fact is that the model of **perfect competition** does not take into account one very important need of real-world **markets**: the institutional arrangements necessary to make them exist. Thus, it is sometimes necessary for governments or private persons to provide these institutional arrangements, which may include buildings, infrastructures, laws, agreements, means of communication, or other things needed for transactions to occur. One very basic example is that **markets** ordinarily won't work in the way described here unless a government is in existence that can protect property rights.[7]
10. A final basic fact is that the model of **perfect competition** does not take into account **dynamic efficiency** over time. It may be in a particular **market** that social losses caused by short-run supracompetitive prices are offset by the social gains from dynamic efficiencies resulting from the profits thereby earned. For example, a drug company may elevate prices for patented drugs, but it might also reinvest in research and development that result in better drugs, to the benefit of society.

7. *See* Guido Calabresi & Douglas A. Melamed, *Property Rules, Liability Rules, and Inalienability: One View of the Cathedral*, 82 Harv. L. Rev. 1089, 1093-1105 (1972); Harold Demsetz, *Toward a Theory of Property Rights*, 57 Am. Econ. Rev. 347 (1967).

§2.2.2 Getting Our Feet Wet with the Ground Rules

As a way of making the Ground Rules more concrete, work through the following facts and the questions that follow. Ten manufacturers located in the State of Examplestan are engaged in the manufacture of cement mix. Among them they have for some time managed to meet that State's entire cement mix needs. They each need as their central inputs only limestone, clay, and shale, each of which they can secure from a very competitive market for quarry goods. The State of Examplestan also boasts abundant skilled labor. Finally, the process for making cement mix is very simple and all cement mixes are essentially identical. As a result of these various factors, the ten sellers are able to operate quite efficiently, and in fact their production costs are almost identical. They are all about the same size and usually produce almost identical quantities of the product.

The prices at which the manufacturers might sell cement mix in the State of Examplestan are set out in Table 2.1 below. Table 2.1 also shows how much they will sell at various prices, what it will cost them to produce at the different rates of output, and how much money they will earn. A few questions follow Table 2.1 that will help us learn a bit about how the Ground Rules work in application.

2.1 Price, Output, and Profitability in the Production of Cement Mix, State of Examples

1	2	3	4	5	6
Price, in Dollars per Pound	Quantity Consumers Will Buy, in Pounds	The Ten Producers' Total Revenue, in Dollars	Economic Cost of Production, in Dollars per Pound	Total Economic Cost of Production, in Dollars	The Ten Producers' Total Economic Profit, in Dollars
10.00	1,000	10,000	40.00	40,000	–30,000
9.00	2,000	18,000	20.00	40,000	–22,000
8.00	3,000	24,000	15.00	45,000	–21,000
7.00	4,000	28,000	8.00	32,000	–4,000
6.00	5,000	30,000	5.00	25,000	5,000
5.00	6,000	30,000	4.25	25,500	4,500
4.00	7,000	28,000	3.50	24,500	3,500
3.00	8,000	24,000	3.00	24,000	0
2.00	9,000	18,000	3.50	31,500	–13,500
1.00	10,000	10,000	5.00	50,000	–40,000

Even though in the end the lessons to be learned here are straightforward, this example will not be entirely easy to work through. Before we start digging through the numbers, let us observe a few general points that will help. First, notice something about the numbers in column 4. The per-unit cost of producing cement mix starts off very high, rapidly declines for a while, and finally begins going up again. This simply happens to be very common in real markets. Production in very small amounts tends to be extremely costly. Imagine the time and labor intensity if a person were to sell cars by making each one from scratch, one at a time. Savings could be gained quickly by producing more cars at a time, employing a workforce, and training each worker to perform specialized, narrow tasks. But it will also usually be the case that per-unit costs of production will eventually begin rising again as the volume of production gets large. This can reflect several facts. As output expands in a particular industry, some inputs necessary in making its products will start to become a bit scarcer and the price of them will go up. Likewise, there are simply strains involved in running a large organization—at some point, increased size starts to become inefficient.

Now, try your hand at the following questions.

Example

Why do the amounts in column 2 get larger as the amounts in column 1 get smaller?

Explanation

Simple supply and demand. This result is explained by common sense, it is borne out by empirical experience, and it follows from that most basic psychological claim of economic theory: People tend to make choices that maximize their wants. It is simply almost always the case that, other things being equal, consumers will buy more of a good as its price goes down.

Example

What value is reported in column 3? How is it calculated?

Explanation

Revenue means the total amount of money that a seller earns from the sale of a good, before accounting for any costs. So, for each horizontal row in Table 2.1, the number in column 3 is the number in column 1 (price) multiplied by the number in column 2 (quantity sold).

Example

What value is reported in column 5? How is it calculated?

Explanation

This value turns out to be very significant. Note that column 5 reports not just **cost** but ***economic* cost**. Economic theory draws a distinction between **accounting cost** and **economic cost**. **Accounting cost**, which is basically what we mean when we use the word "cost" colloquially, is the cost of the raw materials and labor that go into making a good, the cost of distributing it, advertising, overhead, and so on. A firm that is doing well ought to be able to earn at least some revenue over and above all these costs, and that excess (which is the **accounting profit**) can either be retained by the firm to invest in new projects, or it can be paid out to shareholders or other owners of the firm. But economists look at this somewhat differently. To an economist, some of the excess the firm earns over these costs—some of the excess that it could pay out as profit to its owners—has to be thought of as just another cost of doing business. This is so for a simple reason. Every firm must attract operating funds, and to do that it must pay at least enough of a return on investment to ensure that the investors of those funds won't take their money elsewhere to earn a better return. Under **perfect competition** a firm should only be able to pay investors just enough of a return that it can keep enough capital invested in the firm to keep it operating. And that cost—the cost of all raw materials, labor, equipment, and so on, *plus* a competitive rate of return on the money invested in the firm to keep it going—is **economic cost**.

The significance of this fact cannot be overstated, since it explains why in perfect competition all firms will earn zero **economic profit**. So long as the ideal conditions hold, any increase in **economic profit** above zero will attract new entry that will compete those profits back down to zero.

In any case, the numbers in column 5 are calculated by taking the numbers in column 4—the per unit **economic cost**—and multiplying them by the numbers in column 2—the quantity demanded at any given price.

Example

If the quantity that consumers buy at high prices remains low, those consumers who might have bought cement mix at lower prices will have retained some money that they would otherwise have spent on cement mix. In such a case, what is likely happening with that money?

Explanation

One cannot say for sure, but a good likelihood is that consumers will either save that money or spend it on alternatives to cement mix. They might not otherwise have wanted those alternatives as much as cement mix, but they will make do with them when the price of cement mix goes up. For example, some people might choose to build slate paths instead of cement sidewalks, or they might use metal or wood construction materials in building, in place of cement. Alternatives of this kind are called **substitutes**, and they play an important role in economics and antitrust. We will learn much more about them in the discussion of **market power** in Chapter 4 and elsewhere in the book.

Example

Finally, how much cement mix will be sold, and at what price?

Explanation

On the facts stated in this Example, and assuming that the conditions of healthy competition described in the Ground Rules are satisfied to some reasonable degree,[8] we should see producers offering 8,000 pounds of cement mix at $3 per pound, and consumers buying all the units that are offered.

---

8. The facts here suggest that this should be quite a competitive market—that is, the ideal conditions identified in the Ground Rules should be satisfied pretty well. There are no obvious

We can predict this outcome because at any other price the producers will either earn an **economic profit** that would invite new **entry** or expanded capacity from existing sellers, or they will suffer losses that will cause them to change the amount of the product they put on the market. For example, say the producers offered only 5,000 pounds instead of 8,000. They would then make a positive **economic profit**, and in fact they would make the largest profit possible, given the amount of consumer demand and their own production costs. (See for yourself—the largest positive number in column 6 is $5,000, where producers sell 5,000 pounds at $6 per pound.) You might be thinking that it would only make sense for the producers to try to sell at this level, since we've already stated the basic claim of economics to be that people maximize their own wants. But think about what happens if they try it. It will occur to each of them that if one seller could lower its price just a little bit, then in this well-functioning market consumers should all realize it and quickly switch to that lower-price seller. At a market price of $6, each of the ten sellers (which we're told are the same size) will likely divide the $5,000 **economic profit** in ten roughly equal parts. But if one of them lowers to $5, it should be able to take *all* the business—assuming it could jack up its capacity fast enough to service all the new demand, that seller could sell the entire 6,000 pounds that consumers would want at that price, and therefore keep for itself the entire $4,500 in economic profit. (See again for yourself where these numbers come from in Table 2.1—at a price of $5, consumers will want 6,000 pounds, and the resulting **economic profit** will be $4,500.) But consider what would happen *then*. The remaining nine sellers would see the need to react quickly by lowering their own prices at least down to $4. This process will continue until the sellers have all reached the point of zero **economic profit**.

But then, you might ask, could anything be gained at a price *less* than $3, where **economic profit** is zero? The answer, on a long-term basis, is no. If a seller can't sell at a price that will cover its costs, it will sooner or later quit the business.[9]

---

entry barriers. (The fact that there hasn't been new entry in some time likely just shows that the market is being efficiently served at a competitive price. The easy availability of labor and inputs, the fact that the production process is simple, and the small scale at which producers operate all suggest it should be easy to enter.) The product is fungible and there is no obvious information asymmetry or other information problem. As in all real markets there will be transaction costs, but they should be low in a retail market for a simple good.

9. Readers more familiar with economics might notice that the results described here are "long-term" results. It is true that in some cases sellers will continue in a market incurring some economic losses in the short term. That is so because a seller might continue to cover its "fixed costs"—costs that it is legally obligated to pay for some significant term of, say, a year or more—even though it is actually losing some money on each individual sale. For those interested in more depth on this issue, the short-run/long-run distinction is taken up in §2.3.2(d) and (e).

This result, in which producers sell at $3 per pound and consumers buy up the whole 8,000 pounds offered but seek no more, is likely to be stable so long as costs and demand remain stable. It is therefore called the **competitive equilibrium**. The price of $3 per pound is called the **competitive price** and 8,000 pounds is the **competitive quantity**.

§2.3 BASIC PRICE THEORY, MORE TRADITIONALLY EXPLAINED: USING GRAPHS AND MATHEMATICS TO CAPTURE ECONOMIC CONCEPTS

In a sense this section restates what we learned in the "Ground Rules" approach in §2.2, but it does more than just restate it in some more complicated way. This section introduces the powerful analytic tools of basic price theory. It will show how, with just a few facts about the costs of a firm's production and how much of its good consumers happen to desire, we can make strong analytical and predictive judgments about its behavior and the market in which it operates.

For the sake of discussion, we will analyze the behavior of a hypothetical producer of some good, which we will call Firm X. We will use discussion of Firm X to work through analysis of two basic scenarios that together make up the fundamental core of price theory. In §2.3.2, we will ask how Firm X will behave if it is a competitor in a perfectly competitive market: How much will it choose to produce? And at what price will it sell? Second, §2.3.3 will ask the same questions about the behavior of Firm X if it is an out-and-out monopolist.

But first, it might help to begin with a brief refresher on the use of graphical representation, which we will use to introduce price theory.

§2.3.1 Functions, Curves, and Graphs

Economic theory is basically a theory about how important variables relate to each other, and how variations in some of them cause variations in others. We think that the prices of goods go up and down (i.e., they vary) because they have a relation to the costs of making those goods, and to how much consumers desire them. Economists (borrowing from calculus) refer to these causal relationships by saying that one variable is a "function" of some other variable. If we think that some phenomenon X causes or explains some other phenomenon Y, then we say that "Y is a function of X."

For example, the price that firms charge for a good is thought to depend on how much people want that good and how much it costs to make. If there

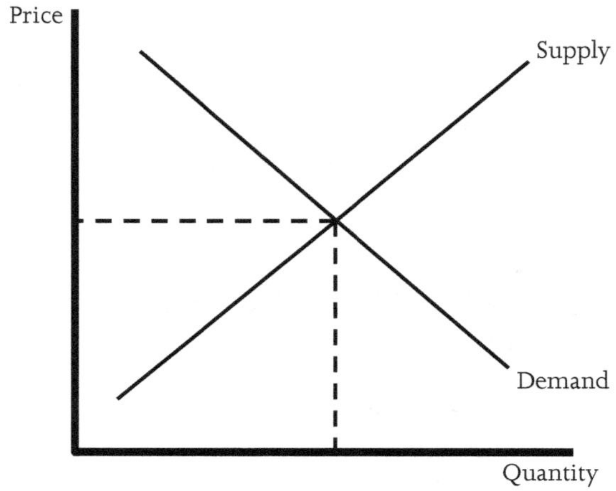

Figure 2.1. A Graph of Competitive Equilibrium as an Example of Graphing "Curves"

is a severe shortage in the supply of an ingredient in fertilizer, that will make fertilizer more expensive and cause the price of corn to go up. Likewise, if scientists discover some important new use for corn—like, say, ethanol gasoline for cars—then there may be an increase in just how much corn various buyers want to buy. That, too, will cause the price of corn to go up. So, we might say that the price of corn is a function of demand and the cost of production.

Economists also often refer to functions as "curves," for the simple reason that you can draw a function on a graph, and it will look like a line or curve. For example, the most familiar graph in economics, a representation of a competitive market in equilibrium, can be drawn as in Figure 2.1.

Here there are lines marked "supply" and "demand." Both lines represent "functions." Demand is a function, because it describes a relationship between two variables. It shows how much of a good consumers will buy at any given price, and so the line marked "demand" displays a relationship between price (the vertical axis) and quantity (the horizontal axis). Supply is likewise a function; it describes how much of a good firms will produce and sell at any given price. So the line marked "supply" again shows a relationship of price and quantity. Because these are functions that are graphically displayed, we could call these two lines the "supply curve" and the "demand curve."[10]

10. You might be thinking, especially if you haven't had math in a while or if you've never had calculus, that these things don't look very much like "curves." Instead they look like "lines," because they are straight. That is true, but economists and others who use calculus in their work have a habit of referring to all two-dimensional functions as "curves," because all of them can be drawn on simple two-dimensional graphs in the same way. Functions that work out on the graph as straight lines are called "linear functions," and those that work out as curved lines are called "curvilinear functions." In the real world it will almost always be the case that cost curves and supply and demand curves will be curvilinear, or will have even more complex shapes.

§2.3.2 How Competitive Markets Reach Equilibrium

We will begin our discussion of substantive price theory by asking how Firm X behaves under *competitive* conditions; that is, in the rest of this section, we will assume that Firm X operates in a perfectly competitive market. (In this discussion, when we say that a market is "competitive," we will mean that it is "perfectly competitive.") By assuming that Firm X's market is competitive, we assume that all the "ideal conditions" of perfect competition described in §2.2 are satisfied here: Entry is free, information is perfect, goods are fungible, and transaction costs are zero.

The quantity that Firm X produces and the price it will charge depend on a few things, and we will approach the analysis of them in five steps. (1) We first have to understand Firm X's *costs*, since a firm can't make profit unless it can earn revenue higher than its costs. (2) We then must work out the other half of the two-part dance that is competition, consumer *demand*. (3) An understanding of those two things together—Firm X's costs and the demand for its product—would actually be enough for a basic answer to the question above: how would Firm X behave under competition. We will put these two ideas together and use them to predict how Firm X will behave to maximize its profits. (4) However, we can learn something more by taking a brief detour to consider an important distinction. Markets behave differently in the *short run* than they do in the *long run*. A firm might be able to operate in a way for a short time (the short run) that will allow it to earn a little bit of supracompetitive profit or suffer some losses, even though neither would be sustainable in the long run. (5) And finally, we will ask: What should Firm X do if it starts to lose money?

§2.3.2(a) How Firms Make Decisions, Part 1: Costs

A firm's basic choice is to decide how much of its product to produce and the price at which it will sell. Those decisions depend first of all on the firm's costs. There are any number of different ways that costs can be measured, but in microeconomic theory there are three measures that are especially important. In just a bit, we will display each of these important cost measures as curves on a graph, and talk about their relationships to each other and their overall significance.

First we care about **average cost** (also known as **average total cost**). Average cost is the total cost of producing some amount of the good, divided by the amount that is produced. If the firm's total outlay for producing 100 units is $1,000, then the average cost at Q = 100 is $10.

Next, we care about **average variable cost**. Here we must distinguish two different sorts of expenses that a firm might incur in doing its business. Some costs are **fixed**, in that a firm must spend these amounts of money just to begin doing business. They must be incurred in that fixed amount without regard to how much of its good the firm actually produces. A firm that intends to manufacture bicycles will have to lease or buy manufacturing space and equipment. That will have some fixed price tag, and it will be the same whether the firm produces ten units or many thousands of units. Other costs, though, are **variable**. They go up or down depending on how many units the firm produces. So, the bicycle company might have to set up a factory and some machinery, but, strictly speaking, it doesn't have to spend any money on the raw metal tubing it will use to make the frames if it doesn't actually produce any bikes. The total amount that it spends on the tubing will go up if it starts producing and will keep going up the more bikes that it makes.

Finally, we care—we care a *lot*—about one last measure of cost that can seem more challenging to understand: **marginal cost**. The firm's marginal cost of production is that additional little bit of cost that it incurs for each additional unit that it produces. As we shall see, firms make their most important decisions by thinking about what will happen to the relationship between marginal cost and price if they make small increases or decreases in their output; that is, considering changes in marginal cost is key to understanding how rational firms make decisions about price and output. This is in effect the central insight of the economics we will study.

Consider how these three measures of costs look when we graph them for one typical firm, Firm X, as in Figure 2.2.

Let us notice a few very important features of these three curves. First, each of them is roughly U-shaped. Each starts off, on the left-hand side of the graph, at a relatively high point. Then, as we move toward the right of the graph, each goes down for a while and then starts going back up again. As we saw in connection with the State of Examplestan scenario in §2.2, a characteristic feature of producing almost any good is that if the firm tries to produce in very small quantities, its costs will be very high—it is inefficient. It would be awfully inefficient to set up a bicycle factory but then make just one or a few bicycles; presumably one would at least have to have a place to do the work and some equipment, and would have to spread that initial capital outlay over just a few units of output. That's why these three cost curves start on the left-hand side at relatively high points. But then, a lot of efficiency can be gained by increasing output just a little. That is why each of these curves slants sharply downward at first. But notice that they also bottom out at a certain point and then start climbing again. As was the case in the State of Examplestan, several facts will ordinarily cause cost curves eventually to become upward sloping in this fashion. As the industry's output expands, inputs needed to make its product will become scarcer, and inefficiencies will creep in in the management of firms, as their own output gets larger.

Next, notice something about the shape of the *AC* and *AVC* curves: They start off fairly far apart from each other, but as we move toward the right of

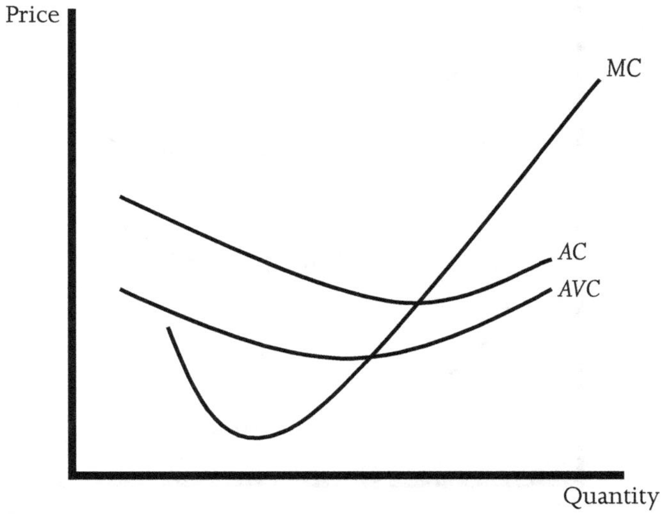

MC = marginal cost
AC = average (total) cost
AVC = average variable cost

Figure 2.2. The Cost Characteristics of Firm X

the graph, they get closer and closer together. In fact, if we stretched them out further, we would see that *AC* and *AVC* just keep getting closer, infinitely, without ever touching. There is a reason for that. *AC* includes both **fixed** and **variable costs**. A fixed cost is a cost that does not vary with output. If manufacturing a good requires some machinery that would be very expensive to remove and resell to another purchaser after it is installed, the purchase is fixed because the expense must be made regardless how many units the firm makes. (There are different kinds of fixed costs and the differences among them matter to some of what we will learn; we will draw some of these distinctions in §2.3.2(d).) A **variable** cost, on the other hand, varies with output. For example, after the firm has purchased the expensive, installed machine, it might also have to buy some raw material that is fed into the machine to make the good, but only so much of it needs to be used for every unit of the good that is produced. So producing more of the good requires more of the raw material; the expense of the raw material is then a variable cost.

And so, at every individual point of output, the *AC* line reports the *sum* of the average fixed cost and the average variable cost at that point of output. But if we graphed average fixed cost as a curve, it would start off relatively high, fall very rapidly for a bit, and then fall more gradually. It would get closer to the horizontal axis—which would represent a cost of $0—but it would never actually reach the axis. If fixed cost is $100, then at Q = 1,

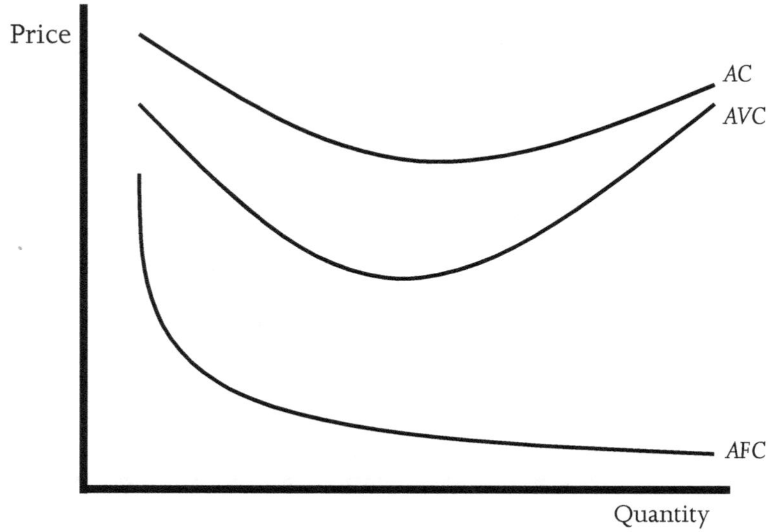

AC = average (total) cost
AVC = average variable cost
AFC = average fixed cost

Figure 2.3. Average Fixed Costs

AFC = \$100; if Q = 2, then *AFC* = \$50, and as we increase Q, *AFC* becomes \$33.33, \$25, \$20, and so on. The slope starts to get flatter and flatter as the average of the fixed cost over the firm's output gets ever closer to \$0, without ever reaching it. So the curves would look like those in Figure 2.3.

The reason this makes *AVC* get ever closer to *AC* is that the distance between those two curves at any point along the graph is just the amount of average fixed cost at that point of output. Average fixed cost gets smaller as output increases, so the space between *AC* and *AVC* gets smaller as well.

Finally, there is an interesting relationship between the MC curve and the *AC* and *AVC* curves. The point where the MC curve crosses each of these two other curves *is at their lowest point*. Consider Figure 2.4.

Notice that there are two points in this figure: AC_{min} (meaning minimum average cost) and AVC_{min} (meaning minimum average variable cost). These are the points at which MC crosses those two other curves. This may seem a little hard to grasp at first, but the reason is really very simple. Remember that marginal cost is the small amount of additional cost that is added to the total with each incremental step that we take toward the right side of the graph. As long as this marginal cost is below an average cost curve, then the addition of a marginal increment of cost will cause the average to go down. So when *AC* and *AVC* are above MC, they are necessarily downward sloping. But as soon as marginal cost is above an average cost curve, then the

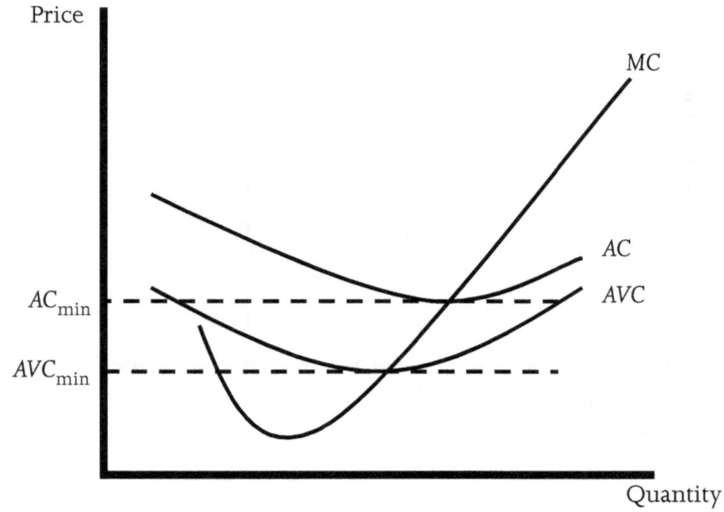

MC = marginal cost
AC = average (total) cost
AVC = average variable cost
AC_{min} = minimum average cost
AVC_{min} = minimum average variable cost

Figure 2.4. Relationship of Marginal and Average Cost Curves

addition of the incremental cost will cause the average to go up. So as soon as MC crosses *AC* or *AVC*, then those curves turn upward sloping. Consider this: You do the 100-meter dash, and you keep track of your times because you want to improve your average. You are pretty fast, and your average after 10 tries is 15 seconds. But then, let's say you have a really good run—13.5 seconds. The addition of this number, which is lower than your existing average, will pull the new average down just a bit.

AC_{min} and AVC_{min} will turn out to be important numbers when we start talking about what a firm should do when it starts losing money. We will get to that in §2.3.2(e). Also, note that in long-run competitive equilibrium, which we will discuss in §2.3.2(d), there are actually three lines that run through the same point: The firm-specific demand curve for every firm that is able to remain in the market is a horizontal line that crosses AC_{min}, and it so happens that the marginal cost curve will cross that point as well. This is so because every firm will have to be able to produce at the lowest technologically feasible cost of production, which is AC_{min}. Because that also happens to be the point at which marginal cost crosses the demand curve, it will be the firm's profit-maximizing choice of output. Even though economic profit at that point is zero, it is profit

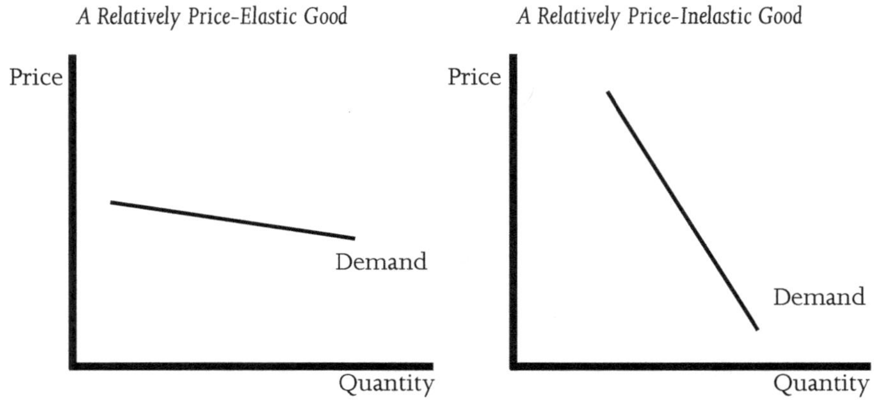

Figure 2.5. The Nature of Demand Curves

maximizing because at any other choice of price or output the firm would actually lose money.

§2.3.2(b) How Firms Make Decisions, Part 2: Demand, Elasticity, and the Firm-Specific Demand Curve

For all their importance, the firm's own cost curves are only one half of what is really a two-character play. We also need to consider one other important factor: demand. Generally, the nature of demand is very intuitive. When something is expensive, fewer people will buy it, and when it is cheap, then more will. So if we graph a demand curve the same way that we graphed Firm X's cost curves, it would look like a line or curve that starts fairly high on the left-hand side of the graph, but then slopes downward as we move to the right. Two examples appear in Figure 2.5.

There is one other feature of demand curves that will be important for us to discuss, before considering the demand for Firm X's product: the *price elasticity of demand*. "Elasticity" is a measurement of how sensitive one variable is to changes in some other variable. So price elasticity of demand (which is often just called "price elasticity") is a measure of how sensitive consumer demand is for a good when the price of that good goes up or down. Technically, price elasticity is the percentage change in the quantity demanded of a good that is caused by a 1 percent change in the price of that good. As a practical matter, if elasticity is a large number,[11] indicating

11. That is, large in absolute value. Elasticity of demand is always a negative number, but the larger the number is in absolute value—for example, –2 as opposed to –1—the more elastic is demand for the good. The more elastic demand becomes, the more that a small change in price will cause a large change in the quantity demanded. A good with an absolute elasticity of more than 1 is said to be "elastic." A good with an absolute elasticity of less than 1 is said to be "inelastic."

that the good is very price elastic, then a small increase in price will cause a large decrease in the quantity consumers will purchase. If elasticity is a small number, indicating that the good is inelastic, then a small increase in price will cause only a small loss in sales.

Elasticity depends on the intensity of consumers' desire for the good and on the availability of substitutes. So, things like medicine and staple food products, for which consumers experience a strong need, are inelastic, whereas nonessential goods like entertainment or snack foods will be more sensitive to price changes. Likewise, highly differentiated goods—those that are carefully branded and imbued with unique characteristics so that consumers do not consider other goods to be easy substitutes for them—are less elastic than fungible goods.

Price elasticity can be nicely conceptualized by thinking about how it affects the shape of the demand curve. If a good is elastic, then a small drop in price (a small move from top toward the bottom on the graph of our market) will cause a large increase in the amount that consumers are willing to buy (a large move from left to right on the graph). So the demand curve will look relatively flat and only shallowly slanted downward. This is shown in the left graph of Figure 2.5. If the good is inelastic, then even large drops in price (large movements from the top toward the bottom) will cause only relatively small increases in quantity (relatively small movements from left to right). This is shown in the right graph of Figure 2.5.

To understand the demand curve faced by Firm X, we also must remind ourselves of something that we noted at the beginning of §2.3.2: Throughout this discussion we have assumed that the market in which Firm X sells its goods is *competitive*. That is, the ideal conditions of perfect competition are satisfied. As one consequence, Firm X has control over only one aspect of its sales. It can choose which quantity to produce, but it cannot choose the price. Recall what we learned in the discussion of the Ground Rules: Under truly competitive conditions, an attempt to raise price above the competitive price will simply drive sales to other sellers.

This fact alone tells us what the demand curve that faces Firm X will look like. Because the market is competitive, if Firm X charges a price higher than the competitive price, it will simply lose sales to its competitors. But so long as it sells at that one, competitive price, it will be able to sell any amount of output that it is physically able to produce.[12] In other words, the

12. Section 2.3.2(d) explains what happens if Firm X can sell at less than that price, and it chooses to do so. But to be clear we might as well point out here that if Firm X discovers some cost-saving technological innovation that allows it to underprice its competitors, under competitive circumstances it won't be able to do so for very long. Existing competitors or new entrants will eventually figure out how to meet X's price.

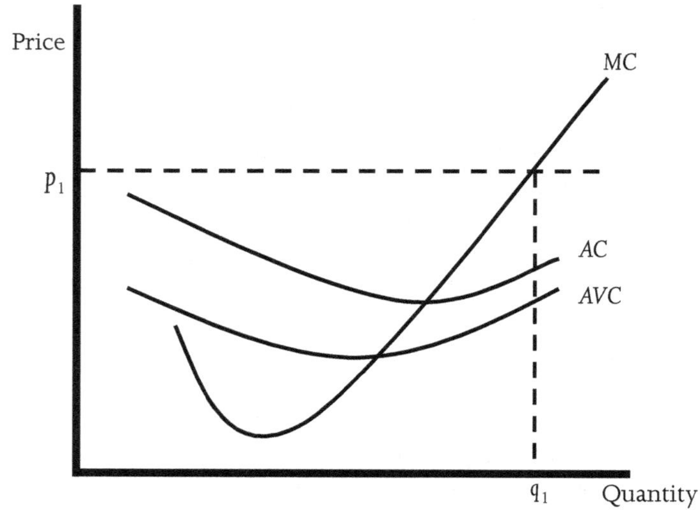

MC = marginal cost
AC = average (total) cost
AVC = average variable cost
p_1 = the price that Firm X will charge in a competitive market
q_1 = the quantity that Firm X will produce at price p_1

Figure 2.6. Pricing and Output Decisions of Firm X

demand curve that faces Firm X is a straight, horizontal line.[13] This is often known as the *firm-specific* demand curve. It is different than the *market* or *industry* demand curve. When we ask what total quantity of the good all the consumers in a market will buy from the entire industry at given prices, we get the industry demand curve. Except in the case of very unusual goods, the industry demand curve will not be a horizontal line. It will be a diagonal, downward-sloping line that slopes down from left to right. For almost any product, the less that a product costs (i.e., as we move from high to low on the graph), the more consumers will buy of it (i.e., we will move from left to right on the graph).

We will therefore assume that upon its entry into the market, Firm X's firm-specific demand curve can be drawn as the horizontal line at p_1 in Figure 2.6.

---

13. This condition is known as "infinite price elasticity of demand"—an infinitely elastic demand curve is horizontal. A firm's firm-specific demand under perfect competition is always perfectly elastic, and the practical consequence is that the firm will be able to sell any amount that it is capable of producing at the competitive price, but zero units at any higher price. It also will find that it will be unable to sell at any price below competitive price and still cover its costs.

§2.3.2(c) How Firms Make Decisions, Part 3: Maximizing Profit

We can now make some predictions about how Firm X will behave, based on the curve MC and the firm-specific, horizontal demand curve at p_1, as they appear in Figure 2.6. As mentioned above, the working of *marginal cost* in the operation of markets is among the most important insights in modern economics. The most important thing to know about it turns out to be extremely simple: *It is profitable to sell an additional unit wherever the marginal cost will be less than the added revenue from the sale.* If you can expand the output of your firm and the additional cost of doing it is less than the price you would get by selling that additional unit, then you should do it. You would make a little more profit; it makes sense. That will continue to be true as the firm expands output outwards along its marginal cost curve until the additional cost just equals the additional revenue. That is, the firm should keep producing more units until the cost of the last additional unit just equals the price. Accordingly, in competitive markets a firm will produce at that quantity where marginal cost equals price. In the case of Firm X, that will be at quantity q_1 in Figure 2.6.

Notice something perhaps a little surprising about how Figure 2.6 is drawn: At the output that Firm X will pick, q_1, the firm-specific demand curve (the dashed line at p_1) is actually higher than its average cost there. This seems like something that shouldn't happen in a competitive market—Firm X will earn a little bit of positive economic profit here because its total revenue (price times quantity at the chosen output, or $q_1 \times p_1$) is greater than its total costs (average cost times quantity). But it is possible, because a firm might enter that has some technological advantage or access to cheaper inputs or some other leg up that allows it to produce more cheaply than other firms in the market. Still, so long as a market is competitive, it will be a short-run outcome only and should not be long lasting, because other firms will figure out Firm X's technological innovation and will reduce their costs too. Economic profit will return to zero in the long run. We will add that distinction next.

§2.3.2(d) How Firms Make Decisions, Part 4: The Short Run, the Long Run, and the Different Kinds of Fixed Costs

The terms **short run** and **long run** are in effect terms of art and have precise meanings. The short run is the period during which some *fixed costs* are not *avoidable*; that is, there are some costs that are not only fixed—they must be paid in some fixed amount, regardless of how much or little of its good the firm actually produces—but the firm can't avoid them, even by going out of business, and can't recover them once they are made. For example, a firm might lease office space or enter into a contract for some input that requires it to take monthly deliveries and make payment on delivery. The ongoing payments are contract obligations that must be complied with regardless how much of its good the firm actually produces, and they cannot be avoided simply by going out of business. Or, a firm might purchase a specialized delivery truck, for which there is no ready resale market, and which has a useful life of two years. That cost, too, is unavoidable, because the value of the truck cannot be gotten back out of it.[14]

The fact that some costs are not avoidable in the short run has two significant consequences. First, it has an effect on the ability of firms to compete with other firms. Even when another firm comes up with a technological innovation that allows it to lower its costs and earn a bit of positive economic profit, it may not be profitable for other firms to mimic that technology immediately, because they would lose more in unavoidable costs than they would gain through the lower cost technology.

This was why, for example, Firm X in Figure 2.6 was able to earn some supranormal profit for a while. For whatever reason, it managed to get its cost curves below its competitors, and for the time being it can either earn a bit of profit on its sales or compete on a price basis with its higher-cost competitors. In the long run, however, when other firms are able to vary their inputs to imitate Firm X's superior technology, price competition will bring price down from p_1 to the point at which all the firms in the market produce at a competitive price. Returning to Figure 2.6, in perfectly competitive long-run equilibrium, every firm that is able to remain in the market will have the same cost curves, and the price that will prevail will intersect the *AC* curve at its lowest point. That is, as we said in the Ground Rules in §2.2, the competitive price will equal the lowest technologically feasible cost of production.

Second, as we shall see next in §2.3.2(e), the fact that some costs are unavoidable in the short run has a consequence for a firm's choices when it is losing money. It may be sensible—though not necessarily—to keep producing at a loss in the short run, because until unavoidable costs have been retired, the firm will lose less by staying in business than it would by exiting.

Finally, we must distinguish one last cost concept, and this one is actually fairly challenging. It takes some work to see why it is different than other cost concepts, and it has a consequence for rational decisionmaking that strikes most people as counterintuitive. A fixed cost that *has already been made and cannot be recovered* is called a **sunk** cost. Say the firm must purchase a piece of heavy equipment that would be prohibitively expensive to try to resell—it has no salvage value once it is purchased. The important fact is not that it is unavoidable, but that the money has already been spent. We

14. Strictly speaking, the short run is a period of time in which at least one factor of production cannot be costlessly varied. The long term is a period in which all factors of production can be costlessly varied. Carlton & Perloff, *supra* at 32.

will consider the effects that this sort of cost has on rational decisionmaking in §2.3.2(e).

So we should distinguish the following kinds of cost:

Fixed Cost: A cost that does not vary with output; it must be spent in a fixed amount in order to enter the business at all. A fixed cost is avoidable if the firm could recover it upon quitting the business. A fixed cost is unavoidable if the firm couldn't recover it even by quitting the business. If it is unavoidable, it is "sunk" from the firm's perspective *only* if it has already been made.

Avoidable Cost: A cost that will no longer be incurred if the business ceases operations. Such a cost could be either fixed or variable. Fixed costs are avoidable, for example, when leases can be subleased or equipment can be resold at fair value. Variable costs are always avoidable, since all variable costs are zero on exit.

Unavoidable Cost: A cost that will continue to be incurred even if the firm ceases operations. By definition, an unavoidable cost is a fixed cost, since all variable costs are zero on exit.

Sunk Cost: A cost that is not only unavoidable, but that *has already been made*.

§2.3.2(e) How Firms Make Decisions, Part 5: Minimizing Loss

Finally, firms sometimes lose money. Obviously enough, firms that lose money don't always just stop production and quit the business immediately. Sometimes they soldier on in the hope that things will improve and the business can be brought back to profitability.

As mentioned above, the decision whether to exit in the face of losses depends on the period in which the decision is made—whether in the short or long term—and just how large the losses are. Only the short-run scenario is a bit difficult to grasp, because the firm will stay in business even though it is losing some money.

Consider Figure 2.7. The figure is drawn in the same way as Figure 2.6, and you will note that price here—the dashed line at p_1—is above average cost. We said this is a short-term result, because as soon as other firms are able to vary their inputs, they will match Firm X's lower-cost technology, pushing price back down so that no one is making economic profit. But the thing is, it is also possible that price could get pushed down even *below* Firm X's costs. It could get pushed down to some point below the dashed line on Figure 2.7 marked AC_{min}, or even below AVC_{min}. Such a thing might happen if, for example, some other new firm enters with even better technology than Firm X has or even cheaper inputs or better management or what-have-you.

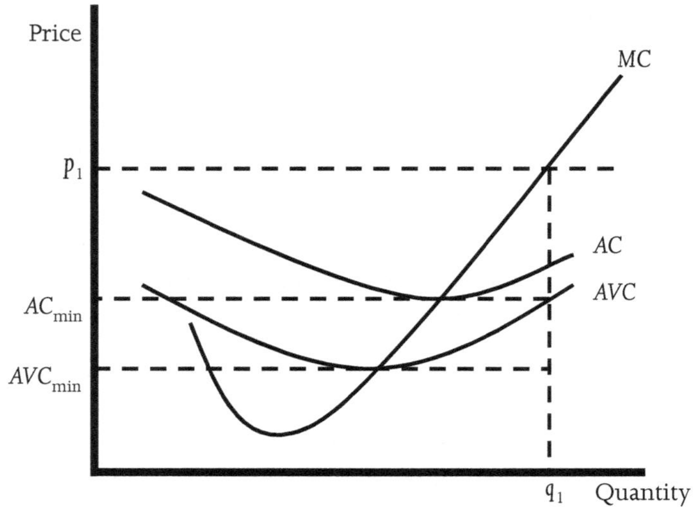

MC = marginal cost
AC = average (total) cost
AVC = average variable cost
p_1 = the price that Firm X will charge in a competitive market
q_1 = the quantity that Firm X will produce at price p_1
AC_{min} = minimum average cost
AVC_{min} = minimum average variable cost

Figure 2.7. Pricing and Output Decisions of Firm X Where the Firm Is Losing Money: When Enough Is Enough

A firm reacts to losses like these differently in the short term than in the long term. In the short run, a firm will continue to produce as long as price is above average variable cost, even if that is below average total cost. That is, Firm X will keep producing in the short run even if price is somewhere below AC_{min}, so long as it is above AVC_{min}. Admittedly, if price is below average total cost, then the firm will be losing some of the money that it has invested to get in the business—some of the firm's fixed costs are not being covered. But the firm still makes enough to cover the variable costs of production, and perhaps then some, and if there is a then some, then that extra can be used to help pay down the fixed costs. If it can cover average variable costs, the firm might lose *some* of the fixed costs, but not *all* of them. But even in the short run, the firm will not remain in the market if it cannot at least cover its variable costs. If price is below AVC_{min}, then Firm X would lose less money by just exiting entirely.

Finally, all this changes in the long run. Once the firm has been in business long enough that it can vary all of its inputs and get out of any fixed costs that were unavoidable in the short run, it will continue only if it can earn at least zero economic profit. In the long run the firm will stay in business only if it can cover *all* of its costs—only if price is greater than or equal to AC_{min}.

§2.3.3 Equilibrium in Monopoly

As mentioned at the beginning, our tour of price theory has basically two components: understanding how firms make decisions in perfectly competitive markets and understanding how they make decisions when they have monopoly power—when they have power over price.

To understand monopoly behavior, we need to introduce another concept: **marginal revenue**. As with marginal cost, marginal revenue is that little bit of additional revenue that the firm earns with each additional unit of sale.

To work through the monopolist's decision making about marginal revenue, we will consider the extreme case, in which one firm has total market power—it is a true monopolist, meaning it is the only firm in a market in which there are no substitutes and no likelihood of competitive discipline through entry. This situation is captured in Figure 2.8.

Though this looks rather different than the situation we considered in Figure 2.6 and §2.3.2(c), the monopolist will employ exactly the same profit-maximizing logic as any other firm to set its price and output. To repeat the decision-making strategy we stated for competitive firms: *It is profitable to sell an additional unit wherever the marginal cost will be less than the added revenue from the sale*. The sole difference in this scenario is that the firm-specific demand curve now facing the firm is no longer horizontal—it is downward-sloping. Accordingly, the additional bit of income that the firm earns from additional sales—its marginal revenue—is not constant. It is a different amount with each unit sold. When the monopolist increases its output, that additional output affects the overall market price. This is different than the circumstance facing competitive firms. Because the firm-specific demand curve under competition is perfectly elastic (horizontal), no output choice by the firm can affect how much consumers are willing to pay. (Accordingly, the marginal revenue curve facing a firm in a competitive market is a horizontal line, and it is identical to that firm's firm-specific demand curve.)

So how does the profit-maximizing logic work when the firm faces a downward-sloping marginal revenue curve? If this were a competitive market, the firm would be forced to set price at p_c and would sell q_c units. (This is because it if the market were competitive, the demand curve depicted in Figure 2.8 would not be this firm's firm-specific demand curve, but rather would be the market demand curve; this firm's firm-specific demand curve would be a horizontal line cutting across the graph at point p_c.) But this all changes when it is one firm that is making all the sales—supplying all

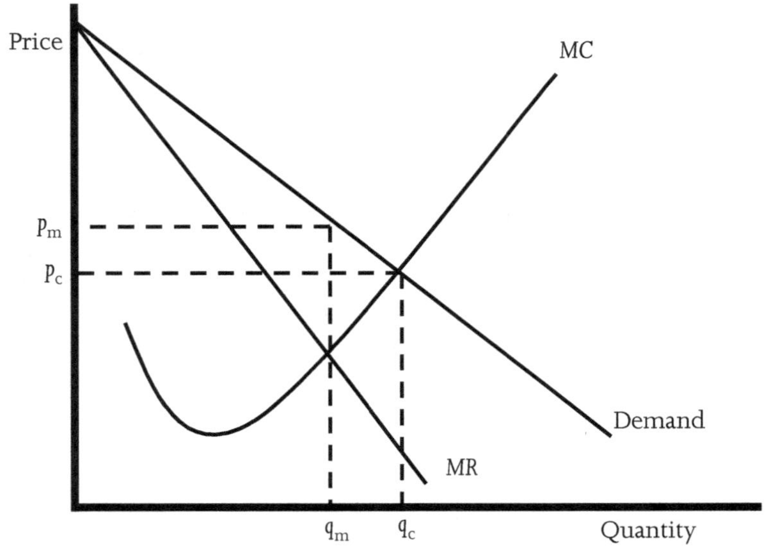

MC = marginal cost
MR = marginal revenue
p_m = monopoly price
p_c = competitive price
q_m = monopoly output
q_c = competitive output

Figure 2.8. Pricing and Output Decisions of Firm X Under Monopoly

the quantity demanded by all the consumers in the market. Notice that in Figure 2.8, at price p_c the marginal revenue that would be earned by the monopolist on the last unit would be substantially lower than the firm's marginal cost for that unit (given by MC at the point $p_c \times q_c$.). That is, sales are being made in this market that, individually, earn less money than they cost the firm to make. It is important to note that this does *not* mean that the monopoly would actually lose money *overall* at the competitive price. Indeed that would almost never be the case.[15] Rather, it means only that its sales *at the margin* cost more to make than the revenue they earn. Accordingly, the firm would then find it sensible to reduce its quantity. As the monopolist reduces output—moves the quantity produced leftward across the graph—the loss

15. The rare exception is the so-called "natural monopoly." A natural monopoly is a market in which fixed costs are so high that even if one firm has all the sales in the entire market it cannot reach a point of sufficient efficiency—a sufficiently low average total cost—that it can reach long-run profitability. It is generally thought that in such markets there is a need for government regulation to set prices; hence, we have long had regulated public utilities through much of the United States.

on individual sales gets smaller and smaller. The loss will eventually reach zero; that point is at p_m, where the marginal cost of the last sale is equal to the marginal revenue of that sale, or MC = MR. But, you might be thinking, why doesn't the monopolist then just keep moving quantity further left? Price would then get even higher, and marginal revenue would get *larger* than marginal cost. Again, it is simple. Remember, no rational firm's goal is to maximize the profitability of individual sales. *Every rational firm's goal is to maximize the total amount of its profit.* Any sale where the marginal revenue exceeds marginal cost—any point on the graph at which the MR curve is higher than the MC curve—is a sale that will add total profit. Accordingly, the monopolist prefers quantity to be set at q_m over any quantity to the left of that point.

But let us notice again that, as a matter of profit-maximizing logic, this does not actually distinguish competitive firms and monopolists at all. Technically, a firm's rational choice under all conditions, including perfect competition, is to set quantity so that MR = MC. In all situations, the profit-maximizing choice is MR = MC, even in perfect competition. This will seem surprising, because earlier we said that in perfect competition, P = MC. But again, this is because in perfect competition, in which the firm faces a horizontal firm-specific demand curve, the demand curve *is* the marginal revenue curve. Where the demand curve is horizontal, each additional unit sold always adds the same amount to revenue, and that amount is simply the price being charged. Therefore, in perfect competition, P = MC = MR. It might also seem surprising to describe this competitive outcome as "profit maximizing," since in long-run competitive equilibrium economic profit is zero. But remember, that result is still the best the firm in competition can do—any lower price loses money, and any higher price loses all sales.

This then leads to a powerful, fundamental conclusion of price theory: *All rational firms under all circumstances attempt to set MC = MR, and where they do the market will be in equilibrium.*

§2.3.4 Price as a Normative Argument: Calculating the Areas of Consumer Surplus, Producer Surplus, and Deadweight Loss

Now that we have completed our tour of the basic price-theory model of behavior within markets, we can consider one other use of price theory that has been influential in antitrust law. Price theory is not only a descriptive theory of market behavior, it is also a normative theory.

The basic normative commitment in price theory begins with the idea of "utility" or "welfare." These synonymous terms describe the good that

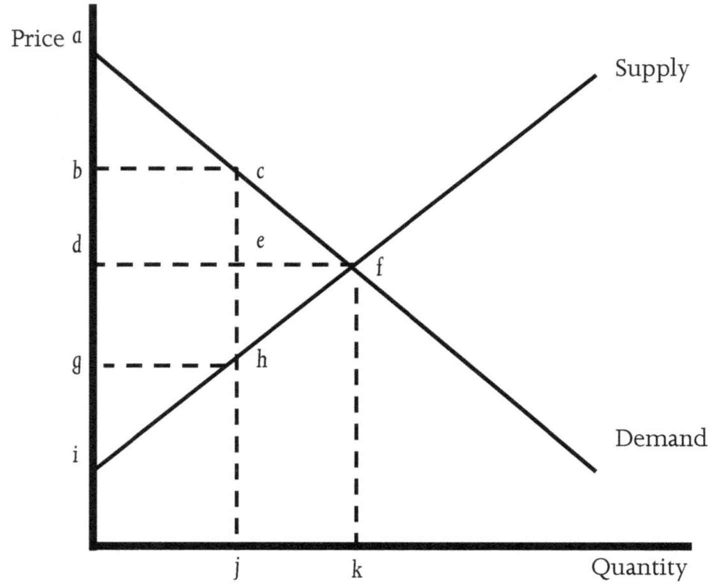

Figure 2.9. Welfare Analysis—Consumer and Producer Surplus Under Competition and Monopoly

you get out of having something. Say that I want to buy a new book that costs \$10. If I am willing to buy the book, that logically shows that the good that I experience from having the book is greater than the good that I experience from having \$10. If I am not willing to buy it at that price, then I must value my \$10 more than I would value having the book.[16]

The normative argument continues with another concept, which we first encountered in the Ground Rules in §2.2: **allocational efficiency**. Economists argue that *that policy is superior that gives people greater total utility*. That is, that policy is best that allocates resources in such a way that the most people have the most of what they want.

Working with these two commitments, it can be shown that under perfectly competitive conditions free-market competition produces the greatest possible allocational efficiency. We will consider a simple market graph, set out on Figure 2.9.

16. Let us note one important clarification, though one that is not technically relevant in antitrust law: However useful these concepts may be, we can only measure utility by measuring *willingness to pay*. If person *A* is willing to spend \$1 for a slice of pizza, but person B would be willing to spend \$2, economic theory presumes that B actually enjoys the pizza more. But this is not necessarily true, and indeed we can be sure it is true only if *A* and B have exactly the same number of dollars before purchasing the slice. It may be that *A* is willing to pay less only because he does not have as much money as B. This point is explored further in the discussion of the inequality of **distribution** in §2.4.

If this market behaves competitively, then output will be set at the point *k* and price will be set at the point *d*. But let us notice something about the demand and supply curves. As you move to the left of the competitive equilibrium point, which is at quantity *k*, notice that the demand curve goes up and the supply curve goes down. That means that there are some consumers that *would have* bought the good at more than the competitive price, and there are some producers that *would have* produced at less than the competitive price. In fact, *all consumers and producers except for those at the very margin would still have done business at some point to the left of the equilibrium point*. The producer and the consumer who are at the very margin—the consumer that would only buy the good at the competitive price or something less, and the producer that would only produce at the competitive price or something higher—are called the **marginal** consumer and producer. The consumers and producers that are to the left of the equilibrium point are called **inframarginal**.

The reason this matters is that every inframarginal participant in a market gets more benefit from participating than the marginal participants do, and so to estimate the true social value of this market, we have to sum up all of that additional benefit. The added benefit to an inframarginal consumer is that he or she would have been willing to buy the good for more than the competitive price, but because the competitive price is all one must pay, that consumer gets to keep that amount of money and spend it on something else. An inframarginal producer gets a similar benefit, because it would have been willing to sell for less than it actually gets at the competitive price.

For example, consider the consumer that would have been willing to buy the good at price *b*. That consumer gets the good and gets some utility from having it. But that consumer also gets to keep the extra money that he or she would have been willing to spend on the good and can spend that money on something else. That amount happens to be measured precisely by the line between points *c* and *e*. Likewise, the producer that would have been willing to sell even if price had gone down all the way to *g* gets to sell at the competitive price. That extra revenue is measured exactly by the line between points *h* and *e*.

The word for the added benefit is **surplus**. Inframarginal consumers enjoy **consumer surplus**, and the entire amount of consumer surplus that all consumers in the market will enjoy can be measured by calculating the area in the triangle *a-d-f*. Inframarginal producers enjoy **producer surplus**, and the entire amount of that value is the triangle *d-f-i*.

Now imagine what happens if the entire market is captured by a monopolist. We will assume that the quantity at which the monopolist's *MC* = *MR*—the point at which it maximizes its profits, as explained in §2.3.3—is at quantity *j*. That causes price to go up to *b*. Only consumers who would have been willing to pay *b* or higher will be able to get the good. And, because they must now actually pay the higher price *b*, they lose all the consumer surplus in the area below the line between the points *b* and *c*. That is, the added profits that the monopolist gets by raising its price up to *b* is simply a confiscation of what had been consumer surplus. In this case the amount of surplus the monopolist captures is represented by the rectangle *b-c-d-e*.

But that is not the only consequence. The reduction in output from *k* to *j* means that there are some sales that won't occur, and therefore that there is some surplus that no consumer or producer will enjoy. The loss of this surplus is known as **deadweight loss**, and here, the amount of the deadweight loss is the area in the triangle *c-h-f*. Deadweight loss is not just a transfer — it is not just a change in how much individual participants benefit from trade. It is an actual *loss* to society. When the monopolist confiscates consumer surplus, at least somebody in society is still getting the benefit of economic activity — some participant earns a surplus from buying and selling. In fact, according to many economists, society should really be indifferent to transfers of surplus between consumers and producers. They are just a wash, the argument goes, from the social perspective. But deadweight loss is truly a loss. It represents economic value that could have been enjoyed under competition that is now lost to anyone.

Given that, you might wonder why the monopolist would bother. The reason is that while deadweight loss may be a loss to *society*, the monopolist's portion of that loss will ordinarily be dwarfed by the amount of consumer surplus that it is able to confiscate by raising its prices. It will be more than the amount of deadweight loss that constitutes the monopolist's lost *producer* surplus, which here is the triangle *e-f-h*.

§2.4 FINALLY, A DOSE OF REALISM, AND SOME IMPORTANT LIMITATIONS OF PRICE THEORY

Whatever usefulness there might be in the model of perfect competition, we should remember that it is strictly a theoretical exercise. Opinions vary over how much it matters that the model is artificial, but there are at least a few important points that an antitrust student should understand, as this section will explain.

Most people involved in antitrust find at least some diagnostic value in a model that can approximate how real-world markets would work if they were working ideally. In particular, it helps to know which features a market would need to operate that way — low-cost information and fungibility, for example. But few doubt that its artificiality must also be borne in mind, or that expecting real-world markets to follow it very closely would be misleading at best. To some, the model's unrealistic nature renders it very unreliable indeed.

The points that antitrust students should understand are at least two.

First, there are important respects in which no real-world firm behaves as predicted by the theory, and their failure to do so does not prove that their markets are not competitive. Most importantly, within the economic model, it is axiomatic that firms in competition price at marginal cost, and earn zero economic profit. In real-world practice, no firm would do this even if it were possible. For one thing, the economist's concept of "marginal cost," while it is definitely a real phenomenon, is useful only as a concept, because it cannot really be measured directly. Accordingly, no real-world firm is typically certain what its own marginal costs even are, much less does any firm deliberately set prices equal to them. In part the problem is just an accounting difficulty. The data are rich, changing, and pose measurement problems. Moreover, most firms produce more than one product, and it is hard to know how much of a firm's overall costs—for bookkeeping, legal services, the CEO's salary, and so on—should be allocated to the marginal cost of any one of them. Separately, real-world firms have very strong incentives to inflate prices over economic cost, and usually find it fairly easy to do so. As a matter of fact, pricing at economic cost is a desperate situation. A firm at sustained zero economic profit is balanced on a razor-thin dividing line between survival and failure. Moreover, any market that operates at zero economic profit in the long-term will pose a serious problem if fixed costs are at all sizeable—marginal cost pricing will fail to recoup them. But as it happens, even in fairly competitive conditions, firms can usually generate at least a little economic profit just by modest product differentiation though product design, intellectual property, or advertising.

And so, in practice, firms don't even try to price at marginal cost, and long-run prices rarely if ever dip that low. Firms follow heuristic rules of thumb to set their prices, which generally consist of some standard, essentially arbitrary markup over an ongoing estimate of accounting cost. That price will routinely generate some cushion of economic profit, even if conditions are quite competitive.[17]

A second important consequence of the model's artificial nature is that it is incapable of accommodating certain values in policymaking. At least two such value problems are substantial and should be understood by antitrust students. Neither of these actually plays much direct role in particular antitrust disputes. Under current law, it would be a rare litigated antitrust matter in which either plaintiff or defendant would raise an argument that the case could generate an externality or a distributional problem. The point of understanding these problems is instead that we cannot simply take the

17. *See generally* Russel Pittman, U.S. Dept. of Justice, *Who Are You Calling Irrational? Marginal Costs, Variable Costs, and the Pricing Practices of Firms* (EAG Discussion Paper 09-3, 2009), available at https://www.justice.gov/sites/default/files/atr/legacy/2009/07/27/248394.pdf.

simple model, with all its apparent confidence and breadth, as actually capturing all values in real-world policymaking.

First, many real-world markets exhibit **externalities.** An externality occurs when the parties to some transaction generate either costs or benefits that are experienced by third parties, but that the parties themselves don't internalize. The problem is that if the parties to the transaction don't personally care about some benefit or cost, then persons in society will have interest in the transaction that won't be reflected in the parties' output decisions. From society's perspective, the parties will engage in the transaction either too much or too little, because society actually cares about the benefits or costs to third parties. The effect is that the market for that transaction will not, on its own, optimize **allocational efficiency**.

A classic example is pollution. Imagine that a steel factory produces harmful air pollution, which impacts residents who live nearby and those who care about environmental conservation. Pollution control technology could mitigate the harm, but it would cost $1 million. Imagine that the steel manufacturer's customer is an auto maker. Neither of them personally bears the full cost of the pollution, because its effects are felt by nearby residents and environmentalists. In fact, neither of them may care at all. So when they negotiate the price of the steel, they won't consider the costs of the transaction that are imposed on others. They will consider only the steelmaker's costs of production, and so the revenue they generate likely wouldn't be enough to pay for the pollution control technology. If the price did in fact reflect the costs felt by third parties, the price would be higher, and the automaker would buy less steel (and therefore, the plant would have lower output and would generate less pollution). You might wonder whether the third parties who experience the pollution could themselves pay for the pollution control technology, but that raises problems of its own. Usually, the problem is that it is hard to get groups of people to work collectively to pay for the cost of some problem, when each of them individually only experiences a small part of the cost.

Pollution is an example of a *negative* externality, because third parties experience a cost that the buyer and seller don't themselves internalize. But externalities can also be positive, in that third parties might enjoy a benefit from some transaction. When that is the case, and the parties to the transaction themselves don't actually enjoy all the benefits that their deals generate, they will tend to engage in too little of the transaction. Examples might include creative works that third parties can take advantage of without paying the creator. Authors of books, for example, might generate value to third parties who borrow books from readers who initially bought them. If the value those third parties get from borrowed books could be captured in some way by authors, then perhaps the authors would produce more books.

Externalities in fact can seem omnipresent in real-world policymaking. Opinions will vary, but to some it will seem that situations are common in which transactions generate costs or benefits for society that markets themselves just can't really take into account. When they do, it seems like an unregulated market may not be the optimal allocator of resources after all.

The second real-world policymaking value that price theory cannot capture is **distributional inequality**. That is, it has no concern for whether individuals are rich or poor or how fairly wealth and income are shared. In fact, price theory systematically privileges the interests of the wealthy, because of a problem known as the decreasing marginal utility of money. Money is like all other goods—the more you have, the less you value any individual unit of it. A wealthy person cares much less about each individual dollar than does a poor person. So, we say that as one gains more dollars, the value one gets from each additional dollar—its marginal utility—decreases. The problem is that when price theory makes its normative arguments—when it argues that a market works better the more that each person gets more of what they want—it cannot directly measure how much subjective benefit each individual person gets from having some good. There is in fact no way to measure such things, or to compare actual utility between persons. The theory's only objective alternative is to ask how much a given person is willing to give in exchange for a good. If one person will give $10 for some good, while another person would give $100, the theory takes it for granted that the second person gets ten times as much utility from it. But that is in fact untrue unless every person has exactly the same number of dollars. The rich person very possibly might pay ten times as much for something than a poor person, but value it less, because the rich person also values his dollars less.

At present, at least, there is no good solution for this problem except to remember that it is a problem. In real-world policymaking, it is not a complete answer to say that a given policy maximizes allocational efficiency, if it also happens to involve unfair distribution.

CHAPTER 3

Part Two of the Two-Part Strategy

Economic Generalizations That Pervade Modern Antitrust

The second part of this book's two-part strategy for explaining antitrust economics is to supplement the basic price theory of Chapter 2 with a set of broad economic generalizations. The courts use each of them in handling antitrust cases, and they pervade the law. Together they go a long way to explaining the modern cases. While the collection of them here might seem a bit miscellaneous, to some degree they are all just manifestations of one central idea, and that idea is what antitrust is now all about: Antitrust does the best it can to preserve conditions for price and quality competition, as those goals are understood in contemporary economic theory. Therefore, it aims to prohibit conduct that could harm competition. It sometimes must compromise in the accuracy it can hope to achieve in its pursuit of these goals, and some of the generalizations go to making those compromises.

The several generalizations are as follows:

1. (a) The central purpose of antitrust law as it now exists is "efficiency," but that word can be confusing. Fortunately, it has a clear meaning in antitrust, but it is usually used without clarification and sometimes in ways that are misleading or inaccurate. Courts and commentators often say that "efficiency" means lower prices and higher output for the benefit of consumers. That is not a terrible rule of thumb, and in most litigated matters it captures the gravamen of the plaintiff's complaint and the law's purpose under the given facts. But there are also cases—especially those where injury is caused by a powerful buyer or occurs at some upstream point in a chain of distribution—in which it is wrong.

   (b) Although it is often said that antitrust protects "consumers" and serves "consumer welfare," the law protects both sellers and buyers, and every other participant in a given market. By and large the analysis of harms to suppliers and other participants is just the same as analysis of harm to downstream consumers. Recognizing this, courts and commentators have begun to shed their use of the misleading traditional phrase "consumer welfare," and say instead that antitrust protects "trading partner" welfare or surplus.
   (c) Within this area of general agreement one technical issue remains. This goal of "efficiency" for the protection of market participants could serve either to *protect trading partners* or to maximize *overall efficiency* (also known as "allocational efficiency," as discussed in Chapter 2). Ordinarily the results reached under the two approaches are the same, but not always. As it happens, there is now broad agreement that in those cases in which the two standards would lead to different results, trading partner protection is to be preferred.
   (d) As mentioned, antitrust must sometimes compromise in its handling of economic facts, because trying to measure them precisely would be too costly and time-consuming. One traditional compromise concerns the handling of efficiencies. Under the "out-of-market efficiencies" rule, a procompetitive benefit alleged in defense of some conduct cannot be raised unless it arises in the same market in which the harm is caused.
2. Antitrust protects "competition on the merits," which is to say that it protects conditions conducive to price or quality competition. The consequence is that there are some sorts of injuries that are not redressable, and some kinds of conduct that are not illegal though they might harm someone. As we shall see, this important idea has several manifestations in current antitrust:
   (a) Antitrust protects competition, not competitors;
   (b) "Social" justifications are not relevant as defenses in antitrust; and
   (c) Antitrust is (almost) always agnostic about actual prices.
3. Finally, there is one special gap in the coverage of our antitrust law that is currently explained by an economic argument. The argument is that collusion is more dangerous than unilateral conduct. The reason this has led to a gap in antitrust is that there is some conduct that most observers acknowledge to be anticompetitive that is nevertheless not illegal. If the conduct is unilateral, even if it leads to higher prices or reduced output, it cannot violate Sherman Act §1, and it will not violate §2 unless the defendant has quite a large amount of market power.

§3.1 THE BASIC PURPOSE OF ANTITRUST: THE MEANING OF "EFFICIENCY"

§3.1.1 "Efficiency," Its Meaning in Contemporary Antitrust, and the Confusing Side-Debate of "Consumer" Welfare

It is now more or less agreed—and so far as the courts are concerned it is the law—that antitrust serves the economic goal of "efficiency."[1] There have been times when it was thought to serve other goals, some of which we tend not to think of as economic.[2] To the extent that those values were once explicitly recognized in the law, like preservation of small business for its own sake, protection of individual liberty, or constraint on the political power of concentrated capital, they are now severely muted if not entirely absent.

If courts agree that "efficiency" is the goal, however, some uncertainty persists. Participants in antitrust affairs use the word constantly, but sometimes they use it pretty loosely and rarely do they explicitly define it. It can cause confusion, and people sometimes use it to mean different things. That is a problem, because in some cases choosing one meaning or the other could affect the outcomes of real disputes.

The following summarizes this important, pervasive, and sometimes controversial issue. The notion of efficiency that now runs through most of antitrust requires that any "efficiency" that is relevant must generate some cost saving or quality improvement, it must be generated in the same market in which the challenged conduct causes harm, and it must benefit participants in the challenged transactions.

1. *Cf. Reiter v. Sonotone Corp.*, 442 U.S. 330, 343 (1979) (identifying the goal as "consumer welfare," as used in Bork's sense, which entails the microeconomic concept of allocational efficiency).

2. This is misleading to some degree. The purpose was always "economic" in some broad sense, because it was always believed that overall prosperity would be served best by whatever particular goal antitrust was thought to serve at a given time. But to modern eyes, the goals served at different points in history can seem more political than economic. Important goals once served include preserving the individual liberty of consumers and small producers, and opposition to large firms for the threat they pose to political institutions. *See generally* Herbert Hovenkamp, *Enterprise and American Law, 1836-1937* (1991); Eleanor M. Fox, *The Politics of Law and Economics in Judicial Decision Making: Antitrust as a Window*, 61 N.Y.U. L. Rev. 554, 563-565 (1986) (recounting changing political motivations in antitrust); David Millon, *The Sherman Act and the Balance of Power*, 61 S. Cal. L. Rev. 1219, 1287-1292 (1988) (summarizing comprehensive historical review, the root consequence of which was that "Congress in 1890 was concerned about power, not efficiency."); Robert Pitofsky, *The Political Content of Antitrust*, 127 U. Pa. L. Rev. 1051 (1979).

§3.1.1(a) Efficiency in General

For what it may be worth, courts now almost always mean one thing when they say that antitrust aims to improve "efficiency." They mean that within a given market the law protects the competitive output and price. So, for example, we think naked price fixing is inefficient because the conspirators seek to produce less and charge more than would occur under unrestrained competition. On the other hand, defendants often argue that challenged conduct will improve efficiency, and those defenses are entertained only if they explain how defendants might produce their goods more cheaply or in some superior way.

Competitive price and output are goals of antitrust because we think competitive markets produce the best social results. Those results are the outcome that is meant by the term "efficiency." As explained in Chapter 2, the means by which markets produce them is through the process of price competition. Wherever one firm can figure out a way to sell a product at a lower price than another, then it should do so, and everyone benefits (even the competitors, so long as they can manage to keep their costs down to those prevailing in the market, because they will continue to cover economic costs, including a competitive return on investment).

Sometimes this can be confusing, because courts characterize some other things as aspects of "efficiency" or as important goals in antitrust, like improved product quality, safety, or variety. *See, e.g., Ohio v. American Express Co.*, 585 U.S. 529, 549-50 (2018) (finding that challenged restraint was procompetitive because, in addition to increasing output, it increased quality); *United States v. Continental Can Co.*, 378 U.S. 441, 455-456 (1964) (holding that quality competition, as well as price competition, is important in antitrust). But that simply reflects the fact that "price" competition in reality is not usually competition exclusively over price. Two products may be close substitutes for one another and therefore exert price-competitive pressure on one another's prices, and yet compete on quality as well. In other words, the ideal condition of fungibility that is assumed to characterize perfect competition is neither fully realized in practice nor very desirable to most of us. For example, you might be considering the purchase of a new car and are torn between two models that are very similar. They are each compact, fuel-efficient, four-door sedans. One of them is a fair bit more expensive than the other, but it also has a better reputation for quality, durability, and resale value. Plainly these two products compete for your attention on grounds other than literal price—the lower-priced car is not a slam dunk just because it costs less. But this doesn't mean they compete in some way fundamentally different from the price competition described in economic theory. It is the same sort of competition and it works in the same way. The only difference is that where products are not perfectly fungible, consumers must compare them on the basis of which combination of price and quality attributes gives the consumer more for the purchase price. Economists refer to this phenomenon as "quality-adjusted price competition." In real-world markets, price competition almost always means competition between products that each represent differing combinations of price and quality.

And so, one might hear courts describe restraints as harming or improving "efficiency," even though the concern may seem to involve quality or other superficially non-price aspects. But remember that the mix of price and quality attributes in real-world products can always be understood as part of the same, essentially price-competitive process.

In any case, for all these reasons, when improvement of "efficiency" matters in a given antitrust case, the efficiency in question must actually improve a competitor's ability to produce a better product or produce it more cheaply. As a practical matter, that requires that the benefit will in fact be passed on to their trading partner. So, for example, if a rule-of-reason case under Sherman Act §1 reaches the point of balancing the harms and benefits of some challenged restraint (*see* §7.1), the defendant can rebut the plaintiff's evidence of anticompetitive harm only by showing that its conduct would somehow allow it to improve its products or reduce its prices. Likewise, in principle, efficiency gains can be raised in defense of an anticompetitive merger, but only if they generate costs savings or quality improvements that will be passed on to the same trading partner threatened by the merger's anticompetitive potential (*see* §17.8).

§3.1.1(b) Antitrust Protects All Trading Partners: The Side-Debate over "Consumer" Welfare

One confusing challenge in recent years has concerned polemics over a particular phrase often used in antitrust to refer to efficiency: *consumer welfare*. A reform movement of the past decade or so sought to strengthen antitrust enforcement and claimed that an important way to do it would be to reject consumer welfare as a goal. It would be replaced with some purportedly more traditional goal.[3] That reform movement itself was controversial, and disagreement on the issue was sharp. This book is not the place for taking sides on it, and you are very welcome to feel about it as you choose. The only point here will be to explain the conflict simply to help avoid the confusion it can cause. As it happens, the critique of the term "consumer welfare" turns out to be probably overstated and to some degree mistaken, no matter what your point of view might be, and a point to be made here is to explain why. In any event, partly to avoid further confusion and controversy around the term, many courts and commentators appear to be dispensing with it. Though no substantive change follows from the different

---

3. You may be familiar with a particular law journal article on this subject, because it enjoyed

terminology, it may be less confusing now that, instead of saying "consumer surplus" or "consumer welfare," folks are saying "trading partner surplus" or "trading partner welfare."

Both the conservative advocates of the 1960s and 1970s and their later critics bear blame for the confusion. Robert Bork himself introduced the problem. In attacking what he believed were illicit goals in the antitrust caselaw of his time, he described his revised goal by the phrase "consumer welfare." But his use of it was misleading at best. Some critics allege he deliberately chose it to make his quite conservative re-design of the law more politically palatable, at a time when popular opinion was favorable to consumer and small-business interests.[4] What he actually advocated, in the terms ordinarily used by economists, was that antitrust should serve *total* welfare—it should seek to maximize the combined welfare of both sellers and buyers in any given transaction. As explained in §3.1.1(c), that means that antitrust should make conduct illegal only where its *net* welfare effect is negative. If the gain to producers from some trade restraint outweighs the harm to consumers, it could still be legal.

Moreover, advocates of the conservative revolution had a strong tendency to speak of their "consumer welfare" ideal in ways that cause further confusion. Bork and all who followed his views refer routinely to the goals of antitrust being *lower* prices and *higher* output. Oftentimes that accurately describes the law's aims in individual cases, but it is not always the case at all, and it is precisely the opposite where monopoly power is exploited by a *buyer*. Where a buyer is a monopsonist, the harm they will cause with market power is to pay *lower* prices or force expanded output.

But that said, Bork's modern critics also bear some blame for adding to confusion. Their key frustration seems to have been driven by something that neither Bork nor other serious conservatives actually said. Admittedly, some advocates of the conservative antitrust revolution tended to speak quite loosely, and they may be to blame for having contributed to the misunderstanding. But the key frustration of the modern critics seems to be that conservative antitrust only served the interests of *retail, end-use consumers*. Admittedly, if antitrust really served only to protect low prices for end-use consumers, important categories of anticompetitive activity would be very difficult to challenge or perhaps beyond the law's reach entirely. For

---

a generally historic career in the popular media: Lina M. Khan, Note, *Amazon's Antitrust Paradox*, 126 Yale L.J. 710 (2017). The paper originated the critique of "consumer welfare" that would drive the reform movement mentioned in the text. If any other law student paper in history has ever been featured in the *New York Times*, there've surely been very few of them, and over its remarkable career this paper has been cited in the popular and academic press tens of thousands of times. During the Biden administration, Ms. Khan would serve as among the youngest Chairs of the Federal Trade Commission in its history and she is now a professor of law at Columbia University.

4. *See, e.g.*, Lande, *supra* note 2.

example, a big firm, like a powerful retailer or an agribusiness that buys from small farmers, might use its power to force low prices on its workers or suppliers, without any visible effect downstream.

The problem is that to attack "consumer welfare" and define it as a preoccupation with end-use buyers confuses what even Bork advocated, and it does not capture rules as they have existed for many decades and up until the present time. The law in fact does apply to market power abuses against labor, small suppliers, and other non-consumer parties. In such cases the law requires no proof of harm to downstream consumers.[5] And indeed, the total welfare standard that Bork favored and that is widely shared by economists would generally support such rules.

Moreover, in fairness, neither Bork's total welfare standard, nor other models of economic "efficiency," nor current antitrust rules would protect labor, small business, or other less powerful groups from *competition*, in the form of price rivalry. That may be the real basis of the new movement's concern. If competition is defined only as price competition (or even quality-adjusted price competition), it may systematically advantage larger firms. It might also favor an organization of society that limits individuals' entrepreneurial freedom and jeopardizes some social values, like local communities and Main Street businesses, the creation of art or rarified intellectual endeavors, or other matters that can be difficult to make commercially viable.

That critique seems important, and thinking through the underlying conflicts is important for any serious student of antitrust. The deep value judgments and empirical uncertainties at stake are really beyond this book, which mainly aims at a neutral statement of existing law.[6] Suffice to say that, for better or worse, the protection of small business, labor, or other concerns *against* price competition is emphatically not possible under current law. That theme is explored in §3.2.1.

§3.1.1(c) The Traditional Bork-Lande Controversy: Total Welfare vs. Coerced Welfare Transfers

Even if the law is coalescing around the consensus of "trading partner welfare," there are few different things that it might mean. It might mean either (1) that antitrust is meant to maximize total allocational efficiency, as explained in §2.3.4, which is the central normative goal usually stated in economic theory, or (2) that antitrust is meant to protect weaker trading partners, even though it may sometimes be at the expense of allocational efficiency. Ordinarily the two approaches will not differ from one another. Most conduct that could cause prices to go up—and therefore transfer a

5. *See generally* Natalie Rosenfelt, *The Verdict on Monopsony*, 20 Loy. Consumer L. Rev. 402 (2008).
6. For readers interested in more, I explore these themes in Chris Sagers, *United States v. Apple: Competition in America* (2019).

weaker partner's wealth—will cause output to fall, resulting in a deadweight loss and reduced allocational efficiency. (*See* §2.3.4.) But, as we shall see, the two goals sometimes do lead to different results.

At present that particular debate appears to have settled down, and the consensus view has come to be that antitrust is meant to prevent *wealth transfer from weaker trading partners*. The change in view began with a widely cited 1982 article by Professor Robert Lande,[7] and it appears to have become the mainstream view.[8] Lande's work has been taken by most to have undermined the argument famously made by Robert Bork, that the legislative history of the Sherman Act disclosed an intent to preserve total allocational efficiency.[9]

Ordinarily the results will be the same under either standard, but not always. There are some cases in which overall allocational efficiency might be unchanged or even increased by conduct that also confiscates consumer wealth. Notably, there are some arrangements that might both increase market power and produce cost savings. For example, suppose that two head-to-head competitors merge. Their merger might give them market power. If they raise their prices, that will cause a loss of some output and therefore a deadweight loss—a loss of consumer *and* producer surplus that is not just a wash—and it is a loss to society. To that extent the merger would be objectionable even from the overall efficiency perspective. However, the merged firm might also be a more efficient producer as a result of the merger, and therefore have lower costs. The savings it enjoys from lower costs would be an overall efficiency *gain* to society, even if none of the savings are passed on to consumers through lower prices. If that gain is larger than the deadweight loss, the overall efficiency view would permit the merger even though consumers lost as a consequence. The trading-partner protection view would not.[10]

The same could be true of many other arrangements that might generate both pricing power and cost savings, like production or research joint ventures. Likewise, "price discrimination" can have the effect of transferring wealth from consumers while not affecting output, and therefore it need not reduce allocational efficiency. (*See* Chapter 16.)

---

7. Robert H. Lande, *Wealth Transfers as the Original and Primary Concern of Antitrust: The Efficiency Interpretation Challenged*, 34 Hastings L.J. 65 (1982).

8. Notably, it was recently endorsed by a Republican office-holder, in sharp contrast from his party's traditional commitments. Mark R. Meador, Comm'r, F.T.C., *Antitrust Policy for the Conservative* 13-18 (May 1, 2025). For some time it has been conceded by academics of varying ideologies to be the consensus. *See, e.g.*, Lawrence A. Sullivan & Warren S. Grimes, *The Law of Antitrust: An Integrated Handbook* 116 & n.20 (2d ed. 2006); Aaron S. Edlin, *Stopping Above-Cost Predatory Pricing*, 111 Yale L.J. 941, 947 & n.24 (2002); Einer Elhauge, *Tying, Bundled Discounts, and the Death of the Single Monopoly Profit Theory*, 123 Harv. L. Rev. 397, 435-439 (2009); Daniel J. Gifford & Robert T. Kudrle, *The Law and Economics of Price Discrimination in Modern Economies: Time for Reconciliation?* 43 U.C. Davis L. Rev. 1235, 1240-1241 & n.21 (2010).

9. *See generally* Robert Bork, *The Antitrust Paradox: A Policy at War With Itself* ch. 2 (1978).

10. This point is explained in Lande, *supra* note 2, at 142-150.

In any event, as one consequence of the law's concern with coerced welfare transfers, pro-competitive benefits that are alleged in defense of challenged conduct generally cannot be raised unless those benefits will be passed on to the trading partners who've been injured. For example, say that a merger creates both market power and some productive efficiencies. In principle, those efficiencies are relevant to judging the merger's legality, but they will be legally relevant only if it can be shown that they will be passed on to the merged firm's trading partners in the form of improved prices. *See* FTC & U.S. Dep't of Justice, *Merger Guidelines* §3.3 (2023).

§3.1.1(d) The Out-of-Market Efficiencies Rule

One issue concerning the handling of efficiencies in antitrust requires a compromise as to which ones are allowed to matter. For better or worse, courts in litigation cannot consider *all* efficiency consequences of a defendant's conduct, and they don't try.

At least as the law has traditionally been understood, efficiency gains relevant in an antitrust dispute must not only represent cost or quality improvements passed on to weaker trading partners (*see* §3.1.1(c)), but they must occur in the same market as any injury caused. This is often known as the "out-of-market efficiencies" rule.

The rule was traditionally founded on two main authorities. First, in the merger decision *United States v. Philadelphia National Bank*, 374 U.S. 321 (1963), the Court found a horizontal merger of two Philadelphia banks to be illegal. The Court rejected two arguments that the merger, even if it caused harms in local banking markets, should be saved by benefits it provided elsewhere. First, defendants argued that by strengthening their position in Philadelphia (where the merger might cause anticompetitive harm to local borrowers or depositors), they would be better able to compete against bigger banks in other cities. The Court found that point irrelevant, writing that:

> [i]f anticompetitive effects in one market could be justified by procompetitive consequences in another, the logical upshot would be that every firm in an industry could, without violating §7, embark on a series of mergers that would make it in the end as large as the industry leader. For if all the commercial banks in the Philadelphia area merged into one, it would be smaller than the largest bank in New York City. This is not a case, plainly, where two small firms in a market propose to merge in order to be able to compete more successfully with the leading firms in that market.

Id. at 370-371. Second, the Court rejected the idea that having a bigger bank would be beneficial to the city of Philadelphia, even if it injured some banking customers, because a bigger bank would "bring business to the area and stimulate its economic development." The Court said that:

> a merger the effect of which "may be substantially to lessen competition" [in violation of §7] is not saved because, on some ultimate reckoning of social or economic debits and credits, it may be deemed beneficial. A value choice of such magnitude is beyond the ordinary limits of judicial competence, and in any event has been made for us already, by Congress when it enacted the amended §7. Congress determined to preserve our traditionally competitive economy. It therefore proscribed anticompetitive mergers, the benign and the malignant alike, fully aware, we must assume, that some price might have to be paid.

Id. at 371.

Second, *United States v. Topco Associates, Inc.*, 405 U.S. 596 (1972), involved a cooperative among several small grocery chains that produced private-label food products. At issue was a rule in the cooperative agreement giving each member exclusive territory in which only it could sell the cooperative's products. The Court held that rule to be a per se illegal market allocation. The member grocery chains argued that they were individually too small to produce their own in-house products, and that they needed them to compete effectively with the private label products that major grocery chains produced. They claimed they needed exclusive territories for these products so that they could develop their own brand identities as grocers—to compete with national chains, they needed store-brand products of their own that only they could sell in a given territory. In other words, they needed to end a certain kind of competition among themselves to improve their ability to provide a different kind of competition against bigger competitors. The Court was unmoved, writing that competition "cannot be foreclosed with respect to one sector of the economy because certain private citizens or groups believe that such foreclosure might promote greater competition in a more important sector of the economy." Rather, "[i]f a decision is to be made to sacrifice competition in one portion of the economy for greater competition in another portion, this . . . is a decision that must be made by Congress and not by private forces or by the courts. *Id.* at 610-611.

The rule has faced some academic criticism, and it is arguably jeopardized by *Ohio v. American Express Co.*, 585 U.S. 529 (2018). The Court there recognized a certain specialized kind of market, described by the Court as a "simultaneous transaction platform," in which some product is jointly consumed by more than one consumer. *American Express* itself concerned credit card transactions, in which a jointly demanded product—a card swipe, representing a payment processing service to support one consumer purchase—is simultaneously consumed by both the cardholder and the merchant that accepts the card. (For further discussion *see* §4.2.5.)

Importantly, the Court held that harms caused to one side of a two-sided platform—say, the merchants—could not be judged in isolation from benefits that might accrue to the other side—the cardholders. While *American Express* may ultimately remain a specialized decision narrowed to its factual context, it is perhaps some support for the idea that harms can be balanced against benefits enjoyed by persons other than those who suffer harm.

When the issue has been raised in the most recent litigation, courts have found ways to avoid it, and whether the rule will be preserved is not clear. *See, e.g., Epic Games, Inc. v. Apple, Inc.*, 67 F.4th 9469, 989 (9th Cir. 2023); *United States v. Google LLC*, 747 F. Supp. 3d 1, 175 (D.D.C. 2024). It retains support among some academics and some surprising political quarters. *See* Meador, *supra* note [CROSS REF], at 27.

§3.2 WHAT ANTITRUST REALLY CARES ABOUT NOW: "COMPETITION ON THE MERITS"

If efficiency is the goal, courts often say that antitrust serves it by requiring *competition on the merits*. That is, its purpose is to ensure as much as possible that the only way firms can get ahead is to make a better product or make it more cheaply.

This idea finds expression in at least three major doctrines that run throughout antitrust: (1) Antitrust does not protect competitors themselves, for their own sake; (2) "social justifications" for otherwise anticompetitive conduct are not relevant—the only relevant justifications are those that show how the challenged conduct actually improves competition on the merits; and (3) antitrust is agnostic about actual prices—prices charged are almost never in themselves illegal.

§3.2.1 Antitrust Protects Competition, Not Competitors

In often cited language, the Court in *Brown Shoe Co. v. United States*, 370 U.S. 294 (1962), wrote that Congress's "concern [was] with the protection of competition, not competitors, and its desire [was] to restrain [conduct] only to the extent that [it] may tend to lessen competition." *Id.* at 320. Thus, antitrust will not afford a remedy where the only injury claimed is to a competitor, and it will not have an effect on price or output. In practice, this circumstance almost always occurs where the injury alleged is really just a consequence of price competition itself. After all, competition is a rough affair and less efficient firms will be forced out of business. That surely is a harm to such firms in some sense, but not one with which antitrust is concerned. (Indeed, the exclusion of less efficient firms through price competition is seen as a *good* thing.)

The idea manifests itself in a variety of ways. Most obviously, private antitrust plaintiffs are required to show that the conduct they challenge caused them "antitrust injury." They must show not only that they suffered some injury but that the injury was of a kind that the antitrust laws seek to prohibit. Again, it cannot be just the ordinary hardship imposed on firms by price competition itself; it must be a harm that will keep firms from forcing down prices or decreasing output. This issue is explored at length in §19.1.1. But the idea appears in substantive rules as well. It played a role in the Supreme Court's decision to make unilateral conduct substantially harder to challenge than multilateral conduct, in that the Court thought that unilateral conduct that harmed a competitor was most likely to be just desirable competition on the merits. *See Copperweld Corp. v. Independence Tube Corp.*, 467 U.S. 752, 767-768 (1984). It is the reason the Court has made it very difficult for plaintiffs to show monopolization through "predatory pricing"—drastically low pricing intended to kill off entrants or existing competitors that constrain the monopolist's pricing discretion long-term. In the Court's view, such conduct will be very difficult to distinguish from plain old vigorous price competition, and so to make it illegal might often just shield competitors from the very forces that antitrust is supposed to preserve. *Brooke Group Ltd. v. Brown & Williamson Tobacco Corp.*, 509 U.S. 209 (1993). And it now drives much of the Court's thinking on vertical restraints. The Court is of the view that the only harm likely from most vertical restraints will be harm to distributors or retailers excluded by the restraints. Because the Court believes that that exclusion will ordinarily not harm consumers, it treats that harm as outside the protection of antitrust. *See Leegin Creative Leather Prods., Inc. v. PSKS, Inc.*, 551 U.S. 877, 906 (2007). (Vertical restraints and the economics of vertical relationships are discussed more fully in Chapter 10 and in the appendix.)

Example

Bob's Hardware is a local home improvement store that had been locked in stiff price competition with another local business called Gene's DIY. The proprietor of Bob's Hardware, one Bob, won this battle when Gene's was forced into bankruptcy. Bob raised his prices a bit, enjoying a little freedom now that competition had abated. But after a calm two months or so since Gene's insolvency, Bob was horrified to learn that Gene's DIY, along with all its inventory, was purchased out of bankruptcy by a nationwide home improvement superstore. Bob believes the acquisition of Gene's DIY was a merger in violation of Clayton Act §7. He sues, arguing primarily that the superstore will be able to use its significant cost advantages to drive Bob out of business, thereby reducing competition.

What result?

Explanation

Bob will probably lose. The injury he complains of—that he will be driven out of business—is an injury that results from competition, not from anticompetitive restraints on competition. If it is true that the superstore will be able to defeat him through "cost advantages," that implies that by being a producer of superior efficiency, it will be a more effective competitor on a price basis.

These are the essential facts of *Cargill, Inc. v. Monfort of Colorado, Inc.*, 479 U.S. 104 (1986) and *Brunswick Corp. v. Pueblo Bowl-O-Mat, Inc.*, 429 U.S. 477 (1977), in both of which the Court held that a plaintiff making this allegation would be unable to show "antitrust injury." That doctrine is discussed in §19.1.1.

§3.2.2 "Social" Justifications Are Not Relevant in Antitrust

As long as there has been antitrust, defendants have sought to defend their conduct by saying that, in their particular circumstances, it was needed to avoid some bad result that would occur if unbridled price competition were allowed to proceed without any restraints. This argument essentially always fails. The courts are now very strongly of the view that the antitrust laws adopt unfettered competition as a fundamental policy of the United States. Accordingly, while defendants are ordinarily permitted to offer "business justifications" or "procompetitive justifications" for otherwise illegal conduct, the theory of the justification must be that the conduct *improves price or quality competition*. The theory cannot be that under the circumstances the best interests of society require an evasion of competition. As the Supreme Court has written, "That kind of argument is properly addressed to Congress and may justify an exemption from the statute for specific industries, but it is not permitted [in antitrust litigation]." *Nat. Socy. of Profl. Engrs. v. United States*, 435 U.S. 679, 689-690 (1978).

A leading example of the argument and of the courts' disregard for it is in *United States v. Socony-Vacuum Oil Co., Inc.*, 310 U.S. 150 (1950). There the government prosecuted a criminal conspiracy by which the country's major crude oil producers and refiners sought to "support" the price of gasoline. Their concern, they said, was that unfettered price competition was making production so unprofitable that many oil wells would be abandoned, and once abandoned would be lost forever. In effect, they argued that a price support scheme to keep the wells running at reasonably remunerative rates was needed to conserve natural resources.

The Court was unimpressed:

> [S]uch defense[s][are] typical of the protestation usually made in price-fixing cases. Ruinous competition, financial disaster, evils of price cutting and the like

> appear throughout our history as ostensible justifications for price-fixing. If the so-called competitive abuses were to be appraised here, the reasonableness of prices would necessarily become an issue in every price-fixing case. In that event, the Sherman Act would soon be emasculated; its philosophy would be supplanted by one which is wholly alien to a system of free competition; it would not be the charter of freedom which its framers intended.
>
> Congress has not left with us the determination of whether or not particular price-fixing schemes are wise or unwise, healthy or destructive. It has not permitted the age-old cry of ruinous competition and competitive evils to be a defense to price-fixing conspiracies. It has no more allowed genuine or fancied competitive abuses as a legal justification for such schemes than it has the good intentions of the members of the combination. If such a shift is to be made, it must be done by the Congress. Certainly Congress has not left us with any such choice. Nor has the Act created or authorized the creation of any special exception in favor of the oil industry. Whatever may be its peculiar problems and characteristics, the Sherman Act, so far as price-fixing agreements are concerned, establishes one uniform rule applicable to all industries alike.

United States v. Socony-Vacuum Oil Co., Inc., 310 U.S. 150, 220-222 (1940).

The Court has reached this same result in many other cases. In *Nat. Socy. of Profl. Engrs.*, the Court found illegal an ethical rule imposed by a leading professional association for engineers which prohibited them from negotiating fees for their work prior to entering into contracts. The Court found the agreement nearly tantamount to a price-fixing agreement, but the engineers claimed that in fact it was necessary for the public safety. They argued that price pressures would lead engineers to do shoddy work or to propose construction designs that would be unsafe. The Court rejected that argument as in essence the argument that competition itself was the problem. Likewise, in *FTC v. Superior Court Trial Lawyers Assn.*, 493 U.S. 411, 423-424 (1990), the Court considered a "strike" organized by lawyers who earned their living in the District of Columbia by taking court-appointed criminal defense work, the purpose of which was to force the DC government to increase the rates it paid for that work. The Court expressed some sympathy for the lawyers' cause and presumed for purposes of decision that an increase in the fees would improve the constitutionally mandated services that indigent clients receive. The Court did not in principle reject the defendants' view that if they were left only to price competition, there would be no political constituency that could effectively lobby for those better services. But the Court considered all such matters irrelevant to its decision. As a naked, horizontal boycott the Court found the conduct to have been illegal per se.

It also helps to consider those cases in which business justifications have persuaded the Court, because the Court has only ever accepted them when it could characterize them as genuinely procompetitive. In *Chicago Bd. of Trade v. United States*, 246 U.S. 231 (1918), the Court considered an agreement reached among commodities brokers as a rule of the exchange of which they were all members, which concerned the pricing of grain. The rule was a horizontal price-fixing conspiracy, though not a "naked" one.[11] Still, one might have expected some suspicion on the Court's part given the explicitly price-restraining nature of the rule. But the Court upheld the rule under rule of reason analysis on its view that it would improve the competitive process for the sale of grain in Chicago. The Court thought the rule would improve the flow of information on the market and would reduce the amount of fraud and abuse exercised by some of the traders on out-of-town farmers, who otherwise were at an informational disadvantage. This would be procompetitive if it would result in more grain being shipped to the exchange by the increasingly confident farmers. Likewise, in *Broad. Music, Inc. v. Columbia Broad. Sys.*, 441 U.S. 1 (1979), the Court considered a trade group of composers of music. The group's major purpose was to market its members' compositions, license customers to perform that music, and enforce the members' copyrights against infringers. However, the group licensed compositions on a blanket basis—for a fixed fee, customers could perform any composition within a large pool of compositions. Formally that sort of arrangement closely resembles a naked horizontal price-fixing conspiracy. And yet the Court applied only a deferential rule of reason analysis, and strongly implied that the arrangement was reasonable because of its procompetitive virtues. Namely, the joint licensing and enforcement of copyrights would lead to huge transaction cost savings and ultimately to more production and sale of music. All but the most famous individual composers would find it prohibitively expensive to negotiate individual licenses on a nationwide basis, and police their rights on such a basis, but in collection the many thousands of them might find it economical to do so.[12]

---

11. That is, the restraint was an "ancillary" one, as is much more fully explained in §7.2. While the agreement related to price and was among horizontal competitors—people who bought and sold grain for their living—it was part of a larger arrangement that itself seemed like a good thing for commerce: the commodities exchange itself. When arrangements like this include rules or side agreements that might have been illegal standing alone, but might also lead to benefits as a part of the arrangement, we call them "ancillary" restraints. The legal consequence is that the restraint will be judged under the rule of reason even if it might have been per se illegal standing alone.

12. There is one exception to this claim that the Court has only ever accepted justifications that genuinely improve price competition, and it remains nominally good law, *Appalachian Coals v. United States*, 288 U.S. 344 (1933). However, the case is not now followed and almost certainly does not state the law. *See, e.g.*, William L. Reynolds & Spencer Weber Waller, *Legal Process and the Past of Antitrust*, 48 SMU L. Rev. 1811, 1812 (1995) (noting that *Appalachian Coals* was "extraordinary" and "makes sense only when placed in the context of the country's disillusionment with capitalism during the depths of the Great Depression").

§3.2.3 Antitrust Is (Almost) Always Agnostic About Prices

We very frequently say in antitrust that its underlying policy is to protect consumers, by ensuring that producers are not able to increase price or (what is effectively the same thing) to reduce output. In other words, there is some sense in which this law is fundamentally *about* prices. And yet it is virtually unheard of anywhere in the law of antitrust for a court to consider actual prices charged by a defendant, or to measure whether those prices were "right" or "reasonable" according to any substantive measure.

In only two scenarios does antitrust ever directly consider actual prices charged, and really only in one of those—one narrow area in all of antitrust law—do the courts ever consider whether the actual prices charged were the "right" prices or not. First, certain rules in antitrust deal with "price discrimination." Sometimes a buyer will attempt to charge two different customers different prices for the same good or service. They might do this for various reasons; on the one hand, differing prices may reflect actual differences in the costs of serving different customers, but on the other hand, discrimination can sometimes be part of an anticompetitive scheme. Price discrimination is discussed at length in Chapter 16. Second—and it is in this one area that the propriety of prices themselves is considered by a court—it is illegal for either a monopolist or a group of horizontal competitors to engage in "predatory pricing." A dominant firm or group might attempt to destroy competitors by setting prices so low that those competitors cannot meet them and will be forced out of business. That may be anticompetitive if the predator's goal is thereafter to raise price to supracompetitive levels. The reason consideration of predation involves judgments about whether prices were "right" is that the courts now very firmly hold that prices cannot be illegally predatory unless they are below the *predator's* own costs. The courts in these cases must therefore make a usually laborious and elaborate factual study of prices charged and their relation to costs. Predatory pricing is discussed in §13.3.3.

Courts maintain this great hesitation to judge prices themselves for two reasons. First, they believe that assessing prices would be prohibitively difficult, and would also imply an ongoing, essentially regulatory job of oversight for the judiciary for which it is poorly suited. Then-judge William Howard Taft (later President, Chief Justice, and one of the country's first great antitrust scholars) addressed this point more than a century ago in *United States v. Addyston Pipe & Steel Co.*, 85 F. 271 (6th Cir. 1898). Defendants there formed a price-fixing cartel, and they defended against Sherman Act prosecution by arguing that their prices—though fixed—were "fair and reasonable." Judge Taft answered in now-famous words: For courts to judge the propriety of prices actually charged would be to "set sail on a sea of doubt. . . ."

3. Part Two of the Two-Part Strategy

In another important early case—*United States v. Socony-Vacuum Oil Co., Inc.*, 310 U.S. 150 (1940), which for all time established that horizontal price fixing is always illegal—the Court elaborated further:

> The reasonableness of prices has no constancy due to the dynamic quality of the business facts underlying price structures. Those who fixed reasonable prices today would perpetuate unreasonable prices tomorrow, since those prices would not be subject to continuous administrative supervision and readjustment in light of changed conditions. Those who controlled the prices would control or effectively dominate the market. And those who were in that strategic position would have it in their power to destroy or drastically impair the competitive system. But the thrust of the rule is deeper and reaches more than monopoly power. Any combination which tampers with price structures is engaged in an unlawful activity. Even though the members of the price-fixing group were in no position to control the market, to the extent that they raised, lowered, or stabilized prices they would be directly interfering with the free play of market forces. The Act places all such schemes beyond the pale and protects that vital part of our economy against any degree of interference. Congress has not left with us the determination of whether or not particular price-fixing schemes are wise or unwise, healthy or destructive. It has not permitted the age-old cry of ruinous competition and competitive evils to be a defense to price-fixing conspiracies. It has no more allowed genuine or fancied competitive abuses as a legal justification for such schemes than it has the good intentions of the members of the combination. If such a shift is to be made, it must be done by the Congress.

Id. at 221-222.

Second, at least nowadays, the courts are exceptionally cautious about interfering with the system of setting prices, which is thought to be very delicate. All government intrusions are feared inadvertently to confuse the signals that control the allocation of resources, and to produce price and output results different than would have occurred under fully free competition. Intrusions are thought to be most risky as to pricing behavior. Even where some pricing practice might theoretically be anticompetitive, it will ordinarily *look* simply like aggressive or otherwise rational pricing. Predatory pricing, in particular, is thought to be difficult to distinguish from mere aggressive price competition—and price competition is precisely the behavior most valued by antitrust. Likewise, price discrimination might be part of aggressive or innovative competition.

So, to generalize, while the goal of antitrust is unequivocally to keep price down and output up, in almost all cases what the courts attempt to do is merely to preserve the *system* for the setting of prices. They leave the prices themselves alone. In this as in other respects, antitrust may seem to some a heavy-handed tool of government, but it aspires at least to serve very free-market values.

§3.3 UNILATERAL VERSUS MULTILATERAL AND THE *COPPERWELD* GAP: ANTITRUST CARES MORE ABOUT CONSPIRACY THAN ABOUT INDIVIDUAL ACTION

Finally, an important distinction runs throughout modern antitrust law between unilateral and multilateral action. The most basic consequence of this distinction is that *there is a gap in the coverage of the Sherman Act*. Concerted activity must be shown for a §1 violation, but unilateral conduct is illegal under §2 only where there is some large amount of market power. Therefore, some conduct might very well be harmful but also be beyond the reach of antitrust. Namely, unilateral conduct in concentrated industries can mimic the behavior of explicit cartels. Where only a few firms are competing in a given sector, they may simply mimic one another's prices, even if they are supracompetitive. This "oligopoly" pricing, as it is called, may very well be more harmful than many cartels that are per se illegal under §1. (The "oligopoly theory" explaining how this behavior can occur is laid out in the appendix.) But because there is no actual conspiracy in such cases, and assuming none of the firms has enough market share to violate §2, the conduct is legal. This result is said to arise from the language of Sherman Act §§1 and 2, which after all seem to distinguish "conspiracies" from "monopolies."[13] But in its modern case law the Supreme Court has also defended this result on economic grounds. The Court defends it according to an economic perspective that it perceives to underlie antitrust generally, and that perspective fits within the overall theme of this chapter.

The Court first recognized the gap in *Copperweld Corp. v. Independence Tube Corp.*, 467 U.S. 752 (1984). There the Court decided that a corporation and its wholly owned subsidiary could not conspire for purposes of Sherman Act §1. The Court emphasized its view that Congress itself required this result, having intended there to be a sharp distinction in the antitrust treatment of unilateral and multilateral action. The legal details of this rule are discussed more fully in §12.2, but the Court in that case also set out an important economic explanation for its view that there is *and should be* this gap in the law: "Subjecting a single firm's every action to judicial scrutiny for reasonableness would threaten to discourage the competitive enthusiasm that the antitrust laws seek to promote." 467 U.S. at 775.

In any case, the gap is not entirely unfilled, because a few other rules in antitrust do have some bearing on harmful unilateral conduct. First, a fundamental purpose of the regulation of horizontal mergers under Clayton Act §7 is to constrain added concentration that could facilitate the kind of interdependent pricing that is predicted by oligopoly theory. (Merger law is

13. That there was such a distinction in the statute itself was not always so clear. *See* §12.2.

discussed in Chapter 17; interdependent price and oligopoly theory are discussed in the appendix.) Likewise, since *United States v. Container Corp. of America*, 393 U.S. 333 (1969), it has been held that agreements for the exchange of price information can violate Sherman Act §1. While mere exchange of information itself is not illegal, if market circumstances indicate that the firms in the market are oligopolists and the sharing of price information would help them price interdependently, then it can be. (The law of information exchange is discussed in Chapter 9.)

CHAPTER 4

The All-Important Concept of Market Power

§4.1 THE OMNIPRESENCE OF MARKET POWER IN ANTITRUST LAW

§4.1.1 Market Power: What It Is

As the law currently stands, most antitrust causes of action require the plaintiff to show that the defendant holds "market power" in some "relevant market." One could say a lot, and people frequently do, about what market power is, how various definitions of it might differ, and how its meaning may vary when used by economists and when used by lawyers. But a rough and ready definition that will suffice is that it is the power of a seller of some good or service to charge a price higher than the price that would prevail under healthy competition. Normally, a seller should be unable to do this. In a healthy market, any attempt to raise price above the competitive price should just cause the seller to lose business (and in a perfectly competitive market it should cause the seller to lose all of its business immediately).[1]

1. One clarification bearing mention is that sometimes some writers distinguish between "market power" and "monopoly power." Namely, "monopoly power" is sometimes used to mean an amount of market power sufficient to render a particular seller a monopolist. But because the terms are often used interchangeably and because the more commonly used term in antitrust is "market power," we will use that term exclusively in this book.

§4.1.2 Why and When Market Power Matters in Antitrust Law

The reason that most causes of action require proof of market power is that, as you will recall, the Sherman Act prohibits not *all* interferences with markets, but only *unreasonable* ones; that is, it is not illegal to restrain trade in a way that doesn't harm competition. In theory, sellers of goods and services should not be able to do any damage to markets if those markets are performing in a healthy way and the sellers themselves lack market power. In other words, even if a seller deliberately tries to harm a market, the attempt should have no effect. Even a group of sellers who work together to constrain some market in some way ought to be unable to have an effect, if the market in which they compete is a healthy, competitive one and the sellers lack market power. However, at least some actors in some markets hold some market power—they hold some power to raise price or restrict output without losing business to competitors.

A running theme in the history of antitrust doctrine is the struggle over when a plaintiff should be required to prove market power. The reason the stakes are so high is that proof of market power is expensive and difficult. The evidentiary case that must be put on to prove market power will typically involve thousands of pages of documents—data concerning the defendant's sales, the nature of its product, and the other competitors thought to be in its market—and will call for testimony of at least one economist for each party. Putting on such a case is expensive. In particular it makes litigation difficult for the plaintiff attorneys who bring much of the antitrust litigation in the United States,[2] who often seek to represent class plaintiffs on a contingency basis. (It is difficult for them because even where they succeed in litigation they must bear this cost on their own at least until the time of final judgment before the trier of fact, and often for some years thereafter while a verdict is on appeal.) Moreover, as we shall see, a defendant will always have a variety of arguments to challenge any demonstration of market power, even when it enjoys a very large portion of the sales of the product it produces. For example, a defendant can say that the "relevant market" is not properly defined, and that in fact its ability to raise price is constrained by the availability of substitutes for its product, or that entry by new competitors into the market is very easy, and that if price is raised above a competitive price, new competitors will just enter and steal

2. For at least the past four decades or so, private plaintiffs have brought an average of about 95 percent of civil antitrust litigation. *See* William Kolasky, *Antitrust Litigation: What's Changed in Twenty-Five Years?*, Antitrust, Fall 2012, at 9.

away the defendant's business. For these reasons it has been said that when the plaintiff must prove market power, the plaintiff almost always loses.[3]

All is not lost for plaintiffs, however, because not all antitrust causes of action require proof of market power. First, some conduct is said to be "per se" illegal. When that is true, the plaintiff merely must prove that the challenged conduct occurred. If the plaintiff can make that showing, then the case is over—the plaintiff wins, and the defendant's market power or lack thereof is irrelevant. Nowadays, however, there are few per se antitrust offenses. For the most part, only if the plaintiff can show that the defendant engaged in a naked, horizontal agreement to fix prices or allocate markets can it be said that the plaintiff's action is for per se liability.[4]

But second, plaintiffs in recent decades had some luck convincing the courts that certain special kinds of conduct should fall in an intermediate category between per se and rule-of-reason treatment, and in such cases the plaintiff need not put on a full factual demonstration of market power. In those cases, the plaintiff can show that the challenged restraint is unreasonable on some lesser showing, which may consist of persuasive, purely a priori economic reasoning, or empirical evidence from other, similar markets that the kind of conduct in question can be harmful. The courts say that the kinds of conduct for which they recognize this more permissive treatment usually are not as unambiguously anticompetitive as naked price fixing, but are also less ambiguous than possibly procompetitive restrictions like covenants included in employment contracts or joint venture arrangements. For example, the Supreme Court used an approach like this in dealing with an agreement among competing dentists under which they refused to provide X-rays to their patients' insurers. *See FTC v. Indiana Fedn. of Dentists*, 476 U.S. 447 (1986) (this case is discussed further in Chapter 8). This trend is still in development, and the rules that have developed remain uncertain. The rules go by a few different, essentially vernacular names—the kinds of conduct that are involved are said to be judged under the "quick-look rule of reason" or an "abbreviated" rule of reason.

Finally, on occasion a plaintiff can avoid the burden of a full market power demonstration even in pure rule-of-reason cases, if the plaintiff can show "direct" evidence of harm to the market. Direct evidence means some clear showing that the challenged conduct did in fact cause an injury to the market, like an increase in prices or a reduction of output.

To see the distinction between direct proof of harm and proof through the market share proxy, remember that both ways of showing harm are ways

---

3. *See* Stephen Calkins, *California Dental Association: Not a Quick Look But Not the Full Monty*, 67 Antitrust L.J. 495, 522 & n.130 (2000).

4. These causes of action are discussed in Chapter 6. Strictly speaking, the courts still describe "tying" as a per se violation, but plaintiffs in those cases in fact must prove that defendant has some power in the one of the markets involved. Tying is discussed in Chapter 11.

to show that harm *actually happened*. That is, the market share proxy is not just a way of showing that harm might occur or that it is likely but that in fact it occurred. The difference is that the market share proxy is *circumstantial* evidence that harm did in fact occur.

Direct proof is less common and can be difficult to come by. Typically, it requires a set of facts under which the plaintiff can make some before-and-after comparison, or can make a comparison between otherwise very similar markets, one of which was affected by the challenged conduct and the other of which was not. A nice example is *FTC v. Indiana Fedn. of Dentists*, 476 U.S. 447 (1986). There the Federal Trade Commission challenged a refusal by a group of dentists to supply X-rays of their patients to the patients' insurers. The Court found the dentists liable in part because the X-rays were in fact withheld, whereas under competition dentists would have competed with respect to their policies as to insurers. *Id.* at 452. In that case there was a before-and-after comparison of a market in which an actual change was observable that could be said to be caused, with confidence, by the defendants' conduct. Another nice example is in *FTC v. Staples, Inc.*, 970 F.2d 1066 (D.D.C. 1997). There the Commission challenged a merger between the office supply chains Staples and Office Depot. The Commission was able to make this showing: In cities in which the two chains both had stores that were geographically close, the prices they charged were significantly lower than in cities where only one of the chains had a store.

So in summary, a plaintiff must put on a demonstration of market power in every antitrust case except for a per se cause of action under §1, a "quick-look" cause of action under §1, or a case in which the plaintiff can show actual harm to a market through direct evidence.[5] These exceptions are really a pretty narrow slice of possible antitrust causes of action, and leave the following as cases in which market power must be shown: all rule-of-reason actions under §1; some boycott cases under §1; all monopolization, attempted monopolization, and conspiracy to monopolize actions under §2; "tying" and exclusive dealing claims under either §1 or Clayton Act §3; actions against mergers or acquisitions under Clayton Act §7; merger review under the Hart-Scott-Rodino Act; and predatory pricing or price discrimination claims under the Sherman Act or the Robinson-Patman Act.

---

5. Technically, there is one other antitrust cause of action that does not require proof of market power, but it has almost never been enforced and is effectively a dead letter: the rule against interlocking directorates under Clayton Act §8.

§4.2 DOCTRINAL TESTS FOR MARKET POWER: THE TRADITIONAL MARKET SHARE PROXY AND THE NEW RULE FOR TWO-SIDED MARKETS

§4.2.1 The Test and Its Origins

Where direct proof of anticompetitive harm is unavailable, as it often will be, the plaintiff must prove harm circumstantially, through evidence that the defendant held market power. Again, the reasoning is that, even if the challenged conduct could in principle increase price or reduce output, it probably wouldn't be effective unless defendants have the protection from competitive discipline that market power represents. The problem is that in practice it would be difficult to measure market power directly. It will normally be quite difficult to put on any persuasive proof that a defendant is in fact able to raise its prices without losing market share. This is so because even in very competitive markets prices will fluctuate, and it would be hard to prove that any given price increase was a grab for more profit rather than an innocent reaction to changing market conditions beyond the defendant's control. The fact that a defendant's prices were rising over time might simply mean that its costs were rising (and proof of costs can itself be difficult and hotly contested) or that demand was increasing (perhaps because the defendant's product had recently been found to have some desirable quality or because the price of some substitute good is going up). Even the fact that a defendant's prices are rising at the same time that its market is becoming more concentrated might simply indicate changes in cost or demand.

To avoid these problems, the courts have developed a test to estimate market power from the defendant's *market share*. "Market share" means the percentage of the sales in a given market that go to a particular seller. This test is sometimes known as the "market share proxy," because the courts take the defendant's share in some market as indirect evidence that the defendant does or does not have power in that market.

The test has three parts. The plaintiff must first define the *product* market in which the defendant competes: that collection of products to which the defendant's customers could turn if the defendant tried to raise its prices. Second, the plaintiff must define the *geographic* market in which the defendant competes: the collection of sellers or potential sellers over some geographic range to which the defendant's customers could turn if the defendant raises its prices. Finally, the plaintiff must show that given all other characteristics of the relevant market, the defendant's market share suggests that it could raise its prices without losing business.

To understand this test, it helps to remember its underlying purpose. What the courts really want to know is just how much power a defendant has to raise its prices. So the market share proxy attempts to identify all sources of competitive discipline the defendant would face if it tries to raise price or reduce output.

§4.2.2 Defining the Product Market: The *Cellophane* Test

The plaintiff must first identify the products that compete with the defendant's product, and which therefore constrain its ability to behave anticompetitively. Defendants will almost always desire to show that the relevant market includes more, rather than fewer, products. The more products there are competing in the same market, the smaller the defendant's share of it will be. For the same reason, plaintiffs will want to limit the product market to as few products as possible.

Because the relevant market should include all constraints on the defendant's pricing freedom, it is made up not only of producers of goods identical to the defendant's product, but also those that are good *substitutes* for it: products to which the defendant's customers could turn if the defendant's prices go up. Product market definition therefore turns on the question whether a particular good is an appropriate substitute for the defendant's good. Probably the most famous case on point is *United States v. E.I. du Pont de Nemours & Co.*, 351 U.S. 377 (1956), a case normally known as the "*Cellophane* case" because the defendant was alleged to have monopolized the market for cellophane. The Court there set out a rough-and-ready test for substitutability that remains in use today:

> [Whether products are substitutes] depends on how different from one another are the offered commodities in character or use, [and] how far buyers will go to substitute one commodity for another. . . . [But] no more definite rule can be declared than that commodities reasonably interchangeable by consumers for the same purpose make up that "part of the trade or commerce," monopolization of which may be illegal. . . . [I]t is the use or uses to which the commodity is put that control[,][and therefore the] market is composed of products that have reasonable interchangeability for the purposes for which they are produced—price, use and qualities considered.

351 U.S. at 393-396, 404. As they have applied it, the courts have approached this "reasonable interchangeability" test through a combination of economic theory, data, and pragmatic judgment. On the pragmatic level, courts simply ask subjectively whether they think consumers might substitute one product for another if prices change. In *Cellophane*, for example, the defendant's product, cellophane, was held to be reasonably interchangeable with other "flexible packaging materials" because the Court found that for each of cellophane's various purposes—like wrapping meat at the grocery store

butcher counter or wrapping packages of cigarettes—there were other products that were reasonably similar in their characteristics and not too different in their going price that purchasers might switch to them if du Pont raised its price. This was so even though the various "flexible packaging" products—including other transparent films, grease-proof paper, and aluminum foil—all had varying degrees of product characteristics that purchasers demanded.

On the more theoretical level, courts often consider evidence relevant to a phenomenon known as "cross-price elasticity of demand." (The concept of elasticity is considered further in the economics chapter, in §2.3.2(b).) Generally speaking, "elasticity" in economics means the likelihood that one thing will change when some other thing changes. For example, "price elasticity of demand" for a particular good is an estimate of how consumers' desire to purchase it will change if the price goes up or down. Food, shelter, and medicine are often cited as inelastic goods, because even if prices go up a fair bit, consumers will still buy about the same amount of them, given their importance. Other measures of elasticity abound. "Income elasticity of demand," for example, measures how much less of a given product consumers will buy when their overall income goes down, and "price elasticity of supply" measures how much more of a product producers will offer for sale if market price goes up. The measure of elasticity important to us here is *cross*-price elasticity of demand: a measure of how demand for one product changes when the price for some other product goes up. For example, there is a good chance that if the price of butter goes up, and all other things remain the same, consumers will buy more margarine. The cross-price elasticity that likely exists between the two goods suggests that consumers consider them substitutes, and therefore that the availability of the one will constrain the ability of sellers to raise the price for the other.

Elasticity is an important concept in economics, but cross-price elasticity plays a problematic role in antitrust cases. While it would be very useful to have accurate measures of it in any market definition exercise, actually measuring it requires data that may not be available and is expensive, labor intensive, and contested in any event. For that reason, courts generally say that proof of elasticity by quantitative evidence—that is, statistical analysis based on actual sales data estimating the effects on one product of price changes in the other—is not mandatory.[6] Therefore, when they discuss it the courts often make use of rough and pragmatic estimates of cross-price elasticity based on the available evidence.

Second, cross-price elasticity estimates can sometimes be seriously misleading. This fact led the *Cellophane* Court itself into a mistake so well known

6. *McWane, Inc. v. FTC*, 783 F.3d 814, 829–830 (11th Cir. 2015); *United States v. Google LLC*, 747 F. Supp. 3d 1, 109 (D.D.C. 2024).

that it is now called the "*Cellophane* fallacy." The Court defined the defendant's product market broadly and therefore found that the defendant held a market share too small to support the government's cause of action. The Court did so in part by relying on data tending to show a high cross-price elasticity between cellophane and other flexible wrapping materials. The problem was that the Court did not ask whether that elasticity measure might merely be the result of already high, supracompetitive prices that du Pont charged because it was in fact a monopolist. That is, the Court failed first to compare du Pont's price for cellophane to the cost of producing it, or to otherwise ask whether the going price was already a monopoly price. Any monopolized product will begin to show some cross-price elasticity with other products once the monopolist has raised the price for it to some significantly supracompetitive price. This will be so even if those other products wouldn't ordinarily be considered good substitutes—their cross-price elasticity with the defendant's product might be low if they were all priced competitively.

Example

Dr. Bartholomew P. Headoftheclass, III, famed professor of economics at Highfalutin University, has been called to testify as an expert witness in a Sherman Act §2 monopolization trial. The parties have contested certain market definition issues, and Dr. Headoftheclass is now attempting to explain to the jury that when the price of the defendant's sole product goes up, demand for aluminum foil goes up as well.

Was Dr. Headoftheclass more likely called by the plaintiff or the defendant?

Explanation

By the defendant. Defendants will almost always want to convince the trier of fact that the relevant market includes more, rather than fewer, products. This is so because, necessarily, the more products there are in the market, the smaller the defendant's share of it will be. Showing cross-price elasticity between the defendant's product and aluminum foil would suggest that the two are substitutes and that aluminum foil should be included in the defendant's product market.

§4.2.3 Defining the Geographic Market

A seller should be included in the defendant's geographic market if it currently sells an identical or substitute product to customers in the same territory as the defendant, or if it easily could do so if the defendant's price goes up. If the defendant's price increase either causes customers to travel to purchase alternatives or invites other sellers to transport more of their goods into the defendant's territory, then those alternatives should be included. Typically an important issue in geographic market definition is transportation cost. If existing or potential producers of good substitutes not currently serving the defendant's territory could cheaply ship goods there (or if consumers could cheaply travel to buy those alternatives and bring them home) those sellers should probably be included.

§4.2.4 Counting Market Participants and Weighing Likely Entry

Once the relevant market is defined in product and geographic terms, one must identify the firms operating within it. For the most part this problem is straightforward, because any firm currently selling or earning revenue in the market will be included. Uncertainty arises as to those that don't currently compete against the defendant, but easily could. They might produce similar products or have similar facilities, and could easily switch to producing the relevant product if the defendant raises its prices, or they might produce the relevant product in some other territory. The problem they pose for market definition is whether to consider them current participants in the defendant's market or merely potential future entrants. If a firm could quickly and easily enter, then it might already exert disciplinary influence on the defendant's pricing behavior. But if entry would take a long time or is uncertain, it probably doesn't currently affect the defendant too much.

The distinction can sometimes have real significance. Remember, under *Philadelphia National Bank*, plaintiff's prima facie showing is made on concentration statistics, so including potential entrants as current market participants will lower the pre-merger and post-merger concentration estimates and make the plaintiff's prima facie case more difficult to show. Choosing not to include them as current participants, and only as potential entrants at some future time, increases those numbers and increases the likelihood of making the prima facie showing, and also shifts the duty to the defendant to come forward with evidence that entry will be likely and will meaningfully constrain any market power created by the merger. (It does not change the burden of *proof*, however, on any issue, because that burden always remains with the plaintiff. *United States v. Baker Hughes, Inc.*, 908 F.2d 981, 983 (D.C. Cir. 1990).)

There is no hard and fast rule on which firms should be considered present competitors and which should be considered likely future entrants, but generally entry must be likely and quick for a firm to be considered a present participant. For what it is worth, the agencies' current *Merger Guidelines* include firms as current participants only if they have committed to imminent entry or could very likely enter very rapidly and without significant sunk costs. FTC

& U.S. Dep't of Justice, *Merger Guidelines* §4.4.A (2023).[7] Other possible entrants can be made part of the defendant's rebuttal, but even then, the evidence should show that entry will be quick and effective. *See id.* at §3.2 (requiring that entry be "timely, likely, and sufficient" to provide effective rebuttal).

An emerging issue in high technology markets is when new technologies should be included in a defendant's market. They can develop quickly and disrupt market arrangements. The problem has been that a developing technology could be relevant both to calculating the defendant's current market share and to conduct by the defendant to exclude that technology. Courts have tended to consider the exclusionary conduct to be legally relevant and have held it illegal, so defendants have argued that those technologies should count as current competitors. The courts so far have disagreed and held that emerging threats can be protected by antitrust without considering them sufficiently close substitutes to defendant's product to exert the kind of discipline on it that current competitors do. *See United States v. Microsoft Corp.*, 253 F.3d 34, 53-54 (D.C. Cir. 2001) (excluding emerging "middleware" technologies as current market participants, even while holding Microsoft's exclusionary acts against those technologies illegal); *United States v. Google LLC*, 747 F. Supp. 3d 1, 113 (D.D.C. 2024) (excluding the possibility that non-search firms like Meta or Amazon could develop.

Example

Before the makers of today's smart phones and tablets transformed the world of mobile computing, antitrust controversy raged over a product known as the "household digital organizer" (HDO). In the year 2010, plaintiff Insignificon, Inc., sued defendant Big Sucker Industries (BSI) for monopolizing the HDO market in violation of Sherman Act §2.

HDOs were similar to handheld personal digital assistants, or PDAs, and could run software and provide online connectivity. Most, however, were physically larger than PDAs, with screen sizes of around six to eight diagonal inches, and were designed to be stationary. Marketing campaigns for HDOs cast them as organizational tools to be kept in some central place in the home, to organize schedules, to let family members communicate, and to keep track of household finances and other affairs. Families might like such a thing but would neither want a full-size desktop computer on the kitchen counter nor want to pay for such a thing when they likely also have a desktop or laptop for other work spaces in the home. BSI alleged in

7. The agencies won't consider a firm a present participant if entry requires significant sunk costs—costs that cannot be recovered if the firm decides to quit and exit the market—because sunk costs make entry less likely.

court papers that the following companies marketed HDO products or other products similar to HDOs:

Manufacturer	Average Annual Unit Sales (Thousands), 2005-2010
BSI (defendant)	1,400
Whammo	500
Avionix	300*
Jaspers Electronics	200
Insignificon (plaintiff)	100
Big Kidz	100
Total	2,600

*Based on 2002-2003 sales.

BSI's product was very similar to Insignificon's. Avionix and Jaspers are both large electronics manufacturers with ranges of consumer products, and they each sold a household organizer product with a six-to-eight-inch screen, Internet connectivity, and the ability to run HDO and PDA software. Avionix actually sold its product for only one year, roughly calendar year 2002. However, it earned a very large amount of sales that year, so its average sales of 300,000 units perhaps understates the threat the firm would pose if its product continued. Interestingly, Whammo and Big Kidz are actually toy companies. Their products were made to look like small laptop computers (the Big Kidz product was even sold in boys' and girls' versions, the one in blue with licensed Hot Wheels race cars depicted on it, the other in pink with a licensed Barbie theme), and they contained the guts of a small computer and could be connected by cable to the Internet. Software, including mainly learning games for young children, could be loaded on these devices only through the companies' proprietary cartridges. (They could not receive computer disks or CD-ROMs or the like, and there was no way to download software to them.) All of these products sold for roughly equivalent retail prices, except for the Whammo and Big Kidz products, which were cheaper.

When BSI first introduced the very first HDO product in 2000, it made commercial sense: Personal computers remained physically large and expensive, and all but the most expensive PDAs at that time were still fairly unsophisticated, little more than glorified calculators with no phone or Internet capability. However, there is no real doubt that the average annual sales figures above are somewhat misleading, in that sales of all HDOs fell over the relevant period (except for the Whammo and Big Kidz products, whose sales held steady).

What was BSI's market share?

Explanation

Even if a court considered only the evidence presented by BSI, the odds are that its share was pretty substantial. However, that share really could not be judged in isolation from the pace of technological change, as the growth of smart phones and tablet computers would shortly eclipse the parties' products altogether.

The first step would be to define the relevant product market. The similarity of the BSI, Insignificon, Avionix, and Jaspers products suggests that they are reasonable substitutes. The Whammo and Big Kidz products pretty obviously are not, for two reasons. They seem inadequate substitutes in terms of capabilities and intended use, and they apparently sold at lower price without stealing HDO sales. So, from the data above, the market could include at least the products produced by BSI, Insignificon, Avionix, and Jaspers, with a combined annual sales of 2 million units.

Each of those firms participated in the market except for Avionix. It is a judgment call whether to include Avionix as a current competitor. It did not sell any HDO product at the time of litigation, but it had done so, and as a large, diversified electronics maker, it presumably could begin producing them again pretty quickly if it were profitable to do so. Sunk costs might include advertising to introduce a new product, purchase of specialized manufacturing equipment that wouldn't be useful to other manufacturers, or training of workers in skills not transferable to other tasks. Whether they are significant is a fact question.

In any event, if the relevant market were defined to include all these sellers, BSI's 1.4 million unit share of that market would be 70 percent. That is a sizeable market share, and might support monopolization liability under Sherman Act §2, depending on all the facts.

However, even when this suit was brought in 2010, the products that BSI and Insignificon were producing were probably seriously challenged by smart phones and tablets, which plainly are close and superior substitutes. Whether those products should have been considered current substitutes when the case was brought is a fact question. For what it is worth, the first of today's smart phones, the iPhone, was introduced in 2007, but in many ways its small size and other limitations might make it an imperfect alternative to the products of BSI and Insignificon. The first tablet computer, the iPad, was not introduced until 2010. Nevertheless, those technologies and the rapid pace of change suggest that one or both of them should be included as a current competitor, or else figure as a significant component of BSI's rebuttal case that current market shares in 2010 did not capture the real state of competition.

§4.2.5 Two-Sided or "Platform" Markets

The Supreme Court introduced a new idea into the measurement of market power in its 2018 decision in *Ohio v. American Express Co.*, 585 U.S. 529 (2018) (*Amex*). The Court found that some markets have the peculiar feature that the seller must simultaneously sell the same product to more than one person. Those persons consume the same unit of the product, together and at the same time, and they must both be persuaded to consume it if it is to be sold at all. Economists began to speculate in the mid-1970s that such markets—which they described as "platforms" or "two-sided" markets—have special characteristics and require special antitrust treatment.

It can seem very confusing that *Amex* described the problem as a matter of market definition. The "market" that is defined will seem to include two or more products that may seem very different, and not at all interchangeable as substitutes. In *Amex* itself, the defendant was a credit card company. On the one hand, it provides a service to cardholders that essentially consists of a short-term line of credit, and, on the other hand, a service to merchants consisting of payment processing. The two services are not even distant substitutes. A merchant who is unhappy when fees for payment processing go up cannot solve its problem by signing up for its own credit card instead. So why did the *Amex* Court say the two services must be combined in one market?

The key to the puzzle is that the only product of interest is the *jointly demanded product*. A platform operator will usually provide different things to participants on different sides of its platform, but the relevant antitrust market is actually for the one, solitary thing that they consume *together*. In *Amex*, that product was neither the consumer line of credit nor the merchant payment processing, distinct products that each were consumed by only one side of the platform. The product they consumed together was *card swipes*. That is, the product was individual payment transactions, and for each transaction to occur, it was necessary that exactly one consumer purchase the short-term credit (by using the card) and one merchant purchase the payment processing (by accepting it). In other words, the market that is legally relevant when *Amex* applies is not a market for the individual components that are provided to one side or the other. It is for the thing that the different participants consume together. As the Court noted, the separate services purchased by the two sides of the platform can be thought of as "inputs to this single product." *Id.* at 545 n.8.

According to the *Amex* Court and the economists whose views it adopted, two-sided markets exhibit certain significant peculiarities that require special antitrust treatment. First, they generate "indirect network effects." You may already be familiar with simple **network effects** (defined more fully in the Glossary): Simple network effects occur when the value of a product increases as more people use it. Common examples are telephones and social media networks. The more people that use a device or service that can communicate with the one that you use, the more valuable it will be to you to use it. Indirect network effects, then, are benefits to users of one product when more people use some *other* product. For example, a merchant gets more benefit from accepting American Express cards if more shoppers use them, and shoppers get more benefit from using them if more merchants there are willing to accept them.

A second economic peculiarity follows from the first. The platform owner who raises price to one side may affect demand on the other. If American Express raises its merchant fees, for example, it may lose some merchants who had been willing to accept its cards. That will make the cards less desirable to cardholders, and so American Express may lose cardholder customers as well. In the worst case scenario, losses on one side generate losses on the other, which in turn generate further losses on the first side, and so on. The result could be a "feedback loop of declining demand." *Id.* at 544. Accordingly, because the platform owner must be sensitive to the cross-platform effects of price changes on one side, its interests in serving the desires of each side constrain its ability to abuse the other. As the *Amex* Court put it, "[p]rice increases on one side of the platform . . . do not suggest anticompetitive effects without some evidence that they have increased the overall cost of the platform's services." *Id.* And finally, on the Court's view, this mutually constraining effect of the two sides on each other leads to this remarkable result: "Only other two-sided platforms can compete with a two-sided platform for transactions." *Id.* at 546.

To address these problems, *Amex* adopts special antitrust rules. First, if a court determines that a market is two sided, the plaintiff must have pleaded the relevant product market as consisting of the jointly demanded good. If plaintiff presented its case as if the market were one-sided, the case can be dismissed. Likewise, once the market is defined as two-sided, plaintiff's evidence must in one way or another demonstrate that price for the jointly demanded product will go up or its output will go down.

Amex has other substantive consequences, discussed at various points in this book, including most importantly that restraints within it are very likely judged under the rule of reason (*see* Chapter 6).

Not every business that connects multiple parties, or otherwise looks like a "platform," will be subject to *Amex* treatment. By its terms, *Amex* applies only to "simultaneous transaction platforms." Those are platforms that "facilitate a single, simultaneous transaction between participants," such that the platform "can sell its services only if [participants on each side] simultaneously choose to use the network." *Id.* at 545. One thing that remains somewhat unclear is whether the transactions in question must be literally, temporally "simultaneous." What seems more important, given the Court's reasoning, is just that the ratio of uses of the platform between each side of the platform be exactly 1:1—that is, for every transaction, there must be exactly one user on each side of the platform jointly consuming the transaction. That is true of credit cards, for example: for every card swipe, there is exactly one use of the platform by a merchant and one use by a cardholder. But transactions could be "simultaneous" in this sense even if they do not happen at the same time. Every sale by an Amazon Marketplace merchant, for example, requires exactly one purchase by an Amazon customer. (This fact in itself raises a serious question about the plausibility of the *Amex* rule, and it is the basis of much growing criticism: If that is they case, then why isn't every sale of food at a grocery store also a simultaneous, two-sided transaction?)

In any case, the Court stressed that its rule does *not* apply to all products, even though they may seem plausibly similar to two-sided platforms. The rule is especially likely not to apply where indirect network effects are minor on one side. As an example, the Court mentioned advertiser-supported newspapers. Advertisers care how many readers there are, but readers do not ordinarily care how much advertising there is. Accordingly, the *Amex* opinion explicitly reaffirms the Court's own antitrust precedents involving newspaper defendants, in which it had treated them as ordinary businesses and considered competitive effects only as to one of their constituencies. *Id.* at 544-545.

As of this writing, *Amex* remains new and surrounded by uncertainties (and much controversy and criticism). It is difficult to predict how widely its rule may be applied, and how many different kinds of things will be held to be "simultaneous transaction platforms."

§4.2.6 Measuring Share Once the Market Is Defined

Once a product and geographic market have been defined there remains the calculation of the defendant's share within it. Usually this poses no real problems and the court will simply tally up the sales of each seller within the market and ask what portion of the total goes to the defendant.

An occasional issue is how share should be calculated when products have been included in the product market that differ significantly in price. Notice that this should not ordinarily occur. If two products sell for substantially different prices, they probably should not be considered reasonably interchangeable substitutes. But where a court does find products to be substitutes despite different prices, a problem of share measurement arises. If share is measured by comparing total revenues of the various sellers in the market, the share would be exaggerated for the seller with the more expensive product. Courts can easily avoid this problem by simply measuring share according to units sold or some other measure of volume not connected to price itself.

§4.2.7 Assessing Other Indices of Market Power

In recent decades perhaps the most important element in the market share proxy test has come to be the third: Courts have become quite concerned that even large market shares do not logically prove that a defendant holds pricing freedom. In principle, a defendant might have a large share in a market in which participants have good information, the product is quite fungible, and entry barriers are low. In such a case, it stands to reason that if the defendant charges a supracompetitive price other sellers and new entrants may find it profitable to expand their own production and steal its business. Therefore, even if a plaintiff has shown that within its relevant product and geographic market the defendant holds a large percentage of sales, a court will still ask whether other facts—and in particular, whether low entry barriers—cast doubt on the defendant's market power.

In effect, in this stage of the market share proxy, the courts engage in very pragmatic estimation of certain elasticities. They want to test the likely consequences of price increases given other known facts, so, first, they want some estimate of consumers' price elasticity of demand (as opposed to the *cross*-price elasticity between the defendant's product and substitutes for it). If the product is one that consumers can easily do without, then market share may not prove so much. Second, they want to estimate the elasticity of supply of existing competitors and likely entrants. If circumstances indicate that a price increase by the defendant would likely invite new sources of supply from competitors, then even a large market share may not show market power.

Example

Assume that the domestic market for rubber bands is properly defined to include "all flexible fastening products suitable for office use." (Demand for rubber bands, perhaps not surprisingly, is quite elastic. That result is a consequence of the fact that several potential substitutes are properly included in the market.) In its geographic aspect the market comprises the United States. This market is dominated by two firms, Stretchy, Inc., and Boingy, Inc., though there are several small manufacturers also selling such products, which effectively constitute a "competitive fringe." Boingy began operations about five years ago by acquiring a few of the fringe operators and recapitalizing them with an additional $50,000,000. The average annual gross revenue for the entire industry during the past ten years was about $200 billion. Stretchy on average earned $150 billion of this and Boingy earned $30 billion.

Does Stretchy hold market power?

Explanation

Probably, but perhaps not. Admittedly, Stretchy holds a very large market share. Based on gross revenues, it holds about 75 percent. The market is also highly concentrated. Stretchy is only challenged by Boingy, which has about 15 percent of the market, and by "several small manufacturers" who among them divide the remaining 10 percent of all sales. However, the fact that Boingy could acquire 15 percent of the market after entering only recently and with only a modest investment (the acquisition cost of the firms it bought plus $50,000,000, which in a multi-billion dollar industry seems small), suggests that entry is easy. Therefore, Stretchy's ability to abuse consumers ought to be pretty effectively disciplined by competitive market forces.

In the frequently cited *United States v. Syufy Enters.*, 903 F.2d 659 (1990), the court on similar facts held that even a very large market share was not enough to support the government's cause of action. Not long after his entry in the Las Vegas movie theater business, defendant Syufy embarked on a series of acquisitions of competitors giving him a very high market share—briefly 100 percent, and for sometime thereafter nearly that much. By the time of trial his share of box office receipts was still 75 percent. However, the government was unable to show more than modest entry barriers. Also, the court was impressed that, shortly after gaining his 100 percent share, Syufy attempted to force one of the major motion picture distributors to license its films to him at a lower price, and that distributor simply refused to do business with him any longer. Thereafter, other theater owners entered the Las Vegas market again, and some of them began gaining significant market share. And on top of it all, Syufy never raised his prices to consumers for tickets or concession items.

§4.3 MEASURES OF CONCENTRATION: THE *MERGER GUIDELINES* AND THE HERFINDAHL-HIRSCHMAN INDEX

Finally, in connection with market power, we should consider one separate but related idea, which is also very general: *concentration*. The concentration of a given market is a measure of how many firms there are in that market, and how much of it each of them controls. A market in which there are only a few firms, or in which there are several but one or a few of them hold very large market shares, is said to be highly concentrated.

Concentration is an estimate of market power in the same sense as the market share proxy, but it is less commonly used in antitrust law. Concentration is customarily calculated only in merger challenges under Clayton Act §7 and in the merger preclearance review process that the federal enforcement agencies conduct under the Hart-Scott-Rodino Act. Concentration matters in that context because under current merger case law, a plaintiff can create a presumption of anticompetitive effect merely by showing that a transaction will significantly increase concentration in an already concentrated market. (These matters are discussed in Chapters 17 and 18.)

Traditionally, concentration was measured simply by calculating the market shares of the firms in a given market and then comparing them directly. This approach is known as calculating the market's "concentration ratio." In its most common form, which was used more or less exclusively by the courts and enforcement agencies throughout the 1960s and 1970s, it appears as the "four-firm" concentration ratio. Under that test, one first defines the relevant market and then adds up the market shares of the four largest firms. The reason for focusing on the four large firms is that under traditional economic theory the risk of price fixing and other collusion is greater where there are fewer significant firms.

Concentration ratios have been largely replaced by a test known as the Herfindahl-Hirschman Index (HHI). Conveniently, the HHI happens to sound a lot like a limerick. Though you can decide for yourself whether the following mnemonic device is exactly *funny*, you are not likely to forget the HHI. Here goes:

> There once was a measure of markets,
> precise, so we need not ballpark it.
> It's *the sum of the squares*
> *of the market shares*
> *of all of the firms in the market.*

So, to calculate the HHI, one defines a relevant market, measures each firm's share of that market, then *squares* them, and then adds them together. The resulting number, the HHI, will be some number from a maximum of 10,000[8] down to a number infinitely close to 0.[9] The lower the HHI, the less concentrated is the market.

---

8. An HHI of 10,000 would imply total concentration—one firm holding 100 percent market share: $100 \times 100 = 10{,}000$.

9. For example, imagine the absurd but theoretically possible scenario in which there are 1 million firms serving a given market, and that each of them holds an equal market share—that is, they each hold one ten-thousandth of one percent of that market. The HHI would be $0.000001^2 \times 1{,}000{,}000$, or 0.000000000001 (one one-trillionth).

The reason the HHI is now preferred is that it is thought to be precise in a way that mere concentration ratios are not. The HHI can distinguish between two different kinds of seemingly concentrated markets: (1) a market in which there are a comparatively small number of firms that each holds some meaningful market share and (2) a market in which only one or a few firms hold large shares and are faced by competition only from a fringe of much smaller sellers. The latter sort of market is thought by many to be more troublesome. This might be because where there are several firms, even though each is pretty big (i.e., the former kind of market), they will find it fairly difficult to maintain any stable cartel. By contrast, in a market with one very large seller that is challenged only by some fringe made up of many small sellers, the powerful firm will be able to engage in "price leadership" under which it can raise its own prices and prevent disciplinary competition from the small rivals by threatening them with retaliation of various kinds.

The HHI can distinguish between these two kinds of markets, but mere concentration ratios cannot. For example, assume there are ten firms in a given market, and four of them are fairly large—each holds a 20 percent market share—while the remaining six firms must divide among themselves the remaining 20 percent of sales in the market. In this example the four-firm ratio and the HHI will give very different measures of the risks posed by the level of concentration. Assuming the six smaller firms are of equal size, then the HHI is about 1,666, which would not be considered really all that high.[10] The four-firm concentration ratio, on the other hand, would be very high—80 percent. But imagine that in the same market there were ten firms, one of them had 80 percent, and the rest each had to share the remaining 20 percent. The two tests now suggest similar results. The HHI is a *dramatically* higher 6,444,[11] but the four-firm concentration ratio would remain about the same—86.6 percent.

10. To calculate the HHI in this market: $20^2 + 20^2 + 20^2 + 20^2 + 3.33^2 + 3.33^2 + 3.33^2 + 3.33^2 + 3.33^2 + 3.33^2 \approx 1,666$.

11. $80^2 = 6,400$, and $2.22^2 \times 9 \approx 44$; $6,400 + 44 = 6,444$.

PART III

Conspiracies in Restraint of Trade

CHAPTER 5

An Introduction to Sherman Act §1

People of the same trade seldom meet together, even for merriment and diversion, but the conversation ends in a conspiracy against the public, or in some contrivance to raise prices.

—*Adam Smith*[1]

Combining an assertion of general antitrust violation with a claim of injury from breach of contract or tort does not automatically make the latter a claim arising under the antitrust laws.

—*Judge Henry Friendly*[2]

§5.1 AN INTRODUCTION TO BUSINESS COLLABORATION AND A FEW PRELIMINARY IDEAS: "HORIZONTAL" AND "VERTICAL" RESTRAINTS, AND PER SE ILLEGALITY VERSUS THE RULE OF REASON

And so we begin our study of the first of the three major causes of action that make up most of antitrust: the law of Sherman Act §1, under which

1. Adam Smith, *An Inquiry into the Nature and Causes of the Wealth of Nations*, vol. 1, bk. 1, ch. 10 (1776).
2. Salerno v. Am. League of Profl. Baseball Clubs, 429 F.2d 1003, 1004 (2d Cir. 1970) (Friendly, J.).

no person may undertake a "contract, combination . . . or conspiracy, in restraint of trade. . . ."[3]

Businesses in fact cooperate with one another—even outright, head-to-head competitors do so—in all kinds of ways, and much of their cooperation is legal. Throughout the history of Western legal systems, business people have joined together to create business firms, even though they might otherwise simply have competed with one another in the same trade. Two lawyers might form a partnership, for example, instead of running competing solo practices. There has long been some incidence of such firms merging together or acquiring one another. During the past century or so, business firms that are separately organized and formally distinct have also increasingly worked together in various ways, through joint ventures, consortia, standard setting bodies, intellectual property pools, and other cooperative arrangements. Cooperative efforts might help the participating firms to make products better or more cheaply, or to develop new ones, or they might operate as trade or professional associations, which lobby on the participants' behalf, provide them with information and professional services, and do other things for them. Surely no one knows just how many such organizations there are, but in the United States alone there are many millions of them.[4] In these various ways, incidentally, businesses also share a great deal of information with one another, and that in and of itself has been of concern in the history of antitrust. In any case, all of these sorts of interaction have at least some claim to be socially beneficial, and essentially all economists and antitrust lawyers now think that at least some business collaborations and information sharing can be procompetitive. (This is in contrast to the views of many lawyers and economists only a few decades ago.) But all of this conduct also raises the potential that the cooperation will violate the antitrust laws. Specifically, by cooperating with each other, firms might find themselves involved in "contract[s], combination[s] . . . , or conspirac[ies]" that unreasonably "restrain[] . . . trade. . . ." Sometimes this might occur because ill-intentioned business people use trade association

---

3. As explained in the introduction in Chapter 1, the other two are the cause of action for unilateral conduct (also known as "monopolization") under Sherman Act §2, covered in Chapters 13 and 14, and the cause of action against mergers and acquisitions under Clayton Act §7, covered in Chapter 17.

4. Counting up all the formal and informal cooperative arrangements that could cause concern under Sherman Act §1 is probably not possible, but the number is surely in the tens of millions. In addition to the 1000 or so very formal standard setting entities active in the United States, *see* http://www.consortiuminfo.org/links/#.Up-Y3KWTOlI, the many thousands of less formal private consortia and IP pools that also issue standards, and the 90,000 or so trade and professional associations, *see* http://www.asaecenter.org/Advocacy/content ASAEOnly.cfm?ItemNumber=16341, we would have to include all the joint ventures, information sharing arrangements and other means of cooperation that businesses now commonly employ. The U.S. Census Bureau reports that there are about 30 million businesses in the United States, *see* http://www.census.gov/econ/smallbus.html, so we would have to add many millions of such arrangements to our estimate.

meetings or the like as a cover for outright price fixing. But often enough antitrust trouble can arise for business people who have merely communicated with one another or attempted to cooperate in ways that they believed to be legal.

Businesses also sometimes cooperate with one another in less ambiguous ways. Namely, they sometimes deliberately agree with one another to restrain trade, perhaps by agreeing on the prices they will charge or dividing markets between them. Nowadays, because this sort of conduct is so obviously illegal (and indeed so likely to invite criminal prosecution), meetings like this are typically carried out in secret. In his 2001 book *The Informant*, for example, journalist Kurt Eichenwald detailed how officials of several major agricultural corporations engaged in a massive, worldwide conspiracy to fix prices in the multibillion-dollar market for the agricultural product lysine. The conspirators—wealthy, high-ranking corporate executives—met in secret in remote locations often under cloak-and-dagger circumstances. The conspiracy was cracked in large part by FBI agents working with an informant who had infiltrated the ring, who attended its meetings wearing a concealed microphone.

In any case, understanding when cooperation is illegal and when it is not calls for drawing a few initial distinctions. We begin with certain background ideas from the operative language of §1. First, the statutory language itself involved a bit of controversy in its early history. Initially it appeared as if the federal courts might read the statute literally—to bar *every* contract that restrained trade—or at least very, very broadly. But over the statute's first few decades the Supreme Court tempered that course. Borrowing from the common law on which the statute was built, the Court ultimately held it to prohibit only those restraints of trade that are *unreasonable*. Next, to implement that broad standard of "reasonableness," the Court has developed a distinction between two sorts of §1 case, a distinction that remains important today—between conduct that is "per se illegal" and conduct that is subject to the "rule of reason." Finally, the courts have long distinguished between two different kinds of combinations under §1—"vertical" combinations and "horizontal" ones. It will serve us well to start with some discussion of what these distinctions mean.

§5.1.1 Limitation of the §1 Prohibition to "Unreasonable" Conspiracies and the Difference Between Per Se and Rule-of-Reason Analysis

In the early history of Sherman Act law, the courts had an important choice to make in their interpretation of §1. Section 1 prohibits "[e]*very* contract, combination . . . or conspiracy, in restraint of trade or commerce. . . ." Read literally, a prohibition on *every* contract that "restrain[s] . . . trade" might be a disaster, since literally every contract could be said to restrain trade in some sense. If I agree to purchase a car from a given car dealership, then I have significantly restrained myself from buying a car from any other seller. Indeed, some seemingly wholesome, well-known kinds of contracts really restrain trade quite a lot. A partnership agreement, for example, almost necessarily involves a naked, horizontal price-fixing agreement. Imagine that two attorneys who previously had competed in the same market as sole practitioners decide to join together and form a law firm partnership. They most likely will agree with one another as to what rates they will charge, as a basic aspect of their firm governance. But no one could seriously take the congressional intent of the Sherman Act to be to outlaw the centuries-old Anglo-American common law of partnerships.

And yet, in only its second decision ever under the Sherman Act, and the first to reach the merits, the Supreme Court held that §1 had to be read literally, and therefore that every contract that restrains trade should be held illegal under Sherman Act §1. *United States v. Trans-Missouri Freight Assn.*, 166 U.S. 290 (1897).[5] The Court argued that even if the effect of such a reading would be widespread economic disaster, it was a problem that Congress would have to solve.

The potentially dramatic sweep of that rule, however, and the consternation it caused at the time, were not to last. Assuming the Court actually intended the most drastic version of the literal reading,[6] it was done away with not too many years later. In the landmark *Standard Oil Co. of New Jersey v. United States*, 221 U.S. 1 (1911), the Court was faced with the federal government's attack on John D. Rockefeller's Standard Oil enterprise. That entity was the paradigmatic "trust," the focus of much public concern over concentrated wealth, and the survivor of several previous government lawsuits. Almost as if it were writing on a clean slate (rather than 15 or so years of its own Sherman Act precedents), the Court noted that its application of the Sherman Act should be "guided by the principle that where words are employed in a statute which had at the time a well-known meaning at common law or in the law of this country, they are presumed to have

5. The Court's first Sherman Act case was *United States v. E.C. Knight Co.*, 156 U.S. 1 (1895), which may be familiar to you from your course in constitutional law. In *E.C. Knight* the Court held that the Sherman Act did not reach the manufacturing of sugar, holding that such conduct was "intrastate" (recall that by their terms Sherman Act §§1 and 2 reach only conspiracies and monopolies in interstate and foreign commerce). The *E.C. Knight* holding obviously reflects a now outdated conception of the reach of "interstate commerce."

6. *See* Donald J. Smythe, *The Supreme Court and the Trusts: Antitrust and the Foundations of Modern American Business Regulation from* Knight *to* Swift, 29 U.C. Davis L. Rev. 85, 107-113 (2005) (arguing that the *Trans-Missouri* Court probably intended no more than that contracts were illegal when they involved interstate businesses like railroads and telegraph, and even then only when the restraint was "direct and immediate").

been used in that sense unless the context compels to the contrary. . . ." 221 U.S. at 59. Accordingly, following a scholarly recounting of the English and American common law of restraints of trade as it existed in 1890, the Court held that "[t]he statute . . . evidenced the intent not to restrain the right to make and enforce contracts . . . which did not unduly restrain . . . commerce, but to protect that commerce from . . . an undue restraint." *Id.* at 60. Noting further that §1 did not specifically enumerate any particular types of contracts that should be held "undue restraint[s]," but rather was "broad enough to embrace every conceivable contract or combination which could be made," the Court presumed that Congress must have intended for the courts to devise the standard by which contracts would be judged. Again convinced that the use of common law terms of art in §1 indicated congressional intent to incorporate common law concepts, the Court decided that "the standard of reason which had been applied at the common law . . . was intended to be the measure [for] determining whether [a given contract represented] the wrong against which the statute provided." *Id.*[7]

And hence was born—or, perhaps, recovered—the rule of reason, a standard under which a "contract, combination . . . or conspiracy" can violate Sherman Act §1 only if it is "unreasonable." As we have hinted before, however, this standard is much easier to state than it is to apply, and a fair bit of this book is devoted to understanding what it means.

One final distinction should be understood at this point. While it is fair to say that all challenges brought under Sherman Act §1 are in some sense subject to the "rule of reason" of *Standard Oil*, which means that the challenged conduct is illegal only if it is "unreasonable," the Court has also held in a number of cases throughout the years that certain classes of conduct are automatically unreasonable. In other words, such conduct is "per se illegal." As we discuss in Chapter 6, there remain basically three categories of conduct that are treated as per se illegal—horizontal price fixing, horizontal market allocations, and some horizontal concerted refusals to deal (or "boycotts"). Once a plaintiff can demonstrate that the challenged conduct falls within one of these per se categories, all the plaintiff need do is prove that the conduct actually occurred. If the plaintiff succeeds in doing that, the case is over, and the defendant is liable. In non-per se §1 cases, by

---

7. To be fair, Justice White, writing for the majority, argued later in the opinion that all of the Court's precedents could be understood as having applied a "rule-of-reason" standard. *See* 221 U.S. at 65-68. And, in any case, some holding like that in *Standard Oil* had to come at some point if the Sherman Act were to persist, since a literal reading of §1 would simply be unworkable. As Justice Brandeis wrote in a somewhat later and still one of the most famous Supreme Court opinions, "[T]he legality of an agreement or regulation cannot be determined by so simple a test, as whether it restrains competition. Every agreement concerning trade, every regulation of trade, restrains. To bind, to restrain, is of their very essence." *Bd. of Trade of the City of Chicago v. United States*, 246 U.S. 231, 238 (1918).

contrast, the plaintiff must not only prove that the defendant engaged in the challenged conduct but also that conduct restrained trade "unreasonably." This is not to say that per se cases are somehow removed from the *Standard Oil* requirement of the reasonableness standard. It is only to say that in per se cases the courts have declared that the challenged conduct, if proven, is so obviously detrimental to competition that it is presumed to be unreasonable as a matter of law.

But, in any case, in the common parlance of antitrust lawyers to describe a case as a "rule-of-reason case" means that the conduct challenged in the case is not per se illegal.

§5.1.2 "Horizontal" Versus "Vertical" Arrangements: The Significance of Product Distribution in the Law of §1

As discussed at much greater length in Chapter 10 and in the appendix, antitrust distinguishes between different kinds of conduct depending on the place of the firms involved in the chain of distribution of their product. Their relationship might be horizontal (if they are head-to-head, competing sellers of the same product, at the same level distribution; an example might be the relationship of Sony and Samsung, which both produce televisions) or vertical (if one of them is an "upstream" participant in the market for the good, and relies on the other to distribute the good; an example would be Sony and its relationship with a retail seller of televisions, like Best Buy). Sherman Act §1 applies to both horizontal and vertical agreements, but it treats horizontal agreements much more harshly.

The courts explain this distinction in the following way. Head-to-head competitors ordinarily have little reason to cooperate or agree with one another about much of anything. Their normal relation is an adversarial one, and their basic task is to make better, cheaper products in order to gain at one another's expense. So unless horizontal competitors can show that some agreement between them will result in some new product or some new, better way of doing things that neither of them could accomplish individually, they are at serious risk of antitrust liability. By contrast, sellers of goods and services *always* have a reason to contract with firms that distribute their goods; it is a fundamental necessity. There is also reason to believe that the consequences of restraints in the vertical context are at least different and more complex. A whole body of economics has grown up around this problem, which is explored in the appendix. Under current law, vertical agreements do not often violate §1. (*See* Chapter 10.)

§5.2 WHY THE PER-SE-VERSUS-RULE-OF-REASON DISTINCTION ISN'T ACTUALLY EASY: THE CHANGING PERSPECTIVE SINCE 1975 AND THE TRADE-OFF BETWEEN FALSE POSITIVE AND FALSE NEGATIVE

Finally, before digging into the substantive specifics of §1 law, it really is necessary to consider some developments in more recent history. As with so many other areas of current antitrust, the law cannot really be understood without some consideration of changes in judicial and economic thinking since the early 1970s. In the law of multilateral restraints in particular—that is, the law of §1—a *lot* has changed since then. The fundamental shifts over this period have all concerned the *plaintiff's evidentiary burden*. The rest of this chapter summarizes this development.

As the legal philosopher Roscoe Pound long ago explained, periods have recurred throughout legal history in which some received doctrinal rule no longer satisfied the needs of the day, but the courts could not yet bring themselves to reject it completely. In those periods, courts have often attempted to stretch or bend a traditional rule to make it fit changing needs, maybe by coming up with new legal fictions or new rationalizations so that new results can be reached even though nominally an old rule is used. The courts' opinions in these cases can seem as much like efforts to convince themselves as the rest of us, even as they insist that they are really just applying the same old legal rule the same way they ever did. In other words, there have been many times when the "law in books" no longer described very well the workings of the "law in action," a process that ordinarily works itself out so that eventually a whole new rule is evolved that better suits ongoing needs.[8] We need not necessarily see this process as a bad thing, however much it might seem intellectually dishonest. It is just the ordinary process of change in a common law system.

That is probably a pretty good explanation for what has happened during the last 40 years or so in the law of multilateral restraints under Sherman Act §1. The courts felt a need to address changing real-world needs, and felt obliged to accommodate that change quite some time before they really had any good theoretical explanation for what they were doing. Just a few years in the 1970s and 1980s saw the rediscovery of the doctrine of ancillary restraints (§7.2), new treatment for horizontal boycotts (§6.2.3), the development of a whole new evidentiary approach in certain

8. Roscoe Pound, *Law in Books and Law in Action*, 44 Am. L. Rev. 12 (1910).

§1 cases, which came to be known as the "abbreviated" or "quick-look" rule of reason (Chapter 8), and the peculiar, possibly *sui generis* rule in *Broad. Music, Inc. v. Columbia Broad. Sys.*, 441 U.S. 1 (1979), under which a horizontal price-fixing agreement might itself *be* the product (§6.2.1(c)). If one unifying need motivated all this bending and stretching of the law of §1, it was the Court's growing concern over *false positives*. The concern became that unduly harsh antitrust rules would impose liability on firms even though they had not behaved anticompetitively and, worse yet, would scare other firms out of engaging in conduct that might be procompetitive but could be misconstrued by antitrust courts.

At least in the law of horizontal restraints under §1, the manner by which the courts attempted to explain all this change led to a fair bit of confusion. For the most part, the "law in books" said that nothing had changed at all, that the courts were just applying the same rules they ever did, even though the "law in action" seemed different indeed. Adding to the confusion was the courts' concern not to go too far the other way. Application of the full rule of reason, with a full-blown market-power analysis, will in effect be a death sentence for many private antitrust plaintiffs and will dissuade even the federal enforcement agencies from challenging many potentially illegal arrangements.[9] For this reason, the courts have struggled to find middle ways, which still give defendants the benefit of some doubt, without inviting the costs and difficulty of the full rule of reason.

This has left some difficulties in the law of §1. At least superficially, many §1 cases still seem to follow the "category" approach that was mentioned in the introductory materials in Chapter 1. That is, they conceive of any particular kind of challenged conduct as falling into one or another particular category, and then they will simply apply the same rules to every case that falls within that category. But the category approach can be quite misleading. Among its most deceptive aspects under §1 is that it makes application of per se rules seem simple. It seems on the surface that a per se case ought to involve only a very simple fact issue: Did the defendant engage in the challenged conduct, or not? One might think there should be no inquiry into market power, market share in a relevant market, or any of the other factual inquiries that make rule-of-reason cases big and expensive. The problem is that except in those cases that are very clear-cut—where head-to-head competitors explicitly agree not to compete, and do nothing

9. *See, e.g.*, Stephen Calkins, California Dental Association: *Not a Quick Look But Not the Fully Monty*, 67 Antitrust L.J. 495, 521-522 (2000) (recounting the expense and difficulty of rule-of-reason litigation; "Making a decision turn on a full, formal proof of market power, the antitrust equivalent of the Full Monty, is a defendant's paradise."); Michael A. Carrier, *The Real Rule of Reason: Bridging the Disconnect*, 1999 BYU L. Rev. 1265 (collecting empirical evidence that rule-of-reason cases are almost always summarily disposed of for defendants because plaintiffs cannot adduce sufficient evidence of market power); Michael A. Carrier, *The Rule of Reason: An Empirical Update for the 21st Century*, 16 George Mason L. Rev. 827 (2009) (updating 1999 study).

else—the courts have found it really quite a challenge to come up with any clear rules about when a case is per se and when it is not. Absent naked horizontal collusion as to price or output, courts typically accord defendants some opportunity to explain how any seemingly per se trade restraint actually poses some procompetitive virtues. In effect, there can be something of a miniature, pretrial trial on the question of whether the challenged restraint is so obviously anticompetitive as to excuse proof of anticompetitive effect. (Of course, this is not really a "trial" in that it ordinarily entails no taking of evidence and does not involve a jury; it will ordinarily take place as a part of pretrial dispositive motion practice, as in proceedings on a motion for summary judgment.)

The Supreme Court explicitly recognized this perhaps first in *Broad. Music, Inc. v. Columbia Broad. Sys.*, 441 U.S. 1 (1979), where it rejected per se treatment for an arrangement that on its surface could have been called horizontal price fixing. The Court wrote that "easy labels to not always supply ready answers," and then offered this important idea:

> [It] is not a question simply of determining whether two or more potential competitors have literally "fixed" a "price." As generally used in the antitrust field, "price fixing" is a shorthand way of describing certain categories of business behavior to which the *per se* rule has been held applicable. . . . [A] literal approach does not alone establish that this particular practice is one of those types or that it is "plainly anticompetitive" and very likely without "redeeming virtue." Literalness is overly simplistic and often overbroad.

Id. at 8-9. In a handful of cases over the following 20 years or so, the Court expanded on this theme. These cases have gradually whittled away the idea that there even is a distinction between per se and rule-of-reason treatment. *Viz.*:

> We have recognized, for example, that "there is often no bright line separating *per se* from Rule of Reason analysis," since "considerable inquiry into market conditions" may be required before the application of any so-called "*per se*" condemnation is justified.

NCAA v. Bd. of Regents of the Univ. of Oklahoma, 468 U.S. 85, 110 (1984). In its most recent major statement on point, the Court seems to have suggested that there is no distinction among different §1 evidentiary standards at all:

> The truth is that our categories of analysis of anticompetitive effect are less fixed than terms like "*per se*," "quick look," and "rule of reason" tend to make them appear. . . . [W]hether the ultimate finding is the product of a presumption or actual market analysis, the essential inquiry remains the same—whether or not the challenged restraint enhances competition. . . . There is always something of a sliding scale in appraising reasonableness, but

> the sliding scale formula deceptively suggests greater precision than we can hope for. . . . Nevertheless, the quality of proof required should vary with the circumstances. . . . [Thus,] there is generally no categorical line to be drawn between restraints that give rise to an intuitively obvious inference of anticompetitive effect and those that call for more detailed treatment. What is required, rather, is an enquiry meet for the case, looking to the circumstances, details, and logic of a restraint. The object is to see whether the experience of the market has been so clear, or necessarily will be, that a confident conclusion about the principal tendency of a restriction will follow from a quick (or at least quicker) look, in place of a more sedulous one. And of course what we see may vary over time, if rule-of-reason analyses in case after case reach identical conclusions. For now, at least, a less quick look was required for the initial assessment of the tendency of these professional advertising restrictions. Because the Court of Appeals did not scrutinize the assumption of relative anticompetitive tendencies, we vacate the judgment and remand the case for a fuller consideration of the issue.

California Dental Assn. v. FTC, 526 U.S. 726, 779-781 (1999). *See also Polygram Holding v. FTC*, 416 F.3d 29, 35 (D.C. Cir. 2005) ("It would be somewhat misleading . . . to say the 'quick look' is just a new category of analysis intermediate in complexity between 'per se' condemnation and full-blown 'rule of reason' treatment"; the analysis has rather become a "continuum.").

So a first problem that remains with us in the law of §1 is that there is no clear guidance on the applicability of specific levels of the *plaintiff's evidentiary burden*. In what now appears to be something of a case-by-case, fact-specific, and uncertain inquiry, the court must situate every case somewhere on the following continuum:

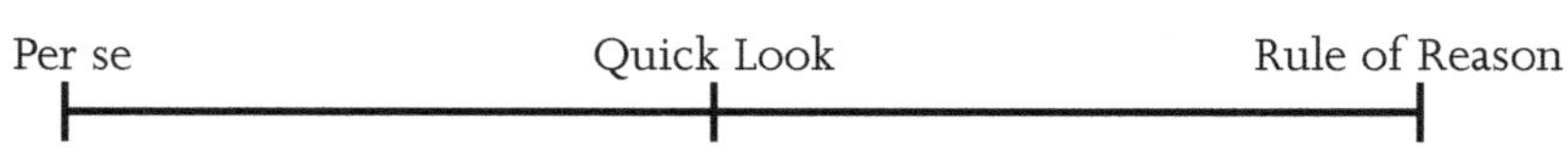

There is one other respect in which the application of per se rules is less certain than it might seem. As the law now stands, vertical restraints are never per se illegal. So it will usually be critical to the parties in a §1 case to know whether the challenged agreement is horizontal or vertical. That distinction might seem like it should be easy to draw, but sometimes it is not. Generally speaking, the issue arises in cases where the plaintiff says that some parties who are in a plainly vertical relationship have also cooperated in some way that has a horizontal aspect. A common scenario is the so-called "hub and spoke" conspiracy. A participant at one level in the chain of distribution might help to coordinate a horizontal conspiracy at another level in the chain, and if it does so it may be per se liable as a participant in the horizontal conspiracy. For example, a distributor might strike a deal with all of its suppliers as to the price at which it will resell their product. Under current law, a vertical resale price agreement is not per se illegal. But if the distributor agreed with each of its suppliers that the resale price would be the same for all of the suppliers' products, and the suppliers agreed among themselves that they would adhere to such an arrangement with the distributor, then the distributor will be complicit in a horizontal conspiracy as well as several vertical arrangements. The arrangement is called a "hub and spoke" conspiracy because each of the vertical agreements with suppliers is like a spoke on a wheel, and the distributor is the hub at the center. (This issue is discussed further in §12.4.)

Example

XYZ, Inc., a manufacturer of washing machines, holds about 35 percent of its market, and is able to wield some influence over the retailers who buy its products. Over the years, XYZ has sought to develop collaborative relationships with its more important retailers, and in particular wants them to devote themselves to promoting sales of its products, rather than engaging in aggressive price competition. XYZ has had a great deal of success in this effort. It has developed essentially informal agreements with several of the leading retail chains to sell its washing machines exclusively. Also, even as to those chains that continue to sell other manufacturer's products, there has developed a policy never to sell below XYZ's manufacturer's suggested retail price (MSRP). In fact, in the past ten years or so, there has never been a single instance of any retailer selling below the MSRP.

Is there any conspiracy in this situation that potentially violates the antitrust laws, and if there is, is it horizontal or vertical? What other facts might be helpful in better answering the question of whether the agreement is horizontal or vertical?

Explanation

Two different kinds of agreements might be at stake here, and both of them might violate antitrust. First, XYZ has engaged in a series of individual, bilateral vertical arrangements with retailers. These arrangements can violate Sherman Act §1 under the standards that apply to vertical restraints (discussed in Chapter 10). Second, depending on what other facts can be adduced, there might be a horizontal price-fixing conspiracy among the retailers. If XYZ had some role in coordinating it, then XYZ might also constitute a "hub and spoke" conspiracy with XYZ as its hub. Either arrangement is per se illegal and if there is a hub and spoke agreement, XYZ is liable for it in the same manner as the retailers.

§5.3 A SUMMARY OF THE LAW OF MULTILATERAL RESTRAINTS

The law of §1 has been in significant flux for a long time, and can be confusing. While some of the following summary may be a bit hard to follow without first reading about all the specific topics, which are covered in later chapters, it may help to start with a simple, big picture summary of the law. This summary will also serve as a road map to the next several chapters of this book.

1. Any agreement among two or more legally distinct entities,[10] as long as the entities are themselves subject to the Sherman Act,[11] is subject to §1 and can potentially constitute a contract, combination or conspiracy that unreasonably restrains trade. All such agreements are analyzed under the following rules.
2. In three specific classes of cases the courts judge multilateral arrangements under the per se standard, all of which are covered Chapter 6:
   a. Horizontal price-fixing arrangements,
   b. Horizontal market allocations, and
   c. Some horizontal refusals to deal (also known as "boycotts").
3. In some small but much less clearly defined class of cases, the courts will apply the so-called quick-look or intermediate rule-of-reason standard of review. The quick-look standard has been applied in cases in which "an observer with even a rudimentary understanding of economics could conclude that the arrangements in question would have an anticompetitive effect on customers and markets."[12] Specific kinds of restraints that have been held subject to quick-look analysis include:
   a. Agreements that would be per se illegal except that some extenuating circumstance causes the court to lack confidence that the practice is invariably harmful;[13]

10. The requirement that there be two or more separate entities involved is discussed in §12.2.
11. The scope of the Sherman Act is discussed in Chapters 20-23.
12. *California Dental Assn. v. FTC*, 526 U.S. 756, 770 (1999).
13. *NCAA v. Bd. of Regents of the Univ. of Oklahoma*, 468 U.S. 85 (1984) (rule of NCAA tightly constraining sale of rights to televise member schools' football games would ordinarily be illegal, but that "would be inappropriate . . . [in a] case[] . . . involv[ing] an industry in which horizontal restraints on competition are essential if the product is to be available at all"); cf. *United States v. Brown Univ.*, 5 F.3d 658 (3d Cir. 1993) (agreement among universities to regulate amount and kinds of financial aid offered was merely horizontal price fixing, but per se would be inappropriate given the publicly oriented nature of the defendant institutions).

b. Agreements to limit advertising, particularly where they relate to advertising of prices;[14]
c. Agreements not to negotiate price or to limit the circumstances under which price would be negotiated;[15]
d. Agreements to refrain from doing something rational competitors would do under free competition, even if that thing does not directly relate to price or output.[16]

While there is no clear guidance as to what the plaintiff must prove in such a case, there must be some evidence showing likely anticompetitive effect, which may consist of theoretical arguments of expert witnesses or evidence of actual effects from similar industries. Most importantly, the plaintiff need not make a full demonstration of market power through proof of market share in a relevant market. The quick-look standard is discussed at more length in Chapter 8.

4. One special class of agreements is subject to an idiosyncratic rule: so-called tying agreements, in which a seller forces buyers to buy two or more separate products even though they might prefer to buy only one of them; the special doctrinal test governing tying arrangements is covered in Chapter 11.
5. In all other cases, the arrangement at issue is subject to challenge only under the full rule of reason. To prevail, the plaintiff must show:
   a. that the conduct could cause price to go up or output to go down, assuming the defendants have market power; and
   b. either that the defendants have market power or direct proof of anticompetitive effect (as explained in §4.1.2).

---

14. *California Dental Assn. v. FTC*, 526 U.S. 756 (1999) (professional association ethical rule prohibiting price advertising subject to quick-look analysis).
15. *Natl. Socy. of Profl. Engrs. v. United States*, 435 U.S. 679 (1978) (professional association ethical rule prohibiting engineers from negotiating price until after entering contract with clients subject to quick-look analysis).
16. *FTC v. Indiana Fedn. of Dentists*, 476 U.S. 447 (1986) (agreement among dentists to refuse to provide patient X-rays to insurers, which insurers would have used to review reasonableness of dentists' medical choices and fees charged, was not per se illegal, but could be condemned without elaborate industry analysis).

CHAPTER 6

Per Se Offenses

§6.1 THE STRUCTURE OF A PER SE CAUSE OF ACTION

Since early in antitrust history the courts have thought that some restraints were so plainly harmful that they could be held illegal without any real inquiry into their purpose or effects. As the Court put it in the following famous language,

> [T]here are certain agreements or practices which because of their pernicious effect on competition and lack of any redeeming virtue are conclusively presumed to be unreasonable and therefore illegal without elaborate inquiry as to the precise harm they have caused or the business excuse for their use.

Northern Pac. Ry. Co. v. United States, 356 U.S. 1, 5 (1958). The Court has stressed that, while new rules of per se illegality may be adopted from time to time, the adoption of new ones is a serious affair. "It is only after considerable experience with certain business relationships that courts classify them as *per se* violations. . . ." *United States v. Topco Assocs., Inc.*, 405 U.S. 596, 607-608 (1972). Per se illegal conduct is also considered the most serious as a matter of policy, and it is now the only conduct that the Justice Department prosecutes criminally.

The Court has also stressed in recent years that it will observe a presumption in favor of rule-of-reason treatment in §1 cases. "[T]his Court," it has explained, "presumptively applies rule of reason analysis, under which antitrust plaintiffs must demonstrate that a particular contract or combination is in fact unreasonable and anticompetitive before it will be found illegal." *Texaco, Inc. v. Dagher*, 547 U.S. 1, 5 (2006). Accordingly, under current law only three classes of conduct remain per se illegal:

- Naked, horizontal price fixing,
- Naked, horizontal market allocations, and
- Some naked, horizontal concerted refusals to deal (a.k.a. "boycotts").

Each of these arrangements is horizontal, and it is per se illegal only if it puts "naked" restraints on price or output. An agreement is "naked" if it involves no more than the trade restraint itself. On the other hand, if the restraint is merely one part of a larger agreement that serves some purpose other than restraining trade, then the trade restraint may be said to be merely "ancillary." If so, it will receive rule of reason treatment. The doctrine of ancillary restraints is discussed in §7.2.

A plaintiff that can convince a court to apply a per se rule (a task that can be more difficult than one might think, as explained in §5.2) has a fairly simple case before it. Most of the modern law of per se liability first appeared in *United States v. Socony-Vacuum Oil Co.*, 310 U.S. 150 (1940). In that case, Justice Douglas packed one long, famous footnote with a series of observations that, though they were largely dicta, would come to dominate per se litigation. He began by summing up the Court's conclusions about the breadth and simplicity of per se prohibitions:

> Whatever economic justification particular price-fixing agreements may be thought to have, the law does not permit an inquiry into their reasonableness. They are all banned because of their actual or potential threat to the central nervous system of the economy.

310 U.S. at 224 n.59. He then made clear the following points:

- There need be no showing of market power or even any ability to cause harm.
- The plaintiff need not prove intent in per se causes of action.
- There need not be any overt act toward carrying out the conspiracy; the agreement itself is sufficient to establish the offense.
- The size of the conspiracy or the commerce involved is irrelevant; at least in the strictest legal sense, there is no de minimis exception to per se illegality under §1.

See id. Accordingly, the structure of a per se cause of action is really very simple. The plaintiff must merely plead that the challenged conduct occurred. If the plaintiff can prove that much, then the defendant is liable.

The only difficult issue in clear-cut per se cases, assuming the basic facts can be shown, will usually be the amount of damages.

Example

John and Joe both operate bait shops in the town of Camden, Maine. Their stores are about ten blocks apart, and they know that they share a number of customers in common. Tired of fighting with each other over every penny, they agree that John will sell Squirmy Wormy brand bait whereas Joe will not, while Joe will sell Shiny Shenanigans lures and John will not. They also agree that when a customer inquires about one of these two brands at the "wrong" store, that owner will direct the customer to the other store. They shake hands on this and call their arrangement a "mutual referral service."

John and Joe are only 2 of probably 40 or so outlets for bait and fishing supplies within the Camden area, and even together they command perhaps 2-3 percent of the relevant market.

Is this illegal? What about the fact that they have no market power? Also, why isn't the arrangement just "ancillary," since John and Joe are also providing a service to customers by advising them where they can find their preferred product?

Explanation

This is a per se illegal market allocation. It is not "ancillary" because there is nothing for it to be ancillary to. In order for a restraint to be ancillary, it must be reasonably necessary as part of a larger, procompetitive arrangement. But here, the only thing to which it is ancillary is an agreement not to compete between two otherwise completely unaffiliated horizontal competitors. It is irrelevant that the parties have no market power. It is even technically irrelevant that the amount of commerce at stake is de minimis, though the likelihood of legal challenge is for that reason very small.

§6.2 CATEGORIES OF CONDUCT THAT REMAIN PER SE ILLEGAL

§6.2.1 Horizontal Price Fixing

§6.2.1(a) In General

The paradigmatic trade restraint is the naked, horizontal price-fixing conspiracy—an agreement between head-to-head competitors setting the price at which they will sell their good or service. Naked, horizontal price fixing has also been long considered the most serious of antitrust offenses, and it is the most harshly punished (in that it is routinely prosecuted by the Justice Department as a crime).

Given the gravity of the offense, courts are generally not inclined to give defendants the benefit of much doubt, wherever it seems like an agreement in one way or another relates to prices or output and is otherwise a naked one. There need be no agreement as to any particular price; there need not even be agreement directly relating to price as such. In *Socony-Vacuum* the defendants did no more than agree to buy up and stockpile some of the product in their market, to cause price to increase.

Agreements as to *terms* of sale can also constitute price fixing, as long as the terms somehow relate to the overall consideration a buyer must give for the good. *Catalano, Inc. v. Target Sales, Inc.*, 446 U.S. 643 (1980), involved a horizontal agreement among beer distributors that they would no longer extend credit to the retail stores that carried their products. Prior to the agreement, they had all routinely delivered beer to retailers before receiving payment, and would usually be paid only after the beer had been sold to retail customers. Though there was no explicit agreement on any price—indeed, the distributors remained free to charge any price they liked for their beer—the Court had no trouble characterizing the arrangement as naked, horizontal price fixing. It first quoted a dissenting judge in the decision below, who wrote that

> [t]he purchase of goods creates an obligation to pay for them. Credit is one component of the overall price paid for a product. The cost to a retailer of purchasing goods consists of (1) the amount he has to pay to obtain the goods, and (2) the date on which he has to make that payment. If there is a differential between a purchase for cash and one on time, that difference is not interest but part of the price.

Id. at 645 (quoting 605 F.2d 1097, 1104 (5th Cir. 1979) (Blumenthal, J., dissenting)). The Court then quoted its own language from *Socony-Vacuum*:

> [T]he machinery employed by a combination for price-fixing is immaterial. Under the Sherman Act a combination formed for the purpose and with the effect of raising, depressing, fixing, pegging, or stabilizing the price of a commodity in interstate or foreign commerce is illegal *per se*.

Id. at 647 (quoting *United States v. Socony-Vacuum Oil Co.*, 310 U.S. 150, 223 (1940)).

§6.2.1(b) Kinds of Conduct Commonly Found to Constitute Per Se Price Fixing

Generally speaking, quite a range of agreements can be found to involve price fixing. The courts are hesitant to require proof of agreement on literal prices, because other kinds of conduct can have the same effects and lack redeeming virtue. So, for example, agreements among competitors to pool their revenues have long been treated as per se illegal price fixing, because they remove the incentive the parties have to compete with one another on a price basis. *See Citizen Publishing Co. v. United States*, 394 U.S. 131, 134-135 (1969). Similarly, a horizontal agreement to take action whose only purpose is to *affect* price in some way is per se illegal. This was the Court's holding in the seminal *Socony-Vacuum* case. In that case, defendant oil producers agreed among themselves to buy up and stockpile agreed upon amounts of oil, to reduce supply and keep prices up. Courts also hold that joint sales or joint licensing agreements are really just naked horizontal price-fixing agreements if they do no more than distribute goods independently produced by the participants. For example, imagine that four makers of televisions agree to create a subsidiary corporation, owned by all of them, to which they will sell all of their product. The subsidiary will then resell their product at one uniform price. This is per se illegal; defendants would surely argue that the joint sales subsidiary was some sort of joint venture that produces efficiencies, but under the circumstances it has no purpose except to fix price.

§6.2.1(c) The Arguably Sui Generis Rule of *BMI*: Price-Fixing Agreements That Are Themselves the Product

The Supreme Court appears to have described one special rule dealing with an unusual and probably rare kind of horizontal restraint, in *Broad. Mus., Inc. v. Columbia Broad. Sys.*, 441 U.S. 1 (1979). That case involved an organization of composers of music which helped them enforce their copyrights. The entity sold licenses to persons who wanted to perform the music, but it did not sell them individually—it sold "blanket licenses" for a flat fee, entitling the licensee to perform all the songs in a library of music, all written by different composer-members of the group. In a technical sense this was horizontal price fixing. The composers, so far as antitrust is concerned, are horizontal price competitors, and by collectively licensing their works at a flat fee, they literally agreed to a particular price. That conduct might be thought per se illegal, and the lower courts so held. The Supreme Court reversed and held that only a rule of reason should apply.

The Court gave two different explanations for this result, one familiar and mundane, the other quite unusual. The familiar explanation was the simple ancillary restraints rule, discussed in more detail in §7.2. Under that rule, an otherwise per se illegal restraint on price or output will be subject to the rule of reason if it is merely part of some larger, desirable arrangement. Here the larger arrangement was the composers' organization itself, and the Court thought it was likely quite desirable for a number of reasons.[1] But the Court appeared to suggest as a different reason for avoiding per se treatment that the licensing practices of the organization in fact created a whole new product. The "blanket license" the organization could sell included *all* songs in its library, and that was something no individual composer could sell. The agreement constituting the price restraint, in other words, was itself a product that purchasers might desire, and the Court suggested that where this is the case, the restraint is not per se illegal. (It should be remembered that this is probably a rare circumstance—it will be the rare case in which a horizontal price or output restraint in and of itself gives consumers something they want but otherwise can't get.)

§6.2.2 Horizontal Market Allocations

Market division cases have sometimes been difficult for the courts because sometimes explicit market divisions accompany otherwise innocent and maybe procompetitive arrangements. For this reason, one of the Court's leading cases on market division, *United States v. Topco Assocs., Inc.*, 405 U.S. 596 (1972), has been criticized. *Topco* is still nominally good law—the Supreme Court has never overruled it. But the restraint at issue was merely one part of a joint venture that arguably might have led to enhanced competition through the introduction of a new brand of products, a fact the dissent stressed vigorously. Critics have said the restraint was probably necessary to make the joint venture financially viable, and so one wonders whether if the case were to come before the Court again it might adopt the "ancillary restraints" approach that has become more prominent in recent decades. (*See* §7.2.)

Still, when market divisions are truly naked, the courts have no trouble finding them per se illegal. The Supreme Court's most recent observation on point, *Palmer v. BRG of Georgia, Inc.*, 498 U.S. 46 (1990), unequivocally reaffirmed that naked horizontal market allocations are per se illegal. There, a

1. The composers would have found it impossible to negotiate individual license agreements with each of the millions of performers, radio stations, movie producers, theaters, bars, and so on that might like to perform their music but could not legally do so without copyright license. They also would find it impossible to police against infringement by those millions of entities. Because the blanket-license innovation made copyright enforcement feasible, it served the procompetitive purpose of encouraging the composers to produce more of their product. Incidentally, this case nicely illustrates a rule, discussed in §3.2.2, that runs throughout antitrust: It is not a defense in antitrust that a restraint might serve some social value other than competition. A defendant can never argue that under the circumstances competition itself would have led to undesirable results. But note that in *BMI* the defendants did not make that argument. They argued that their arrangement allowed them to *improve* competition, because it made it feasible for them to produce more of their product or produce a product they could not individually supply. Courts will always consider it procompetitive to produce more of a product, to sell it more cheaply, or to improve its quality.

leading national provider of bar exam preparation courses—the familiar Bar/Bri firm—agreed with an upstart provider of those courses located in Georgia—defendant BRG of Georgia—that the two of them effectively would no longer compete in that state. The defendants argued that their arrangement was not a simple, naked trade restraint, but was rather an intellectual property deal. Though they had been fierce price competitors when BRG first began operations, they reached an agreement under which BRG would be given an exclusive license to market the Bar/Bri course in Georgia. BRG would pay Bar/Bri a commission on all the Bar/Bri courses it sold and keep the rest. As part of their agreement Bar/Bri promised that it would no longer separately compete with BRG in that state, and BRG promised that it would not compete with Bar/Bri outside of Georgia. The price of the course immediately jumped from $150 to $400 (if those prices seem low, recall that the deal was reached in 1979).

That the deal was styled essentially as an agency relationship, in which the national firm licensed a local one to sell its product, gave the Court no trouble. In a barely three-page, unanimous, per curiam order the Court held that any "agree[ment] not to compete in . . . [one][an]other's territories" is "unlawful on its face." *Id.* at 49-50.

Example

ABC incorporated is a nationwide provider of waste management services. It operates a fleet of garbage trucks in various cities around the country. However, ABC has not yet broken into the waste management business in the state of Oregon, and it desires to do so. Currently, the main provider of such services in the Portland area is a company called XYZ, Inc. The CEO of ABC one day calls the CEO of XYZ, and mentions his interest in establishing a foothold in Portland. One of his suggestions is simply that ABC acquire XYZ by way of a merger. But XYZ's CEO is dead set against any such acquisition, and in fact threatens ABC with "all-out warfare" if it tries to enter Portland.

Things stand on about this footing for a month or so, during which time the two CEOs continue to exchange threats and counterthreats. However, both of them secretly know that the other company is no easy adversary, and that a fight for dominance in Portland could be very costly for both. They finally reach a compromise. Their written contract, styled "Agency Agreement," provides that in lieu of directly providing waste management services in Portland itself, ABC would appoint XYZ to be its "authorized agent" in Portland. In a preamble, the agreement lists several reasons that ABC prefers to operate in Portland by way of an agent.

XYZ promises to supply its own equipment and maintains its existing management team, who operate with ABC's oversight. It continues to issue its own advertising under its own name, and does not amend its contracts with customers to indicate the new agency relationship. The parties do not publicly announce their agency agreement. The major written requirement under the agreement is that XYZ pay ABC a fee, described in the agreement as a "commission," which is a percentage of XYZ's revenue under its service contracts in the Portland area.

First of all, what category of antitrust analysis does this arrangement likely fit into? And is this likely to be legal or illegal?

Explanation

The arrangement is a horizontal market allocation and it is per se illegal. The fact that it is characterized as an agency arrangement is probably of no significance, for the reasons stated in *Palmer v. BRG of Georgia, Inc.*

EXPLANATION

§6.2.3 Concerted Refusals to Deal (a.k.a. "Boycotts")

One final category of conduct can sometimes be illegal per se, though it has caused a lot more confusion than the other two: concerted refusals to deal, sometimes known as group "boycotts." The law in this area is complicated by the fact that the term "boycott" itself can mean so many different things. In everyday speech, it connotes a political demonstration—people unhappy with some company or some organization might collectively refuse to patronize it. To suggest that such things could violate antitrust would seem pretty surprising, since collective, nonviolent protest seems like such a part of American culture and one that is valued by many. And, whether they are valued or not, consumer or politically oriented protests sometimes enjoy protection under the First Amendment. Nevertheless, sometimes some things that look similar to such boycotts not only violate antitrust but are per se illegal.

§6.2.3(a) Distinguishing Per Se and Non-Per Se Boycotts

The conduct with which antitrust is most concerned does not really look much like the essentially political consumer boycott that the word normally implies. The conduct we care about in antitrust normally involves an agreement among competitors or some other participants in a given market under which they refuse to do business with some other party who is also involved in that market. For such an arrangement to be of interest to antitrust law, it usually must somehow serve the parties' own *commercial* advantage.

But even where boycotts are clearly commercially motivated, it can still be hard to say just how they should be treated in antitrust, and this is because boycotts can come in a lot of different forms. For example, in *Blue Shield of Virginia v. McCready*, 457 U.S. 465 (1982), the plaintiff alleged that her insurer had agreed with a trade association of *psychiatrists* that the insurer would not reimburse the services of *psychologists*. This was an agreement among two participants in a market for mental health services (insurers and psychiatrists) under which the insurers would boycott another participant (psychologists), and it was a direct interference with price competition between psychiatrists and psychologists. A somewhat different boycott was alleged in *Associated Gen. Contractors of California, Inc. v. California State Council of Carpenters*, 459 U.S. 519 (1983). There a union of carpenters claimed that a group of construction firms (i.e., the union members' employers) had coerced third parties not to give their business to construction firms that hired union carpenters. This too was a direct interference with the system of individual choices made on the basis of price and quality.

How to handle these arrangements has caused substantial trouble in antitrust. There was a time, prior to the 1970s, when the Supreme Court held in broad language that *all* multilateral refusals to deal should be per se illegal.[2] Even now, some arrangements that come within the very loose definition of "boycott" are so blatantly anticompetitive that no one is likely to believe they should be legal, but there are many others where the consequences are more ambiguous. For example, one common problem is in "standard setting." Many private groups exist that devise agreed-upon standards for the making of products or the performance of various functions. The membership of those groups often includes representatives from industries that may be affected by the standards produced. If the group produces a standard for the design of a given product, and that design becomes widely adopted by makers and buyers of the product, that might disadvantage some maker who happens to prefer an alternative design (perhaps it owns intellectual property in that other design or has significant investments in plant and equipment to make that other design). The standard could be said to be a boycott of that alternative product. That is, the group's members could be said to have pressured buyers of the product not to do business with makers of the disfavored design. But it is thought that standardization can also be procompetitive, and in particular in recent years the "interoperability" of technological goods has been thought to improve price and quality competition. Another common problem involves cooperatives and trade associations. Imagine that a group of small retailers agree to combine their resources to form a wholesale purchasing cooperative that will allow them to enjoy volume discounts on purchases of the items that they will each sell.

---

2. *See, e.g.*, *Radiant Burners, Inc. v. Peoples Gas, Light & Coke Co.*, 364 U.S. 656 (1961); *Klor's, Inc. v. Broadway-Hale Stores, Inc.*, 359 U.S. 207 (1959).

The arrangement might have procompetitive advantages. It allows the small retailers to provide more vigorous price competition to the large retailers who already enjoy their own scale efficiencies. But what if the retailers establish membership rules and because of those rules one of their own small competitors is excluded from the cooperative? Has that retailer been boycotted in a way that should be considered illegal?

The Supreme Court addressed all these issues in its seminal decision in *Northwest Wholesale Stationers, Inc. v. Pacific Stationery & Printing Co.*, 472 U.S. 284 (1985). There, several small retail sellers of stationery items set up a purchasing cooperative to acquire inventory for them. They had trouble meeting the cost advantages of their larger competitors, who could buy in volume at lower prices. Buying together, the group of smaller retailers could get their own volume up and get discounts. The case arose when the cooperative expelled one of its members for violation of a membership rule. There was no doubt that in some sense this was a "boycott" or a "refusal to deal." But to hold that any exclusion—any membership rule—is per se illegal would likely make the venture unworkable. There was also no doubt that that the venture could pose procompetitive benefits.

The Court therefore explained something of a new test for application of its traditional per se rule relating to boycotts:

> Cases to which this Court has applied the *per se* approach have generally involved joint efforts by a firm or firms to disadvantage competitors by either directly denying or persuading or coercing suppliers or customers to deny relationships the competitors need in the competitive struggle. In these cases, the boycott often cut off access to a supply, facility, or market necessary to enable the boycotted firm to compete, and frequently the boycotting firms possessed a dominant position in the relevant market. . . . In addition, the practices were generally not justified by plausible arguments that they were intended to enhance overall efficiency and make markets more competitive. Under such circumstances the likelihood of anticompetitive effects is clear and the possibility of countervailing procompetitive effects is remote.
>
> Although a concerted refusal to deal need not necessarily possess all of these traits to merit *per se* treatment, not every cooperative activity involving a restraint or exclusion will share with the *per se* forbidden boycotts the likelihood of predominantly anticompetitive consequences.

Id. at 294-295 (citations and quotation marks omitted).

So when, under this standard, is a boycott per se illegal? While the test is hardly cut and dried, in cases following *Northwest Wholesale Stationers* the courts have almost always reserved per se treatment for boycotts that involve a few elements. They must be:

(a) horizontal agreements among competitors,
(b) that are naked, and not ancillary to a procompetitive arrangement, and

(c) that target other horizontal competitors of the group's membership, with the goal to raise prices or restrict output.

Again, notwithstanding *Northwest Wholesale Stationers*, when the Court is confronted with a serious, naked, horizontal boycott case, it has no trouble finding it per se illegal. The Court's most recent case on point, *FTC v. Superior Court Trial Lawyers Assn.*, 439 U.S. 411 (1990), involved an agreement among lawyers who represented the bulk of indigent criminal defendants in the District of Columbia. Dissatisfied with the pay they received from the courts, they refused to take any more cases until the fee was raised. Though the Court expressed some sympathy with the partially political motivation of the boycott, the Court also noted that it was an agreement among horizontal competitors that was naked of any procompetitive goals. Its only purpose was to coerce an increase in the price to be paid for the conspirators' services. Accordingly, the conduct was per se illegal.

§6.2.3(b) The First Amendment Issue

As will be explained at more length in §21.4.5, boycott cases raise a special First Amendment issue, and *Superior Court Trial Lawyers* is again a leading case. When people get together to state their views, either publicly or to their government, they may be engaging in conduct that is constitutionally protected as speech or petition of government for redress of grievances. Thus, at least in theory any concerted refusal to deal might enjoy constitutional protection from antitrust.

The issue was raised squarely in *NAACP v. Claiborne Hardware Co.*, 458 U.S. 886 (1982). There, a group of NAACP activists literally boycotted retail stores in a particular town in Mississippi that they alleged to have behaved in racially discriminatory ways. They refused to patronize those stores, and they encouraged others to do so as well, until that discriminatory conduct ended. The stores sued under state tort theories and recovered damages and injunction in the state courts, but the Supreme Court reversed. The Court wrote that the "right of the States to regulate economic activity could not justify a complete prohibition against a nonviolent, politically motivated boycott designed to force governmental and economic change and to effectuate rights guaranteed by the Constitution itself." *Id.* at 914.

However, when the defendants in *Superior Court Trial Lawyers* raised the same constitutional argument, alleging that they were in the same shoes as the *Claiborne Hardware* defendants, the Court disagreed. Despite its sympathy with these defendants, the Court found their boycott to be predominantly "commercial" and therefore entitled to no constitutional protection at all. *See also Allied Tube & Conduit Corp. v. Indian Head, Inc.*, 486 U.S. 492, 508 (1988) (holding *Claiborne Hardware* inapplicable to a boycott conducted by business competitors who "stand to profit financially from a lessening of competition in the boycotted market").

Example

A group of retail chain stores has gotten together and decided that they are fed up with Walmart, since it is a very successful price cutter. They decide that they will collectively visit the major manufacturers whose products they sell and tell them that they will no longer carry those products unless the manufacturers stop selling to Walmart. Is that conduct illegal, and if so why?

Would it be different if instead of boycotting the manufacturers, the retailers formed a lobbying group and argued to Congress that unless it passed legislation that would make it more difficult for Walmart to compete, they would simply stop selling products that were also retailed by Walmart?

Explanation

The initial boycott is per se illegal. It is a horizontal concerted refusal to deal that seeks to injure a horizontal competitor by denying to it a needed resource for effective competition. The situation would be different if the group acted by lobbying Congress, even though the outcome of their effort might be just the same. On the one hand, it does not clearly appear that this boycott would qualify for the protection of the First Amendment under *Claiborne Hardware*, because it is commercially motivated. However, as we discuss at length in §21.4, this would constitute "petitioning" conduct that enjoys a special exemption from antitrust under a judge-made doctrine known as the *Noerr-Pennington* immunity. So in the second scenario, the retailers' conduct would not violate antitrust.

Example

A group called the Lutheran Mother's Association, consisting mainly of women of the Lutheran faith who are mothers, issue a press release demanding that manufacturers of home video games reduce the violence and provocatively dressed characters in the games they market to children. The press release states that the Association's 10,000 members nationwide will refuse to buy any goods from any store that sells games that the Association finds either too violent or too sexually suggestive. Does this violate antitrust?

Explanation

No. This boycott has no commercial component and is essentially the same as that in *NAACP v. Claiborne Hardware*.

§6.3 DO PER SE RULES APPLY IN TWO-SIDED MARKETS?

In its 2018 decision in *Ohio v. American Express Co.*, 585 U.S. 529 (2018) (*Amex*), the Supreme Court introduced an idea new to antitrust, in recognizing that some markets have "two-sided" or "platform" properties. *Amex* poses some uncertainties for application of per se rules.

Where a market is two-sided, its real product — the relevant product market of antitrust interest — will be some thing that is consumed by two different parties, *together*. In *American Express* itself, the defendant was a credit card company that maintains a platform for payment transactions. It sells its service both to cardholders, on one side, and merchants, on the other. The jointly demanded product was card swipes — individual purchase transactions. Because the Court thought that trade restraints affecting one side could not properly be considered in isolation from their effects on both sides, it held that the only relevant product of a truly two-sided platform is the jointly demanded product. (For further discussion, *see* §4.2.5.)

While this new law on two-sided markets poses some uncertainties, it seems clear that agreements *within* platforms will be subject to the rule of reason, while agreements *between* competing platforms can still be per se illegal in appropriate circumstances. This is because relationships between the owner of the platform and a party on one side will be treated as vertical. *Id.* at 541. All agreements among them will therefore be governed under the rule of reason, *id.*, which will be applied under the new rule that the relevant market is the market for the jointly demanded product. Thus, there is legally relevant harm only if the price of the jointly demanded good goes up or its output goes down. On the other hand, agreements between owners of different, competing *platforms* seem likely to be treated as horizontal. As the Court stressed, "[o]nly other two-sided platforms can compete with a two-sided platform for transactions." *Id.* at 546. So, if an agreement between platform owners entails a naked restraint on price or output, it stands to reason that it will be subject to per se treatment. The underlying economic literature identifies restraints on inter-platform competition as harmful and presumably no less so than any other horizontal restraints.[3]

3. *See, e.g.*, William F. Baxter, *Bank Interchange of Transactional Paper: Legal and Economic Perspectives*, 26 J. L. & Econ. 541, 586-587 (1983).

CHAPTER 7

The Rule of Reason and the Doctrine of Ancillary Restraints

§7.1 WHAT THE RULE OF REASON IS REALLY ABOUT AND THE ELEMENTS OF A RULE-OF-REASON CAUSE OF ACTION

It is worth noting again a point made before. In principle, the substantive question to be asked in any §1 case is always the same: It is not whether there was some multilateral restraint of trade, but whether some such restraint was *unreasonable*. Therefore, while the choice to apply the per se or rule-of-reason label to a given case is of great practical significance to the parties, the difference between them is in some sense only procedural or secondary. It is only a matter of which questions are left open for the trier of fact, and what evidence the plaintiff has to put on. As the Supreme Court has explained,

> [W]hether the ultimate finding is the product of a presumption or actual market analysis, the essential inquiry remains the same—whether or not the challenged restraint enhances competition. Under the Sherman Act the criterion to be used in judging the validity of a restraint of trade is its impact on competition.

NCAA v. Bd. of Regents of the Univ. of Oklahoma, 468 U.S. 85, 104 (1985).

Moreover, though we often think of the per se rule and the rule of reason as clearly distinct rules, they are not. This is so for two reasons. First, despite the apparent simplicity of the "category" approach (explained in

Chapter 1), and the apparently simple distinction between the per se rule and the rule of reason, it can be hard to know in a particular case which of them should apply. As we shall see, there will be times when the courts devote quite a bit of fact-sensitive analysis to a given situation before deciding to apply the per se rule, even where there may be some conduct that looks like a horizontal restraint on price or output. It sometimes is a little hard to see how this analysis is so different from traditional rule-of-reason analysis, even if the court ultimately decides to apply a per se rule.

Second, it turns out that the per se rule and the rule of reason are not so much distinct rules as opposite points on a continuum, and that the level of analysis that a court decides to impose (i.e., the kinds of evidence the plaintiff must put on and the sorts of questions that are left open for the trier of fact) can fall at points on the continuum between these two poles.

Again, the Supreme Court put it this way (quoting earlier cases and a leading treatise):

> [I]t does not follow that every case attacking a less obviously anticompetitive restraint [than naked horizontal price fixing] . . . is a candidate for plenary market examination. The truth is that our categories of analysis . . . are less fixed than terms like "per se," "quick look," and "rule of reason" tend to make them appear. We have recognized, for example, that there is often no bright line separating per se from rule of reason analysis, since considerable inquiry into market conditions may be required before the application of any so-called "per se" condemnation is justified. . . . [Moreover,][t]here is always something of a sliding scale in appraising reasonableness, but the sliding scale formula deceptively suggests greater precision than we can hope for. . . . Nevertheless, the quality of proof required should vary with the circumstances.

California Dental Assn. v. FTC, 526 U.S. 756, 779-780 (1999) (internal citations and quotation marks omitted). (This issue of the continuum or "sliding scale" of §1 is further discussed in §§8.2-8.3.)

In any case, a true rule-of-reason case almost always requires that the plaintiff put on either direct evidence of actual harm—which normally means some compelling proof of a sustained increase in price or decrease in output clearly caused by the challenged restraint—or proof of market power through the market share proxy test discussed in Chapter 4. But even proof of market power under the market share proxy is not necessarily enough. The plaintiff ultimately must convince the trier of fact that the defendants were able to use their combined market power to *harm* the market and that the harm outweighs any benefit.

Still, knowing just what the rule of reason requires can be a challenge. One leading treatise rather understates things when it says that, "[a]lthough the rule of reason has long been part of Sherman Act jurisprudence, the precise analysis . . . remains somewhat indistinct." 1 Am. Bar Assn., *Antitrust Law Developments (Sixth)* 56 (6th ed. 2007). That was in part because some traditional formulations were extremely open-ended, so much so that they were hardly legal tests at all. Most famously, in the influential early case *Bd. of Trade of the City of Chicago v. United States*, 246 U.S. 231 (1918), Justice Brandeis wrote this:

> The true test of illegality is whether the restraint imposed is such as merely regulates and perhaps thereby promotes competition or whether it is such as may suppress or even destroy competition. To determine that question the court must ordinarily consider the facts peculiar to the business to which the restraint is applied: its condition before and after the restraint was imposed; the nature of the restraint and its effect, actual or probable. The history of the restraint, the evil believed to exist, the reason for adopting the particular remedy, the purpose or end sought to be attained, are all relevant facts.

246 U.S. at 238. He added, moreover, something important about the role of intent in rule-of-reason analysis. Noting that evidence of intent was important but not controlling, he wrote:

> This is not because a good intention will save an otherwise objectionable regulation or the reverse; but because knowledge of intent may help the court to interpret facts and to predict consequences.

Id.

But this famous statement of the test came under heavy criticism because it was so very broad. It made virtually everything relevant, which could be a problem for businesses trying to plan their affairs and for plaintiffs trying to make their cases. It seemed like parties had to prove or disprove an unlimited range of relevant facts.[1]

That problem has abated to a large degree. Lower courts gradually developed a more precise test, and while the Supreme Court made no comment on it for many years, the Court eventually adopted it, first in *Ohio v. American Express Co.*, 585 U.S. 529, 541-542 (2018), and again in *NCAA v. Alston*, 594 U.S. 69, 96-97 (2021). As the Court has stated it, the test has these elements:

> [(1)] the plaintiff has the initial burden to prove that the challenged restraint has a substantial anticompetitive effect." [(2)] Should the plaintiff carry that burden, the burden then shifts to the defendant to show a procompetitive rationale for the restraint. [(3)] If the defendant can make that showing, the burden shifts back to the plaintiff to demonstrate that the procompetitive efficiencies could be reasonably achieved through less anticompetitive means.

Id. (citations omitted).

---

1. *See, e.g.*, Peter C. Carstensen, *The Content of the Hollow Core of Antitrust: The Chicago Board of Trade Case and the Meaning of the "Rule of Reason" in Restraint of Trade Analysis*, 15 Res. L. & Econ. 1 (1992); Maurice E. Stucke, *Does the Rule of Reason Violate the Rule of Law?* 42 U.C. Davis L. Rev. 1375 (2009).

Still, some real uncertainties remain. For their part, the lower courts had stated roughly the same test, over dozens of opinions and many years, but their formulations differed in their details, and the differences could drive different outcomes.[2] Some lower courts still state formulations that are not identical to the Court's test in *Amex* and *Alston*, and it is not clear which if any of them are really the law. *See, e.g., United States v. Am. Airlines Grp., Inc.*, 675 F. Supp. 3d 65, 109 (D. Mass. 2024). Importantly, as commentators have noted,[3] the second and third elements of the Court's formulation might imply that a defendant can rebut the prima facie case by identifying *any* procompetitive benefit, even one that is substantially smaller than the anticompetitive harm. Plaintiff must then show some less harmful means of achieving *that* benefit, however small or however greatly outweighed by the harm, or else lose its case. In other words, it seems possible that under this formulation a restraint could be very substantially anticompetitive but still be legal, so long as there is some benefit to be gained and no less harmful way to get it. If so, apparently, then any amount of anticompetitive harm would be permitted so long as there is any procompetitive benefit that can't be gotten more cheaply.

If that really was the Court's intent, it would seem a significant departure. For what it is worth, the Court has not directly answered whether it meant to do away with a final balancing step. The entire discussion of the rule of reason in *American Express* was essentially dicta, because the Court held that plaintiff failed to meet even the prima facie showing. The courts in *Alston* never reached a balancing step because each of them found defendants to have failed at step two. Moreover, there are reasons to believe the Court did not intend to reject balancing. For one thing, the dissenters in *American Express* stated their own three-step version of the rule of reason, without suggesting that it differed in substance, and it followed the more traditional understanding. They would permit a plaintiff to overcome the showing of competitive benefit at stage two by showing "that the legitimate objective does not outweigh the harm that competition will suffer, i.e., that the agreement 'on balance' remains unreasonable." *American Express*, 585 U.S. at 553-554 (Breyer, J., dissenting) (citing 7 Philip I. Areeda & Herbert Hovenkamp, *Antitrust Law* ¶ 1507a (4th ed. 2013)). And in fact, many of the authorities cited by the *American Express* majority in setting out its test themselves include a traditional balancing element of the kind captured in the dissent's formulation. So how exactly the Court's formulation affects these details remains unknown. *See, e.g., Am. Airlines Grp.*, 675 F. Supp. 3d at 110-111 (explaining the

2. *See generally* Gabriel A. Feldman, *The Misuse of the Less Restrictive Alternative Inquiry in Rule of Reason Analysis*, 58 Am. U. L. Rev. 561 (2009).

3. *See, e.g.*, Andrew I. Gavil & Jordan L. Ludwig, *The Many Sides of* Ohio v. American Express Co., Antitrust, Fall, 2018, at 8, 10-11.

parties' competing visions of the test's details, and stating in dicta that the test does include a balancing step).

Moreover, we don't know much about how the rule of reason test works on any formulation, because rule-of-reason cases so rarely reach the merits. In practice, virtually all of them—97 percent according to one well-regarded study[4]—are disposed of on motion to dismiss or summary judgment, for the plaintiff's failure to properly allege or produce sufficient initial evidence to suggest that the challenged restraint *could* harm competition.[5] When plaintiffs can survive that early stage, courts also sometimes summarily rule for the plaintiff when the defendant cannot show some procompetitive justification for the restraint. In the end, only about 2 percent of rule-of-reason cases ever reach the final stage of balancing or consideration of less restrictive alternatives by a trier of fact. So, written opinions are vanishingly rare that even reach the merits, much less explain how courts should weigh the later factors, like less-restrictive-alternative analysis and balancing of costs and benefits.

§7.2 THE DOCTRINE OF ANCILLARY RESTRAINTS

Finally, one other specific issue has developed over the years that sometimes modifies the application of per se rules. The doctrine of "ancillarity" governs cases in which some arrangement overall is procompetitive—like the creation of a new business or the sale of an existing one—but some small part of it, in isolation, might seem anticompetitive. The doctrine provides that where that small part of it—the "ancillary" part—is reasonably related to the overall purposes of the procompetitive arrangement and not unreasonably harmful to competition, it will be subject only to the rule of reason. The rule is an old and venerated one, though it lay dormant for a long time. It was resurrected only during the 1970s, at about the same time the Supreme Court was limiting its traditional per se rules and introducing more supple approaches to apply them.

Almost as long as there has been a Sherman Act, and as long as it has been clear that naked horizontal price and output restraints are strictly forbidden, there has also been an awareness that some positive commercial arrangements might contain aspects that, taken alone, would resemble the horizontal constraints that are forbidden. A classic example is a covenant not to compete contained in a contract for the sale of a business. Suppose

4. *See generally* Michael A. Carrier, *The Rule of Reason: An Empirical Update for the 21st Century*, 16 George Mason L. Rev. 827 (2009); Michael A. Carrier, *The Real Rule of Reason: Bridging the Disconnect*, 1999 BYU L. Rev. 1265 (1999).

5. Carrier, *The Rule of Reason: An Empirical Update*, *supra* note 2.

a barber has had a successful business in a particular location in a small town, but desires to sell. The building he owns and the equipment within it would be worth something, but not as much as the going business as a whole, meaning the profit-making value he has enjoyed by virtue of his location and his established clientele. The problem is he may not be able to sell the business for what it is really worth to any other barber if there is a risk that he will just set up a new shop somewhere nearby and compete with his buyer for the same customers. That risk might diminish the value to any buyer. So in exchange for a sale price reflecting the business's real worth, the barber might have to agree not to compete directly with the buyer for some period and within some geographical territory. Suppose the selling barber agrees not to ply his trade for one year within ten miles of the old shop. Now, taken alone, this agreement—an agreement between two horizontally competitive sellers of the same service not to compete in the same area—might seem like a market division, and therefore to be per se illegal (as explained in §6.2.2). The problem is that the covenant in this case is probably also a healthy, competitive one; that is, it will facilitate the sale of a business by one person who no longer values it at its true worth to a person who does. The doctrine of ancillarity was devised to address this kind of problem.

Determining whether a restraint is "ancillary" or "naked" has engendered a lot of litigation, and the courts have used many formulations to describe the test. One leading treatise gathers the following many different formulations:

- An ancillary restraint "contributes to" or is "subordinate and collateral to" the efficiency enhancing purposes of a beneficial arrangement.
- A restraint is ancillary if it "is an inherent feature of the [beneficial arrangement]," as opposed to "an unnecessary, output-limiting appendage."
- A restraint is ancillary if it is "reasonably related to . . . and no broader than necessary to effectuate" the beneficial arrangement's purposes.
- A restraint is ancillary only if there is no "substantially less restrictive alternative[] available to achieve th[e] objectives" of the beneficial arrangement.
- An "ancillary restraint is subordinate to and collateral in the sense that it serves to make the main transaction more effective in accomplishing its purpose."
- An ancillary restraint must be "reasonably related to [some] integration and reasonably necessary to achieve its procompetitive benefits."

1 Am. Bar Assn., *Antitrust Law Developments (Sixth)* 466 (6th ed. 2007) (collecting cases and other authorities). Putting them all together, the common theme appears to be that, in order for a restraint to be "ancillary"

to a beneficial arrangement, the restraint must be *reasonably related to it*, and *reasonably necessary for its purposes*. In other words, it can't just be some unrelated price-fixing agreement or the like between parties that happen also to be in a joint venture, and, even if it is more closely related to the venture it cannot achieve the venture's aims in some way that is unnecessarily harmful. A court is likely to hold that a restraint is unnecessarily harmful if there are fairly obvious, feasible alternative ways of achieving the same results without causing as much limitation on healthy price and output.

Accordingly, as it now exists, the doctrine provides that where a defendant can prove the following elements, the challenged conduct will be judged only under the full-blown rule of reason, even if, standing alone, the conduct would otherwise have been per se illegal:

- The restraint is "ancillary," meaning that it is essential or somehow closely related to some arrangement that is itself beneficial, like a new partnership or joint venture, or the sale of a business; and
- The restraint is not unreasonably restrictive of competition in light of other alternatives that might reach the same results.

(The ancillary restraints rule and its relationship to the overall law of §1 are summarized in a chart in §§7.2 and 8.3.)

Example

The American Toilet Seat Institute is a nonprofit organization made up of academics, industrial engineers, government officials, and representatives of the toilet seat manufacturing industry. ATSI's mission is to study the design and manufacture of toilet seats to make sure that they are as safe and well functioning as can be. Among many other things, ATSI issues an annually updated list called the "Toilet Seat Design and Function Specifications." This book-length document sets out a long list of minimum performance requirements to which toilet seats must conform in order to receive the ATSI seal of approval.

ATSI is not itself a government entity or affiliated with any government. The Toilet Seat Design and Function Specifications do not have the force of law, and they are published only as the organization's opinion. However, the ATSI seal of approval has come to possess surpassing dominance. It is well known to consumers and some state and local building codes actually require toilets to comply with the ATSI specifications. Failure to secure the ATSI seal is usually the kiss of commercial death.

Recently, at ATSI's annual meeting to consider revisions to the Toilet Seat specifications, the organization considered a petition from a manufacturer concerning a new product, to be known as the "power-down" toilet seat. The seat is equipped with a small motor that causes the seat automatically to go down after use. Upon consideration, the ATSI membership decided that the power-down product is unsafe, and should not be permitted under the ATSI specifications.

It turns out that the organization's decision, which was made by majority vote of the entire membership sitting as a body, was influenced by a report submitted by one Michael Heaster. Heaster is the CEO of one of the country's largest toilet seat manufacturers, and a fierce competitor of the producer of the new power-down design. Could ATSI's decision violate the Sherman Act? Under what standard would any challenge to the ATSI press release be judged under §1?

Explanation

This conduct is in effect a concerted refusal to deal, and because some participants in it are themselves sellers of the product that is disfavored here, it is a horizontal one. Some horizontal concerted refusals to deal are per se illegal, as explained in §6.2.3. Under other circumstances this one could qualify, given Heaster's commercial motivations and ATSI's "surpassing dominance." However, the standard setting function, especially as undertaken by a group with such diverse and well-qualified members, likely serves important procompetitive functions. Therefore, the fact that sometimes ATSI standards exclude some competitors probably does not make them automatically illegal.

CHAPTER 8

Section 1 Now

The Long Struggle to Define an Intermediate Rule of Reason and the Law of the Sliding Scale

§8.1 INTRODUCTION

The courts spent several of the decades since the antitrust revolution of the 1970s developing a middle range of analysis for some horizontal restraints, which exists between per se and full rule-of-reason treatment. The cases in which they sought that middle way were often known as the "quick look" or "abbreviated rule of reason" cases. The idea began to surface in a trio Supreme Court decisions in a short period between the mid-1970s and the mid-1980s: *United States v. Natl. Socy. of Profl. Engs.* (decided in 1978), *NCAA v. Bd. of Regents of the Univ. of Oklahoma* (decided in 1984), and *FTC v. Indiana Fedn. of Dentists* (decided in 1986). Many lower courts would then apply such a standard and the Federal Trade Commission also played an important role in its development. As for the Supreme Court, its next statement on the issue would not come until 15 years later, in *California Dental Assn. v. FTC* (decided in 1999).[1] The Court has not very explicitly addressed the question since then, though its summaries of §1 standards in recent cases reveal something of its thinking on these matters. *See NCAA v. Alston*, 594 U.S. 69, 96-97 (2021).

At length, though, it may be that the quick-look standard is no longer really a distinct test and perhaps was never meant to be. It is probably fairer

1. Prior to 1999 it was not actually that clear which of the Court's §1 decisions were quick-look decisions and which ones expressed some other new elaboration on §1. But the Court itself finally identified that trio of cases as its decisions on the issue. *See California Dental Assn. v. FTC*, 526 U.S. 756, 769-770 (1999).

to say that there really is only one test for §1 liability, applicable to all cases, and it happens to be quite flexible. It exists as a continuum, with per se cases at one end and "full" rule of reason cases at the other. In between are all the other cases in which a restraint is neither certainly illegal nor so uncertain that it requires a full analysis of defendant's market. The difference in each case is an evidentiary one—how much proof a plaintiff must adduce to show that the defendant's restraint really caused harm.

§8.2 THE QUICK-LOOK RULE AND ITS ORIGINS

Understanding the quick look really poses two problems, but only the first of them is particularly tough. That harder question is when the quick-look approach should be used. Much easier is the question of what structure of analysis applies once a quick-look approach is adopted. That much is reasonably straightforward from the cases.

§8.2.1 When Is a Case a Quick-Look Case?

§8.2.1(a) The Case Law

The first case commonly thought of as a quick-look case was *United States v. Natl. Socy. of Profl. Engs.*, 435 U.S. 679 (1978). There the Justice Department sued an old, very eminent professional organization for an ethical rule it imposed on its members, under which they were prohibited from negotiating their prices with customers prior to receiving a contract for engineering work. Writing for the majority, Justice Stevens explicitly noted that there was no allegation of an actual price-fixing conspiracy. However, in practice, the rule prohibited members from even submitting any sort of price information to clients or discussing price before a contract was awarded. The defendants argued that "bidding on engineering services is inherently imprecise," and that price competition "would lead to deceptively low bids, and would thereby tempt individual engineers to do inferior work with consequent risk to public safety and health." *Id.* at 693. Justice Stevens characterized the question before the Court this way:

> [W]hether the [restraint] may be justified . . . because it was adopted by members of a learned profession for the purpose of minimizing the risk that competition would produce inferior engineering work endangering the public safety.

Id. at 681.

Justice Stevens' analysis began with the observation that the defendants' restraint required "no elaborate industry analysis . . . to demonstrate [its] anticompetitive character," *id.* at 692, a holding that seemed to indicate his view that it was per se illegal. However, the majority then elaborately considered the defendants' proposed procompetitive justification—that its rule was required to prevent shoddy or dangerous engineering work—before ultimately rejecting it. That analysis would not seem necessary if the restraint were really per se illegal.

The Court's only explanation for giving these defendants the benefit of rather more doubt than usual was that the defendants were engaged in a learned profession. The Court made reference to a footnote in an earlier opinion, which had concerned the legal profession. There the Court had written that it "is, of course, relevant in determining whether [a] particular restraint violates the Sherman Act" that the "restraint operates upon a profession as distinguished from a business. . . ." That is so because

> [i]t would be unrealistic to view the practice of professions as interchangeable with other business activities, and automatically to apply to the professions antitrust concepts which originated in other areas. The public service aspect, and other features of the professions, may require that a particular practice, which could properly be viewed as a violation of the Sherman Act in another context, be treated differently.

Id. at 686-687 (quoting *Goldfarb v. Virginia State Bar*, 421 U.S. 773, 788 n.17 (1975)). The *Professional Engineers* majority then expressed its "adherence" to "the view expressed in *Goldfarb* that, by their nature, professional services may differ significantly from other business services, and, accordingly, the nature of the competition in such services may vary. Ethical norms may serve to regulate and promote this competition, and thus fall within the Rule of Reason."

The Court again considered this issue of intermediate analysis a few years later, in two different cases decided in quick succession. The first, *NCAA v. Bd. of Regents of the Univ. of Oklahoma*, 468 U.S. 85 (1984), was quite a different case from *Professional Engineers*, and it had something interesting to add about when a case would be a quick-look case. The Court there considered a rule of the NCAA prohibiting its member schools from selling television rights to football games. The rule was a naked, horizontal output restraint that under other circumstances would have been pretty clearly per se illegal. But this case involved an unusual product—athletics. As the court wrote, "a certain degree of cooperation is necessary if the type of competition that petitioner and its member institutions seek to market is to be preserved." *Id.* at 118. The case "involve[d] an industry in which horizontal restraints on competition are essential if the product is to be available at all." *Id.* at 101. As the Court explained, "[a] myriad of rules affecting such matters as the size of the field, the number of players on a team, and the extent to which physical violence is to be encouraged or proscribed, all must be agreed upon, and all restrain the manner in which institutions compete." *Id.* That did not mean that *any* agreement reached among the members would be legal, and indeed the Court held that the television output limitation was illegal, and would be even had there been no proof of market power. It was, however, a sufficient basis for giving the defendants the benefit of more doubt than under a pure per se analysis.

Importantly, the Court added that certain facts in the case were *not* relevant to application of the quick look. The decision was not based on "a lack of judicial experience with this type of arrangement, on the fact that the NCAA is organized as a nonprofit entity, or on . . . the NCAA's historic role in the preservation and encouragement of intercollegiate amateur athletics." *Id.* at 100-101.

Shortly thereafter, the Court decided another case rather similar to *Professional Engineers*. In *FTC v. Indiana Fedn. of Dentists*, 476 U.S. 447 (1986), the Court considered an agreement among a number of Indiana dentists under which they refused to supply their patients' X-rays to dental insurers. Their goal was to thwart the insurers' efforts to contain their own costs, as insurers had begun to review the dentists' medical decisions before actually paying for the work done. The Court again found this to be a restraint as to which "no elaborate industry analysis" was required, but also explicitly stated that it was not applying a per se rule. Rather, the Court wrote:

> A refusal to compete with respect to the package of services offered to customers, no less than a refusal to compete with respect to the price term of an agreement, impairs the ability of the market to advance social welfare by ensuring the provision of desired goods and services to consumers at a price approximating the marginal cost of providing them. Absent some countervailing procompetitive virtue—such as, for example, the creation of efficiencies in the operation of a market or the provision of goods and services—such an agreement limiting consumer choice by impeding the "ordinary give and take of the market place," cannot be sustained under the Rule of Reason.

Id. at 459. Since no plausible justification was offered, the restraint was illegal. As for why it did not apply a per se rule, the Court again noted its reluctance to impose per se rules against professional groups, *id.* at 458, but added that per se rules are also inappropriate in "the context of business relationships where the economic impact of certain practices is not immediately obvious." *Id.* at 458-459.

The Court's final statement on the issue so far, *California Dental Assn. v. FTC*, 526 U.S. 756 (1999), was in another case rather like *Professional Engineers*. At issue was another restraint on price information. A professional association of dentists prohibited its members from advertising claims that asserted cheaper prices or superior quality. The FTC and the Ninth Circuit on appeal applied a quick look to the restraint, under which it would be illegal on its face without an adequate procompetitive justification. Both the agency and the court of appeals rejected the defendants' justification—that the advertising restraints constrained fraud and addressed the imbalance of information as between dentists and their patients. The Supreme Court reversed and remanded for further analysis by the Ninth Circuit.

The majority in *California Dental* was eager to give some further clarity about when a case is a quick-look case and what happens when it is, and this time the Court had to explain itself against the backdrop of an intervening 15 years of commentary and lower court case law that struggled to work out just what the Court had been getting at in the initial trio of cases. What the Court had to say is unquestionably important, but it also remains fairly Sphinx-like and laconic. The Court's only real explanation was that some intermediate analysis should apply where "an observer with even a rudimentary understanding of economics could conclude that the arrangements in question would have an anticompetitive effect on customers and markets," or where "the great likelihood of anticompetitive effects can easily be ascertained." *Id.* at 770. However, the majority gave one other clue for why more than per se analysis was appropriate:

> [T]he relevant output for antitrust purposes here is presumably not information or advertising, but dental services themselves. The question is not whether the universe of possible advertisements has been limited (as assuredly it has), but whether the limitation on advertisements obviously tends to limit the total delivery of dental services.

Id. at 776. Perhaps by this the Court meant that some naked horizontal restraints should get less than full rule-of-reason scrutiny—because a person with rudimentary economics training could predict their competitive impacts—but not per se treatment because they are not *direct* restraints on price or output. This might help explain the result in *Indiana Federation* and *Professional Engineers*, both of which involved conduct that seemed highly suspicious but that did not directly fix prices or output.[2]

2. The Court has mentioned abbreviated treatment once since *California Dental*, in its recent decision in *FTC v. Actavis*, 570 U.S. 136 (2013). However, its thoughts in that case were essentially in dicta, and if anything they added even less clarity than did *California Dental*. The *Actavis* Court held illegal a certain kind of anticompetitive agreement between drug manufacturers. Specifically, existing makers of patented drugs would pay potential entrants to stay out of their markets, in exchange for not suing to challenge the incumbent firms' patents. The Court explicitly refused to hold these agreements subject either to a "quick-look" standard or a presumption of illegality, and insisted that they would be judged under a structured rule of reason. But it is hard to read the Court's explanation of the structured rule of reason that it described as anything other than some sort of strict, nearly per se quick-look approach. The Court held that in any case where the payment made to the would-be entrant was "large," the deal would be illegal, without proof of either firm's market power, so long as the firms could not make out certain defenses that would all seem unlikely whenever the payment was "large." Moreover, the Court explicitly said that on remand, even though the lower courts would apply a full rule of reason, they could "structure antitrust litigation so as to avoid . . . consideration of every possible fact or theory," since rule-of-reason litigation is "always something of a sliding scale." *Id.* at 159. It is unclear how there could be some separate rule that is a clearly distinct from this one and also recognizable as the "quick look."

During the period since *Professional Engineers* the lower courts and the Federal Trade Commission have applied quick-look rules many times. For what it may be worth, the Commission has in a series of cases developed a detailed framework for the analysis of quick-look cases, and that framework contains its own gloss on when a restraint should be treated as quick look. The Commission will apply quick-look analysis when a restraint is "inherently suspect," meaning that it "appears likely, absent an efficiency justification, to restrict competition and decrease output. . . ." *In re Massachusetts Bd. of Optometry*, 110 FTC 549, 561 (1988). Sometimes the Commission has also described "inherently suspect" conduct as that which "past judicial experience and current economic learning have shown to warrant summary condemnation." *In re Polygram Holding, Inc.*, 136 FTC 310, 344-345 (2003).

§8.2.1(b) So When Is a Case a Quick-Look Case?

Again, the harder of the two major questions under the quick-look doctrine is how one knows when the doctrine applies. The best we can do at present is to approach the problem with two different strategies. First, we can attempt a broad generalization, as best we can, from the case law: A quick-look restraint is a naked restraint—that is, not ancillary to some separate, procompetitive arrangement—among horizontal competitors[3] that poses a likelihood of an increase in price or reduction in output, but it is more than a simple price or output restraint among ordinary, for-profit trade competitors.

Second, we can try to be more concrete by identifying the specific circumstances in which courts have found the doctrine applicable. There are at least three paradigm scenarios:

1. The defendants are members of a learned profession and the challenged restraint is colorably for their self-regulation. Three of the Supreme Court's four quick-look cases relied on this fact. However, it seems important not to overstress this criterion, since the other of the Court's opinions, *NCAA v. Bd. of Regents*, did not involve it at all, and the lower courts have considered a number of other bases for applying quick-look treatment. Moreover, the Court has applied per se treatment to professional defendants where their conduct is truly unadorned horizontal price or output restraint. *See, e.g., FTC v. Superior Court Trial Lawyers Assn.*, 493 U.S. 411 (1990); *Arizona v. Maricopa County Med. Socy.*, 457 U.S. 332 (1982).
2. The agreement is an explicit horizontal agreement on price or output, but some economic feature of the product casts doubt on the

3. Though the Supreme Court has not so held, at least one court of appeals has now strongly indicated that quick-look agreements must be horizontal. *See In re Insurance Brokerage Antitrust Litig.*, 618 F.3d 300, 318 (3d Cir. 2010); *Gordon v. Lewiston Hosp.*, 423 F.3d 184, 210 (3d Cir. 2005).

competitive effects of the restraint. For example, in *NCAA v. Bd. of Regents*, the Supreme Court explained that it would have applied a rule of per se illegality to what was otherwise a naked, horizontal output restriction, but for the peculiar economics of sports as a business. As the Court wrote, the production of the product there—sporting events—appears to require some horizontal cooperation at a minimum, and so even otherwise naked, horizontal restraints will get a bit more deference than they might in other markets. The same was a driving rationale in the majority opinion in *California Dental*—the Court was insufficiently certain that the harms of advertising restraints outweighed their benefits. Several lower courts have relied on this point of view.

3. The agreement is *not* an explicit horizontal agreement on price or output, but it relates to the "output" of something that is not "the relevant output for antitrust purposes," *California Dental Assn. v. FTC*, 526 U.S. at 776. This was true in both *California Dental*, where the restraint was a limitation on advertising (not dental services), and *Indiana Federation of Dentists*, where the restraint was a refusal to provide X-rays to insurers (not, again, a limitation on dental services).

Example

The National Academy of Phlebotomy Arts & Sciences, or NAPAS, is a non-profit organization whose members are all professional phlebotomists—that is, they are the people who stick a needle in your arm and draw your blood at the hospital or when you donate blood to organizations like the Red Cross. NAPAS does not sell any product or service and depends on its members' annual dues to cover its operating costs.

In all states phlebotomists are required to undergo some minimum training and testing. However, membership in the NAPAS is not required in any state. Still, about 65 percent of the working phlebotomists in the United States are NAPAS members, in large part because they receive certain benefits from membership. In particular, they receive free continuing education services that they need in most states to keep their licenses current. They can also purchase cheap insurance through NAPAS and receive certain other promotional benefits.

NAPAS maintains a short list of membership rules, and not infrequently expels members for failure to comply with them. Among other things, the rules require that no member phlebotomist may work more than 40 hours per week. NAPAS defends this rule by pointing out that, in the organization's view, overly tired phlebotomists are at a greater risk of injuring patients and committing malpractice.

Does the NAPAS rule violate federal antitrust?

Explanation

This is probably per se illegal, unless it qualifies for the so-called labor exemption from antitrust (*see* Chapter 23). The analysis would be as follows. First, the restraint is of a kind that would ordinarily be per se illegal: It is a horizontal restraint on output (which in this case is labor). It is probably not ancillary to anything. The NAPAS itself might constitute a "larger procompetitive arrangement." However, restraints on conduct imposed by trade or professional groups have not usually been considered ancillary, because they are not reasonably connected to the group's existence or reasonably needed to achieve its benefits.

Even so, NAPAS might argue that the association is "professional" in nature, and therefore that restraints it imposes as a matter of self-regulation are entitled to quick-look treatment. This raises a bit of an uncertain question. In none of the quick-look cases involving professions has there been any serious doubt that the defendants were truly "professionals." Here, though, the work in question seems to be only a moderately skilled nonprofessional occupation. While it is hard to say, it seems unlikely a court would find industry restraints here to enjoy quick-look treatment on this ground. If not, then the restraint would seem per se illegal.

Again, though, that leaves open the significant question whether the labor exemption would apply. Assuming the member phlebotomists are "employees" of the hospitals where they work, they are likely permitted to adopt restraints relating to hours and working conditions. *See* Chapter 23.

Example

Three different companies in the city of Akron, Ohio, provide auctioneer services. When some person or entity needs to sell some collection of property, and wants to do it by auction, any one of these three companies will provide an auctioneer and other services to help run the auction.

The three companies share a common problem: A number of their clients have engaged in fraudulent representations about some of the items they've sold at auction, inflating the prices. The auctioneers fear that sooner or later they will be held liable for these frauds, but more importantly they fear that publicity about the frauds will discourage the public from attending and participating in auctions. They get together and decide on a joint policy for verifying the authenticity of the items for sale, which consists of a series of procedures for valuation, and a list of minimum evidence requirements for to show the authenticity of especially valuable items, like fine art and antiques. They agree that none of them will auction items claimed to have value that cannot be verified according to the agreed upon procedures. This joint agreement is later challenged by the Justice Department as in violation of the Sherman Act.

Is it illegal?

Explanation

It's a hard question. The arrangement is horizontal, and it is not clearly ancillary to any other arrangement. It also arguably involves a concerted refusal to deal—the firms won't auction items that can't meet minimum standards of authenticity. And the firms may together have market power, as they are the only firms in Akron. But even assuming the case meets the criteria for per se treatment under *Northwest Wholesale Stationers*, there are facts that would weigh in favor of some treatment other than per se. Arguably, the restraint does not concern "the relevant output for antitrust purposes," but rather has to do with the firms' gathering of information. Second, the nature of the market is one in which a court may feel that it is not sufficiently clear what the competitive effects of the restraint might be. It seems plausible that the purpose and the effect of the restraint are to improve information for all market participants, which should be procompetitive. Also, it seems like any competitive harms should be small. Unless the agreement includes some sort of unduly restrictive provisions, the effects seem likely at most to involve some loss of price competition for sale of high value items the sellers are unable or unwilling to authenticate.

§8.2.2 What Happens When the Quick Look Applies?

The second of the two major questions that arise as to the quick-look standard is what happens when it is decided that the quick look applies. As mentioned, this is the easier of the two questions, since the structure of quick-look analysis is now reasonably clear.

Restraints subject to the quick look require "no elaborate industry analysis . . . to demonstrate [their] anticompetitive character," *Professional Engineers*, 435 U.S. at 692, and therefore, while they are not automatically illegal in the manner of per se restraints, they "require[] some competitive justification even in the absence of a detailed market analysis." *NCAA v. Bd. of Regents*, 468 U.S. at 110. The Court has also given this now-critical elaboration:

> The truth is that our categories of analysis of anticompetitive effect are less fixed than terms like "*per se*," "quick look," and "rule of reason" tend to make them appear. We have recognized, for example, that "there is often no bright line separating *per se* from Rule of Reason analysis," since "considerable inquiry into market conditions" may be required before the application of any so-called "*per se*" condemnation is justified. . . . There is always something of a sliding scale in appraising reasonableness. . . . [T]he quality of proof required should vary with the circumstances. . . . [T]here is generally no categorical line to be drawn between restraints that give rise to an intuitively obvious inference of anticompetitive effect and those that call for more detailed treatment. What is required, rather, is an enquiry meet for the case, looking to the circumstances, details, and logic of a restraint. The object is to see whether the experience of the market has been so clear, or necessarily will be, that a confident conclusion

> about the principal tendency of a restriction will follow from a quick (or at least quicker) look, in place of a more sedulous one.

California Dental, 526 U.S. at 779-781 (internal citations and quotation marks omitted).[4] In applying this sliding-scale approach to the case before it, the *California Dental* majority felt that there was some obligation to "give a more deliberate look than a quick one," though not "necessarily . . . the fullest market analysis." *Id.* at 779. The Court also strongly indicated that the problem in the case was not the record. The FTC might very well have put on enough evidence, but the court below just failed to analyze it to the Court's satisfaction. Had the Ninth Circuit just given a more thorough written analysis of the evidence in the record—like the one that Justice Breyer gave in dissent—the majority might have affirmed.

It has never been terribly clear what form the evidence in these cases can or must take, but the *California Dental* opinion gave an important hint when it *rejected* quick-look analysis as to "question[s] susceptible to empirical but not *a priori* analysis." 526 U.S. at 774. In other words, the Court thinks that at least sometimes the courts *may* perform quick-look analysis entirely as a matter of *economic theory*.[5]

All that, though, so far as it goes, does not actually tell us that much about actual quick-look litigation. More details have been filled in by the Federal Trade Commission and the lower courts. In a series of decisions dating to *In re Massachusetts Bd. of Registration in Optometry*, 110 FTC 549 (1988), the Commission gave the analysis more structured content. In these cases the Commission set out a multistep, burden-shifting analysis, which the Commission and some courts refer to as the "*Mass. Board* standard." Importantly, you will note that it closely follows the multi-step framework for full rule of reason cases, as explained in §7.1, and really differs only in a key detail of its first element. This point will be examined fully in a bit.

Even though the *Mass. Board* decision predated *California Dental*, the Commission has argued aggressively that it can accommodate *California Dental*'s insistence that the §1 evidentiary burden must be assessed on a case-by-case, sliding scale basis. Several federal courts of appeals, in post-*California Dental* opinions, have now affirmed that the *Mass. Board* framework is consistent with the guidelines of the Supreme Court's quick-look case law.

Under this approach, the structure of a quick-look case is as follows:

1. If the plaintiff can make a prima facie case by showing that the restraint is "inherently suspect," under the test explained in §8.2.1, then a presumption arises that the restraint is anticompetitive.

4. *See, e.g.*, *N. Car. St. Bd. Dental Exs. v. FTC*, 717 F.3d 359, 374 & n.11 (4th Cir. 2013); *North Texas Specialty Physicians v. FTC*, 528 F.3d 346, 361 (5th Cir. 2008); *Polygram Holding, Inc. v. FTC*, 416 F.3d 29, 35 (D.C. Cir. 2005). *See also In re Realcomp II, Ltd.*, No. 9320, at 21 & nn.16, 18 (FTC, Oct. 30, 2009), available at http://www.ftc.gov/os/adjpro/d9320/091102realcompopinion .pdf (canvassing other evidence that Commission's Mass. Board framework captures current law).
5. "Empirical" means "based on evidence." A person makes an empirical judgment after having looked at some actual proof. "A priori" means "based on reason, not on evidence."

2. The burden then shifts to the defendant to put forward some *plausible, legally cognizable* theoretical justification for the restraint. That the defense must be *legally cognizable* means that it must show both how the justification flows from the agreement itself and promotes a value of competition—that is, that it could improve the defendants' ability to engage in price competition by improved product quality or information, reduced costs, or otherwise. *See* §3.2.2.
3. The plaintiff can then show that the justification is inadequate and that the restraint likely will harm consumers, either as a matter of theory or on such evidence as is needed to show that harm is "likely." If the plaintiff succeeds, then the defendant must put on a full evidentiary showing to prove that its justification is adequate.
4. However, if the plaintiff fails to show that the initial justification is inadequate, then the case becomes a full-blown rule-of-reason case. To proceed, the plaintiff will have to prove market power in a relevant market or put on direct evidence of actual anticompetitive effects.

See, e.g., Polygram Holding, Inc. v. FTC, 416 F.3d 29, 35-36 (D.C. Cir. 2005) (summarizing FTC's *Mass. Bd.* rules and affirming them as accurately capturing the law of the quick-look standard).

Notice something crucial about this analysis. It is almost identical to the four-step analysis courts now follow for full rule of reason cases, as explained in §7.1. The only real difference is in element number 1, in the proof required for plaintiff to make the prima facie case of substantial anticompetitive harm. Namely, under the full rule of reason, a plaintiff must actually show, with either direct evidence or the indirect proof of the market share proxy (*see* §4.2), that the defendant holds market power (along with some reason to believe that the challenged restraint would injure competition if undertaken with market power). The difference in those cases that are neither full rule of reason nor per se is that this same element is required but can be met with less demanding proof.

How much proof is needed in those cases is a different question, and it appears now to be subject to the "sliding scale." In fact, it is increasingly said that the sliding scale has really replaced the quick look as an independent standard. This issue is discussed in the next section.

§8.2.3 The Rise of the Sliding Scale and the Structure of Cases in the Middle

As mentioned at the beginning of this chapter, while the quick look or abbreviated rule of reason was an important development in the law, it really has been overtaken by the Supreme Court's recent preference for a "sliding scale" approach.

In every recent occasion for comment, the Court has stressed that the rule of reason is neither "a rote checklist" nor "an inflexible substitute for careful analysis." *NCAA v. Alston*, 594 U.S. 69, 97 (2021). It requires "an enquiry meet for the case," that is tailored in every individual dispute to "the circumstances, details, and logic of a restraint." *California Dental Assn. v. FTC*, 526 U.S. 756, 781 (1999).[6] In fact, the Court has all but explicitly rejected the idea that there is any discrete "quick look" category at all.[7] In so doing, it has endorsed a position favored by many commentators and long advocated by the country's leading antitrust treatise.[8] Lower courts have increasingly interpreted the Court as having rejected the idea of any one, unique intermediary standard.[9]

How much this actually matters in practice is an interesting question. After all, as mentioned, the only difference between a "quick look" case and cases more loosely distributed along a continuum is what are presumably small variations in how much proof is required as to one element. But in fact it does matter on some level, perhaps in significant ways. If there is one specific standard, and it applies only to cases for which it is appropriate, then courts and parties will spend a lot of time fighting about whether the standard applies, and undue pressure will rest on the question. Whole cases could turn on whether trial courts pick the right standard or not.[10]

§8.3 SECTION 1 NOW, IN SUMMARY: THE SLIDING SCALE AND THE RULE OF ANCILLARY RESTRAINTS

The following chart summarizes the state of §1 law as it currently exists. The chart includes both the sliding scale treatment of section one cases and compares it to the separate but somewhat distinct rule that often appears in §1 cases, the rule of ancillary restraints. (Ancillary restraints are discussed in §7.2.)

6. *See also FTC v. Actavis, Inc.*, 570 U.S. 136, 159-160 (2013); *Am. Needle, Inc. v. NFL*, 560 U.S. 183, 203-204 (2010).

7. *Cal. Dental*, 526 U.S. at 780-781 ("there is generally no categorical line to be drawn between restraints that give rise to an intuitively obvious inference of anticompetitive effect and those that call for more detailed treatment").

8. *Alston*, 594 U.S. at 88-89 (citing 7 Philip E. Areeda & Herbert Hovenkamp, *Antitrust Law* ¶1507 (2013)); Actavis, 570 U.S. at 159 (same); *Cal. Dental*, 526 U.S. at 779–780 (same).

9. *See, e.g., United States v. American Airlines Grp., Inc.*, 121 F.4th 209, 221-222 (1st Cir. 2024); *Polygram Holding, Inc. v. FTC*, 416 F.3d 29, 35 (D.C. Cir. 2005) ("It would be somewhat misleading [to] . . . suggest the Court has [simply] moved from a dichotomy to a trichotomy, when in fact it has backed away from any reliance upon fixed categories and toward a continuum.").

10. *See, e.g., American Airlines Grp.*, 121 F.4th at 221-222 (rejecting defense argument that trial court improperly applied quick-look standard; implying that a sliding-scale approach avoids undue pressure on the question of selecting right test).

The Sliding Scale of §1 Evidentiary Requirements

Ancillary Restraints Cases	"Full" Rule of Reason Cases	Cases in Between (Sometimes Known as "Quick Look" Rule of Reason Cases)	Per Se Cases
1. Plaintiff challenges a restraint that ordinarily would be per se illegal, like horizontal price fixing or market allocation. 2. Defendant shows that: (a) The restraint is associated with some separate, discrete arrangement that in itself is pro-competitive—like a joint venture, an employment contract, or a sale of property, and (b) the challenged restraint is reasonably necessary to achieving the benefits of that other arrangement. 3. The challenged restraint is then analyzed under the "full" rule of reason, as summarized in the next column.	1. Plaintiff makes a prima facie showing that the challenged restraint causes substantial anticompetitive harm. Typically requires: (a) Reason to believe that the challenged conduct could cause harm, if undertaken with market power, and (b) Proof that defendant holds some market power. 2. Burden of production shifts to Defendant to show some pro-competitive purpose served by the challenged restraint. 3. Burden shifts back to Plaintiff to show a less restrictive alternative to achieve Defendant's proffered justifications. 4. Plaintiff may attempt to show that any proffered justification causes more harm than benefit ("balancing").	1. Plaintiff makes prima facie showing that the challenged restraint causes substantial anticompetitive harm. The amount of proof required will vary by case and depends on whether the restraint is more obviously anticompetitive (more like a per se case) or less so (more like a full rule of reason case). Can generally be shown either by compelling economic reasoning, evidence of harm from similar restraints in other markets, or perhaps other proof. 2. Burden of production shifts to Defendant to show some pro-competitive purpose served by the challenged restraint. 3. Burden shifts back to Plaintiff to show a less restrictive alternative to achieve Defendant's proffered justifications. 4. Plaintiff may attempt to show that any proffered justification causes more harm than benefit ("balancing").	1. Plaintiff proves that conduct occurred that is subject to a per se rule (naked, horizontal price-fixing or market allocation, or some concerted refusals to deal). 2. The restraint is conclusively presumed to be unreasonable.

CHAPTER 9

One Further Problem in Horizontal Cooperation

Exchanges of Information

§9.1 THE TRADITIONAL BOOKENDS APPROACH

Antitrust has struggled for a long time to cope with the problem of exchanges of information among competitors. Policy makers have always believed that at least sometimes the sharing of information is dangerous to the system of competition, but a tension inheres in that view. Admittedly, there is something a little suspicious about this behavior at least some of the time. Normally, companies consider their internal information proprietary and they go to great lengths to keep it to themselves. They patent it, copyright it, and trademark it when they can, and when they can't they conceal it, keep it in a safe, discipline their employees for disclosing it, sue their competitors for stealing it, and claim their constitutional rights are violated when they are forced to reveal it.[1]

In this day and age, some of them also engage in outright espionage to discover their competitors' secrets. Information about a competitor's costs, sales, revenues, processes, and so on can be competitively valuable. Inside information can also be embarrassing to a company, especially when the company is performing poorly, and that is another reason for suspicion when a company just happens to give away its information freely.

1. *See, e.g.*, *Ruckleshaus v. Monsanto Co.*, 467 U.S. 986 (1984) (considering company's argument that requirement of revealing research data concerning a pesticide, in exchange for a federal license to sell that pesticide under the Federal Insecticide, Fungicide and Rodenticide Act, would effect a taking of private property in violation of the Fifth Amendment).

But on the other hand, information is the lifeblood of competitive markets. One of the ideal conditions we've stated for perfect competition is that all market actors have *perfect* information (*see* §2.2), and so it may seem odd that exchanges of information could ever be bad things. After all, our extensive system of federal securities regulation exists solely to enforce disclosures of information; it does this by requiring periodic reporting by public companies (of information they would often enough *really* like to keep from capital markets and securities analysts) and by rules against insider trading and securities fraud.

Well, despite the importance of information to well-functioning markets, there are at least a few arguments that at least some exchanges among competitors are dangerous to competition. First, they might indicate that the competitors in fact have reached an actual price-fixing conspiracy. Obviously enough, two competitors cannot agree on a price without revealing to one another what the price will be. More importantly, a well-regulated price-fixing conspiracy requires a fair bit of ongoing information sharing, since a cartel's main problem is to ensure that its members do not cheat by secretly undercutting the cartel price. Accordingly, the courts now frequently treat exchanges of price information as a "plus factor" in proving conspiracy with circumstantial evidence. (Proof of conspiracy and the "plus-factors" test are discussed in Chapter 12.) Second, even in the absence of actual price-fixing conspiracy, some markets may be especially prone to inflated oligopoly pricing. An agreement to share information in such a market might be an "unreasonable" one under §1. The "contract, combination . . . or conspiracy" in this case is not an agreement to fix prices, but the information sharing arrangement itself.

The law of information exchange remains fairly uncertain and can be a very delicate problem for businesspeople, who have a difficult time knowing what it is okay for them to talk about when they attend conferences or trade association meetings or otherwise mingle with their competitors. For this reason businesspeople often need the advice of antitrust counsel when representing their firms at professional functions or when they are solicited by competitors to share information. Trade associations typically have their own in-house antitrust counsel or rely fairly extensively on outside advice. Indeed, the newsletter of the witty folks over at the Trade Association Committee of the ABA Section of Antitrust Law is known as *The Information Exchange*.

A bit of background helps. The early law of information exchange grew out of the first few decades of the twentieth century. Economically times had been difficult up until the turn of the century, and major changes in technology and industry had bred concern that the changing world economy could no longer be captured in the prosaic economic theory of Adam Smith's day. As one result, many came to believe that in order for industry to survive under new competitive conditions, and to avoid continuing economic distress, there would have to be some way to coordinate production and prices. That control, some feared, would either have to come from some socialist or fascist government intervention of the kind then rising in Europe, or through private rationalization of production, which would mean either consolidation or some sort of multilateral agreements to coordinate particular industries. A cornerstone of such cooperative efforts at this time was information sharing, and a common program recommended at the time was the "open price association." This meant a trade association in which the members shared their pricing and sales data.

The antitrust law that arose to deal with these new phenomena was expressed most prominently in two Supreme Court opinions of the 1920s, both dealing with open price associations. We might think of these two roughly as bookends or as opposite ends of a continuum of what is permitted in the exchange of information. Importantly, these early decisions seemed predominantly concerned with *intent*—the Court seemed to ask, on the basis of the kind and amount of information that was being shared, whether the defendants intended to raise prices. If so, the arrangement would be held illegal.

First, *American Column & Lumber Co. v. United States*, 257 U.S. 377 (1921), involved an arrangement among lumber manufacturers. They agreed to form a trade association that would be administered through a fairly sophisticated central secretariat. All members were required to submit detailed information not only about the prices they had charged and the sales they had enjoyed in the past, but also to make projections about future sales. The central administrative body not only collected this information but analyzed it and used it to make detailed predictions about *future* sales trends, including predictions of future prices. The group circulated these forecasts to its members, and it also distributed detailed information about the members' actual sales, identifying the seller, buyer, and price of individual sales. The Court found this arrangement an unreasonable restraint of trade.

By contrast, *Maple Flooring Mfrs. Assn. v. United States*, 268 U.S. 563 (1925), found no liability for a superficially similar arrangement. Again a group of lumber manufacturers formed a trade association with fairly elaborate information gathering facilities, and again the group's central administrative body distributed reports about the performance of the industry. But in this case the information distributed was retrospective only and was in the form of summaries and general statistics. It provided no specifics about particular sellers or particular transactions.

Understanding the difference between these two cases explains a lot about the current law of information exchange, and shows the Court trying to weigh the policy balance between encouraging information that will aid the machinery of price competition and constraining information that will aid collusion.

9. One Further Problem in Horizontal Cooperation

One further early case has some continuing significance, *Cement Mfrs. Protective Assn. v. United States*, 268 U.S. 588 (1925). The defendants there were a group of cement manufacturers who used their trade association to gather and disseminate information about which of them was selling how much cement to whom, and at what price. The defendants said their agreement was needed to protect them from a certain kind of fraud that arose because of the particular nature of the contracts used in their trade,[2] and the Court agreed. We shall see momentarily why *Cement Mfrs.* has continuing importance.

§9.2 THE STRUCTURAL APPROACH OF UNITED *STATES v. CONTAINER CORP.* AND THE LAW AS IT STANDS

While *American Column* and *Maple Flooring* (and a number of other early trade association cases) remain good law, the law in this area is fact bound and unpredictable. The only very clear rule is that, as the courts often say, mere exchange of information is not in and of itself illegal, even if the information concerns prices. In any event, the uncertainty exists in large part because of the Supreme Court's last major statement on the issue, *United States v. Container Corp. of America*, 393 U.S. 333 (1969).

Container Corp. was at a minimum quite a shift of emphasis from the Court's traditional focus on intent in the old bookends cases. The Court did not inquire at all into the parties' intent, and was not even particularly concerned about the amount or kind of information being shared. Rather, the Court focused on the structure of the industry itself and the likelihood that shared price information would facilitate higher prices. The defendants were several manufacturers of cardboard boxes. While they had no formal agreement to share information, an informal tradition had grown up in the industry in which any one of them could ask any other for information about its recent sales. The Court first held that the informal tradition

---

2. Cement was predominantly used by construction contractors who had to bid for the construction projects they worked on. In their bids they had to estimate the price they would have to pay for cement to be used in the job. So, for the contractors' protection, it had become common in the industry for cement manufacturers to offer cement at a specific price for a specific project when the contractor prepared the bid. The manufacturer would agree to supply at that price if the contractor secured the bid, even if the market price went up, but also to free the contractor to procure cement elsewhere if the market price went down. This put the cement manufacturers at the risk of a certain kind of abuse by the contractors: A contractor could set a price in its bid but then secure several different contracts from different contractors for the full amount of cement needed for the job. If the price of cement then went up, the contractor could call for delivery of all the cement, use what it needed for the job, and then resell the rest at a profit. To protect against this, the manufacturers shared information with one another as to specific sales.

was enough to satisfy the contract, combination or conspiracy requirement under §1. Second, the Court focused on the competitive risk of shared price information. Specifically, the Court was concerned that the market was concentrated, the product was fungible, and demand was inelastic. Those conditions could nurture interdependent behavior in which the defendants could cause their prices to rise even without an explicit agreement to do so, at least so long as they had good information about prices being charged. Under those circumstances, the Court held an agreement to share price information illegal.

Container Corp. had little to say about the continued vitality of the old bookends approach under *American Column* and *Maple Flooring*, though it cited *Cement Mfrs.* with approval. So it would appear that where a plaintiff could show an information-sharing arrangement like the one in *American Column*, it could still prevail under the rule of reason even without a showing of any market structure evidence like that at issue in *Container Corp.* Or a plaintiff could put on a case to show that structural factors make a given market like the one in *Container Corp.*, and if so the plaintiff could establish illegality under what is in effect a rule of reason.[3] Finally, a defendant can try to rebut either theory by identifying some purpose to be served other than restraining competition, like the prevention of fraud as in *Cement Mfrs.* Note that in this latter scenario, the purpose will have to be one that supports *competition* and not just any social value. As explained in §3.2.2, it is never relevant in antitrust to say that some restraint is needed because competition itself would have produced an undesirable outcome. The prevention of fraud in *Cement Mfrs.* can be defended as procompetitive because, by protecting market participants from strategic abuses, it encouraged them to be more active in the market.

Example

Let us imagine that you are the CEO of a company that manufactures paper clips. You are a small company, and no one in your industry has more than a small percentage of the market. You've been asked by some of your

3. There was uncertainty in the *Container Corp.* opinion itself over whether the majority had found the information exchange before it to be per se illegal. Some language in the majority opinion seemed to indicate that. A concurrence by Justice Fortas stressed that he did not understand the Court so to hold, and it is now taken for granted that the case merely set out a rule-of-reason cause of action. *See* 1 Am. Bar Assn., *Antitrust Law Developments (Sixth)* 92-93 (6th ed. 2007). To be sure, it is unlike most other rule-of-reason actions in that it is not clear that the plaintiff must prove market power in some relevant market. It appears that as long as the plaintiff can show evidence consistent with oligopoly behavior—like concentration, some entry protection, inelastic price, fungibility of products (which makes "cheating" on the basis of quality harder), numerous customers and frequent transactions, and other matters that tend to make coordination easier and "cheating" easier to detect—a price-sharing agreement may be illegal.

competitors to form an organization with them. Among other things, being a member of the organization would require you to supply information about your customers and the prices you charge. Would joining the organization be illegal? What facts would you want to know before you get your company involved in such an organization?

Explanation

Joining the organization is not illegal, at least not solely because of the information sharing aspect. However, it would be wise to follow up on two separate questions. First, what kind of information will be required and how will it be used? Will it be disseminated in a way that will facilitate price fixing? Second, are the general circumstances of this industry such that collusion or interdependent oligopoly pricing behavior would be likely? On the latter question, the facts already give a significant indication. We're told that no firm has more than a small market share, suggesting that oligopoly interdependence is unlikely. Liability under *Container Corp.* is therefore not much of a concern.

Example

ABC, Inc., is one of seven major manufacturers of a special kind of woven cotton textile that is used in the making of medical supplies. There is no good substitute for this textile in many of the uses to which it is put. Together, the seven makers of this textile have about 90 percent of the relevant market. The product is undifferentiated. That is, buyers of the product are largely indifferent as to which of the seven producers' product they buy.

ABC and its competitors routinely exchange information concerning their sales. In fact, they have each often responded to requests from one another to provide information about particular sales, prices and customers. While there is nothing in writing, there is something of a "gentleman's agreement" in the industry that such information will be provided when requested.

Is there anything illegal going on here?

Explanation

These are essentially the facts of the *Container Corp.* case. Because the industry is concentrated, the basis of competition is price alone, and "cheating" by lowering price is easy to detect, this is an industry already prone to interdependent oligopoly pricing behavior. Therefore, agreements to share price information, especially if the information is not made public, will be much more suspect and may violate the rule of reason.

PART IV

Vertical Restraints

CHAPTER 10

Antitrust and the Distribution of Goods

§10.1 VERTICAL RELATIONSHIPS IN GENERAL

This book so far has discussed mainly horizontal restraints. But antitrust also concerns itself with "vertical" relationships, which means roughly relations between buyer and seller. Vertical restraints law, in other words, is the law of antitrust as it relates to *distribution*.

Antitrust is concerned with distribution arrangements for one simple reason. When a seller of a good parts company with it to some intermediary—some intermediary who will then provide it to the ultimate purchaser—the seller will have some interest in having a say in the means by which the good is then resold. The original seller will be quite concerned with the retail price at which the products are ultimately sold and also with what steps the intermediary might take to convince buyers to buy the product. The volume and price at which the intermediary sells will affect what profits the original maker can earn.

Judicial thinking on vertical restraints has changed drastically in the past 50 years. Time once was that vertical restraints were taken to be just as serious as horizontal ones, and they were frequently held illegal in antitrust law. In particular, the courts were concerned about efforts to control downstream prices, conduct that was thought to be harmful both to intermediate distributors and to consumers. Some economists began to challenge that judicial approach, starting in the 1960s, and by the mid-1970s antitrust saw a sea change in the treatment of vertical restraints.

On the surface, the current law of vertical restraints is pretty easy to state: All vertical restraints are subject to the full-blown rule of reason, with only one real exception. "Tying" arrangements—in which the manufacturer refuses to sell one product unless the buyer takes some other product along with it—are judged under a structured rule-of-reason standard still sometimes called the "per se" rule for tying. Some other arrangements are treated like ties, like the "bundling" of various products or "full-line forcing." Still, even the cause of action for tying is not so different than the ordinary rule of reason. The only significant difference is that once a plaintiff can make a showing of market power in one market, there is no requirement of proving that that market power could have anticompetitive effect.

This chapter lays out the current law of vertical restraints in general. This turns out to be largely a history lesson, because so much has changed in a relatively short time. Historical or no, however, it remains important to understand the past of this law in some depth. In ways that remain somewhat difficult to predict, some old rules within it may remain quite significant, notwithstanding the sea change in the law worked by *Leegin Creative Leather Prods., Inc. v. PSKS, Inc.*, 551 U.S. 877 (2007). Importantly, even though *Leegin* broadly authorized essentially all vertical restraints, and federal actions to challenge them are now essentially unheard of, it is even now critical to understand the hoary old rule of *United States v. Colgate & Co.*, 250 U.S. 300 (1919). One particular vertical restraint—minimum vertical price fixing or "resale price maintenance"—remains sharply prohibited under some state antitrust laws, and avoiding liability there likely requires observing the *Colgate* rule. Other rules from this long history could plausibly regain importance as the law evolves.

Section 10.3 also addresses one special technical rule in vertical restraints law, which is how to distinguish vertical and horizontal conspiracies. That distinction can be harder to draw than it might seem. Particularly now that no vertical restraints are subject to per se treatment, plaintiffs challenging them will almost always try to show that they are in fact horizontal in nature or have some horizontal aspect that would justify per se treatment. Chapter 11 covers the law of tying and bundling.

§10.2 THE LAW OF VERTICAL RESTRAINTS IN GENERAL

§10.2.1 Varieties of Vertical Restraint

Distribution restraints come in a wide variety, and the differences among them have some significance for their likely competitive effects.

On the simplest level, a supplier and its buyer might agree to prices at which the good will be resold, a practice commonly known as "vertical price fixing" or "resale price maintenance" (and among antitrust lawyers inevitably shortened to RPM). Pricing restraints might set maximum or minimum resale prices.

Non-price restraints are at least superficially different, though they may serve the same purposes and have the same effects. A manufacturer might give its distributor an exclusive resale territory—that is, it may agree with the distributor that it will not allow any of its other distributors to sell its product in the same geographical territory. But this may have effectively the same consequence as minimum RPM. Either way, the manufacturer might in effect be granting the distributor some amount of supranormal profit on sales of its product by protecting the distributor from *intrabrand* competition. For example, the Sony company might promise a retailer that no other retailer in its geographic area will be permitted to carry Sony televisions. If the Sony brand has some differentiated value—consumers will pay a bit more for the Sony brand, on their view that it has a quality advantage—then the retailer will be able to raise prices a bit on its Sony TVs that won't be competed away by other nearby Sony dealers. That would have an effect similar to Sony simply requiring all its retailers to sell at a minimum, supracompetitive retail price.

Some say that a basic distinction among kinds of vertical restraint is between those likely to serve upstream interests (and so likely imposed by sellers) and those likely to serve downstream interests (and so likely imposed by buyers). Those that favor sellers, and reflect upstream power, will tend to enforce competitiveness at the retail level, but those that favor retailers likely reflect retailer market power and will result in higher consumer prices without a compensating increase in quality or service.[1]

§10.2.2 Vertical Restraints in Historical Perspective: The Long Road from *Dr. Miles to Continental T.V.* to *Leegin*

For the time being, the story of vertical restraints is one that is mostly told historically. It is told as a long-time development, with a continuously evolving underlying philosophy, but, also one that has changed a lot quite recently and likely will change more in the near future. Until recently, the law of vertical restraints under §1 was rather complex. Several different substantive rules might apply depending on how a restraint was characterized, and a set of technical pleading rules applied to proof of vertical conspiracy, making it harder to prove than horizontal conspiracy. However, mainly

1. This distinction is elaborated in Lawrence A. Sullivan, Warren S. Grimes & Chris Sagers, *The Law of Antitrust: An Integrated Handbook* 301-379 (3d ed. 2015).

because of one decision—*Leegin Creative Leather Prods., Inc. v. PSKS, Inc.*, 551 U.S. 877 (2007)—this all appears to have gotten much simpler.

For the better part of a century the law of vertical restraints was dominated by one much older decision, *Dr. Miles Med. Co. v. John D. Park & Sons Co.*, 220 U.S. 373 (1911). In that case, plaintiff Dr. Miles was a manufacturer of medicines the formulas for which it owned and kept secret, but which it had not patented. Dr. Miles sold its products through distribution contracts requiring them to be sold at a minimum retail price and prohibiting their sale to any other sellers that would undercut that price. Defendant John D. Park was a third-party distributor that had managed to get its hand on stocks of Dr. Miles's medicines at cut rates. Dr. Miles sued it for tortious interference with its distribution contracts.

The Court found the contracts illegal. It was moved neither by the defendant's stated desire to protect its secret formulas nor by its essentially libertarian argument that, as the maker and owner of the products in question, it ought to be able to control its own retail prices. Because of the case's posture, the Court's ultimate holding was not that Dr. Miles had violated antitrust per se; rather, it held that the consignment contracts were unenforceable under the doctrine of illegal contracts, and therefore that Dr. Miles's tort cause of action must fail. But from the Court's reasoning, all later courts took *Dr. Miles* to state a rule of per se illegality, at least as to vertical minimum price fixing. In later decades the courts extended this rule to other kinds of vertical restraints, including those not explicitly involving price at all.

However, because most manufacturers are acutely concerned with their own retail prices and with the behavior and diligence of their distributors, and because the courts have always shown intuitive sympathy for manufacturers' right to choose with whom they will do business, *Dr. Miles* spawned a difficult jurisprudence full of exceptions and special rules. Importantly, in a decision that is still influential in areas well beyond vertical restraints, *United States v. Colgate & Co.*, 250 U.S. 300 (1919), the Court issued a major clarification to *Dr. Miles*. Under *Colgate*, a manufacturer is free to announce the terms on which it is willing to sell its products, and remains free to stop doing business with any distributor, even if its reason for doing so is a refusal to comply with suggested resale prices. The distinction proved very difficult to apply since unilateral insistence on retail price and conspiracy to fix retail price will typically look very similar.

The Court further narrowed *Dr. Miles* in *United States v. General Electric Co.*, 272 U.S. 476 (1926). In that case the government challenged a nationwide plan set up by the General Electric company for the distribution of its light bulbs. The arrangement consisted of a network of "agency" agreements with wholesale distributors and retail electric supply stores. G.E. delivered the bulbs to these agents on a consignment basis, meaning that though they stored the bulbs in their own inventories, the agents did not pay for the bulbs up front, sold them only for a commission on each sale, and remitted the remaining proceeds to G.E. The agents never took formal title to the bulbs, did not carry insurance on them, were protected from most risk of damage to them, and returned unsold bulbs to G.E. In other words, the facts indicated that the relationships really were common law "agency" relationships and not sales disguised as agency. *General Electric* established a rule, which is still good law, that a principal is legally incapable of conspiring with its agent under Sherman Act §1.

This rule was moderated to some extent over the years, as in *Simpson v. Union Oil Co. of California*, 377 U.S. 13 (1964), where the Court found illegal an RPM plan operated through a series of purported consignment arrangements. The Court found that, in substance, the "consignees" were really independent entrepreneurs, except for the fact that they were not free to set their own prices. In such a case,

> [where the]"consignment" device is used to cover a vast gasoline distribution system, fixing prices through many retail outlets, the antitrust laws prevent calling the "consignment" an agency. . . . [Otherwise,] . . . the end result of [per se illegality for price fixing] would be avoided merely by clever manipulation of words, not by differences in substance. The present, coercive "consignment" device, if successful against challenge under the antitrust laws, furnishes a wooden formula for administering prices on a vast scale.

Id. at 21-22. Still, even now, it appears that where a supplier operates through arrangements that in their substance really are agency consignment arrangements, restraints it sets with those distributors cannot violate §1. *See Valuepest.com of Charlotte, Inc. v. Bayer Corp.*, 561 F.3d 282 (4th Cir. 2009). The relevant factual inquiries in distinguishing true agencies from mere sales are whether there is a formal parting of title, whether the manufacturer or the distributor bears the risk of loss to the goods while they are in the distributor's possession, and which of them bears the risk of unsold inventory. It also matters whether the distributor deals only in the supplier's goods, or rather carries other products. In the latter case, the distributor is less likely to be an agent, even if other terms of the agreement are agency-like. *See Simpson*, 377 U.S. at 22-24 & n.10.

Over the years, the law arising under *Dr. Miles*, *Colgate*, and *General Electric* became elaborate and unpredictable.[2]

Non-price vertical restraints were also treated fairly harshly through much of the twentieth century, and by mid-century the Court had decided

---

2. In particular, cases applying the distinction between RPM agreements that were per se illegal under *Dr. Miles* and mere unilateral refusals to sell except according to preannounced resale terms, immune from antitrust under *Colgate*, were metaphysical and hard to explain. Matters grew worse in recent times as the courts became more convinced that *Dr. Miles* was actually incorrect—that RPM might actually have some procompetitive virtues and not deserve per se condemnation. But *Dr. Miles* proved resistant to either legislative or judicial undoing, and so instead the courts made it increasingly hard for plaintiffs to prove that there

to hold them all per se illegal, *see United States v. Arnold Schwinn & Co.*, 388 U.S. 365 (1967), *rev'd, Continental T.V., Inc. v. GTE Sylvania, Inc.*, 433 U.S. 36 (1977). However, those rules too came under heavy pressure by the 1970s. *Schwinn* concerned a distribution plan under which a manufacturer sold some of its output by outright sales, but required those distributors only to sell within specified territories and not to resell to unauthorized retailers. The Court held that non-price vertical restraints imposed on an outright sale to a distributor—as opposed to restraints imposed on an agent—should be per se illegal. The only real explanation the Court gave was its concern that such restraints "would violate the ancient rule against restraints on alienation. . . ." 388 U.S. at 380. Strictly speaking, the Court had before it only one specific sort of territorial limitation. But language in the opinion seemed to cut more broadly, and would seem to make all non-price vertical restraints per se illegal: "If the manufacturer parts with dominion over his product or transfers risk of loss to another, he may not reserve control over its destiny or the conditions of its resale." *Id.* at 379.

Schwinn was an unpopular decision, only partly because it broke with another Supreme Court opinion then only four years old (*White Motor Co. v. United States*, 372 U.S. 253 (1963)), which had refused to hold vertical territorial restraints per se illegal. Critics disapproved of the *Schwinn* Court's focus on the essentially uneconomic concerns for restraints on alienation and the common law distinction between outright sale and consignment. And so, only ten years later, the Court took the unusual step of reversing itself yet again, in *Continental T.V., Inc. v. GTE Sylvania, Inc.*, 433 U.S. 36 (1977). There the Court considered another distribution plan that permitted retailers to sell only within specified geographic territories, a restraint that would have been pretty squarely within the rule of *Schwinn* had the Court not decided to reverse itself.

The Court began by observing that "[r]ealities must dominate the judgment. . . . The Anti-Trust Act aims at substance," *id.* at 47, and accordingly that antitrust law "must be based upon demonstrable economic effect rather than . . . formalistic line drawing," *id.* at 59. The Court also offered the following, which would come to represent an epochal change in focus: "Interbrand competition . . . is the primary concern of antitrust." *Id.* at 51 n.19. *Intra* brand competition, by contrast, was apparently to be given much less concern.

---

had been any vertical price arrangement at all. First, *Monsanto Co. v. Spray-Rite Service Corp.*, 465 U.S. 752 (1984), instituted certain new ideas about proof of conspiracy, and strongly suggested the Court's concern not unduly to interfere with vertical relationships. Later, in *Business Electronics v. Sharp Electronics*, 485 U.S. 717 (1988), the Court introduced an entirely new pleading standard for vertical price fixing. Thereafter, a plaintiff would have to put on some more or less particularized evidence that the defendant had conspired as to an actual, specific resale price in order to invoke per se illegality. No requirement even remotely similar is imposed in horizontal price-fixing cases.

Contrary to the reasoning in *Schwinn*, the *Continental T.V.* majority thought there might be substantial consumer benefits from limits on intrabrand competition. In effect, the Court thought the restraints might allow manufacturers to give their distributors a small bonus or incentive to encourage them to help the manufacturer enter a new market or compete more effectively in its current markets. As the Court explained:

> [N]ew manufacturers and manufacturers entering new markets can use the restrictions in order to induce competent and aggressive retailers to make the kind of investment of capital and labor that is often required in the distribution of products unknown to the consumer. Established manufacturers can use them to induce retailers to engage in promotional activities or to provide service and repair facilities necessary to the efficient marketing of their products. Service and repair are vital for many products, such as automobiles and major household appliances. The availability and quality of such services affect a manufacturer's goodwill and the competitiveness of his product. Because of market imperfections such as the so-called "free rider" effect, these services might not be provided by retailers in a purely competitive situation, despite the fact that each retailer's benefit would be greater if all provided the services than if none did.

Id. at 54-55.

Similar changes occurred in other areas of vertical restraints law. During the same year as *Continental T.V.*, the Court fairly drastically loosened rules on tying arrangements, rejecting what had once been a genuine per se rule for what can only really be called a structured rule of reason. *See U.S. Steel Corp. v. Fortner Enterprises, Inc.*, 429 U.S. 610 (1977). Likewise, there had been a long period during which it was thought that one special class of vertical restraints—exclusive dealing contracts, under which the buyer is forbidden to take some of its product from the seller's competitors—would be subject to a sui generis, relatively pro-plaintiff rule. Though the Supreme Court has not addressed the question in a very long time, even its last statement on point—more than 50 years ago—indicated that it intended the courts to find exclusive contracts illegal only in the presence of significant market power, and with due sensitivity to specific market conditions. *See Tampa Electric Co. v. Nashville Coal Co.*, 365 U.S. 320 (1961). Since then lower courts have treated the question not only as an ordinary rule-of-reason problem, but have suggested that there may even be certain safe harbors in which an exclusive dealing arrangement cannot be challenged at all. (Tying and exclusive contracts are dealt with separately in Chapter 11.)

And finally, trends in thinking about vertical restraints recently brought about the end of *Dr. Miles* itself. Many observers have argued that the same policy justifications that swayed the Court in *Continental T.V.* actually apply to vertical price restraints as well, and that they should get the same legal treatment. Even in *Continental T.V.* the Court was urged by some to go further and overrule *Dr. Miles* as well, though the Court declined. 433 U.S. at 51 n.18. But after that decision, it was probably only a matter of time before *Dr. Miles* would be reversed. In 1997 the Court held vertical *maximum* price fixing subject to the rule of reason, leaving only vertical minimum price fixing still per se illegal. *State Oil v. Khan*, 522 U.S. 3 (1997). In 2007 the Court did away with even that last vestige of *Dr. Miles.* in *Leegin Creative Leather Prods., Inc. v. PSKS, Inc.*, 551 U.S. 877 (2007). (In one other recent development in vertical restraints law, the Court also limited tying law just a bit, in *Illinois Tool Works, Inc. v. Independent Ink, Inc.*, 547 U.S. 28 (2006) (holding that the mere possession of intellectual property in the "tying" good is not sufficient in itself to show that a defendant holds "power" in that product sufficient for the tying cause of action, as explained in Chapter 11).)

In summary, after *Leegin*, all vertical restraints are subject to the rule of reason, with only one limited exception: If a plaintiff challenging a tying arrangement can show that the defendant held market power in the tying product market, a rebuttable presumption arises that it caused anticompetitive effects. (Recall that, in any ordinary rule-of-reason case under §1, the plaintiff must show not only that a restraint occurred and that the defendants had market power but that as a matter of theory the restraint could in fact cause an increase in price or a decrease in output. Tying is considered more fully in Chapter 11.)

§10.2.3 Doctrinal Elaborations Following *Leegin*'s Universalization of Rule-of-Reason Treatment

The state of RPM law and the use of RPM arrangements in America following *Leegin* both developed in ways that were somewhat unexpected. Federal oversight of RPM has developed very little since *Leegin*, because there has been very little federal RPM litigation since then. That was somewhat unexpected, because *Leegin* itself acknowledged ways that RPM might still be harmful, and seemed to anticipate that noxious RPM would face appropriate challenge. *See Leegin*, 551 U.S. at 893, 897-898. After all, the Court in *Continental T.V.* and *Leegin* merely held vertical restraints subject to a rule of reason, and the Court has never held any restraint, vertical or otherwise, to be per se legal. Observers expected ongoing RPM litigation as well, and elaborated on theories of liability under the new rule of reason.[3] And yet, challenges to RPM under federal law have become effectively non-existent. Plaintiffs enjoyed one substantial success immediately after *Leegin*, but since

3. *See, e.g.*, Warren S. Grimes, *The Path Forward After* Leegin: *Seeking Consensus Reform of the Antitrust Law of Vertical Restraints*, 75 Antitrust L.J. 467 (2008) (summarizing "points of consensus in vertical restraints policy," and listing among them these ideas).

then the cases have become so rare and ineffectual that as a matter of federal policy RPM is for practical purposes less per se legal.[4]

But on the other hand, a few states have preserved strict laws against RPM. It remains per se illegal under California[5] and Maryland law,[6] and some other states apparently still treat it more harshly than does federal law. That perhaps accounts for the fact that real-world use of RPM is still not that common, even though *Leegin* so broadly authorized it.[7] (That said, there definitely are other possible explanations. For example, RPM turns out to be a difficult and expensive policy for manufacturers to maintain, because retailers have strong incentives to secretly violate RPM terms. Manufacturers must invest resources and personnel in monitoring distributors and punishing those that disobey. Moreover, it is often said that there are other, more effective ways for manufacturers to achieve the goals they commonly claim to desire as their reason for adopting RPM.[8]) For what it may be worth, it appears that antitrust practitioners now advise clients who desire to use RPM that they can avoid most risk so long as they can either avoid distribution in California and Maryland or satisfy themselves that their RPM programs comply with the *Colgate* doctrine—the longstanding rule that there is no vertical agreement where manufacturers merely announce their preferred resale prices and choose not to deal with distributors who charge less.

All that said, it seems worth understanding those theories that might be used by plaintiffs in federal RPM litigation, since RPM remains subject to challenge in principle. Generally speaking, it appears to be acknowledged that vertical price restraints are of more concern than non-price restraints, despite the fact that they are superficially subject to the same standard under §1. First, it is widely acknowledged that vertical restraints could be used as a component of horizontal price-fixing conspiracy at either the upstream or

---

4. The one substantial success was *Toledo Mack Sales & Service, Inc.*, 530 F.3d 204 (3d Cir. 2008) (reversing judgment as a matter of law for defendant, finding sufficient evidence of unreasonably anticompetitive vertical restraints to reach jury). The plaintiff in the *Leegin* case itself lost on remand without consideration of the merits because it had pled the case as a per se case, without alleging a relevant market or competitive injury, *see PSKS, Inc. v. Leegin Creative Leather Prods., Inc.*, 615 F.3d 412 (5th Cir 2010), and only a smattering of district court opinions have otherwise considered the issue, *see* 1 *Antitrust Law Developments (Ninth)* ch. 1.D (9th ed. 2022) (discussing cases).

5. *Alsheikh v. Superior Court*, No. B249822, 2013 WL 5530508, at *3 (Cal. Ct. App. Oct. 7, 2013); *see also Alan Darush MD APC v. Revision LP*, No. CV 12-10296, 2013 WL 1749539, at *6 (C.D. Cal. Apr. 10, 2013) (citing *Mailand v. Burckle*, 20 Cal. 3d 367 (1978) ("Under current California Supreme Court precedent, vertical price restraints are per se unlawful under the Cartwright Act. There is no indication that precedent is changing.")).

6. Maryland explicitly amended its antitrust law after *Leegin* to reaffirm that RPM is per se illegal under Maryland law. Md. Code Ann., Com. Law §11-204(b). The U.S. Supreme Court has made clear that states are permitted to differ in their antitrust rules from federal law.

7. *See* James Mulcahy & Filemon Carrillo, Leegin, *Ten Years Later: Did Vertical Agreements Remain Unlawful Per Se Where Adopted to Facilitate A Price-Fixing Horizontal Scheme?*, 38 Franchise L.J. 119 (2018).

8. *See generally* Grimes, *supra* note 3.

downstream level. An upstream cartel could use minimum RPM agreements to help police a price-fixing agreement. A downstream cartel with some power might impose RPM agreements on its suppliers, to prevent cheating among its own ranks. Where a plaintiff could show that a minimum RPM agreement is part of an illegal horizontal conspiracy at either level, the vertical restraint itself would violate the rule of reason. *See Leegin*, 551 U.S. at 893.

Second, RPM can be a tool for abuse by either a manufacturer or a buyer that has market power. A manufacturer with market power could use minimum RPM as a tool of foreclosure—the reward of RPM could be used in effect as a bribe to keep distributors from carrying its competitors' products. A retailer with market power might coerce a supplier into imposing RPM agreements on its other retailers, in order to fend off any risk of price competition to itself. In either case the necessary showing of market power would presumably be of the sort ordinarily required in §1 rule-of-reason cases (*see* Chapter 4). The *Leegin* Court noted that the *source* of the restraint is relevant, because it should be of more concern if the impetus for the restraint comes from retailers. The argument is that manufacturers should ordinarily want price competition among their distributors. The lower the retail prices charged for a manufacturer's goods, the higher the volume of its retail sales will be and, other things equal, the higher its profits. So, if the manufacturer originated the restraints, they are more likely to have some legitimate purpose. *See* 551 U.S. at 897-898.

While the law is still developing, these points have already had influence in rule-of-reason vertical restraints reasoning. *See, e.g.*, *Toledo Mack Sales & Service, Inc. v. Mack Trucks, Inc.*, 530 F.3d 204, 225 (3d Cir. 2008) (noting that the restraint in question was of concern because the manufacturer appeared to have market power and because it appeared to be adopted at the behest of the retailers). The economic reasoning likely to surround the developing law of vertical restraints, after *Leegin*, is explored in more detail in the appendix.

§10.3 DISTINGUISHING HORIZONTAL AND VERTICAL CONSPIRACIES

As one might guess, following *Leegin*, any plaintiff injured by what really is a vertical restraint will likely try to characterize it as horizontal, or as having horizontal elements. By doing so a plaintiff might be able to take advantage of a per se rule. In principle, any vertical arrangement might have horizontal aspects. For example, either one of the parties could be vertically integrated into the other party's market, such that they are in both a horizontal and a vertical relationship. Likewise, buyers and sellers that are not vertically integrated might nevertheless agree to vertical restraints for the purpose of facilitating some other, horizontal conspiracy.

The most common form of the latter sort of agreement is the so-called "hub-and-spoke" conspiracy. A powerful player either at the upstream or downstream level orchestrates a series of vertical arrangements with participants at the other level that facilitates a horizontal conspiracy at that level. In a leading case on point, *Toys "R" Us v. FTC*, 221 F.3d 928 (7th Cir. 2000), the toy retailer Toys "R" Us was accused of having approached its major suppliers to secure their agreement to limit the products they were willing to supply to competing, discount retailers. Had each individual supplier merely agreed to that bilaterally, only with Toys "R" Us, the arrangement would have been at most a non-price vertical exclusivity deal subject to the rule of reason, and there might have been an absolute defense under the *Colgate* rule (which is explained in §10.2.2). However, the Federal Trade Commission adduced evidence that the suppliers had secured assurances from Toys "R" Us that it would enter into a similar arrangement with each of them. In other words, they employed Toys "R" Us as the facilitator of what was effectively a horizontal agreement among them to boycott the discount retailers. The court held this to constitute a horizontal conspiracy the purpose of which was to keep prices up, and found it to be a per se illegal restraint for which Toys "R" Us could be liable as well. *See also United States v. Apple*, 791 F.3d 290 (2d Cir. 2015).

CHAPTER 11

Tying and Exclusive Contracting

§11.1 INTRODUCTION

§11.1.1 A Special Problem in Distribution

Antitrust has for a long time carved out special treatment for a particular category of non-price vertical restraint: arrangements that cause a buyer to take something from a seller that they otherwise might not. They can be thought of as in three categories. First are "tying" arrangements, in which a buyer must take at least one additional product to get the one that they actually want. Second are various variations on the tying theme, like bundling of several products together or "full-line forcing." Finally, "exclusive dealing" contracts require some downstream buyer not to buy from other suppliers. Each of these categories of conduct can be challenged under different statutory provisions. Each of them is a "contract" and therefore can violate Sherman Act §1 (even where the buyer is coerced into it in some sense by the buyer's market power), each can constitute exclusionary conduct in a §2 monopolization claim, and each of them can violate a separate provision of the Clayton Act, §3, which is designed specifically to address these kinds of sales arrangements.

It now seems safe to say that each of these three categories of restraint is treated more harshly than the rest of vertical restraints, though only slightly. They are subject to their own special rules, and generally speaking the rules simplify the showing plaintiffs would otherwise have to make. All other vertical restraints are subject to the full-blown rule of reason.

Whether they really should be treated differently is an open question. The roots of this special treatment may lie in essentially noneconomic political values. To the courts of the early twentieth century, it seemed wrong for sellers to limit the commercial freedom of buyers. That may have reflected not so much a concept of social efficiency, as a defense of individual liberty. As antitrust became more and more driven by economic theory, critics argued that these restraints actually might be procompetitive and at any rate were unlikely to be harmful. For many years there has been agitation to relax these rules. However, more recent economic theory has begun to suggest that, like other vertical restraints, tying and exclusive contracts really might in fact be economically harmful. And it has also been argued that tying, at least, really does pose special problems calling for idiosyncratic rules. (For further explanation, see the discussion of the economics of distribution in the appendix.)

§11.1.2 The Limitations and Peculiarities of Clayton Act §3

Part of the congressional motivation for adopting the Clayton Act in 1914 was the belief that certain kinds of abuses were going unchecked because of unduly narrow judicial constructions of the Sherman Act, and among the several specific substantive sections was §3, prohibiting exclusive contracts and ties. This section is beset by several peculiarities, and for that reason it is used less often to challenge ties and exclusive contracts than Sherman Act §§1 and 2. All or most tie-ins that could be challenged under Clayton Act §3 could be challenged under Sherman Act §1, and so they are.[1]

In any case, Clayton Act §3, 15 U.S.C. §14, makes it unlawful

> to lease or make a sale or contract for sale . . . or fix a price charged therefor, or discount from, or rebate upon, such price, on the condition . . . that the lessee or purchaser thereof shall not use or deal in the goods . . . of a competitor . . . of the lessor or seller, where the effect . . . may be to substantially lessen competition or tend to create a monopoly in any line of commerce.[2]

---

1. Clayton Act §3 was probably necessary in its day if tie-ins were to be subject to legal challenge at all. Just a few years before its adoption, the Supreme Court had upheld tying arrangements involving power arising from patents, and had suggested that ties might be difficult to challenge under the antitrust laws. *See Henry v. A.B. Dick Co.*, 224 U.S. 1 (1912).

2. Note that while this section does not explicitly use the word "tie" or "tying," it prohibits sales made on "condition" that the buyer will not purchase a product of the seller's competitor. That language has been read to reach any sort of agreement that causes a buyer to take something from the seller they otherwise would not.

The peculiarities of the provision are these. First, §3 applies only to "person[s] engaged in commerce," and as explained elsewhere in this book this has been held to mean that the sale or lease must involve two or more states (*see* §20.2.2). Second, §3 applies only to "goods, wares, merchandise, machinery, supplies, or other commodities. . . ." Therefore, the section does not apply to any tying arrangement where either the tied or tying product is a service or is an intangible thing, like credit or intellectual property.

Under present law, the only advantage to a plaintiff in Clayton Act §3 might be that it prohibits arrangements whose effect "may be to substantially lessen competition or tend to create a monopoly in any line of commerce." The courts are split as to whether this standard requires a lesser showing by the plaintiff than proof of "unreasonableness" under Sherman Act §1, and the Supreme Court has not answered the question. However, given the common criticism that the per se tying test under §1 is already too plaintiff-friendly, and the increasingly common view that vertical restraints are usually not harmful, that distinction seems unlikely to persist even in those circuits that have suggested it.

§11.2 TYING

§11.2.1 What Tying Is

A "tying" arrangement is one in which a seller coerces a buyer to take two or more products rather than just one. There may be situations in which buyers desire a given product so much that they will buy an additional product with it in order to get the one they really want. (In the parlance of the tying case law, the product that consumers want is called the "tying" product, and the one they are forced to take with it is the "tied" product.) Early on the reaction of the courts to tying arrangements was quite negative and they held them illegal under the Sherman Act. Their hostility reflected a few concerns. The predominant theoretical concern was that a seller who already had monopoly power in one market might use it to "leverage" increased market share in another, so as to earn monopoly profits there too. But the courts also seemed to harbor the moral or populist instinct that tying affronted personal liberty. In any case, the early tying case law was extremely uncompromising. As we shall see, that strictness was softened over time, so that the tying test courts now employ—though it is still known as a "per se" test—leaves a fair bit of room for ties the courts think are not harmful, and is effectively just a structured rule of reason.

§11.2.2 The So-Called Per Se Tying Test

The tying cause of action is commonly said to have five elements, and they do not differ depending on whether the action is brought under Sherman Act §1 or Clayton Act §3:[3]

- Plaintiff must show that:
  1. There were two different products,
  2. The plaintiff was required to buy both to get the one it wanted,
  3. The defendant had some "power" in the tying product market, and
  4. The arrangement affected a "substantial" amount of commerce.
- If those elements are shown, then:
  5. The defendant may attempt to rebut with business justifications.

§11.2.2(a) Separate Products

The tying cause of action begins with a subtle philosophical problem: Where is the boundary between two products? The question can seem fairly obvious where the products are tangible and physically separate objects, especially if they are not complementary to one another. But those tying arrangements that have been challenged have almost always involved complementary items. A leading early case, for example, involved the sale of large stationary computers that used paper punch cards. Defendant IBM required purchasers of its computers also to buy its cards. *Intl. Bus. Mach. v. United States*, 258 U.S. 451 (1936). But where the products are complementary, as in that case, is it so obvious that they are separate products just because they have separate physical existence? What about a desktop computer and its peripherals (the monitor, mouse and keyboard)? On the one hand, they might seem like one product because a person can't really use a computer without a keyboard. But on the other hand, maybe it would be to the consumer's benefit if they were marketed as separate products. Perhaps one could shop around for the best price or the best features on each part of the system. Anyway, similar problems abound in other marketing scenarios. Is a car a separate product from its radio, for example? What about from its tires? These problems are then exacerbated where the allegedly separate products are intangible, as with software code, or where one of them is a service, as with anesthesiology or radiology or the like and the hospital where they are performed.

---

3. As mentioned, ties can also be challenged under Sherman Act §2, but in that case the cause of action differs. The plaintiff must show a very substantial amount of market power, sufficient to constitute "monopoly power" under §2, and that the tying arrangement was "exclusionary." *See* §13.3.5.

The Supreme Court has attempted in its most recent decisions to fashion a test that is removed from attempted metaphysical distinctions between discrete "things," and driven instead by evidence of producer behavior and consumer demand. In two recent decisions, the Court has said that the separate products inquiry "turns not on the functional relation between the[] [products], but rather on the character of the demand for the[m]," *Jefferson Parish Hosp. Dist. No. 2 v. Hyde*, 466 U.S. 2, 19 (1984), and therefore that there can be separate products only where there is "sufficient consumer demand so that it is efficient for a firm to provide [them] separately," *Eastman Kodak Co. v. Image Technical Servs., Inc.*, 504 U.S. 451, 462 (1992).

Under this test, products are "separate" if they could profitably be marketed separately. This can be shown even if no one would want one of the products without the other. No one would want surgery without anesthesia, for example, but they were found to be separate products in *Jefferson Parish*. *See also Jefferson Parish*, 466 U.S. at 19 n.30 ("We have often found arrangements involving functionally linked products at least one of which is useless without the other to be prohibited tying devices."). So, it is not a question whether consumers need or want both products or even whether consumers would want one without the other. So long as there could be a viable market for sales of one of the products alone, the products are separate. Thus, cars and car tires are separate, even though the first set of tires one buys for a car will come with it from the dealer. There is separate consumer demand for replacement tires. In the case law it has often been significant if the plaintiff could put on evidence that one of the products had in fact been sold separately sometimes. The fact that sellers have been willing to do it in itself tends to show that it can be profitable and therefore that consumers desire it.

Beware, however, that merely because products are separate does not mean that selling them together, and even refusing to sell one without the other, is illegal. The other elements of the cause of action must also be met.

§11.2.2(b) Coerced Purchase of Both Products

This element is probably the simplest. There must be some refusal by the seller to provide the products separately, or some onerous penalty for buyers who elect to take them separately.

§11.2.2(c) Power in the Tying Product

The logic of the harm caused by tying requires that buyers are actually forced to buy the tied product. That implies that the seller must have power in the tying product market. Strictly speaking, the Supreme Court's cases only require "appreciable economic power" in the tying market, *Eastman Kodak Co. v. Image Technical Servs., Inc.*, 504 U.S. 451, 461 (1992), and there was a time when the courts were lax in demanding proof of it.[4] More recent decisions, however, have made clear that "power" in the tying market means "market power" of a kind sufficient to satisfy §1 rule-of-reason causes of action. *Kodak*, for example, held that the "market power" that must be shown is "the ability of a single seller to raise price and restrict output," a power that "ordinarily is inferred from the seller's possession of a predominant share of the market." 504 U.S. at 464.

§11.2.2(d) "Substantial" Amount of Commerce Affected

This element is essentially vestigial in most circuits. In the Supreme Court's earlier tying cases, the Court had held that the tying arrangement must affect a "not insubstantial amount of commerce," *Northern Pac. Ry. Co. v. United States*, 365 U.S. 1, 11 (1958), but, critically, substantiality is measured only by absolute dollar amount, regardless how large or small the relevant market is. The Supreme Court has held amounts as low as $60,000 to be "substantial." *United States v. Loew's, Inc.*, 371 U.S. 38, 49 (1961). Most ties challenged in federal litigation will meet this low threshold easily.

§11.2.2(e) Business Justifications

If a plaintiff can make out the other elements of the per se claim, the defendant can still respond with justifications indicating its tie is procompetitive. The most common defense is that the tie is necessary to preserve the quality and brand image of the seller's product. For example, a seller of some durable and long-lasting good, like a high-end photocopier, might tie sale of the copier to a long-term contract for supply of toner cartridges. It might defend that arrangement if it could show that the use of cartridges from third parties causes its machines to perform poorly, weakening its brand image. This sort of defense has held some sway, particularly where the defendant could show that it instituted the policy in response to customer quality complaints.

Example

XYZ, Inc., manufactures a special machine used by auto mechanics to refurbish old piston heads. The machine is very popular, and currently it faces

4. Indeed, until a few years ago it had been a longstanding rule that the holding of *any* intellectual property in the tying product was sufficient to show "power" there. But many patents and copyrights give their holders little or no market power because there are close substitutes for the protected property. *Illinois Tool Works, Inc. v. Independent Ink, Inc.*, 547 U.S. 28 (2006), reversed that rule.

no competition from substitutes because XYZ has a patent on the machine, and no one has figured out any way to refurbish piston heads through any process that wouldn't infringe the patent. While XYZ's machine is popular, many users of it have grown frustrated with some of XYZ's policies. In particular, the machine requires the use of a special solvent which is produced and packaged separately by XYZ. Several other solvent products are available that could be used in the machine, but XYZ requires all users to sign an agreement requiring them to use only XYZ solvent in the XYZ machine.

Is this legal?

Explanation

Probably not. The fact that the machine is patented and has no close substitutes suggests a substantial amount of market power in the tying product—the refurbishing machine. There seems little doubt that the special solvent is a "separate product," as it is packaged and available separately, and there is also little doubt that the purchase of the solvent is "coerced," since it is a condition for access to a desired product (the refurbishing machine). The "substantial amount of commerce" is basically a vestigial requirement in any event, and since this product is apparently mass produced that requirement would presumably be no problem. The only question whether this is illegal will turn on whether XYZ could muster a convincing "business justification." It might be able to do so if it can document evidence that consumers prefer the product when used only with XYZ's solvent.

Example

Bazoomer Software, Inc., is the maker of a popular suite of business productivity applications, which includes a word processing program, a spreadsheet, a slideshow program for presentations, and some other tools. Bazoomer sells this package as a unit and does not sell the programs separately. (Bazoomer believes significant technological advantages follow from including all programs in one suite—the programs run better, because they take up less computer memory than they otherwise would.) A would-be competitor introduced its own slideshow program and attempted to sell it for about two years, but sales were weak and the company went insolvent. It has sued Bazoomer, alleging that the inclusion of all its products in one package—including its overwhelmingly dominant word processor—precluded independent markets for any of the other products in its suite.

Has Bazoomer engaged in an illegal tie?

Explanation

It is hard to say, but defendant Bazoomer has a number of arguments on its side. Admittedly, the plaintiff can probably satisfy the requirement of power in the tying product (the word processor), and if it can show that the products are distinct, then the requirement that consumers were forced to buy both products is straightforward. However, there would seem to be a question as to whether there are separate products here. Products are separate only if they can profitably be produced that way, but the plaintiff's own experience perhaps shows that these products cannot be. Moreover, even if these products are separate, Bazoomer could put on a case for business justification—apparently, combining the programs makes them work better.

§11.3 EXCLUSIVE CONTRACTS

There was a fairly long period during which it was thought that a special, more plaintiff-friendly rule applied to one particular sort of distribution arrangement: the exclusive dealing contract. These arrangements limit the buyer's freedom to purchase the good from other suppliers as well. They might take the form of a requirements contract requiring the purchaser to take its entire need for the good from a single supplier, a contract forbidding purchases from the supplier's competitors, an outputs contract requiring the customer to take all of the supplier's output, or a contract with penalties for purchasing elsewhere. It is now clear that these arrangements are subject to what is effectively a rule of reason, requiring proof of market power in a relevant market and likely anticompetitive effects.

The traditional pro-enforcement rule was based on one of the Supreme Court's few decisions on point, *Standard Oil Co. v. United States (Standard Stations)*, 337 U.S. 293 (1949). There the Court stressed its intent to allow the plaintiffs to challenge large-scale exclusive dealing plans under a simpler standard than full rule of reason. The Court believed they posed special competitive risks when they were widely used, but also wanted to shield them from the then-very harsh rule against tying. The Court suggested that exclusive contracts should be illegal where they foreclose some "substantial" percentage of distribution in a given market, and held illegal a foreclosure of 6.7 percent.

That rule began to meet its end in the Court's only other major ruling on the issue, *Tampa Elec. Co. v. Nashville Coal Co.*, 365 U.S. 320 (1961). There the Court introduced a more fact-rich inquiry than the simple focus on percentage foreclosure in *Standard Stations*. The Court wrote that it must

> weigh the probable effect of the contract on the relevant area of effective competition, taking into account the relative strength of the parties, the proportionate

> volume of commerce involved in relation to the total volume of commerce in the relevant market area, and the probable immediate and future effects which pre-emption of that share of the market might have on effective competition therein. It follows that a mere showing that the contract itself involves a substantial number of dollars is ordinarily of little consequence.

Id. at 329. Accordingly, even a large percentage foreclosure of distribution might not be illegal if the plaintiff cannot also show that it would likely impede entry or expansion by existing competitors.

Since *Tampa Electric*, courts have developed this "qualitative substantiality" test further and often describe it as just an application of the rule of reason. *See, e.g., McWane, Inc. v. FTC*, 783 F.3d 814, 835 (11th Cir. 2015); *ZF Meritor LLC v. Eaton Corp.*, 696 F.3d 254, 271 (3d Cir.2012). However, they continue to apply *Tampa Bay*'s requirement of "substantial foreclosure" and recognize that it is both special to the law of exclusive contracts and arguably anachronistic. *McWane*, 783 F.3d at 835. In the ordinary case, it is now fairly clear that the plaintiff must show that the challenged contracts cover about 40 percent of the market or more. Some courts have found illegality on less,[5] but in more recent years it has been rare,[6] and given the modern emphasis on qualitative rather than quantitative factors, sometimes foreclosures significantly higher than that have been held legal.[7] In particular, if an exclusivity arrangement—even one foreclosing a very large share—has either a short term or is easily terminated, it is very unlikely to be illegal. In some courts, contracts with terms of less than one year are presumed legal. *See, e.g., Roland Mach. Co. v. Dresser Indus., Inc.*, 749 F.2d 380, 395 (7th Cir. 1984).

---

5. *See, e.g., Am. Motor Inns, Inc. v. Holiday Inns, Inc.*, 521 F.2d 1230 (3d Cir. 1975) (foreclosure of 14.7 percent not necessarily unlawful if other factors indicate no substantial impact on interbrand competition).
6. *See, e.g., Ryko Mfg. Co. v. Eden Servs.*, 823 F.2d 1215 (8th Cir. 1987); *Satellite Television & Associated Res., Inc. v. Contractual Cablevision, Inc.*, 714 F.2d 351 (4th Cir. 1983) (foreclosure of 8 percent of households lawful); *Twin City Sportservice, Inc. v. Charles O. Finley & Co.*, 676 F.2d 1291 (9th Cir. 1982) (long-term foreclosure of 24 percent unlawful).
7. *See, e.g., Omega Envtl., Inc. v. Gilbarco, Inc.*, 127 F.3d 1157 (9th Cir. 1997) (foreclosure of 38 percent found lawful); *Kuck v. Bensen*, 647 F. Supp. 743 (D. Mo. 1986) (foreclosure of 37 percent lawful); *Gonzalez v. Insignares*, Civil Action No. C84-1261A, 1985 WL 2206 (N.D. Ga. 1985) (foreclosure of 40 percent lawful).

PART V

Proof of Conspiracy

CHAPTER 12 Proof of Conspiracy Under Sherman Act §1

§12.1 WHY CONSPIRACY IS HARD TO PROVE

All Sherman Act §1 causes of action—that is, most antitrust actions other than for monopolization or unlawful merger—require the plaintiff to prove the existence of a "contract, combination, . . . or conspiracy" in restraint of trade. In recent times the Supreme Court has stressed the fundamental significance of this requirement:

> The meaning of the term "contract, combination . . . or conspiracy" is informed by the "basic distinction" in the Sherman Act "between concerted and independent action" that distinguishes §1 of the Sherman Act from §2. [*Copperweld Corp. v. Independence Tube Corp.*, 467 U.S. 752, 767 (1984)] (quoting *Monsanto Co. v. Spray-Rite Service Corp.*, [465 U.S. 752, 761 (1984)]). Section 1 applies only to concerted action that restrains trade. Section 2, by contrast, covers both concerted and independent action, but only if that action "monopolize[s]," 15 U.S.C. §2, or "threatens actual monopolization," *Copperweld*, 467 U.S., at 767, . . . a category that is narrower than restraint of trade.

Am. Needle, Inc. v. Natl. Football League, 560 U.S. 183, 190 (2010). However, this seemingly straightforward requirement that there be multilateral action can be difficult to understand and difficult for the plaintiff to prove. It is also a high-stakes issue over which parties litigate fiercely. Per se and quick-look rules in antitrust are available only under §1, so if the plaintiff fails to prove conspiracy, its only hope will be to make the much more difficult showing of market power large enough to support a §2 monopolization claim.

There are really three reasons the conspiracy element can be challenging. First, and perhaps surprisingly, it can be hard to know whether the entities involved in a transaction are even separate from one another. Of course in many cases this will be no problem, as when the defendants are natural persons not employed by the same firm. But it can easily get quite complex, especially where one of the defendants is a corporation and another defendant owns some stock in it. This recurrent problem, which is often referred to as the "single entity" or "intraenterprise conspiracy" problem, occasioned important Supreme Court decisions in 2006 and 2010 and has been the subject of much controversy. (*See* §12.2.)

Second, evidence of conspiracy in violation of antitrust can be hard to come by. Conspiracies in restraint of trade are illegal and can constitute crimes subject to severe penalties. Hard-core conspirators, knowing that their conduct is illegal, will normally try to keep it as secret as possible. Nowadays, smoking gun evidence of conspiracy is rare except where government investigators have gotten it through undercover agents or cloak-and-dagger techniques. So a plaintiff must often seek to prove conspiracy with purely circumstantial evidence. The courts, however, fear that if they make it too easy for plaintiffs to prove conspiracy with nothing more than circumstantial evidence, they will deter innocent, procompetitive conduct. (*See* §12.3.2.)

Finally, there will often be cases in which the behavior of firms within a concentrated industry really *seems* like there must be some sort of agreement among them, but there really just isn't. As explained in depth in §12.3.3 and in the appendix, a running problem in antitrust is how to deal with the behavior of "oligopolists," and their behavior poses a particular problem for plaintiffs trying to prove conspiracy. It may be rational under the right circumstances for oligopolists to raise their prices above the competitive price, quite unilaterally, as they will be able to predict that their competitors will all do the same. This "interdependent" pricing is thought to be a fairly common occurrence, but in and of itself it involves no "conspiracy" and cannot violate §1. Still, it will often produce what appears to be persuasive circumstantial evidence that there *was* such a conspiracy, despite the lack of any direct evidence. The courts therefore have had to develop rules for handling this sort of case. (*See* §12.3.3.)

Example

A manufacturer of computer printers has acquired about 60 percent of its market. A would-be competitor files suit, arguing that the defendant has violated the antitrust laws by using its market power to force software companies to design operating systems that will be compatible only with its patented printer design. The plaintiff raises both a §1 claim and an attempted monopolization claim under §2. The defendant files a motion to dismiss both claims. The court grants the motion as to the §1 claim. Was that decision correct?

Explanation

Yes. Here the only conduct challenged was the defendant's unilateral conduct. Section 1 claims require that there be some "contract, combination, . . . or conspiracy," meaning that the defendant must have acted along with at least one other person.

§12.2 THE SINGLE ENTITY PROBLEM: *COPPERWELD, DAGHER*, AND *AMERICAN NEEDLE*

However much uncertainty there may be as to proof of conspiracy, there is at least one clear black letter rule, set out in *Copperweld Corp. v. Independence Tube Corp.*, 467 U.S. 752 (1984). *Copperweld* seems to state a very simple rule indeed, and it is one that in many cases will be quite easily applied: A corporation may not "conspire" with its wholly owned subsidiary for purposes of Sherman Act §1. The rule might seem almost painfully obvious, in that simple internal pricing and marketing decisions in any corporate family would seem likely to involve significant trade restraints, and if the Sherman Act were to apply to such decisions the very idea of the corporate subsidiary would be more or less outlawed. A related rule is that a firm's officers and employees cannot conspire with one another, and neither can unincorporated internal divisions of the same firm.

And yet, it is interesting to consider just how provocative are the issues raised by this seemingly simple rule. For one thing, *Copperweld* overturned a different black letter rule that had been in place for about 40 years and that had been reaffirmed in a number of previous Supreme Court opinions. Whatever may be the correctness of the *Copperweld* result, it is intriguing to see how quickly the decision raises basic and fundamental issues of the nature of business firms and the organization of the economy. Tellingly, in his vigorous dissent in *Copperweld*, Justice Stevens quoted the following language, in which he defended the 1947 Supreme Court decision in *United States v. Yellow Cab Co.*, 332 U.S. 218 (1947). *Yellow Cab* was the leading case for the so-called "intra-enterprise conspiracy" doctrine, which was jettisoned in *Copperweld*. Justice Stevens quoted the following:

> The central message of the Sherman Act is that a business entity must find new customers and higher profits through internal expansion—that is, by competing successfully rather than by arranging treaties with its competitors. This Court has held that even commonly owned firms must compete against each other, if they hold themselves out as distinct entities. "The corporate interrelationships of the conspirators . . . are not determinative of the applicability of the Sherman Act."

467 U.S. at 783 n.7 (Stevens, J., dissenting) (quoting *United States v. Citizens & Southern Natl. Bank*, 422 U.S. 86, 116-117 (1975), and citing *United States v.Yellow Cab Co.*, 332 U.S. 218, 227 (1947)).

Admittedly, the "intra-enterprise conspiracy" rule that predated *Copperweld* was particularly despised by critics. To make a long story short, for a period of about 40 years prior to *Copperweld* it was technically possible under U.S. law that a corporation and its wholly owned subsidiary could conspire in violation of Sherman Act §1. That occasioned a whole subgenre of scholarly criticism, and strenuous efforts by the lower courts to avoid ever finding a parent-subsidiary conspiracy. The intra-enterprise conspiracy doctrine was honored by the lower courts, of course, but almost exclusively in the breach.

Also admittedly, *Copperweld* laid out a lengthy policy analysis to explain its rejection of intra-enterprise conspiracy, and many subsequent observers have taken it as an important gloss on the fundamental theoretical basis for the §1 multilateral conduct requirement. The essence of the Court's guidance was that separate firms have separate "interests." While the Court never precisely explained which "interests" mattered or why, it apparently meant that those firms separate enough to conspire under §1 do not share in the same profits and losses. This stands to reason because only firms "separate" in this sense will gain from underselling one another. They will attempt to steal sales from one another, and they will do so through price competition. That redounds to the common good because it forces them to produce as efficiently as they can. But where two entities have the same economic incentive—which they do when they merely earn money for one common fund, as was the case in *Copperweld*—then their independent action will probably benefit society no more than their joint action, because in neither event would they willingly fight to steal business from one another. The Court also offered the separate policy point that a rule that discourages productively efficient integrations would impose some costs. In any case, while *Copperweld* technically only answered a narrow question about the 100 percent subsidiary situation, the Court seemed to offer this analysis as a guide for lower courts to follow in fashioning a new single entity case law.

The problem is that in practice, the reasoning laid out in *Copperweld* has not added much clarity at all. In fact, the lower court case law has been basically indistinguishable from the pre-*Copperweld* cases. Except as to the ultimate result in *Copperweld* itself—the holding that a corporation and its *wholly* owned subsidiary are a "single entity"—the courts are left to make more or less a priori judgments, usually at a fairly early pretrial stage, about complex, speculative and fact-bound issues. And while no one seems to doubt the wisdom of the *Copperweld* reasoning, it has proven too abstract to decide subsequent cases wherever they pose issues that are difficult at all. Perhaps it is fairly easy to say that an 80 percent shareholder is as much in "control" of a subsidiary as a 100 percent shareholder. But what about a 49 percent shareholder? Or a 35 percent shareholder? Or what if neither owns any of the other, but the two of them have joined together in a "joint venture" to produce some new product or service? Is the joint venture a conspiracy of the two of them, or is it an entity separate from them whose actions are unilateral? What about a cooperative association of independent firms formed to buy some input from them, or formed to jointly market their products? In cases like these, both before *Copperweld* and after it, lower courts have been left without much clear guidance except their own intuitions. To borrow from a great scholar of business law, *Copperweld* has left the courts in these cases with words rather than rules.[1]

Indeed, the Court's own next decision on point was one of the stranger and more inscrutable cases in the area. In *Texaco, Inc. v. Dagher*, 547 U.S. 1 (2006), the Texaco and Shell oil companies formed a joint venture between them, a separate corporation they both would own. The venture would refine gasoline and then sell it, under the two parents' separate brands but at one price set by the venture. The Court's basic holding was that, under the circumstances, the agreement on price could not be challenged as a per se illegal price conspiracy. The Court made repeated references in dicta to the firm as a "single entity," even though many prior decisions had applied §1 to the internal conduct of joint venturers.[2] Still, even for that its holding might have seemed just an ordinary, humdrum application of familiar law: Its basic rule seemed to be that where an arrangement is a "lawful [and] economically integrated joint venture," *id.* at 3, that is not a "sham," *id.* at 5 n.1, and where the challenged conduct is a "core activity of the joint venture," like an "internal pricing decision," then the per se rule does not apply. The Court explicitly reserved the question whether the price agreement could separately be challenged under the rule of reason.[3] But what made the opinion so confusing was that the Court explicitly reversed the

---

1. Adolph A. Berle, Jr., *The Theory of Enterprise Entity*, 47 Colum. L. Rev. 343, 346 (1947).
2. *See, e.g.*, *United States v. Topco Assocs., Inc.*, 405 U.S. 596 (1972); *United States v. Sealy, Inc.*, 388 U.S. 350, 352-354 (1967); *Timken Roller Bearing Co. v. United States*, 341 U.S. 593, 598 (1951) ("agreements . . . to suppress competition . . . can[not] be justified by labeling the project a 'joint venture.' Perhaps every agreement and combination to restrain trade could be so labeled.").
3. The failure of that issue to arise was fortuitous; the plaintiffs had simply failed to plead any rule-of-reason theory of liability, so the Court refused to address the possibility of rule-of-reason liability. 547 U.S. at 7 n.2.

court of appeals for having applied the rule of ancillary restraints, holding that the rule "has no application . . . where the business practice being challenged involves the core activity of the joint venture itself—namely, the pricing of [its] very goods. . . ." *Id.* at 7-8. The problem this raised was that on one plausible reading of the opinion, *Dagher* seemed to hold that the "internal" conduct of "economically integrated" joint ventures was simply immune from §1 entirely, as the conduct of a "single entity."[4]

But in any case, whatever concerns *Dagher* might have raised were put to rest a few years later in *Am. Needle, Inc. v. Natl. Football League*, 560 U.S. 183 (2010). Defendant National Football League was an unincorporated association of teams, each team being a separately organized business entity, and there was no common ownership among them. The teams collectively agreed to license their logos to makers of team memorabilia through a joint sales agency—an arrangement that ordinarily could constitute per se price fixing. The peculiar economic nature of professional sports, however, and the joint-venture nature of the NFL led many to believe that the league's joint activities should be subject at least to deferential antitrust review. In this particular case, in part on reliance on the reading of *Dagher* just suggested, the NFL argued that it was a "single entity" and therefore simply immune from §1 altogether. Both lower courts agreed. The lower court opinions demonstrated just how pliable the economic reasoning in *Copperweld* could be. The court of appeals based its decision on very little more than its view that the "NFL teams share a vital economic interest in collectively promoting NFL football," and accordingly "that only one source of economic power controls [that] promotion. . . ." 538 F.3d 736, 743 (7th Cir. 2008).

4. This is so because if the ancillary restraints rule *had* applied—and the case seemed to most antitrust observers like a straightforward ancillary restraints case—the result could easily have been the same one that the Court reached. If the conduct was a "core activity" of the venture, as the Court held, then one presumes it must have been "ancillary"—it must have been "reasonably related" to the venture's purposes and "reasonably necessary" to achieve its procompetitive benefits. *See* §7.2. In other words, the basis for reversing the Ninth Circuit's application of a rule of per se liability might just have been a mistaken decision as to whether the price restraint was "ancillary" to a procompetitive arrangement, not a mistake in applying ancillary restraints at all. So the fact that the Court held *both* the restraint could not be per se illegal *and* that the ancillary restraints doctrine was inapplicable logically seems to imply only one thing: that the restraint is immune from §1. Many have suggested that this was simply a doctrinal mistake, since the case seemed so plainly ripe for ancillary restraints treatment. For what it is worth, the Court may have meant to introduce a new wrinkle in that doctrine. Following *Dagher*, perhaps it was intended that ordinary joint ventures—unlike the Texaco-Shell venture—could adopt horizontal limitations on price or output so long as they are "ancillary" to the venture's purpose and comply with the rule of reason; that is, they could adopt restraints reasonably related to the venture and reasonably necessary to achieve its benefits, so long as they do not unreasonably restrain trade. But "economically integrated" joint ventures—like the Texaco-Shell venture—can impose restraints that are not "ancillary" but are nevertheless "core activities." The problem then is simply the doctrinal one: What sort of restraint could that possibly be?

Justice Stevens—who dissented in *Copperweld*—wrote for a unanimous Court, and reversed. The opinion resoundingly reaffirms *Copperweld*, and largely restates the economic analysis there, but rejects single-entity treatment for the NFL. According to the Court,

> [t]he fact that NFL teams share an interest in making the entire league successful and profitable, and that they must cooperate in the production and scheduling of games, provides a perfectly sensible justification for making a host of collective decisions. But the conduct at issue in this case is still concerted activity under the Sherman Act that is subject to §1 analysis.

Id. at 202-203.

One is left to wonder how much guidance there is even after *American Needle*. The Court stressed at length that the ability to conspire must be judged on a "functional analysis," but explained that it just depends on consideration of the defendants' economic interests, as under *Copperweld*. In short, both before and after *Copperweld* the lower courts have been resigned to making the single entity decision according to a loose, a priori judgment whether the defendants are sufficiently "integrated" or have sufficiently "unified" economic interests that the specific agreement would not deprive markets of price competition. But however much intuitive sense the reasoning in *Copperweld* and *American Needle* might seem to make, this is really no guidance at all. After all, aren't the economic interests within naked, horizontal price-fixing cartel "unified" to some pretty substantial degree?

Having said that, a few specific rules emerge. For the most part, the courts have said that where one corporation *controls* another, the two cannot conspire for purposes of Sherman Act §1. "Control" plainly can exist where a firm owns some majority share in another firm, even though it is less than 100 percent. Presumably it could even include situations in which one firm owns less than a majority, where other indications suggest that it exercises control. Likewise, subsidiaries with a common parent cannot conspire horizontally with each other.

It can also often be fairly easy to say that a given arrangement is *not* a single entity and that participants within it can conspire. A common situation has been the production joint venture in which the venture is organized as a separate entity, but the members impose some membership or conduct rules through the venture agreement, or cause the venture to take some other action affecting competition. The fact that the venture is a legally separate entity does not mean that the members have not conspired with each other in taking those actions. *See, e.g., United States v. Topco Assocs., Inc.*, 405 U.S. 596 (1972); *United States v. Sealy, Inc.*, 388 U.S. 350, 352-354 (1967). Another common scenario has involved trade or professional associations that impose rules on their members. On the one hand, "a trade association is not by its nature a walking conspiracy," *Consolidated Metal Prods., Inc. v. Am. Petroleum Inst.*,

846 F.2d 284, 293-294 (5th Cir. 1988), and so in order to be responsible for its actions an individual member must have had some role in taking them. But where its actions clearly are the actions of all the members—as with the adoption of binding ethics or membership rules—then every member is party to a conspiracy as to those actions. It is clear that "[w]hen an organization is controlled by a group of competitors, it is considered to be a conspiracy of its members," *North Texas Specialty Physicians v. FTC*, 528 F.3d 326, 356 (5th Cir. 2008). It does not matter that the members are not direct competitors, so long as they have "substantially similar economic interests." *Hahn v. Oregon Physicians' Serv.*, 868 F.2d 1022, 1029 (9th Cir. 1988).

§12.3 PROVING CONSPIRACY

§12.3.1 The Basic Framework and the Law as It Once Was

Once it is clear that a plaintiff has identified two or more defendants who are separate entities, the question still remains whether there was an agreement among them constituting a "contract, combination, . . . or conspiracy." A leading statement on point holds that there need be merely some "unity of purpose or a common design and understanding, or a meeting of minds in an unlawful arrangement." *Am. Tobacco Co. v. United States*, 328 U.S. 781, 810 (1946).

In meeting this standard, by no means must there be a "contract" in the ordinary common law sense. There is no need for any exchange of consideration or other indices of a formal common law contract. Likewise, "whether an unlawful combination or conspiracy is proved is to be judged by what the parties actually did rather than by the words they used." *United States v. Parke, Davis & Co.*, 362 U.S. 29, 44 (1960). Accordingly, "[w]hether the conspiracy was achieved by agreement, by tacit understanding, or by acquiescence . . . coupled with assistance in effectuating its purpose is immaterial." *United States v. Bausch & Lomb Optical Co.*, 321 U.S. 707, 723 (1944). Thus, there need be no writing or formalities of any kind, and conspiracy can be inferred from nonverbal conduct such as a course of dealing.

A paradigm case was *Interstate Circuit, Inc. v. United States*, 306 U.S. 208 (1939). One defendant was an owner of movie theaters. He sent copies of a letter, on his company's letterhead, to eight large movie distributors, listing each of them as addressees and urging them to agree to certain terms that effectively constituted price fixing and market allocations. Despite the total lack of evidence of any communication among the distributors, each complied with uncannily identical behavior. The Court noted that each of the distributors had an economic motive for concerted action, and held that on all these circumstances the distributors should be held to have conspired. *American Tobacco*, too, involved the parallel pricing behavior of the three leading U.S. tobacco companies, which together produced about 90 percent of all U.S. cigarettes. While there was no evidence of explicit price fixing, the Court found their behavior too improbably identical for there to have been no conspiracy. Their prices had been practically identical for 25 years and they had raised prices in lock-step fashion, sometimes on the same day, even during the Depression, when their own costs were falling. Also damning was that the defendants could offer no economic justification for their behavior. Likewise, in *United States v. Container Corp. of America*, 393 U.S. 333 (1969), the Court found there to have been an agreement among several producers in a given industry, sufficient to constitute a "contract, combination, . . . or conspiracy" under §1, to share price information with one another. But the only evidence of such an agreement was specific instances in which one defendant asked another about the price charged in a particular sale, and the other defendant provided the information. That a pattern of such exchanges occurred was enough to prove that there was an agreement among them to share the information. *Id.* at 335.

Moreover, there is no requirement that the parties have some naturally sympathetic interests with one another. There can be a "unity of purpose or a common design and understanding" even where there is acrimony or conflict of interest among them. "[A]s a question of law, . . . [an] attitude of suspicion, wariness and self-preservation of the parties [does not] negate[] a conspiracy." *United States v. Singer Mfg. Co.*, 374 U.S. 174, 192-193 (1963). It would be rather bad policy if the rule were otherwise, because the members of the most anticompetitive cartels by the very nature of such arrangements have some conflicting interests. Indeed, a conspiracy can be held to exist even if some of the members (indeed, even if all of them but one) were coerced into joining it.

However, the cases have always been careful to point out that *mere* parallel behavior is not enough, by itself, to prove conspiracy circumstantially. In *Theatre Enter. v. Paramount Film Distrib. Corp.*, 346 U.S. 537 (1954), the plaintiff owned a suburban movie theatre. Each of the several defendant movie distributors refused to grant the plaintiff the right to show "first-run" movies in its theatre. The defendants all denied collaboration and they also put on a plausible economic explanation for why they each had independently refused the plaintiff's request (namely, that it was more profitable for them to restrict their first-run films to other locations). The Court found that no reasonable trier could find a conspiracy on the plaintiff's showing. The Court wrote that "[c]ircumstantial evidence of consciously parallel behavior may have made heavy inroads into the traditional judicial attitude toward conspiracy; but 'conscious parallelism' has not read conspiracy out of the Sherman Act entirely." 346 U.S. at 541.

Often the plaintiff's chief evidence will be the fact that over some period of time prices among the defendants were similar, and that when they changed they changed in a parallel fashion. That would normally be the result where the defendants have engaged in a successful price-fixing conspiracy. This is often called proof of conspiracy through evidence of "conscious parallelism." But as may be fairly obvious, the big problem with this approach is that the same result should often be observed in competitive markets too. Indeed, the more competitive the market, the more precisely similar should be the sellers' prices. Similarly, in the common scenario of "oligopoly," where prices may be supracompetitive even in the absence of price agreement, prices will tend to be similar throughout the market much of the time. (*See* §12.3.3.) Therefore, while the courts have long permitted plaintiffs to show agreement through evidence of conscious parallelism, they have tailored the plaintiff's burden so that triers do not infer conspiracy in cases where parallel pricing has simply arisen through competition.

To deal with this problem, the courts have devised the so-called "plus-factors" test for proof of conspiracy. Over the years, they have built up a framework under which to infer conspiracy from circumstantial evidence, and they have held that where the plaintiff's proof is based on evidence of parallelism, there must also be some "plus factor" suggesting that it wasn't *mere* parallelism. Before getting to that, however, we must consider the consequences of a new, rather stricter theoretical approach adopted by the Supreme Court during the past few decades. We turn to that development next.

§12.3.2 Proving Conspiracy Under *Twombly, Monsanto,* and *Matsushita*: The Pretrial Requirement of "Economic Sense"

§12.3.2(a) The Economic Sense Test

Notwithstanding what may appear to be the fairly permissive definition of "contract, combination, . . . or conspiracy," under *American Tobacco*, and the freewheeling approach of some of the older case law just discussed, the law of conspiracy has arguably changed quite a bit since the days of *Interstate Circuit*. As so often seems to be the case in recent antitrust, the changes have been driven by growing judicial reliance on economic theory. The change came as the result of a trio of Supreme Court opinions: *Monsanto Co. v. Spray-Rite Serv. Corp.*, 465 U.S. 752 (1984), *Matsushita Elec. Indus. Corp. v. Zenith Radio Corp.*, 475 U.S. 574 (1986), and *Bell Atl. Corp. v. Twombly*, 550 U.S. 544 (2007). Together, these decisions adopted a new standard for proof of conspiracy through circumstantial evidence. Henceforth, in every §1 case in which the plaintiff seeks to prove conspiracy without direct evidence, the trial court must perform an a priori theoretical analysis to determine whether the conduct alleged to have occurred would be *economically rational.*

Strictly speaking, the proof-of-conspiracy cases had for a long time contemplated a rationality inquiry of this sort. *Interstate Circuit* and *American Tobacco* both took it as proof that there *was* a conspiracy that the parallel conduct shown by the plaintiff would have been economically irrational in the absence of conspiracy. Likewise, *Theatre Enterprises* took it as evidence that there was *not* a conspiracy that the parallel conduct would have been rational even if it were entirely unilateral. But the trio of cases that began in 1984 made this inquiry substantially more rigorous, and made it clear that a case alleging a conspiracy that would be irrational—in the mind of one district court judge, applying only economic theory—must be dismissed as a matter of law in the absence of direct proof.

Monsanto began the development. The Court wrote that

> [t]he correct standard is that there must be evidence that tends to exclude the possibility of independent action by the [alleged conspirators]. That is, there must be direct or circumstantial evidence that *reasonably tends to prove* that the[y] had a conscious commitment to a common scheme designed to achieve an unlawful objective.

465 U.S. at 768 (emphasis added). *Matsushita* then made clear that whether circumstantial proof *reasonably* shows such a common scheme depends on economic rationality. The Court explained:

> [A]ntitrust law limits the range of permissible inferences from ambiguous evidence in a §1 case. Thus, . . . conduct as consistent with permissible competition as with illegal conspiracy does not, standing alone, support an inference of antitrust conspiracy. . . . [Accordingly,] plaintiff . . . must present evidence that tends to exclude the possibility that the alleged conspirators acted independently. . . . [I]n other words, . . . [the] conspiracy [must be] reasonable. . . .

475 U.S. at 588 (citations omitted). The *Matsushita* Court then held that the alleged conspiracy in that case had not been proven because, in the Court's view, it would have been economically irrational. The Court did not hold that it would have been impossible, but rather that in order for it to have been profitable to the defendants, they would have had to undertake a difficult and risky strategy with uncertain benefits. Because the Court felt that a rational, profit-maximizing firm would not have taken such a risk, the plaintiff could prove such a conspiracy only by putting on some truly substantial showing that it occurred.

§12.3.2(b) When and How the Test Is Applied

As a matter of civil procedure, there are several points during a lawsuit at which this requirement of economic sense can be applied, and a case is dismissible at any of those points if the plaintiff's evidence is insufficient. At any one of those points, under the evidentiary standards that apply at that point, the plaintiff must show that the alleged conspiracy would have been economically rational. Following the trio of cases discussed here, the test can be applied at the pleadings stage, at the summary judgment stage, and at the directed verdict stage.

The major innovation of *Bell Atl. Corp. v. Twombly*, 550 U.S. 544 (2007), was to clarify that the economic sense test applies even at the earliest of these stages: at consideration of a motion for dismissal under Federal Rule of Civil Procedure 12(b)(6). The *Twombly* question therefore is whether the plaintiff's bare, initial allegations, taken as true, are sufficient "to state a claim on which relief can be granted." That judgment necessarily will be made before the plaintiff has had opportunity for discovery and before the defendant is even required to serve an answer admitting or denying the plaintiff's allegations.[5]

Twombly actually went a fair bit further than that, in that it modified the interpretation of two other federal procedural rules, Rules 8(a)(2) and 9(b). They provide in relevant part as follows:

> **Rule 8. General Rules of Pleading**
>
> (a) Claim for Relief. A pleading that states a claim for relief must contain:
>
> . . .
>
> (2) a short and plain statement of the claim showing that the pleader is entitled to relief . . .
>
> **Rule 9. Pleading Special Matters**
>
> . . .
>
> (b) Fraud or Mistake; Conditions of Mind. In alleging fraud or mistake, a party must state with particularity the circumstances constituting fraud or mistake. Malice, intent, knowledge, and other conditions of a person's mind may be alleged generally.
>
> . . .

---

5. Only "parties" may take discovery under the Federal Rules, and the plaintiff does not become a "party" until the complaint is filed. The defendant's answer or a motion under Rule 12(b) must be filed within 20 days of service of the complaint. Therefore there will be no time for the plaintiff to conduct discovery prior to filing of a 12(b) motion, and the defendant necessarily will file the motion before filing any responsive pleading or any of the mandatory evidentiary disclosures required by the Rules.

As acknowledged by language in both the majority and dissent in *Twombly*, these pleading rules were meant to make pleading a simple process, and to prevent pretrial practice from becoming a strategic game of lawyerly technicalities (which it had been before the innovation of modern pleading in the nineteenth century). The significance of Rule 9(b) is that it had traditionally been taken to mean that *only* fraud or mistake must be plead with "particularity." And in fact, the dominant Supreme Court guidance on the question had for many years required only enough explanation of the plaintiff's claim to "give the defendant fair notice of what the . . . claim is and the grounds upon which it rests. . . ." *Conley v. Gibson*, 355 U.S. 41, 78 (1957). *Conley* made clear the Court's intent that this required only a basic, simple statement of the plaintiff's claims, and over the years, hundreds of federal opinions quoted its rule that a 12(b)(6) motion should be denied "unless it appears beyond doubt that the plaintiff can prove no set of facts in support of his claim which would entitle him to relief." *Id.* at 45-46. *Twombly* reversed *Conley*, 550 U.S. at 562-563, and in its place adopted a new "plausibility" standard for pleading in all civil cases under Rule 8. In the case of pleading of conspiracy in a §1 case, plausibility requires the pleading of "enough factual matter (taken as true) to suggest that an agreement was made." It does not "impose a probability requirement at the pleading stage," according to the Court, and only requires "enough fact to raise a reasonable expectation that discovery will reveal evidence of illegal agreement." As a consequence, in a §1 case, "an allegation of parallel conduct and a bare assertion of conspiracy will not suffice." Accordingly, "when allegations of parallel conduct are set out in order to make a §1 claim, they must be placed in a context that raises a suggestion of a preceding agreement, not merely parallel conduct that could just as well be independent action."

The practical consequence of this ruling, at least in antitrust cases, is that the *Monsanto-Matsushita* economic sense standard now applies at the pleading stage, and it is to be applied on such particularized facts as the plaintiff is able to plead at that stage. The problem for most plaintiffs will be that at that stage, they will have had no discovery. They therefore will likely have no direct proof of conspiracy, and such circumstantial evidence as they have will likely be only what is available from public sources, like the newspapers or corporate filings with the Securities and Exchange Commission. So they are unlikely to have much clear evidence of anything other than parallel behavior. As a practical matter, this will make §1 lawsuits very difficult for consumers or others in arm's-length relationships with the defendants. The only plaintiffs not so constrained are the federal agencies, which have certain pretrial investigative powers, and those who have done business in some more direct way with the defendants or have access to insider whistleblowers.

Just as *Twombly* imposes the economic sense test at 12(b)(6), *Monsanto* and *Matsushita* apply it at the stages of summary judgment and directed verdict. Strictly speaking, the question of whether or not the defendants conspired is for the finder of facts, but recall that Federal Rule of Civil Procedure 56, which sets out the standard for summary judgment, requires the court to ask whether, drawing all reasonable inferences in favor of the non-moving party, there is any genuine issue of material fact requiring trial. Unlike the *Twombly* analysis, this test will be applied only after the plaintiff has had a chance to develop its case through some months or years of discovery—depositions, interrogatories, mandatory disclosures under the Federal Rules, and affidavits prepared by the plaintiff's own witnesses. At both stages, the plaintiff must again show that the conspiracy it alleges makes "sense" as a matter of mainstream economic theory. Likewise, even if the plaintiff survives summary judgment, it may be required to show that there is a genuine issue at the directed verdict stage on the basis of the additional evidence it has put on at trial.

When *Twombly* was decided, there was concern that it had substantially restricted plaintiffs' access to antitrust litigation,[6] and it remains controversial and the subject of many proposals for reform. But for what they may be worth, some lower court decisions since 2007 have suggested that, at least in antitrust, things may not be so dire as they first seemed. Several §1 conspiracy allegations have made it past the *Twombly* pleading stage, and there have been indications that allegations fitting the traditional "plus-factors" pleading approach for proof of antitrust conspiracy are still adequate, so long as they are stated with some particularity.[7]

§12.3.3 The Significance of Oligopoly Theory

As mentioned, the law on proof of conspiracy has been significantly influenced by "oligopoly theory." An oligopoly is a market dominated by only a few large firms. Economists have long thought that such markets might behave differently than competitive ones, and in particular that oligopolist firms will make decisions based on their *predictions* of what their competitors will do. Most importantly, oligopolists can foresee that if they cut their prices they may increase their sales in the short term, but will then just

6. *See, e.g.*, Chris Sagers, *A Tale of Two Panels: The Size of the Chancellor's Foot in* Text Messaging *and* Potash, CPI Antitrust Chronicle, Nov. 2011; Kevin M. Clermont & Stephen C. Yeazell, *Inventing Tests, Destabilizing Systems*, 95 Ia. L. Rev. 821, 823 (2010) (arguing that *Twombly*, and the follow-up decision in *Ashcroft v. Iqbal*, 556 U.S. 662 (2009), "destabilized the entire system of civil litigation," creating a "revolutionary" new "civil procedure hitherto foreign to our fundamental procedural principles"); *see also* Linda Greenhouse, *Roberts Court Is a Conservative's Dream*, N.Y. Times, July 1, 2007 (quoting Yale Law Professor Judith Resnik, who called 2007 "the year they closed the courts").

7. *See, e.g.*, *Minn-Chem, Inc. v. Agrium, Inc.*, 683 F.3d 845, 859-860 (7th Cir. 2012) (en banc); *In re Text Messaging Antitr. Litig.*, 630 F.3d 622 (7th Cir. 2010).

face their competitors' corresponding price cuts, and that if such a process continues all competitors will be reduced to zero economic profits. A better solution for all of them would be to set prices higher, and to refrain from poaching competitors' sales. That way, they each could earn some supra-competitive profits indefinitely. This produces the same result as an explicit price-fixing cartel, but with the crucial difference that it can be reached without any agreement at all. Without agreement, this behavior does not violate Sherman Act §1, and unless one of the oligopolists has enough market share to demonstrate monopoly power, there can be no violation of §2.

Several factors are thought to make this "interdependent pricing" behavior more feasible in any given market. First, the market must be concentrated. In more competitive markets it is just too risky for any one firm to raise price in the hope that all other firms will follow. Second, it helps the oligopolists if they can easily detect "cheating"—the charging of lower prices by some firms who hope to keep their price cuts secret, so as to avoid retaliation. Cheating is thought to be easier to detect where there are frequent sales to many sellers and relatively undifferentiated (i.e., relatively fungible) products. Interdependent pricing is also easier where demand is inelastic, because any price increase will be more profitable the less elastic is the demand.

The theory has significance for proof of conspiracy, but the direction it points in any given case can be hard to predict. The same market features that facilitate interdependent oligopoly pricing will also facilitate explicit cartel agreements. So depending on what other facts a plaintiff can plead, the presence of features facilitating oligopoly may either help or hurt the plaintiff's effort to show conspiracy.

On the one hand, if there are some meaningful indications of conspiracy over and above mere parallelism in prices, the pleading of oligopoly factors will tend to add further support to the conspiracy allegation. In effect, oligopoly industry features are additional "plus factors." *See, e.g.*, *In re Text Messaging Antitr. Litig.*, 630 F.3d 622, 627-629 (7th Cir. 2010) (finding that oligopoly industry structure "constitutes supporting evidence of collusion" where plaintiff also plead parallel prices and evidence of substantial communications among defendants).

But on the other hand, where the plaintiff's only evidence other than oligopoly factors is *mere* parallelism in price or other behavior, then oligopoly factors may actually *hurt* the plaintiffs' case on conspiracy. Large, parallel movements in price or other behavior might be suspicious in competitive markets. In a price-competitive market made up of many small sellers, it would be surprising to see the sellers making sudden, parallel movements in price or other terms, in the absence of some actual conspiracy or coordination among them. But oligopoly firms might do such things through purely independent action. For example, in the well-known *In re Petroleum Prods. Antitrust Litig.*, 906 F.2d 432 (9th Cir. 1990), the Ninth Circuit

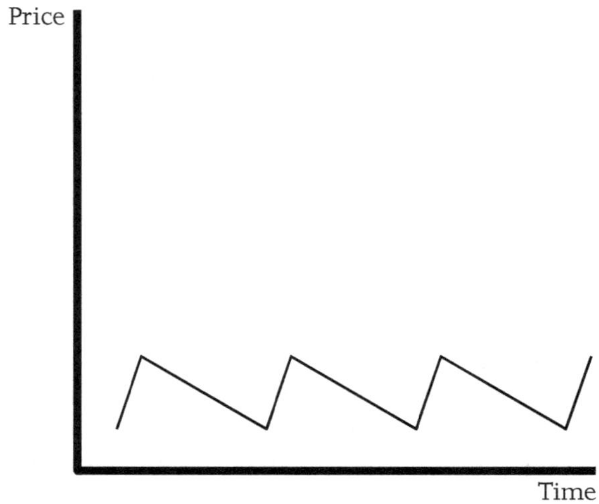

Figure 12.1. The "Sawtooth" Pricing Pattern of *In re Petroleum Products*

considered evidence that prices charged by several oil companies for refined gasoline followed a "sawtooth" pattern. All of their prices would sharply increase at the same time, then gradually decline over a period of several weeks, and then sharply increase again. Graphically, the pattern looked like Figure 12.1.

The plaintiffs argued that in the absence of an agreement, competitive forces would prevent such behavior. It would be irrational for any one firm independently to make repeated, sharp price increases, and so the plaintiffs argued that there must have been some underlying agreement. The court disagreed, because it found the market sufficiently concentrated and sufficiently susceptible to interdependence that this pattern might have arisen through purely independent action. *Id.* at 444-445. It is worth noting, however, the court's explicit observation that had the market been highly competitive, this pricing behavior, even standing alone, might prove conspiracy.

Oligopoly theory is explored in more detail in the appendix.

§12.3.4 The Continuing Framework for Proof of Conspiracy with Circumstantial Evidence: The "Plus-Factors" Test as It Is Now Applied

Even before the *Monsanto-Matsushita-Twombly* trilogy, the lower courts had developed a standard for judging circumstantial evidence of conspiracy, and it incorporated to some degree the same essential reasoning that the trio would later make more rigorous. As mentioned several times already, this standard has come to be known as the "plus-factors" approach. As early as 1954 it was clear that evidence of mere parallel conduct, without more, could not prove conspiracy. *Theatre Enter. v. Paramount Film Distrib. Corp.*, 346 U.S. 537, 541 (1954). Therefore, the courts' test provided that where the plaintiff begins with evidence of parallel behavior, it must also adduce evidence of some additional factors that make that parallel behavior appear to be more consistent with conspiracy than with unilateral action.

Even before *Monsanto* the plus-factors test had a flavor of economic theory, as the courts often implied that the strongest plus factors would be those suggesting that the parallel behavior would have been irrational had there been no conspiracy. In the classic case on point, *American Tobacco*, three oligopolist cigarette manufacturers engaged in a long period of almost precisely coordinated price changes. Most important to the Court was that they continually raised their prices throughout the Great Depression, a time when other economic factors should have caused a rational firm acting alone to cut its prices to compete for the dwindling demand. *See Am. Tobacco Co. v. United States*, 328 U.S. 781, 805 (1946).

Not all plus factors are necessarily driven by this point of economic theory, however, and effectively any evidence can be relevant so long as it tends to make the existence of conspiracy more likely. Evidence of large amounts of communication or information sharing among horizontal competitors is ordinarily thought indicative of conspiracy, especially when the interactions are closely followed by some parallel conduct. Other evidence of conduct that could facilitate collusion is relevant, like public price announcements that are followed by parallel price changes, or the creation of industry manuals or formulas for the calculation of input or transportation costs, or anything else that could permit competitors to predict one another's prices. Likewise, evidence consistent with a cartel's enforcement of its prices against its own members can be useful. For example, if there is some evidence of predatory price responses or refusals to deal, followed by return of the victim's prices to the overall parallel pricing, that would tend to suggest that the defendants are enforcing a price-fixing agreement.

Example

Air travel between New York and Washington, D.C., ought to be fairly competitive, by all appearances. Numerous flights are offered every day by the major carriers, and they face competition from no-frills discount carriers and several smaller-scale shuttle services. Nevertheless, a class of plaintiffs have adduced evidence, including a statistical analysis by an economist, showing that airfares in that market were remarkably uniform during the past few years. They further point out several erratic price increases during that period, and the fact that all of the carriers made similar jumps at almost the same time. The plaintiffs argue that this behavior would not be observed absent some price-fixing arrangement and have sued to challenge it under Sherman Act §1.

The defendants move to dismiss the complaint, arguing that the plaintiffs have failed to plead enough evidence of conspiracy. Will the court grant the defendants' motion?

Explanation

It is a close question. The plaintiffs have rested mainly on proof of parallel pricing, which in and of itself is insufficient to prove conspiracy. Even evidence of erratic shifts in prices, like that stressed by the plaintiffs here, is not necessarily sufficient if there is also evidence that makes interdependent oligopoly behavior plausible. However, here the plaintiffs have alleged that the market is a competitive one and therefore that any repeated pattern of sharp price increases would be irrational in the absence of agreement. This complaint should probably survive an initial motion to dismiss and should also go to trial unless the defendants can produce enough evidence of either interdependent price or some other explanation for the pricing behavior that precludes a genuine fact issue as to the existence of a conspiracy.

Example

The plaintiff, a purchaser of professional photocopying equipment, has alleged that two major photocopier manufacturers—ABC, Inc., and XYZ, Inc.—conspired to fix their prices. The proof is indisputable of consistency in their prices over a long period (though their prices are also largely parallel with prices of their several minor competitors). The plaintiff also adduced evidence that marketing and sales personnel from both firms communicated frequently, as well as evidence of a series of "retreats" organized by the two firms, at which executives of both firms met, purportedly for team-building and management training purposes. During discovery, the plaintiff also identified damaging e-mails, and executives of both companies made certain rather incautious statements in deposition. In one example, a sales executive's exasperated response to questions about the purpose of certain phone call was "Well, how else would I know what price was going to do?" Finally, the plaintiffs developed evidence that during the period of the alleged conspiracy there was a span of several weeks during which the two firms' prices fluctuated fairly drastically, and were not parallel. During that period there was also evidence of meetings between the two firms' CEOs. Shortly thereafter, this rare event of serious discrepancy in their pricing ended, and their prices returned to near-unison.

The defendants seek summary judgment, arguing that the plaintiff has not shown conspiracy. Will the court grant the defendant's motion?

Explanation

Probably not, as the plaintiff has put on enough proof of conspiracy. First, there is direct proof in this case. The plus-factors test and all of the reasoning in the *Monsanto-Matsushita-Twombly* trilogy only apply to *circumstantial* evidence. Here, the plaintiff has direct proof in the form of the executives' admissions in deposition. Assuming those admissions are admissible and they are not countered by overwhelming defense evidence, they could support a triable issue as to conspiracy.

But even without that proof, the plaintiff has put on a substantial circumstantial case of conspiracy. To begin with, there is evidence of parallel pricing. The plus factors that the plaintiff adduces in addition to parallelism include substantial interfirm communications and meetings among the firms' executives, and the meeting between CEOs during a period of apparent price competition. The latter evidence might well suggest that one firm engaged in retaliatory attack for a deviation from agreed upon prices, or that the two firms reached a peace accord to settle one brief bout of price competition.

§12.4 SPECIAL PROBLEMS IN PROOF OF VERTICAL CONSPIRACY

In principle, proof of vertical conspiracy is the same as proof of horizontal conspiracy. It is subject to the same basic standard as set out in *American Tobacco*, and it is subject to the economic sense test of *Monsanto*, *Matsushita*, and *Twombly* (indeed, *Monsanto* was a vertical restraints case). Thus, it can be proven by either direct or circumstantial evidence, but if the evidence is only circumstantial, the plaintiff must adduce some plus factors that exclude the possibility of independent action. But at least since the seminal vertical restraints decision in *Continental T.V., Inc. v. GTE Sylvania, Inc.*, 433 U.S. 36 (1977) (discussed in Chapter 10), the courts have been more cautious about inferring vertical conspiracy. This has at least two explanations. First, recall the emphasis in *Continental T.V.* on keeping antitrust primarily focused on *inter*brand competition, while giving restraints on *intra*brand competition the opportunity to drive innovation in distribution and marketing. Second, communications and cooperation among horizontal conspirators are rather inherently suspect. In most cases, in the absence of some joint-venture style arrangement, there is no especially procompetitive reason such things should occur. But in the vertical context, some level of ongoing communications are an essential part of the process of buying and selling the good.

The major consequence of this distinction is that courts are much more hesitant to take evidence of significant communication or other interactions as evidence of an anticompetitive agreement. In *Monsanto*, for example, the plaintiff was a price-cutting distributor that had been terminated by its supplier. The plaintiff alleged the termination was a consequence of a resale price-fixing agreement with the supplier's other dealers and that the plaintiff was terminated because the other dealers complained about its price cutting. The Court was skeptical of mere evidence of dealer complaints, however, because again, communications in vertical relationships are an ordinary part of business. Given the nature of the relationship, the Court suggested that mere dealer complaints alone, even complaints about another dealer's price cutting, cannot in themselves prove a vertical price-fixing conspiracy.

PART VI

Confronting Mr. Big: The Law of Monopoly

CHAPTER 13

The Offense of Monopolization

> Unless you become more watchful in your states and check the spirit of monopoly and thirst for exclusive privileges you will in the end find that . . . the control over your dearest interests has passed into the hands of these corporations.
>
> —*Andrew Jackson*[1]

> Great cases, like hard cases, make bad law.
>
> —*Oliver W. Holmes, Jr.*[2]

> Go to jail. Go directly to jail. Do not pass go. Do not collect $200.
>
> —*Charles Brace Darrow*[3]

And so we turn to the second of the three major theories of liability in U.S. antitrust law, unilateral anticompetitive conduct: the law of Sherman Act §2.[4] Section 2 is generally thought to set out three causes of action: monopolization (discussed in this chapter), attempted monopolization (*see* §14.1), and conspiracy to monopolize (*see* §14.2).

1. Andrew Jackson, *Columbia World of Quotations* (1996).
2. *N. Secs. v. United States*, 193 U.S. 197, 400 (1904) (Holmes, J., dissenting) (one of the first major cases to find a violation of Sherman Act §2).
3. Charles Brace Darrow (1889-1967), U.S. inventor (instruction in the game "Monopoly" (1933)).
4. As explained in the introduction in Chapter 1, the other two are the cause of action for multilateral conduct (also known as "contract, combination . . . , or conspiracy") under Sherman Act §1, covered in Chapters 5-12, and the cause of action to challenge mergers and acquisitions under Clayton Act §7, covered in Chapter 17.

It has been clear almost since the beginning of U.S. antitrust that the mere possession of a large market share, and even a very large amount of market power, cannot in itself violate §2. Even the exercise of market power to raise prices, in and of itself, is not illegal. There is evidence in the legislative history of the Sherman Act that this was intended, and it follows from the common law definition of "monopoly" predating 1890. Mere bigness, in other words, is not illegal. Rather, the monopolization defendant must have *done* something to acquire or maintain its monopoly position, and that something must have been more than mere competition on the merits. Even to acquire genuine market power is permissible if, in order to do it, the defendant did no more than ensure that it was the most efficient producer of the good or service in question.

One modern statement of this fundamental policy came in *United States v. Grinnell Corp.*, 384 U.S. 563 (1966), where the Court declared that a monopolization plaintiff must prove: "(1) the possession of monopoly power in the relevant market and (2) the willful acquisition or maintenance of that power as distinguished from growth or development as a consequence of a superior product, business acumen, or historic accident." *Id.* at 570-571. Proof of element one is almost always made using the market share proxy test discussed in Chapter 4, though as we shall see, a §2 plaintiff must prove a very high market share under that test in order to show a §2 violation. As for the second element, in subsequent case law it has come commonly to be known as the "exclusionary conduct" element, since the plaintiff is normally called on to prove that the defendant *excluded* competitors from what would otherwise have been normal competition or competitive entry into the monopolist's market. As we shall see, there has always persisted a great deal of controversy and uncertainty about what can constitute "exclusionary" conduct, and generally speaking, it is difficult for plaintiffs to prove. The large majority of our discussion of §2 will consist of working out the meaning of the phrase in contemporary law.

Example

The making of "airframes"—that is, the structural part of an aircraft, excluding the propulsion and all the internal gadgets and appointments—is a concentrated industry, and in the entire United States only four manufacturers are currently in the business. There is also little doubt that the incumbent firms have some pricing discretion, because entry barriers are high. Because of the huge initial start-up costs, an entrant would have to be able to enter at a large scale in order to produce efficiently. Demand is inelastic, however (there are only so many airplanes and helicopters the world really needs), so it would be hard for an entrant to price low enough on entry to steal away or generate enough business. Anyway, one of the incumbent firms, Behemocon, Inc., is by far the largest, with a market share of about

65 percent. The industry experiences only infrequent bouts of price competition, mainly because with its massive scale and resources Behemocon has been able to respond to price cuts with fearsome and immediate pricing reprisals. In fact, following the last major round of serious price competition, which was more than 20 years ago, the only firm to have attempted entry in the industry in living memory was forced into insolvency. And so, at present, if you want to buy an airframe you'll pretty much pay the same for it from any of the incumbents.

Does any conduct in this scenario violate Sherman Act §2?

Explanation

Probably not. Admittedly, Behemocon may hold "monopoly power" under the first element of the test quoted from *Grinnell*, above. But recall that §2 also calls for proof of some exclusionary *conduct*, and here the only apparent conduct has been sloth during less competitive periods, and price reductions to meet competition when it arises. True, Behemocon apparently does not customarily underprice its rivals, and does so only to keep them from cutting their prices, and indeed at least once it did so severely enough to cause a firm's exit. That is less than ideal, but it is not ordinarily illegal because cutting prices to meet the lower prices of one's competitors is the usual nature of competition. And the exit of firms that cannot meet their competitors' prices is an ordinary consequence of competition, and accordingly it is not the basis for antitrust liability. As long as Behemocon's conduct could not be shown to be "predatory" pricing (*see* §13.3.3), all it has done through its price responses is to "compete on the merits" (*see* §3.2).

Note, incidentally, that this conduct also does not violate Sherman Act §1 on the facts stated. Section 1 requires proof of "contract, combination, . . . or conspiracy," which seems to be absent here. That fact highlights an interesting problem in antitrust law: There is a gap in the Sherman Act. Interdependent oligopoly pricing is unambiguously anticompetitive and socially harmful, but it is also not illegal. In and of itself, it constitutes neither the conspiracy necessary for §1 nor "exclusionary" conduct necessary for §2. (The "gap" and the problem of oligopoly are explored in §3., §12.3.3, and the appendix.)

§13.1 EARLY CASE LAW AND ITS CURRENT SIGNIFICANCE: *ALCOA, UNITED SHOE*, AND THE MANY FORMS THE LAW COULD HAVE TAKEN

Section 2 monopolization cases were brought almost as soon as the Sherman Act was adopted, but the early Supreme Court case law lacked any clear theoretical guidance. The Court failed to specify with any clarity exactly what were the elements in the cause of action, and seemed ambivalent over the importance of matters like intent and whether there was any requisite showing of monopoly power. Thus a series of the Court's early opinions, even though we often hear about them as foundational decisions in the law of monopoly, cannot really tell us that much about the modern law of §2. In essence most of what the Court had to say up until and including *United States v. United States Steel*, 251 U.S. 417 (1920), is now of mainly historical interest.[5] Following *United States Steel* the Court then went nearly silent on the matter for many years.

Among the first really important cases, in terms of its long-term impact on the law, did not come until decades later: *United States v. Aluminum Co. of Am.*, 148 F.2d 416 (2d Cir. 1945) (*Alcoa*). Though *Alcoa* is a Court of Appeals decision, for a special procedural reason it has effectively the status of a Supreme Court decision.[6] Also, the panel that decided it happened to be something of a dream team: Learned Hand, his first cousin Augustus Hand, and Thomas Swan.

Alcoa was (and remains) a mammoth corporation responsible for a large portion of the production of aluminum in the world. Alcoa was the holder of the very first patents for commercially viable aluminum production, which were granted in the 1880s and 1890s, and expired around 1909. In this civil monopolization claim the government alleged that after the patents expired Alcoa took a series of actions to ensure that it remained the sole or dominant producer in the United States.

Among the most important holdings in the *Alcoa* opinion was the court's insistence on evidence of exclusionary conduct. Even though Alcoa arguably had a roughly 90 percent market share during much of the relevant period, and even though the Justice Department urged that merely holding such a large share should be sufficient for §2 violation, the court reaffirmed that mere size alone was not enough. As Learned Hand famously put it:

> It does not follow because "Alcoa" had such a monopoly, that it "monopolized" the ingot market: it may not have achieved monopoly; monopoly may have been thrust upon it. . . . [Likewise,][a] single producer may be the survivor out of a group of active competitors, merely by virtue of his superior skill, foresight and industry. . . . The successful competitor, having been urged to compete, must not be turned upon when he wins.

---

5. *See, e.g.*, *United States v. Am. Tobacco Co.*, 221 U.S. 106 (1911); *Standard Oil Co. v. United States*, 221 U.S. 1 (1911); *Northern Securities v. United States*, 193 U.S. 197 (1904). *See generally* Lawrence A. Sullivan, Warren S. Grimes & Chris Sagers, *The Law of Antitrust: An Integrated Handbook* 91-95 (3d ed. 2015).

6. Because four members of the Supreme Court were disqualified, the Supreme Court was required to apply the provisions of a statute known as the Expediting Act, now codified at 28 U.S.C. §2109, to certify the case to the three most senior judges of the relevant circuit. Under the Expediting Act, the decision of that court was "final and conclusive," thus equating it to a decision of the Supreme Court.

148 F.2d at 429. Also of lasting significance was Judge Hand's view that when a §2 monopolization plaintiff seeks to prove monopoly power through market share, the plaintiff must demonstrate a very high percentage share as an absolute minimum requisite showing of the §2 cause of action. In establishing a set of benchmarks that is still very frequently cited by the courts, Judge Hand wrote that "[Alcoa's 90% share of the relevant market] is enough to constitute a monopoly; it is doubtful whether 60 or 64% would be enough; and certainly 33% is not." 148 F.2d at 424. His rough guidelines have held up pretty well.

On the other hand, *Alcoa* also set out one of the more criticized holdings in modern antitrust law, and most observers do not much agree with it anymore. Judge Hand held that it could be evidence of the bad conduct necessary for §2 violation that the defendant merely expanded its output to meet any new demand. This was so despite the court's acknowledgement that Alcoa itself had "stimulated demand and opened new uses for the metal," because before it did so it "ma[de] sure that it could supply [the demand] it had evoked." *Id.*

Anyway, one other fairly early lower court opinion has had a lasting effect on the law of monopolization. In *United States v. United Shoe Machinery*, 110 F. Supp. 295 (D. Mass. 1953), the well-regarded district judge Charles Wyzanski considered a civil §2 claim against United Shoe Machinery, a very large manufacturer of equipment used in the making of shoes and itself the lineal descendent of the defendant corporation in a monumental early monopolization case, *United States v. United Shoe Machinery Co. of N.J.*, 247 U.S. 32 (1918). Of lasting significance was Judge Wyzanski's consideration of what sort of conduct could satisfy the conduct element of the §2 claim. He noted that cases up until that time had taken three separate approaches to exclusionary conduct. (1) Early cases had required that monopoly be acquired or maintained by conduct that would itself constitute an unreasonable restraint of in violation of §1. (2) Later, "[a] more inclusive approach was adopted," under which "an enterprise has monopolized in violation of §2 if it (a) has the power to exclude competition, and (b) has exercised it, or has the purpose to exercise it. The least that this conclusion means is that it is a violation of Sec. 2 for one having effective control of the market to use, or plan to use, any exclusionary practice, even though it is not a technical restraint of trade." 110 F. Supp. at 342. (3) Finally, there was the approach of Judge Hand in *Alcoa*, under which "one who has acquired an overwhelming share of the market 'monopolizes' whenever he does business, apparently even if there is no showing that his business involves any exclusionary practice." The only exception would be where the defendant can prove "that it owes its monopoly solely to superior skill, superior products, natural advantages, (including accessibility to raw materials or markets), economic or technological efficiency, (including scientific research), low margins of profit maintained permanently and without discrimination, or licenses conferred by, and used within, the limits of law (including patents on one's own inventions, or franchises granted directly to the enterprise by a public authority)." *Id.* As suggested, it was alternative number 2 that has prevailed with the courts.

§13.2 THE BASIC CAUSE OF ACTION AS IT EXISTS: "MONOPOLIZE" IS A VERB

We are now in a position to formalize the monopolization cause of action as it currently exists. We should add that in addition to the two elements already discussed—proof of monopoly power and exclusionary conduct—courts have now recognized the possibility of a "procompetitive justifications" defense, and some have explicitly incorporated it into their framing of the monopolization cause of action. So the basic cause of action for monopolization now requires the plaintiff to prove:

1. that the defendant "possess[ed] . . . monopoly power in the relevant market,"
2. that the defendant engaged in "willful acquisition or maintenance of that power as distinguished from growth or development as a consequence of a superior product, business acumen, or historic accident," and
3. that such countervailing benefits as are said to flow from that anti-competitive conduct are either pretextual or outweighed by their anticompetitive harms.

United States v. Grinnell Corp., 384 U.S. 563, 570-571 (1966).

As to the first element, proof of monopoly power, it is ordinarily shown through the market share proxy. The only difference between proof of "monopoly" power and the market power showing commonly required under §1 is that, in §2 cases, the amount of market share that must be shown is much higher. The Supreme Court has never stated minimum share percentages plaintiffs must show to prove monopoly power. In the absence of that guidance, as mentioned, courts now roughly follow the benchmarks set out in Judge Hand's *Alcoa* opinion. In other words, a monopolization plaintiff ordinarily must prove something in the range of about 70 percent or so of a relevant market, plus evidence that the defendant enjoys some protection from entry or other conditions that would permit the defendant to raise price and reduce output.

Proof of the second element, "exclusionary conduct," has been by far the most difficult and hotly contested of the three elements. Sections 13.3.3-13.3.8 detail the many ways that plaintiffs may try to prove exclusion, and they compose the large majority of this chapter. Finally, §13.4 discusses such case law as there is on the procompetitive justifications element.

§13.3 PROVING EXCLUSIONARY CONDUCT UNDER §2

§13.3.1 The (So Far) Unsuccessful Search for a General Theory of Exclusion

Courts and commentators have long sought some theoretically coherent explanation for why some conduct should be considered exclusionary but other conduct should not. The effort has not gone well, at least insofar as the goal is to find one, unified theory. Instead, as we shall see, the courts for now are resigned to judging exclusion according to the same category approach that we saw in the law of §1. A court first asks what *kind* of conduct is at issue, and then applies whatever doctrinal test applies to all other conduct in that category.

After laying out some background behind the exclusionary conduct element, this section considers the long effort to devise a unifying theory of exclusion and the most elaborately developed of the candidates, the so-called "profit sacrifice" test. It then summarizes the default alternative with which we are still left, the category approach (§13.3.1(c)), and briefly considers the special problem of intent in monopolization cases (§13.3.2). We then move on to the specific categories of exclusionary conduct as the courts now see them, in §§13.3.3-13.3.8.

§13.3.1(a) Background

The courts have summarized the test for exclusion in any number of ways. In one leading case the Supreme Court said that exclusion is conduct undertaken "to foreclose competition, to gain a competitive advantage, or to destroy a competitor." *United States v. Griffith*, 334 U.S. 100 (1948). But taken literally, that formula is too broad. It might outlaw plainly procompetitive conduct. Innovations that reduce cost, for example, would produce "a competitive advantage" and might very well "destroy a [less efficient] competitor," but encouraging that conduct is a core goal of antitrust.

Accordingly more modern decisions focus not only on injury to rivals, but also require that the injury is caused in some way other than by competition on the merits. It is insufficient if the only harm a plaintiff can allege results from the lower prices or better quality the defendant has achieved through efficiencies or innovation. This sense was captured in another well-known definition, from a leading treatise: "exclusionary comprehends at the most behavior that not only (1) tends to impair the opportunities of rivals, but also (2) either does not further competition on the merits or does so in an unnecessarily restrictive way." 3 Philip Areeda & Donald F. Turner, *Antitrust Law* ¶626b (1978). That sense of it has been echoed repeatedly in the modern case law.[7]

But no general statement could really do justice to the difficulty of the matter, and indeed most discussions of it begin by explaining how hard it is to come up with good monopolization standards. In part the problem has been that so many different sorts of conduct could arguably exclude competition, at least when engaged in by a seller with monopoly power. For this reason, exclusionary acts have been difficult to categorize. As the D.C. Circuit noted in *United States v. Microsoft Corp.*, 253 F.3d 34 (D.C. Cir. 2001):

> Whether any particular act of a monopolist is exclusionary, rather than merely a form of vigorous competition, can be difficult to discern: the means of illicit exclusion, like the means of legitimate competition, are myriad. The challenge for an antitrust court lies in stating a general rule for distinguishing between exclusionary acts, which reduce social welfare, and competitive acts, which increase it.

Id. at 58. Likewise, the Third Circuit has said that: "'Anticompetitive conduct' can come in too many different forms, and is too dependent upon context, for any court or commentator ever to have enumerated all the varieties." *LePage's, Inc. v. 3M*, 324 F.3d 141, 152 (3d Cir. 2003) (en banc) (quoting *Caribbean Broad. Sys., Ltd. v. Cable & Wireless PLC*, 148 F.3d 1080, 1087 (D.C. Cir. 1998)). Accordingly, the Supreme Court has said:

> In [Sherman Act] cases, plaintiffs should be given the full benefit of their proof without tightly compartmentalizing the various factual components and wiping the slate clean after scrutiny of each.

Continental Ore Co. v. Union Carbide & Carbon Corp., 370 U.S. 690, 699 (1962).

§13.3.1(b) The Ambiguous Reception of "Profit Sacrifice" and "No Economic Sense" Tests

While courts and commentators have never successfully devised any general test to explain exclusion, there has been no shortage of efforts. One of the most discussed of them has its roots in *Aspen Skiing Co. v. Aspen Highlands Skiing Corp.*, 472 U.S. 585 (1985), and it resembles some other tests the Supreme

7. *See, e.g.*, *Aspen Skiing Co. v. Aspen Highlands Skiing Corp.*, 472 U.S. 585, 605 n.35 (1985) (quoting the Areeda-Turner statement verbatim); *Taylor Publg. Co. v. Jostens, Inc.*, 216 F.3d 465, 475 (5th Cir. 2000) (same); *Catch Curve, Inc. v. Venali, Inc.*, 519 F. Supp. 2d 1028, 1036 (C.D. Cal. 2007) (same).

Court has devised in its antitrust case law. While the Court itself has never explicitly adopted the test, language in *Aspen* has led some to believe that exclusion requires some showing of *profit sacrifice*. That is, for the conduct to be illegal, it should be shown to be economically irrational unless the monopolist could stand to gain even more profit by excluding a rival.

Aspen, decided in 1985, made probably the most systematic effort to synthesize a single standard for §2 exclusion of any decision since Judge Hand's famous *Alcoa* decision of 1945. In so doing, however, the Court introduced an ambiguity. On the one hand, the Court, quoting the Areeda treatise mentioned above, wrote that

> "exclusionary" comprehends at the most behavior that not only (1) tends to impair the opportunities of rivals, but also (2) either does not further competition on the merits or does so in an unnecessarily restrictive way.

Id. at 605 n.32 (quoting 3 Phillip I. Areeda & Donald Turner, *Antitrust Law* 78 (1978)). Quoting another famous book on antitrust, the Court added that "[i]f a firm has been attempting to exclude rivals on some basis other than efficiency, it is fair to characterize its behavior as predatory." *Id.* at 605 (internal quotation marks omitted; quoting Robert Bork, *The Antitrust Paradox* 138 (1978)). Either of those definitions could be read fairly broadly. Under them, just about anything a monopolist could do to hurt a competitor could be said to be exclusionary, so long as it doesn't boil down to just making a product better or more cheaply.

But then the *Aspen* Court laid heavy emphasis on its view that the challenged conduct in that case would have been *economically irrational* in the absence of an exclusionary goal. The plaintiff and defendant were the owners of adjoining ski resorts, and the defendant held monopoly power in their market. They had engaged for some years in a cooperative arrangement under which they would each sell passes to skiers that would give them access to both resorts. At a certain point, however, the monopolist resort decided no longer to participate and refused all alternative arrangements that the plaintiff proposed, causing the plaintiff severe financial losses. In finding the refusal to deal an actionable act of anticompetitive exclusion, the *Aspen* Court elaborately explained that a rational firm would have seen the plaintiff's alternative shared-access plans as an opportunity for profit. The refusal was therefore irrational unless the defendant hoped to make even more money by killing off the plaintiff and earning monopoly returns. The resulting ambiguity is whether §2 plaintiffs must show not only conduct that harms rivals that does not constitute competition "on the merits" but also that that conduct would have been *economically irrational* in the absence of a motive to exclude. In effect, this would end the possibility of liability for "costless" exclusion—conduct that may not be competition on the merits, but is also low cost and therefore may not be irrational even if it does not lead to monopoly profits.

The Court added to this impression in *Verizon Commcns. v. Law Offices of Curtis V. Trinko*, 540 U.S. 398 (2004). In that case, which also involved a monopolist's refusal to deal with a rival, the Court relied heavily on *Aspen*. While again the Court did not clearly require a showing of profit sacrifice, it went even farther than *Aspen* on that score. It found the defendant's refusal to deal not exclusionary, in large part on the ground that it involved no loss of profits.[8] In any case, the enforcement agencies have also sometimes urged some form of no economic sense test in their own litigation and in amicus briefs.[9]

Still, while it is now surely sufficient under §2 to put on proof that conduct would be irrational in the absence of anticompetitive motive, it is not at all clear that a mandatory profit-sacrifice test has become the law of §2. Neither *Aspen* nor *Trinko* explicitly required it, and it has been rejected by at least one court of appeals, in a prominent opinion. *See LePage's, Inc. v. 3M*, 324 F.3d 141 (3d Cir. 2003) (rejecting argument that a defendant selling above its costs cannot violate §2, as a matter of law). There is also much academic debate, and leading commentators have been sharply critical of the profit-sacrifice test.[10] For the time being, at least, no such test appears to have been adopted as mandatory.

§13.3.1(c) The Current State of Play: Analyzing Exclusion Through the Category Approach

Accordingly, we have been left to address exclusion under §2 through a category approach. There is no standard classification for these various categories of liability, and it also has been suggested that separating them out as separate theories of liability may not be that helpful analytically.[11] However there is at least one major reason to believe that there is a distinction among

8. *Trinko* added a new ambiguity as well, which is limited to the special case of the refusal to deal: The Court seemed to indicate that the plaintiffs might be required to show that the monopolist refused to engage in conduct that it had already, voluntarily engaged in before. This point is discussed further in §13.3.4.

9. *See* Gregory J. Werden, *Identifying Exclusionary Conduct Under Section 2: The "No Economic Sense" Test*, 73 Antitrust L.J. 413, 413-414 (2006) (describing these efforts).

10. *See, e.g.*, Eleanor M. Fox, *Is There Life in Aspen After Trinko? The Silent Revolution of Section 2 of the Sherman Act*, 73 Antirust L.J. 153, 161-162 (2005) (*Trinko*'s evident profit-sacrifice standard was a "heroic inference to draw" from prior case law, in which Professor Fox could find no such limitation); Steven C. Salop, *Exclusionary Conduct, Effect on Consumers, and the Flawed Profit-Sacrifice Standard*, 73 Antitrust L.J. 311 (2004); cf. Spencer Weber Waller, *Microsoft and Trinko: A Tale of Two Courts*, 2006 Utah L. Rev. 741, 741-742 ("Sometimes there is an opinion[,][like *Trinko*,] that is so profoundly wrong that Mary McCarthy's famous quote about Lillian Hellman comes to mind: '[E]very word she writes is a lie, including *and* and *the*.' . . . [*Trinko*] is wrong on the law, wrong on the facts, wrong as a matter of procedure, wrong as a matter of economics, wrong as a matter of institutional competencies, and a poor contrast with the way section 2 legal standards have been [previously] articulated.").

11. *See, e.g.*, Andrew I. Gavil, *Exclusionary Distribution Strategies by Dominant Firms: Striking a Better Balance*, 72 Antitrust L.J. 3, 24 (2004).

some of the theories of exclusionary conduct. Exclusion that is alleged to have occurred through the monopolist's *pricing* decisions appears to be substantially more difficult to prove. For that reason, we discuss it first, in §13.3.3. Thinking of the categories as separate is also at least a useful way of organizing a large body of cases. With that in mind, we can think of them as falling into five rough categories:

1. Exclusionary *pricing* (*see* §13.3.3). A monopolist might try to exclude its rivals by setting its own prices so low that they cannot survive if they try to meet those prices. This strategy could come in a few variations:
   a. Garden variety predatory pricing, which is price so low that it excludes rivals,
   b. Predatory *buying*, which means raising the price of necessary inputs so high that rivals can't afford them, or
   c. Discount programs couched as loyalty or promotional efforts, but which really are just price predation.[12]
2. Exclusionary *refusal to deal* (*see* §13.3.4). There might be times when a monopolist can hurt its rivals by just refusing to do business with them. For example:
   a. It might be such an important player in a market that rivals cannot do business without some sort of collaboration with it,
   b. It might be a vertically integrated seller of an input that rivals need, or
   c. It might have control over some resource, like a communications network or a railroad station, to which competitors need access.
3. Exclusionary *distribution* (*see* §13.3.5). A monopolist might try to exclude its rivals by closing off channels in the chain of distribution, denying them access to either customers or suppliers. For example, the monopolist might:
   a. engage in exclusive contracts with suppliers or customers, or it might impose penalties or restrictions to discourage suppliers or customers from switching, and thereby foreclose opportunities to its would-be rivals, or
   b. it might tie other products to the one over which it holds monopoly power, or engage in related conduct like bundling of products or discount programs for volume or full-line purchases.

---

12. At one time it had been thought that an additional price-related theory of exclusion could be the "price squeeze," in which a vertically integrated monopolist sells the monopoly input to rivals only at a very high price, but then competes against them in the downstream market at a low price. The Supreme Court did away with this possibility in *Pac. Bell Tel. Co. v. linkLine Commcns., Inc.*, 555 U.S. 438, 442 (2009).

4. Exclusionary *misuse of institutions* (*see* §13.3.6). Often enough, if you want to have a monopoly, the government can be a great ally. A monopolist could abuse the processes of government or the processes of government-like entities to cause harm to its rivals. For example, it might:
   a. Bring frivolous lawsuits or file administrative complaints against rivals, or
   b. It might try to manipulate the setting of rules by government bodies or private standard setters in ways that hurt its rivals.
5. Exclusionary *innovation* (*see* §13.3.7). Finally, when a company largely controls a market, it may be able to disadvantage rivals by introducing technological changes or otherwise using technology strategically to make it more difficult for them to compete. For example:
   a. It might try to change the design of its product or introduce a new product altogether as a way of keeping rivals from offering good substitutes, or
   b. It might try to use intellectual property in strategic ways to stifle competition.

Finally, in §13.3.8 we consider that range of case law showing how courts try to identify exclusionary conduct that may not fit within these neat categories. There is less clear guidance in these more miscellaneous areas, and the case law is sparser, but themes do emerge.

We discuss each of these possible showings of exclusionary conduct in turn. But before turning to them, we begin in §13.3.2 by discussing one evidentiary issue that cuts across all theories of exclusion: whether evidence of intent has any particular importance. It turns out that intent evidence, while not strictly necessary in §2 cases, can play some role in them, and it always plays more or less the same role, regardless what theory of exclusion the plaintiff asserts.

§13.3.2 The Role of Intent

Evidence of the defendant's intent to monopolize or otherwise harm competition is relevant to the plaintiff's case on monopolization, but it is neither necessary nor sufficient to prove that the defendant violated §2. Technically, the offense of outright monopolization under §2 (as opposed to the offenses of attempted monopolization and conspiracy to monopolize, which are discussed in Chapter 14) contains no requirement that the plaintiff prove any particular intent on the part of the defendant. Moreover, it is clear under modern law that mere evidence of intent to monopolize, even on the part of a defendant that holds monopoly power, is not enough to satisfy the "exclusionary conduct" element.[13]

But on the other hand, intent evidence undeniably plays a role in many monopolization cases. There were some indications in the early case law that it would play a big role. Some of the Supreme Court's early cases focused on intent almost exclusively, and in *Alcoa* Judge Hand offered this famous though rather ambiguous observation:

> In order to fall within §2, the monopolist must have both the power to monopolize, and the intent to monopolize. To read the passage as demanding any 'specific' intent makes nonsense of it, for no monopolist monopolizes unconscious of what he is doing.

United States v. Aluminum Co. of Am., 148 F.2d 416, 432 (2d Cir. 1945). The implication seemed to be that *some* showing of intent was in fact a requisite element for liability.

That no longer states the law, and present law is probably best captured by saying that evidence of anticompetitive intent is not necessary but can support the plaintiff's case of exclusionary conduct. Intent evidence plays the same role in monopolization cases that it does in rule-of-reason cases under §1. Recall (as discussed in §7.1) Justice Brandeis's oft-cited observation in *Bd. of Trade of the City of Chicago v. United States*, 246 U.S. 231 (1918). Intent evidence is useful in rule-of-reason cases, "not because a good intention will save an otherwise objectionable regulation or the reverse; but because knowledge of intent may help the court to interpret facts and to predict consequences." *Id.* at 238. Likewise, in the D.C. Circuit's influential *Microsoft* opinion, the court wrote that "[e]vidence of the intent behind the conduct of a monopolist is relevant only to the extent it helps us understand the likely effect of the monopolist's conduct." *United States v. Microsoft Corp.*, 253 F.3d 34, 59 (D.C. Cir. 2001).

Not all intent evidence is persuasive. The evidence of intent that the courts now mostly care about is not the mere desire to harm rivals. As the Supreme Court has explained:

> Even an act of pure malice by one business competitor against another does not, without more, state a claim under the federal antitrust laws; those laws do not create a federal law of unfair competition or "purport to afford remedies for all torts committed by or against persons engaged in interstate commerce."

---

13. *See* 1 Am. Bar Assn., *Antitrust Law Developments* (Ninth) 241-242 (9th ed. 2022) (collecting cases).

Brooke Group Ltd. v. Brown & Williamson Tobacco Co., 509 U.S. 209, 225 (1993). Rather, the relevant evidence is proof that the defendant intended to accomplish the specific anticompetitive actions alleged, as where evidence shows that the defendant intended to foreclose rivals' access to needed technology or distribution channels.

§13.3.3 Exclusionary Pricing: Price Predation and Its Variations

Among the most commonly asserted theories of exclusion is predatory price cutting. It stands to reason that a firm trying to ward off potential challengers might try a really aggressive price response, and if the effect of it is to kill off those challengers, it might be a tool to get or preserve market power. Say that a seller has gained a monopoly position over a fairly large geographical area, but then is challenged by a would-be new entrant in, say, Mesa, Arizona. The monopolist might simply reduce its own prices in Mesa to some point it knows to be below the challenger's costs of producing the product. If the monopolist can keep it up for long enough, it may force the challenger out of business, and then return to its own comfortable monopoly status. This might be true even if that low price is below its *own* costs, because the monopolist could fund the losses associated with that predation in one of two ways. It might either charge supracompetitive prices in other markets where it is not facing challenge, or bring prices back up in Mesa after the rival is defeated. This strategy might ultimately be profitable if the monopolist can go back to charging supracompetitive prices in Mesa long enough to cover its losses and turn a profit.

However, two serious problems confront any attempt to address predatory pricing through law. Both ideas originate in an article by the economist John McGee, and were supported by a body of theory in articles and judicial opinions.[14] First, at least in those cases where price cutting is plainly anticompetitive—where it is below the seller's own costs, and therefore rational *only* if it eventually leads to some supracompetitive pricing power—it is a risky strategy. The seller necessarily loses money on each unit that it sells. If it kills the would-be rival it then must not only recover all the money that it lost but more on top of that, or else it would have been better just to price competitively. The problem then is that by charging high post-predation prices, the seller would attract new entry unless there are some large entry

14. McGee's original article was John S. McGee, *Predatory Price Cutting: The Standard Oil (N.J.) Case*, 1 J. L. & Econ. 137 (1958). Other contributions include Robert Bork, *The Antitrust Paradox* 149-155 (1978), Richard S. Posner, *Antitrust Law* 191-193 (2d ed. 2001), and Frank H. Easterbrook, *Predatory Strategies and Counterstrategies*, 48 U. Chi. L. Rev. 263 (1981).

barriers. This is sometimes known as the "long purse" strategy because the predatory seller who tried it would have to have a big purse—a lot of money on hand—to burn in funding it.[15]

Second, even if price predation does occur, there is a policy challenge in trying to prevent it. Competing for sales through lower prices is what firms are supposed to do in healthy competition. So even the possibility of treble damages litigation in response to merely lowering one's prices could discourage the activity that antitrust is supposed to encourage. Moreover, even as to claims of plainly anticompetitive price—where price is deliberately below "cost"—there remains the problem of measuring costs. Measuring the costs of production is difficult and uncertain, so there is a risk that the courts will get it wrong, overestimate a defendant's costs, and end up punishing the defendant even though it was merely competing at some price equal to or above its costs.[16] For these reasons, the courts have fashioned rules for price predation that make it very difficult to prove (as explained shortly, in §13.3.3(a)).

Still, there remain many who believe price predation is a serious problem, and an academic literature now exists that attempts to show how it might occur. Perhaps no other topic in the law of monopolization has occasioned quite such a voluminous and controversial debate, and in §13.3.3(c) we consider some evolving trends and the possibility that proof of predation might eventually become easier.

§13.3.3(a) The Present Price-Cost Standard Under *Brooke Group*

The leading price predation case is now *Brooke Group Ltd. v. Brown & Williamson Tobacco Co.*, 509 U.S. 209 (1993). Plaintiff Liggett was a cigarette manufacturer that had pioneered low-cost, generic cigarettes in the early 1980s. In the highly concentrated national market for cigarettes, defendant Brown &

15. *See* Lester G. Telser, *Cutthroat Competition and the Long Purse*, 9 J.L. & Econ. 259 (1966).

16. Strictly speaking, a firm might be behaving anticompetitively even if its prices are above its own costs. If the firm *could* charge a higher price than it is charging, given its market power, but it decides not to do so for the purpose of excluding new rivals or preventing expansion by existing challengers, the cumulative long run effect might be to preserve more pricing power for the firm than if it had just used the market power it has. Imagine that the incumbent firm lowers price every time a new firm tries to enter, but even then price is above its own cost. It might still drive out the entrants if they are less efficient. The exclusion of those less efficient entrants might be anticompetitive if it prevents them from achieving efficiency by competing for expanded output, as seems not unlikely. If they could achieve efficiency but upon every attempt are forced out by the incumbent's above-cost price cutting, the incumbent will profitably preserve its own market power. Still, to be clear, this sort of above-cost predation is *not* illegal under current law. As a matter of law, prices cannot be predatory in violation of Sherman Act §2 unless they are below the defendant's costs. *See* §13.3.3(a).

Williamson was the third-largest producer, but a distant third. In its best years its market share was about 12 percent. The plaintiff was quite a bit smaller yet, with an annual market share between 2 percent and 5 percent. There seems little doubt that the industry had at least sometimes earned supracompetitive profits through oligopoly pricing or outright collusion (recall the Supreme Court's decision in *Am. Tobacco Co. v. United States*, 328 U.S. 781 (1946), discussed in §12.3). The plaintiff's introduction of generic cigarettes was an attempt to save itself from financial ruin. It priced them substantially below going rates and gave distributors rebates for volume purchases. The program was successful, and the largest losses of business it caused to competitors was to the relatively low-priced defendant Brown & Williamson. Price competition ensued from all of the other major cigarette producers, but only Brown & Williamson actually beat the plaintiff's prices with a new line of generics that it introduced to compete with the plaintiff. Liggett found it could not persist in competition with Brown & Williamson, and it brought suit alleging that the defendant's purpose was to bring it back into compliance with a well-disciplined structure of oligopoly pricing.

The Supreme Court affirmed a judgment notwithstanding the verdict (the jury found liability and awarded Liggett $150 million after trebling) on the finding that the plaintiff could not show that the alleged scheme could produce any long-term injury to competition. As the Court wrote: "No inference of recoupment is sustainable on this record, because no evidence suggests that Brown & Williamson—whatever its intent in introducing [generic cigarettes] may have been—was likely to obtain the power to raise the prices . . . above a competitive level." 509 U.S. at 229. Ultimately, the Court set out a two-part test for a showing of actionable price predation under Sherman Act §2:

> First, a plaintiff seeking to establish competitive injury resulting from a rival's low prices must prove that the prices complained of are below an appropriate measure of its rival's costs. . . . The second prerequisite to holding a competitor liable under the antitrust laws for charging low prices is a demonstration that the competitor had . . . a dangerous probability, of recouping its investment in below-cost prices. "For the investment to be rational, the [predator] must have a reasonable expectation of recovering, in the form of later monopoly profits, more than the losses suffered." . . . Recoupment is the ultimate object of an unlawful predatory pricing scheme; it is the means by which a predator profits from predation. Without it, predatory pricing produces lower aggregate prices in the market, and consumer welfare is enhanced.

509 U.S. at 224. Subsequent courts have begun referring to the *Brooke Group* standard as the "price-cost" test for exclusionary pricing. *See, e.g., ZF Meritor, LLC v. Eaton Corp.*, 696 F.3d 254 (3d Cir. 2012).

Neither in *Brooke Group* nor elsewhere has the Supreme Court itself identified the "appropriate measure of . . . costs," and the lower court case law has produced some confusion on that point. Theoretically, the appropriate measure is usually said to be "marginal cost," since a producer will earn zero or greater economic profits by charging any price equal to or greater than its own marginal cost.[17] The problem is that marginal costs are even more difficult to measure in litigation than other measures of cost. There is some general agreement, following an influential law review article, that an adequate alternative standard would be "reasonably anticipated marginal cost" as estimated by measuring average variable cost.[18] *See* Philip Areeda & Donald F. Turner, *Predatory Pricing and Related Practices Under Section 2 of the Sherman Act*, 88 Harv. L. Rev. 697 (1975); *see generally* 1 Am. Bar Assn., *Antitrust Law Developments* (Ninth) 290-299 (9th ed. 2022).

§13.3.3(b) When Does the Price-Cost Test Apply?

Since *Brooke Group*, defendants have argued that its very demanding price-cost test, requiring proof of conduct on which the defendant actually *lost* money on individual sales and had a reasonable expectation of recoupment, should apply more broadly than just to literal prices. Other kinds of practices are common that could have the same effect as just lowering price. Manufacturers might give rebates based on sales volume or market share, for example. Say that a manufacturer holding a monopoly share in retail sales of its product initiates a program in which it will pay its distributors year-end rebates if they hit annual volume sales targets. That may be exclusionary in the sense that it will pressure the retailers to devote at least as much of their retail sales to the monopolist's product as needed to hit the sales targets, and so they may reduce their purchases from the monopolist's rivals. But the effect may be no different than if the monopolist had simply lowered its prices in the first place. After all, on these facts it sounds like the competitors could keep up their sales just by matching the effective price of the monopolist's goods after rebate. And if the monopolist can afford its discounted prices because the volume stated in its sales goals lowers its costs, well, that in itself isn't anticompetitive exclusion, it's the efficiency that antitrust is supposed to encourage. Arguably, therefore, the same policy concerns driving *Brook Group* are at issue. Making this conduct illegal or even open to too much uncertainty might chill procompetitive conduct. And so, defendants

---

17. Marginal cost is the increase in cost that results from producing each additional unit of output. *See* §2.3.

18. Average variable cost is the average of all costs that vary with output—that is, all prices over and above a firm's fixed costs. To calculate the AVC, one sums up the total variable costs and divides by the number of units produced. *See* §2.3.

have argued that *Brook Group* should apply in all cases in which challenged conduct really just amounts to price cutting. Indeed, some defendants have argued it should apply even more broadly than that and, for example, they have argued that it should apply to conduct like exclusive contracting, tying, or bundling, such that that conduct would be legal so long as the prices the defendant charges are still above its costs.

So far the lower courts have only obliged and applied the price-cost test where the challenged conduct truly aids the defendant through nothing but lowering its actual price. The test will apply where the theory of exclusion is that the defendant offers rebates, discounts, or other promotional terms that result in prices its rivals can't meet, even though they may expand the defendant's market share at its rivals' expense.[19] Application of the test does not depend on how the plaintiff characterizes its theory of exclusion. For obvious reasons, plaintiffs will try if they can to characterize their theories of exclusion as involving something other than mere price discounting, because if they can show some exclusionary mechanism other than price, they will not be subject to the very demanding price-cost test. *ZF Meritor, LLC v. Eaton Corp.*, 696 F.3d 254, 273-275 & n.11 (3d Cir. 2012).

Some courts, however, notably the Third, Ninth, and Eleventh Circuits, have refused to apply the price-cost test in cases in which the challenged conduct seemed price-like, but in which "price itself was not the clearly predominant mechanism of exclusion. . . ." *ZF Meritor*, 696 F.3d at 277. In both *ZF Meritor* and *LePage's, Inc. v. 3M*, 324 F.3d 141 (3d Cir. 2003) (en banc), the Third Circuit held that the price-cost test did not apply to "bundled discount" programs—programs in which the defendant sells some collection of goods for less than it would cost to buy each of the items individually. The practical effect may seem very similar to a simple price discount—if I give you the option of buying products A and B together for less than the price of buying them separately, maybe all I've really done is reduced the price. And so, the defendants in both cases said that a price-cost rule should apply. Recognizing that such programs are common and often harmless (e.g., season tickets or all-in-one home theater systems), the court nevertheless held that when employed by a firm with a monopoly in one of the products, they might exclude rivals that seek to sell one of the non-monopoly products. In both cases the court therefore rejected defense arguments that the discount programs could not be illegal if the defendants' prices were above their

19. *See, e.g., NicSand, Inc. v. 3M Co.*, 507 F.3d 442, 451-452 (6th Cir. 2007) (applying price-cost test to a challenge to up-front payments offered by a supplier to several large retailers on the basis that such payments were "nothing more than 'price reductions offered to the buyers for the exclusive right to supply a set of stores under multi-year contracts'"); *Concord Boat Corp. v. Brunswick Corp.*, 207 F.3d 1039, 1060-1063 (8th Cir. 2000) (applying price-cost test to volume discounts and market-share discounts offered by a manufacturer); *Barry Wright Corp. v. ITT Grinnell Corp.*, 724 F.2d 227, 232 (1st Cir. 1983) (applying the price-cost test to uphold discounts linked to a requirements contract).

costs. Instead, the courts applied what were in effect standards for exclusive contracts, asking how much distribution had been foreclosed to the monopolists' rivals, and whether that foreclosure was impermissibly exclusionary. *See also McWane, Inc. v. FTC*, 783 F.3d 814, 833-835 (11th Cir. 2015) (applying similar analysis to rebates for exclusive purchases of monopolist's product).

Similarly, in *Cascade Health Solutions v. PeaceHealth*, 515 F.3d 883 (9th Cir. 2008), the Ninth Circuit required something less than the strict price-cost test in a similar bundled discount situation. While the court held that there really must be some consideration of the defendant's costs, it refused to require that a defendant actually lose money on the bundle. Rather, it adopted a test under which a bundle could be actionably exclusionary even where the overall price charged for the bundle is above the monopolist's costs for producing all the products in the bundle.[20]

§13.3.3(c) Evolving Trends in Predation Law

There may be some reason to believe that courts may be slowly moving toward somewhat more pro-enforcement predation standards, even with respect to simple predatory pricing. This has mainly to do with the endless theoretical ferment over the topic among legal academics and economists. McGee's initial paper and the very influential Areeda and Turner paper of 1975 both spurred whole genres of economic and legal literature attempting to explain how, despite the early theoretical doubts, predation might be rational and effective. That literature made large strides during the past few decades, and there is now a fairly broad consensus among academics that the early theoretical thinking was too skeptical of the practice.

To simplify a large and complicated literature, it has basically identified a series of possible predation strategies that would not pose such substantial

20. The test the court adopted, which has come to be known as the "discount attribution" test, was recommended by the Antitrust Modernization Commission in 2007 and by several commentators. It is a little complex, but its rationale is just that even an above-cost price for a bundle of products can be exclusionary, because it might exclude a single-product seller of one of the goods in the bundle. It can do that even though that seller can produce the good more efficiently than the monopolist. Here is the reasoning: It is possible that I could be a monopolist of product A, but also sell product B, even though I am not a very efficient producer of B. Another seller might produce only product B, but be much more efficient at doing it than I am. My profits on A might be sufficiently large that I could afford to sell a bundle of products A and B at a bundled discount low enough that the effective price of B is lower even than my own costs of producing B. The discount attribution test attempts to deal with this problem in the following way. It takes the entire amount of discounts offered for all products in the bundle, adds them up, and subtracts the total discount from the price charged under the bundle for the non-monopoly product sought to be supplied by a competitor. If subtracting the total discount from that one product would cause it to be sold at less than the monopolist's costs of producing that product, then the bundle is exclusionary. The idea, ultimately, is that we do want antitrust to protect those would-be competitors that can produce the product at least as cheaply as the monopolist can.

risks to the predator. Much of this literature has focused on the possibility that a predator could develop a *reputation* for aggressive price retaliation. If so, it might be able to convince potential entrants (or what may be more important, their capital financiers) that the predator could engage in quick bouts of predatory, costly retaliation but then enjoy sufficient recoupment when new entrants or small challengers succumb. So long as potential challengers believe the predator could do that profitably, they might be too afraid to challenge its ordinary, supracompetitive prices. In effect, the reputation for predation creates the entry barrier (and therefore recoupment) of which *Brooke Group* was so skeptical.

In any case, this new thinking has not borne case law fruit so far, but there have been occasional inklings that it may do so one day. Notably, the Tenth Circuit once wrote:

> Recent scholarship has challenged the notion that predatory pricing schemes are implausible and irrational. . . . [E]conomists have theorized that price predation is not only plausible, but profitable, especially in a multi-market context where predation can occur in one market and recoupment can occur rapidly in other markets. . . . Although this court approaches the matter with caution, we do not do so with the incredulity that once prevailed.

United States v. AMR Corp., 335 F.3d 1109, 1114-1115 (10th Cir. 2003). Still, that court went on merely to apply the *Brooke Group* standard in a more or less traditional fashion, examining the government's cost evidence with an exceptionally critical eye and ultimately finding no predation or any other wrongdoing.

Finally, it is worth noting that the predation literature has not only offered criticisms. It has also offered alternative doctrinal approaches, some of which pose interesting possibilities for addressing deficiencies in the *Brooke Group* approach. Several economists have proposed variations on a "dynamic" approach to predation, which would dispense with price-cost comparisons altogether. They would instead use rules keyed to the alleged monopolist's *conduct*, as a sort of proxy for predation. Generally speaking, they would seek to force the monopolist itself to pick prices that are not predatory, without any subsequent inquiry into whether the prices were predatory or not.[21] Approaches like these might have the effect of providing

---

21. *See* William J. Baumol, *Quasi-Permanence of Price Reductions: A Policy for Prevention of Predatory Pricing*, 89 Yale L.J. 1 (1979) (making price reductions, when made in response to new entry, "quasi-permanent"); Aaron S. Edlin, *Stopping Above-Cost Predatory Pricing*, 111 Yale L.J. 941 (2002); Oliver E. Williamson, *Predatory Pricing: A Strategic and Welfare Analysis*, 87 Yale L.J. 284 (1977) (prohibiting output increases by monopolist after entry, for 12 to 18 months; consequence would be to force monopolist to choose appropriate output *prior* to entry).

some breathing room for new entry,[22] and also offer the possibly very desirable feature of remaining agnostic about price (like most of the rest of antitrust but unlike *Brooke Group*; *cf.* §3.2.3).

§13.3.4 Exclusionary Refusals to Cooperate

Section 2 plaintiffs sometimes argue that a monopolist's rivals cannot survive unless it somehow does business with them. For example, say the monopolist owns or has control over some technological infrastructure that its competitors need, like a seaport or a railway switching facility, or like a network of electrical lines that reach the homes and businesses of electricity consumers. If that facility is very expensive to duplicate, then the monopolist's competitors may not be able to compete unless they can negotiate with the monopolist to provide them access to it. In the case of the seaport, perhaps the monopolist is an importer of some commodity that has also gotten control of the port or facilities needed to unload the commodity; in the case of electrical wires, perhaps the monopolist both owns the wires and is a generator of electricity transmitted across them. Either way, the monopolist might have competitors—other importers of the same commodity, or other generators of electricity—who don't own similar facilities and need access to them to compete. Or, say the monopolist is a supplier of an important input in the making of computers, and it holds 80 percent of the relevant market for that good. Perhaps it has had some long term, mutually satisfactory relationship with a given buyer, but then discovers that the buyer has filled some of its needs for the input from the monopolist's competitors. If the monopolist retaliates by cutting that customer off, and perhaps adds a bit of zing by making it known to its other customers that it will do the same to them if they are disloyal, that might constitute an anticompetitive exclusionary act aimed at the competing suppliers.

The courts have addressed refusal-to-deal scenarios in two different ways. First, the Supreme Court and lower courts have recognized in a number of cases that, sometimes, a monopolist's refusal to do business with someone is anticompetitive. Second, while the Supreme Court has never explicitly recognized it, the lower courts have sometimes applied the so-called "essential facilities" doctrine to deal with cases in which a monopolist controls some important facility.

---

22. The concern is that if a monopolist could quickly respond to small entrants, it could kill them off before they have a chance to reach an efficient level of production (on the reasonable assumption that entrants will produce more efficiently as they increase output). If so, a large seller in a concentrated industry might be able to stave off the only serious ongoing threat to sustained supracompetitive pricing, and might be able to do so without ever pricing below cost.

§13.3.4(a) Refusals to Deal in General

Monopolists have been held to violate §2 when they refuse to deal with customers or suppliers who frequent their rivals,[23] and when they refuse to do business with the rivals themselves in ways that injure the rivals' ability to compete.[24]

In some cases this theory of exclusion has become very difficult to prove. However, as we shall see, understanding it requires a distinction that is sometimes ignored or misunderstood: the harsh rule, making the claims difficult to prove, applies only to monopolists' refusals to deal with their *rivals*. Most courts now recognize that those cases are economically quite different than refusals to deal with customers or suppliers.

In any case, modern courts have found refusal-to-deal claims in tension with a rule first recognized in *United States v. Colgate*, 250 U.S. 300 (1919) (discussed in more detail in Chapter 10). There the Court considered a claim that a manufacturer had agreed with its distributors to fix the prices at which they would resell its products to consumers, conduct that would have been illegal if proven.[25] The Court, stressing what it saw as the inherent freedom of businesses to choose how to manage their affairs, found there to be no violation at all. The Court wrote:

> In the absence of any purpose to create or maintain a monopoly, the [Sherman] act does not restrict the long-recognized right of trader or manufacturer engaged in an entirely private business, freely to exercise his own independent discretion as to parties with whom he will deal.

Id. at 307. *Colgate* was actually a §1 case, and its basic holding was that a manufacturer's mere refusal to deal was not a "contract, combination . . . or conspiracy." It was merely a unilateral refusal to sell to distributors it did not favor (because they would not sell at the desired resale price). *Colgate's* §2 relevance is that the courts have drawn from it a general principal that private persons have a right to choose with whom they will deal. The important decision in *Verizon Commcns. v. Law Offices of Curtis V. Trinko*, 540 U.S.

---

23. *See, e.g., Lorain Journal Co. v. United States*, 342 U.S. 143 (1951) (monopolist newspaper refused to sell advertising space to businesses that also purchased advertising on local radio station).
24. *See, e.g., Aspen Skiing Co. v. Aspen Highlands Skiing Corp.*, 472 U.S. 585 (1985) (monopolist that had engaged in a collaborative joint sales program with a smaller competitor refused to engage in it any longer, the only logical goal of which being to drive the competitor out and take full monopoly); *Eastman Kodak Co. v. Southern Photo Materials Co.*, 273 U.S. 359 (1927) (monopolist supplier of photographic supplies that wanted to integrate vertically into retail sales, and refused to sell its products any longer to a retailer that refused to sell its business to the monopolist).
25. The practice had only recently been held to be per se illegal in *Dr. Miles Med. Co. v. John D. Park & Sons Co.*, 220 U.S. 373 (1911). The *Dr. Miles* rule itself was overturned in 2007, and vertical price fixing is now judged only under the rule of reason. *See* Chapter 10.

398 (2004) described §2 liability for refusal to deal as a very narrow exception to the general freedom under *Colgate* to choose one's business associates.[26] However, as commentators[27] and even lower courts have noted,[28] the *Trinko* opinion rather conspicuously edited out a part of the *Colgate* formulation—that it is only "*[i]n the absence of any purpose to create or maintain a monopoly* [that] the [Sherman] act does not restrict" this freedom. *Colgate*, 250 U.S. at 307 (emphasis added). The Supreme Court itself had on prior occasions pointed to this same qualifying language as creating a substantial exception to the general rule of *Colgate*. *See Lorain Journal v. United States*, 342 U.S. 143, 155 (1951). Perhaps *Trinko* meant to signal a deliberate intent to make *Colgate* even more strict than the *Colgate* Court had intended, though it did not say so explicitly.

In any case, confusion also followed from *Trinko*'s reliance on *Colgate* because *Trinko* involved a refusal to deal with a rival but *Colgate* did not. (*Colgate* involved a manufacturer's refusal to sell to distributors who would not abide by specified minimum resale prices.) By citing *Colgate* without commenting on the distinction, some take *Trinko* to mean that its very strict treatment of refusals to deal applies regardless whether the injured party is the monopolist's rival.

As the lower courts have begun to apply it, they do in fact draw that distinction, and the law is quite different where the victim of the refusal is not the monopolist's competitor.

Refusal to Deal With Rivals. Where the target of the refusal to deal is a rival, *Trinko* implied a rule something like the *Brooke Group* price-cost test for predatory pricing, discussed in §13.3.3. *Trinko* called for proof that logically excludes purposes other than an anticompetitive one. *Trinko* made a significant point of the facts of *Aspen Skiing Co. v. Aspen Highlands Skiing Corp.*, 472 U.S. 585 (1985), a case *Trinko* described as "at or near the outer boundary of §2 liability." 540 U.S. at 409. The Court's concerns mainly had to do with economic incentives, again echoing the policy concerns stated in *Brooke Group*. Namely, if firms are required to share valuable resources with their own competitors, it will decrease the value to them of those resources and may discourage them from making desirable investments. *Id.* at 407-408. The

---

26. *See Trinko*, 540 U.S. at 408-409 (Court is "very cautious in recognizing . . . exceptions" to the *Colgate* rule; the "limited exception" to the right recognized in the Court's leading case on point was "at or near the outer bound of §2 liability."); *Aspen Skiing Co. v. Aspen Highlands Skiing Corp.*, 472 U.S. 585, 601 (1985) (placing a "high value . . . on the right to refuse to deal with other firms").

27. *See, e.g.*, Andrew I. Gavil, *Exclusionary Distribution Strategies by Dominant Firms: Striking a Better Balance*, 72 Antitrust L.J. 3, 46 (2004).

28. *Viamedia, Inc. v. Comcast Corp.*, 951 F.3d 429, 454 (7th Cir. 2020); *Steward Health Care System, LLC v. Blue Cross & Blue Shield of Rhode Island*, 311 F. Supp. 3d 468, 481 n.15 (D.R.I. 2018).

Trinko ruling was so strict that for many years it basically ended refusal-to-deal as a theory of liability for competitor plaintiffs.[29]

Even as to refusals to deal with rivals, some uncertainty remains about what a plaintiff must show, and it follows from some discussion in *Aspen Skiing*. As discussed above (*see* §13.3.1(b)), while the Supreme Court has apparently never required a profit-sacrifice showing as mandatory in §2 cases, *Aspen* seems possibly to have indicated that a §2 plaintiff must show that the challenged conduct would be economically irrational in the absence of anticompetitive purpose. *Trinko* if anything amplified that impression. Moreover, *Trinko* added an additional ambiguity unique to the case of refusals to deal. The Court distinguished *Aspen* not only on the ground that the refusal to deal in that case was irrational (in the absence of anticompetitive motive) but also because the defendant there had for some time voluntarily engaged in just the conduct the plaintiff wanted to continue. That corroborates the idea that the desired dealing would be profitable to the monopolist, and that refusal to do it would be irrational in the absence of anticompetitive motive.

In the abstract, all agree that a refusal to deal with a rival is actionable if it ends an existing, voluntary arrangement and it would be irrational in the absence of an anticompetitive motive. What is less clear is whether that showing is now mandatory. The *Trinko* Court distinguished *Aspen* in part on the ground that, in *Trinko*, the defendant had never before engaged in the conduct that the plaintiff desired. The significance of that distinction was that in *Aspen* the prior course of dealing gave us confidence that the refusal to deal was anticompetitive in purpose. The argument was that a rational firm would continue an existing, profitable course of business, and wouldn't stop it unless it would be even more profitable to exclude the competing business. *Trinko* did not explicitly require such a showing, but some lower courts have taken it now to be a requirement, notably one written by then-Judge Gorsuch before his elevation to the Supreme Court.[30] In fact, some courts have implied that not only must plaintiff show that the refusal to deal was irrational, because dealing would have been profitable, but that the refusal must discontinue an existing course of conduct.

More recently some lower courts have taken a narrower view of *Trinko*. Significantly, *Duke Energy Carolinas, LLC v. NTE Carolinas, LLC*, 111 F.4th 337 (4th Cir. 2024) suggested that *Trinko* may not apply or may be more limited outside of regulated markets. (*Trinko* concerned telephone markets, which were regulated by the Federal Communications Commission and subject to competition protections enforced by that agency.) *Viamedia, Inc. v. Comcast Corp.*,

---

29. Until very recently no such plaintiff since *Trinko* had won more than the most limited success. Erik Hovenkamp, *The Antitrust Duty to Deal in the Age of Big Tech*, 131 Yale L.J. 1483, 1490 n.26 (2022).

30. *See, e.g.*, *Novell, Inc. v. Microsoft Corp.*, 731 F.3d 1064, 1075 (10th Cir. 2013) (Gorsuch, J.). *See also Covad Commcns. Co. v. Bell Ad. Corp.*, 398 F.3d 666, 675 (D.C. Cit. 2005).

951 F.3d 429, 455-459 (7th Cir. 2020), seemed to consider the range of possible liability fairly broad, and *Steward Health Care System, LLC v. Blue Cross & Blue Shield of Rhode Island,* 311 F. Supp. 3d 468, 483-485 (D.R.I. 2018), suggested that there is no strict requirement to show profit-sacrifice, and that the standard may actually be a fair bit less demanding than *Brooke Group.*

Academic proposals for further refinement show promise.[31]

Refusal to Deal With Non-Rivals. This situation is simpler and now seems straightforward. First, a number of courts have made clear that *Trinko* does not apply. *E.g., Chase Mfg. Co. v. Johns Manville Corp.,* 84 F.4th 1157, 1173 (10th Cir. 2023); *United States v. Google LLC,* 778 F. Supp. 3d 797, 865-867 (E.D. Va. 2025). As a number of courts have now noted, this kind of refusal-to-deal is effectively just a tying or exclusive dealing arrangement, and they treat it as such.[32] To be clear, a mere refusal to deal with a non-rival—like a choice not to sell to a given customer or buy from a given supplier—must be more than a simple choice not to sell or buy, without more. In itself that choice is effectively per se legal. To be an actionable refusal to deal, it must be *conditional* in some way or be part of some plan to injure a rival and thereby restrain competition. But where a monopolist refuses to sell or buy from a third party for the purpose of injuring the monopolist's own horizontal competitor, it can be actionable under §2 and will generally be analyzed as a demand for exclusive dealing or a tie.

§13.3.4(b) The Essential Facilities Rule

In addition to the idea in *Aspen Skiing*—that refusals to deal can sometimes be actionably "exclusionary"—the courts have sometimes employed a more detailed doctrine known as the "essential facilities" rule. This doctrine appears to be reserved for those cases in which the defendant holds some technological resource or some input that is very special, not duplicable, and essential to competition. If one or more competitors control such a thing, and if they exclude access to would-be competitors, their conduct may violate the Sherman Act.

Technically the Supreme Court itself has never applied the essential facilities doctrine by name, and has given some indications that if squarely faced with the issue it will hold that the doctrine is not the law.[33] But the

31. *See, e.g.,* Hovenkamp, *supra* note [CROSS REF] (identifying cases in which a monopolist's refusal to supply access to its "primary" product, in which it built market power through its own difficult-to-duplicate investments, is needed to protect those investments and cases in which it is not; urging that the latter cases be treated akin to tying or exclusive dealing contracts).

32. *See, e.g., Chase Mfg. Co. v. Johns Manville Corp.,* 84 F.4th 1157, 1173 (10th Cir. 2023) (so noting, and holding *Trinko* applicable only to refusals to deal with competitors).

33. While the doctrine finds its origin in early Supreme Court case law, the Court has never actually approved its use in §2 monopolization cases. The Court's early cases on point all concerned §1 claims in which some group of competitors refused access to their jointly operated facility to some other competitor. *See Associated Press v. United States,* 326 U.S. 1 (1945); *United States v. Terminal R.R. Assn.,* 224 U.S. 383 (1912).

Court also has never held that it is *not* the law, and arguably has applied the doctrine in everything but name, as a number of its (now aging) opinions in fact ordered powerful firms to provide nondiscriminatory access to some facility. In fact, the case that gave birth to the doctrine also sets out a paradigm factual case for a facility that might seem "essential." The defendants in *United States v. Terminal R.R. Assn.*, 224 U.S. 383 (1912), were several railroads that jointly owned a "terminal" facility in St. Louis that trains crossing west or east had to use; it so happened that their terminal was the only one that could feasibly accommodate eastbound traffic from the western United States. The Court held that it would violate the Sherman Act if the defendants refused their competitors access to the terminal on reasonable terms, finding such access essential to their ability to compete. The Court has applied similar reasoning in a handful of other cases, including some §2 cases, though admittedly it has never explicitly stated that it meant to apply the essential facilities doctrine by name.

The doctrine, like most other theories of anticompetitive exclusion, has proven controversial. In addition to the concerns discussed above as to any sort of refusal-to-deal liability—that it intrudes on the right recognized in *Colgate* to choose with whom one will deal—the major policy concern with the essential facilities doctrine has been that it will impede *innovation*. The doctrine almost by definition governs important pieces of technology, which more or less by definition will be very expensive (for, if they were not, then competitors could just duplicate them). But to create such things, firms that own them ordinarily will have had to invest large amounts of money and time. If they know that following the creation of some really unique facility they are forced to share it with their rivals, it may dampen an otherwise efficient incentive to create such things.

Nevertheless, the lower courts have applied the essential facility doctrine, by name, with some frequency. In one leading case, *MCI Commcns. Corp. v. AT&T*, 708 F.2d 1081 (7th Cir. 1983), the Seventh Circuit identified four necessary elements to establish liability under the doctrine, and they are now widely followed by other courts. They are:

> (1) control of the essential facility by a monopolist; (2) a competitor's inability practically or reasonably to duplicate the essential facility; (3) the denial of the use of the facility to a competitor; and (4) the feasibility of providing the facility.

Id. at 1132-1133. Each of these elements has been given further content in the subsequent case law. The facility must actually be in the control of the monopolist, and the monopolist must have refused to supply it on reasonable terms. (It bears observing that the essential facilities doctrine would likely never require that access to a facility be given for *free*, or even for less than a competitive rate of return. If some competitor were unable to pay such a rate, that in and of itself would not constitute an anticompetitive denial of access.) The facility must be "essential" in the sense that there is no other alternative through which competitors can provide a competing good or service. It is not sufficient that other alternatives are less economical or that duplicating the facility would cost rivals more than paying for access to the defendant's facility. And it must be feasible for the defendant to provide access, meaning that it is physically feasible and that doing so would not be unreasonably costly. *See generally* 1 Am. Bar Assn., *Antitrust Law Developments* (Ninth) 275-281 (9th ed. 2022).

Finally, there is reason to believe that in order for the doctrine to be available, at least in a §2 case, the defendant in control of the essential facility must also be a competitor of those firms seeking access to it. That is, the defendant must be in both a horizontal and a vertical relationship with the would-be rivals. For example, in MCI, defendant AT&T owned the physical system of wires that made up the U.S. telephone network. Plaintiff MCI wanted to create a competing technology for long-distance communications based on wireless, microwave transmissions between microwave towers, but it still needed access to AT&T's local networks to get its signals to the telephones in people's homes and businesses. Thus, the parties were in both a vertical relation—if the plaintiff had its way, the defendant would sell local network access to it—and a horizontal one, as the plaintiff proposed to become the defendant's competitor in the long-distance telephone market. At least one case seems to have held that this hybrid vertical-horizontal relationship is required as a matter of law. *Alaska Airlines, Inc. v. United Airlines, Inc.*, 948 F.2d 536 (9th Cir. 1991). Whether or not that relationship is a formal requirement, it surely makes a case more persuasive, and most cases that have found an essential facility have involved such a relationship.

Example

Two online merchants of used books are locked in a close competitive struggle. The first of them, SecondStory.com, currently holds about 60 percent of online used-book purchases. It has managed to knit together a large network of brick-and-mortar used-book store "distribution partners." Those stores digitally catalog their inventories and upload their inventory information to SecondStory.com. SecondStory.com is then able to provide to its online customers a huge, searchable database of used books, which they can conveniently purchase by a one-click system, with one simple payment window (making it appear that the purchase comes directly from SecondStory.com rather than a disperse and unconnected web of independent stores).

Setting this up turns out to have been pretty expensive. SecondStory.com not only had to identify the many thousands of distribution partners with whom it now works, and negotiate an individual contract with each one of them (which in each case included a ten-year arrangement that the stores would not provide similar comprehensive inventory information to other online booksellers, renewable by the parties), it also had to set up a substantial technological infrastructure. That infrastructure, SecondStory.com's innovative new Virtual Warehouse system, required it to provide each distribution partner with special labeling and packaging equipment and UPC-code scanner devices, as well as software and a system for automatically printing postage payable by SecondStory.com for shipment of books directly to customers.

The second largest seller in the market, ChapterTwo.com, has so far made no fewer than four separate entreaties to SecondStory.com to provide it some sort of access to the Virtual Warehouse system. ChapterTwo.com is increasingly sure it needs that access to survive. Among its offers was one made complete with letters of intent from a syndicate of banks, indicating they would finance a partnering agreement between ChapterTwo.com and SecondStory.com, under which ChapterTwo.com would invest to maintain and improve the Virtual Warehouse network. SecondStory.com has refused steadfastly.

ChapterTwo.com has sued in §2 to challenge SecondStory.com's refusals to deal. What result?

Explanation

Even assuming that "online used-book purchases in the United States" is a relevant product market, and therefore that SecondStory.com could hold a market share large enough to establish §2 monopoly power, it seems unlikely that mere refusal to sell access to the Virtual Warehouse system is actionable under §2. The policy arguments in *Trinko* should weigh against it. Likewise, it seems unlikely that Virtual Warehouse is an "essential facility." Three of the four elements seem relatively easy to satisfy, but the fourth—inability of ChapterTwo.com to duplicate the facility—may be difficult to show. Indeed, that ChapterTwo.com was able to secure substantial commitments of capital finance for expansion and improvement to the existing system undercuts the nonduplicability argument. It suggests that ChapterTwo.com might be able to secure enough capital to develop its own rival system.

As we shall see, ChapterTwo.com would probably have a better argument to challenge the ten-year exclusivity arrangements with the distribution partners. But that will have to await §13.3.5.

Example

Let us modify the facts in the prior example. Assume that, once again, SecondStory.com had developed the Virtual Warehouse system, along with its expensive infrastructure program and the exclusivity deals with distribution partners. But it was also clear that SecondStory.com meant to provide access to the network to other booksellers. In investor calls and press releases it described the plan to sell access as a major new revenue generator. And let us say that SecondStory.com and ChapterTwo.com in fact engaged in some initial negotiations and entered into a nonbinding memorandum of understanding indicating their intent that ChapterTwo.com would purchase access in the Virtual Warehouse system once it was up and running. But then, let us say, ChatperTwo.com itself began to gain market share, or the deal otherwise became less appealing to SecondStory.com, and so it rescinded its MOU with ChapterTwo.com, and refused any further requests for access.

Does this change the result in the prior example?

Explanation

Here there is a much better case that the refusal to deal is exclusionary. These facts would make out a good case of exclusion on the "profit sacrifice" theory. The major case lending support would be *Aspen*. Here, as in *Aspen*, SecondStory.com had already engaged in voluntary dealings with ChapterTwo.com, as part of a business model it was actively building, implying that it anticipated that relationship to be profitable. It ended the relation for no clear reason except to avoid competition. As in *Aspen*, unless some other facts emerge to explain it otherwise, that decision would seem irrational in the absence of anticompetitive purpose.

§13.3.5 Exclusionary Distribution: Exclusive Contracts, Tying, Bundling, Full-Line Forcing, Loyalty Discounts, and the Many Other Faces of Vertical Foreclosure

Next, a monopolist might use various kinds of vertical restraints, which we've already seen in connection with Sherman Act §1 (*see* Chapter 10), to exclude its rivals from necessary avenues of distribution.

To a large extent the law of exclusionary distribution under §2 is the same as the law that applies under §1. For example, the law of exclusive contracting under §1 and the law of tying under §1 and Clayton Act §3 are both applied in pretty much the same way in §2 cases. The one possibly significant difference is the indication made by a number of courts that these rules should be applied more stringently against a monopolist than against defendants who together only represent enough market share to support a §1 claim. The reason is simple. As explained in Chapter 10 and further in the appendix, the reason that the courts have become more tolerant of vertical restraints in §1 cases is their belief that *intra*brand competition should not ordinarily be able to harm consumers wherever the parties to the arrangement face strong *inter*brand competition. But where a firm holds market power at the upstream level significant enough to satisfy §2, then almost by definition there is no serious interbrand competition, and in such cases anticompetitive effects should be plausible. *See, e.g., United States v. Dentsply, Inc.*, 399 F.3d 181, 191-196 (3d Cir. 2005).

But other than the general indication that distribution restraints will be taken more seriously where the defendant is a monopolist, it appears that doctrinally they are usually handled in the same way.

Garden variety exclusive contracts—that is, agreements that explicitly require someone to deal only with the monopolist—are analyzed as they are under §1 (as explained in Chapter 11). The court first asks how much trade is "foreclosed"—how much needed resources the contracts exclude from the monopolist's rivals—and then applies the standard rule of reason burden-shifting formula (as explained in §7.1). However, courts take exclusionary contracts more seriously where the defendant is a monopolist. For one thing, the usual requirement of a 40 percent foreclosure share is relaxed in §2 cases. *United States v. Microsoft Corp.*, 253 F.3d 34, 69-70 (D.C. Cir. 2001) (finding exclusive contracts that did not violate §1 for lack of foreclosure percentage did violate §2, because the monopolist's power made even less prevalent exclusivity deals likely harmful). For another, courts in §2 cases are generally unmoved by the fact that an arrangement is not literally exclusive or leaves some freedom of action. They look instead to practical effects. *Id.* at 75-76; *United States v. Google LLC*, 747 F. Supp. 3d 1, 146, 156 (D.D.C. 2024). Likewise, courts in §1 cases often follow rules of thumb under which they uphold deals whose surface features make them seem innocuous, like short duration or easy terminability. *See, e.g., Omega Envtl. v. Gilbarco, Inc.*, 127 F.3d 1157, 1163 (9th Cir.1997) (holding contracts that are short in duration to be presumptively legal); *Roland Mach. Co. v. Dresser Indus., Inc.*, 749 F.2d 380, 395 (7th Cir.1984) (same). But in §2 cases, most courts ignore such formalistic rules and examine the practical, economic substance of exclusivity arrangements, regardless of appearances. *See, e.g., McWane v. FTC*, 783 F.3d 814, 834 (11th Cir. 2015) (courts should examine "the practical effect" of an arrangement and hold it illegal if the effect is "to make it economically infeasible" for the monopolist's trading partners to switch). Courts show especial concern for exclusivity where peculiarities of the market leave rivals with no easy alternatives to the distribution or input that the monopolist has foreclosed. *See, e.g., McWane*, 783 F.3d at 839-840; *United States v. Dentsply Int'l, Inc.*, 399 F.3d 181, 193 (3d Cir. 2005).

Other arrangements are sometimes made that are not exactly in the form of exclusive dealing or requirements arrangements, but that have similar effect by making it costly for customers to switch to competitors' products. "Loyalty" discounts or volume rebates to distributors who take all or substantial parts of their product from a monopolist can be exclusionary. Most courts will analyze these contracts' economic substance to ask whether they could frustrate entry or expansion by the monopolists' rivals. *See, e.g., McWane*, 783 F.3d at 833-835; *ZF Meritor, LLC v. Eaton Corp.*, 696 F.3d 254 (3d

Cir. 2012). Arrangements like these are ordinarily analyzed like exclusive contracts: if they foreclose undue portions of the market from the monopolist's rivals, and the monopolist cannot demonstrate a procompetitive justification that outweighs the harm of exclusivity, they are illegal. (Defendants have argued that rebates and discounts are simply price competition and should be analyzed under the much more defense-friendly price-cost test of *Brooke Group Ltd. v. Brown & Williamson Tobacco Co.*, 509 U.S. 209 (1993). Courts accept that argument only if they determine that price was the only or dominant means of exclusion. This issue is discussed in §13.3.3(a).)

Likewise, a long-term lease of a product can have an exclusionary effect, at least if the product is a high value and long-lasting one. If the lease imposes some mandatory duration or imposes a penalty for early return, it has the same effect as an exclusive contract. If the lessee had simply been able to buy the equipment, then when it seeks to switch to some competitor's product it could at least sell the original product to recoup some of the cost. *See United States v. United Shoe Machinery Corp.*, 110 F. Supp. 295 (D. Mass. 1953).

Likewise, where the monopolist has tied or bundled products and forced buyers to take all of them, for the most part they will be handled in just the same way as under §1 and Clayton Act §3. For example, in *Eastman Kodak Co. v. Image Technical Servs., Inc.*, 504 U.S. 451 (1992), the Court found evidence of a tying arrangement imposed on customers by a monopolist to satisfy both a tying theory under §1 and a monopolization theory under §2. (For discussion of the elements of tying and bundling claims, *see* Chapter 11.)[34]

However, having said all that, there is one final qualification that may be more significant. Again, a theme running throughout the law of exclusion under §2 is that the kinds of conduct that can be exclusionary are highly varied and can be hard to distinguish. The courts treat some of them as really just aggressive pricing, to be judged under the *Brooke Group* predatory pricing standard. Consider again volume discounts that a monopolist might give its dealers. Even if such a deal mandated no exclusivity, one might argue that it discourages entry or expansion because it may make small-firm competition more expensive. But its procompetitive potential is also obvious—assuming that the dealers themselves don't have market power, a volume discount even by a monopolist should tend to push costs down and reflect only the large-volume monopolist's efficiency advantages. So the problem with analyzing these somewhat more complex arrangements is that their effects are less straightforward, they pose real prospects of consumer

---

34. There may be some differences. As with other distribution restraints, the courts have indicated some willingness to find §2 exclusion for tying conduct that might not satisfy a §1 or Clayton Act §3 claim, as for example they may not require so clear a showing that the products are separate or that there was an agreement concerning the tie. Likewise, tying violates §1 or §3 only if it affects a substantial amount of commerce in the tied product market, but the same conduct could violate §2 if it affects competition in either the tying or tied markets. *See generally* 1 Am. Bar Assn., *Antitrust Law Developments (Ninth)* 258-259 (9th ed. 2022).

benefit, and the courts are very hesitant to deter possibly procompetitive conduct. Generally speaking, if the arrangement does not have the effect of ensuring exclusivity, the courts hold that it is really just a form of aggressive pricing, and therefore it is analyzed not as a non-price vertical restraint, but as predatory pricing under *Brooke Group*. In such a case, the arrangement could violate §2 only if the initial showing of monopoly power is made, the discount program renders the monopolist's price below its costs, and there is a dangerous probability that the monopolist will recoup its losses through later, supracompetitive pricing. *See generally* 1 Am. Bar Assn., *Antitrust Law Developments* (Ninth) 259-260 (9th ed. 2022).

Example

Consider again the example from the last section: SecondStory.com, the largest online seller of used books in the United States, has managed to capture sales by knitting together a network of brick-and-mortar used-book stores that make their inventories available to SecondStory.com's online customers—a system called the Virtual Warehouse. Those "distribution partners" do so subject to ten-year contracts that prohibit them from supplying their inventory information to SecondStory.com's competitors.

The question in the prior example was whether SecondStory.com's refusal to sell access to the Virtual Warehouse was an illegal refusal to deal. But what about the long-term exclusive dealing contracts?

Explanation

Here ChapterTwo.com's argument is probably a fair bit stronger than its refusal-to-deal theories. Recall from Chapter 10 that, in general, courts are pretty tolerant of vertical restraints. Even exclusivity arrangements with suppliers or customers—the sort of contract most likely to "foreclose" one's horizontal competitors—are unlikely to be illegal unless foreclosure is extensive and long-lasting. But in this case, two facts are striking. First, the agreements are for long terms. Courts frequently say that duration is a key concern in the legality of exclusive dealing contracts (*see* Chapter 11). Second, the amount of foreclosure is probably pretty large. There is probably a fairly solid case here that the contracts are meant to keep ChapterTwo.com or other competitors from developing systems that could compete with the Virtual Warehouse.

One interesting issue in this case is that the plaintiff could benefit from the rule of *Continental Ore Co. v. Union Carbide & Carbon Corp.*, 370 U.S. 690, 699 (1962), mentioned above, under which a §2 plaintiff should be allowed to stitch together all the evidence of exclusion it has, rather than be forced to challenge specific acts in isolation. Here, each individual exclusivity arrangement presumably forecloses only a de minimis amount of commerce. But in combination, the thousands of identical contracts might foreclose a very substantial portion of the supply of an essential input.

§13.3.6 Exclusionary Misuse of Institutions: Exclusion Through Public and Quasi-Public Instrumentalities

In various ways one firm might try to enlist the government or some other institution to help in the fight against its competitors. The firm might lobby for a law that would prohibit or disadvantage a competitor's product, or tax the competitor disproportionately or impede it in some other way. The firm might also try to block government action favorable to a competitor, like the granting of a license to do business to that competitor, or the grant of a patent or permission to market a new drug. Sometimes competitors can make use of other institutions that are not technically the government, but perform similar functions. Any such conduct could harm competition, to the benefit of the firm that undertook it, and so in principle any of it could constitute predatory or exclusionary conduct under §2.

However, the major problem for such a theory is that the challenged conduct might qualify for an exemption from antitrust law under the so-called *Noerr-Pennington* immunity. Where a party is trying to encourage some action by government, no matter how malevolent its motives might be, this doctrine normally renders its conduct immune from antitrust. (The *Noerr-Pennington* doctrine is covered in Chapter 21.) To make a long story short, a plaintiff trying to make out a §2 case on abuse of public or quasi-public instrumentalities will have to show either that the conduct wasn't really petition of government at all—for example, that the petition was made indirectly, perhaps to an influential but formally private standard setting organization—or that the petitioning was actually just a "sham." It is a sham where the defendant didn't actually care about the government action for which it petitioned, but only wanted to use the *process* of petitioning itself to injure a rival or delay new entry or the like.

Abuse of institutions theories can come in a lot of forms. We will consider three common scenarios—lobbying before policy makers or standard-setting bodies, filing bogus lawsuits or administrative petitions, and deliberate enforcement of bogus intellectual property.

§13.3.6(a) Standard Setting and Government Rule Making

Markets tend to be surrounded by all kinds of rules and institutions. There are rules to govern the ownership of things and the making of deals to buy and sell them, to govern disclosures of information, to limit transactions that threaten safety or the environment, and any of thousands of other things. Since these rules can limit the choices marketplace actors might otherwise make, they can limit competition. To the extent a competitor can manage to influence them, they can be used strategically as weapons against marketplace rivals.

Someone has to make all these rules. The government, of course, is omnipresent in the making of them. Most governments set the fundamental rules for commercial dealing, the rules of contract, property and tort, and in modern times they have also set the health, safety, and public welfare rules we now take for granted. While a competitor might try to secure government rules like these that would disadvantage its competitors, generally speaking the attempt to get them cannot be the basis of antitrust liability. Where a firm merely asks a legislature to adopt a law that hurts its competition, the *Noerr-Pennington* doctrine makes it very difficult to challenge that petitioning conduct in antitrust.

However, there are two major ways that abuses of rule-making processes can still be challenged as in violation of antitrust. First, not all government rules for the marketplace are set by legislatures. Administrative agencies are also often empowered to make rules, and, though the Supreme Court has not yet reached the question, there is growing authority that *Noerr* does not always protect nefarious conduct in these contexts. In particular, there is authority that in contexts that are "less political" than the legislative arena—including at least some administrative rule making—*misrepresentations* are not protected by *Noerr* (as explored further in §§13.3.6(b) and 21.4.1(c)). So if a monopolist were to mislead an administrative agency into adopting rules that help it to acquire or maintain monopoly power, that might form the basis of a §2 cause of action.

Second, there are also literally hundreds of thousands of other organizations active in the U.S. economy that make rules of various kinds. Most such groups are purely private. Often known as "standard setting organizations," they can have a great deal of influence in the marketplace. With surprising frequency, their standards are adopted directly into state and local laws. Often enough, however, they are influential simply because of their own reputation, or because their standards are incorporated by reference in private contracts. And a given standard may become dominant because of a "network" effect—once a given technology becomes widely adopted, it may be that in order for competitors to stay in that market they must make their products compatible with it. The classic example of such a case was the industry-wide dominance of the VHS videotape standard, which destroyed the rival Beta standard.

Anticompetitive attempts by a monopolist to abuse any such standard setting process might violate §2. Generally, where such a group is wholly private and the theory of liability is based on the influence the SSO has through its own reputation or by the use of its standards by other marketplace actors, there is no likelihood of *Noerr* immunity. And where the standard is influential in that way, the theory of liability is a standard boycott theory—the idea is that the defendant has used the offices of the SSO to persuade or coerce others into refusing to deal with its rivals.[35]

Still, some such groups are not entirely private, and where anticompetitive conduct involves a quasi-public group, more complex *Noerr-Pennington* issues arise. Sometimes the standards they produce are adopted verbatim into law. Sometimes otherwise private groups are even appointed, more or less formally, to do a government job. For example, most states require applicants for the bar exam to graduate from an ABA-accredited law school, or, if they didn't, to jump through additional, more onerous bureaucratic hoops. Likewise, Congress has provided that any hospital approved of by the Joint Commission on Accreditation of Hospitals, a private group, will be automatically eligible to receive payments under the Medicare and Medicaid programs.

Whether petitioning to quasi-public groups enjoys *Noerr* immunity was addressed in *Allied Tube & Conduit Corp. v. Indian Head, Inc.*, 486 U.S. 492 (1988).[36] There, a member of an influential SSO secured the adoption of a fire safety standard that would prohibit use of a new competitor's product in buildings. It got that result by packing the meeting at which the standard was approved with its own paid agents—in effect, by defrauding the SSO. Even though technically the SSO was wholly private, the defendant raised a *Noerr* defense on the theory that its standard was routinely incorporated into state and local laws verbatim. In fact, said the defendant, because the SSO's standard was simply rubber-stamped in many jurisdictions, the only way to have any impact on actual laws to be adopted was to lobby the SSO itself. While the Court expressed sympathy for that argument, it ultimately held that "[t]he scope of [*Noerr*] protection depends . . . on the source, context, and nature of the anticompetitive restraint at issue." Furthermore, "in less political arenas," which is to say, outside the context of lobbying an actual legislature, "unethical and deceptive practices can constitute abuses of administrative or judicial processes that may result in antitrust violations." *Id.* at 499-500. An important issue in the case was that, while the Court refused to find any *Noerr* protection and it upheld a jury finding of liability, the only theory of harm for which the defendant was found responsible was for the standard's independent impact in the marketplace, not for its adoption by any government. Thus, where an otherwise private SSO holds some formal policymaking role or is otherwise quasi-public, the "source, context, and nature"

35. *See, e.g.*, *Allied Tube & Conduit Corp. v. Indian Head, Inc.*, 486 U.S. 492 (1988); *Am. Soc. of Mech. Engrs., Inc. v. Hydrolevel Corp.*, 456 U.S. 556 (1982); *Radiant Burners, Inc. v. Peoples Gas, Light & Coke Co.*, 364 U.S. 656 (1961).

36. Technically, *Allied Tube* was a §1 case, and the conduct at issue was orchestrated among several members of the SSO. There is no apparent reason why its reasoning as to *Noerr* would apply differently in the §2 context.

of that scenario may call for a different result. Some lower courts have so held.[37] (For more on the *Noerr-Pennington* doctrine, *see* §21.4.)

§13.3.6(b) Exclusionary Litigation and Administrative Complaints

A similar theory of exclusion, which raises similar *Noerr* issues, is that a firm might file frivolous lawsuits or take frivolous administrative actions against a competitor, solely for the purpose of impeding the competitor's ability to compete. As one common example, a party might fraudulently procure intellectual property or some other exclusive government right to do something, and then enforce that right through litigation against its competitors. Or a party might use lawsuits or filings before regulatory tribunals to keep a competitor from acquiring license rights or some other thing the competitor needs to compete. Parties might be tempted to bring claims like these even when they have no real basis, because the very pendency of the judicial or agency proceeding might delay a competitor's entry or otherwise injure it.

It has been clear at least since *California Motor Transport Co. v. Trucking Unlimited*, 404 U.S. 508 (1972), that any such conduct can be anticompetitive and can in principle satisfy the conduct element of a §2 claim. The plaintiff's problem ordinarily will be to overcome the *Noerr* immunity. Again, it is difficult to show that lobbying publicly directed toward legislators or government administrators is a "sham," and unless it is a sham, the petitioning is immune. (*See* §21.4.) However, there may be substantially more room to challenge this sort of abuse when it occurs in administrative or judicial settings (as apparently it often does), even where it is not a "sham." This is so because the Supreme Court has said that *misrepresentations* are less tolerable in that context than they are in traditional legislative lobbying.

First of all, in the foundational *Noerr* cases themselves, the Court made clear that, in the traditional context of petitioning legislators, falsehoods are legally irrelevant.[38] However, in subsequent cases the Court has said that fraudulent conduct is less tolerable outside the "political arena," especially

37. *See, e.g.*, *Massachusetts Sch. of Law at Andover, Inc. v. Am. Bar Assn.*, 107 F.3d 1026 (3d Cir. 1997) (holding American Bar Association immune for law school accreditation activities where theory of harm was reliance by state bar regulators on accreditation decision); *Sessions Tank Liners, Inc. v. Joor Mfg. Co.*, 17 F.3d 295 (9th Cir. 1994) (immunizing deliberate misrepresentations to an SSO as valid attempts to influence government action, where theory of harm was government adoption of the resulting standard).

38. *See Eastern R.R. Presidents Conf. v. Noerr Motor Freight, Inc.*, 365 U.S. 127 (1961) (finding it "legally irrelevant" that the petitioning conduct had included a deceitful publicity campaign, featuring newspaper articles supposedly written by concerned citizens, but actually written by the defendants' publicity firm).

where it occurs in adjudicatory and administrative contexts.[39] A substantial body of lower court case law now holds that there is a misrepresentation exception to the *Noerr* immunity, which is triggered in "less political arenas. . . ."[40]

The most thorough analysis of the issue remains *In re Union Oil Co. of California*, 138 FTC 1 (2004). There the Federal Trade Commission accused defendant Unocal of monopolizing the market for gasoline compliant with California emissions standards. The Commission alleged that Unocal had defrauded a state agency called the California Air Resources Board (CARB), which had authority under state law to mandate technological standards for gasoline to protect the environment. Specifically, defendant Unocal was said to have encouraged the CARB to adopt standards that would require a certain technology in petroleum refining, but failed to disclose that it held patents in that technology. After adoption of the standard, Unocal announced that it held the patents and aggressively sought royalties from other firms producing under the new standard. The Commission ruled that at least under the facts alleged in the agency staff complaint,[41] there would be no *Noerr* immunity. Maybe the most useful portion of the Commission's analysis was its summary of the facts courts have considered in deciding whether a case involves one of the "less political arenas": (1) whether the government actor would expect truthfulness, which is most likely in judicial and agency adjudicatory contexts (where falsehoods can be crimes or ethical violations) and somewhat less so in administrative rule makings; (2) the amount of the government decision maker's discretion, more discretion implying more likelihood of *Noerr* immunity (since the rationale of the misrepresentation exception is that it helps preserve the integrity of proceedings that place

39. *California Motor Transport* wrote that "[m]isrepresentations, condoned in the political arena, are not immunized when used in the adjudicatory process." 404 U.S. at 513. In *Allied Tube* the Court wrote that "in less political arenas, unethical and deceptive practices can constitute abuses of administrative or judicial processes that may result in antitrust violations." 486 U.S. at 489. And perhaps most important, in *Profl. Real Estate Investors, Inc. v. Columbia Pictures Indus.*, 508 U.S. 49 (1993), the Court considered a lawsuit in federal court that was alleged by the defendant in that suit to have been itself exclusionary. The Court took the opportunity to explain what constitutes a "sham" in the context of litigation and held that the suit in that case had not been a "sham." But what is important is that the Court explicitly explained that it was *not* deciding whether there was a general misrepresentation exception to *Noerr* in adjudicatory or administrative contexts. Quoting the string of its own prior holdings discussed here, the Court left open the question "whether and, if so, to what extent *Noerr* permits the imposition of antitrust liability for a litigant's fraud or other misrepresentations." *Id.* at 61 n.6.

40. *See* C. Douglas Floyd, *Antitrust Liability for the Anticompetitive Effects of Government Action Induced by Fraud*, 69 Antitrust L.J. 403 (2001) (collecting cases).

41. The matter never reached a final judgment before the Commission. While proceedings were pending before an agency Administrative Law Judge, Unocal was acquired by Chevron. As part of the Commission's approval of the acquisition, Chevron entered a consent decree with the Commission in which it agreed to substantial limits on use of the patents that were the subject of the CARB dispute.

a high value on truthfulness); (3) the extent to which the government decision maker must rely on participants for its access to information; and (4) whether the circumstances allow the antitrust tribunal to determine that the petitioner's misrepresentations caused the plaintiff's alleged injury.

§13.3.6(c) Enforcement of Bogus Patents: The *Walker Process* Cause of Action

A special rule governs §2 exclusion by enforcement of bogus patents, which was set out in *Walker Process Equipment, Inc. v. Food Machinery & Chemical Corp.*, 382 U.S. 172 (1965). In that case, one company sued another for infringement of a patent covering sewage treatment technology. The defendant counterclaimed, saying that the patent itself was gotten by fraud on the Patent Office. Therefore, said the defendant, a lawsuit to enforce it was an anticompetitive effort to monopolize the market for that technology under Sherman Act §2. The Supreme Court said that the antitrust counterclaim could proceed, holding that attempts to enforce a fraudulently procured patent (or even threats to do so) could constitute the "exclusionary conduct" element of a §2 claim. (This rule is discussed at much more length in Chapter 15.) The *Walker Process* Court did not consider whether *Noerr* or *Pennington*, both of which had already been decided, were relevant. That presumably was because it was not clear until *California Motor Transport* in 1972 that lawsuits and other adjudicatory petitions were protected by *Noerr*.

§13.3.7 Exclusionary Innovation

Plaintiffs sometimes try to show exclusion by virtue of the fact that the monopolist has exclusive access to some special technology. It might have intellectual property that it has refused to share, or it might design a monopolized product in such a way that competitors just find it too difficult to make meaningful substitute products. The courts have been very skeptical of such theories. They pose an irony for a body of law the goal of which is to force competitors to try to make their products better and more cheaply.[42] The courts' reluctance also reflects the strong, essentially libertarian impulse underlying the *Colgate* rule, mentioned above: Even a monopolist ordinarily has no duty to cooperate with other firms.

---

42. *See, e.g.*, *Verizon Commcns., Inc. v. Law Offices of Curtis V. Trinko*, 540 U.S. 398, 407 (2004) ("To safeguard the incentive to innovate, the possession of monopoly power will not be found to be unlawful unless it is accompanies by an element of anticompetitive conduct."); *Berkey Photo, Inc. v. Eastman Kodak Co.*, 603 F.2d 263, 281 (2d Cir. 1979) ("[A]ny success that [even a monopolist] may achieve through the process of invention and innovation is clearly tolerated by the antitrust laws.").

Still, there remains some possibility that innovations and design changes can be actionably exclusionary, particularly as high technology industries have come to prominence, and the importance of the interoperability among high tech products has come to be an important part of competition in those industries. This was seen perhaps most prominently in the D.C. Circuit's influential en banc opinion in *United States v. Microsoft*, 253 F.3d 34 (D.C. Cir. 2001). *See* 1 Am. Bar Assn., *Antitrust Law Developments* (Ninth) 283-288 (9th ed. 2022).

§13.3.7(a) Refusals to License Intellectual Property

Of doctrines relating to innovation, this is the simplest, because in all but one circuit it is now effectively per se legal for a given firm to refuse to license its intellectual property. While refusals to deal not involving intellectual property can sometimes constitute unlawful exclusion (*see* §13.3.4), the courts have fashioned this special exception, again, to protect the policy in favor of innovation. *See generally In re Indep. Serv. Orgs. Antitrust Litig.*, 203 F.2d 1322 (Fed. Cir. 2000). The only clear exception is in the Ninth Circuit. In *Image Technical Servs. v. Eastman Kodak Co.*, 125 F.3d 1195 (9th Cir. 1997), the court held that an intellectual property owner merely enjoys a presumptive right to refuse to deal.

§13.3.7(b) Product Design

Theoretically, a monopolist could stifle competition by introducing a new product or changing an existing one to make it hard for competitors to produce effective substitutes. Even if the monopolist lacks a patent, it might be that in order to compete with the monopolist's products, competing products must be compatible with it in some way or must be able to perform functions that, through technological manipulation by the monopolist, they cannot perform. This theory appears to be nearly as difficult as challenge to refusal to license intellectual property. While no court appears to have said explicitly that product design choices are per se legal, and a number of courts have suggested in dicta that they could conceivably constitute exclusion, only one opinion appears ever to have held that a design choice was in fact exclusionary—the D.C. Circuit's monumental *Microsoft* opinion.

Among the first cases to consider the theory, and still the leading opinion, was *Berkey Photo, Inc. v. Eastman Kodak Co.*, 603 F.2d 263 (2d Cir. 1979). The plaintiff was a small processor of photographic film (in those days, the only way to develop photographs was to pay a company like Kodak or Berkey to develop the film for you), which also had a small camera manufacturing operation. According to the plaintiff, because defendant Kodak held a monopoly share of film manufacturing, and because different kinds of film could be made to work only in cameras in which they fit properly, Berkey and other camera makers depended for their existence on the ability to make cameras that would be compatible with Kodak's film. In 1972 Kodak introduced the hugely popular 110-speed "Instamatic" series of cameras, and simultaneously introduced a new and superior kind of color film. Kodak heavily marketed the new film as a technological breakthrough for the quality of the resulting pictures, but it made the film compatible only with its own new Instamatic cameras. The plaintiff claimed this excluded it from making compatible cameras. The court was unreceptive, writing that "any firm, even a monopolist, may generally bring its products to market whenever and however it chooses," *id.* at 286. But for all its skepticism, the *Berkey* court did not rule out the possibility of a product design theory of liability. The court wrote:

> This is not to say, of course, that new product introductions are *ipso facto* immune from antitrust scrutiny, and we do not agree with Kodak's argument that they are; in all such cases, however, it is not the new product introduction itself, but some associated conduct, that supplies the violation.

Id. at 286.

In subsequent cases the theory has generally failed, but *Microsoft* is a major exception. Defendant Microsoft was held to have monopoly power in the market for "Intel-compatible PC operating systems," and to have taken a number of steps to protect that power. Among those steps were features Microsoft built in to its Windows operating system and its Internet Explorer web browser, and in particular its "integration" of the browser into the operating system. Microsoft had made it difficult for users to remove or deactivate the preloaded Internet Explorer and to replace it with the rival browser Netscape. Its motivation, according to the court, was to thwart Netscape not as a rival browser, but as a substitute *operating system*, which might have occurred had Netscape prospered and third-party programmers become interested in developing software to run upon it. Noting that "[a]s a general matter, courts are very skeptical about [such] claims," the court found that "Microsoft's conduct, through something other than competition on the merits, has the effect of significantly reducing usage of rivals' products and hence . . . is anticompetitive. . . ." While Microsoft offered some general business justification for the technological value of this software integration, its justifications were not "specifie[d] or substantiate[d]. . . ." *United States v. Microsoft Corp.*, 253 F.3d 34, 64-66 (D.C. Cir. 2001).

§13.3.7(c) Failure to Predisclose

A closely related theory of harm is that a monopolist introducing a new product should give its technical specifications to those competitors who would be harmed by it, to help them gear up their own response. As one might guess, this theory has not fared well.

Berkey Photo again remains a leading case. The plaintiff there alleged that Kodak should have predisclosed to it the technical details of its new Instamatic camera and the film that would work with it. The plaintiff put on evidence that Kodak had, in fact, long had a policy of making selective predisclosures when they would serve the company's interests. For example, during the 1960s Kodak developed the now familiar "Super 8" film, which would allow amateurs to make home movies. Kodak itself did not have much presence in the making of movie *cameras*, however, and so it was in the company's best interests to make sure that those companies that could mass produce amateur movie cameras had enough information about the new film to make cameras that could use it. That would maximize Kodak's own sales of the new movie film, which was its chief objective. In fact, Kodak's CEO admitted at trial that the company made just this sort of judgment call at every such occasion to determine whether disclosure was in the company's own pecuniary self-interest.

The *Berkey* court rejected any duty of even a monopolist to predisclose design specifications, and though the argument has been made elsewhere, it appears that no court has yet found liability on it. The *Berkey* court again began by stressing the risk this theory of liability would pose to innovation. The court further observed that it would be very difficult even for Kodak—"accustomed though it is to making business decisions with antitrust considerations in mind"—to know to which firms it would be legally bound to make disclosure, or when such disclosure would be required. That obligation, too, thought the court, would chill innovation.

It is unclear at present whether this theory of liability will ever be successful, but no court has fully ruled it out.

§13.3.8 The Unlimited Range of Other Conduct That Can Be "Exclusionary" and Judicial Reluctance to Consider It

As mentioned, exclusionary conduct can be essentially anything a monopolist might do that impedes entry or expansion by rivals, unless that conduct is simply competition on the merits—making the product better or more cheaply. Moreover, there is as yet no general theoretical explanation to govern when any such conduct is exclusionary or not. There is no requirement that the conduct be otherwise illegal. "Legal actions, when taken by a monopolist, may give rise to liability if anticompetitive." *Image Technical Servs., Inc. v. Eastman Kodak Co.*, 125 F.3d 1195, 1207 (9th Cir. 1997); *see also Eastman Kodak Co. v. Image Technical Servs.*, 504 U.S. 451, 488 (1992) (Scalia, J., dissenting) ("Behavior that might otherwise not be of concern to the antitrust laws—or that might even be viewed as procompetitive—can take on exclusionary connotations when practiced by a monopolist."). As long as the plaintiff can show in some plausible way that conduct has made it more difficult to compete, and that conduct is not itself competition on the merits, that conduct at least in theory could be part of the showing of exclusion. For example, *Multistate Leg. Studies v. Harcourt Brace Jovanovich*, 63 F.3d 1540 (10th Cir. 1995) involved competition between the dominant national provider of bar exam study courses and a smaller firm trying to sell a supplemental course, which it hoped would be available to students in any general bar course. (Allegedly, the monopolist saw the plaintiff as a threat because it wanted to offer its own, competing supplemental course.) Among other steps the monopolist took to injure the plaintiff was to schedule its general study courses at times that would make it inconvenient for students to also purchase the plaintiff's course. The court found that allegation sufficient to raise a triable issue of fact.

Among the more commonly asserted forms of miscellaneous conduct are actions that could in themselves violate §1, like various kinds of boycotts, or business torts like intentional interference with contracts. Deception is also fairly commonly alleged, like falsely disparaging a rival's products or otherwise spreading falsehoods that harm a rival.[43] Likewise, though it has been rare for plaintiffs actually to uncover such conduct, there is no doubt that physical destruction of a competitor's facilities or other sabotage or violence can constitute "exclusion." For example, in *Conwood Co. v. U.S. Tobacco Co.*, 290 F.3d 768 (6th Cir. 2002), defendant U.S. Tobacco—a monopolist with a market share in excess of 70 percent—used its staff of field representatives to destroy the in-store display racks used by plaintiff Conwood to sell its tobacco products. The plan of sabotage was large, resulting in about $100,000 per month of costs to Conwood. It was held sufficient to constitute "exclusion" under §2. Likewise, in *Dooley v. Crab Boat Owners Assn.*, No. C 02-0676 MHP, 2004 WL 902361 (N.D. Cal. April 26, 2004), the court found an issue of fact sufficient to reach a jury where the defendant fishing operator cut competitors' crab lines and assaulted crew members.

§13.4 THE LEGITIMATE BUSINESS JUSTIFICATION

Finally, even if the plaintiff can prove that the defendant held monopoly power and took anticompetitive action to acquire or maintain it, the defendant can put on evidence that there was some legitimate business justification

43. *See, e.g., Natl. Assn. Pharm. Mfrs., Inc. v. Ayerst Labs.*, 850 F.2d 904 (2d Cir. 1988) (letter sent by monopolist maker of branded drug to pharmacists, falsely disparaging product of plaintiff generic drug manufacturer); *Intl. Travel Arrangers, Inc. v. Western Airlines, Inc.*, 623 F.2d 1255 (8th Cir. 1980) (falsely disparaging advertisements).

for that conduct. If the defendant can come up with such evidence, it will be up to the plaintiff to show either that the justification was pretextual or that, even if not pretextual, the harms caused by the conduct outweigh any benefits it could deliver. A justification is "legitimate" where it explains how the conduct helps the defendant compete as to price or quality. That is, the justification must be that the challenged conduct improves consumer welfare. It must also be "specifi[c][and] substantiate[d]"; it is insufficient to offer generalities. *United States v. Microsoft*, 253 F.3d 34, 66 (D.C. Cir. 2001). As in any other antitrust context, it is not sufficient to advance "social justifications" or arguments that competition itself would produce bad results. (*See* §3.2.2.)

As we learned in connection with rule-of-reason analysis under §1 (*see* §7.1), while courts often describe the final stage in the analysis to be a "balancing" of pro- and anticompetitive effects, it is misleading to suggest that the courts actually balance anything. Instead, they ask whether the conduct was "unnecessarily restrictive," *Aspen*, 472 U.S. at 605 n.32, or was "more restrictive than reasonably necessary" to achieve "competition on the merits," *Multistate Legal Studies v. Harcourt Brace Jovanovich*, 63 F.3d 1540, 1550 (10th Cir. 1995).

Example

Consider again the previous example of SecondStory.com and its Virtual Warehouse system. Again, SecondStory.com was an online seller of used books, and in order to secure access to a large inventory it set up a network of "distribution partner" agreements with individual, brick-and-mortar used-book stores. The used-book stores agreed to ten-year exclusive arrangements with SecondStory.com that they would not supply inventory information to other online booksellers, and also that they would keep confidential the details of the Virtual Warehouse system and its technology. SecondStory.com also refused to give its faltering smaller rival ChapterTwo.com access to the Virtual Warehouse system, despite several requests.

Assuming ChapterTwo.com could make out the other elements of a §2 claim, might SecondStory.com nevertheless have any business justification?

Explanation

One would think SecondStory.com would have a colorable business justification, at least if the challenge is to its exclusive contracts and confidentiality agreements. It ought to be able to show that the Virtual Warehouse itself was a procompetitive innovation. It allowed SecondStory.com to capture a lot of market share quickly, and apparently only on the basis of cost or quality advantages—that is, it gained market share by competition on the merits, not anticompetitive exclusion. And it ought to be able to show that its large investment in creating the system would be jeopardized by lack of exclusivity or confidentiality. Imagine that individual distribution partners were allowed first to use SecondStory.com's equipment to digitally inventory their stocks of books, with nicely printed UPC labels or the like, and create detailed databases of their stock, and then also allowed to sell that information to Second Story.com's competitors, like ChapterTwo.com. Then ChapterTwo.com might have gotten a valuable competitive asset for much less than it cost SecondStory.com, and SecondStory.com's incentive to create the desirable innovation might be seriously diminished. This would constitute a straightforward free-riding justification for SecondStory.com's exclusivity and confidentiality requirements (as explained in Chapter 10 and further in the appendix). Still, the exclusivity restriction is for a *very* long time. While it is ultimately a fact question, it seems unlikely that a ten-year term is really justified on this ground.

Moreover, the justification seems less plausible as to SecondStory.com's refusal to deal with ChapterTwo.com, particularly if, as suggested in the second example in §13.3.4, SecondStory.com had in fact sold access to Virtual Warehouse to other booksellers in the past. If it could be shown that the refusal was exclusionary—because the Virtual Warehouse really was an essential facility or because SecondStory.com's real purpose was not competition on the merits, but harm to a competitor—then it is hard to see how SecondStory.com's arrangement is really only needed to improve competition on the merits. Again, as suggested in the example in §13.3.4, a real exclusionary purpose might be present if SecondStory.com really has foreclosed a large percentage of the supply of an essential input and then denied it to a competitor.

CHAPTER 14

Attempted Monopolization and Conspiracy to Monopolize

Sherman Act §2 prohibits not only "monopoliz[ation]," but two other things as well. Recall that under its terms, no "person . . . shall monopolize, or *attempt* to monopolize, or *combine or conspire* with any other person or persons, to monopolize any part of . . . trade or commerce. . . ." 15 U.S.C. §2 (emphasis added). In some ways these causes of action for attempt and conspiracy are problematic for plaintiffs, and they are less often litigated than the regular monopolization claim. They impose some elements of proof on plaintiffs not required for monopolization or under §1, and they offer only the same remedies as any other cause of action under §1 or §2. However, they remain useful strategic tools for plaintiffs, because they tend to fill some gaps in the law that would otherwise exist. They are useful for plaintiffs who have some evidence of wrongdoing and injury, but may not be able to make out a case for monopolization or for violation of §1.

§14.1 THE §2 ATTEMPT CAUSE OF ACTION

Under contemporary law, the attempt cause of action is essentially the same as the monopolization cause of action, except for two things. First, the plaintiff need show only some lower threshold of market power. Second, however, in addition to exclusionary conduct, the plaintiff must show that the defendant specifically intended to acquire monopoly power.

Probably the two most important cases on attempted monopolization are an old one, *Swift & Co. v. United States*, 196 U.S. 375 (1905), and a recent one, *Spectrum Sports, Inc. v. McQuillan*, 506 U.S. 447 (1993). In *Swift*, Justice Oliver Wendell Holmes wrote for the Court that by using the phrase "attempt to monopolize" in §2, Congress meant to incorporate the requirement from the common law of attempts that the defendant specifically intended to accomplish the illegal result that was allegedly attempted. That is, the plaintiff must show that the defendant had a "specific intent" to attain monopoly power. *Spectrum Sports*, now the dominant authority on point, is influential for two reasons. First, the Court crystallized the cause of action into a three-element test. Under *Spectrum Sports*, all §2 attempt plaintiffs must "prove (1) that defendant has engaged in predatory or anticompetitive conduct with (2) a specific intent to monopolize and (3) a dangerous probability of achieving monopoly power." 506 U.S. at 456.

Second, *Spectrum Sports* made clear that each of these three elements was separate and necessary and, above all, that the "dangerous probability" requirement demanded some showing that the defendant holds power in some relevant market. The Court took the case to resolve an uncommonly unbalanced circuit split. The court below—the Ninth Circuit—had reaffirmed one of its own early rulings, *Lessig v. Tidewater Oil Co.*, 327 F.2d 459 (9th Cir. 1964). But since *Tidewater* was decided, literally every other federal circuit had gone the other way on the central question it raised. Specifically, *Tidewater* read *Swift & Co.* to permit proof of both dangerous probability of success and specific intent to monopolize upon a mere showing of predatory conduct. Though no other court outside the Circuit agreed, when the Ninth Circuit considered the issue again in *Spectrum Sports*, it reaffirmed *Tidewater*. The Supreme Court reversed, holding that all three elements are necessary and some proof must be adduced as to each. As we shall see, it is not clear that specific intent is so divorced from the predatory conduct requirement—it appears that proof of the latter can also be submitted as evidence that the defendant held the former. But it is *very* clear that it is distinct from the dangerous probability requirement.

§14.1.1 Predatory Conduct

The sort of conduct that can satisfy the first element of the attempt cause of action—that the defendant engaged in predatory or exclusionary conduct designed to acquire monopoly power—is exactly the same as that which could satisfy the conduct element of the full-blown monopolization claim. Courts have frequently held that conduct which could not satisfy the conduct element of the monopolization claim also cannot satisfy the conduct element of the attempt claim. *See* 1 Am. Bar Assn., *Antitrust Law Developments (Ninth)* 332-340 (9th ed. 2022) (collecting cases). The sort of conduct that can satisfy this conduct requirement, for both the monopolization and attempt causes of action, is discussed in §13.3.

§14.1.2 Specific Intent

As in the law of criminal attempts, proof of attempted monopolization requires proof that the defendant acted with "specific intent." In this case, the defendant must have had the specific intent to acquire a monopoly. Specific intent differs from the sort of general intent evidence commonly introduced in antitrust cases, which usually consists of no more than the intent to engage in some exclusionary act. (*See* §7.1 and §13.3.2.) Indeed, Judge Hand famously wrote in *Alcoa* that, in an attempted monopolization case, specific intent is not the intent merely to harm a competitor by undercutting its prices or denying it access to a useful resource or any of the other things that can satisfy the §2 conduct element. Rather, it is the intent to use that conduct to *acquire a monopoly*. *United States v. Aluminum Co. of Am.*, 148 F.2d 416, 431-432 (2d Cir. 1945).

The reason for the intent requirement is simple. By definition, an attempt is an unsuccessful effort to accomplish an offense. Specifically, in the case of attempted monopolization, the defendant wanted to get a very large market share but didn't, or hasn't yet. So basically, by definition, attempts do less overt harm than successful offenses. Without the confirming, real-world consequences that follow from outright monopolization, there is some risk that attacking mere attempts will stifle competitive conduct. Requiring evidence of specific intent helps to limit this risk. As Justice Holmes explained in *Swift & Co.*, it is virtually by definition that acts constituting an attempt, without some evidence of intent, would just be a collection of lawful acts. As he wrote:

> Intent is . . . essential to such an attempt. Where acts are not sufficient in themselves to produce a result which the law seeks to prevent—for instance, the monopoly—but require further acts in addition to the mere forces of nature to bring that result to pass, an intent to bring it to pass is necessary in order to produce a dangerous probability that it will happen.

196 U.S. at 396.

But what proof is needed is less certain. The Supreme Court has said little more than that it must be "something more than an intent to compete vigorously. . . ." *Spectrum Sports*, 506 U.S. at 459. *Spectrum Sports* explicitly suggested that proof of the defendant's 'unfair' or 'predatory' tactics . . . may be sufficient to prove the necessary intent to monopolize. . . ." 506 U.S. at 459. A safe generalization is that direct evidence of intent is probably sufficient, and intent can also be inferred in cases involving substantial and grossly anticompetitive predatory or exclusionary conduct.[1]

§14.1.3 Dangerous Likelihood of Success

In most cases, the "dangerous likelihood" element boils down to a market power showing through evidence of high market share protected by entry barriers. As in most other antitrust contexts, there is no bright-line test for how much power is enough. However, it appears that a 50 percent share is ordinarily sufficient, a share between 30 percent and 50 percent is occasionally sufficient but usually not, and a share below 30 percent is almost surely insufficient. *See M&M Med. Supplies & Servs., Inc. v. Pleasant Valley Hosp., Inc.*, 981 F.2d 160, 168 (4th Cir. 1992) (establishing these parameters for the Fourth Circuit); 1 Am. Bar Assn., *Antitrust Law Developments (Ninth)* 343-348 (9th ed. 2022) (collecting cases and synthesizing these guidelines).

Example

The CEO of Behemoth Air, Inc., a commercial airline with its most significant base of operations at the Dallas-Fort Worth (DFW) airport, has tired of the price competitiveness at DFW, especially between his firm and its closest rival, Ginormous Airlines Corp. Together, the two firms held about 90 percent of all nonbusiness travelers there, and so were primed for very profitable operations, if they could only temper their price war. He therefore finally called his counterpart at Ginormous, hoping to put it finally to rest. A fairly tense conversation ensued (as one might expect, given that most competitors are acutely aware they are not allowed to discuss competition with one another), in which Behemoth's CEO lamented the profits being lost through the two firms' price warfare. "Do you have a suggestion for me?" asked the Ginormous CEO. "Yes," was the reply, "I have a suggestion for you. Raise your goddamn fares 20 percent. I'll raise mine the next morning. You'll make more money, and I will too." Ginormous Airlines' CEO politely declined and immediately hung up. Unfortunately for Behemoth's CEO, his counterpart had had some inkling that such a call might be coming. He had already contacted the FBI, which had already installed a recording device on his telephone. The conversation was recorded, and the Justice Department brought suit against Behemoth and its CEO. Needless to say, however, there was no actual conspiracy here.

Has anything illegal occurred?

1. *See generally* Lawrence A. Sullivan, Warren S. Grimes & Chris Sagers, *The Law of Antitrust: An Integrated Handbook* 151-152 (3d ed. 2015) (making this point).

Explanation

These were the essential facts in *United States v. Am. Airlines, Inc.*, 743 F.2d 1114 (5th Cir. 1984). American Airlines CEO Robert Crandall called his counterpart, the CEO of Braniff Airlines Howard Putnam, and had the conversation above. Putnam's phone was tapped. The court found that these facts made out a case for attempted monopolization, on the theory that Crandall hoped to combine the two firms' market shares to wield true monopoly power. The court held that the fact that no actual agreement was reached was irrelevant. The facts made out a case for attempted monopolization.

Note that there is no §1 cause of action here, because there is no such thing as a §1 "attempt." Because there was no completed "contract, combination, . . . or conspiracy," there can be no violation of §1.

§14.2 THE §2 CONSPIRACY CAUSE OF ACTION

The §2 conspiracy plaintiff must show that (1) two or more defendants conspired, (2) with specific intent to secure a monopoly, and (3) took at least one overt act in furtherance of their conspiracy. Proof of the conspiracy element is identical to that under Sherman Act §1, and the specific intent requirement is the same as that for attempted monopolization. However, this theory differs in two ways from a claim for either §1 conspiracy or §2 attempted monopoly, and they are ways that at least in some jurisdictions could make §2 conspiracy an important strategic alternative for some plaintiffs.

First, the "overt act" requirement is not the same as the exclusionary conduct element of other §2 causes of action. The act need not even be independently harmful, and in principle can consist of any conduct whatsoever, so long as it could plausibly be part of putting the conspiracy into effect. Maybe more importantly, the courts are split as to whether the plaintiff must show monopoly power or even dangerous probability of success. Prior to *Spectrum Sports*, and following more traditional concepts from the common law of conspiracy, courts ordinarily said there was no requirement to show even dangerous probability of success. Since *Spectrum Sports*, a number of courts have taken that opinion to require proof of dangerous probability (typically meaning that the defendants together hold at least 50 percent of the market in question) or at least that, if the conspiracy were successful, monopolization would be the result. But other courts have continued to hold that there need be no proof of dangerous probability. In those jurisdictions it is not entirely clear how much if any market power must be shown, but presumably a market share less than 50 percent would suffice and possibly even less than might be required for a §1 claim under the rule of reason.

Accordingly, it may be that in some jurisdictions a plaintiff with proof of no more than an actual conspiracy, a specific intent to monopolize, and one overt act might have enough to prove a violation, even if the conspiracy was of a sort that would not trigger a per se rule under §1.

See generally 1 Am. Bar Assn., *Antitrust Law Developments* (Ninth) 348-353 (9th ed. 2022).

§14.3 EVIDENCE OF BUSINESS JUSTIFICATION

Though it is less clear in this context, it appears that the defendant can rebut either an attempt or conspiracy claim under §2 with the same sort of business justification it might put on for a full-blown monopolization case. For example, in *Multistate Leg. Servs. v. Harcourt Brace Jovanovich*, 63 F.3d 1540 (10th Cir. 1995), the only §2 claim before the court was an attempt claim, but the court nevertheless entertained a series of the defendant's proposed business justifications, and ultimately held that some of them raised triable issues of fact. The court did not address the issue of whether they were even relevant in an attempt claim, and simply wrote that the defendant's justifications "can sometimes be a defense to a section 2 claim." Id. at 1550-1552. There is no apparent reason to suspect that the same would not go for conspiracy claims as well.

§14.4 THE PRACTICAL IMPORTANCE OF THE ATTEMPT AND CONSPIRACY THEORIES: PLEADING STRATEGY

One might wonder what good these causes of action do for anybody. The attempt cause of action requires a large showing of market power and accordingly an expensive fact case to put on from the plaintiff's perspective. The conspiracy action requires a showing of multilateral action, with all the difficulties such a showing poses in §1 cases, plus the added challenge of proving subjective intent. Section 2 conspiracy also affords the plaintiff no access to the per se or quick-look treatment available in some §1 cases. And neither theory would entitle the plaintiff to remedies not available for the more familiar §1 or §2 claims.

But in fact these alternative theories can be quite important to plaintiffs. They help to fill in the gap in the Sherman Act between garden-variety conspiracy on the one hand, and full-blown, single-firm monopoly on the other. For this reason plaintiffs alleging the more familiar §1 conspiracy claims or a §2 monopolization claim routinely add either or both a §2 attempt count and a §2 conspiracy count. The idea is that if during the course of litigation the plaintiff fails to show some particular element needed for the more familiar counts, it might still be able to show §2 attempt or conspiracy.[2] If the plaintiff fears it cannot make out the market power showing needed for monopolization and cannot show multilateral conduct under §1, but has some good evidence concerning intent and conduct, it might have an attempt theory as a backup. Likewise, imagine that the plaintiff has evidence of conspiracy but fears it can neither make *any* substantial showing of market power nor allege a per se theory of liability under §1. If the plaintiff has uncommonly good evidence of specific intent to monopolize and some predatory conduct, then at least in some jurisdictions, it might have a §2 conspiracy claim.

2. In antitrust litigation, theories of liability not plead early enough will usually be lost. So, for example, if a plaintiff who has pled only full-blown monopolization loses at the summary judgment or directed verdict stage for failure to prove monopoly power, it will be too late to try to replead the case as an attempt or conspiracy case. The plaintiff will have lost.

PART VII

Antitrust, Innovation, and Intellectual Property

CHAPTER 15

Antitrust, Innovation, and Intellectual Property

§15.1 THE RATIONALIZATION OF TWO POLICIES

Two strong policies in American law are relevant to innovation by private business, and they are in at least some tension. First of all, we actively support innovation, in many ways. A primary support is through intellectual property (IP) law. Technological innovations and business methods can be patented, artistic works can be copyrighted, brands can be trademarked, and various kinds of IP enjoy trade secret and other common law protection. We support it in many other ways. Governments directly subsidize all kinds of research, and they also subsidize it indirectly through tax benefits and many other ways.

The reasons we encourage innovation are essentially economic. Innovation leads either to better products—things people will want more than what is currently available—or ways to make them more cheaply. In effect, innovation leads to better quality-adjusted price competition. The problem is that it may be difficult to make innovations commercially viable, and this is because of a characteristic inherent in the nature of innovation. Once a person has created or invented something, it is difficult to keep other people from copying it. But in creating the thing, the creator will likely have invested some time and money. If other people can just copy the thing when it is made public, and start producing it for sale themselves, they will be able to sell it at the cost of producing it. The creator will then be forced to meet that competition, and will only be able to cover production costs, without being able to recoup the initial investments in research and development.

Under that state of play, the incentive to innovate might be diminished, especially in sectors in which research and development is expensive or uncertain.[1] The basic purpose of our IP law is to deal with these issues. By preventing competitors from immediately copying an IP-protected innovation, we allow the creator to earn some margin of supracompetitive profits for a time, to cover the initial cost of research and development.

But another strong federal policy is in tension with innovation policy. Antitrust (and some other laws) strongly encourages price competition. Price competition in and of itself will eat away at those same profits that IP law seeks to preserve. Even with patent protection, margins that otherwise might encourage investment in innovation might be too small to support research and development work. At least where markets are very competitive, there might be little incentive for innovation, except for innovation in the production process and distribution of goods. (Those innovations can reduce cost and help secure new business through lower prices.)

To clarify one thing, all these problems of policy are hugely controversial and depend on empirical questions that remain unanswered and may be unanswerable. First, despite decades of empirical research, no one knows whether innovation is better encouraged by protection from price competition—as implied in IP policy—or whether it might be better encouraged by regular old competition itself. After all, as explained in Chapter 2, one key mechanism by which competition is thought to improve the working of markets is that it continually pressures firms to improve their product quality or find cheaper production processes.[2] Second, even if innovation does call for some shelter from direct price rivalry, it entails trade-offs of competing values that probably cannot be measured. How far must competition be limited to reach a desirable amount of innovation investment? How much will that innovation be worth, and is it worth more than the harm caused when the innovator is protected from competition? How much consumer harm can we live with just to get better products for people who can afford them? These and similar questions probably can't even be measured empirically, much less will there ever be any real consensus.

Whatever might be the right answer to those broad policy questions, there is a more direct and technical conflict between IP and antitrust. The very tool through which IP law encourages innovation is to give some measure of market power through the exclusive right to produce the innovative

1. In other words, there is an *externality* here. Innovation creates a positive externality, a benefit that other people can take without paying for. That is thought to be bad for allocational efficiency because knowing they won't be able to fully exploit the returns on their investment, creators will create less than might have been desired by society. Externalities are discussed in §2.4 and the Glossary.

2. *See generally* Richard Gilbert, *Looking for Mr. Schumpeter: Where Are We in the Competition-Innovation Debate*, in Innovation Policy and the Economy 159 (Adam B. Jaffe, Josh Lerner & Scott Stern, eds. 2005) (summarizing empirical literature).

thing. Antitrust takes market power as its central enemy. This opposition of the two policies has led to a number of specific antitrust doctrines, and they will be the subject of this chapter. In most cases where IP and antitrust conflict, the courts' concern will be whether the IP holder has taken some improper action to expand the scope of its IP. It is the nature of IP to restrain competition, but the courts have said that antitrust is a countervailing policy which makes it illegal to stretch the restraint beyond the specific grant of IP rights granted by the government. *See, e.g., Walker Process Equip. v. Food Mach. & Chem. Corp.*, 382 U.S. 172, 180 (1965) (Harlan, J., concurring) (stating the need to "achiev[e] a suitable accommodation in this area between the differing policies of the patent and antitrust laws").

§15.2 SPECIFIC ANTITRUST APPLICATIONS

On the one hand, it is clear that conduct affirmatively *permitted* by the IP laws is immune from antitrust. Most obviously, creating something and protecting it with IP is per se legal, as is producing the creation and a lot of the ways in which one might sell the right to do it. *See generally Unitherm Food Sys. v. Swift-Eckrich, Inc.*, 375 F.3d 1341, 1356 (Fed. Cir. 2004), *rev'd on other grounds* 546 U.S. 394 (2006) ("As a general rule, behavior conforming to the patent laws oriented towards procuring or enforcing a patent enjoys immunity from the antitrust laws."). Likewise, courts will generally read antitrust rules to be relaxed where needed to permit firms to use their lawfully acquired IP as they like. In one famous observation, which is perhaps a bit excessive in its Latin, the Supreme Court wrote that "[t]he patent laws which give a 17-year monopoly on 'making, using, or selling the invention' are *in pari materia* with the antitrust laws and modify them *pro tanto*." *Simpson v. Union Oil Co. of California*, 377 U.S. 13, 24 (1964). The phrase "in pari materia" is a reference to the rule of statutory construction under which two statutes on the same subject matter must be read together to achieve harmony where possible, and one read to modify the other where they irreconcilably conflict. *See* 2B *Sutherland on Statutes and Statutory Construction* §51:2 (Norman J. Singer & Shambie Singer, eds., 7th ed. 2010). "Pro tanto" just means "to the extent of." So, *Simpson* held that the patent and antitrust laws must be construed together, and that where there is an inconsistency between them the patent laws modify the antitrust laws to the extent of the inconsistency.

But this simple immunity only goes so far. The courts have observed a whole range of ways in which a person might use IP that go too far, invade competition policy too much, and violate antitrust. "It is . . . well settled," one court said, "that concerted and contractual behavior that threatens competition is not immune from antitrust inquiry simply because it involves the exercise of [IP] privileges." *Data Gen. Corp. v. Grumman Sys. Support Corp.*, 36 F.3d

1147, 1185 n.63 (1st Cir. 1994). As one court rather more colorfully put it, the view of many IP holders that their IP gives them immunity just to do whatever they want "is no more correct than the proposition that the use of one's . . . baseball bat cannot give rise to tort liability." *United States v. Microsoft Corp.*, 253 F.3d 34, 63 (D.C. Cir. 2001).

In the remainder of this section we will consider the most prominent scenarios in which the use of IP might violate antitrust.

§15.2.1 Acquisition of Legitimate Intellectual Property as an Antitrust Violation

IP is an "asset" within the meaning of Clayton Act §7, and so acquisitions of IP whose effect "may be substantially to lessen competition, or to tend to create a monopoly" are illegal. As such, acquisitions of IP that are large enough to trigger the filing thresholds are subject to pre-acquisition review under the Hart-Scott-Rodino Act. (*See* Chapters 17 and 18.) Patterns of acquisitions that create market power and exclude competitors can also violate Sherman Act §1 or §2. For example, in *Kobe, Inc. v. Dempsey Pump Co.*, 198 F.2d 416, 423-424 (10th Cir. 1952), the Tenth Circuit found a §2 violation where the defendant acquired every important patent in a given field—dozens of them over a significant period—but failed to produce anything under most of them and merely enforced them against would-be competitors. *See generally* 2 Am. Bar Assn., *Antitrust Law Developments (Sixth)* 1083-1085 (6th ed. 2007).

That said, this theory of liability plainly applies only to *acquisitions* of IP previously granted to someone else. It seems extremely unlikely that one's own creative activities, and legitimate steps to protect them with IP, could ever violate antitrust. Clayton Act §7 and the Hart-Scott-Rodino Act would presumably have no applicability, as they apply only to "acquisitions." Likewise, one's own inventions and a firm's internal research and development efforts would lack the multiplicity of actors required for Sherman Act §1, and §2 never applies to a firm's growth through "superior skill, foresight, and industry." *See generally Unitherm*, 375 F.3d at 1356.

It is at least conceivable that *joint* research and production work shared among two or more firms could give rise to §1 or §7 liability, but it seems unlikely that it could arise from the innovation work itself. Where firms set up R&D joint ventures, they might share substantial amounts of information or agree to restraints not directly related to the work of the venture, and those activities might be illegal. But so long as the venture's claims for IP to cover its work are legitimate as a matter of IP law, it is in effect impossible that those claims could generate §1 liability. And even if a §1 plaintiff might like to try, the venturers would likely enjoy the protection of the National Cooperative Research and Production Act, 15 U.S.C. §§4301-4306.

The NCRPA provides: (a) that the conduct of R&D joint ventures can be challenged only under the rule of reason modified by a special, very pro-defendant standard for market definition; (b) that, as long as the venturers have filed a special notice with the enforcement agencies, the plaintiff can recover only single damages and attorney fees; and (c) that if the plaintiff loses, the defendants can recover their attorney fees.

§15.2.2 Improper Extension or Abuse of Otherwise Legitimate Intellectual Property

§15.2.2(a) Nonuse

If a firm acquires an IP right in some new innovation, but then simply refuses to produce anything under the right or to allow anyone else to do so, we might think that is both an anticompetitive outcome and a subversion of IP policy. However, the holder of an IP right may choose simply not to use it, and unilateral nonuse in itself cannot violate antitrust. *See Hartford-Empire Co. v. United States*, 323 U.S. 386, 432-433 (1945) ("A patent owner is not in the position of a quasi-trustee for the public or under any obligation to see that the public acquires the free right to use the invention. He has no obligation either to use it or to grant its use to others."); *Standard Oil Co. v. United States*, 283 U.S. 163, 179 (1931). But as mentioned above, some case law holds that acquisition of patents from others, for the purpose of excluding substitute products from a monopolist's market, could constitute actionable exclusion under Sherman Act §2. *See Kobe, Inc. v. Dempsey Pump Co.*, 198 F.2d 416, 423-424 (10th Cir. 1952).

§15.2.2(b) Objectively Baseless Infringement Claims

IP is enforced, as a practical matter, by the bringing of lawsuits. If the IP holder brings an infringement action against a competitor asserting rights under the IP that are plainly beyond the rights actually given, that in principle might seem anticompetitive. The courts have never disagreed with that idea. However, an infringement action, like other lawsuits, is a "petition of government" and will enjoy antitrust immunity under the *Noerr-Pennington* doctrine unless it is a "sham." (*See* §21.4.) In fact, the Supreme Court has made it very difficult to show that a lawsuit is a sham. In *Profl. Real Estate Investors, Inc. v. Columbia Pictures Indus., Inc.*, 508 U.S. 49 (1993), the Court held that a lawsuit is a sham only where (1) the legal claim is objectively baseless (meaning that no reasonable litigant could expect recovery under it) *and* (2) the plaintiff's subjective motivation in bringing the suit was anticompetitive.

In a leading case, the Federal Circuit stated in dicta that the bringing of a sham infringement claim could constitute the "exclusionary conduct" component of a Sherman Act §2 claim. *Nobelpharma AB v. Implant Innovations, Inc.*, 141 F.3d 1059 (Fed. Cir. 1998). Importantly, this is to be distinguished from the special case in which the IP holder brings an infringement action on a patent that was procured from the federal Patent and Trademark Office through deliberate fraud. If the infringement defendant can show that species of fraud, then the antitrust counterclaim, known as a *Walker Process* claim, becomes much easier than the showing of sham under *Professional Real Estate Investors*. This is further explained in §15.2.4. (*See also* §13.3.6(c).)

§15.2.2(c) Standard Setting and the Patent Hold-Up Problem

Since the explosion in high technology that began in the 1980s, the work of standard setting organizations (SSOs) has become omnipresent in technology sectors. SSOs are usually privately organized, not-for-profit entities whose purpose is to issue formal guidance about the doing of various things. There are tens or hundreds of thousands of them at work in the United States now, and their work touches upon matters literally throughout the U.S. economy. Their standards can become influential in a variety of ways. They can be incorporated into law, and they are with surprising frequency, often with very little substantive oversight by the governments that adopt them. But they can also become influential through their own independent force. Technology sectors often experience a need for "interoperability." A fax machine has little value if it cannot communicate with other fax machines, because of incompatible software. The value of a computer peripheral device might be diminished if the plug that connects it to a computer is incompatible with most computers. The value of software applications is drastically improved by standards that allow them to work on or communicate with different devices and platforms. For these reasons, high tech manufacturers have for some decades worked collaboratively through SSOs to design technological standards to ensure interoperability.

In any case, the work of SSOs has raised another issue at the IP-antitrust interface. Because SSOs' members commonly include representatives from the industries affected by their standards, much of their conduct is at least nominally subject to antitrust. Adoption of a standard can violate antitrust, especially when it amounts to an unjustified boycott of the product of a competitor to the SSO's own members.[3] More recently one specific sort of

---

3. Two well-known cases were *Allied Tube & Conduit Corp. v. Indian Head, Inc.*, 486 U.S. 492 (1988), and *Am. Socy. of Mech. Engrs. v. Hydrolevel Corp.*, 456 U.S. 556 (1982), in both of which the Court upheld antitrust liability where manufacturers who were SSO members used SSO procedures to injure competitors. Going back a bit further, in *Radiant Burners, Inc. v. People's Light & Coke Co.*, 364 U.S. 656 (1961), the Court permitted an antitrust action to proceed against an SSO itself where there were allegations that its repeated refusals to approve a new technology were anticompetitively motivated.

standard-setting conduct has become of keen interest, and it is relevant to the IP related issues: the so-called "patent hold-up."

A patent hold-up occurs when an SSO participant either fails to disclose that it owns patents that would be infringed by the adoption of a standard, or refuses to license them after they are included in a standard. Assuming a standard becomes significant in the industry, that participant may then acquire a significant degree of market power it otherwise would not have. To prevent such abuses, SSOs commonly require members to disclose IP they own that could be covered by a standard under consideration, and to license any IP that is incorporated in a standard on terms that are "fair, reasonable, and non-discriminatory" (FRAND). Notwithstanding these policies, however, abuses still occur, and they can generate antitrust liability.

In recent years the Federal Trade Commission has taken the lead in enforcement against this sort of conduct, and in several cases the Commission has succeeded in imposing liability. These cases, however, must be balanced against two major monopolization actions that the Commission ultimately lost, and that will pose major challenges for hold-up cases. First, *Rambus, Inc. v. FTC*, 522 F.3d 456 (D.C. Cir. 2008), characterized the question before it as whether *deception* could constitute actionable "exclusion" under §2. The Commission sued Rambus for failing to disclose that it owned patents that would be covered by the adoption of a standard by an SSO of which it was a member. The court emphasized that defendant Rambus was "an otherwise lawful monopolist," because its power emanated from legitimate patents, and held that "use of deception simply to obtain higher prices normally has no particular tendency to exclude rivals and thus to diminish competition." *Id.* at 439. The court believed that it had not been adequately shown that the SSO in that case would not have adopted Rambus's technology as its standard had Rambus disclosed its patent rights. That being the case, the court believed that the only harm was that Rambus would earn more money from the licensing of its rights than it would had the SSO been aware of the patents and had it required Rambus to accept some reasonable royalty rates prior to adoption of the patents. As to that, the court applied its general understanding of the law under §2—that merely to exact higher profits via lawfully acquired market power is never in itself an antitrust violation.

Ten years later, *FTC v. Qualcomm, Inc.*, 969 F.3d 975 (9th Cir. 2020) again rejected a hold-up claim, and expressed similar skepticism that hold-up threatens anticompetitive harm. *Qualcomm* is a factually dense, complicated case, and several of its holdings are likely to remain controversial. But at least some of them will probably be important going forward. Qualcomm, a dominant maker of computer chips used in cellphones, secured inclusion of its patents in standards with which as a practical matter every cellphone must comply. Qualcomm disclosed those patents during the standard setting process and agreed to license them on FRAND terms. However, it took a very aggressive view of its own FRAND duties. First, it refused to license its patents to any other makers of computer chips, and instead licensed only the makers of the cellphones that would incorporate them. That was to increase its profits: because the retail price of a cellphone is much higher than what any manufacturer would pay for the components that go into it, end-product manufacturers can be coerced to pay much higher royalties than an upstream chip maker would be willing to pay. According to the FTC and the lower court, the policy was also designed to frustrate the entry and growth of rival chip makers. Second, Qualcomm refused to supply its own chips to cellphone makers unless they first agreed to license its patents as well. (Recall that Qualcomm was also a dominant manufacturer of the cellphone chips themselves.) The license it required them to take was actually unnecessary, because under patent law's "exhaustion" doctrine, an initial sale of the chips to the cellphone maker would extinguish all of Qualcomm's patent rights in them. The Ninth Circuit held both practices legal. It found no antitrust duty to license patents to rival chip makers, even though Qualcomm had made FRAND commitments.[4] It likewise found no injury caused by the demand that end-use cellphone makers take chip licenses. The court reasoned that someone somewhere in the process of making cellphones would have to pay Qualcomm a royalty, since no cellphone could be made without infringing its patents. On the court's view of the facts, Qualcomm's policy would not make rival chip makers' chips more expensive than Qualcomm's chips, and it also imposed to different cost on cellphone makers, regardless whose chips they bought.

§15.2.3 Licensing Issues as to Legitimate Intellectual Property

§15.2.3(a) Licensing or Refusal to License

The grant of a license to use legitimate IP cannot in itself violate antitrust. Likewise, some lower courts now mostly recognize a rule of per se legality for unilateral *refusals* to license IP rights, although the Supreme Court has never quite so held. If this rule in the lower courts accurately states the law, then it is an exception to the general rule on refusals to deal. Recall that while a single firm acting unilaterally has a broad freedom to choose with whom it will do business, *United States v. Colgate*, 250 U.S. 300 (1919), there is an exception where the firm holds monopoly power and its refusal amounts to "exclusionary" conduct. While the modern Court takes the view that the right to refuse to deal is very broad, *see, e.g., Verizon Commcns. Inc. v. Law Offices of*

4. For this ruling, the court relied primarily on *Verizon Commcns. Inc. v. Law Offices of Curtis V. Trinko, LLP*, 540 U.S. 398 (2004), as to which, *see* §13.3.4.

Curtis V. Trinko, LLP, 540 U.S. 398 (2004), it is not unlimited. Where it is unduly exclusionary, the refusal can violate Sherman Act §2. (*See* §13.3.4.)

There have been indications over the years that despite language in the Supreme Court's earlier opinions, which had suggested that the right to refuse a license is unqualified, sometimes an IP holder's refusal to license can be part of an antitrust violation. The lower courts are currently split on the question. The First and Ninth Circuits have held that a refusal to license IP is presumed to be permissible, but the presumption can be rebutted by evidence that the defendant's explanation for its refusal was pretextual. *See Image Technical Servs. v. Eastman Kodak Co.*, 125 F.3d 1195 (9th Cir. 1997); *Data Gen. Corp. v. Grumman Sys. Support Corp.*, 36 F.3d 1147 (1st Cir. 1994). As an example of evidence that the explanation is pretextual, the *Image Technical Services* court pointed out that the defendant had a blanket policy refusing any licensing of certain replacement parts for its machines, when in fact only 65 percent of the parts were covered by any patent. 125 F.3d at 1219. In any event, another circuit has held that refusals to license otherwise lawful IP are per se legal. *In re Indep. Serv. Orgs. Antitrust Litig.*, 203 F.3d 1322 (Fed. Cir. 2000).

The matter is entirely different with a *concerted* refusal to license IP. Such agreements are taken quite seriously and are sometimes held to be per se illegal. Even where a court believes there might be some redeeming virtue, an agreement restraining the members' freedom to license their IP will be subject to rule-of-reason challenge. *See* 2 Am. Bar Assn., *Antitrust Law Developments (Sixth)* 1127-1128 (6th ed. 2007).

§15.2.3(b) Trade-Restraining License Terms

Whatever may be the freedom of the IP owner to license or refuse to license, the *terms* agreed to between licensor and licensee can violate antitrust.

In its earliest cases, the Supreme Court suggested that an IP holder can include such terms as it likes in a license. In *United States v. Gen. Elec.*, 272 U.S. 476 (1926), for example, the Court so ruled on a greater-includes-the-lesser line of reasoning. Since G.E. was free not to license at all, it could license with such restrictions as it saw fit. (In that case, the Court upheld minimum resale price terms included in a license to make light bulbs.) Likewise, early decisions recognized very broad freedom to adopt territorial or customer restraints on licensees. *Ethyl Gasoline Corp. v. United States*, 309 U.S. 436 (1940). The courts have also always broadly upheld "field of use" restrictions—license terms that permit the licensee to produce the technology for only one particular purposes. *See, e.g., Gen. Talking Pictures Corp. v. W. Elec. Co.*, 304 U.S. 175 (1938) (upholding a term limiting the production of sound amplifier technology only for public theater use, and not for home use).

In later cases, however, the Court began to find some distinctions from these early, very broad rules, and in particular from the rule of per se legality for price restraints in *General Electric*. The first important distinction was drawn in *United States v. Line Material Co.*, 333 U.S. 287 (1948), where the Court described *General Electric* as "directed at agreements between a patentee and a licensee to make and vend. [The opinion] carr[ies] no implication of approval of all a patentee's contracts which tend to increase earnings on patents." Accordingly, *General Electric* does not require "otherwise than that the precise terms of the grant define the limits of a patentee's monopoly and the area in which the patentee is freed from competition of price, service, quality or otherwise." *Id.* at 299-300.

Over time, the courts have recognized several specific arrangements under which the terms of a license can be challenged under antitrust. First, ever since *General Electric* was decided, there has been agitation to find exceptions for *price* restraints. It remains the law under *General Electric* that a patentee may put resale price restraints on a licensee that is licensed to produce and sell the patented technology. However, *Line Material* and several other cases have clarified that price restraints cannot be made in coordination with *other* patentee firms. Two firms, for example, might have patents covering what could be competing and noninfringing technologies. If, acting in concert, they agree to impose minimum resale prices on their licensees, there is a per se violation of §1. *See, e.g., United States v. New Wrinkle, Inc.*, 342 U.S. 371 (1952). Similarly, if they "cross-license" their patents to one another, and agree that each of them may then sublicense all of their patents as one package, but only subject to minimum resale price terms, they have violated §1. *Line Material*, 333 U.S. at 287.

The early rule on territorial and customer restraints has fared better than the *General Electric* rule, probably because language in the Patent Act seems specifically to contemplate such licensing restrictions. However, there have been cases finding that a license with a territorial restriction is really just a disguised horizontal market allocation, in which case the arrangement is likely per se illegal. For example, say that two manufacturers of sporting goods are in the process of developing a new inflatable ball technology. They both manage to secure patents on their differing designs. Fearing competition among their substitutable new products, they agree each to grant the other a license to produce both technologies, but subject to the condition that one sells in the western United States and the other in the eastern United States. Such an agreement is illegal.

Exclusivity terms can also be illegal in at least two ways. First, where the patentee agrees with the licensee that it will not license the patent to others, and where they might have been competitors or where other potential licensees would have been competitors, the enforcement agencies have treated the agreement as an "acquisition" by the licensee of an "asset" subject to Clayton Act §7 and the pre-acquisition filing requirements of the Hart-Scott-Rodino Act (*see* Chapters 17 and 18). Second, if the patentee prohibits the licensee from using competing technologies, the arrangement can be challenged like other exclusive dealing contracts, under the rule of reason. *See* 2 Am. Bar Assn., *Antitrust Law Developments (Sixth)* 1103-1104 (6th ed. 2007).

Example

Next Frontier Technology, Inc. (NFTI) is a nonprofit corporation established by participants in the telecommunications industry to develop the next generation of electronic communications. NFTI itself has no significant resources and does not perform its own technological research, but NFTI members agree to disclose to one another discoveries they desire to be included in NFTI designs. Their main goal is to agree among themselves as to software designs they each will employ, to achieve "interoperability"—to ensure that buyers of the devices they produce will be able to communicate with each other.

NFTI members agree that they will disclose the fact of any IP they own that might be infringed by any product design to be adopted by NFTI, whether the design is adopted at their own urging or that of another member. They agree that if they own IP included in a design they will license it to any other member on reasonable and nondiscriminatory license terms, and that when they produce a product on a NFTI design that incorporates another member's IP, they will not produce products on competing designs.

Does any aspect of the NFTI arrangement violate antitrust?

Explanation

Yes, the agreement not to produce competing designs is likely illegal. On the one hand, insofar as NFTI members "disclose . . . discoveries" for inclusion in shared software designs they will incorporate in their products, NFTI is just a garden-variety SSO. Likewise, the agreements that members will disclose their IP and license it when it is included in NFTI product design standards are *pro*competitive. They ensure that no member can squeeze more supracompetitive profitability out of their IP than would otherwise be available.

On the other hand, the agreement not to make noninfringing products on a non-NFTI design, just because some NFTI design happens to incorporate a member's IP, is likely illegal. It constitutes an agreement not to compete—NFTI members appear to be horizontal competitors, and when competitors agree to make only certain products and not others, they ordinarily will have made a per se illegal horizontal agreement not to compete. A case on point would be the *New Wrinkle* decision, mentioned above. Arguably this agreement might be ancillary to the creation of the NFTI itself, and therefore might enjoy rule-of-reason treatment, but it is hard to see why. Agreements are ancillary where they are reasonably related to some larger procompetitive arrangement and reasonably needed to achieve its procompetitive advantages. NFTI is surely a procompetitive arrangement, but an agreement not to produce products that would compete with NFTI members' IP seems only useful to preserving the profitability of that IP. Therefore, it is likely not ancillary. (The ancillary restraints rule is discussed in §7.2.)

Example

Far-Fri, the nation's leading provider of bar exam preparation courses, sold its courses profitably in the state of Idaho for several years, as until recently it faced no competition there. But an upstart firm, launched by recent law school graduates disgruntled at the high prices of Far-Fri's product, has begun offering its own Idaho bar course, and the two firms for a few years have been locked in fierce price competition. At length, representatives of both firms meet, and they agree to an arrangement to calm the ferocity between them: In exchange for the local firm's agreement not to sell bar prep courses outside of Idaho, Far-Fri will appoint that firm its exclusive agent for sales within Idaho. That is, the upstart firm will thereafter actually start selling the Far-Fri product in Idaho, and even Far-Fri itself will no longer sell that course in Idaho. The agreement also provides that for every Far-Fri course that the local firm sells in Idaho, it will pay Far-Fri a royalty of $100 (which, at the time of the agreement, is about 40 percent of the going price of the Far-Fri course).

Is there any violation of antitrust law?

Explanation

Yes. These were the facts in *Palmer v. BRG of Georgia, Inc.*, 498 U.S. 46 (1990). The Court had no difficulty discerning that though the agreement in that case was fashioned as a license for the upstart firm to sell the national firm's product, it was in substance just a market allocation agreement. The Court held it per se illegal.

§15.2.3(c) Blocking Patents, Cross-Licensing, and Patent Pools

A common problem in patent law has been that a particular technology, in order to work well or to be commercially viable, must be made in such a way that it would be covered by more than one patent. Unless all of the covering patents are owned by one person, there may be a frustration of the ability of any of the patentees to exploit the value of their patents. They cannot themselves produce a viable product without infringing other patents, and they cannot license their patents to a licensee unless that firm can also get licenses for all the other covering patents. In cases such as these the patents are known as "blocking patents." The common solution has been for the patentees to negotiate an arrangement called a "cross-license" or "patent pool." Under such a deal, they each agree to license their own patents to the other members of the pool, with permission to sublicense all the blocking IP required so that their own licensees can produce viable and noninfringing products.

In keeping with the general view in antitrust that multilateral conduct is of more concern, licensing and other restraints adopted in pools of IP are subjected to more antitrust scrutiny than a firm licensing its own IP unilaterally. First of all, patent pools or cross-licensing of any kind are received with much suspicion unless they include *only* blocking patents. That is, there is no accepted justification for creating any sort of cross-licensing arrangement between the holders of IP for competing products. The only exception would be for those cases, as in *Broad. Music Inc. v. Columbia Broad. Sys.*, 441 U.S. 1 (1979) ("BMI"), in which the holders of small-dollar-value IP would have very difficult problems negotiating licenses and enforcing the payment of royalties. (*See* §6.2.1(c).) But note that even groups like these—groups organized collectively to license and enforce small-value IP, often known as "collective rights organizations" or "collective management organizations"—are subject to a fair degree of suspicion. The defendants in the BMI case, for example, have faced antitrust challenge many times, and have operated under antitrust consent decrees continuously overseen by judges of the Southern District of New York since the 1940s.

Where a pool covers blocking patents, the arrangement itself is likely permissible. However, restraints imposed on the use of the cross-licensed patents can violate antitrust. The courts are most concerned about price or other restraints that will allow the individual patentees to extend the trade restraining power granted under their own patents. As mentioned above, courts have found it illegal for the cross-licensees in a patent pool to include resale price restraints in their sublicenses of the patents. By doing so, the members would be imposing restraints under patents that they do not personally own, but are merely licensed to sell through sublicenses.

§15.2.3(d) The "First Sale" Doctrine and the Tying Rule

Two other important doctrines constrain the power of IP holders to extend their lawful IP monopoly. First, in patent law, while there is some broad freedom to impose restrictions through *licenses*, there is no freedom to impose any restrictions on the use or resale of patented products that the patentee itself makes *and then sells*. For example, in the leading case of *United States v. Univis Lens Co.*, 316 U.S. 241 (1942), a manufacturer held patents for multifocal eyeglass lenses. It manufactured glass "blanks," which were disks made of two different kinds of glass fused together, and which could be finished into multifocal eyeglasses. The blanks would work as eyeglass lenses only when ground and polished according to prescription for each individual patient, and the manufacturer did not perform that work on its own. Rather, it employed a network of distributors and optometrists that had facilities for finishing the blanks according to prescription. The manufacturer sold the blanks to those firms outright, along with a license to employ its process for the finishing, but also required them to sell at no less than a minimum resale price.

The Court held this illegal, because a restraint was imposed on resale of a good that the patentee had already manufactured under its patent. Because "[t]he full extent of the monopoly is the patentee's exclusive right to make use, and vend the invention," wrote the Court,

> [t]he patentee . . . surrender[s] his monopoly in whole by the sale of his patent or in part by the sale of an article embodying the invention. . . . [S]ale of it exhausts the monopoly in that article and the patentee may not there after, by virtue of his patent, control the use or disposition of the article. Hence the patentee cannot control the resale price of patented articles which he has sold, either by resort to an infringement suit, or, consistently with the Sherman Act . . . , by stipulating for price maintenance by his vendees.

Id. at 250.

A conceptually similar rule is that the general doctrine of tying applies even though the "tying" product happens to be protected by IP. In these cases the courts justify application of antitrust to an IP license by pointing out that the IP holder is attempting to extend the restraining power of its lawful IP beyond the terms of the grant of IP. As long as the plaintiff can make out the other elements of a tying cause of action, the fact that the tying good is protected by IP is irrelevant. (As to tying generally, *see* Chapter 11.)

§15.2.3(e) Settlements of IP Litigation and the "Reverse Payments" or "Pay for Delay" Problem: *FTC v. Actavis*

Finally, there is one special antitrust problem surrounding IP-related settlements of litigation. Because of special statutory provisions governing pharmaceutical patents, a pattern arose during the past three or four decades in which makers of patented drugs reached agreements with other drug makers that might like to enter their markets, in which the incumbent would make large payments to keep them out.

On that description such an agreement might seem pretty obviously illegal, as a market-allocation scheme in violation of straightforward cases like *Palmer v. BRG of Georgia, Inc.*, 498 U.S. 46 (1990) (*see* §6.2.2). But it turns out that these deals were a fair bit more complex than this description makes them sound, mainly because of a special statutory scheme surrounding pharmaceutical patents. The irony is that the statute was designed to make drug markets *more* competitive, in large part by encouraging entrants to challenge questionable patents. But inadvertently the statute invited patented incumbents and would-be entrants simply to reach agreements in which the incumbent paid the entrant in exchange for the entrant's agreement not to challenge the validity of the incumbent's patent.[5] Importantly, these deals—which came to be known as "reverse payment" settlements—are unusual in one key sense. They are "reverse" settlements because it is the incumbent manufacturer that pays the would-be entrant to settle the lawsuit. But, strictly speaking, the incumbent in these lawsuits is the *plaintiff*, alleging that entrant (who is the defendant in the suit) will infringe the incumbent's patent by entering the market. The parties to them nevertheless argued that they were just settlements of legitimate patent litigation, and not the naked market allocations that their critics said they were. Because of their reverse nature and allegedly anticompetitive effect, critics called them not "reverse payments," but "pay for delay."

Most lower courts to consider these deals found them to be legal, and indeed a few found them nearly per se legal. But the Supreme Court recently disagreed, in *FTC v. Actavis*, 570 U.S. 136 (2013), finding that they are likely illegal in any case in which the payment made by the incumbent is "large," in comparison to the costs of litigation and the value of the underlying patent. Strictly speaking, the *Actavis* Court claimed that it was only announcing a full-blown rule-of-reason standard, and explicitly refused to adopt any rule of "quick-look" review or presumptive illegality. However, while it is too soon really to tell how its standard will play out in litigation, the details of the Court's opinion again suggest that it had in mind a specialized, structured cause of action in which a plaintiff needs to show only that there was some payment, which was "reverse" (which, again, means that in some other, prior lawsuit, a *plaintiff* made a payment to a *defendant*, in exchange for dropping a lawsuit), and which was "large" in relation to the costs of the underlying litigation. If a party challenging such a settlement can make those showings, then it need not make any showing of market power or anticompetitive injury, and the defendant can defend only on narrow grounds.

---

5. Specifically, a statute known as the Hatch-Waxman Act provides that where a would-be entrant would like to begin making a drug, but an incumbent manufacturer of it has a patent covering the drug, the entrant may make a special filing with the Food and Drug Administration indicating its intent to challenge the validity of the patent. That filing triggers a holding period in which no other person may attempt to enter the market, and in which the entrant and the incumbent are supposed to resolve the issue of patent validity. Again, the goal of the statute was procompetitive in that it was meant to encourage challenges to patents that might be invalid. But in practice, the parties realized that the filing automatically put them in the posture of parties to patent validity litigation, which they claimed merely to "settle" by reaching agreement not to compete.

§15.2.4 Enforcement of Wrongfully Acquired Intellectual Property

Separate questions arise where a person tries to take advantage of IP rights that turn out to be unenforceable. Antitrust has been especially concerned where a firm acquires a patent through fraud on the government. In the leading case, *Walker Process Equip. v. Food Mach. & Chem. Corp.*, 382 U.S. 172 (1965), a firm allegedly procured a patent from the federal Patent and Trademark Office by concealing the fact that the invention had already been publicly available for a time before the patent application (and therefore was unpatentable). The firm then brought an infringement action against a competitor, which in a counterclaim argued that the enforcement of a fraudulently acquired patent was an effort at monopolization. The Court held that an attempt of this nature, to enforce a patent procured by fraud, could itself be "exclusionary conduct" supporting a cause of action under Sherman Act §2.

This *Walker Process* cause of action poses a minor logic problem under the *Noerr-Pennington* antitrust immunity. (*See* §21.4.) The filing of a patent infringement action, like the filing of any other lawsuit, constitutes a "petition of government" and is protected by *Noerr-Pennington*. The *Walker Process* decision was handed down before the *Noerr-Pennington* rule had been fully elaborated through caselaw, and before it had become clear that lawsuits, too, could constitute "petitions." Moreover, while there is an exception to *Noerr-Pennington* wherever a petition is really just a "sham," the Supreme Court in *Professional Real Estate Investors, Inc. v. Columbia Pictures Indus., Inc.*, 508 U.S. 49 (1993), made it extremely difficult to demonstrate a "sham" where the petitioning in question is a lawsuit. So the problem is that *Walker Process* seemed to commend enthusiastically a cause of action that would almost always be barred by *Noerr-Pennington*.

But as it happens, *Professional Real Estate Investors* appears to have carved out a fairly large exception for conduct in adjudicatory contexts that is *deceptive*. The Court reserved the question "whether and . . . to what extent *Noerr* permits the imposition of antitrust liability for a litigant's fraud or other misrepresentations," and specifically noted that it was not deciding whether a *Walker Process* claimant must show that the patent infringement claim brought against it was "objectively baseless" and subjectively ill-motivated. *Id.* at 61 n.6. (Those are the two requirements that the Court *does* impose to prove that nondeceptive lawsuits are "shams" under *Professional Real Estate Investors*. They are very difficult to establish.) In the leading lower court opinion to reach the issue after *Professional Real Estate Investors*, the Federal Circuit held that a party could challenge enforcement of a fraudulently procured patent if it could show *either* that the patent was acquired through "knowing and willful fraud"—the *Walker Process* standard—or that the lawsuit was a sham under *Professional Real Estate Investors*. The practical effect of this holding is that there are two different ways that an infringement defendant can challenge the infringement action as an antitrust violation. First, if there was fraud on the PTO, the infringement defendant may have a *Walker Process* counterclaim. Second, even if there is no evidence of any misconduct before the PTO, and the patent is otherwise valid, the infringement defendant might argue that the legal theory on which the infringement claim is based is so faulty, and the infringement plaintiff's subjective motivations so anticompetitive, that the infringement claim is simply a "sham" under *Professional Real Estate Investors.* In that case, the filing of the suit itself might constitute the exclusionary conduct element of a §2 claim. *See Nobelpharma AB v. Implant Innovations, Inc.*, 141 F.3d 1059 (Fed. Cir. 1998).

PART VIII

Price Discrimination

CHAPTER 16

Price Discrimination and the Robinson-Patman Act

§16.1 THE PHENOMENON AND ITS COMPETITIVE SIGNIFICANCE

Price discrimination means charging different buyers different prices for the same thing. (That is actually a bit imprecise, but we will add more precision below.) Where it can be accomplished it can be profitable, and it can cause two harms that are both of concern to antitrust law: It reduces consumer surplus and under some circumstances it reduces overall economic welfare. The reason that price discrimination can be so profitable is that, on the one hand, it may transfer surplus from the consumer to the producer, but on the other hand, it does not necessarily cause any decrease in the output demanded. Let us consider an example.

Suppose that a seller could somehow develop really sophisticated information about each specific consumer's willingness to pay for a good. If the seller could get each consumer to pay the most that they are willing to pay for the good, the seller could make more profit than otherwise would be the case, and possibly a *lot* more. In any market, there are likely to be some sellers who are willing to pay only the bare minimum price needed to cover the cost of producing the thing. That is, at least a few buyers would be willing to buy the thing only at the competitive price. But at least some of the buyers for any good—and ordinarily, it is thought, most of the buyers—would probably be willing to pay at least a little bit more for it. They might just like it more, or they might be wealthier, and other things being equal a person with more wealth should be willing to pay more for any good. As explained in §2.3.4, when the good is sold at the competitive price, there is a special little bonus enjoyed by all those consumers who would have been willing to pay more for the good. They get the good, *and* they get to keep the extra money they would have been willing to pay for it. Economists call that extra bonus "consumer surplus." But consumers get to keep that extra little bonus only if the seller sells at one, fixed price. If the seller can figure out what each consumer is actually willing to pay, and then actually get them to pay it, the seller would extract that bonus from them without losing the sale. If the seller could figure out the one special, maximum price that *every* consumer is willing to pay, and charge the special price to each consumer, then it could extract all of their consumer surplus *without losing any of its sales.*

But notice something else. While there is a transfer of wealth here that consumers themselves might consider undesirable, the fact that there are no lost sales has a surprising consequence for the social desirability of the practice. Because there are still exactly as many units being sold, the only economic effect is a transfer of wealth from consumers to producers. Recall that the normative goal most prevalent in current economics is to maximize "allocational efficiency." But as explained in Chapters 2 and 3, allocational efficiency has nothing to do with the *distribution* of wealth. So under the commonly accepted normative view of most economists, price discrimination that only transfers consumer surplus does not cause any loss of overall efficiency. In fact, assuming that the market is otherwise perfectly competitive, allocational efficiency will still be *optimal*—as good as it could possibly be—even though the price discriminating monopolist confiscates all consumer surplus.

A response from the antitrust perspective might be that, while that might very well be, the now commonly accepted view of the congressional intent of the antitrust laws is to prevent abuse of consumers. Antitrust does not primarily aim to maximize allocational efficiency; it primarily aims to prevent confiscations of consumer surplus. *See* §3.1.1(c).

However, attempts to control price discrimination through law have been controversial, and legal challenges to it are now very difficult to make. The economics of price discrimination are among the more complex and hotly disputed in economics. And even as to such consensus as there may be that price discrimination causes any cognizable harm, the main tools in U.S. law to deal with it are now heavily criticized. The most important of the tools for our purposes, the Robinson-Patman Act (RPA), which appears as Clayton Act §2, 15 U.S.C. §13, is an awkward, complicated, and poorly designed statute. (The other major effort to control discrimination in U.S. law has been through economic regulatory laws that set the prices of public utilities. Since the era of "deregulation" began in the 1970s, that approach too has fallen far out of favor.)

This book's approach to this complex problem will be in two parts. Section 16.2 will first lay out the economic theory of price discrimination as it now exists. Sections 16.3-16.6 will then work through the various causes of action currently available under the RPA to deal with it.

§16.2 THEORETICAL PERSPECTIVES

§16.2.1 Price Discrimination in Economic Theory

§16.2.1(a) What It Is

Strictly speaking, it is not always "discriminatory" to charge one buyer a specific dollar price and then charge another a different dollar price for the same good or service. This is so because, depending on the good or service, it might be more expensive to serve some customers than it is to serve others. For example, it is usually more expensive to provide utilities services to residents of sparsely populated rural areas than to city dwellers. Some products also involve significant transport costs, which may vary a lot depending on how far a given customer is from the place where the good is produced. So charging one customer a price that is really *different* from the price charged to another means charging the first customer a price that gives the seller a larger margin over the cost of selling to that customer. If one customer is more expensive to serve than another, then charging them the same price actually gives the more costly customer a discount. For this reason, economists usually define "price discrimination" to mean charging prices to different customers that aren't directly related to the costs of serving them.

In American law, price discrimination is usually defined much more simply. A price can be "discriminatory" under our primary price discrimination law, the RPA, wherever two similar customers are charged different dollar-amount prices for the same good. Cost differences (and other justifications) enter into it only if the defendant can sufficiently prove that they exist, in putting on a defense. *See* §16.5.2.

§16.2.1(b) The Practical Prerequisites for Effective Price Discrimination and the Incidence of It in the Real World

Price discrimination in some forms is thought to be very common.[1] Pennysaver coupons in the Sunday circular, senior citizen discounts on breakfast,

1. *See, e.g.*, Hal Varian, *Price Discrimination*, in 1 *Handbook of Industrial Organization* 597, 598-599 (Richard Schmalensee & Robert Willig, eds. 1989) (noting the frequency and variety of price discrimination).

and student discounts on computer software are all probably mainly designed as price discrimination plans. But there are also thought to be more complex and powerful modes of price discrimination, which probably require at least some market power and lead to supracompetitive profits.

However, there are three reasons to believe that supracompetitively profitable price discrimination is fairly difficult to pull off, and that in many markets it should be self-defeating and unlikely. First, producers face a serious information problem. The only way to charge a person more than the competitive price without reducing output is to find out how much more that person is willing to pay. But for obvious reasons, consumers do not volunteer that information and ordinarily would not share it very willingly. Sometimes some outwardly obvious trait, such as age, distinguishes different consumers. Student discounts and senior citizen discounts are common for this reason. Both very young and elderly consumers are more price elastic, so sellers may find that they can increase sales while still covering costs if they can attract those consumers with discounts but maintain higher prices to their regular customers. (Price elasticity is discussed in §2.3.2(b).)

Where producers cannot rely on such an outward trait, they must find some way to force or trick consumers into revealing their preferences. One well-known technique is the coupon. Consumers willing to go to the trouble of seeking out coupons and working to redeem them are thought to be more price sensitive, and might not have bought the product but for the discount. There are many variations. Sometimes a producer charges all consumers an up-front, lump-sum fee just to participate in the market, and then charges a fixed price to all purchasers for all purchases. This has the effect of price discriminating, because the average cost of each unit will be lower for higher-volume purchasers.

To enjoy truly significant supracompetitive profits, however, probably requires more significant information. Some sellers have devised ingenious strategies for this purpose. The airlines, for example, discovered ways to distinguish business travelers from leisure travelers, the former being much less price elastic and therefore willing to pay much higher fares. But the technology they have developed to do it has been enormously expensive. Indeed, the airlines' information processing needs became so voracious that they drove one of the world's most significant advances in computer processing power.[2]

Because of the cost of the sophisticated information needed to make substantial profit from discrimination, and because less sophisticated

2. *See* T.A. Heppenheimer, *Turbulent Skies: The History of Commercial Aviation* (1995).

discrimination schemes impose some real costs on sellers because of their inaccuracies, charging uniform prices is ordinarily just the more efficient choice for most sellers.[3]

Second, in addition to the seller's information problem, price discrimination only works if buyers are prevented from engaging in *arbitrage*. It won't work if some buyers are able to buy the product at a low price and then resell it to consumers who value it more highly. Imagine that airline tickets could be freely resold after they are purchased. (They are not resellable, in fact. That is not a coincidence.) Airfares are usually much lower when they are purchased in advance, precisely because the airlines mean to price-discriminate between leisure and business travelers. If I know that there is heavy demand among business travelers for weekday flights between New York and Boston, I might buy up a lot of tickets for those flights well in advance. I could then turn a profit by reselling them to business travelers close in time to the departure date, charging them more than I paid but less than the airline would charge. Over time, the airline would have to respond to the price pressure I impose through my arbitrage efforts, lowering its business fares to meet mine. Assuming the market is otherwise competitive, highly effective arbitrage should eventually bring the prices that all consumers face down to a competitive price.

Arbitrage can sometimes be prevented by sellers by contract. Again, entertainment promoters and the airlines often prohibit resale of their tickets. Arbitrage can also be practically infeasible in some markets. Some products are very difficult to resell, especially if they are quickly perishable or expensive to store, and personal services are ordinarily impossible to resell. Likewise, if the markets being discriminated are separated geographically, the cost to the arbitrageur of transporting the product to the higher value buyers might make the arbitrage not worth it.

Finally, in order for price discrimination to be substantially *profitable*, it is ordinarily thought to call for some market power. In perfectly competitive markets, price discrimination is impossible. If a seller of a good is selling it at two different prices, one of the prices must be above cost. If so, a competitor will lose those customers to whom it offered the higher price. Even in less competitive markets, so long as entry is not uncommonly difficult, any substantial profits from discrimination should invite disciplinary competition. As soon as some consumers are charged a higher price, even if arbitrage is prevented, there is nothing to stop competitors from offering those consumers a bit lower price.

---

3. Daniel J. Gifford & Robert T. Kudrle, *The Law and Economics of Price Discrimination in Modern Economies: Time for Reconciliation?* 43 U.C. Davis L. Rev. 1235 (2010) (making this point).

§16.2.2 Its Peculiarity in a System of Competition

Even aside from the problem that significantly profitable discrimination is probably fairly rare, and even aside from the fact that it might not harm overall efficiency, there are peculiarities with a system of competition law that tries to prevent it.

First, at least in this country the political concern with price discrimination has never been over either allocational efficiency or consumer welfare, at least not directly. Rather, the congressional and popular hostility to price discrimination that was prominent during the early twentieth century was driven by animosity to bigness in and of itself, and a desire to preserve small firms for their own sake. Much of this agitation centered on the growth of large and powerful chains of retail stores, and the threat they posed to small, local retailers. The concern was that the chain retailers, with their purchasing power, could extract lower prices from suppliers. Local stores were then stuck with discriminatorily high prices.[4] But, for better or worse, antitrust has now largely given up on the concern for particular forms of organization—that is, it does not for the most part take a position on whether small firms or big ones are inherently preferable.

Likewise, animosity was driven by simple fairness concerns. Antimonopoly agitation of the early twentieth century took as a major harm of concentrated power just that prices could be arbitrary and abusive. This concern drove not only the RPA, but also the many economic regulatory statutes of the time that constrained discrimination by regulated firms.[5] But that, too, sits uncomfortably with modern antitrust law. For better or worse, its normative commitments are no longer driven by traditional moral concerns.

Second, a real problem with any approach on price discrimination is that, as discussed more fully in §3.2.3, antitrust is almost always agnostic about price. The courts rarely consider prices themselves as any component of liability. In its earliest years antitrust law made clear that to consider the legality of prices themselves would be to "set sail on a sea of doubt."[6] In other words, courts eschew analysis of prices themselves because of the complexity of analyzing them and making judgments about them. The main problem with respect to judging *discriminatory* pricing is that price differences as between customers might be tools of simple price competition.[7]

---

4. *See* Gifford & Kudrle, *supra* note 3, at 1255-1259 (discussing this history).
5. *Id.*
6. This was famously explained by Judge, and later both President and Chief Justice Taft, in the influential early opinion *United States v. Addyston Pipe & Steel & Co.*, 85 F. 271, 283 (6th Cir. 1898). *See also Atl. Richfield Co. v. USA Petr. Co.*, 495 U.S. 328, 354 n.12 (1990) (quoting *Addyston Pipe* in support of courts' unwillingness to consider the "reasonableness" of prices).
7. *See* Gifford & Kudrle, *supra* note 3, at 1250-1255.

They might reflect cost differences between serving different customers, for example.

§16.3 THE STATUTE, ITS ORIGINS, AND ITS PECULIARITIES

Strictly speaking, price discrimination can be challenged in a few different ways in current antitrust law. Where discriminatory prices are part of a predatory pricing scheme, they can be challenged under Sherman Act §1 (if there is more than one firm joined in a conspiracy to price predatorily) or Sherman Act §2 (if the firm charging the predatory prices is a monopolist). Discrimination is also still sometimes prohibited by regulated firms. It was part of the traditional "common carrier" duty to charge similarly situated customers the same price, and preventing price discrimination was a major purpose of the long-standing, pervasive economic regulation to which such firms were subject. (On common carriers and traditional economic regulation, *see* §22.1.) However, the main tool to challenge price discrimination under current law is the Robinson-Patman Act (RPA), which appears as an amendment to the Clayton Act and is codified at 15 U.S.C. §§13-13c. In very broad terms, the RPA makes it illegal for a seller in domestic commerce to charge similarly situated customers different prices for the same good, where the plaintiff can show that the discrimination will cause *competitive* injury, unless the seller can make out one of several specific defenses.

Most discussions of the RPA begin by observing that it is a disfavored statute, which is drafted in a complex and confusing way and adopts a policy at odds with other policies in antitrust law. Specifically, the RPA was designed to protect certain *competitors* from vigorous competition, whereas, the courts often remind us, the rest of antitrust protects only competition, and *not* competitors. *See* §3.2.1. And yet, since its adoption in 1936, the RPA has withstood all of the many attempts to repeal it.

The RPA sets out four civil causes of action,[8] as follows: The most important and common of them is the action for simple price discrimination, set out in RPA §2(a). The three others play supporting roles, and aim to support the primary objective of stopping simple discrimination. Section 2(c) prohibits fictitious brokerage or commission fees that are just disguised discrimination, §§2(d) and 2(e) prohibit promotional allowances that are really just disguised discrimination, and §2(f) prohibits buyers from knowingly inducing or receiving discriminatory benefits.

8. A fifth cause of action provides for criminal penalties for specified kinds of knowing price discrimination. Robinson-Patman Act §3, 15 U.S.C. §13a. However, this provision has not been enforced in nearly 40 years.

The RPA can be enforced in basically the same ways as any other antitrust provision, though as a practical matter all RPA claims are now brought by private plaintiffs. Only the FTC has brought any federal enforcement during the past few decades, and even its efforts have dwindled to effectively nothing. Private plaintiffs can bring RPA challenges under Clayton Act §§4 and 16 (*see* §19.2.2).[9]

Case law under the RPA has become complex, for two reasons. First, the statute itself is drafted in a very complicated way—for no clear reason—with multiple reticulated qualifications and provisos. Second, the statute has been so persistently unpopular with the courts and commentators that the case law has found dozens of limitations to narrow the circumstances in which the act can even apply and the substantive theories of harm on which defendants can be liable. Indeed, while the survey of the law below is more than complex enough, it necessarily leaves out quite a lot of the detail that is to be found in the cases.

§16.4 PREREQUISITES TO RECOVERY

In a few respects the RPA limits the persons and transactions to which any of its four causes of action can apply.

§16.4.1 Narrowed Jurisdictional Reach

§16.4.1(a) "In Commerce": Proof of Physical Transfer of Goods Across State Lines Is Required in All RPA Actions (Probably)

By its terms, the primary offense under RPA—garden-variety price discrimination under §2(a)—and most of the subsidiary offenses apply only if at least one of the challenged transactions literally involves more than one state. That is, the commodity in that transaction must physically cross a state line. This is to be distinguished from the ordinary "interstate commerce" requirement that applies to claims under the Sherman Act and Clayton Act §7, and to other federal laws, by virtue of the Commerce Clause of the U.S. Constitution. The constitutional requirement is satisfied wherever a transaction "touches on" or "affects" interstate commerce. Even transactions that physically take place entirely within one state are in "interstate commerce" so long as they have some nontrivial relationship to the larger economy.

9. Recall that the state attorneys general acting in *parens patriae* can only sue under the Sherman Act. The RPA appears as §2 of the Clayton Act, and so the in *parens patriae* plaintiff cannot enforce it.

(*See* §20.2.) The RPA, by contrast, specifically requires that the defendant be "engaged *in* commerce" and that the challenged conduct occur "in the course of such commerce" (emphasis added). Section 2(a) adds that "either or any of the purchases involved . . . [must be] *in* commerce" (emphasis added). The Supreme Court has taken this language to require that, in a §2(a) case, at least one of the sales must involve goods that physically cross a state line. *Gulf Oil Corp. v. Copp Paving Co.*, 419 U.S. 186, 195 (1974). Moreover, while the "purchases involved" language of §2(a) does not appear in either the causes of action for fictitious commissions under §2(c) or the discriminatory promotional allowances, the lower courts since *Copp* have held that the same requirement applies there as well. And finally, the §2(f) cause of action for the knowing receipt of discriminatory benefits is derivative of the other causes of action—the buyer cannot be liable for receiving benefits unless the seller violates §2(a), 2(c), 2(d), or 2(e) in making them. And since the in-commerce requirement applies to all of those causes of action, it applies to §2(f) as well. *See* 1 Am. Bar Assn., *Antitrust Law Developments (Ninth)* 529-530 (9th ed. 2022) (collecting and summarizing cases).

So, under current law, all RPA causes of action require proof that in at least one of the transactions, goods were transferred across a state boundary.

§16.4.1(b) Section 2(a) Cases Only (Probably): Domestic Consumption or Resale

Furthermore, §2(a) requires that the commodities be sold "for use, consumption, or resale within the United States." This language has been construed to mean that *both* of the transactions in question occurred within the U.S. and were sales for use or subsequent resale within the U.S. So, export transactions from the U.S. cannot violate the RPA, and the fact that a seller charges one price for exports and a different price for domestic sales is not relevant. As to whether this requirement can apply to the subsidiary causes of action under §2(c), 2(d), or 2(e), the Supreme Court has not spoken, but the lower courts have indicated it does not. However, logically, the requirement should apply to §2(f) cases where the challenged sales are only simple price discrimination. A §2(f) action will lie only where there could be liability for the seller as well, and if the only challenge to the seller's conduct is under §2(a), then §2(f) liability should require that the sales in question were for domestic use or resale.

§16.4.2 Scope of the RPA

Once it is determined that the challenged transactions are within the RPA's jurisdictional scope, it should be asked whether the persons and transactions involved are of the kind to which the RPA applies.

§16.4.2(a) Legal Persons Exempted from RPA Coverage

Two specific kinds of legal persons enjoy narrow RPA exemptions: cooperative associations and nonprofit entities. *See* 15 U.S.C. §13b, §13c. These provisions turn out to be more complex than one might expect.

First, the cooperatives exemption is for those associations sometimes formed among consumers or competitors to jointly purchase or produce some thing, for their mutual use. A common example would be a purchasing cooperative among small, competing retail stores, in which they combine their resources to purchase in bulk and enjoy volume discounts they otherwise could not get. But the exemption applies only to:

> [a] return[] to [the cooperative's] members, producers or consumers the whole, or any part of, the net earnings or surplus resulting from its trading operations, in proportion to their purchases or sales from, to, or through the association.

15 U.S.C. §13b. It does *not* apply either to receipt of discriminatory benefits or to the work the members do to generate their earnings. So, imagine that a purchasing cooperative among retailers were to purchase supplies, and make them available both to members of the cooperative and nonmembers at the same price. But then, at the end of each year, the cooperative might have profits from the year's sales, which it might then distribute to the members. That would be literally "discriminatory," in that it would have the effect of giving the products to member customers at a lower price than nonmember customers. But that is precisely what the RPA's cooperatives exemption permits. *See Nw. Wholesale Stationers v. Pac. Stationery & Printing*, 472 U.S. 2984, 286 n.2 (1985). However, the same cooperative is not exempt from RPA for the actual prices that it charges for things that it sells, or the prices it receives for things that it buys.

Likewise, the RPA is inapplicable to the "purchases of their supplies for their own use" by the following institutions: "schools, colleges, universities, public libraries, churches, hospitals, and charitable institutions" so long as they are "not operated for profit." 15 U.S.C. §13c.

§16.4.2(b) Commodities

Like Clayton Act §3 (*see* §20.2.2), the RPA applies only to sales of "commodities." In effect, that means it applies only to sales of tangible goods. Therefore, it does not apply at all to sales of services or intangible goods.

§16.5 THE FOUR RPA CAUSES OF ACTION

The RPA's four civil causes of action can be thought of as one primary cause of action, for simple price discrimination, plus three causes of action that merely support the primary cause by closing loopholes.

1. By far the most important and common RPA cause of action is for ordinary *price discrimination* under RPA §2(a). In short, §2(a) makes it illegal to sell the same commodity within interstate commerce to separate buyers at a different price, if it can be shown that the discrimination injured competition, and unless one of a handful of defenses can be made out.
2. Second, it is effectively per se illegal to try to disguise a discriminatory price by concealing it as a *brokerage payment* under RPA §2(c). It is "effectively per se" because the plaintiff need not show competitive injury, and §2(c) is not subject to the defenses that apply to the §2(a) cause of action.
3. Likewise, it is effectively per se illegal to try to disguise discrimination by way of discriminatory *promotional allowances* under RPA §§2(d) and 2(e). Again, the plaintiff need not show injury to competition, and there is only one available defense.
4. Finally, a buyer can violate the RPA through the knowing *inducement or receipt of discriminatory benefits* under RPA §2(f).

§16.5.1 The Primary Offense: Ordinary Price Discrimination Under RPA §2(a)

The RPA identifies §2(a) as setting out a "prima facie" showing, which the plaintiff must first establish and the defendant can rebut only by making out one of a handful of specified defenses. The prima facie case consists of a set of factual predicates—basically, that there were two comparable sales to different buyers at different prices—and a requirement of proof of competitive injury.

§16.5.1(a) The Factual Predicates of the §2(a) Cause of Action

Laying out the basic factual case for a §2(a) violation requires a series of specific showings:

1. *Reasonably contemporaneous.* First, the transactions at issue must occur at roughly the same time. Otherwise, changing market conditions might make them not fairly comparable, and price differences might be based on goals other than competitive injury.
2. *Outright sales.* They must also be outright and completed sales. They cannot be leases, licenses, agency or consignment arrangements, or other transactions that do not pass title. They also cannot be inchoate efforts to sell, such as offers or options.
3. *Like grade and quantity.* Next, the commodities at issue must be "of like grade and quality." This requirement is straightforward. If the

products are physically the same, then they are of like grade and quality. If there is a physical difference between them that is relevant to their value to buyers, then they are not. For example, if a manufacturer produces two lines of tennis shoes, but one is made with lower quality materials and craftsmanship, they are not "of like grade and quality." The major limitation has been that the commodities are *not* of different grade or quality just because they are separately branded. If the seller has merely put different labels on identical products, and marketed them differently, they are still "of like grade and quality."

4. *Same seller, different buyers.* The sales also must be to two different buyers, and they must be made by the same seller.
5. *Different price.* Finally, the sales must have been at different prices. The plaintiff must only show that there is a difference in *absolute* price. The question is a simple comparison of dollars and cents, and if the plaintiff can make this initial showing—that a single seller made outright sales of commodities of like grade or quality, in commerce, to two separate buyers, and there was a difference in the absolute, simple price—then there arises a presumption of illegality. However, if there really are significant cost differences in serving two customers, the defendant may be able to make out a "cost justification" defense.

§16.5.1(b) Causing Competitive Injury

Having shown the requisite factual basis, the §2(a) plaintiff must also show that the discrimination caused a competitive injury. Technically three theories of competitive injury are now available, though usually only one of them sees much use.

Oddly enough, one widely conceded harm of price discrimination, which might have been thought to be within the normative goals of antitrust as they are now understood—the extracting of "surplus" from consumers and transferring it to producers—is not redressable under RPA. Instead, a §2(a) plaintiff must show that there will be indirect harm to consumers because the discriminatory pricing will injure the ability of a disfavored firm to engage in price competition. Specifically, price discrimination violates §2(a) where its

> effect . . . may be substantially to lessen competition or tend to create a monopoly in any line of commerce, or to injure, destroy, or prevent competition with any person who either grants or knowingly receives the benefit of such discrimination, or with customers of either of them.

RPA §2(a), 15 U.S.C. §13(a).

The courts have read this language to countenance three theories of competitive injury under §2(a). First, "primary line" injury is injury to the seller's own competitors. For example, a seller might cause primary line injury to one of its own competitors by reducing the price it charges only to those customers that also might patronize the competitor. The problem for plaintiffs is that the Supreme Court considers a primary line RPA case to be so similar to a predatory pricing case under the Sherman Act that it has made the RPA and Sherman Act actions largely the same. *See Brooke Group v. Brown & Williamson Tobacco Corp.*, 509 U.S. 209 (1993). Accordingly, the plaintiff must show that (1) the discriminatory price the seller charges to its competitor's customer was so low that it was actually below the seller's own costs (i.e., it was actually at a loss) and (2) there is a likelihood that the seller will be able to recoup the losses of its predatory campaign. (*See* §13.3.3.) The *Brooke Group* standard has made primary line injury very hard to prove (under either the RPA or Sherman Act §2), and plaintiffs now effectively never see courtroom success on such claims.

"Secondary line" injury is injury to competitors of the seller's favored buyer. This theory is the only one that is ordinarily viable, and it is driven mainly by concern for the purchasing power of powerful buyers. The plaintiff must meet a few requirements to show secondary line injury. The challenged sales must discriminate as between two buyers that are actually in competition with one another, in one geographic market.

Finally, "tertiary line" injury is injury to the customers of the defendant seller's distributors. The reasoning in such cases is the same as for secondary line injury. For example, a buyer that buys directly from a manufacturer might be in competition with the *customers* of a distributor that gets favored treatment from the same manufacturer. The injured buyer in such a case would have to show that it is in competition with the favored distributor's customers, in one geographic market.

In secondary and tertiary line cases, evidence of §2(a) injury can be shown either by direct evidence, which will consist of lost sales to the competitor who is injured, or by a special inference that is permitted under the Supreme Court's decision in *FTC v. Morton Salt Co.*, 334 U.S. 37 (1948). *Morton Salt* held that an inference of injury to competition is shown where a substantial price difference has been maintained over a substantial period of time. However, the *Morton Salt* inference can be rebutted by evidence showing that any sales lost to the injured buyer were actually caused by something else. (The *Morton Salt* inference is not available in primary line cases. There, there must be proof of price below cost and a likelihood of recoupment.)

So while more than one theory of injury is technically available, the only one that is ordinarily viable is for injury to competitors of the *favored buyer*. This makes sense in light of the original purpose of the RPA, which was to curtail the power of large retail chains. Accordingly, the most common scenario in which a §2(a) claim might succeed will involve discounts given by a manufacturer to one distributor but not others, which might give the distributor an advantage in taking sales from competing distributors. For example, a manufacturer might consider a large retail chain to be a more important customer than a smaller, family business, and so it might try to secure that larger retailer's business by giving it preferential discounts. But in doing so, the manufacturer might undercut the smaller retailer's ability to compete for business and, ultimately, to survive. That form of injury is the sort most commonly challenged, and the plaintiff will attempt to show that the injury occurred either by putting on direct evidence of sales lost because of the inability to enjoy discounts or by drawing an inference of lost sales from evidence of a long period of substantial price difference.

§16.5.2 The §2(a) Defenses (Which Also Apply in One Other Case)

Three defenses appear in the RPA's language itself. The defenses apply in different ways to the four RPA causes of action. They each are available to defendants in ordinary §2(a) cause of action, and, because the §2(f) action is entirely derivative of the §2(a) claim, they are all also available in defense of a §2(f) claim. However, none of them apply to the §2(c) claim, and only the "meeting competition" defense is available as to the promotional allowance causes of action under §§2(d) and 2(e).

In every case, the defendant bears the burden of proving any of these defenses.

§16.5.2(a) Meeting Competition

A separate RPA subsection, §2(b), provides this defense. By its terms, this defense is available to defendants sued under both §2(a) and §§2(d) and 2(e)—it may be raised after a prima facie case is made of "discrimination in price or services or facilities furnished. . . ." To make out this "meeting competition" defense, the defendant must show that the discrimination was undertaken "in good faith to meet an equally low price of a competitor, or the services or facilities furnished by a competitor." Moreover, the seller must show that its pricing was "a genuine, reasonable response to prevailing competitive circumstances." *Falls City Indus. v. Vanco Beverage, Inc.*, 460 U.S. 428, 450-451 (1983). Defendants have had difficulty in making the defense where they have not systematically documented that their discriminatory choices were driven by competition. For example, where a defendant only shows in a general sense that competition was increasing, without putting on evidence of specific prices sought to be met or specific communications with customers asking for matching prices, the defense may not be available.

The courts have also held that the price charged to meet competition must *only* meet it, and not beat it. A price that *beats* it can be discriminatory in violation of RPA. *Falls City Industries*, 460 U.S. at 446.

§16.5.2(b) Cost Justification

A proviso to §2(a) itself permits

> differentials [in price] which make only due allowance for differences in the cost of manufacture, sale, or delivery resulting from the differing methods or quantities in which such commodities are to such purchasers sold or delivered.

RPA §2(a), 15 U.S.C. §13(a). The cost justification has proven very difficult for defendants, because it requires proof of actual costs and the burden of making the showing is on the defendant.

§16.5.2(c) Changing Conditions

Another proviso, also contained in §2(a), permits

> price changes from time to time where in response to changing conditions affecting the market for or the marketability of the goods concerned, such as but not limited to actual or imminent deterioration of perishable goods, obsolescence of seasonal goods, distress sales under court process, or sales in good faith in discontinuance of business in the goods concerned.

RPA §2(a), 15 U.S.C. §13(a). Although the list of specific changing circumstances identified in the proviso is explicitly nonexclusive, most cases finding the defense to be made out have involved one of the enumerated concerns; that is, the case has in fact involved distress sales of food or other perishable items made to prevent imminent loss.

§16.6 THE SUBSIDIARY RPA CAUSES OF ACTION

§16.6.1 Brokerage Payments Under RPA §2(c)

RPA §2(c) prohibits the giving or receiving of a "commission, brokerage, or other compensation, or any allowance or discount in lieu thereof, except for services rendered. . . ." The purpose of this provision, as with the prohibition on discriminatory promotional allowances under §2(d) and 2(e), is to close loopholes; that is, Congress adopted what is in effect a kind of per se rule for these kinds of behavior, with the purpose of making it even more legally risky to engage in disguised price discrimination through phony commissions or side payments. The §2(c) cause of action requires no showing of competitive injury, and it is not subject to any of the defenses that are otherwise available under the RPA.

§16.6.2 Promotional Materials Under RPA §§2(d) and 2(e)

Some kinds of promotional allowances must be offered on nondiscriminatory terms to distributors who are in actual competition with one another, wherever sales are made to those distributors contemporaneously. Again, this rule is designed to penalize attempted evasions of the RPA through disguised discounts. As with §2(c), the cause of action under §§2(d) and 2(e) requires no showing of competitive injury, and it is subject to only one defense: the meeting competition defense.

The kinds of allowances subject to this rule include any sort of payment or assistance that could help *resell* the goods, such as payments to fund advertising or in-store marketing support. They do not include programs designed to encourage the initial sale of the goods to the buyer, such as favorable credit terms or delivery services.

§16.6.3 Inducing or Receiving Discriminatory Benefits Under RPA §2(f)

Finally, the RPA makes it illegal for a buyer knowingly to induce or receive a discriminatory benefit. This liability is entirely derivative of the seller's liability, because §2(f) makes it illegal to induce or receive only those benefits that are "prohibited by this section." So if the seller in the relevant transaction would have had any defense, or if the plaintiff's case against the seller would be missing any necessary element, then there also will be no §2(f) action against the buyer.

PART IX

Antitrust Aspects of Mergers and Acquisitions

CHAPTER 17

Antitrust Aspects of Mergers and Acquisitions

And finally, we turn to the third of the three major causes of action that make up most of antitrust: the law of Clayton Act §7, under which an *acquisition* can be illegal if it could lead to market power.[1] Antitrust has always put some limits on mergers and other business acquisitions (M&A), and technically there are several theories under which M&A can be challenged. Any acquisition transaction involves a "contract" and therefore could theoretically be challenged under Sherman Act §1. Likewise, if an acquisition or a series of them gives one firm a truly commanding position there may be a violation of Sherman Act §2. By 1914, however, Congress felt that the courts were unduly lax in applying the Sherman Act to M&A, and so it included an M&A provision in the Clayton Act of that year. As a practical matter acquisitions are now mainly challenged under Clayton Act §7. As we shall see, in most cases in which there would be any viable challenge, plaintiffs enjoy certain advantages under §7.

Section 7 is a surprisingly complex provision, though in its most pertinent parts, it may seem simple enough. It makes it illegal for one person to "acquire" the "stock," the "share capital," or the "assets" of another person, if to do so "may . . . substantially . . . lessen competition, or . . . tend to create a monopoly." And yet the substantive antitrust law of mergers and acquisitions turns out to be very complex, and this is so for two broad

1. As explained in the introduction in Chapter 1, the other major causes of action are the action for multilateral conduct (also known as "contract, combination . . . or conspiracy") under Sherman Act §1, covered in Chapters 5-11, and the action for unilateral conduct (also known as "monopolization") under Sherman Act §2, covered in Chapters 13 and 14.

reasons. First, the statute itself is surrounded by a profusion of nit-picky doctrinal details. This is in some part because over its long history §7 has been the focus of a great deal of controversy, and it has been amended a number of times during struggles between the courts and Congress. It is Moby Dick-like in the scars it bears from these many battles: a profusion of provisos, exceptions, and other little curlicues that can raise a myriad of (usually nonsubstantive) issues in litigation. Second, as the law has evolved, the substantive theory of liability under §7 has gone from simple to more complex. The Celler-Kefauver Amendments of 1950 were initially read as a strong bar against mergers of any real magnitude, in effect putting almost all of the risk of uncertainty on the merging parties.[2] That made the law simple. Any merger in a moderately concentrated market that increased concentration more than trivially was illegal, and the courts were deaf to defenses based on procompetitive benefits. However, the trend began reversing itself as early as the mid-1970s, and the courts have come to place more and more of the onus of substantive merger law on plaintiffs. They now demand an elaborate demonstration of both market circumstances and the theory on which the plaintiff alleges harm will ensue.

If there is one defining theme that will be with us throughout our discussion, it is the need to balance the risks posed by merger law as between plaintiffs and defendants. A simple test for liability tends to put the risk mostly on the merging parties (i.e., the defendants), whereas a more open-ended, facts-and-circumstances test puts the risk on the plaintiff (and, arguably, on society). This is so because, even more than elsewhere in antitrust, merger law concerns *predictions about future events*, and predictions about things that are inherently uncertain. Importantly, §7 as currently worded prohibits acquisitions not only where they are "unreasonable," but where their "effect . . . *may* be substantially to lessen competition, or to *tend* to create a monopoly" (emphasis added). The courts have long held that under this language the competitive harms posed by a transaction need not yet have materialized at the time it is challenged. Monopoly need only be its "tend[ency]." For this reason, §7 has often been called "incipiency" regulation.

This chapter begins in §§17.1 and 17.2 with a brief bit of real-world background that will prove helpful in understanding this law. Sections 17.3-17.8 then cover the substantive cause of action under §7—the case that any plaintiff must make out to challenge any acquisition under the basic law of merger and acquisition, whether it is a private plaintiff suing for damages or injunction, the government making a case within the Hart-Scott-Rodino process, or the government seeking to undo a consummated transaction.

2. *See* Derek Bok, *Section 7 of the Clayton Act and the Merging of Law and Economics*, 74 Harv. L. Rev. 226 (1960) (classic article on point, urging a set of bright-line judicial tests under §7 and criticizing the many arguments for more open-ended analysis on cost-benefit grounds).

Finally, Chapter 18 covers the special, nonsubstantive, purely bureaucratic process through which most merger challenges are now handled: the Hart-Scott-Rodino premerger clearance process.

§17.1 SOME BRIEF BACKGROUND

§17.1.1 The Many Ways One Firm Can Acquire All or Part of Another: A Primer on Acquisition Transactions

Among the antitrust bar and the antitrust commentariat, it is routine to refer to all the transactions subject to §7 and HSR as "mergers." This is not that big a deal, because under current law most transactions by which control changes hands are treated the same way. But it is technically inaccurate. This so-called "merger" law actually applies to all kinds of acquisitions, whether of equity securities, physical assets, intellectual property, or other assets,[3] and to call it "merger" law covers up some technical issues. Particularly when one is first learning this law it can be misleading. As we shall see, the degree to which the various kinds of control transactions can be subject to Clayton Act §7 and to HSR can raise complex questions.

Also, for the sake of simplicity this section will introduce only *corporate* acquisitions, governed by state corporation law. Other business acquisitions—the merger of two partnerships, for example—are subject to antitrust to the same extent as corporate acquisitions, but the structure of the transactions themselves will be governed by other bodies of state law, and will differ in some respects from what is described here.

A *merger* is a transaction governed by state corporation law, under which two corporations effectively become one. State law requires that when two companies desire to merge, a plan of merger must ordinarily be approved by the boards of directors of the two companies and then approved by the companies' shareholders. Mergers can be structured in two basic ways: (1) One firm can be merged into the other, so that the target firm merges out of existence and simply becomes a part of the surviving, acquiring firm; or (2) the two firms can both merge into one and emerge as a new, third company (following which both of the original firms are considered to have merged out of existence). *See* Figure 17.1.

3. In fact, as we shall see, transactions can be "acquisitions" under §7 that do not involve exchange of outright ownership. The antitrust law of mergers and acquisitions is really most interested in "control," but arrangements we might not ordinarily consider "acquisitions"—like leases, licenses, or contractual rights to use some asset—can trigger §7. Because for now we are concerned only with more traditional acquisition transactions, we will discuss those more exotic issues later. *See* §17.3.

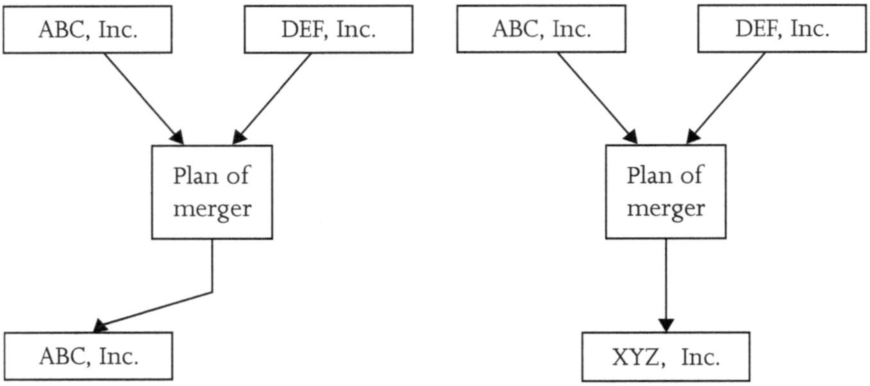

Figure 17.1. Two Basic Merger Structures

Acquisitions of control can be accomplished through means other than merger. First, the acquiring firm can simply acquire all or a controlling portion of the shares of the target firm, following which the target would be a subsidiary of the acquiror. In most such cases, the acquiror will quickly replace the target firm's board with its own nominees (which it can do, because it will have become the controlling shareholder), and the new board may make other changes in the management team. Many state corporation statutes now provide that stock acquisitions such as this can be accomplished through negotiations with the target firm's board of directors and shareholder approval.[4] Second, the acquiring firm might simply buy all the assets of the selling firm. After such a deal, the acquiror will hold a large new clump of assets, while the seller will still exist but just as an empty shell with one asset—the money or other consideration paid to it for the sale of its assets. In principle, the selling firm could continue to exist indefinitely and could even reinvest the proceeds in some new business endeavor. But in the usual case the firm will simply distribute the proceeds to its shareholders and then dissolve.

The reason there are so many ways to accomplish the same substantive result—the transfer of the business from one firm to another—is that different transactional forms pose different pros and cons in terms of tax and corporate law. Mergers, for example, can pose tax benefits for

4. That is to say, the transaction works in basically the same way as a merger, but instead of combining the two companies into one, it results in the acquiring firm owning the target firm as its subsidiary. The acquiring firm will negotiate a price and a plan of share exchange with the selling firm's board of directors, the board will recommend the plan to the shareholders, and if the shareholders approve it (usually by a simple majority), shares will be exchanged according to the plan. If approved, the acquiring firm will acquire shares even from those shareholders who voted against the plan, just as in a merger.

shareholders, but they have the downside that the acquiring firm takes on all of the acquired firm's liabilities. Depending on the facts, merger, share exchange, or assets acquisition may be judged the best from the firms' particular perspectives.

Finally, one rather different sort of acquisition deserves special comment: the *tender offer*. Sometimes one company (or, in the unusual case, a wealthy individual or group of individuals) will desire to acquire another company, but will be unable to negotiate any friendly arrangement for it, such as a merger or a contractual purchase of shares or assets. Those other kinds of transactions are "friendly" because they call for board approval of the target firm before they are submitted for shareholder vote. Tender offers are therefore often called "hostile" takeovers, and indeed they often are hotly opposed by the incumbent management, who ordinarily fear for their jobs if the takeover is successful. Thus, the tender offer proponent goes directly to the shareholders of the company and offers to purchase their shares. A successful tender offer will result in the acquiror holding a controlling percentage of the target company's voting stock (and sometimes 100 percent of it, though frequently it will be to the acquiror's strategic advantage to acquire only a bare majority of the stock). For purposes of antitrust law, tender offers are treated in basically the same way as other control acquisitions, but there are several technical differences in their treatment in the HSR process. *See* Chapter 18.

§17.1.2 The Competitive Relationship Between the Merging Firms: Horizontal, Vertical, and Conglomerate Mergers and the Significance of These Distinctions

Antitrust law makes important doctrinal consequences depend on the competitive relationship between the merging entities. As far as antitrust is concerned, that relationship will be one of three possibilities: *horizontal*, *vertical*, or *conglomerate*. The terms horizontal and vertical have the same meaning here as they do in the law of conspiracy under Sherman Act §1. A horizontal merger is between two companies that are at the same level in the chain of distribution of some good or service, while a vertical merger is between two companies that are at different levels in the same chain of distribution. For example, a merger between the Sony electronics company and the Samsung electronics company would be horizontal. They produce an overlapping range of consumer electronics, such as televisions and stereo equipment. But if Sony were to merge with the Best Buy company, a retailer of consumer electronics, that would be a vertical merger. Finally, a conglomerate merger is between two companies that are in different lines of business. They are in neither a horizontal nor vertical relationship in any chain of distribution. It would be a conglomerate merger were Sony to merge with, say, Gillette, the maker of shaving products. (For discussion of special economic problems concerning the horizontal-vertical distinction, see the appendix.)

"Conglomerate" acquisition is a bit of a loose term, and it is used to mean different things. Roughly, it connotes an acquisition between companies not currently in either horizontal competition or vertical relation, though they might be some day. But this could describe at least three kinds of transactions. The parties might be producers of the same good or service but not in the same geographical area. Or, they might produce products that do not compete with one another (i.e., consumers do not perceive the products as substitutes), but as to which there are some similarities or affinities. A good example of this sort of merger was at issue in *FTC v. Proctor & Gamble Co.*, 386 U.S. 568 (1967). The merging parties were Purex, a large producer of bleach, and Proctor & Gamble, a dominant maker of household cleaning products. Though P&G did not make bleach, its manufacturing and marketing facilities were similar to those used in the making of bleach. P&G might therefore have entered into bleach production quite a bit more easily than, say, a maker of golf clubs. This fact, as we shall see, has a consequence for whether a merger can be challenged legally. Finally, what we might think of as "true" or "pure" conglomerate mergers are those between firms that do not and likely will never compete, as they produce products with no similarities or affinities of any kind. One might wonder why firms like that would merge in the first place, but there was a time when they did with frequency. In fact, during the late 1960s there was a huge wave of mergers, and many of them were truly conglomerate. There is dispute as to why so many of these mergers occurred, though there was some support in economic thought for advantages they might pose. In practice, however, many of them were ill-fated, as they produced unmanageable firms that called for one centralized management to oversee the making and doing of widely varying lines of business. The conglomerate mergers of the 1960s wound up failing in large numbers, and many of the firms spent much of the 1970s and 1980s unwinding combinations that proved unwise. All that said, though, true conglomerations still occur. For example, the Altria Group, Inc., a holding company formed in 1985 to own the Phillip Morris cigarette company, also happened to own Kraft Foods, the maker of such things as Kraft cheese, Oreo cookies, and Jell-O pudding. Perhaps tellingly, however, Altria eventually spun off Kraft to its shareholders, following which Kraft became again an independent company with its own management.

§17.2 SOURCES OF THE LAW OF MERGER AND ACQUISITION: WHENCE §7, HART-SCOTT-RODINO, AND THE *GUIDELINES*, AS WELL AS THE PECULIAR QUASI-IRRELEVANCE OF THE SUPREME COURT

For the most part, antitrust courses focus on the case law of the U.S. Supreme Court because, for the most part, that is where antitrust is made. Not so in mergers and acquisitions. The Supreme Court has not decided a merger case on the merits since *United States v. Citizens & S. Natl. Bank*, 422 U.S. 86 (1975). One key reason for the Court's silence is that in the following year Congress revolutionized the administration of M&A law by adopting the Hart-Scott-Rodino Antitrust Improvements Act (HSR). HSR set up a system of "pre-clearance" review, which usually requires both parties to any large acquisition to make a filing with both of the antitrust enforcement agencies, and then wait for the agencies to approve or disapprove the transaction. The HSR process will be examined in full in Chapter 18. Usually, would-be M&A parties either make changes to their plan to try to satisfy the enforcement agencies or, in cases in which the agencies are strongly opposed to their deal, give up completely. Accordingly, most large merger controversies don't make it to court anymore.

That hardly means, however, that the M&A case law has become irrelevant. For several reasons it remains very relevant. First, the basis on which the enforcement agencies make their decision under HSR as to any proposed transaction is whether it would violate §7 as the courts have interpreted it. Moreover, cases are still tried under §7, and they can get started in several ways. First, some acquisitions are exempt from HSR or fall below its filing thresholds (HSR requires preclearance review of only larger transactions), but nevertheless private parties, state attorneys general, and the federal enforcement agencies still challenge them through litigation.[5] Second, sometimes a merger subject to HSR filing is disapproved by the enforcement agencies, and yet would-be merger proponents who happen to be really feeling their oats will go ahead with it anyway. They remain perfectly free under the HSR to proceed with their transaction, but they take the risk

5. Private persons and state attorneys general can bring civil actions to enforce §7 by way of the private causes of action in Clayton Act §§4 and 16, and under Clayton Act §4a the Justice Department can seek money damages for §7 violation if the violation injures the United States in its business or property. (Note that the states cannot enforce Clayton Act provisions through *parens patriae* actions; *see* 15 U.S.C. §15c(1).)

that the agencies will then seek to enjoin it through a federal court action under the standards that govern §7.

The problem is that while the case law matters, the Supreme Court's cases on point are now all old and state views that many consider out of harmony with other developments in antitrust. We will examine the consequences in the sections to follow.

§17.2.1 The Long Legislative History of §7 and the Coming of HSR

§17.2.1(a) Statutory Origins

While federal law has governed M&A for 120 years, the development of the law has been a long and tortuous struggle, punctuated with frequent disagreements between the courts and Congress. Though the Clayton Act appeared in 1914, the law as it now exists really is barely 50 years old, as a major statutory amendment of 1950 was not given life until certain Supreme Court opinions of the 1960s, which in turn were significantly modified by later decisions in the 1970s.

Arguably the most important single event in this history was the adoption of that 1950 amendment, which is still known by the names of its cosponsors—the Celler-Kefauver Act. On its surface the amendment might not seem exactly epochal. Its two primary changes were merely to close long-standing loopholes—the amendment made §7 applicable to assets acquisitions as well as stock acquisitions, and made it applicable to vertical and conglomerate deals as well as horizontal ones. But more important was the clear message, contained mainly in the statute's legislative history, indicating the intent of Congress to make M&A *much* more difficult.

§17.2.1(b) The Creation of Modern Merger Law by the Warren Court

For all the undoubted significance of the Celler-Kefauver amendment, modern merger law did not really begin until more than a decade later, with two important Supreme Court decisions of the early 1960s. The first was *Brown Shoe Co. v. United States*, 370 U.S. 294 (1962), the Court's first significant post-Celler-Kefauver case. There, the country's third largest shoe maker acquired the eighth largest. Both companies manufactured shoes, and both were also integrated forward into retail. That is, they not only made shoes, they also sold them directly to customers in retail stores that they owned and operated.

In *Brown Shoe* the Court took its first opportunity for extended consideration of the 1950 amendments. Probably more important than any doctrinal result the Court reached in the case was its long, detailed examination of the Celler-Kefauver amendment and its legislative history. Among the long shadows that Chief Justice Warren cast in this opinion, one of the most important was the following summary:

> The dominant theme pervading congressional consideration of the 1950 amendments was a fear of what was considered to be a rising tide of economic concentration in the American economy. . . . Statistics . . . were cited as evidence of the danger to the American economy in unchecked corporate expansions through mergers. Other considerations cited in support of the bill were the desirability of retaining "local control" over industry and the protection of small businesses. Throughout the recorded discussion may be found examples of Congress' fear not only of accelerated concentration of economic power on economic grounds, but also of the threat to other values a trend toward concentration was thought to pose.

Id. at 315-316 (footnotes omitted). He also gave content to this generalization by laying out an influential list of specific congressional objectives he found in the statute and its legislative history:

- Because Congress closed two specific loopholes that had undermined §7 before 1950—by making clear that the statute applied to assets acquisitions and to competitive harms in addition to those between acquiror and acquiree—§7 was meant to apply to all sorts of acquisitions—horizontal, vertical, and conglomerate.
- The Court also found a strong Congressional desire to halt competitive injuries as soon as they were reasonably likely, even if they had not yet materialized.
- As the Court said, mergers should be stopped "at a time when the trend to a lessening of competition in a line of commerce was still in its incipiency"; because §7 bans transactions whose effect "*may* be substantially to lessen competition," the statute is concerned "with probabilities, not certainties." *Id.* at 323.
- However, the Court cautioned that this incipiency standard not be carried too far; its concern is captured in the following frequently quoted view of the Senate Judiciary Committee: "The use of these words ['may be'] means that the bill, if enacted, would not apply to the mere possibility but only to the reasonable probability of the pr[o]scribed effect. . . ."[6]
- Still, for all that, the Court stressed its view that antitrust remained fundamentally committed to price competition, and not to the preservation of individual businesses for their own sake. To make its point the Court set out among the more famous and frequently cited observations in antitrust, that by adopting the antitrust laws

---

6. S. Rep. No. 1775, at 6 (1950).

Congress was concerned only with the "protection of competition, not competitors. . . ." *Id.* at 320.

- Finally, the Court set out the doctrinal approach that it intended to be applied in merger cases, an approach now often called the "functional test." The Court wrote that, while market share statistics are relevant, "only a further examination of the particular market—its structure, history, and probable future—can provide the appropriate setting for judging the probable anticompetitive effect of the merger." *Id.* at 322 n.38.

See generally id. at 316-323.

A decision followed only one year later that was, if anything, even more important: *United States v. Philadelphia National Bank*, 374 U.S. 321 (1963). Probably its single most important contribution was its adoption of what amounts to a quasi per se rule for some horizontal mergers. Justice Brennan began by explaining that "[the] intense congressional concern with the trend toward concentration," as demonstrated in the Celler-Kefauver Act, "warrants dispensing, in certain cases, with elaborate proof of market structure, market behavior, or probable anticompetitive effects." *Id.* at 363. This concern produced the following holding, which for many years was the most important statement in merger law:

> [W]e think that a merger which produces a firm controlling an undue percentage share of the relevant market, and results in a significant increase in the concentration of firms in that market is so inherently likely to lessen competition substantially that it must be enjoined in the absence of evidence clearly showing that the merger is not likely to have such anticompetitive effects.

Id. As interpreted in the subsequent case law of the 1960s, *Philadelphia National Bank* stated a strong presumption of illegality for horizontal mergers creating even relatively small increases in concentration.

§17.2.1(c) The Sea Change of the 1970s and the Coming of HSR

The case law of the 1960s, which mostly applied the *Philadelphia National Bank* presumption quite strictly, came to be warmly criticized, because it was thought to be too harsh and conflicted with then-developing trends in economic theory. During the 1960s, the Supreme Court often prohibited mergers that would not even raise concern today,[7] and indeed, for more than a

---

7. *See, e.g., United States v. Von's Grocery*, 384 U.S. 270 (1966); *United States v. Pabst Brewing Co.*, 384 U.S. 546 (1966); *United States v. Aluminum Co. of Am.*, 377 U.S. 271 (1964).

decade following *Brown Shoe,* the government won fully a dozen merger cases before the Supreme Court and lost none.[8]

In part in response to this criticism, and in part through efforts of the enforcement agencies themselves, the courts by the early 1970s began to infuse their §7 case law with the then growing body of economic thinking in favor of many mergers. The new thinking most prominently influenced one of the Court's last §7 opinions, *United States v. Gen. Dynamics,* 415 U.S. 486 (1974). While the case depended on certain unique facts that might seem to limit its applicability, most observers believe it marked an important shift in the Court's thinking. That case and a few others of the time probably reflected the thinking of several newly appointed Justices,[9] and they appear to have marked a significant change. In short, the Justice Department in that case sought to stop a merger using the same simple concentration statistics it had been using for about ten years under the *Philadelphia National Bank* framework, as in effect its only evidence. Writing for a Court divided 5-4, Justice Stewart found that the particular industry there (coal mining) was characterized by unusual economic circumstances that made retrospective concentration statistics unreliable. The Court also set out a general analysis of the *Philadelphia National Bank* approach, explaining its view that concentration evidence alone should be viewed with more caution. Most observers believe that the *General Dynamics* Court meant to make a major statement effectively rejecting the strongly presumptive approach of *Philadelphia National Bank.*[10]

This turn of events posed a problem for the enforcement agencies. The agencies had already faced important challenges in their duty to enforce §7. Prior to HSR, agency challenges almost necessarily occurred after a deal had been consummated—in the planning stages, corporate acquisitions are almost always kept as secret as the law will allow, and they tend to move quickly. This proved a serious bar to effective remedy. While there is no legal requirement that a §7 challenge be brought prior to consummation, courts

8. Eleanor M. Fox, *Antitrust, Mergers, and the Supreme Court: The Politics of Section 7 of the Clayton Act,* 26 Mercer L. Rev. 389, 396-397 (1975).

9. *See, e.g.,* Howard R. Lurie, *Mergers Under the Burger Court: An Anti-Antitrust Bias and Its Implications,* 23 Vill. L. Rev. 213 (1978); Chris Sagers, *#LOLNothingMatters,* 63 Antitrust Bull. 7, 20-21 (2018). The arguably changing judicial politics of this era are further discussed in §§1.1 and 1.2.

10. *See, e.g., United States v. Baker Hughes, Inc.,* 908 F.2d 981, 984-985 (D.C. Cir. 1990) (finding *General Dynamics* to require "a totality-of-the-circumstances approach," under which courts must "weigh[] a variety of factors to determine the effects of particular transactions on competition"); 1 Am. Bar Assn., *Antitrust Law Developments (Ninth)* 373 (9th ed. 2022); Note, *Horizontal Mergers After* United States v. General Dynamics Corp., 92 Harv. L. Rev. 491 (1978). *Cf. Hosp. Corp. of Am. v. FTC,* 807 1381 (7th Cir. 1986), where Judge Posner noted that none of the Supreme Court's 1960s merger case law had been overturned, and cast some doubt on whether *General Dynamics* even limited them. He noted as well, however, that in other decisions, the Supreme Court, echoed by the lower courts, has said repeatedly that the economic concept of competition, rather than any desire to preserve rivals as such, is the lodestar that shall guide the contemporary application of the antitrust laws, not excluding the Clayton Act. *Id.* at 1386.

are very hesitant to enter any meaningful relief against a consummated transaction. But following *General Dynamics*, the agencies would be charged not only with trying to find legally significant transactions early enough to get meaningful relief, they would also be required to develop much more sophisticated factual cases to challenge them. That problem at least was significantly mitigated by a congressional response, in the Hart-Scott-Rodino Act of 1976. In fact, going back to at least the 1930s there had been frequent calls, often enough from the enforcement agencies, for some sort of federal, pretransaction review power. Congress finally heeded in 1976, not coincidentally following *General Dynamics*.

Anyway, at about the same time, and abruptly, the Supreme Court went silent. The Court has not said a thing about merger law in more than 40 years. It has never been exactly clear why, though two explanations present themselves. First is the very practical fact that, following HSR, most merger cases just don't get that far in the courts. Nowadays any merger large enough to be reportable will either be approved during HSR, and thereafter fairly unlikely to face any challenge, or opposed by the agencies, an event that usually causes the parties to abandon the merger.[11] A second, more speculative possibility is just that the Court and Congress had for so long played out the same struggle in merger policy, and the Court finally gave up. At several different points since 1914, Congress has attempted to set out clear rules making M&A more difficult, but the Court then gradually ate away at those reforms through narrow constructions, following which Congress amended the law again to restate its intent to constrain mergers, and so on.[12]

In any case, the effect of the Court's silence is that the story of merger law since 1975 has been written in the U.S. Courts of Appeals. Although since 1975 certiorari has been sought in several litigated merger cases, the Court has so far turned all of them down.

---

11. One separate statutory explanation might be that Congress effectively repealed the Expediting Act in 1974. For most of the twentieth century, that statute had made government antitrust cases appealable directly to the Supreme Court and, by contrast with most of its docket, left the Court less discretion to choose which antitrust cases it would hear. The 1974 amendment made government antitrust appeals ordinarily work like all others. *See* Pub. L. No. 93-528, §5, 88 Stat. 1706, 1709 (1974), codified at 15 U.S.C. §29, as amended. That said, reform of the Expediting Act can't be a full explanation for the Court's silence on merger law, because the Court has continued to hear all other kinds of antitrust cases without much change.

12. In fact the Court may have given up after one last explicit warning from Congress. In 1975, *United States v. American Building Maintenance Industries*, 422 U.S. 271 (1975), read §7 to apply only to mergers in which both parties were engaged literally in interstate commerce, meaning that their businesses crossed state lines. Congress explicitly reversed that decision a few years later, Antitrust Procedural Improvements Act of 1980, Pub. L. No. 96-349, 94 Stat. 1154 (1980), noting that it had generated much criticism, and reaffirming the traditional understanding that §7 reaches as far as the Sherman Act. H.R. Rep. No. 96-871, 96th Cong. 2d Sess., 4-7 (1980).

§17.2.2 The *Merger Guidelines*

Over the past several decades, the antitrust enforcement agencies have sought to clarify the law of §7 by systematically laying out their own understanding of it in a series of guidance documents called the *Merger Guidelines*. The *Guidelines* have been influential, particularly because of the agencies' predominant role in merger review under HSR and because the *Guidelines* in each of their many revisions have been the collaborative work of influential academics, veteran lawyers, and federal policy makers. Understanding them is indispensable in understanding the antitrust law of mergers and acquisitions.

In response to criticism of the pro-enforcement merger doctrine of the 1960s, which was said to be unprincipled and too chaotic to provide guidance to courts or business, the Justice Department began this long project with its first set of *Guidelines* in 1968. The 1968 document was welcomed in many ways but was criticized for retaining a still strict policy against even fairly small mergers.[13] Since then, the *Guidelines* have undergone a handful of major revisions. Each revision was the work of a new federal administration, but it is clear that they have not simply correlated with different political perspectives. The document was not changed until fairly major revisions that occurred early in the Reagan administration, in 1982 and then again in 1984.[14] They were again substantially revised in 1992 by the incoming Clinton administration, though the revisions were designed by the predecessor administration.[15] For what it may be worth the 1992 *Guidelines* appear to have been designed specifically to respond to a string of courtroom defeats during the 1980s, at a time when the courts seemed determined to scale back §7 dramatically.[16] In any case, the 1992 *Guidelines* are generally said to have been more permissive of mergers, and somewhat more so than the case law had been,[17] though again this may have reflected the agencies' desire to accommodate the harsh judicial criticism they endured during the 1980s. They are also significant in several other respects. The 1992 *Guidelines* were

---

13. U.S. Dep't of Justice, *Merger* Guidelines (1968) [hereinafter "1968 *Merger Guidelines*"]. As of this writing, the current *Guidelines* and all historic merger policy documents are available at www.justice.gov and www.ftc.gov. For discussion of the judicial and public reception, see Steven A. Newborn & Virginia L. Snider, *The Growing Judicial Acceptance of the Merger Guidelines*, 60 Antitrust L.J. 849 (1992).

14. U.S. Dep't of Justice, *Merger Guidelines* (1982) [hereinafter "1982 *Merger Guidelines*"]; U.S. Dep't of Justice, *Merger Guidelines* (1984) [hereinafter "1984 *Merger Guidelines*"].

15. FTC & U.S. Dep't of Justice, *Horizontal Merger Guidelines* (1992) [hereinafter "1992 *Horizontal Merger Guidelines*"]; The 1992 document was significantly revised in 1997. FTC & U.S. Dep't of Justice, *Horizontal Merger Guidelines* (1997) [hereinafter "1997 *Horizontal Merger Guidelines*"].

16. *See* John B. Kirkwood & Richard O. Zerbe, Jr., *The Path to Profitability: Reinvigorating the Neglected Phase of Merger Analysis*, 17 Geo. Mason L. Rev. 39 (2009) (making this point and explaining the background).

17. *See, e.g.*, 4 Phillip E. Areeda & Herbert Hovenkamp, *Antitrust Law* ¶901b3 (2d ed. 2006).

the first set issued jointly by both the Justice Department and the Federal Trade Commission. They also added an entirely new theory of harm from merger, the so-called "unilateral effects" doctrine (*see* §17.7). Interestingly, the 1992 *Guidelines* had nothing whatever to say about vertical or conglomerate mergers. They explicitly preserved the rules governing those transactions under the 1984 *Guidelines*. During the George W. Bush administration, the agencies supplemented the 1992 *Guidelines* with a significant joint commentary in 2006, and then they substantially revised them with new *Guidelines* in the Obama administration in 2010[18] and the Biden administration in 2023.[19]

The development of these documents over the years was mostly marked by bipartisan and interagency cooperation and consensus, with one significant exception concerning the treatment of non-horizontal deals,[20] but that appears to have been resolved with bipartisan support for the new treatment of those deals in the 2023 *Guidelines*.[21]

If there is one overriding theme in the history of the *Guidelines*, it is one that mirrors the development of substantive merger law itself. The original *Guidelines* were simple and harsh. Over time they have grown consistently more flexible and much more complex and, possibly with the exception of the 2023 *Guidelines*, they have also grown more permissive.

The *Guidelines* are not federal "rules" as that term is used in administrative law. That is, they are not regulations that have the force of federal law, issued pursuant to a grant of statutory rule making authority from Congress. Accordingly, they are not binding on merging parties or any other private persons, and they do not bind the courts (which instead must apply the law of §7 as they understand it from judicial precedent, not the *Guidelines*). Technically, they do not even bind the agencies. They are merely guidance documents intended to advise the public about the agencies' opinions as to which transactions will likely be subject to legal challenge by the agencies. Moreover, because the *Guidelines* are not "rules" with the force of law, they cannot be reviewed by the federal courts in the same way that actual federal

---

18. FTC & U.S. Dep't of Justice, *Horizontal Merger Guidelines* (2010) [hereinafter "2010 *Horizontal Merger Guidelines*"].
19. FTC & U.S. Dep't of Justice, *Merger Guidelines* (2023) [hereinafter "2023 *Merger Guidelines*"].
20. Late in the first Trump administration, the agencies issued the first new guidelines for non-horizontal mergers since 1982. Up until that time, they had simply preserved the parts of the 1982 Guidelines that applied to non-horizontal deals as their latest statement on the issue. *See supra* note [XXX]. Very shortly thereafter, the incoming Biden administration rejected those new guidelines and reverted to the prior policy pending revisions that they intended to include in the next iteration of overall merger guidelines. They included those revisions in the 2023 *Merger Guidelines* and, contrary to some predictions, the new guidelines have been endorsed by the second Trump administration.
21. 2023 *Merger Guidelines* §§ 2.4-2.5.

rules can be.[22] Importantly, the *Guidelines* do not purport to change the law or state any new rules of law, but only to state the agencies' understanding of the current case law under §7 as the courts have stated it. Technically, the *Guidelines* merely restate the law as it exists.

That the *Horizontal Merger Guidelines* have had a large influence is undeniable, but the influence is also somewhat ambiguous. While the courts often express high regard for them and cite them as authority[23] (indeed, courts have castigated the agencies for *failing* to follow them[24]), there is reason to believe that many courts just fail to understand them or, while expressing respect for them, fail to apply them or do so incorrectly.[25] But all that aside, the *Guidelines*' real significance reflects simply the power the agencies hold within the HSR process. Most large transactions are now reviewed by the agencies under HSR, and the vast majority of them are approved by the agencies with no challenge. Some small percentage receive more critical analysis, but most of those are also resolved by negotiation between agency and parties. In the small handful of cases each year in which an agency strongly opposes a transaction, the parties often abandon their deals rather than face the agencies in court. All of the decisions in all of these cases made by the agencies and by the parties are made in the shadow of the *Guidelines*. In other words, even though judicial reception of the *Guidelines* has been somewhat equivocal, the vast bulk of the application of §7 to American M&A transactions occurs under the framework of the *Guidelines* and such other enforcement intentions as the agencies may have. And, since they know this, there is little doubt that the small army of defense-side antitrust counselors

---

22. When a federal agency makes a rule with the force of law, a person aggrieved by that rule normally can sue the agency in federal court in a process known as "judicial review." If a court finds a rule to be in conflict with the statute that it implements or otherwise to have been adopted improperly, the court can hold the rule unenforceable. But in fact, federal agencies very commonly issue mere guidance documents intended to advise the public or state their enforcement intentions. At least as the law currently stands, mere guidance documents are not reviewable by the courts, even though they are often quite influential. *But see* Richard J. Pierce, Jr., *Merger Law Is Dante's Inferno Revisited*, The Reg. Rev., Mar. 13, 2023 (arguing that ongoing changes in administrative law could render them subject to review).

23. *See, e.g.*, Chi. Bridge & Iron Co. N.V. v. FTC, 534 F.3d 410, 431 n.11 (5th Cir. 2008) ("Merger Guidelines are often used as persuasive authority when deciding if a particular acquisition violates the antitrust laws."); Steven A. Newborn & Virginia L. Snider, *The Growing Judicial Acceptance of the Merger Guidelines*, 60 Antitrust L.J. 849, 851 (1992) (noting that between issuance of the revised *Guidelines* of 1982 and the revisions of 1992, the 1982 *Guidelines* were cited by federal courts in more than 75 cases).

24. *See United States v. Baker Hughes, Inc.*, 908 F.2d 981, 985-986, 988 & n.13 (D.C. Cir. 1990); *United States v. Syufy Enters.*, 903 F.2d 659, 664 & nn.11, 21 (9th Cir. 1990); *United States v. Waste Mgt., Inc.*, 743 F.2d 976, 982-983 (2d Cir. 1984).

25. *See, e.g.*, Kirkwood & Zerbe, *supra* note 12 (analyzing every judicial opinion in a litigated government merger case since adoption of 1992 *Horizontal Merger Guidelines* to test their compliance with or use of *Guidelines* approach to "entry" issues; finding that all opinions expressed respect for *Guidelines* on this issue, but few actually employed them and several misunderstood them).

who advise merging firms rely extensively the *Guidelines* and on whatever other insight they can glean of the agencies' enforcement intentions.

§17.3 THE SUBSTANTIVE LAW OF CLAYTON ACT §7: SCOPE AND APPLICABILITY

As it now exists, the scope of Clayton Act §7 is complex, though at least it can be stated with reasonable confidence. Under current law the statute applies to:

- Any "acquisition" (a somewhat murky but very broad term meaning any transaction in which a bundle of legal rights relating to some thing of value is transferred),
- in which either:
  - any
    - "person" (meaning an individual, any business entity, and essentially any other legally recognized form of association), acquires
    - "stock or share capital" (meaning any voting interest),
  - or any
    - "person" that is "subject to the jurisdiction of the Federal Trade Commission" (meaning a for-profit business, except for banking, transport, or communications firms regulated by another federal agency, or a nonprofit that provides financial benefits to its members) acquires
    - "assets" (meaning essentially any thing of value),
- from any other "person,"
- as long as both parties to the transaction are within the interstate commerce jurisdiction of the U.S. Congress.

A few of the relevant terms call for elaboration. Section 7 applies where a person "acquire[s]" either any "assets" or any "stock or other share capital." None of these terms is defined by statute, but, in part as the result of several corrective congressional interventions, they are all now read very broadly, to reflect §7's prophylactic purpose and to deter formalistic evasions through clever lawyering.

First, an "acquisition" is a transaction involving some sort of reduction of an asset to the acquiror's *control*. A well-known early statement is in *United States v. Columbia Pictures Corp.*, 189 F. Supp. 153 (S.D.N.Y. 1960), where the court found the purchase of a long-term, exclusive license to the copyrights in motion pictures to constitute an "acquisition." In general terms, the court explained:

> As used here, the words "acquire" and "assets" are not terms of art or technical legal language. In the context of [Section 7], they are generic, imprecise terms encompassing a broad spectrum of transactions whereby the acquiring person may accomplish the acquisition by means of purchase, assignment, lease, license, or otherwise. The test is pragmatic. The final answer is not in the dictionary.

Id. at 181-182. Accordingly, the court wrote that an acquisition means the "transfer of a sufficient part of the bundle of legal rights and privileges from the transferring person to the acquiring person to give the transfer economic significance and the proscribed adverse 'effect.'" *Id.* at 182. Accordingly it is clear that garden-variety purchases are "acquisitions"—like a transfer of a thing for value in exchange for cash, for securities, or for some other asset traded in kind. But courts have also found much more exotic arrangements to be "acquisitions," such as an agreement between an Internet bookseller and a brick-and-mortar bookseller, that the former would manage the latter's website (which the court analogized to an acquisition of the latter firm's online presence);[26] the creation of a standard-setting joint venture among computer manufacturers for the development of certain standard software designs, where the participants joined by contributing initial funding and were given certain management rights;[27] and a management agreement under which the owner of one business is hired to manage—to make business decisions, including price and output decisions for—a horizontal competitor.[28] The central idea in all these cases seems to be that there must be some transfer of rights to control a thing, so that the acquiror gets the economic benefit from it.

Importantly, the *creation of a new* entity may constitute an "acquisition." For example, in *United States v. Penn-Olin Chem. Co.*, 378 U.S. 158 (1964), two existing corporations involved in chemical manufacturing agreed to cooperate in the production of a new product. To set up their joint venture, they created a new corporation they would own jointly. The Court held the deal subject to §7 because the two joint venturers had "acquired" stock in the newly formed corporation.

Likewise, "assets" and "stock or other share capital" are not defined by statute, but as with "acquisition," they are read broadly to deter formalistic evasions. "Stock or other share capital" is the somewhat simpler term. Naturally, it includes all voting securities in corporations as well as equity ownership interests in other business entities, such as partnerships or limited liability companies. "Assets" is more vague but is in any case read very

---

26. *Gerlinger v. Amazon.com, Inc.*, 311 F. Supp. 2d 838, 853 (N.D. Cal. 2004).
27. *Addamax Corp. v. Open Software Found., Inc.*, 888 F. Supp. 274, 285 (D. Mass. 1995).
28. *Hosp. Corp. of Am. v. FTC*, 807 F.2d 1381, 1387 (7th Cir. 1986).

broadly. Again, the *Columbia Pictures* opinion has been influential, with the court writing:

> Consistent with the broadly-drawn language is the word "assets." It is not a word of art, nor is it given a built-in definition by statute. As used in this statute, and depending upon the factual context, "assets" may mean anything of value.
>
> The fact that an item of value may not be treated as an asset for purposes of taxation or bookkeeping, while having some evidential significance, is not conclusive. The word "assets" usually has a technical connotation in the field of taxation and accounting. There is nothing in the legislative history of Section 7 to justify the defendants' viewpoint that the word "assets" is to be interpreted through the eyes of tax experts or accountants rather than business men, or that "assets" means only "capital assets."

189 F. Supp. at 182. Accordingly, any sort of ordinary asset used in the doing of business is unproblematically an "asset," such as a factory, inventory, or equipment. Courts have also found more exotic, intangible things such as the following to constitute "assets": patents,[29] trademarks,[30] and trade routes or customer lists.[31]

Finally, the "persons" to whom the statute applies and the sort of "commerce" they must engage in are also now read broadly. "Person" is subject to one technical curlicue that relates to the jurisdiction of the Federal Trade Commission to enforce the Clayton Act under Clayton Act §11. Because of that curlicue, §7 applies when:

- The *acquiring person* is either:
  - Any "person" in cases involving acquisition of "stock or other share capital," or
  - A "person" that is not among the banking or common carrier entities specifically excluded from Clayton Act §11 enforcement, in cases involving acquisition of "assets," and
  - The *acquired person*—that is, the firm that is being acquired or is selling some of its stock or assets—is a "person" as defined in the Clayton Act.

In other words, §7 applies very broadly to all kinds of acquisitions, except that it does not apply to asset acquisitions by banks or regulated common carriers.

---

29. *SCM Corp. v. Xerox Corp.*, 645 F.2d 1195, 1205 (2d Cir. 1981).
30. *United States v. Beatrice Foods Co.*, 344 F. Supp. 104, 114 (D. Minn. 1972).
31. *United States v. ITT-Continental Baking Co.*, 485 F.2d 16, 20 (10th Cir. 1973), *rev'd on other grounds*, 420 U.S. 223 (1975).

"Commerce," too, though it was once the subject of some controversy, is now very broad, and in effect is just as broad as the "trade or commerce" to which the Sherman Act applies.

Example

Gorman Bros., an Ohio partnership, has been an uncommonly successful competitor in the distribution of restaurant supplies and equipment in Northeastern Ohio, and now accounts for a large part of that business, enjoying annual sales in excess of $10 million. One of its major competitors, Fizzypop, Inc., happened recently to falter, and ultimately was liquidated in bankruptcy. Gorman immediately made contact with another Ohio company, the investment firm Whitman & Assocs., LLC. Among other things it does to earn its bread, Whitman is active in purchasing assets from bankruptcy estates and reselling them. Gorman's particular hope was that Whitman might be able to get its hands on a jewel of an asset from the Fizzypop liquidation proceeding, a set of ongoing service arrangements, all identified as "agency appointments," under which Fizzypop was to be on call to fix the soda-fountain distribution systems maintained by restaurants. Whitman did not exactly "buy" the agency appointments, but rather reached a deal with the bankruptcy trustee under which it would broker the reassignment of the agreements to a new service company. Following some negotiations, Whitman was able to get each of the agency deals reassigned by each restaurant to Gorman Bros., much to the satisfaction of all involved. Whitman's not insubstantial fee for performing this service was paid by Gorman Bros.

Is this transaction subject to Clayton Act §7?

Explanation

Probably. First, there is no doubt that the transaction is in or affecting commerce in the United States. Second, the fact that one party to the sale is a general partnership and the other is an LLC is irrelevant; both are now clearly "persons" under the Clayton Act and subject to §7. Next, there is probably not much doubt that the service arrangements are "assets" within the meaning of §7. Under the *Columbia Pictures* opinion discussed above, the term means roughly anything of value. Probably somewhat more difficult is whether the renegotiation of existing service contracts constituted an "acquisition." The renegotiation of existing service contracts seems a fairly exotic "acquisition" if it is one. But, again, *Columbia Pictures* stressed the importance of reading these terms broadly, and indicated that any transaction resulting in a transfer of control over some "asset" is an "acquisition."[32]

32. A technical point is that while this acquisition is probably subject to Clayton Act §7, it would not be subject to the pre-acquisition reporting requirements of the Hart-Scott-Rodino

§17.4 THE §7 SUBSTANTIVE CAUSE OF ACTION

Once it is determined that a transaction is subject to §7, the question becomes whether it is illegal. The substantive cause of action under §7 is roughly the same regardless what sort of transaction is being challenged, though its details vary somewhat depending on whether the transaction is horizontal, vertical, or conglomerate. Claims against horizontal deals are the most common and the most commonly litigated, and therefore are the best understood. Claims against vertical and conglomerate deals are both more uncertain legally. There just isn't that much guidance from either the courts or the agencies on how they should be approached, and they tend to be much more fact intensive and complex as a matter of economic theory.

In summary, the plaintiff in any §7 case bears the burden to show that a challenged deal will facilitate conduct by the merging parties that will harm competition. In principle, the cause of action that still applies is a burden-shifting formula under which the plaintiff can make its case on a prima facie showing of likely harm, plus a rebuttal of any defense evidence that the prima facie case mischaracterizes the likely effects of the merger. In horizontal deals, plaintiff can make the prima facie case just by showing that concentration will increase significantly. The prima facie showing is more complex and less certain in non-horizontal deals, and can't consist of mere increase in concentration. By definition vertical and conglomerate deals do not in themselves change concentration in either the acquiring or target firm's market. That said, in every case the theory of harm will be based on some *horizontal* impact. That is, even if the transaction is not a horizontal one, the plaintiff's explanation of the harms that will flow from it must be based on some new ability it will give one of the merging parties to harm its own horizontal competitors. For that reason, all currently viable non-horizontal theories of harm—and therefore the plaintiff's prima facie case—will involve market definition and proof of power in a relevant market.

The cause of action has three basic elements. One influential opinion explains it this way:

> [(1)] By showing that a transaction will lead to undue concentration in the market for a particular product in a particular geographic area, [or by making an initial demonstration that a non-horizontal merger could cause harm,]

Act, even if it is large enough to meet the dollar-value filing thresholds of that statute. Because Whitman & Assocs. is an "investment firm" that, as a part of its business, buys bankruptcy assets and holds them only for resale, sales by it are in the "ordinary course of business" and therefore exempt from HSR. *See* Clayton Act §7a(c)(1), 15 U.S.C. §18a(c)(1). HSR exemptions are explained further in §18.2. Clayton Act §7 itself contains no "ordinary course of business" exception.

> the government establishes a presumption that the transaction will substantially lessen competition. [(2)] The burden of producing evidence to rebut this presumption then shifts to the defendant. If the defendant successfully rebuts the presumption, [then (3)] the burden of producing additional evidence of anticompetitive effect shifts to the government, and merges with the ultimate burden of persuasion, which remains with the government at all times.

United States v. Baker Hughes, Inc., 908 F.2d 981, 982-983 (D.C. Cir. 1990) (citing, among others, *Philadelphia National Bank*).[33]

Breaking it down a little further, the elements work this way:

1. *Prima Facie Case.* In horizontal cases, plaintiff's prima facie showing will rely heavily on market definition and evidence that the merger will increase concentration in an already concentrated market. Nominally, that evidence alone can satisfy the prima facie showing and create a presumption of anticompetitive effect, but ordinarily plaintiff will have put on other evidence supporting an inference of anticompetitive harm. That may include evidence of entry barriers or evidence of past conduct within the market.

   In non-horizontal mergers the prima facie showing is somewhat different, because non-horizontal mergers in themselves do not change concentration in any present market. Plaintiff's prima facie showing will nevertheless consist of evidence that some relevant market is concentrated, because all non-horizontal theories of harm depend on market power in a relevant market. *See* §17.5.
2. *Rebuttal Evidence.* Following prima facie showing, a burden of production shifts to defendant to put on evidence rebutting it. This will ordinarily consist of challenge to plaintiff's market definition and evidence that, regardless how the market is defined, easy entry would undermine and likelihood of market power. Defendants also often adduce evidence at this stage that their merger will generate pro-competitive efficiency benefits, but this theory has proven much more difficult for them. *See* §17.6.
3. *Additional Evidence and the Theory of Harm.* If defendant rebuts the prima facie showing, plaintiff must make its ultimate case and carry the burden of showing anticompetitive harm. To do this, plaintiff will need to demonstrate some theory under which the transaction will harm competition. This so-called "theory of harm" will vary by type of transaction.

---

33. Technically, *Baker Hughes* was a horizontal merger case, and identified this as the test for challenge to horizontal mergers. It now seems clear, however, that the same basic framework appears to apply in non-horizontal merger cases as well (i.e., as to vertical and conglomerate mergers). *United States v. AT&T, Inc.*, 916 F.3d 1029, 1032 (D.C. Cir. 2019).

a. *Horizontal.* As a practical matter, two theories of harm are available to challenge horizontal deals, both of which are discussed in §17.7.1:
   i. *Coordinated effects*
   ii. *Unilateral effects*
b. *Vertical.* Quite a variety of theories of harm are available to challenge vertical deals. Those most clearly viable at present, both of which are discussed in §17.7.2, are:
   i. *Foreclosure*
   ii. *Access to Competitively Sensitive Information*
c. *Conglomerate.* The only theory of harm currently available to challenge conglomerate deals is that they will forestall what would have been "potential competition." *See* §17.7.3.

4. *The Failing Firm Defense.* Finally, in some cases an otherwise illegal merger might be excused if the defendant can show that the value of some procompetitive advantages to be gained through the transaction outweigh whatever anticompetitive harms it may pose. Perhaps surprisingly, given much of what we learn elsewhere in antitrust law, the courts and agencies have long been sharply hostile to this defense, and it remains very difficult to prove. *See* §17.8.

We ought to notice one interesting issue front and center. This standard for challenging mergers, including horizontal mergers of competitors, is often quite a bit more permissive than the law relating to horizontal restraints under Sherman Act §1. Two head-to-head competitors can merge all their operations completely and not face per se illegality, even where the merger significantly increases single-firm market power. Moreover, the merged firms will thereafter set only one price for the product the parties had previously produced separately. And yet, if the same two firms remained separate but agreed as to the price at which they would sell, the agreement would be per se illegal (and a few corporate executives might even go to prison). This might all seem pretty counterintuitive, and critics of antitrust have often pointed to this apparent tension as proof of the law's fundamental lack of cohesion.

But courts and commentators have come up with several explanations for this result. First, and most obviously nowadays, mergers are thought by many to produce efficiencies—there may be economies of scale or scope or other benefits that can't be realized when the parties continue on as separately organized businesses. Some also believe there is social value in what has come to be known as the "market for corporate control." Controlling interests in businesses can be valued just like any other thing that can be bought or sold, at least where there is a healthy market for those interests. As a simple argument of economics, if control of a business is for sale in a healthy, competitive market, then it will be purchased by those who value it most. Those who value it most will be those who can use that control most profitably. Running a business in the most profitable way, barring market imperfections or some sort of fraud or wrongdoing, is the best for society (so say some economists). So if a business is bought by someone who values it more than its current owner, that buyer may then put in place more effective managers, cut out wasteful programs, and improve the efficiency of the operation. Likewise, if existing managers of a company know that their firm is perpetually at risk of being bought out from under them, they will be pressured to run the company as well as they can to keep that from happening. (You see, if the company is being run as well as possible, then shareholders will already enjoy the highest possible value for their shares, assuming the market for their shares is itself functioning properly, and there should be no buyer willing to pay more for them than the price at which they are already valued.) But the market for corporate control will not function well if the law somehow seriously deters mergers and acquisitions. If it does, that would give poor, inefficient, or evilly intentioned managers government protection from what could otherwise be the healthy disciplinary force of competition.

Now ask yourself whether these facts meaningfully distinguish merger from the kinds of horizontal agreement that are treated more harshly under antitrust. At least in the case of naked, horizontal price agreements or market allocations or the like, the answer seems pretty obviously to be yes. It may be true that mergers can result in identical pricing of products that otherwise would compete, but in the case of the naked multilateral agreement, that is the *only* thing the agreement accomplishes.

§17.5 THE SUBSTANTIVE CAUSE OF ACTION, STEP 1: MARKET DEFINITION AND THE *PRIMA FACIE* CASE

In every §7 case, the plaintiff will bear the initial burden to show that the merged entity could cause harm through market power. The Supreme Court has always declined to specify any minimum measure of market power to be shown in merger cases, and most lower courts continue to hold that, technically, there is no fixed threshold of concentration or other evidence that will satisfy the plaintiff's initial burden.[34] As we'll see, the threshold has grown over time, and is certainly something higher than the 30 percent market share showing found sufficient in *Philadelphia National Bank*.

34. *See, e.g.*, *FTC v. Staples, Inc.*, 970 F. Supp. 1076, 1082 (D.D.C. 1997) (citing *United States v. Philadelphia Natl. Bank*, 374 U.S. 321, 363-365 (1963)).

At this initial stage, plaintiff often will show more than mere concentration numbers, and in all non-horizontal cases must show some evidence of anticompetitive harm other than increasing concentration, because by definition non-horizontal mergers do not increase it. But in effectively all cases the prima facie case will depend heavily on market demonstration of significant concentration, because all presently viable theories of harm depend on it. In merger cases, courts and the agencies examine concentration using Hirschmann-Herfindahl Index (HHI), described in detail in 4.3.

§17.5.1 Horizontal Cases

The plaintiff's initial showing is the most straightforward in horizontal cases. The plaintiff's prima facie showing can depend mainly or entirely on concentration evidence, and it shifts the burden to the defendant to produce evidence that the deal is not anticompetitive.

The antitrust agencies' *Merger Guidelines* codify this test and supplement it with specific HHI benchmarks. That is, the *Guidelines* set out specific concentration levels at which the agencies are more or less likely to challenge a horizontal merger.

The agencies' views on this point have varied over time. In their current iteration, the 2023 *Merger Guidelines* consider any market with an HHI higher than 1800 to be "highly concentrated," and any HHI increase of more than 100 to be "significant," and presume that any merger that significantly increases a market to render it "highly concentrated" is illegal. Moreover, if the increase is "significant" and creates a merged entity with a market share of 30% or more, that too is presumed illegal. *Id.* at §2.1. These points return the *Guidelines* to the thresholds that appeared in the 1992 *Horizontal Merger Guidelines,* and reverse a course taken in the 2010 *Horizontal Merger Guidelines,* which had increased them substantially.[35]

However, these numbers must be taken with a large grain of salt, because in practice the agencies very rarely challenge mergers without much more serious concentration evidence. Even the 2010 revision did not capture actual practice. It has been shown that in recent history, the agencies have ordinarily challenged deals only at much higher concentration numbers. *See* John Kwoka, *Mergers, Merger Control, and Remedies* (2014).

---

35. *See* 2010 *Horizontal Merger Guidelines* §5.3 (providing that mergers resulting in an HHI below 1,500 ordinarily require no further analysis; those that involve HHI increase of more than 100 points and result in HHI between 1,500 and 2,500 "raise significant competitive concerns and often warrant scrutiny"; those resulting in HHI above 2,500 will raise significant concern if the increase is over 100 points; and those resulting in HHI above 2,500 are presumed anticompetitive if the increase is over 200 points.).

The 1992 document raised the numbers quite a bit from where they'd been in 1984, *see* 1984 *Merger Guidelines* §3.1, and drastically higher than in 1968, *see* 1968 *Merger Guidelines* §5.

Moreover, as mentioned, the strong trend since 1975 has been to reduce the power of the *Philadelphia National Bank* presumption, initially in *General Dynamics* and even more stridently in lower court case law during the 1980s and 1990s. In these cases the courts have been skeptical of bare concentration statistics, and in particular they have stressed the care with which courts must review defendants' rebuttal evidence.[36] Some in fact have implied that mere evidence of a certain increase in concentration is, as a matter of law, insufficient to prove a §7 violation.[37] One opinion, *United States v. Baker Hughes, Inc.*, 908 F.2d 981 (D.C. Cir. 1990), has been considered especially important in that it was written by then-Judge Clarence Thomas and was joined by then-Judge Ruth Bader Ginsburg. *Baker Hughes* stressed at length that since *General Dynamics* the inquiry under §7 has become a "totality of the circumstances" test, and accordingly even very high concentration statistics will not support a challenge unless there is also substantial evidence of entry barriers and a convincing theory of harm.

All that said, though, it remains the case that the large majority of merger challenges will be against horizontal deals and depend heavily on concentration numbers. It just so happens that the numbers will almost always be quite high. As something of a rule of thumb or folk wisdom among antitrust lawyers, the agencies typically challenge horizontal mergers only if they are "4-to-3" or larger. That is, if the market contains only four major competitors and one of them proposes to acquire another, that would be a change from four major firms to three, and the agencies will bring challenge. If the pre-merger market has more than four competitors and the merger would leave it with four or more, the agencies will not. Assuming firms of equal size and assuming that the four firms control the entire market, a 4-to-3 deal would have a pre-merger HHI of 2500, increase it by 1250, and leave a post-merger HHI of 3750.[38]Most successful horizontal merger challenges for the past few decades have involved comparable numbers.

Like other rules of thumb, this one does not always hold. The agencies do sometimes challenge mergers leaving four or more competitors, and they win some of those cases. Those exceptions tend to prove the rule, however, because they usually involve unusual market structures that generate

---

36. *See FTC v. H.J. Heinz Co.*, 246 F.3d 708, 720 (D.C. Cir. 2002); *United States v. Baker Hughes, Inc.*, 908 F.2d 981, 990 & n.12 (D.C. Cir. 1990); *Hosp. Corp. of Am. v. FTC*, 807 F.2d 1381, 1386 (7th Cir. 1986); *United States v. Waste Mgt., Inc.*, 743 F.2d 976, 981-983 (2d Cir. 1984).

37. *See H.J. Heinz*, 246 F.3d at 716 n.11.

38. Recall that the HHI is "the sum of the squares of the market shares of all the firms in the market." If four firms divide an entire market equally, they each have 25% market share. The pre-merger HHI is therefore $4(25)^2 = 2500$. If two of the firms merge, their combined market share is 50%, and the post-merger HHI is $50^2 + 2(25)^2 = 3750$, for an increase in HHI of $3750 - 2500 = 1250$.

high HHI results. For example, in *United States v. Bertelsman SE & Co., KGaA*, 646 F.Supp.3d 1 (D.D.C. 2022), the government successfully blocked acquisition by the publisher Penguin Random House of its rival Simon & Schuster, even though it was a 5-to-4 deal. But the concentration numbers were unusual because Penguin Random House was already much larger than any other competitor. Recall that the HHI formula is designed to give more weight to deals in markets that have one or a few large competitors. (*See* §4.3.) Before the merger, Penguin Random House held 37% of the relevant market, a much larger share than any of the other major firms. The deal would leave the merged firm with about half the relevant market, and the four major firms left after the deal would control 91% of it. The resulting HHI numbers were an increase of 891 from 2220 to 3111. 646 F.Supp.3d at 37. Those are large numbers, comparable to those in a typical 4-to-3.

§17.5.2 Vertical Cases and Conglomerate Cases

While the cause of action for non-horizontal merger has never been as clearly defined as for horizontal ones, some substantial clarifications were recently made in *United States v. AT&T, Inc.*, 916 F.3d 1029 (D.C. Cir. 2019), and new guidance was provided in the 2023 *Merger Guidelines*. *AT&T*, the government's first vertical merger challenge in more than 40 years and the first litigated vertical merger case of any kind in decades, required the courts seriously to consider what the vertical merger cause of action should look like, in light of other changes in merger law.

Again, a vertical merger does not *change* concentration in any market. By definition, the target firm and the acquiring firm are in different product markets, and therefore the concentration levels in their two markets will be the same before and after the acquisition. Accordingly, a vertical merger plaintiff must make its prima facie case with some other "fact-specific showing that the proposed merger is likely to be anticompetitive." *Id.* at 1032. So even at the prima facie stage, plaintiff will need a theory of harm—a theory to explain how plaintiff's initial evidence demonstrates likely anticompetitive harm.

Likewise, a conglomerate acquisition does not change concentration in any present market, although if the target firm would otherwise have entered the acquiring firm's market, then it might make that market more concentrated than it would otherwise have been in the future.

All that said, market definition is still centrally important in any vertical or conglomerate challenge that is likely to be brought, and it will effectively always be part of the plaintiff's prima facie case. Theories of non-horizontal harm that are currently viable all rely on the merged firm holding market power in some relevant market. Non-horizontal theories of harm are discussed in §17.7.

§17.6 THE SUBSTANTIVE CAUSE OF ACTION, STEP 2: REBUTTAL EVIDENCE

If the plaintiff makes its prima facie case, a burden of production shifts to defendant to rebut that showing. In principle, under the test as described in *Philadelphia National Bank* and *Baker Hughes*, the plaintiff could win at this stage if defendant produces no evidence at all. Some courts seem to have suggested otherwise, and in any even it never happens in practice. The defense will effectively always come forward with rebuttal evidence.

§17.6.1 Market Definition and Entry

Two key and common bases on which defendants rebut the initial showing are to attack plaintiff's market definition and to show that, regardless how markets are defined, easy entry would undercut any likelihood of market power.

As for market definition issues, they are handled as they are in other antitrust cases, as explained in Chapter 4. When defendants put on evidence of likely entry, courts and the agencies require it to show that entry would be "timely, likely, and sufficient." *FTC v. Sanford Health*, 926 F.3d 959, 965 (8th Cir. 2019); 2023 *Merger Guidelines* § 3.2. As the agencies describe them, these factors seem fairly difficult to meet. In effect it must be shown that entry will be so certain and effective that it will "replace lost competition before any effect from the loss of competition due to the merger may occur." *Id.* Moreover, what the defendant must put on in rebuttal varies with the strength of the prima facie case. If the concentration and other evidence at the initial stage is very strong, then the rebuttal showing must be as well. *Sanford Health*, 926 F.3d at 963.

§17.6.2 Efficiencies

No one doubts that, in principle, business consolidations can lead to efficiency gains. They can help the joined firms make their product better or more cheaply. The merged firms might use merger to reduce their costs in any number of ways—they might combine or reorganize production facilities, combine their promotional efforts over a broader range or larger volume of products, ship their goods in larger volume, or use their consolidation in any number of other ways to rationalize their operations.

Much more controversial has been whether such gains should play any role in assessing legality under §7. While defendants have long argued that efficiency gains should be available as a defense, the courts, enforcement agencies, and most commentators remained very skeptical until recently. The Supreme Court has never fully resolved the issue, and in fact its most recent statements on point seem to have been that they could not, as a matter of law. In *FTC v. Proctor & Gamble Co.*, 386 U.S. 568 (1967), the Court wrote that "[p]ossible economies cannot be used as a defense to illegality. Congress was aware that some mergers which lessen competition may also result in economies, but it struck the balance in favor of protecting competition."[39]

Indeed, the *Proctor & Gamble* Court seemed to hold—in a passage that has been much criticized—that the advantages the merged firms might gain through efficiency increases could be held *against* them in §7 litigation.[40] Plaintiffs and the Federal Trade Commission argued as recently as the early 1990s that efficiencies were no defense whatsoever, as a matter of law,[41] and even more recently some courts have expressed continuing uncertainty.[42]

The strict rule of *Procter & Gamble* probably no longer states the law. Hostility to efficiencies had a basis in theory and the legislative history,[43] but it was the subject of much criticism, and it has been at least partially

---

39. 386 U.S. at 579. Other language to similar effect can be found in a few of the Court's other cases, including the frequently quoted view that "an otherwise illegal merger cannot be saved merely because, on some ultimate reckoning of social or economic debits and credits, it may be deemed beneficial. A value choice of such magnitude is beyond the ordinary limits of judicial competence, and in any event has been made for us already, by Congress when it enacted the amended §7. Congress determined to preserve our traditionally competitive economy. It therefore proscribed anticompetitive mergers, the benign and the malignant alike, fully aware, we must assume, that some price might have to be paid." *United States v. Philadelphia Natl. Bank*, 374 U.S. 321, 371 (1963). *See also Ford Motor Co. v. United States*, 405 U.S. 562, 570 (1972) (rejecting efficiency arguments, mainly on citation to *Philadelphia National Bank*).

40. The acquiring company in *Proctor & Gamble* was a large, diversified manufacturer of household cleaning goods, and it sought to acquire a prominent manufacturer of one household good it did not make, liquid bleach. The Court found that the acquiror's large advertising budget and its ability to advertise a large range of goods in high volume—that is, the efficiencies it enjoyed in the marketing of its products—would create entry barriers giving the merged firm market power. 386 U.S. at 579.

41. *See, e.g., FTC v. Univ. Health, Inc.*, 938 F.3d 1206, 1212, 1222 (11th Cir. 1991) (noting the FTC's argument that "there [is no] efficiency defense to section 7 challenges").

42. *See, e.g., FTC v. Staples, Inc.*, 970 F. Supp. 1076, 1088 (D.D.C. 1997) ("Whether an efficiencies defense showing that the intended merger would create significant efficiencies in the relevant market, thereby offsetting any anti-competitive effects, may be used by a defendant to rebut the government's prima facie case is not entirely clear.").

43. The Court's early hostility was founded on the uncommonly strong language of §7, under the Celler-Kefauver amendments, and the Court's view of the legislative history. Efficiencies also pose problems of proof—they typically must be shown on a prospective and speculative basis, and were they more freely entertained they surely could be the subject of abuse by defendants and defense experts. On a separate point, efficiencies are implicitly recognized in contemporary §7 law already, in that horizontal combinations are not banned outright but are subject to challenge only under a relatively permissive standard. This is the flip side of an observation made in §17.4 that even large horizontal mergers are treated much more leniently than the most de minimis horizontal price fixing, because the law recognizes that mergers pose potential efficiency gains.

eroded. As early as the 1982 *Merger Guidelines* the Justice Department recognized a very narrow efficiency defense, which was preserved in the 1992 *Horizontal Merger Guidelines* and expanded in the revisions of 1997 and 2010. The lower courts likewise have mostly now held that there is at least theoretically some possibility of defending an otherwise illegal merger on efficiency grounds.[44] Still, defendants have had significant trouble making the defense. Efficiencies have sometimes weighed in favor of out-of-court resolutions in the HSR process, but, to date, no court in a litigated merger case has approved an otherwise illegal merger on this basis. *See* 1 Am. Bar Assn., *Antitrust Law Developments* (Ninth) 385 & n.222 (9th ed. 2022) (collecting cases and so stating).

One technical point the courts have not resolved is whether efficiencies evidence is part of defendant's rebuttal of plaintiff's prima facie case, or rather a defense that is separate from the plaintiff's case in chief. Some courts that have directly addressed it have held that they are only rebuttal evidence and cannot be raised in defense of an otherwise illegal merger.[45] While the *Guidelines* have recognized efficiencies since 1982, they never commented on this particular issue until 2023. The 2023 *Merger Guidelines* imply that efficiencies are *not* a defense and are considered only in connection with the prima facie case.[46]

That seemingly academic distinction could matter a lot. If efficiencies can be used only to rebut the prima facie case, then they can only put the plaintiff to its proof and not win the case in themselves. In other words, even a very persuasive demonstration of efficiency gains could do no more than show that a merger is not illegal solely because it significantly increases concentration. If the plaintiff's further proof then shows that the merger would cause harm, the efficiency evidence could not render it legal.

We will consider the efficiencies issue here, as part of defense rebuttal to the prima facie case, because that is how they've most often been handled.

---

44. *See, e.g.*, *FTC v. H.J. Heinz Co.*, 246 F.3d 708, 722 (D.C. Cir. 2001); *FTC v. Tenet Health Care Corp.*, 186 F.3d 1045, 1054 (8th Cir. 1999); *FTC v. Univ. Health, Inc.*, 938 F.2d 1206, 1222 (11th Cir. 1991); *FTC v. Staples, Inc.*, 970 F. Supp. 1066, 1088-1089 (D.D.C. 1997).

45. Not many cases have clearly, directly addressed this question, but *United States v. Anthem, Inc.*, 855 F.3d 345 (D.C. Cir. 2017), did, and it held efficiencies relevant only as rebuttal to the prima facie showing. *Id.* at 353-55. Other courts to have given efficiencies serious consideration have done at the prima facie stage, and without deciding the issue have recognized that they might be prohibited as defense. *See, e.g.*, *Heinz*, 246 F.3d at 720; *Univ. Health*, 938 F.2d at 1222. Some courts have been entirely unclear on the issue. *See, e.g.*, *Tenet Health Care*, 186 F.3d at 1054-55.

46. *Compare* 2023 *Merger Guidelines* § 3.3 (so noting; citing *Proctor & Gamble* as holding that "economies [from a merger] cannot be used as a defense to illegality," but acknowledging that they might be considered in rebuttal to prima facie evidence) *with* FTC & U.S. Dep't of Justice, *Horizontal Merger Guidelines* § 10 (2010), FTC & U.S. Dep't of Justice, *Horizontal Merger Guidelines* § 4 (1992, rev. 1997), and U.S. Dep't of Justice, *Merger Guidelines* § 3.5 (1982, rev. 1984).

A defendant raising efficiency evidence must make several showings. First, efficiencies must be "merger-specific," which means "they must be efficiencies that cannot be achieved by either company alone because, if they can, the merger's asserted benefits can be achieved without the concomitant loss of a competitor." *FTC v. H.J. Heinz Co.*, 246 F.3d 708, 722 (D.C. Cir. 2001); 2023 *Merger Guidelines* §3.3. Next, they must be "verifiable," using "reliable methodology and evidence not dependent on the subjective predictions of the merging parties." *Id.* On this, though the courts and the agencies have stated no particular standard of proof, their expectations are high. Because efficiencies arguments are necessarily forward-looking predictions, they are received with skepticism and must be based on a substantial amount of evidence. Defendants are most likely to meet the showing if the claimed efficiency is of the kind that the parties had previously achieved in past transactions, or if there is some other real-world basis for the argument. The 1992 *Horizontal Merger Guidelines*, which have been influential with courts in weighing efficiencies arguments, added this useful perspective:

> The Agency has found that certain types of efficiencies are more likely to be cognizable and substantial than others. For example, efficiencies resulting from shifting production among facilities formerly owned separately, which enable the merging firms to reduce the marginal cost of production, are more likely to be susceptible to verification, merger-specific, and substantial, and are less likely to result from anticompetitive reductions in output. Other efficiencies, such as those relating to research and development, are potentially substantial but are generally less susceptible to verification and may be the result of anticompetitive output reductions. Yet others, such as those relating to procurement, management, or capital cost are less likely to be merger-specific or substantial, or may not be cognizable for other reasons.

Id. at §4.

Finally, efficiencies must be "cognizable," meaning that they must lead to benefits of the kind antitrust seeks to generate. For example, the merging parties cannot assert a cost savings that might arise because of a reduction in output or their own ability to charge higher prices. Likewise, effects that benefit only the merged firm, like costs savings from productive efficiency improvements that the firm will not pass on to customers, are not cognizable. 2023 *Merger Guidelines* §3.3.

Example

National Auto Parts, Inc. (NAPI), a manufacturer of replacement parts for automobiles, has acquired a distribution firm known as American Auto Supply (AAS). Though NAPI is by a substantial margin the largest producer in its field, it faces competition from about a dozen other manufacturers, three of them fairly large. All of them sell their products either through AAS or one of the other nationwide auto parts distributors. Those nationwide distributors in turn sell the products to retail stores and to local distributors that sell parts to garages and mechanics. It turns out that *retail* sales, directly to car owners and mechanics, are quite competitive. Nationwide distribution, however, is not. Only three firms exist in the United States that perform that function. AAS has about 53 percent of that market, whereas its two competitors have 33 percent and 14 percent, respectively.

The acquisition is challenged by one of NAPI's competitors. As part of its response, NAPI argues that whatever competitive harms might arise will be outweighed by the acquisition's efficiency enhancements. Specifically, NAPI says, there will be savings from the improved ability of NAPI managers to oversee the firm's distribution directly. Moreover, NAPI believes that AAS has been "overcommitted" and is producing at an inefficiently high volume; as AAS's new owner, NAPI will achieve some cost savings by scaling back AAS's volume a bit.

Does the acquisition violate Clayton Act §7?

Explanation

EXPLANATION

While one should always recall that vertical mergers such as this one are rarely challenged and almost never see courtroom consideration, this one seems fairly egregious. Both markets at issue appear to be significantly concentrated, so whichever one is the "primary" market (i.e., whichever one is the market in which it is thought there might be competitive problems), there may well be sufficient concentration to support liability. While we can't tell from these facts what the concentration statistics would be in NAPI's market, it sounds like they could be fairly high. NAPI is dominant by a "substantial margin" and three other firms are "fairly large," so the fact that there are still eleven other competitors may not represent much competitive power—it sounds as though those eleven firms are pretty small. And AAS's market is massively concentrated—the HHI in the target market is 4,094. Various theories of harm might be alleged as to either market, depending on what other facts can be shown. The acquisition might be part of a facilitation of collusion at either level or a means of securing competitors' sensitive information at either level. It seems that it might also be a foreclosure strategy at either level; either NAPI or AAS, by having established a tight relationship with the dominant firm at the other level, might have set up a major barrier to entry at its own level.

As for NAPI's efficiency justifications, they will probably not be very successful. First, the agencies have indicated that the efficiencies most likely to be persuasive are those arising from directly measurable scale economy improvements, such as cost savings from combining production in a smaller number of plants. Less promising are speculative efficiency claims, such as improvements in management of the kind suggested by NAPI. Second, NAPI says it will achieve cost savings from reducing AAS's volume, but even if that were true that is not a "cognizable" savings. Since it results from a unilateral reduction in output, it is not the sort of justification that can be raised in antitrust litigation.

§17.7 THE SUBSTANTIVE CAUSE OF ACTION, STEP 3: PLAINTIFF'S THEORY OF HARM

If defendant rebuts plaintiff's prima facie case, the burden then shifts back to plaintiff to prove that the merger will likely cause anticompetitive harm. This requires above all a theory on which the merger would be harmful, and evidence supporting it sufficient to meet the plaintiff's burden of proof.

In principle there are any number of ways a plaintiff could show that a merger is harmful. The 2023 *Merger Guidelines* preserve a view always stated in the *Guidelines*, that the theories of liability it lists are not exhaustive.[47] This edition in fact introduces quite a range of innovative new theories of harm and suggests they might be tried in litigation. 2023 *Merger Guidelines* §§ 2.6-2.11. However, the courts, for better or worse, have been less susceptible to innovation or creativity than the agencies might prefer, and even the agencies have occasionally suggested that they will limit themselves.[48] So the discussion here will focus on those theories that are presently most viable.

§17.7.1 Theories of Harm from Horizontal Merger

The two theories of harm most commonly asserted in horizontal merger cases are as follows. (1) *Coordinated effects:* Because acquisitions among competitors tend to increase concentration in a given industry, they might facilitate either collusion (collusion being easier the fewer members there are in any given conspiracy) or oligopoly pricing behavior even in the absence of agreement. (2) *Unilateral effects:* In some markets—in which products are "differentiated" or branded—increasing concentration might support

47. *Compare* 2023 *Merger Guidelines* at 29 *with* FTC & United States Dep't of Justice, *Horizontal Merger Guidelines* § 1 (2010) ("merger analysis does not consist of uniform application of a single methodology," so the agencies "apply a range of analytical tools to the reasonably available and reliable evidence"); *and* FTC & United States Dep't of Justice, *Horizontal Merger Guidelines* §2.0 (1992) (Guidelines lay out only "some of" the possible theories of anticompetitive harm, and insisted that "mergers will be analyzed in terms of as many potential adverse competitive effects as are appropriate").
48. Specifically, see FTC & U.S. Dep't of Justice, *Commentary on the Horizontal Merger Guidelines* 2-3 (2006) (stating that the agencies would only challenge horizontal mergers under the coordinated effects theory and the unilateral effects theory, both discussed here).

unilateral pricing power. As a practical matter, the unilateral effects theory has become more important and is more often asserted by the agencies.[49]

First, the coordinated effects theory is based on the idea that anticompetitive cooperation is easier when there are fewer firms in a given market. The idea is that, other things being equal, when the number of firms in any market shrinks, it will be easier for the remaining firms to collude explicitly or to engage in interdependent pricing behavior (also known as "oligopoly pricing" or "conscious parallelism"). The reason it is easier is mainly that "cheating" from cartel agreements or from interdependent oligopoly behavior becomes more difficult when there are fewer firms. The theory appeared as early as the 1982 *Horizontal Merger Guidelines*, and reflects the theory of oligopoly pioneered in a famous paper of the 1960s by economist George Stigler. (The theory is explored in detail in the appendix.) For this reason, §7 plays one special role within antitrust law, in that at least in principle it could help close a gap that otherwise exists in the Sherman Act. Recall that interdependent oligopoly behavior might be quite effective in raising prices, but in the absence of some agreement it does not violate Sherman Act §1. Likewise, merely using one's market power unilaterally to charge supracompetitive prices—which is what interdependent oligopolists do—does not constitute monopolization or any other violation of Sherman Act §2. So one of the few antitrust tools available to combat interdependent pricing is §7 merger enforcement against horizontal mergers on the coordinated effects theory.

This theory requires evidence not only that the merger will increase concentration, but also that postmerger conditions will be conducive to coordinated interaction. Most obviously, the plaintiff can put on evidence that conditions will be like those originally identified by Stigler as conducive to coordination. In addition to a reduction in the number of firms, coordination is thought to be encouraged by any number of other factors that can make cheating difficult to detect, such as product heterogeneity and competition on nonprice factors, or a pattern of sales that are infrequent and confidential. Second, the *Guidelines* have long adopted the "maverick" theory. Based on a widely read law review article,[50] the idea is that in some markets one firm may have a history of consistently bucking pricing norms. That is, it may have shown itself to be willing to "cheat" from coordinated behavior. If that firm is to be acquired, it might increase the risk of coordinated effects.

49. You might be thinking that the most obvious concern should really be that M&A might create outright monopolies. That would surely be a concern of antitrust, and transactions such as that would certainly be illegal under contemporary law. But merger-to-monopoly has been for so long and so obviously illegal that it is very rarely even attempted, and is not very often talked about as a serious concern of antitrust policy.

50. Jonathan B. Baker, *Mavericks, Mergers, and Exclusion: Proving Coordinated Competitive Effects Under the Antitrust Laws*, 77 N.Y.U. L. Rev. 135 (2002).

For what it may be worth, concentration statistics are more important where the theory of harm is coordinated effects. As we shall see, the whole idea in a unilateral effects case is that the merged firm could exercise some pricing power because it will *not* face a competitive response from firms in its market other than the one with which it has just merged, and therefore overall concentration is less important. Higher concentration statistics may therefore be called for to establish the prima facie case in coordinated effects cases.

Second, the unilateral effects theory posits that in some markets, the increased concentration caused by a horizontal deal will facilitate unilateral price increases by the merged entity, acting on its own. The *Guidelines* suggest this could happen in two ways. First, it is thought that there could be markets in which there are several sellers, but that some of the sellers sell uncommonly "differentiated" products. That is, their products may be sufficiently different from other products within the relevant market that they enjoy some margin of pricing discretion. This follows from economic theorizing that began in the 1930s and came to be known as the "theory of monopolistic competition."[51]

A second theory of unilateral effects is that where remaining firms in a given market are capacity constrained, they may be unable to respond to price increases. This theory is conceptually simpler and has fared well when it has been used. *See* 1 Am. Bar Assn., *Antitrust Developments (Ninth)* 379-380 (9th ed. 2022).

Example

Since childhood Bob Cochran has proven to be both a born salesman and an extremely shrewd competitor. As a man he put these skills to use in the world of commerce (in his native Boise, Idaho). Noticing one day the price of nails in his neighborhood hardware store, he saw his opportunity. He opened first one small, competing store, and then another, and then another. By the time of his first acquisition of a competing hardware store, Bob had managed to secure about 8 percent of hardware sales in Boise, but by then the swashbuckling derring-do of corporate acquisition had set a fire in his soul. Bob's ultimate goal had come to be some sort of vertical integration, as his major difficulty running his chain in Boise was the persistent threat of expansion there by the national hardware retailers.

---

51. *See* Roscoe B. Starek III & Stephen Stockum, *What Makes Mergers Anticompetitive? "Unilateral Effects" Analysis Under the 1992 Merger Guidelines,* 63 Antitrust L.J. 801, 806 n.20 (1995) (noting that the theory originated in the economics literature in 1929).

Bob did not stop until he had made himself the fourth largest hardware store in Boise, with his eyes set on acquisition of the third.[52] By then Bob's stores held about 16 percent of the Boise market, whereas the largest three firms held 21 percent, 23 percent, and 40 percent. And Bob would have gone guns a-blazin' for that next competitor. He had already secured the financing commitments (Bob had always found that the easy part—entering a new or acquiring an existing firm was not terribly costly, in the larger scheme of things, and there seemed to be plenty of private investors in Boise willing to take a bet on retail acquisitions) and gotten the ball rolling on the deal. But before he could move forward, he received a civil investigative demand from the Justice Department indicating that it was investigating his pattern of acquisitions as a violation of §7.

Would Bob's planned acquisition of the third largest firm in Boise violate §7?

Explanation

It is a close question, but arguably it may not. Admittedly, depending on how the market is defined, this may be a highly concentrated market and the acquisition would increase concentration substantially. If the market is "retail hardware sales in Boise, Idaho," then the premerger HHI is 2,826, and the acquisition would increase it by 672 points, to 3,498. Those are very high numbers and they would surely be high enough to trigger the interest of the enforcement agencies and satisfy the prima facie case under the *Philadelphia National Bank* standard. However, the facts suggest that entry is easy and that existing competitors are constrained by the threat of entry by national retail chains. That casts doubt on whether there really will be market power, even at very high concentration.

Moreover, there are some problems with the theory of harm. There could conceivably be theories here based on either unilateral or coordinated effects, though a unilateral theory seems unlikely. Perhaps a unilateral theory could be made out to analogize this case to the *Staples* case (discussed above), but nothing suggests that these hardware stores are different from others except perhaps in their size, and size alone is unlikely to make any retail store sufficiently differentiated to satisfy the *Staples* theory. A coordinated effects theory would make more sense, given the very high level of concentration and the transparency of pricing. This market seems fairly well suited to oligopolistic interdependence. Purchases are extremely high volume and prices are transparent. Products are probably not highly differentiated in terms of quality between the four stores, or at least not so much that price

52. Let us assume, quite reasonably, that none of Bob's acquisitions would have been large enough to trigger reporting duties under the Hart-Scott-Rodino Act. HSR is discussed in detail in Chapter 18.

comparisons are infeasible. One store's wrenches and nails and so on are probably pretty feasibly comparable with another's, and indeed they likely carry many of the same brands. Consumers therefore have good information, and "cheating" would be very easy to detect. However, again, ease of entry would arguably undermine efforts at coordination.

Roughly similar facts were before the court in *United States v. Syufy Enter.*, 903 F.2d 659 (9th Cir. 1990). The market there was first-run showings of films in Las Vegas movie theatres. But the result should be similar. The *Syufy* court stressed at length its view that, despite a period of very high concentration, there should be no serious entry barriers in that market. The court was very much persuaded by the fact of some actual new entry during the period of the defendant's dominance, and the refusal of one of the major movie distributors to deal with him any longer when he tried to use his position in Las Vegas to leverage more favorable terms on his access to films.

§17.7.2 Theories of Harm from Vertical Merger: "Ability and Incentive" to Foreclose, and Access to Information

For many years prior to *United States v. AT&T, Inc.*, 916 F.3d 1029 (D.C. Cir. 2019), the agencies had challenged only one or a few vertical merger cases per year during Hart-Scott-Rodino review. None went to trial, and in all of them the parties either abandoned their deals or resolved the agency objections by concessions.[53] Since *AT&T* the agencies have revived a small vertical enforcement program, with some success,[54] though the cases have proven challenging and the government has lost some major litigated matters.[55] Much uncertainty remains as to the substantive law. This is so because current economic thinking about vertical merger is complex, and because there had been so little judicial or agency guidance on them for so long.[56] Those

---

53. *See* M. Howard Morse, *Vertical Mergers: Recent Learning*, 53 Bus. Law. 1217 (1998) (noting the upsurge in enforcement actions that began in the mid-1990s and discussing evolving theoretical bases for liability and innovations in remedies sought).

54. Most importantly, *Illumina, Inc. v. FTC*, 88 F.4th 1045 (5th Cir. 2023), reversed the Commission's finding of § 7 liability in a vertical deal, but only on one particular element, and upheld enough of its determination that parties abandoned their deal. The parties abandoned deals in several other post-*AT&T* matters in which the government filed complaint or objected during HSR review, including Visa's acquisition of the financial technology provider Plaid, Nvidia's acquisition of the computer chip design firm Arm, and Lockheed Martin's acquisition of a maker of missile engines called Aerojet Rocketdyne.

55. The government fully litigated and lost in two major vertical cases. *FTC v. Microsoft Corp.*, 136 F.4th 945 (9th Cir. 2025); *United States v. UnitedHealth Group, Inc.*, 630 F.Supp.3d 118 (D.D.C. 2022).

56. As mentioned above, between 1984 and 2023, the agencies operated under the portion of the1984 Merger Guidelines that related to non-horizontal mergers. When the 1984 Guidelines were superseded by the 1992 Horizontal Merger Guidelines, the agencies simply preserved that part of the 1984 Guidelines that had applied to vertical and conglomerate

difficulties and the government's resounding loss in *AT&T* may cast some doubt on the plausibility and political likelihood of future challenges. For now at least it appears that vertical enforcement is still on the table.

The principal theory of harm remains "foreclosure." Plaintiff will claim that merger would give the merged entity control over an asset at one level of the vertical relationship that is needed by competitors at the other level. The theory traces its origins to the Supreme Court's early vertical merger decisions, even though they are few and the most recent was decided more than 40 years ago.[57] But while those cases themselves were much criticized and largely ignored during the conservative antitrust revolution, the theory of harm from vertical merger has been revived and has grown much more sophisticated.

For example, *Illumina, Inc. v. FTC*, 88 F.4th 1036 (5th Cir. 2023), involved Illumina, a maker of gene sequencing platforms that are used in a variety of medical research applications. Illumina sought to acquire Grail, which had developed a promising, innovative cancer treatment. Grail's product depended on access to Illumina's platform technology, and so did Grail's competitors—other firms developing similar cancer treatments. In fact, Illumina was the only supplier of that product, and it had no substitutes. The FTC alleged that if Illumina owned Grail, it would refuse to sell its platform technology to Grail's competitors. The Fifth Circuit agreed.[58]

It appears that going forward, foreclosure in these cases will be judged under a test coming to be known as the "ability-and-incentive" test. *Illumina*, 88 F.4th at 1051-54; 2023 *Merger Guidelines* §2.5.A.1. Ability to foreclose is largely a question of market definition. The merged firm won't be able to foreclose rivals from a product unless the merger would leave it with a large market share in the product, with few substitutes and low likelihood of entry. Incentive depends on whether the foreclosure

---

deals, and they did the same in 2010. The agencies' guidance on non-horizontal deals therefore remained in force as the law of vertical and conglomerate deals for more than 30 years, until they were replaced in 2023.

57. *Brown Shoe Co. v. United States*, 370 U.S. 294, 323-324 (1962) (citation and footnote omitted). In that case, the country's third largest shoe maker acquired the eighth largest. Both companies manufactured shoes, and both were also integrated forward into retail—that is, they not only made shoes, they also sold them directly to customers in retails stores that they owned and operated. The Court applied foreclosure reasoning and found the acquisition illegal. *See also Ford Motor Co. v. United States*, 405 U.S. 562 (1972) (holding illegal Ford's acquisition of spark plug manufacturer, largely on simple foreclosure theory); *United States v. E.I. du Pont de Nemours & Co.*, 353 U.S. 586 (1957) (holding illegal du Pont's acquisition of large bloc of General Motors voting stock, because du Pont was a major supplier of automotive fabrics and finishes; introducing simple foreclosure theory).

58. 88 F.4th at 1051-54. The court nevertheless reversed and remanded on one issue in the Commission's handling of rebuttal evidence, but the parties then abandoned the deal before the Commission could take further action. They did so presumably because the Fifth Circuit and found most matters so heavily in the Commission's favor.

would make economic sense for the merged firm. After all, by refusing to sell its product to rivals, the firm will lose the profits it could have made from those sales. Foreclosure still makes sense if the profits of building a monopoly by excluding rivals generates more gain than what's lost by not selling to them. Much of the evidence in *Illumina*, for example, would lose more not selling its gene-sequencing platform to competitors who were designing their own cancer therapies than it would gain if it could get a monopoly over a cancer therapy product itself. The court considered expert views and other evidence supporting this incentive theory, including the projected size of the cancer treatment market if the product could be developed, and Illumina's documented plan to revise its business model to focus mainly on Grail's new product rather that Illumina's platform technology.

As is probably obvious, the ability-and-incentive test depends on forward-looking predictions that will remain fact-sensitive and uncertain. For what it may be worth, the prediction is not quite so speculative and subjective as this discussion may make it seem. The expert testimony on which it is based will usually depend on a complex quantitative model known as bargaining theory. Still, the cases will boil down to the competing views of expert witnesses and which of them the factfinder considers more persuasive. The Fifth Circuit found for the Commission in *Illumina*, but the courts ruled against the government on the same theory in *AT&T*, 916 F.3d at 1029, *FTC v. Microsoft Corp.*, 136 F.4th 945 (9th Cir. 2025), and *United States v. UnitedHealth Group, Inc.*, 630 F.Supp.3d 118 (D.D.C. 2022).

The 2023 *Merger Guidelines* preserve one other primary theory of harm from vertical merger—that by integrating vertically, and becoming a supplier or customer of some asset to its own competitors, the merged firm will gain access to sensitive information that it could use for anticompetitive purposes. *Id.* at § 2.5.B. For example, *UnitedHealth Group* involved the acquisition by a health insurer of a firm that provided claims processing technology to itself and other insurers. The government claimed that the insurer would get access to its competitors' claims processing history, and also that its access to data would discourage other claims processing firms from innovating in their own technologies. Theories of this nature are even more speculative than the ability-and-incentive test of foreclosure. So far, the only court to have considered such a theory in a fully litigated matter rejected it as unsubstantiated. *UnitedHealth Group*, 630 F.Supp.3d at 140-52.

§17.7.3 Theories of Harm from Conglomerate Merger

Challenges to conglomerate merger are now rare in the United States. though they still can be made. The basic theory of harm remains grounded in the possibility of "potential competition."[59] The idea is that, but for the merger, the acquiring firm might have entered the market "de novo"—it might have entered just by setting up its own facilities to make the products produced by the incumbents. If that potential entrant instead acquires an existing firm in the market, the deal might have much less potential to stimulate competition. Moreover, prior to that acquisition, the potential entrant—assuming it was known to be a potential entrant—may have exerted a constraining influence on oligopoly behavior within the market. 2023 *Merger Guidelines* § 2.4.[60]

Other theories have evolved in recent economics literature, and to some extent they appear to have been incorporated in some regimes overseas, though they've shown no sign of life in the United States so far.[61]

As was the case with vertical mergers, the Court's early case law on conglomerate merger stated simple theories of harm and applied them

---

59. It has been observed that, technically, the theory of "potential competition" is not a conglomerate theory, but a horizontal one. The potential competition argument is that, but for the merger, the acquiror would have entered and made a product horizontally competitive with existing firms, and the projected harm is the loss of price constraining power such entry would have. In effect, the theory really just reconceives the acquiring firm as if it were already a horizontal competitor and asks whether, if it were presently in the market, its acquisition of the target firm would be illegal under horizontal merger standards. U.S. Dept. of Justice & FTC, *Non-Horizontal Merger Guidelines* §4.133 (1984), available at http://www.justice.gov/atr/public/guidelines/2614.htm; Jeffrey Church, *Conglomerate Mergers*, in 2 *Issues in Competition Law & Policy* 1503, 1508 n.18 (ABA Section of Antitrust Law 2008). But that said, this is also the only presently available theory to challenge acquisitions by firms not already actual horizontal competitors, and for the most part it is thought of by practitioners as a theory of harm from conglomerate merger.

60. At one time, two other, distinct theories were prominent in U.S. law, but they are both now effectively dead. First, it was thought that conglomerate mergers could lead to the problem of "reciprocal dealing." The idea is that where a firm, A, does business with another firm, B, A might be able to achieve an advantage if it buys up another firm, C, which just happens to do business with B. Imagine that A sells something to B, and then B sells something else to C (the second product need have no particular relationship to the first one). It was thought that if A bought C, A could then say to B: "If you want to continue selling your product to C, you need to buy my product exclusively from me." The theory was approved of by the Supreme Court in *FTC v. Consol. Foods Corp.*, 380 U.S. 592 (1965), but was harshly criticized for the unlikelihood that reciprocity could harm consumers. It is no longer meaningfully used in U.S. law. *See* Jeffrey Church, *Conglomerate Mergers*, in 2 *Issues in Competition Law & Policy* 1503, 1510-1511 (ABA Section of Antitrust Law 2008). Second, there was the thought that if any firm was acquired by a much larger firm, even if they had no competitive overlap, the acquisition might "entrench" the acquired firm as the new leader in its market, through greater marketing power or the new power to behave predatorily that could come with access to the acquiring firm's deeper pockets. This theory too fell in to quick disfavor. Critics felt that the harms said to follow from "entrenchment" were really just healthy, competitive advantages that should not be discouraged. *See id.* at 1511-1514. Both of these theories were included in the original 1968 *Merger Guidelines*, but were then dropped when the *Guidelines* were revised in 1982, and have had no effective life since then.

61. *See* Jeffrey Church, *Conglomerate Mergers*, in 2 *Issues in Competition Law & Policy* 1503 (ABA Section of Antitrust Law 2008) (explaining those theories and the recognition given those theories in recent enforcement actions by the European Commission).

quite harshly, and as with vertical mergers, that approach was much criticized.[62] But again, the 1984 *Non-Horizontal Merger Guidelines* preserved a rather more nuanced "potential competition" theory. When the government finally introduced new guidance on non-horizontal deals in the 2023 *Merger Guidelines*, it reincorporated the 1984 rules for conglomerate mergers largely as they were. *See id.* at §2.4.

The Supreme Court, in its last statement on the issue, indicated that once a plaintiff has made some minimum showing of concentration in the market to be entered, the theory of harm from conglomerate merger has two further elements. *See United States v. Marine Bancorp.*, 418 U.S. 602, 624-625 (1974). First, the plaintiff must show that "the acquiring firm has the characteristics, capabilities, and economic incentive to render it a perceived potential *de novo* entrant. . . ." The courts are split as to the standard for determining whether de novo entry would have occurred, but there is some reason to believe it is a heightened standard. While some only require that the acquired would "probably" have entered absent the merger, *FTC v. Steris*, 133 F.Supp.3d 962, 966, 977-78 (N.D. Oh. 2015), others require that entry be "likely" or "very likely" or meet other standards, 1 Am. Bar Assn., *Antitrust Law Developments (Ninth)* 399-400 (9th ed. 2022). The 2023 *Merger Guidelines* require a "reasonable probability" of entry, *id.* at § 2.4.A, but it remains to be seen whether that formulation will satisfy courts.

Second, the plaintiff must show that "the [entering] firm's premerger presence on the fringe of the target market in fact tempered oligopolistic behavior on the part of existing participants in that market." *Marine Bancorp.*, 418 U.S. at 625. The 2023 *Merger Guidelines* capture this requirement by considering the degree of concentration in the market to be entered and any practical evidence that the target firm's entry might have increased competition there. 2023 *Merger Guidelines* §2.4.

Finally, it bears observation that this area of conglomerate merger enforcement is one of the few in §7 law in which subjective intent plays a significant role. Because a plaintiff must prove that but for the merger the acquiring firm would have entered the market on its own there likely must be some proof of the subjective intent of the acquiring firm. Those courts that have entertained potential competition theories have stressed the importance of subjective intent evidence. *See Steris*, 133 F.Supp.3d at 977-84; 1 Am. Bar Assn., *Antitrust Law Developments (Ninth)* 400-401 (9th ed. 2022). Evidence of subjective intent is relevant to both of the *Marine Bancorp.* factors

62. *See, e.g.*, Robert Bork, *The Antitrust Paradox* 246 (1978) ("Perhaps no more disheartening evidence of antitrust's intellectual decline can be cited than the government's demonstrated ability to win conglomerate merger cases without ever advancing a plausible economic argument. Basic analysis shows that there is no threat to competition in any conglomerate merger.").

just mentioned.[63] Proof of that nature will come from live witnesses interviewed during the HSR process and from review of the acquiring firm's documents.

§17.8 THE "FAILING FIRM" DEFENSE

Finally, it remains possible that in rare cases defendants could defend an otherwise illegal merger if one of them is seriously likely to fail without it.

Even during the 1960s, when the Court applied its merger policy most strictly, the law permitted parties to a challenged merger to defend by showing that, in its absence, one of them would fail financially. The doctrine was first recognized in *Intl. Shoe Co. v. FTC*, 280 U.S. 291 (1930), and subsequently approved of in the legislative history of the Celler-Kefauver Amendment in 1950. The doctrine was given substantially more content in the 1969 decision in *Citizen Publg. Co. v. United States*, 394 U.S. 131 (1969). There the Court held that to establish this defense the merging parties must show that the target firm is in "imminent danger" of failure, a test that has been applied on a fact-sensitive analysis of cash flow, balance sheets, and relations with lenders. Second, the failing firm must have no realistic prospect for reorganization (e.g., through the Chapter 11 proceedings of federal bankruptcy law). Finally, there must be no viable alternative purchaser that poses less anticompetitive risk. Typically, the courts have asked in this respect whether the failing firm undertook reasonable and good faith efforts to find an alternative buyer but was unsuccessful. *See generally* 2023 *Merger Guidelines* §3.1.

---

63. A distinction is sometimes drawn between two different potential competition scenarios. First, a market might exist in which a firm outside the market is commonly perceived as a likely entrant. If this is the case, the risk that that firm might enter may act as a deterrent to price collusion or oligopoly pricing by firms already in the market. Therefore, it could be argued that merger between that firm and one already in the market should be blocked, as such a merger would cause the loss of a procompetitive disciplinary force. Courts and commentators have referred to this as "perceived potential competition." This situation is much more commonly alleged by plaintiffs, and it is more easily proven. Second, a market might exist in which some particular firm is not generally perceived as a possible entrant and the risk of its entry imposes no constraint on pricing in that market, but nevertheless that firm subjectively intends to enter. Theoretically, if that firm merges with a firm already in the market a plaintiff might show that it would be competitively superior if the merger were blocked and the acquiror required to enter on its own. The reason this second theory is more difficult for plaintiffs is that there must be contemporaneous evidence of the acquiring firm's intent to enter, which it will have an incentive to deny and which likely can be shown, if at all, only by the firm's own internal documents. *See generally* Lawrence A. Sullivan & Warren S. Grimes, *The Law of Antitrust: An Integrated Handbook* 655-666 (2d ed. 2006).

CHAPTER 18

Merger Review Under Hart-Scott-Rodino

§18.1 1976: HSR AND THE REVOLUTION OF BUREAUCRATIC MERGER REVIEW

§18.1.1 Introduction

As mentioned previously (*see* Chapter 17), the antitrust law of merger and acquisition is now predominantly a bureaucratic practice that occurs within the offices of the federal enforcement agencies, and does not often see time in the courtroom. This is a result of the Hart-Scott-Rodino Antitrust Improvements Act of 1976 (HSR). The new system of review rests predominantly on two major innovations: (1) It automatically freezes most large acquisitions for a period of at least one month, and during that period gives the agencies powerful civil investigative tools to collect information about them; and (2) it provides the agencies with tools for securing preliminary injunctive relief, *before* a transaction is consummated. These innovations were thought to be needed because of a confluence of factors during the 1960s and 1970s that were making the government's job of merger enforcement unmanageable. First, once the more analytical, less enforcement-friendly M&A case law of the 1970s had gotten under way, the government lost the advantage of the straightforward structural presumptions of *Philadelphia National Bank*. (This development is explained in §17.2.1.) The agencies found themselves faced with the burden of developing much more complex factual cases. Second, even before that development, at a time when the government had enjoyed favorable substantive law, the agencies struggled with serious problems of effective remedy. The courts only very reluctantly order the unwinding of corporate transactions after they have already been undertaken, and since most §7 actions prior to HSR could not be brought to final judgment before the parties had consummated, the government was ordinarily denied any effective relief. In fact, though the agencies scored many victories during the 1960s under the *Philadelphia National Bank* regime, it turns out that in most of those cases they were awarded either no relief or only very limited relief.[1] HSR addresses these problems by giving the agencies some breathing room within which to gather evidence and decide how a given acquisition should be judged.

In practice, the typical HSR review goes roughly like this: The parties to the acquisition will typically spend a period of some months negotiating their arrangement. By the time they present it to the agencies under the HSR, they will have developed a large amount of factual and financial information, and will be able to make a substantial, fact-rich case to the agencies about the deal's effects on competition. They then will make the filing required by the HSR, which triggers a statutory minimum period during which they must wait before consummating their transaction.[2] The filing itself is a costly, burdensome and undesirable affair. The disclosure of information itself is generally not the problem merging parties are really worried about. Unlike a securities filing with the Securities and Exchange Commission and some other regulatory filings, information submitted pursuant to HSR is ordinarily confidential. Also, strictly speaking, the mere fact of reportability under HSR does not put a transaction at any greater risk under the antitrust laws; the standard that applies is still only whether the transaction violates Clayton Act §7. But the process is expensive in absolute dollars and cents, both because it requires a large filing fee and because it requires the production of information, and it poses serious strategic risks for the parties. In any case, during the process the FTC and the Antitrust Division perform their review on the basis of their understanding of the case law of §7. HSR itself creates no substantive law. It is purely a procedural mechanism that allows the agencies to decide whether any particular transaction might violate §7. However, the leading statement of the law of §7 is now probably the detailed guidance document that the agencies jointly issued for use during HSR review, known as the *Merger Guidelines (see* §17.2.2). Though they purport only to capture the law of §7 as received

1. *See* Lawrence A. Sullivan & Warren S. Grimes, *The Law of Antitrust: An Integrated Handbook* 578-579 (2d ed. 2006).

2. The two agencies have coextensive authority to review transactions under HSR, but only one of them will review each filed transaction. By agreement between them they decide, as to each proposed transaction, which agency will review.

from the courts, in many respects the *Guidelines* approach is more subtle and sophisticated.

Strictly speaking the agencies can institute an actual antitrust challenge to a transaction at any time, either before or after the expiration of HSR's waiting periods. But as a practical matter, when the agencies believe a transaction is problematic, they normally use up all the time they possibly can under the HSR framework before bringing challenge. The reason is simple: While the HSR clock is still ticking, the agencies have the upper hand. They have powerful tools to demand information—failure to comply with which can result in federal court injunctive orders, rescission of any transaction undertaken, and severe money penalties for each day of continued violation—and they can delay a transaction for a fairly long time if the parties are recalcitrant.

§18.1.2 Unpacking HSR

With that big picture as our introduction, it is time to face certain facts: The terms and inner workings of the premerger review system under HSR are complex, thorny, and meticulous. The system has also evolved an elaborate informal culture that can be somewhat difficult to understand just from reading the statute and rules but is nevertheless important to understanding HSR's operation in practice. The rest of this chapter will attempt to unpack HSR in what hopefully will be a straightforward way. It will work through the same analytical process that an antitrust counselor would undertake when a client asks whether some proposed transaction raises antitrust problems.

A lawyer asked to advise as to antitrust aspects of any sort of deal must work through a series of fairly detailed little questions. In the abstract the most important question is whether, as a matter of substance, the deal would violate Clayton Act §7. Again, the process of HSR review is really only a chance for the agencies to decide whether they would challenge the deal under §7.

If the lawyer thinks the deal would survive challenge as a matter of substance (or, if not, has advised the client how to fix the deal so that it will), the next problem is whether an HSR filing is required. Whether or not it is, from the client's perspective, is a big deal, for the reasons mentioned above. In answering this big question, the first issue is whether the deal is even covered by HSR. That means asking whether it is among the class of transactions to which HSR applies, whether any of HSR's several exemptions might be available, and whether the size of the transaction meets HSR's filing thresholds. Reportability under HSR is covered in §18.2. Second, if the deal is reportable, the lawyer needs not only to begin preparing the filing itself and the presentation of the case the parties may have to make to the agencies, but to advise the client on certain preconsummation conduct that can lead to legal problems during HSR. First, the parties should take care in the production of sensitive documents relating to the transaction. Some items of the HSR Form (the basic document that must be filed as the notification that is required by HSR) require the initial filing to include copies of strategically sensitive documents that analyze markets and competitive issues surrounding a deal.[3] This poses a special counseling problem for the M&A lawyer. On the one hand, the parties must prepare internal analyses as part of their investigation and negotiation of potential deals. But on the other hand, they must be advised that much of what they write will be disclosed to the government and so must avoid giving any appearance of illegality. Likewise, it is illegal for parties to a reportable deal to engage in preapproval "gun jumping," which means the coordination of their operations or sharing of information. Again, the generally nonlawyer managers who will be in charge of the firms must be so counseled, and a plan must be in place to keep operations separate during the HSR waiting period.

And then, once preparations are made, the form is filed and the HSR "clock" starts ticking. In about 95 percent of HSR filings the agencies are able to give early termination. They can tell even before the expiration of the initial HSR waiting period that the deal will not raise legal concerns under §7, and so they give the parties their approval. But in the remaining 5 percent or so, the agencies find more to be concerned with. Many of those cases will result in a so-called "second request." After the expiration of the initial HSR waiting period—a period of 30 calendar days from the date of the initial filing—the responsible agency will submit a demand to the merging parties for more information, which usually will be quite substantial. A second 30-day waiting period is triggered by the second request, but it does not begin until the parties have fully complied with production of the information requested. Since production can be onerous and can result in disputes between the parties and the agency, the total length of the HSR process in these unusual cases can last much longer than the 60 calendar days of the two mandatory waiting periods. It commonly lasts four or five months or so, and occasionally it can last a year or more. (The agencies

---

3. As of this writing the rules governing pre-merger notification are in flux, but the changes will not affect anything written here. In late 2024 the FTC, which has rulemaking authority to regulate HSR procedures, adopted a substantially revised set of premerger notification rules. FTC, *Final Rule: Premerger Notification; Reporting and Waiting Period Requirements*, 89 Fed. Reg. 89216 (Nov. 12, 2024) (amending 16 C.F.R. Parts 801-03(2024)). Under the prior rules, merging parties were required to file so-called "4(c) documents," named for box 4(c) on the HSR Form, consisting of strategic planning documents that might have been created in preparation for the transaction. The new rules expanded the amount of information required in a number of areas and may call for more sensitive material than had been required under box 4(c).

The new rules have been challenged in litigation that, as of this writing, has not been resolved. *Chamber of Commerce v. FTC*, Case No. 6:25-cv-009 (E.D. Tex. Jan. 10, 2025). All points made in the text will be unaffected by the results of that litigation.

can also informally ask the parties for more time once the second statutory waiting period has begun, and parties ordinarily give it—since the alternative is a fairly certain agency lawsuit charging violation of §7.) Anyway, once the participants reach the end of that long and often contentious process in second-request cases, there typically will be something of an ultimatum. The agency will state its concerns about the deal, and will usually indicate corrections the parties can make to resolve them. (In horizontal merger cases the agencies usually desire divestitures of particular assets held by the parties, which they think will pose particular problems if they are still held by the merged entity. In vertical and conglomerate merger cases, the agencies often desire restrictions on conduct.) When some satisfactory corrections can be agreed to, the agency and the parties will enter into a negotiated order making it effective. The deal, as modified, can then be consummated. Sometimes, though, no such compromise can be reached. When that is the case, only one of two things can happen: The parties can either give up or go ahead with their deal despite government opposition. Going ahead means the risk, expense, and public exposure of litigating a §7 case against the federal government, and also continued delay of a merger deal that is inherently time-sensitive. Also, parties that are publicly traded will typically see a significant drop in share price on the mere announcement of government opposition. Accordingly, when the government threatens suit the parties will often just abandon their deal. In those few cases where the parties proceed, the first step will be an immediate government lawsuit for preliminary injunction. If preliminary relief is granted, especially if it is upheld on the invariably expedited appeal, that will kill off some deals that haven't yet been abandoned. If the parties nevertheless persist, the case then enters ordinary §7 litigation—in the case of the DOJ, in a federal district court, and in the case of the FTC, in administrative litigation before an agency Administrative Law Judge (*see* §19.2.1). At this point, the deal can be consummated only if the parties succeed and the agency unsuccessfully exhausts or abandons its appeals.

§18.2 COVERED TRANSACTIONS

Again, the first question to ask is whether a deal is subject to HSR at all. This can be thought of in three parts: (1) Is the form of the transaction (such as a merger, a purchase of assets or shares, or a tender offer) of the kind subject to HSR? (2) If so, might this particular deal nevertheless enjoy one of HSR's several exemptions? (3) If the answer to question 1 is yes but the answer to question 2 is no, is the deal large enough to satisfy the HSR filing thresholds? If the answer to question 3 is yes, then the parties to the deal must comply with HSR.

The general scope of HSR—the kinds of persons and transactions to which it applies—is essentially the same as that of §7 (*see* §17.3). HSR applies whenever a "person . . . acquire[s]" the "assets or voting securities" of any other person, so long as one of them is "engaged in commerce or in any activity affecting commerce. . . ." (Note that, unlike Clayton Act §7, which applies only if both parties to a deal are within Congress's "interstate commerce" power, HSR applies when either of them is. 15 U.S.C. §18a(a)(1)). In particular, "person," "acquisition," and "assets" have the same statutory meaning as they do in §7. "Securities" has largely the same meaning as "stock or other share capital" under §7.

Importantly, as with §7 (*see* §17.3), HSR can apply to acquisitions of *newly created* persons, including persons created as a part of the deal constituting the covered transaction itself. So, for example, imagine that two existing firms believe that although outright merger would not be in their best interests, they might both benefit from joining forces with respect to some specific project. The firms could proceed in various different ways, but if they contribute significant assets to the project and retain ongoing managerial involvement in it, and assuming the deal is a large one, the odds are that they will be required to make an HSR filing. They might choose actually to create a new corporation or an LLC or some other formal entity to act as their joint venture, and by assigning themselves stock or voting ownership interest in it they will be "acquiring securities" of another "person." Or, they might simply agree by contract to contribute assets, and then to share in the management and profits of the effort, but in that case they will have just created a general partnership between them, in which case they again will both be considered acquiring persons of the entity under HSR.

HSR also contains a long series of exemptions, all of which appear in §7a(c), 15 U.S.C. §18a(c). These exemptions fall in three general categories: (1) noncontrol transactions, such as a purchase of nonvoting preferred stock or an acquisition that is in the ordinary course of business and not made for control; (2) transactions in sectors that are regulated by some other federal agency, such as banking or ocean shipping; and (3) miscellaneous areas exempted by the FTC by rule making.

Finally, if an acquisition is of a kind subject to HSR and does not qualify for any exemption, it must be determined whether the transaction meets HSR's filing thresholds. While we shall see in a second that in its precise terms the filing threshold is pretty complex, we can state it in rough terms like this: A transaction otherwise subject to HSR is usually reportable if the value of the stock or assets that will be acquired are worth more than $126.4 million.[4] That said, stating the threshold rule precisely is quite a bit

4. The HSR filing threshold is adjusted annually to reflect growth of the economy. As originally enacted, HSR required a filing if the thing being acquired were worth more than $50 million. As of 2025, that number had been adjusted to $126.4 million. Federal Trade

more of a mouthful. Under the language of HSR, a transaction is reportable if:

§18a. Premerger Notification and Waiting Period

(a) . . .

(2) as a result of such acquisition, the acquiring person would hold an aggregate total amount of the voting securities and assets of the acquired person—

(A) in excess of [$505.8 million[5]] . . . ; or

(B) (i) in excess of [$126.4 million] . . . but not in excess of [$505.8 million] . . . ; and

(ii) (I) any voting securities or assets of a person engaged in manufacturing which has annual net sales or total assets of [$25.3 million] . . . or more are being acquired by any person which has total assets or annual net sales of [$252.9 million] . . . or more;

(II) any voting securities or assets of a person not engaged in manufacturing which has total assets of [$25.3 million] . . . or more are being acquired by any person which has total assets or annual net sales of [$252.9million] . . . or more; or

(III) any voting securities or assets of a person with annual net sales or total assets of [$252.9 million] . . . or more are being acquired by any person with total assets or annual net sales of [$25.3 million] . . . or more. . . .

This test breaks down into basically two fact questions: (1) how large the transaction will be and (2) how large the parties to it are.[6]

First, as to the size of the transaction: Some transactions are so large or so small that they are either automatically reportable or automatically nonreportable regardless how big the parties are. A transaction is always reportable if the acquiring person will hold voting securities or assets of the acquired person worth more than $505.8 million. Likewise, all transactions resulting in holdings less than $126.4 million are nonreportable.

Second, the size of the parties becomes relevant where the value of the holdings will be between $126.4 million and $505.8 million. Here

---

Commission *Revised Jurisdictional Thresholds for Section 7A of the Clayton Act*, 90 Fed. Reg. 7697 (Jan. 22, 2025).

5. The dollar amounts given in this excerpt from §18a and in the remainder of the discussion are as adjusted for 2025. *See supra* note XXX.

6. Prior to 2000, there had been a third requirement. In all cases it was required that the acquiring person would hold at least 15 percent of the shares and assets of the acquired person, or a total value of shares and assets of the person of at least $15 million. This requirement was removed by amendments to HSR in 2000. *See* Pub. L. No. 106-553, tit. VI, §630(a), 114 Stat. 2762A-108-2762A-111 (Dec. 21, 2000).

the inquiry seems more complex because it depends to some extent on whether the acquired person is "engaged in manufacturing," and because a thorny little web of distinctions is drawn on the parties' varying sizes. But this part of the test too can be broken down into more manageable parts. Generally speaking, a transaction in this size range is reportable where either the buyer or the seller is very large. First we will consider those transactions where the buyer is large. These are the cases in which it matters whether the seller is "engaged in manufacturing" or not. Wherever the buyer has total assets or annual net sales of $252.9 million or more, the deal will be reportable if the seller is worth anything more than about $25.3 million. The value of that second number—the amount that the seller is worth—will be measured differently depending on whether the seller is in manufacturing. If it is, the deal is reportable if *either* its total assets or its annual net sales are $25.3 million or more. If not, the deal is reportable only if the seller's total assets are $25.3 million or more. Second are those transactions where the seller is large, and this test can be stated more simply. Wherever the seller has total assets or annual net sales of $252.3 million or more, a deal is reportable if the buyer has total assets or annual net sales of $25.3 million or more.

This test is often summarized somewhat differently, as consisting of a "size-of-the-transaction" test and "size-of-the-parties" test. The size-of-the-transaction test requires that the acquiring person will hold voting securities or assets of the target firm greater than $126.4 million. The size-of-the-parties test requires that either the acquiring or acquired person has annual net sales or total assets of at least $252.9 million and the other has annual net sales or total assets of at least $25.3 million. The size-of-the-parties test does not apply if the value of the transaction is over $505.8 million. *See, e.g.*, 1 Am. Bar Assn., *Antitrust Law Developments (Ninth)* 413-414 (9th ed. 2022); 1 Stephen M. Axinn et al., *Acquisitions Under the Hart-Scott-Rodino Antitrust Improvements Act* §§5.04, 5.04 (2009).

So, to summarize:

- *Transactions producing holdings less than $126.4 million are never reportable.*
- Transactions producing holdings of more than $505.8 million are always reportable.
- Transactions producing holdings between $126.4 million and $505.8 million are reportable in either of two situations:
  - The buyer is large—it has total assets or annual net sales of $252.9 million or more—and the seller is worth $25.3 million or more, as measured in the following way:
    - for sellers in manufacturing, either by total assets or annual net sales;
    - for sellers not in manufacturing, by total assets.

- The seller is large—if it has total assets or annual net sales of $252.9 million or more—and the buyer has total assets or annual net sales of $25.3 million or more.

Oddly enough, it turns out that this very complex test can be practically summarized in pretty down-to-earth terms, and it all boils down to the following bottom line: Big firms—those that are worth more than $252.9 million—must report most of their big purchases and their big sales. Any time they *acquire* an interest in any one person worth more than $126.4 million they will have to report it, unless the deal is worth less than $505.8 million and the seller is small—worth less than $25.3 million (measured in different ways, depending on whether the seller is a manufacturer). Any time they *sell* an interest in themselves worth more than $94 million they will have to report it, unless the deal is worth less than $505.8 million and the buyer is worth less than $25.3 million.

Example

Piper Aeronautics, Inc., a Delaware corporation headquartered and doing business in Maine, is a manufacturer of engine parts and other components for light aircraft. Piper happens to be a subsidiary of another Delaware Corporation, Wilson Industries, a diversified holding company with headquarters in New York City. Wilson owns 60 percent of Piper's voting stock. Anyway, Piper holds 8 percent of the voting common stock of one of its own chief competitors, the Prisonic Manufacturing Corp. After an uncommonly profitable period this past year, Prisonic's board chose to pay its common shareholders an "in kind" dividend, which consisted of the distribution of a one-half common share for each common share currently held by the common shareholders. In part because of this turn of events but also because Piper itself had been performing quite well, Wilson decided to increase its own holdings in Piper, buying another 5 percent of its outstanding voting shares.

Assuming it meets the HSR filing thresholds, is any transaction in this scenario reportable under HSR?

Explanation

No. Because the in-kind dividend necessarily affected all the shareholders the same, it did not change Piper's percentage ownership of Prisonic. The dividend is therefore exempt from HSR under §18a(c)(10). Likewise, Wilson was already Piper's controlling shareholder—it already owned more than 50 percent of Piper's voting stock. The acquisition of an additional 5 percent of Piper's stock is therefore exempt from HSR under §18a(c)(3).

Example

The cognac tasted sweet as the two corporate presidents toasted the final culmination of the long and sometimes difficult negotiation between their two firms (which happened to be horizontal competitors). They could now look forward to what should be a much more fruitful and easier period of productivity, given that the research they expected to produce together was in their mutual interest. For the duration of the agreement they have reached (which is initially to last five years, though it is renewable for two-year periods on the agreement of both firms), it promised to give each of them a technological superiority over their respective competitors. Still, as the two of them glanced wistfully over at the chalet fireplace, neither could shake that feeling. . . . Shouldn't we have filed under HSR? Shouldn't we?

Explanation

The odds are that they should have filed, assuming their joint project was large enough to satisfy the HSR filing thresholds. It sounds as though their two firms have agreed to create a joint venture for research and development, and ordinarily they would have set it up as a corporation or partnership between them. The venture is therefore a third "person" in whom they each will have acquired an ownership interest.

Example

Your client is flabbergasted and outraged that you would suggest an HSR filing, more or less openly accusing you of trying to run up a legal tab through unnecessary work. After all, he says, the firm he's buying is in Florida, and he's only ever done business in Idaho. He's a bit cranky, this one, a self-made man who still runs a business worth nearly $30 million as a sole proprietorship. Now, as you patiently try to explain to him why the form must be filed, ask yourself: How big must the seller be, and how much must the transaction be worth for you to be right on this one? Or is he right? Is there some aspect of the deal that would make his instinct correct?

Explanation

None of the facts suggest that the deal would not be reportable if the filing threshold is met, though in fairness, meeting the threshold will require the target to be quite large.

The fact that the businesses are in different states is irrelevant. It would be irrelevant even if they were in totally separate geographic and product markets. HSR requires the filing whenever one "person" makes an acquisition from any other "person" if the filing thresholds are met and the deal is not exempt under one of the HSR exemptions. As for the filing thresholds, the acquiror appears to have either annual net sales or total assets of more than \$25.3 million. Therefore, the deal is reportable if the stock or assets to be acquired are either worth more than \$505.8 million, or worth more than \$126.4 million and the seller has annual net sales or total assets of more than \$252.9 million.

§18.3 WHAT HAPPENS ON MERGER REVIEW

Once it is determined that a transaction is reportable, the next step is to prepare and file the notification materials—the HSR Form—and wait for the agencies to perform their review. The filing of the form triggers the complex series of procedural steps that basically make up the HSR process.

§18.3.1 The Initial Filing and the HSR Clock

Note that although the HSR waiting period does not begin until the necessary HSR Forms are filed, the automatic stay feature of HSR applies as a matter of law, whether or not any form is filed. If the parties consummate a reportable deal without filing notice and waiting for expiration of the waiting period, they are subject to large civil money penalties and injunctive relief to halt their transaction.

Once a satisfactory HSR Form is filed by every party that is required to file, there begins a statutory "waiting period," which is sometimes called the HSR "clock"—the all-important rules by which the agencies calculate the period of time that the parties must wait before consummating their transaction. The clock starts ticking in most cases as soon as *both* agencies have received, from *both* parties, either a complete HSR Form or an incomplete Form and a statement satisfactorily explaining the noncompliance.

Incidentally, we shall see at several points a series of special HSR rules that relate to tender offers and sales of assets by a company in bankruptcy. The first of them appears here: Because tender offers are almost always time sensitive and "hostile"—they are almost always opposed by the target company's management[7]—the HSR clock is triggered as soon as the *acquiror's* HSR Form is received by both agencies. Requiring both parties to file in order to trigger the waiting period would give the target management an easy way to stymie any tender offer that would meet HSR filing thresholds. Still, target management cannot avoid filing an HSR Form altogether. They must file no later than the fifteenth day after receipt by the agencies of the acquiring person's filing, or, in the case of a cash tender offer, on the tenth day thereafter. Failure of the target firm to file does not affect the running of the HSR clock, but it constitutes a violation of the HSR itself and is subject to civil penalties.

As it happens, while a special timing rule also applies to sales by a bankruptcy trustee,[8] the agencies have interpreted the rule still to require that both the bankruptcy trustee and the acquiring person file the HSR Form and that the HSR clock begins only when both agencies have received the form from both parties. *See* 1 Stephen M. Axinn et al., *Acquisitions Under the Hart-Scott-Rodino Antitrust Improvements Act* §7.03[3][b][iii] (2009).

In most transactions, the *initial* waiting period lasts for 30 calendar days from the date on which the clock starts. If that period expires with the responsible agency having taken no action, then the HSR process concludes and the parties may go ahead with their transaction.

Again, special timing rules apply in tender offers and bankruptcy. In the case of *cash* tender offers, the initial waiting period lasts 15 days from the date of receipt by both agencies of the acquiror's HSR Form. (In noncash tender offers—which is to say, those in which the consideration to be paid for the target company's shares is something other than cash—the ordinary 30-day initial waiting period applies.) Likewise, where a corporation going through bankruptcy is under the control of a bankruptcy trustee, the initial

7. A "tender offer" is simply an open-market offer to purchase securities directly from shareholders. Tender offers are almost always "hostile" transactions in the sense that the management of the target corporation will almost always oppose them. "Friendly" change-in-control transactions, like mergers and purchase of all of a target-firm's assets, require the approval of the target company's board. *See* §17.1.1.

8. There are some cases in bankruptcy in which no trustee is appointed, and so the special HSR timing rules for bankruptcy do not always apply. When a company is liquidated under Chapter 7 of the bankruptcy code, it is always placed in the hands of a bankruptcy "trustee," who in some cases is a government official and in all cases acts only as a fiduciary of the firm's creditors, with the sole purpose of maximizing the value of the firm's assets. Likewise, since it is often the management of an insolvent firm who are to blame for its insolvency, bankruptcy law often requires that a firm in Chapter 11 reorganization be put under control of a trustee. Sometimes a Chapter 11 debtor's management can remain in control, and in such cases the company is known as the "debtor-in-possession." The special HSR timing rules applicable to bankruptcy only apply where the HSR Form is to be filed by a trustee. In other words, where no trustee has been appointed, and the Form must be filed by the debtor-in-possession, the ordinary HSR timing rules apply.

waiting period is 15 days from receipt of the HSR Form by both agencies from both the trustee and the acquiring party.

§18.3.2 The Second Request and Further Extensions of Time

The agencies approve the vast majority of reported transactions during the initial 30-day waiting period. But in about 5 percent of filings, the agencies determine that a transaction poses significant competitive concerns and that they cannot approve it without further information. In those cases the agencies issue the all-important "second request"—a request for further information and documentary evidence that automatically has the effect of triggering a second statutory waiting period, which usually runs 30 days from the agencies' receipt of the information requested.

Compliance with a second request is much more expensive and time-consuming than the ordinary HSR filing resolved by early termination, routinely consuming many months and millions of dollars in fees and expenses. It is so expensive in large part because the volume of documents and other information needed to comply with the agency's request will be dramatically larger than that produced with the initial HSR Form. There also typically will be a substantial amount of negotiation and push and pull between the agency and the parties' counsel, all of which is time consuming and expensive. Technically the second request may be made on any day before the expiration of the initial waiting period, but, understandably, the agencies will ordinarily issue it on the last day of the waiting period. Waiting until the end maximizes the amount of time the agencies have for their review.

Again, a few special rules apply to tender offers and sales by a bankruptcy trustee. First, in all tender offer cases (including cash and noncash cases), the second waiting period is triggered when the agency receives substantial compliance from the *acquiring* person (as opposed to non-tender offer cases, in which the period begins only when the requested information is received from all parties who received requests). 16 C.F.R. §803.20(c). Again, the rationale is to deny the target firm management an opportunity hold up the whole process by just failing to comply.[9] Second, in both cash

9. That is, in any case in which the agency has sent a second request to the target firm or its officials, as well as the acquiring firm, the target firm could hold up the process by just dragging its feet. Again, the target firm's management will almost always be quite hostile to a takeover. *See* §17.1.1. In any event, HSR and the implementing rules deal with this problem in two ways. As mentioned in the text, the second request waiting period begins as soon as the acquiring firm complies with the request. Second, 16 C.F.R. §803.21 requires all parties who have received a second request to respond within a "reasonable time," and failure to do so is subject to HSR civil penalties.

tender offers and sales by a bankruptcy trustee, a second request extends the waiting period for only ten days. *Id.*

Finally, the agencies can in fact secure additional time even beyond the 30-day second request period (or 10 days, in the case of cash tender offers and sales by bankruptcy trustee). First, under §18a(g)(2), the agency can request a court order extending the waiting period if it can show that, before the expiration of the waiting period, "any person . . . fail[ed] substantially to comply" with any aspect of the second request. More commonly, the parties and the agency may simply negotiate to give the agency more time. After all, the agency wields significant leverage—if it has significant concerns over the deal's legality, and the parties are unwilling to give it more time, its alternative is simply to sue.

§18.3.3 Disputes Within the HSR Process

Ordinarily the parties can and must resolve their differences within the HSR process without resort to the courts.

The first serious dispute that may arise is whether the initial HSR Form is a complete and adequate filing. In principle, HSR permits a party to submit an incomplete filing coupled with an explanation of noncompliance. However, the government can assert that the filing is not "substantially complete" and therefore that it does not trigger the HSR clock. The government takes a strict view of noncompliance, and considers it excusable only when full compliance would be truly impossible—as for example if full disclosure as to some particular issue requires confidential information in the possession of some other party. *See* 1 Stephen M. Axinn et al., *Acquisitions Under the Hart-Scott-Rodino Antitrust Improvements Act* §9.05 (2009) ("Both the FTC and Antitrust Division staff have equated 'substantial compliance' with 'absolute compliance.'"). Strictly speaking, the onus is on the government to prove the inadequacy of a party's filing, because the government's remedy is to seek injunctive relief from a federal district court under §18a(g)(2). However, the agencies can and do informally reject filings as inadequate, including some accompanied by statements explaining noncompliance. In such a case the filing party can be in a bit of a bind. HSR provides for no internal review process for the adequacy of initial filings—like the one provided for second request disputes, described below—and a mere rejection of the filing as incomplete is likely not "final agency action" that can be reviewed as a matter of administrative law. But the parties also cannot simply go forward with their transaction. If the transaction is in fact reportable, consummating without undergoing the HSR waiting period is a civil violation of HSR subject to serious penalties. The parties will likely have no realistic alternative except to refile a more complete HSR Form. Surely the wisest course is simply to file the most complete possible Form wherever one can.

Second requests will frequently entail much more significant disagreements between the agencies and parties before them. The most common dispute of all will be whether the scope of the information requested is reasonable. First of all, the parties may negotiate with the agency on this matter, and the agency may be willing to reduce the scope of the request. If they cannot reach agreement, HSR provides for an internal dispute mechanism. Section 18a(e)(1)(B) requires each agency to "designate a senior official who does not have direct responsibility . . . concerning the transaction at issue" to resolve disputes as to whether the agency's request is "unreasonably cumulative, unduly burdensome, or duplicative," or whether the request, once the person has attempted to comply, has been substantially complied with. The FTC has designated its General Counsel; the Justice Department assigns each appeal to a Deputy Assistant Attorney General who has no enforcement responsibility as to the particular transaction. If that process is decided unfavorably to the filing party, it appears that the decision can be reviewed in court as a matter of administrative law.

A separate sort of dispute arises if the parties attempt to comply with the second request, or only partially comply and submit a statement of reasons for noncompliance (as permitted by 16 C.F.R. §803.3), and the agency then determines that the parties' attempted compliance with the second request was incomplete. This sort of dispute can also be submitted for resolution by the "designated senior official," as set out in §18a(e)(1)(B), and the official's decision is again reviewable as a matter of administrative law.

But if a person simply refuses to comply with a §18a(e)(1) request, the agencies may seek a federal district court injunction to enforce compliance under §18a(g)(2). Likewise, even parties attempting to comply with a second request are required by 16 C.F.R. §803.21 to do so within a "reasonable time," and failure to do so can also be the basis of a §18a(g)(2) order.

Example

Your boss, J. Worthington Dalrymple III, partner in the firm of Difficult, Feckless & Cheep, can no longer contain his fury over not one but two rejections of an HSR Form by the Federal Trade Commission. He (acting through you) has attempted to file the form on behalf of a corporation attempting to acquire a small competitor, but the agency has objected to his explanation that no Item 4(c) documents were generated in the case. So he has directed you to draft a complaint to initiate proceedings to force the agency to accept the filing, though he's not exactly sure how to go about it. What should you do?

Explanation

There is likely nothing you can do. The rejections probably do not constitute "final agency action" for purposes of administrative law, and so there probably could be no action for judicial review. Likewise, HSR and the implementing rules do not provide for any internal dispute resolution concerning rejections of the initial form. While technically the parties are under no present obligation to refile if they choose not to, they cannot consummate their transaction without HSR compliance. So your only realistic option is to return to the client for a further, more diligent search for 4(c) documents (i.e., analyses of the transaction prepared for management), and then attempt to file again, perhaps with a more elaborate explanation of steps taken to locate them.

§18.3.4 The Problem of "Gun Jumping"

It is illegal for parties to a reportable transaction to coordinate their activities or engage in illegal information sharing—also known as "gun jumping"—prior to agency approval. Doing so can violate HSR itself, in that it prohibits consummation of a reportable transaction before the end of the waiting period, and if there is some premerger agreement as to prices, market allocations, information, or other anticompetitive matters, there may be a violation of Sherman Act §1. Accordingly, where gun-jumping is discovered, the agencies can recover both the severe civil penalties available for HSR noncompliance, and injunctive relief for Sherman Act violations.[10] Clients often will not understand the breadth and severity of this rule, and they will also be very anxious to get started with the large and time-sensitive job of meshing their two companies together, so they need to be counseled carefully not to engage in prohibited preparations.

---

10. *See, e.g., United States v. Gemstar-TV Guide Intl., Inc.*, No. Civ. A. 03-0198(JR), 2003 WL 21799949 (D.D.C. July 16, 2003) (assessing $5.67 million in HSR money penalties and an injunction for violation of Sherman Act §1 where parties entered into trade-restraining agreements prior to expiration of waiting period); *United States v. Titan Wheel Intl., Inc.*, No. Civ. A. 1:96CV01040, 1996 WL 351143 (D.D.C. May 10, 1996) (imposing $130,000 in HSR civil penalties against acquiring firm for 13-day period during which it took operational control of facilities of target firm before expiration of waiting period); *see generally* 1 Stephen M. Axinn et al., *Acquisitions Under the Hart-Scott-Rodino Antitrust Improvements Act* §9.05[3][b][iii].

§18.3.5 What Happens at the End

Again, HSR review ends in the vast majority of cases with little consequence. The merger will either be approved by early termination or the initial waiting period will be allowed to expire with no action from the agencies.

Even in that small proportion of cases in which a second request is issued, the agencies rarely oppose a deal outright. Much more commonly, the agencies identify specific issues within a proposed transaction that they consider to cause competitive problems, and the parties will then negotiate a voluntary settlement under which some assets are divested to satisfy the agencies' concerns. For example, in a deal between two retail chains selling similar products, the agency might feel that the overall merger is not in itself problematic, but that in certain specific cities there would be an impermissible increase in concentration. In such a case, the agency and the parties will likely negotiate an agreement that in the specific problem areas, one of the merging parties would sell its store to a third-party competitor. When such deals are reached, they are memorialized in a "consent decree," which is simply a settlement agreement, and it will be filed in court simultaneously with a complaint by the agency asserting a violation of §7. This has the effect of ensuring that the settlement agreement will be binding on the parties, enforceable by the court's contempt powers.

In the rare cases in which an agency opposes a deal outright, and no consent decree can be worked out, the opposition often causes the parties to abandon the deal. But occasionally the parties in such a case will attempt to go ahead with their deal, knowing that they will have to successfully defend a lawsuit under §7. In those lawsuits, the agencies enjoy first of all a special, unusually powerful preliminary injunction remedy. Technically, the two agencies' requests for preliminary injunction are subject to different statutory standards, and the standard for FTC injunctions would appear to be more favorable to the agency.[11] However, in both cases the courts have generally adopted a standard for approving the injunction that is more favorable to the agency than would be the case under the standard that usually applies to preliminary civil relief. The agencies usually only need to show something like a "reasonable probability" of success on the merits, and if they can do so, the courts will usually presume that the granting of the order is in the public interest. Private equities—the harm to the parties—are given little weight. *See* 1 Am. Bar Assn., *Antitrust Law Developments* (Ninth) 432-436 (9th ed. 2022). Again, the grant of a preliminary injunction will usually be the death knell for those deals that have made it that far, but the denial of the injunction will usually end the agencies' action against it.

---

11. The Justice Department's power to get this relief appears in Clayton Act §15, 15 U.S.C. §25. The FTC's power appears in FTC Act §13(b), 15 U.S.C. §53(b).

Sometimes, though, the entry or denial of such an order is not the end of the case. First of all, there may be appeal to a court of appeals, which usually proceeds on an expedited basis, and, particularly if a preliminary injunction is entered at that level, there may then be substantive litigation on the merits.

§18.3.6 Special Treatment for Cash Tender Offers and Bankrupt Entities

Because the details are fairly complex and scattered, it might be helpful just to review all the special procedural rules that apply to HSR review of tender offers and sales from bankruptcy.

- *Tender offers:*
  - *Starting the HSR clock:*
    - In all tender offers, the HSR clock is triggered by the filing of an HSR Form by the acquiring firm.
  - *Target firm's HSR Form:*
    - In cash tender offers, the target firm must file its own HSR Form within 10 days of the acquiror's initial filing.
    - In noncash tender offers, the target firm must file its own HSR Form within 15 days of the acquiror's initial filing.
  - *Initial waiting period:*
    - In cash tender offers, the initial waiting period is 15 days.
    - In noncash tender offers, the initial waiting period is 30 days.
  - *Second request waiting period:*
    - In all tender offer cases, the second request waiting period is triggered upon substantial compliance by the acquiror.
    - In cash tender offers, the second request waiting period is 10 days.
    - In noncash tender offers, the second request waiting period is 20 days.
- *Sales from bankruptcy:*
  - *Starting the HSR clock:* In all cases, the initial waiting period begins only when an HSR Form is received from the debtor-in-possession or the bankruptcy trustee, as the case may be, *and* the acquiring person.
- *Initial waiting period:*
  - Where a trustee has been appointed, 15 days from the date of receipt by both agencies of an HSR Form from both parties.

- Where the debtor remains in possession, in a Chapter 11 reorganization, 30 days from the date of receipt by both agencies of an HSR Form from both parties.
- *Second request waiting period:*
  - Where a trustee has been appointed, 10 days from the date of substantial compliance by all persons who received the request.
  - Where the debtor remains in possession, in a Chapter 11 reorganization, 30 days from the date of substantial compliance by all persons who received the request.

Example

The management of your client Havenahardtime Industries, Inc., is overjoyed to be nearing the end of a Chapter 11 reorganization proceeding. The company's CEO calls you to report the great success he and his team have had negotiating the sale of the last significant asset they were required to sell as part of the Chapter 11 plan of reorganization negotiated with Havenahardtime's creditors. They are aware that the sale is probably reportable under HSR, but he would like you to give him some rough sense how long the delay caused by HSR will be; in particular, he'd like you to give him some estimate of the *minimum* time the delay could be. What do you tell him?

Explanation

Probably something approaching 30 calendar days.

Strictly speaking, there is no minimum period; technically, the agencies could grant early termination immediately and may very well do so within a few days of the filing. But assuming the deal raises even minimal competitive issues, the agencies would likely use up a fair bit of at least the initial waiting period. In this case, both the initial waiting period and any second request waiting period will last 30 calendar days. In this case it appears that no bankruptcy trustee was appointed, as the CEO and other managers of Havenahardtime are still in control. The firm is therefore a debtor-in-possession and the special timing rules for bankruptcy trustees do not apply.

So a reasonable prediction of the minimum time would be something in the range of three to four weeks. In the unlikely event that a second request is issued (because they are always unlikely), a minimum estimate would be 60 calendar days plus the time it takes Havenahardtime (and the acquiring firm, assuming a second request is issued to it as well) to comply with the request. So, in that case, an estimate would be something on the order of three months or more.

Example

P. Boone Chickens, the notorious corporate takeover artist and scourge of incumbent management everywhere, has announced a hostile, "all-cash, all-shares" offer to acquire Sittingduck, Inc., a publicly traded Delaware corporation. On the same day as his announcement, Chickens delivers his HSR Form to the Federal Trade Commission and the Justice Department. Sittingduck's management, however, have decided to oppose the transaction in any way conceivable, including by taking any steps they can to frustrate the HSR process. For now they intend to refuse to comply with any HSR procedures and to bring injunctive action in federal district court to get the HSR process stopped.

What result? Also, when will the initial waiting period for Chickens's HSR review expire?

Explanation

The result is surely a negative one for Sittingduck's management. First, they cannot refuse to comply. Failure of the target firm to comply "within a reasonable time" with either the initial HSR filing obligation or any second request that may issue is a civil violation of HSR subject to hefty money penalties. The agencies may also procure a federal injunction ordering HSR compliance by Sittingduck.

Chickens's initial waiting period expires 15 calendar days after the date his HSR Form was received by both the FTC and DOJ, regardless of what Sittingduck might do or not do. His offer is a cash tender offer, triggering the 15-day waiting period, and because it is a tender offer, the target firm's failure to comply does not affect the HSR clock.

PART X

Institutions and Procedures in Antitrust

CHAPTER 19

Institutions and Procedures in Antitrust

Antitrust is surrounded by a set of idiosyncratic ancillary rules. They govern the ways that antitrust policy is enforced and many of them seek to ensure that antitrust serves only its intended purposes. In particular, a set of fairly complex procedural rules surround the enforcement of antitrust through private lawsuits. Congress, and much more so the federal courts in recent years, have been concerned to ensure that private persons do not use these lawsuits for improper reasons. As we will see, a running theme throughout the law of antitrust is the suspicion of the courts that private antitrust claims are brought mainly by businesspersons only to injure their own competitors and not to protect the health of markets. This concern drives many of the rules we study in this chapter.

To a large extent the typical antitrust lawsuit looks like other lawsuits. They always occur in federal courts[1] (although, when they are brought by the Federal Trade Commission, they sometimes begin with trial before an administrative court called an Administrative Law Judge), and so they are subject to the general rules of civil and criminal procedure that govern other federal trials. Though it may be surprising, given the complexity of the issues to be resolved, antitrust cases are often tried to a jury, and it appears that both parties in civil antitrust litigation have a Seventh Amendment right to jury trial.[2]

1. *Marrese v. Am. Acad. Orthopaedic Surgeons*, 470 U.S. 373, 379-380 (1985); *Gen. Inv. Co. v. Lake Shore & Michigan S. Ry.*, 260 U.S. 261, 286-288 (1922).

2. *See Beacon Theatres, Inc. v. Westover*, 359 U.S. 500, 504 (1959) (dicta); *Fleisman v. Welsbach St. Lighting Co. of Am.*, 240 U.S. 27, 29 (1916) (dicta); *In re Japanese Elec. Prods. Antitrust Litig.*,

As we have seen already, a plaintiff normally must prove that the defendant's restraint of trade was "unreasonable," and that normally requires proof that the defendant holds market power. So at the end of the day, civil antitrust actions that reach the merits often will boil down to the reaction of 12 ordinary people to a "battle of the experts." Jurors will be asked to decide whether they believe either the economist called to testify for the plaintiff or the economist called to testify for the defense as to what may be a series of complicated fact questions.[3]

In any case, however much they may resemble other lawsuits on the surface, antitrust trials are also subject to a collection of peculiar ancillary rules and institutions. First, we will consider the specialized set of rules mentioned above that surrounds litigation by private plaintiffs. There are several. Again, they all seem ultimately designed to make sure that antitrust suits are brought only by those plaintiffs most likely to serve the underlying purposes of antitrust, and less likely to abuse it for commercial advantage. Second, antitrust is enforced by an uncommon array of enforcers. Antitrust can be enforced through criminal prosecution by the U.S. Attorneys, through civil proceedings brought by either one of two completely separate federal agencies, through civil actions brought by state governments, and through civil actions brought by private plaintiffs. Next, in part because there are such a range of possible enforcers, certain special technical rules govern these suits. First, a special rule of collateral estoppel exists relating to what is colloquially known as "follow-on" litigation. Second, antitrust has its own, rather complex statute of limitations. Finally, we will consider several idiosyncratic issues surrounding antitrust remedies.

---

631 F.3d 1059, 1079 (3d Cir. 1980) (noting that "prior cases have always assumed" the right). Likewise, criminal antitrust defendants have the same Sixth Amendment jury rights as other criminal defendants. Of course, the parties in either sort of action can agree to try a case to the bench. In enforcement actions by the FTC, however, there is no constitutional jury right. This is because the Seventh Amendment preserves civil jury rights only for "suits" that were recognized "at common law," and the courts have interpreted that phrase to embody only such causes of action as existed when the Bill of Rights was introduced in 1789. Section 5 of the FTC Act did not exist at that time, and so it is beyond the scope of the Seventh Amendment. The finder of fact in FTC proceedings is the Commission itself.

3. Criminal antitrust prosecutions are also tried to juries, but because prosecutions are almost never brought except for per se offenses, the only fact issues that criminal antitrust juries usually face are whether the defendant engaged in the challenged conduct. Difficult economic issues—those that are raised when the jury must decide whether the defendant's conduct was "reasonable"—are usually limited or irrelevant in criminal per se cases.

§19.1 LIMITATIONS ON PRIVATE RECOVERY: THE "ANTITRUST INJURY" RULE, THE STANDING REQUIREMENT, AND *ILLINOIS BRICK*

Recall that Article III of the U.S. Constitution, which creates the Supreme Court and sets out the maximum jurisdiction of the federal courts, has been held to require that every plaintiff filing suit in federal court must show "standing." Very generally speaking, to have standing a plaintiff must have suffered some actual injury and must show that the injury was in some way caused by the defendant's challenged conduct. Absent such a showing, to entertain the dispute is beyond the constitutional power of the Article III courts.

Private plaintiffs under Clayton Act §4 must make this minimum showing, no less than any other plaintiff in federal court. But for reasons of their own, the courts for some time have also required antitrust plaintiffs to show a fair bit more, and they predicate that requirement on the language of §4. (Critics have observed that the language can at least arguably be read to require no more than the bare minimum "injury" and "causation" required by Article III itself. After all, §4 requires only that the plaintiff be a "person . . . injured in his business or property by reason of anything forbidden in the antitrust laws. . . ." But the courts have read it to require more.) The courts have also founded their various rules for private plaintiffs on their concern that antitrust could be abused to the detriment of the very markets it is designed to protect if the private cause of action is available too widely. They have developed three general rules to limit the §4 action to only those plaintiffs they believe will serve the law's intended purpose and whom they believe are within the language of §4. The rules are (1) *antitrust injury*, a requirement that the harm complained of be one the antitrust laws were intended to prevent; (2) *antitrust standing*, which is in fact something of a causation rule, requiring a showing that the particular plaintiff is not "too far removed" from the challenged conduct; and (3) the *indirect purchaser* rule (also known as the *Illinois Brick* rule), intended to avoid duplicative recoveries.

§19.1.1 Antitrust Injury

Private plaintiffs must show that the injury for which they seek redress was of a special kind—namely, that it constitutes *antitrust injury*. Clayton Act §4 permits money damages recovery to "any person who shall be injured in his business or property by *reason of anything forbidden in the antitrust laws* . . ." (emphasis added). Likewise, Clayton Act §16 permits injunctive relief for private persons "against threatened loss or damage *by a violation of the antitrust laws* . . ." (emphasis added). Consequently, a private plaintiff must show not only that the defendant violated antitrust law, and that the violation caused the plaintiff some injury in its "business or property," but that the injury was of the kind that the antitrust laws were designed to prevent.

The Supreme Court first introduced this concept in *Brunswick Corp. v. Pueblo Bowl-O-Mat, Inc.*, 429 U.S. 477 (1977). The defendant was among the country's largest makers of bowling equipment, and it had decided to begin acquiring bowling alleys. The plaintiffs were much smaller firms that owned and operated individual bowling alleys. The plaintiffs brought suit under Clayton Act §7 to challenge the defendant's acquisition of competing bowling alleys in cities where they operated, and their only clearly articulated theory of harm to themselves was that had the acquired alleys—all of which were suffering financially—been allowed to fail, the plaintiffs would have earned higher profits. The Court began by assuming *arguendo* that the acquisitions violated §7. Likewise, assuming the plaintiffs could show that the acquired alleys really did provide effective competition and keep prices down, the Court did not doubt that they could show injury to their "business or property." But as the Court explained, the plaintiffs' loss of their ability to raise prices because of an *enhancement* to competition was not the sort of harm that antitrust was meant to remedy. Quite the opposite, in fact, and to grant the plaintiffs their relief would therefore pervert the basic purposes of the statute.

On very similar facts, in *Cargill, Inc. v. Monfort of Colorado, Inc.*, 479 U.S. 104 (1986), the Court reaffirmed *Brunswick* and held that the same rule applies to private plaintiff injunctive actions under Clayton Act §16. The Court has also since held that a plaintiff must demonstrate antitrust injury even when challenging a per se violation, such as horizontal price fixing. *Atl. Richfield Co. v. USA Petroleum Co.*, 495 U.S. 328, 337 (1990).[4]

The antitrust injury requirement is usually only an issue when the plaintiff is a competitor of the defendant. It is generally pretty difficult for a competitor plaintiff to show that one of its competitors engaged in conduct that violated the antitrust laws, that also harmed the plaintiff in some way, and that caused harm by *limiting* competition (rather than by enhancing competition). If the defendant's conduct in some way improved its ability to compete on the merits, in that it is able to offer a better product or sell it at a lower price, that might very well hurt the plaintiff, but not in a way that antitrust was meant to prevent. If the defendant's conduct does genuinely harm competition in a way meant to be prevented by the antitrust

4. Strictly speaking, *Atlantic Richfield* involved a vertical price-fixing conspiracy, not a horizontal one, but under the law at that time vertical price fixing was per se illegal.

laws—for example, if the defendants raise their prices—that will usually actually *help* the plaintiff, because the plaintiff can then either raise its own prices or take business from the defendant. In that sort of case, there is an injury to *competition*, but not to the *plaintiff*, and so again the competitor plaintiff would be unable to show antitrust injury.

There are some clear exceptions to this generalization. First, a competitor plaintiff can challenge price reductions—which ordinarily are thought to be the very soul of competition—if they are *predatorily* low. This is so because the object of a predatory pricing scheme is usually thought to be not just to harm competitors, which in and of itself is perfectly permissible, but to force their exit altogether. The ultimate goal is usually thought to be that on the victim's exit, *the predator can then charge supracompetitive prices. See Cargill, Inc. v. Monfort of Colorado, Inc.*, 479 U.S. 104, 121 (1986). Second, where the challenged conduct is *exclusionary*, a competitor plaintiff is harmed in a way that also harms competition. For example, a monopolist or cartel of the plaintiff's competitors might pressure important suppliers or customers to avoid the plaintiff. That would obviously harm the plaintiff, and it would also harm competition by excluding from the market the benefits of the plaintiff's ability to compete as to price or quality.

Example

For many years Manny has operated one of the only two hardware stores in Muncie, Indiana, and he has been locked in heated price and quality competition with his competitor during that entire time. Finally, this past fall, Manny succeeded—his competitor issued a notice in the local paper indicating its intent to file for bankruptcy liquidation. Manny quickly instituted modest price increases throughout his entire inventory and began turning a comfortable margin.

Much to Manny's horror, a nationwide chain of hardware stores decided to open a location in Muncie, and rather than build a new store, the chain merely bought up Manny's competitor before it was able to take bankruptcy. Manny challenges this acquisition as a merger that will tend to reduce competition and create a monopoly, in violation of Clayton Act §7. What result?

Explanation

Manny likely lacks "antitrust injury," and his suit will be dismissed. Likely his only option is to put on a colorable case that the new entrant has or will engage in predatory pricing, and that showing is very difficult.

Example

ABC, Inc., is a manufacturer of chewing gum. Its two largest competitors, DEF, Inc., and GHI Corp., have met under clandestine circumstances to agree to minimum prices for new products they intend to introduce that feature pictures of popular cartoon characters on the packaging. By bribing some of the conspirators' employees, ABC was able to secure smoking-gun evidence of this agreement. Fearful for the future of its beloved ABC Gum, ABC sues, alleging a horizontal price-fixing conspiracy in violation of Sherman Act §1. Realizing it may have some difficulty proving damages, it seeks only an injunction under Clayton Act §16. The defendants move to dismiss. What result?

Explanation

The plaintiff has failed to show antitrust injury and the matter should be dismissed. (The fact that these are new products, featuring cartoon characters, is a red herring and is irrelevant; this is a garden-variety price-fixing conspiracy.) Assuming the plaintiff's alleged facts are true, the plaintiff has shown a violation of Sherman Act §1. However, in this case, just like in most price-fixing cases, the defendants have agreed only to *raise* their prices. If your competitor raises its prices, that can only help you, by causing consumers to switch from the competitor's goods to yours.

While the Supreme Court has never explicitly held as much, in both *Atl. Richfield Co. v. USA Petroleum Co.*, 495 U.S. 328, 337 (1990), and *Matsushita Elec. Indus. Co. v. Zenith Radio Corp.*, 475 U.S. 574, 582-583 (1986), the Court so stated in strongly worded dicta.

§19.1.2 Standing or "Remoteness"

The courts have long recognized that the broad language of Clayton Act §4 could pose fairly severe and probably unintended effects for antitrust defendants. Nominally, any person who could claim to be "injured in his business or property" by any antitrust violation could sue for treble damages. But that might make the pool of possible plaintiffs very large. Say that a corporation is involved in the making of high-end coffee makers. One of the inputs it must buy to make its product is a small computer chip. It comes to light that most of the makers of these chips have secretly conspired to fix their prices for it. The resulting increase in the corporation's costs caused it to raise its prices, and therefore it lost a substantial number of sales. A Clayton Act §4 claim by the corporation would be no problem. It has plainly suffered harm and it can easily make a showing of antitrust injury. But what about its shareholders? They may have lost value because of the company's diminished performance. Should they also be able to sue? What if the company, because of lost revenues, is unable to service loans it has taken out to fund its operations? Should its creditors have a right to sue the computer chip cartel for three times the unpaid principal and interest? What if, because of lost revenues, the corporation is unable to continue funding its employee benefits program, and as a result that program goes into default and must be rescued by the federal Pension Benefit Guaranty Corporation, resulting in large losses to the taxpayers and to the corporation's employees? Should either the employees or the PBGC have an antitrust suit against the computer chip cartel? The obvious instinct is that Congress could not have intended to give all these various parties three times the value of their losses.

To deal with these problems the courts have required private antitrust plaintiffs, in addition to the showing of antitrust injury, to make a more generalized showing that they are "appropriate" plaintiffs. The test the courts have devised has come to be known as the "antitrust standing" rule or the rule of "remoteness." The primary guidance on the rule remains the Supreme Court's decisions in *Blue Shield of Virginia v. McCready*, 457 U.S. 465 (1982) and *Associated Gen. Contractors of California, Inc. v. California State Council of Carpenters*, 459 U.S. 519 (1983). Those two cases set out and purport to apply a fairly Sphinx-like, multi-factor test that has been much criticized for its lack of clarity.

Interestingly, the Court in *Associated General Contractors* noted "a similarity between the struggle of common-law judges to articulate a precise definition of the concept of 'proximate cause,'" and the struggle for an antitrust standing doctrine. In trying to formulate a rule to identify appropriate plaintiffs under Clayton Act §4, the federal courts found themselves in the same confusing doctrinal morass that the common law courts faced 100 years earlier as to causation in tort law. "It is common ground" between these two judicial struggles, said the Court, that

> the judicial remedy cannot encompass every conceivable harm that can be traced to alleged wrongdoing. In both situations the infinite variety of claims that may arise make it virtually impossible to announce a black-letter rule that will dictate the result in every case.

459 U.S. at 536. Instead, the Court attempted to gather all of the relevant factors that it could, and ultimately identified five. Courts should consider:

1. Whether there is "a causal connection between an antitrust violation and harm . . . allege[d]," and whether "the defendants intended to cause that harm";
2. The "nature of the alleged injury," including whether the plaintiff was a "consumer []or a competitor";
3. The "directness or indirectness of the asserted injury," which is to say, how many "links" there are in the "chain of causation between the . . . injury and the alleged restraint";

4. Whether there is some "identifiable class of persons," other than the plaintiff, with more "direct" injury, because their "self-interest would normally motivate them to vindicate the public interest in antitrust enforcement," and whether "[d]enying [the plaintiff] a remedy" under those circumstances "is not likely to leave a significant antitrust violation undetected or unremedied"; and
5. The "risk of duplicate recoveries . . . or the danger of complex apportionment of damages. . . ."

Id. at 537-544.

As the lower courts have applied this test, they have focused mainly on whether there is some class of persons who have a more direct injury than the plaintiff, and when there is, they are likely to deny standing. One leading treatise summarizes the current state of things this way:

> [W]here a plaintiff's injury is derivative of a more direct injury to some other person, and that person would have a strong incentive to pursue its own antitrust claim against the defendant, standing is not likely to be recognized.

1 Am. Bar Assn., *Antitrust Law Developments* (Ninth) 814 (9th ed. 2022). In fact, rather than working through the five *Associated General Contractors* factors, many courts have simply examined a plaintiff's role in the marketplace as a shorthand way of addressing standing, and will ordinarily deny standing if the plaintiff was neither a competitor of the defendant nor a purchaser from it. *See id.* at 826.

§19.1.3 The Direct Purchaser Rule

A final judicially fashioned rule to limit the availability of private remedies is the so-called "indirect purchaser" rule, also often known as the *Illinois Brick* rule, after the case in which it was announced, *Illinois Brick Co. v. Illinois*, 431 U.S. 720 (1977). *Illinois Brick* was actually the flip side to an earlier decision, *Hanover Shoe, Inc. v. United Shoe Mach. Corp.*, 392 U.S. 481 (1968). In *Hanover Shoe*, the plaintiff was a shoe manufacturer that successfully sued the dominant maker of shoe-making machinery for monopolization under Sherman Act §2. The Court rejected the defendant's argument that the plaintiff suffered no injury because it could just pass on the overcharge to its own customers. The Court thought that such a defense would invite unduly complex litigation and also would leave as the only likely plaintiffs the ultimate retail consumers, whose injuries would be too small to justify litigation.

Ten years later, *Illinois Brick* addressed the flip-side problem. If direct purchasers (like the plaintiff in *Hanover Shoe*) could sue, without any possible deduction in their damages for passing on, could *their* customers also sue for their overcharges? The *Illinois Brick* Court said no. In that case, the state of Illinois sued brick manufacturers that had conspired to fix their prices. Illinois purchased those bricks, but only through the construction contractors that were awarded contracts for state construction projects. It was the contractors who purchased the bricks in the first instance. The state of Illinois, therefore, was not like the *Hanover Shoe* plaintiff. It did not purchase the overpriced goods directly from the defendants that overpriced them. The Court's reasoning was simple. Illinois could not recover—even if the contractors themselves had not yet sued—because *Hanover Shoe* had already made clear that the contractors *could* sue, and therefore allowing an indirect purchaser to sue as well would put the defendants at the risk of duplicative recoveries. Moreover, calculating the actual injury suffered by an indirect purchaser, thought the Court, would be much more difficult than the relatively simple matter of estimating an overcharge to a direct purchaser.

Thus, the simple rule under *Hanover Shoe* and *Illinois Brick* is that where the plaintiff is a consumer, it can sue for damages only if it purchased the good directly from the defendant that committed the antitrust violation. On the one hand, a direct purchaser can recover the entire overcharge, even though it may have passed on some of the overcharge to its own customers. On the other hand, an indirect purchaser cannot sue for money damages at all.

The Supreme Court has held that *Illinois Brick* applies to both Sherman Act §§1 and 2, and lower courts have found it applicable to challenges against mergers and acquisitions under Clayton Act §7. *See, e.g., Lucas Auto Engr., Inc. v. Bridgestone/Firestone, Inc.*, 140 F.3d 1228, 1233-1234 (9th Cir. 1998). One other subsidiary rule is that, though the Supreme Court has not yet addressed it, *Illinois Brick* does not apply to injunctive actions under Clayton Act §16. *Lucas*, 140 F.3d at 1235 (so holding and collecting cases). The Court has resisted limitations or exceptions to *Illinois Brick*, though many plaintiffs have asked it to recognize them. For example, a consumer cannot sue an upstream firm, even if the downstream firm that the consumer buys from is required by a regulator to pass on all of its costs. *Kansas v. Utilicorp United, Inc.*, 497 U.S. 199 (1990). Likewise, it makes no difference if the seller from whom a consumer bought something did not itself set its own retail prices. Even if it sells on a fixed commission, and the retail price is otherwise within some supplier's discretion, its customer is still a direct purchaser. *Apple, Inc. v. Pepper*, 587 U.S. 273 (2019). As the Court has explained, "even assuming that any economic assumptions underlying the *Illinois Brick* rule might be disproved in a specific case, we think it an unwarranted and counterproductive exercise to litigate a series of exceptions." *Utilicorp*, 497 U.S. at 217.

Interestingly, the state courts, in interpreting their antitrust statutes, mostly do not follow the *Illinois Brick* rule. They permit indirect purchasers (like ultimate consumers who claim they are injured by price fixing as to raw materials used in the goods they buy) to bring antitrust actions. For this reason, indirect purchaser litigation is among the claims commonly brought by private plaintiffs under state antitrust law. It is also a source of bitter complaint by antitrust defendants and their counsel, since it seems to result in the duplicative recovery that *Illinois Brick* sought to prevent.

Example

You have just bought a new pair of $400 Nike sneakers that have Floats-Like-a-Dream comfort sole inserts, neon lights in the feet, a USB port, and GPS-ready navigation technology. You learn from an article you've just read in the *Wall Street Journal* that Nike is suspected of fixing the price of so-called "super-premium athletic footwear" with other makers of such shoes. You file a lawsuit immediately, alleging a violation of §1 of the Sherman Act. On these facts alone, will Nike be able to dismiss your lawsuit?

Explanation

Probably. Like most retail products, your shoes were likely purchased at a retail store, and not directly from Nike. If so, your suit could be dismissed under *Illinois Brick* because you are not a direct purchaser. If you bought your shoes directly from Nike in some fashion, as through a company-owned store for example, you would be a direct purchaser and able to sue.

Example

The enforcement staff of the FTC initiates an action under §5 of the FTC Act against a group of ophthalmologists who allegedly have conspired to fix their prices. The defendants move to dismiss the action both for lack of "antitrust injury" and under the *Illinois Brick* rule. What's the result?

Explanation

The motion should be denied. Both the "antitrust injury" and *Illinois Brick* rules apply only to private plaintiffs.

§19.2 THE UNUSUAL VARIETY OF ENFORCERS

Over antitrust's long history Congress has provided a surprisingly wide range of different avenues for its enforcement. This probably reflects the congressional conviction at different times that the statute was being underenforced. For example, the Federal Trade Commission (FTC), a federal agency that is one of the policy's primary enforcers, was created in 1914 after the first 20 years of what many legislators believed was inadequate enforcement and narrow judicial interpretation. Their hope in creating the FTC was that as an expert body with investigative, prosecutorial, and rule-making powers it could give effect to their ideal of an antitrust policy with broader reach.[5]

§19.2.1 Federal Enforcers

Two separate federal agencies enforce the antitrust laws: the Antitrust Division of the Department of Justice (DOJ) and the FTC, an independent agency. The Antitrust Division, headed by a presidentially appointed Assistant Attorney General, investigates and challenges conduct anywhere in U.S. jurisdiction that may violate the Sherman, Robinson-Patman, or Clayton Acts. The Division also shares responsibility with the FTC to perform merger preclearance review under the Hart-Scott-Rodino Act.

§19.2.1(a) The Justice Department, Antitrust Division: Civil Enforcement Powers

While the Justice Department performs a number of special administrative functions in antitrust, for our purposes its role in civil antitrust litigation looks roughly like that of any civil plaintiff. The Division's power to bring civil antitrust actions flows from three provisions—Sherman Act §4, Clayton Act §15, and Clayton Act §4a. The first two of these provisions in effect empower the DOJ to enforce all of antitrust law by bringing injunctive actions in the federal district courts.

The third provision, Clayton Act §4a, is rather different. It empowers the DOJ to represent the federal government in court as, in effect, a private antitrust plaintiff. When the DOJ sues under this rule, it alleges that some person that sold something to the government, or otherwise did business

5. There is a separate theme within this history as well. There was also concern for the risk to business persons of a law so vague and hard to predict, and so an additional motivation of both the Clayton and FTC Acts in 1914 was to provide more detailed guidance to business. For an elaborate history of this period and the concerns leading to the two statutes, *see* Martin J. Sklar, *The Corporate Reconstruction of American Capitalism, 1890-1916* (1988).

with it, hurt the government's interests through some violation of the antitrust laws. A typical case might involve a company that provides cars for the government's auto fleet. The government usually buys such things by issuing a request for sealed bids, and picks the lowest price. If the carmaker agreed with its competitors on the prices they would bid, that violates Sherman Act §1 and the government has a money damages cause of action under Clayton Act §4a. In §4a cases, just like private plaintiff antitrust actions, the government can recover treble damages plus costs, attorneys fees, and interest.

Still, the DOJ is not just any ordinary antitrust plaintiff. Its role is much larger, and it is a fundamentally regulatory one. It shares with the FTC the responsibility of managing the nation's merger preclearance review process under the Hart-Scott-Rodino Act (discussed at length in Chapter 18). Likewise, while the DOJ has no power to make binding substantive regulations as to competition policy, it exercises an influential policy-making function by way of issuing enforcement "guidelines." Technically, these documents are not binding law, and rather only set out guidance about when the DOJ will likely bring an enforcement action against particular conduct. Guidelines have been issued to govern mergers, dealings in intellectual property, international operations, competitor collaborations ("joint ventures"), and health care, and they have exerted significant influence. (The most influential of them, the *Merger Guidelines*, is discussed at length in Chapter 17.) The DOJ will also issue, on request, an informal opinion about the legality of specific, proposed conduct. While the agency's "business review letters" do not bind it, the DOJ will in appropriate cases indicate whether it has any "present enforcement intention" with respect to the conduct described in the request. Finally, Congress has given the DOJ powerful investigative tools. Unlike the ordinary plaintiff, the DOJ can issue discovery orders called "civil investigative demands" prior to the filing of any lawsuit, and through them may require production of documents, answers to interrogatories, or appearance at in-person deposition. 15 U.S.C. §1312. In effect, the DOJ performs an informational investigative function by using these powers that is unlike any mere litigant.

§19.2.1(b) The U.S. Attorneys and Criminal Enforcement

Criminal antitrust prosecutions are brought mainly by the various U.S. Attorneys, and those that are not are handled by Antitrust Division headquarters. The FTC has no role in criminal prosecutions. (Indeed, all federal crimes are prosecuted by the Justice Department—no other federal agency has authority to prosecute crimes.) Strictly speaking, criminal penalties can be sought for any violation of Sherman Act §1 or §2 and for some other antitrust offenses, but as a practical matter the Justice Department does not criminally prosecute any conduct other than naked horizontal price fixing or market allocation. This is so probably for a variety of reasons. Among other things, the Supreme Court has held that the Justice Department must prove (beyond a reasonable doubt, the more demanding standard of proof in criminal proceedings) that the defendant acted with a "criminal intent."[6] That showing would be difficult in light of the factual complexity of most antitrust cases. It would also just be difficult generally to make out a rule-of-reason case under the criminal burden of proof and the constitutional protections of criminal defendants. But the policy also reflects the concern that the stigma of criminal conviction and the severe penalties available for antitrust crimes should be reserved only for those most obviously morally culpable actions, and by general consensus that means naked horizontal restraints on price or output. In any case, for our purposes the main differences between a DOJ civil action and a DOJ criminal action are (1) a criminal action will almost always begin with a grand jury investigation, conducted by DOJ prosecutors; (2) the action will be subject to the Federal Rules of Criminal Procedure, which set out somewhat different rules concerning discovery and pretrial relations among the parties, and the criminal procedure protections of the U.S. Constitution; (3) the government will bear the higher burden of proof for criminal actions; and (4) the government must make the showing of "criminal intent."

Example

The Justice Department brings a civil lawsuit against a group of manufacturers of X-ray equipment. The defendants are alleged to have entered into various trade restraining agreements with each other. They sell their X-ray equipment to various hospitals, including Cedars-Sinai in New York, Brigham & Women's Hospital, which is affiliated with Harvard University, Johns Hopkins, Yale Medical School, the U.S. Army's Walter Reed Medical Center, the Mayo Clinic, and the Cleveland Clinic. What kind of relief can the government get?

Explanation

This is a bit of a trick question. Ordinarily the Justice Department could challenge this conduct only as a crime under Sherman Act §1, or by bringing an injunctive action under Sherman Act §4 to challenge it as a civil violation of §1. However, notice that one of the purchasers here is a hospital owned by the federal government—the Army's Walter Reed hospital. Therefore, the government itself can show injury to its "business or property" and can sue for treble damages plus costs and attorney fees under Clayton Act §4a.

6. *See United States v. United States Gypsum Co.*, 438 U.S. 422 (1978).

§19.2.1(c) The Federal Trade Commission, Its Special Functions, and Its Complicated Jurisdiction

The second federal enforcer is the Federal Trade Commission. The FTC is an "independent agency," which means that the structure created for it by its underlying organic statute shelters it somewhat from the influence of the President. Specifically, the Commission is made up of five Commissioners, and can take most of its major actions only by majority vote among them. Moreover, while the Commissioners are appointed by the President, with Senate confirmation, their seven-year terms overlap one another; by statute no more than three of them can be of the same political party; and the President can fire them only for "inefficiency, neglect of duty, or malfeasance in office. . . ." FTC Act §1, 15 U.S.C. §41. It is difficult for any one President to pack the Commission with loyalists, and the Commissioners need not fear for their jobs merely for the President's disagreement with their decisions.

While the FTC has no role in criminal antitrust prosecutions, it otherwise has a scope of responsibilities that roughly resembles that of the Antitrust Division. Still, the FTC's jurisdiction and powers turn out to be among the more complicated little issues in antitrust. This is so because the FTC has always been a somewhat controversial entity, and various interests have more or less incessantly lobbied Congress to tinker with its powers.

The scope of the agency's jurisdiction is rather complex, but that issue is dealt with in a later chapter along with the overall scope of antitrust (*see* §20.2.3). Its enforcement powers are rather complex as well. The agency has two major substantive enforcement powers in the antitrust area. First, the Clayton Act empowers it to enforce §§2, 3, 7, and 8 (which govern, respectively, price discrimination, tying and exclusive contracts, mergers and acquisitions, and interlocking directorates, all of which are discussed elsewhere in this book). *See* 15 U.S.C. §21(a). Second, §5(a)(1) of the FTC Act, the Commission's organic statute, empowers it to prevent all "[u]nfair methods of competition in or affecting commerce. . . ."[7] The relationship of this provision to antitrust generally is slightly complicated. Strictly speaking, the FTC has no formal power to enforce the Sherman Act, but the Supreme Court has made clear that conduct that violates the Sherman Act also violates FTC Act §5. *See FTC v. California Dental Assn.*, 526 U.S. 756, 763 n.3 (1999) ("The FTC Act's prohibition of unfair competition and deceptive acts or practices . . . overlaps the scope of §1 of the Sherman Act"); *Fashion Originators' Guild, Inc. v. FTC*, 312 U.S. 457, 463-464 (1941). On the other side of the same coin, §5 probably reaches conduct that would not in itself

7. Section 5(a)(1) also prohibits "unfair or deceptive acts or practices"; the Commission has mostly used this separate power as a consumer protection tool, to attack false advertising or consumer fraud or the like.

violate the Sherman or Clayton Acts. *See FTC v. Sperry & Hutchinson Co.*, 405 U.S. 233, 239 (1972) (holding that §5 empowers the agency "to define and proscribe an unfair competitive practice, even though the practice does not infringe either the letter or the spirit of the antitrust laws"). In short, the Commission's antitrust enforcement power is at least as broad as the combined Sherman, Clayton and Robinson-Patman Acts, and perhaps is broader, though as a practical matter the FTC now very rarely makes any effort to use that broader power.

The procedures by which the Commission enforces these substantive provisions are also somewhat complex. In effect, the agency has two different avenues to bring actions under the Clayton Act and FTC Act §5. First, it can proceed through an internal adjudication procedure known as a "Part 3" proceeding,[8] which if successful results in a forward-looking injunction known as a "cease-and-desist" order. To bring this sort of action, the five members of the Commission must first vote to bring a complaint. Having done so the Commission then withdraws, and the case is litigated by "complaint counsel," who are agency staff attorneys. The proceeding in most respects resembles any other civil antitrust action, except that it is before an agency employee known as an Administrative Law Judge (ALJ), and there is no jury. Either the defendant or complaint counsel may appeal an ALJ order to the Commission, which then acts essentially as an appellate body. If the Commission makes a finding of liability, the result is a cease-and-desist order prospectively enjoining the defendant from the challenged conduct. Defendants may appeal full Commission decisions to the federal courts of appeals, in which case the Commission itself is styled as opposing party.

Importantly, when a defendant appeals a cease-and-desist order, statute requires the reviewing court to give the Commission very broad deference. "The findings of the commission, board, or Secretary as to the facts, if supported by substantial evidence, shall be conclusive." 15 U.S.C. §§21(c), 45(c). On this point, Judge Posner once began a discussion of this deference with a rather surprising bit of self-effacement:

> One of the main reasons for creating the Federal Trade Commission and giving it concurrent jurisdiction to enforce the Clayton Act was that Congress distrusted judicial determination of antitrust questions. It thought the assistance of an administrative body would be helpful in resolving such questions and indeed expected the FTC to take the leading role in enforcing the Clayton Act, which was passed at the same time as the statute creating the Commission.

8. Part 3 proceedings are so named because the procedures governing them are set out in Part 3 of the Commission's Rules of Practice, codified at 16 C.F.R. §§3.1-3.83.

Hospital Corp. of Am. v. FTC, 807 F.2d 1381, 1387 (7th Cir. 1986). Accordingly, a court's "only function is to determine whether the Commission's analysis of the probable effects of [the challenged conduct] . . . is so implausible, so feebly supported by the record, that it flunks even the deferential test of substantial evidence." *Id.* at 1385.

The FTC, like the DOJ, also has a number of powers that are more regulatory in character. Again, the Commission shares oversight with the DOJ of the HSR merger preclearance program. But the FTC also has authority to make regulations to prohibit violations of §5; that is, the FTC can promulgate rules that have the force of federal law to determine which conduct violates §5.[9] This rule-making authority is, like so much else about the Commission, complicated, but for what it may be worth, rule making has never played a very significant role in the agency's work. More important has been the Commission's panoply of special investigative powers. It has not only the DOJ's power to issue precomplaint civil investigative demands, it can also employ a series of nonlitigation investigative powers to compel production of information merely for the purpose of preparing reports on various industries.[10] Finally, like the DOJ, the Commission can issue informal "business advisory opinions" on the request of private parties.

§19.2.2 Private Plaintiffs and the Rule of Treble Damages

Unlike the competition laws of virtually every other country in the world, U.S. antitrust permits private persons to bring causes of action for injuries caused by antitrust violation. Indeed, ever since its first adoption, U.S. antitrust has permitted not only private money damages but enhanced, additional damages as a sweetener to encourage them to act as "private attorneys general." When it was first adopted in 1890 Sherman Act §7 provided that any person personally injured by any violation of the act could recover *three times* the actual injury they suffered. This is the so-called "treble damages" rule. Original Sherman Act §7 also provided that successful private plaintiffs could recover attorneys fees and costs. *See* ch. 647, 26 Stat. 290, §7 (1890). Interestingly, the legislative history suggests that the original drafters probably misperceived just how sizable treble damages would one day become. They feared that the primary victims of the massive "trusts" they sought to restrain would be retail consumers whose individual injuries

---

9. The Commission can make rules governing unfair competition under FTC Act §6(g), 15 U.S.C. §46(g), and rules governing deceptive acts or practices under FTC Act §18, 15 U.S.C. §57a.

10. The Commission's C.I.D. power is set out in FTC Act §20, 15 U.S.C. §57b-1. It can also issue more mundane, somewhat less powerful subpoenas under FTC Act §9, 15 U.S.C. §49. The Commission's nonlitigation investigative powers appear in FTC Act §6, 15 U.S.C. §46.

would be too small to justify a lawsuit without the encouragement of treble damages and attorney fees. (In those days the class action had not yet been invented—class actions are now probably the primary tool by which small consumer injuries are redressed.) In fact, treble damage awards now frequently run into the many millions of dollars.

Original Sherman Act §7 was replaced by Clayton Act §§4, 4a, and 4c, which preserve the treble damages remedy and attorney fees and added a provision for prejudgment interest, as well as Clayton Act §16, which provides that any state government or private person entitled to seek money damages can also seek injunction of antitrust violations.

So, for example, imagine that a cartel of manufacturers of acetylsalicylic acid, the basic ingredient in aspirin, have entered into a stable and long-lasting price-fixing conspiracy. The plaintiff, a manufacturer of aspirin that must buy its raw material from members of the cartel, shows in litigation that the cartel was able to raise the price of acetylsalicylic acid by 10 cents per pound. The plaintiff also shows that it bought 1 million pounds during the period of the challenged conduct. The plaintiff's injury during that period would therefore be \$100,000, and if the plaintiff successfully shows liability, it will be awarded \$300,000 plus its attorney fees and costs.

The private treble damages remedy remains controversial. Its critics believe it incentivizes frivolous litigation and overdeters violations, perhaps chilling procompetitive conduct. Critics are in particular hostile to the fact that private plaintiffs may bring money damages actions following successful criminal or civil actions by the Justice Department and that when they do so they enjoy a special statutory collateral estoppel effect (which is discussed further below). These so-called "follow-on" suits are frequently brought by class action plaintiff attorneys who themselves can earn very large fees if they succeed. However, defenders of this remedy are also vocal, and they say that given the extraordinary difficulty of bringing private antitrust actions—especially on a contingency basis—it is necessary to preserve meaningful enforcement of competition policy. Moreover, there is emerging empirical evidence that in fact at least some anticompetitive conduct—and especially horizontal price fixing—is much more profitable than was previously thought, so much so that treble damages liability may be not nearly *enough* to discourage it adequately.[11]

---

11. John M. Connor & Robert H. Lande, *Cartels as Rational Business Strategy:* Crime *Pays,* 34 Cardozo L. Rev. 427, 474-476 (2012) (presenting results of large empirical study of cartel behavior, finding that cartel penalties might need to be made many times larger than they currently are in order to be "optimal").

§19.2.3 State Governments: As Private Plaintiffs and in *Parens Patriae*

State governments have played a large role in enforcing federal antitrust policy. They have been fairly frequent litigants and they have formed an influential professional association, the National Association of Attorneys General (NAAG), which among other things has issued its own nonbinding but fairly influential set of model enforcement guidelines.

State governments can act as antitrust plaintiffs in two ways. First, they can sue in their own right as "persons," if they are injured in their business or property, using Clayton Act §4 just as private individuals do. Though the term "person" as used in §§4 and 16 is not explicitly defined to include state governments as persons,[12] the courts have held them to be "persons" for purposes of private enforcement. *See Georgia v. Pennsylvania R.R. Co.*, 324 U.S. 439, 447 (1945) (holding that state of Georgia, suing to enjoin injury to itself as proprietor of a railroad, was "person" within meaning of Clayton Act §16). For that matter, cities and other political subdivisions can sue for both injunctive and treble damages relief in their personal capacities as "persons." *See* 1 Am. Bar Assn., Section of Antitrust Law, *Antitrust Law Developments* (Ninth) 799 (9th ed. 2022).

Second, state governments can also bring a special sort of representative action called the "*parens patriae*" (meaning roughly "in place of the parent"). The *parens patriae* action was created by Clayton Act §4c, added as Title III of the Hart-Scott-Rodino Antitrust Improvements Act in 1976, to reverse *California v. Frito-Lay, Inc.*, 474 F.2d 774 (9th Cir. 1973). *Frito-Lay* held that state governments had no power to enforce federal antitrust in a representative capacity on behalf of their citizens. Importantly, *parens patriae* actions are subject to certain limitations. Among other things, (1) they may be brought only on behalf of natural persons who reside within the state; and (2) they may be brought only for Sherman Act violations, meaning they cannot be used to enforce the Clayton or Robinson-Patman Acts. There are certain other interesting differences between *parens patriae* actions and ordinary cases, however, and from the perspective of the persons they are intended to benefit they may sometimes be superior to Clayton Act §4 class actions. For example, there is no need to certify the action pursuant to Federal Rule of Civil Procedure 23, a difficult hurdle that is frequently the death of a §4 class action, and if the state succeeds the citizen beneficiaries can avoid what might otherwise be large contingency attorney fees.

---

12. The Clayton Act's definition section defines "person" this way: The word "person" or "persons" wherever used in this Act shall be deemed to include corporations and associations existing under or authorized by the laws of either the United States, the laws of any of the Territories, the laws of any State, or the laws of any foreign country. 15 U.S.C. §12(a).

§19.3 TECHNICAL PROCEDURAL PECULIARITIES

§19.3.1 Follow-On Litigation and Collateral Estoppel

It is common that a federal enforcer will first sue a defendant and secure some injunctive or criminal remedy, and then private persons will realize they have been harmed by the same illegal conduct and sue for money damages. The Clayton and FTC Acts provide several specific benefits for these so-called follow-on plaintiffs. The overall effects of these several specific provisions are that the fact that the government has sued a defendant has no negative consequences for subsequent plaintiffs; the pendency of the government action tolls the private plaintiffs' statute of limitations; and if the government action reaches a final judgment of liability on the merits, that has positive legal consequences for subsequent plaintiffs.

First of all, the two statutes provide that government enforcement has no negative effect on subsequent plaintiffs.[13] The fact that the DOJ or the FTC has already secured some relief does not limit the relief a subsequent private plaintiff may seek.[14] Moreover, the Clayton Act provides in §5(a), 15 U.S.C. §16(a), that where a "final judgment or decree" has been entered in any civil or criminal action "by or on behalf of the United States under the antitrust laws to the effect that a defendant has violated said laws shall be prima facie evidence against such defendant" in any case brought by any other party against that defendant, "as to all matters respecting which said judgment or decree would be an estoppel as between the parties thereto. . . ." In other words, if the Justice Department is successful in securing a verdict or conviction, then a plaintiff in a later civil action challenging the same conduct can use that earlier result to its advantage. Even though the government is no longer a party, the private plaintiff can use the prior proceeding as "prima facie" evidence of any issues tried in the earlier case, including rather the largest looming issue of all, that of the defendant's liability.

This rule is limited in several respects. First, it does not apply to most proceedings brought by the FTC—the statute does not apply to the Commission's "findings," meaning that no factual or legal rulings made in an FTC administrative cease-and-desist proceeding may be used by subsequent plaintiffs. Second, §5(a) applies only where the government

---

13. An exception is for *parens patriae* actions. Where a state brings such a suit and the matter reaches final judgment, no citizen represented in that matter can thereafter file a private Clayton Act §4 action.

14. *See* Clayton Act §11(e), 15 U.S.C. §21(e) (providing that FTC enforcement of the substantive provisions of the Clayton Act has no effect on subsequent antitrust); FTC Act §5(e), 15 U.S.C. §45(e) (providing that FTC enforcement of the substantive provisions of the Clayton Act has no effect on subsequent antitrust).

judgment is "final" and does not apply to judgments secured before the taking of any testimony. This is why many government lawsuits settle consensually in consent decrees and many criminal prosecutions end in pleas of *nolo contendere*—in either case, §5(a) does not apply.

Finally, the antitrust statute of limitations (discussed below) as to both private and state government actions is tolled during the pendency of a Justice Department civil or criminal action (except for a DOJ treble damages claim under Clayton Act §4a) or any FTC action. The tolling period continues for one year after the government action concludes.

§19.3.2 The Antitrust Statute of Limitations

As one might expect, given the complexity of possible violations and the range of enforcers, the antitrust statute of limitations is itself fairly complex. The basic rule appears in Clayton Act §4b, 15 U.S.C. §15b, which subjects most civil antitrust actions to a four-year limitations period. Section 4b explicitly applies to private money damages causes of action (including those brought by states in their personal capacities), Justice Department treble damages cause of action, and state *parens patriae* actions. However, it does *not* apply to Justice Department injunctive actions under Sherman Act §4, FTC cease-and-desist proceedings under FTC Act §5, or any government enforcement of Clayton Act §7. These government civil actions are subject to literally no limitations period.

Section 4b is also silent as to private actions for injunction under Clayton Act §16. However, the lower courts have held them subject to the equitable doctrine of laches, and follow the four-year limitations period of §4b as a guideline in applying laches. *See, e.g., I.T.T. Corp. v. G.T.E. Corp.*, 518 F.2d 913, 926-929 (9th Cir. 1975). Laches does not apply to Justice Department or FTC injunctive actions. Justice Department criminal prosecutions are subject to a separate limitations statute—they must be commenced within five years of the offense, 18 U.S.C. §3282.

The statute of limitations under §4b accrues (i.e., it begins to run) as soon as the plaintiff suffers ascertainable injury. As a practical matter this means that the period does not begin to run even if the injury is known, so long as damages would as yet only be speculative. *See Zenith Radio Corp. v. Hazeltine Research, Inc.* 401 U.S. 321, 338-342 (1971) (permitting recovery on claim filed in 1963 for injuries resulting in 1959-1963 from conduct that occurred prior to 1954, since injuries for which relief was sought would not have been ascertainable at time of the challenged conduct). Recall as well that, as mentioned above, the §4b limitations period is tolled as to any private or state government claim during the pendency of government actions other than DOJ treble damage claims under Clayton Act §4a. *See* Clayton Act §5(i), 15 U.S.C. §16(i).

Example

In January of 1995, the Justice Department instituted proceedings under Sherman Act §4, which led ultimately to a finding of civil liability before a jury, against Megabeast Corporation, a maker of video game software. The government sued for monopolization within a relevant market defined as "violent action online gaming." Most of the challenged conduct involved a complex web of exclusive dealing arrangements with distributors, which the government alleged made it too hard for competing software firms to get their products to market. The most recent of the challenged conduct occurred in about 1991 and 1992. Following the two-year trial of the government's claim, the jury returned a verdict of liability in all respects. Six months later, a private cause of action was filed against Megabeast on exactly the same facts and the same legal theory by a plaintiff class of competing software makers. After two years or more of pretrial practice, including momentous amounts of discovery, Megabeast moves for summary judgment. In its reply, the plaintiff class does not adduce any new facts concerning the relevant market or Megabeast's conduct within it.

Megabeast's motion asserts a variety of theories: (1) that a competing software video game maker is not an appropriate plaintiff under these circumstances, (2) that these plaintiffs failed to put on sufficient evidence to support the §2 cause of action, and (3) that the claims are time barred. Should the defendant's motion be granted?

Explanation

From what we can tell from these facts, there is no reason to believe the claims should be dismissed. First, a plaintiff class composed of horizontal competitors can show antitrust injury under these circumstances. They are injured in fact through lost sales, and the injury is caused not by competition itself but by anticompetitive exclusion. There is no *Illinois Brick* issue—the injury alleged is not through some indirect purchase of a good—and there is no obvious reason to suspect a "remoteness" or "antitrust standing" problem. The injury is direct and the damages ascertainable. (Recall that remoteness is usually at issue only where the plaintiff is neither the defendant's customer nor its competitor.)

Second, while it is true that a plaintiff asserting monopolization under §2 must prove a relevant market and exclusionary conduct within it (*see* Chapter 13), this is a "follow-on" suit following a judgment of liability on the merits brought by or on behalf of the United States. Therefore, under Clayton Act §5(a), the finding of liability is prima facie evidence of liability in the class's subsequent private suit. Unless Megabeast has come up with some evidence at this stage to rebut the earlier finding of liability, its motion should not be granted on this ground.

Finally, the class's claims are not time barred. While this is a Clayton Act §4 cause of action, and is therefore subject to the four-year statute of limitations in Clayton Act §4b, the pendency of a government cause of action tolls the limitations period, per Clayton Act §5(i).

Example

In January of 2002, the Justice Department sues IBM and other computer manufacturers for a conspiracy in restraint of trade. Along with the Justice Department are nine state Attorneys General suing in *parens patriae*. The alleged conduct, which occurred in November and December of 1992, concerns primarily an alleged price-fixing conspiracy and certain market divisions. Can this cause of action proceed?

Explanation

The Justice Department claim may proceed, but the state claims are probably time barred under the statute of limitations in Clayton Act §4b. Recall that there is no statute of limitations on federal government civil enforcement actions (though there are time limits on both criminal prosecutions—five years—and on money damages claims by the Justice Department, which are subject to the same four-year limitations period as other money damages claims). However, Clayton Act §4b, which sets out the primary antitrust statute of limitations, is explicitly applicable to state *parens patriae* actions.

§19.3.3 Government Settlements and the Tunney Act

One final special procedural issue governs settlement agreements entered into by government enforcers. Unlike private antitrust suits, the parties to government antitrust actions cannot just voluntarily settle when they feel it is appropriate.

Under a statute known as the Tunney Act, which now appears as Clayton Act §§5(b)-5(h), 15 U.S.C. §§16(b)-16(h), DOJ settlements require court approval and opportunity for public comment. Once a settlement agreement is negotiated—such agreements being known as "consent decrees"—the DOJ must file the decree with a district court having jurisdiction over the matter, along with a document prepared by the DOJ known as the Competitive Impact Statement. The CIS must describe the defendant, its industry, and the challenged conduct, and explain why the proposed decree is in the public interest. These documents must also be published in the *Federal Register*, and all interested persons are invited to comment on them. It is up to the district court, on reviewing the CIS and comments received, to decide whether the decree should be approved as in the public interest.

Settlements of state government *parens patriae* suits likewise require court approval and notice to represented persons, under the basic authorization for *parens patriae* actions, Clayton Act §4c(c). Unlike the Tunney Act, this provision sets forth no guidance for the court's determination, and it also provides for no notice for public comment or opportunity for public involvement.

The FTC is not subject to the Tunney Act or other statutory restraints on settlement, but has voluntarily adopted procedures for considering settlements that largely map the Tunney Act procedures. *See* 1 Am. Bar Assn., *Antitrust Law Developments* (Ninth) 730-732 (9th ed. 2022).

§19.4 REMEDIES IN ANTITRUST

§19.4.1 Recovery of Money

§19.4.1(a) Money Damages: Private Plaintiffs, States in *Parens Patriae*, and the Federal Government

Private plaintiffs, including the states suing in their personal capacities, the federal government suing for its own injuries, and states in *parens patriae*, can all recover three times the damages they suffer. They are also entitled to attorneys fees and costs. Technically a successful plaintiff may be entitled to prejudgment interest, calculated from the time of filing the complaint until the time of final judgment,[15] but only if the plaintiff can show that the defendant was unusually dilatory, and no plaintiff appears ever to have successfully made this showing.[16]

Damages may be calculated in various different ways depending on the nature of the alleged injury. Where the plaintiff is a customer challenging an overcharge, it can recover the difference between the inflated price and what the price would have been absent the defendant's illegal conduct. Where the plaintiff is a competitor, it can recover lost profits; that is, it can recover the amount it would have made had its business not been injured by the defendant's conduct.

Naturally, all plaintiffs bear the burden of proving the damages to which they are entitled. The plaintiff's proof must be "based on data"[17] and cannot constitute "speculation or guesswork."[18] Moreover, a defendant can rebut the plaintiff's case on damages by showing that some of its losses were

15. All successful plaintiffs in all federal civil actions are entitled to postjudgment interest—it is mandatory under 28 U.S.C. §1961.

16. 1 Am. Bar Assn., *Antitrust Law Developments* (Ninth) 842-843 (9th ed. 2022).

17. *Zenith Radio Corp. v. Hazeltine Research, Inc.*, 395 U.S. 100, 123 (1969).

18. *Bigelow v. RKO Radio Pictures*, 327 U.S. 251, 264 (1946).

caused by mismanagement, ordinary competition, economic downturn, or other lawful factors. A defendant can also rebut by putting on evidence that the plaintiff failed to mitigate its losses.[19]

However, an important and long-standing rule is that plaintiffs will not be forced to prove damages with mathematical precision. The courts recognize that antitrust damages are inherently speculative. They almost inevitably require a finder of fact to determine what the world would have been like in the absence of the defendant's conduct, and there is no certain way to make that finding. As the Supreme Court has said, "The vagaries of the marketplace usually deny us sure knowledge of what plaintiff's situation would have been in the absence of the defendant's antitrust violation."[20] The courts have often said it would be inequitable to allow guilty defendants to benefit from this inherent uncertainty. Therefore, it is enough for the plaintiff to put on "a just and reasonable estimate," as long as it is "based on data,"[21] and that showing can ordinarily be made with expert testimony or knowledgeable lay testimony.

§19.4.1(b) FTC: Disgorgement, Restitution, and Forfeiture in Administrative Proceedings

Ordinarily, the FTC does not seek money damages. It cannot sue to recover harms to the government (i.e., the DOJ's job under Clayton Act §4a) and, in antitrust cases, most often seeks only to enjoin illegal conduct. The Commission can seek equitable money recoveries, however, for violation of antitrust or any other law that it administers. Namely, it can seek restitution for victims or disgorgement of ill-gotten gains, 15 U.S.C. §57b, and it fairly often does so in non-antitrust consumer protection cases. To seek that relief it must first fully conduct an administrative trial before a Commission Administrative Law Judge and then issue an order prohibiting the conduct, and then seek and order in federal court for monetary relief. The Commission cannot unilaterally order monetary relief on its own.

For a number of years the FTC took the view that a separate provision of the FTC Act, 15 U.S.C. §53(b), authorized it to seek equitable money relief in federal court, without invoking the process of an internal administrative proceeding.[22] Beginning in the 1970s and for some decades most federal

---

19. For example, if the plaintiff alleges that the defendant illegally refused to sell it something or terminated some relationship with it, the defendant can put on evidence that the plaintiff had other opportunities open to it. If so, even where there is a violation, the plaintiff's damages will be only the difference between the value of that alternative and the deal the plaintiff could have gotten from the defendant.

20. *J. Truett Payne Co. v. Chrysler Motor Corp.*, 451 U.S. 557, 566 (1981).

21. *Zenith Radio Corp. v. Hazeltine Research, Inc.*, 395 U.S. 100, 123 (1969).

22. *See FTC v. Mylan Labs.*, 62 F. Supp. 2d 25 (D.D.C. 1999); FTC, *Policy Statement on Monetary Equitable Remedies in Competition Cases*, 68 Fed. Reg. 45,820 (Aug. 4, 2003).

courts agreed, but in *AMG Capital Mgt., LLC v. FTC*, 141 S. Ct. 1341 (2021), the Court rejected that interpretation. The Court held that §53(b) authorized only non-monetary injunctions from federal court and held that they were to be used only to support actions in which the Commission initiated administrative proceedings before an ALJ. After *AMG Capital*, the Commission can procure monetary relief only after full administrative proceedings.

§19.4.1(c) Money Penalties for Contempt

A number of the enforcement agencies' equitable powers can be enforced by money penalties for violation of orders or compliance requirements:

- Violation of an FTC cease-and-desist order is enforceable by a civil penalty for every violation or for every day of a continuing violation (the penalty is $10,000 per violation of an FTC Act order and $5000 per violation of a Clayton Act order). FTC Act §5(l), 15 U.S.C. §45(l); Clayton Act §11(l), 15 U.S.C. §21(l).
- Likewise, a failure to comply with the premerger notice requirements of the Hart-Scott-Rodino Act (discussed at length in Chapter 18) is punishable by a penalty of $11,000 per day for each day of noncompliance. In effect, if parties consummate a merger that was reportable under HSR, then every day following consummation until such time as they comply will be subject to that penalty. Clayton Act §7A(g)(1), 15 U.S.C. §18A(g)(1).

To secure any such relief, the agencies must seek court order.

§19.4.2 Structural Relief — Divestiture or Dissolution

In extraordinary cases the courts can enter an equitable "divestiture" order to undo some consummated transaction, to dissolve a business association, or even to break up a company into smaller pieces or dissolve it altogether. Divestitures and dissolutions have occurred on occasion through most of the history of antitrust, and have been ordered in some cases even very recently. Despite the controversy that has always surrounded them, the Supreme Court has more than once stated that they are the most important of antitrust remedies.[23] But the courts enter them in only the rarest and most egregious cases, and claim that they will not do so where any other equitable relief would be satisfactory. Other relief should be satisfactory, for

23. *California v. Am. Stores Co.*, 495 U.S. 271, 281 (1990) ("Divestiture has been called the most important of antitrust remedies"); *United States v. E.I. du Pont de Nemours & Co.*, 366 U.S. 316, 329 (1961) (same).

example, where the plaintiff merely complains of some specific anticompetitive conduct, which can simply be enjoined. Divestiture will come to seem needed only where the defendant holds truly massive market power, and the likelihood of future abuses seems high.

Divestiture is most feasible in cases of recently consummated mergers and acquisitions, particularly if the parties have not yet made significant efforts to integrate their firms. Even there the remedy is disfavored however. Indeed, the difficulty of securing postconsummation divestiture was one driving force behind the adoption of the Hart-Scott-Rodino Act in 1976—the agencies argued that unless they had a chance to review mergers in the proposal stage, and make such challenges as they thought required before deals are consummated, they would never be able to effectively enforce Clayton Act §7. *See* §17.2.1.

However, these remedies remain controversial. The major objection is to their drastic nature, of course, but as to divestiture—which anticipates that following the order, two or more separate firms will continue to operate as going entities—there is an additional problem. For the remedy to be effective on an ongoing basis, the court must make decisions of an inherently nonlegal kind, about how best to structure businesses for their long-term financial viability.

The Justice Department can seek divestiture and dissolution under the broad power granted to it in Sherman Act §4, 15 U.S.C. §4, and Clayton Act §15, 15 U.S.C. §25. The FTC traditionally did not seek structural remedies, and its statutory authority to do so is not clear. However, the agency has recently begun to argue that the power granted under FTC Act §13(b), 15 U.S.C. §53(b), to seek preliminary and other injunctive relief entitles it to seek divestitures at least of consummated mergers. *See Chicago Bridge & Iron Co.*, 138 F.T.C. 1024 (2004) (ordering divestiture in a consummated merger case). Private plaintiffs (including state governments) can seek divestiture under Clayton Act §16. *See California v. Am. Stores Co.*, 495 U.S. 271 (1990).

§19.4.3 Other Injunctions

The same statutory provisions that govern divestiture and dissolution—Sherman Act §4, Clayton Act §15 and 16, and FTC Act §13(b)—entitle parties to a whole variety of other, less drastic injunctive relief to redress their anticipated harm from ongoing antitrust violations. Though technically some of these provisions might not seem by their explicit terms to be so broad,[24]

24. For example, the Justice Department's power to seek injunctive relief under Sherman Act §4 and Clayton Act §15 is nominally limited only to orders "to prevent and restrain . . . violations." One might have read that provision narrowly such that it authorizes only narrow conduct remedies limited to the specific conduct complained of.

the courts have long read them very broadly to authorize "such orders and decrees as are necessary or appropriate" to serve the purposes of antitrust. The power of the FTC to enter cease-and-desist orders, and the power of both agencies to enter into voluntary settlements known as "consent decrees" are also effectively injunctive in nature. Such orders and decrees invariably take the form of fairly detailed, roughly regulatory orders that set constraints on the defendant's ongoing behavior for some specified period of time.

§19.4.4 Remedies in Merger Preclearance Review

In 1976 Congress adopted the Hart-Scott-Rodino Act, which requires that most large merger and acquisition plans be submitted to the federal enforcers before they are consummated. This gives the agencies a chance to determine whether the deals are likely illegal. HSR itself, however, does not set out any rules of substantive liability.[25] Rather, an agency challenge during the course of HSR review is substantively just like any other merger challenge, and ordinarily asserts a violation of Clayton Act §7. To enforce §7 in the course of HSR review, the agencies must ordinarily seek immediate injunctive relief in district court, and this will usually occur under heavy time pressure since there is a premium on stopping the deal prior to consummation. Still, this only occurs quite rarely because in the rare cases in which an agency opposes a deal under HSR review, the parties almost always agree to some remedial conditions prior to consummation or they abandon their deal altogether. In the very rare cases in which an agency indicates that it would challenge the merger, but the merging parties decide to consummate anyway, the agency's only recourse is to seek temporary restraining order, preliminary injunction, and ultimately a permanent injunction through litigation (in the DOJ's case, it will seek all these remedies in federal district court under Clayton Act §15; in the FTC's case, it will seek preliminary relief in district court under FTC Act §13(b), and then begin Part 3 proceedings before an agency ALJ to secure a permanent cease-and-desist order).

25. Except in the sense that failure to comply with HSR itself—failure to report a reportable transaction, for example—is subject to a penalty of $11,000 per day for each day of the period of noncompliance. *See* Chapter 18.

PART XI

The Scope of Antitrust

CHAPTER 20

The Scope of Antitrust Generally

§20.1 ANTITRUST IS THE GREAT SWISS CHEESE

In the abstract, antitrust appears to apply broadly, so much so that it seems at first glance to reach to the full extent of the Congress's constitutional power over interstate commerce. Sherman Act §§1 and 2 by their terms apply to "trade or commerce" that occurs anywhere in the interstate and foreign commerce of the United States, and the federal courts have taken that language to express a congressional intent that antitrust be very broadly applied. The inclusive modern definition is perhaps the natural culmination of the Supreme Court's long-held belief that "Congress intended to strike as broadly as it could in §1 of the Sherman Act,"[1] a view it developed because "[l]anguage more comprehensive" than that in §1 "is difficult to conceive."[2] It probably also reflects the broad definition given to the terms "trade" and "commerce" for various purposes at common law, as the courts have explicitly held that antitrust was meant to incorporate those ideas.

But having said all that, antitrust actually turns out to be subject to quite a bristling profusion of little exemptions and limitations, and each of those limits has spawned its own case law, history, and idiosyncrasies. The *scope* of antitrust, in other words, turns out to be a surprisingly complex little body of law in its own right. Indeed, this book devotes four full chapters to it (Chapters 20-23) and doesn't even cover it all. An interesting fact is that

1. *Goldfarb v. Superior Ct. of Virginia*, 421 U.S. 773, 787 (1975).
2. *United States v. South-Eastern Underwriters Assn.*, 322 U.S. 533, 553 (1944).

this is also true of the competition laws of most nations that have them. The European Union (EU), for example, for as long as it has had a competition law, has had a procedure in place by which specific industries can seek "block exemptions" from EU competition law. As just a few examples, the EU for many years recognized exemptions for insurance and ocean shipping, both of which have also long enjoyed exemptions from U.S. antitrust.

First of all, even the very broad modern conception of "trade or commerce" under the Sherman Act does not reach everything that could be regulated under Congress's power. Notably, it excludes purely charitable or gratuitous exchanges of goods or services, and notoriously, as the lingering result of a historical accident, it excludes the game of professional baseball. It also has international limits. While U.S. antitrust does reach some conduct that occurs overseas, the rules by which it does are complicated and result from a surprisingly political, long-standing compromise involving U.S. importing and exporting interests. Discussing these features of the basic scope of antitrust will consume the rest of this chapter

Moreover, several large carve outs from the scope of antitrust have been developed through a body of purely judge-made case law. The most important of these is a set of rules that prevent antitrust from applying to the *political* process, a problem discussed in Chapter 21. Imagine that the owners of railroads operating in a given state agree to collectively urge the state's legislature to prohibit the shipping of cargo within the state by semi truck. If the legislature complies, the result would be patently anticompetitive and contrary to the policy of the antitrust laws. But for federal antitrust to prohibit it would also be quite a surprising result that was likely unintended by Congress and would also probably impinge on political participation protected by the First Amendment. So, as we will see, the Supreme Court has provided through a set of rules known as the political "immunities" that antitrust mostly does not apply to this sort of thing.

The Court has developed other case-law exemptions, notably for conduct already regulated by some statute other than antitrust (discussed in Chapter 22), and for labor union activities (discussed in Chapter 23).

Finally, Congress has also tinkered quite a lot with the scope of antitrust, usually in much more specific ways than the courts have done. It has done so normally at the request of the affected industry and often over vigorous protest from that industry's customers, the government enforcement agencies, and other observers. There are now upwards of 30 explicit statutory antitrust exemptions. Among a few dozen other things, antitrust does not apply to the "business of insurance," ocean shipping, exporting cartels that send products into foreign commerce, the medical resident matching program, international airline alliances, the granting of need-based financial aid by universities, the fixing of interest rates for charitable gift annuities, or—everybody simply must *love* this one—the marketing of hog cholera serum. Also, in many cases in which antitrust still applies, Congress has modified it by statute. For example, while local government entities can be antitrust defendants, they cannot be sued for money damages. Likewise, research and production joint ventures can be sued only under the rule of reason and can only face single (not treble) damages. The handling and significance of these many statutory exemptions will be discussed briefly in Chapter 22, which more generally addresses antitrust in regulated industries.

§20.2 THE BASIC SCOPE OF ANTITRUST: THE "COMMERCE" REQUIREMENT, THE INTERSTATE REQUIREMENT, AND THE REACH OF THE CLAYTON AND FTC ACTS

§20.2.1 "Trade or Commerce" in General; Its Exclusion of Charity and Gratuity; and That Awkward Orphan of Antitrust, Professional Baseball

While, again, there are many specific exceptions from the scope of antitrust, it remains the case that where no statutory or case-law exemption is available, antitrust cuts very, very broadly. The basic question of its scope is to ask where the boundaries might lie of the "trade or commerce" that occurs "among the several States, or with foreign nations," which is explicitly referenced in Sherman Act §1 and 2.

First, observe that, by the apparent indication of the explicit language, the requirement that the conduct occur in interstate or foreign commerce is logically distinct from the requirement that the conduct constitutes "trade or commerce." The indication seems to be that conduct can be "trade-like" or "commercial" without being in interstate or foreign commerce, and vice versa. Fortunately, at least one of these requirements is easy. It is now clear that domestic conduct is within "interstate" commerce any time it is within the interstate commerce jurisdiction of Congress under the Commerce Clause of the U.S. Constitution. Whether it can be within "foreign" commerce turns out to be a fair bit more complex, but that will be discussed in §20.3.

Whether conduct is "trade or commerce" raises a different question, and it is the question of whether the conduct is the sort that Congress intended to be subject to mandatory competition. Modern courts define the scope of "trade or commerce" very broadly. Even early decisions defined the "commerce" subject to the statute to include any "purchase, sale, or exchange of commodities,"[3] and they said it should be construed liberally,

3. *Addyston Pipe & Steel Co. v. United States*, 175 U.S. 211, 241 (1899).

to give the statute its intended effect—it should "not [be treated as] a technical legal conception, but [as] a practical one, drawn from the course of business."[4] More importantly, modern courts have held generally that any exchange of money for a good or service, between any persons, is in "trade or commerce."[5] In one influential case, *United States v. Brown Univ.*, 5 F.3d 658 (3d Cir. 1993), the Third Circuit held that an agreement among nonprofit universities concerning need-based scholarship funds was a contract relating to "trade or commerce." Despite what might have appeared to be genuine charity, the court had no real trouble with the issue. The defendants conceded that the giving of educational services in exchange for money is "commerce," regardless of the defendants' nonprofit form of organization. And, the court wrote,

> [t]he amount of financial aid not only impacts, but directly determines the amount that a needy student must pay to receive an education at [the defendant schools]. The financial aid therefore is part of the commercial process of setting tuition.

Id. at 665.

In fact, it is really only in limited, exotic circumstances that modern courts have found conduct simply not within "trade or commerce" for antitrust purposes A leading case is *Dedication and Everlasting Love to Animals v. Humane Socy. of the United States, Inc.*, 50 F.3d 710 (9th Cir. 1995). The plaintiff was a California charitable organization devoted to animal welfare. It sued the Humane Society, a national umbrella organization for nonprofit entities committed to similar purposes. The plaintiff's theory of liability was in effect that the Humane Society, a "competitor" for the same charitable donations on which the plaintiff relied to fund its operations, had taken various actions to steal away the "market" for donations. While first acknowledging that no conclusion could be drawn from the fact that the parties were organized as nonprofit corporations, the court seemed fairly appalled at the very idea of the plaintiff's theory of liability. "If statutory language is to be given even a modicum of meaning," wrote the court, "the solicitation of [charitable] contributions ... is not trade or commerce, and the Sherman Act has no application to such activity." *Id.* at 712.

Let us observe one important fact about these definitions of "commerce." They focus on the nature of the *conduct* that is challenged, not the nature of the person or entity that engages in it. The Supreme Court has

---

4. *Swift & Co. v. United States*, 196 U.S. 375, 398 (1905).

5. *See, e.g., Goldfarb v. Virginia State Bar*, 421 U.S. 773, 787 (1975) ("commerce" includes any "exchange of ... a [good or] service for money"); *United States v. Brown Univ.*, 5 F.3d 658 (3d Cir. 1993) (holding the provision of education by nonprofit universities, in return for tuition, to be "commerce" within meaning of Sherman Act).

made very clear that the fact that a party is organized as a nonprofit entity is irrelevant.[6] More generally, the courts and commentators are in wide agreement that "[t]here is no immunity [from antitrust] conferred by the form of the organization."[7] Accordingly, the fact that a party is organized as, say, a not-for-profit entity or an unincorporated association or in some other seemingly noncommercial form is essentially irrelevant. This is so because such entities can have incentives and pose policy concerns that are the same as for-profit businesses. Also, if businesses could avoid antitrust merely by reorganizing in a certain way, it would create a large loophole in antitrust.

Slightly different issues of scope are raised by the language of the Clayton Act, the Robinson-Patman Act, and the FTC Act. One of those provisions, however, and arguably the most important of them—§7, which governs mergers and acquisitions—has basically the same scope as the Sherman Act. There had been some doubt on this score during the mid-1970s, when the Supreme Court indicated its view that Congress meant "engaged in commerce" to limit the scope of these laws. As these decisions applied to §7, however, they were overturned by Congress in 1980. (The treatment of §7 is discussed in greater detail in Chapter 17.)

Finally, let us briefly consider the strangest rule in all of antitrust law, the broad antitrust immunity of professional baseball. The now-infamous *Fed. Baseball Club of Baltimore v. Nat. League of Profl. Baseball Clubs*, 259 U.S. 200 (1922) first adopted this immunity, though for its time *Federal Baseball* was actually sensible enough. In that case—by which time baseball had become truly big business and was organizing itself into essentially the form it would continue to have down to the present—a failing team sued two national league organizations, alleging that they had conspired to drive it out of business. Writing for the Court, Oliver Wendell Holmes simply held that the playing of baseball, even as an exhibition for profit, was not within Congress's Commerce Clause jurisdiction, applying the Court's precedents as they were then understood. Holmes analogized the playing of a sport to other kinds of "personal effort," and at the time he felt it clear that such things were wholly matters of state government regulation. Were the issue decided for the first time today, of course, it would come out differently. Nowadays it is very clear that all other professional sports are fully subject to antitrust law.[8] But so far the Court has steadfastly refused to reverse *Federal*

---

6. *NCAA v. Bd. of Regents of the Univ. of Oklahoma*, 468 U.S. 85, 100 n.22 (1984) ("There is no doubt that the sweeping language of §1 applies to nonprofit entities."); *Am. Socy. of Mech. Engrs. v. Hydrolevel Corp.*, 456 U.S. 556 (1982) (finding it "beyond debate that nonprofit organizations can be held liable under the antitrust laws").

7. *Dedication and Everlasting Love to Animals v. Humane Socy. of the United States, Inc.*, 50 F.3d 710, 713 (9th Cir. 1995).

8. *See, e.g., Am. Needle v. Nat. Football League*, 560 U.S. 183 (2010); *Flood v. Kuhn*, 407 U.S. 258, 282-283 (1972) (so holding).

Baseball, holding as recently as 1972 that the rule must be preserved. *See Flood v. Kuhn*, 407 U.S. 258 (1972). The Court so held even though it had long been clear that other forms of entertainment were "commerce," and even though the Court itself had found *other professional sports* to be in commerce. For what it may be worth, the Court's baseball decisions have continued to uphold *Federal Baseball* only as a matter of *stare decisis*. *See Flood*, 407 U.S. at 282-283. This special exemption has been the focus of intense criticism, and is opposed by probably everyone except for the team owners, and yet even Congress has been unable to undo very much of it.

Example

A Methodist church has begun accepting donations of clothes, blankets, and other used items for distribution to the poor. Two other major charities in town, Goodspirit Industries and the Catholic Ministries Shelter, also collect such items on a donation basis. Goodspirit in turn sells the items in its "Goodspirit Thrift Shops," which sell used items at very low prices. The proceeds of those sales are used to fund programs for the homeless, and Goodspirit also employs disadvantaged people in its thrift shops as a way to provide them with job training. Catholic Ministries simply redistributes the donations it receives, both by giving them directly to the poor and by delivering them to area shelters.

The managers of these two charities learn of the large-scale program begun by the Methodist church, and are concerned about their own access to a continuing supply of donated items. They decide together that will not provide services to those needy persons who also receive services from the Methodist church. Does this arrangement violate antitrust?

Explanation

Probably not. Theoretically, the challenged agreement resembles a horizontal concerted refusal to deal, and under appropriate circumstances could be illegal. But because these are plainly charitable entities, there likely is no "trade or commerce" at stake for purposes of antitrust law.

This is a closer case than one such as *Dedication and Everlasting Love to Animals v. Humane Socy. of the United States, Inc.*, 50 F.3d 710 (9th Cir. 1995), because there is an actual exchange of money at stake, and it arguably is not completely gratuitous. One of the conspirators, Goodspirit, sells donated items for money. Still, presumably, Goodspirit makes those sales at a loss or only covers its costs, and in any case would use its revenues only to provide services to the poor. Nevertheless, depending on the facts that could be adduced, it is at least possible that Goodspirit is engaged in "trade or commerce," and therefore that the boycott could be illegal.

§20.2.2 Clayton Act §3 and the Robinson-Patman Act

As discussed further in §11.1.2 and §16.4, there has been a bit more confusion about the scope of certain provisions of the Clayton Act and the Robinson-Patman Act (RPA), and in some respects their scope is different than that of the Sherman Act. Under current law, these limitations apply to Clayton Act §3 (which governs tying and exclusive dealing arrangements) and the RPA (which appears as Clayton Act §2, and governs price discrimination).

First, these two provisions apply only to transactions in "commodities." As to both statutes this is now commonly understood to include only tangible goods. It therefore excludes any sort of services and also excludes intangible things such as news and information, securities, financial instruments, insurance, and intellectual property. 1 Am. Bar Assn., *Antitrust Law Developments (Sixth)* 174-175, 494-496 (6th ed. 2007). Second, they apply only to transactions in commodities for "use, consumption, or resale within the United States. . . ."[9] While there is less certainty on this point, it appears fairly clear that these statutes require that all sales involved in the challenged conduct take place in this country. In effect, they can only apply to domestic conduct or to imports into the United States. *See id.* at vol. 2, p. 1186.

Finally, during the mid-1970s the Supreme Court issued a handful of opinions in which it stressed certain jurisdictional language that appears in those provisions but does not appear in the Sherman Act. Specifically, as they existed at that time, each of the following statutes applied only to "person[s] engaged in commerce": the Robinson-Patman Act, Clayton Act §3, and Clayton Act §7. The Court's several decisions of that period held that "engaged *in* commerce" meant that the challenged conduct must literally be "in" interstate commerce. This meant that there had to be some component of a challenged transaction that occurred in two or more separate states.

In 1980 Congress amended Clayton Act §7 to provided that it applies to transactions "in ... *or affecting* commerce" (emphasis added), and it is now clear that this had the effect of giving §7 the same broad scope as the Sherman Act. However, the Supreme Court's more restrictive interpretations have so far been left in place as to the Clayton Act §3 and the RPA.

---

9. Technically, this limitation only appears in Robinson-Patman Act §2(a), and so it is possible that other provisions of the Robinson-Patman Act can apply to exports. But §2(a) is by far the most important of the statute's substantive provisions. *See* Chapter 16.

Example

The law firm of Craven, Feckless & Nogüd has come to hold about 50 percent of all of the legal work in the small town of Billings, Montana. Feeling its market-power oats, but somewhat concerned about the growing estate planning practice of another, smaller firm in Billings, CF&N institutes a new policy demanding that all of its clients, in order to employ the firm as to any legal matter, also employ CF&N for their estate planning needs. Can this arrangement violate antitrust?

Explanation

This is a "tying" arrangement, which could be challenged under either Sherman Act §1 or possibly as attempted monopolization under Sherman Act §2 (tying can satisfy the "exclusionary conduct" requirement of the outright monopolization claim, but a 50 percent market share is likely insufficient for anything other than an attempt claim).

However, this arrangement could not violate Clayton Act §3, even though it ordinarily applies to tying. The reason is that Clayton Act §3 applies only to tying that involves "commodities," and professional services such as legal representation are not "commodities."

§20.2.3 The Jurisdiction of the Federal Trade Commission

The FTC has two major antitrust enforcement powers: The power to enforce FTC Act §5, which in practice means power to enforce the Sherman Act, and the power to enforce substantive Clayton Act provisions under Clayton Act §11. These provisions set two kinds of limits on the FTC's jurisdiction.

First, FTC Act §5 applies to "persons, partnerships, or corporations," except for banks and common carriers. But FTC Act §4 defines "corporations" to include only those that are "organized to carry on business for [their] own profit or that of [their] members...." Accordingly, it has jurisdiction over all natural persons and partnerships,[10] and all for-profit corporations, but at least some of the time it lacks jurisdiction over nonprofit corporations. This could be a significant loophole because, despite what some might think, many nonprofit entities engage in massive amounts of commerce, earn huge revenues, and make many of their participants wealthy. However, the Commission has been relatively successful in convincing the courts that particular nonprofit entities operate "for [the] profit ... of [their] members." For example, if a professional association provides

10. By definition, all partnerships are organized for profit. *See* Revised Uniform Partnership Act §202(a) (1997).

some economic benefits to its members, such as helping them secure low-cost malpractice insurance or special discounts on products and services, that will likely establish FTC jurisdiction under §5. *See California Dental Assn. v. FTC*, 526 U.S. 756 (1999).

Second, the Commission's power to enforce the Clayton Act is subject to two different kinds of limits. First, it is subject to the same "in commerce" limit as any other Clayton Act plaintiff—namely, when it attempts to enforce the Clayton Act §3 or the Robinson-Patman Act, it must show that the challenged transaction involves "commodities" and that it directly touches two or more states. (*See* §20.2.2.) Second, the Clayton Act itself provides that while the Commission is generally vested with enforcement of substantive Clayton Act provisions, it cannot enforce them against banks and common carriers (including both transportation companies and communications companies). Clayton Act §11, 15 U.S.C. §21. As to those entities, Clayton Act enforcement is vested in their industry-specific regulators (e.g., banks are mostly subject to Clayton Act enforcement by the Federal Reserve Board of Governors). Interestingly, though, the Justice Department can enforce the Clayton Act against anyone. Even though FTC cannot take Clayton Act action against banks or common carriers, DOJ can, under its power to seek injunction under Clayton Act §15, 15 U.S.C. §25.

Example

The Federal Trade Commission and the state Attorney General of the state of Washington bring a challenge under Clayton Act §7 to undo a consummated acquisition of a major hospital located in Seattle, Washington, by a holding company that operates numerous hospitals in the vicinity of Vancouver, British Columbia. The Seattle hospital was previously operated by the Seventh Day Adventist religious organization and was entitled to nonprofit tax exemption status. The defendants move to dismiss the complaints of both parties on jurisdictional grounds. What result?

Explanation

The motion for dismissal should probably be denied as to both parties. There might first of all seem to be a question of the FTC's power to take action against nonprofit corporations, but observe that that limitation applies only to enforcement of FTC Act §5. (And, in any case, the fact that a hospital is nominally a nonprofit entity is unlikely to satisfy the exemption from §5 for entities not operated "for the profit of [their] members"; hospitals sell a service for money, and earn large revenues.) A separate issue is that the transaction has an international component. On that issue, see below. As a preview, this particular transaction would surely be within the extraterritorial reach of Clayton Act §7. It involves substantial economic impacts within the United States.

§20.3 INTERNATIONAL ANTITRUST: THE REACH OF U.S. LAW OVERSEAS

Obviously enough, anticompetitive conduct can occur in other countries, and sometimes that conduct may have some connection to the United States, or it may cause harms to markets here. When that happens, the question arises whether there is any legal action anyone can take to redress it.

§20.3.1 The International Reach of the Sherman Act

With some exceptions not relevant here, customary international law provides that nations have legislative jurisdiction only over conduct that occurs within their territory or that has some substantial and foreseeable consequences within their territory. *See Restatement (Third) of the Foreign Relations Law of the United States* §402 (1987). Accordingly, as a matter of international law U.S. antitrust can only apply to overseas conduct when that conduct actually causes some harm within the United States. Moreover, U.S. courts routinely observe a principle known as "comity" when they entertain lawsuits involving foreign persons or foreign conduct. Comity is a judge-made principle of respect for the sovereignty of other nations, and counsels courts to use caution before taking jurisdiction over foreign conduct. Prior to 1982—the year in which Congress adopted an important statute to be discussed shortly, which was meant to clarify some aspects of extraterritorial antitrust—the courts employed these doctrines generally to require that U.S. antitrust could apply only if extraterritorial conduct had substantial, reasonably foreseeable consequences within the United States. But upon the adoption of the 1982 legislation, this set of rules got a fair bit more complex.

The current state of affairs can be roughly summarized as a strong presumption in favor of extraterritorial application to foreign conduct that affects domestic commerce, subject to two major exceptions. The two exceptions are imposed by the Foreign Trade Antitrust Improvements Act (FTAIA), 15 U.S.C. §6a, as well as a few other statutory provisions. The exceptions are that U.S. antitrust usually will not apply to foreign *injuries*, and it will usually not apply to harms caused by U.S. *exports*.

First of all, the strong presumption of extraterritoriality comes from a post-FTAIA decision, *Hartford Fire Ins. Co. v. California*, 509 U.S. 764 (1993). The Court there held that overseas conduct by foreign parties that would be illegal here is subject to the Sherman Act so long as the conduct was intended and in fact did hurt domestic commerce. It appears that the only exception the Court would recognize in such cases is outright compulsion to engage in the conduct by a foreign government.

Second, two exceptions follow mainly from FTAIA. That statute provides in full as follows:

15 U.S.C. §6a. Conduct involving trade or commerce with foreign nations

> Sections 1 to 7 of this title [that is, the Sherman Act] shall not apply to conduct involving trade or commerce (other than import trade or import commerce) with foreign nations unless—
>
> (1) such conduct has a direct, substantial, and reasonably foreseeable effect—
>
> (A) on trade or commerce which is not trade or commerce with foreign nations, or on import trade or import commerce with foreign nations; or
>
> (B) on export trade or export commerce with foreign nations, of a person engaged in such trade or commerce in the United States; and
>
> (2) such effect gives rise to a claim under the provisions of sections 1 to 7 of this title, other than this section.
>
> If sections 1 to 7 of this title apply to such conduct only because of the operation of paragraph (1)(B), then sections 1 to 7 of this title shall apply to such conduct only for injury to export business in the United States.

A first consequence under FTAIA is that the Sherman Act does not provide a remedy for foreign *injuries*. The Supreme Court's most recent statement on point held that the "substantial and reasonably foreseeable injury" required for Sherman Act applicability must be the same injury for which the plaintiff seeks a remedy. The plaintiffs in *F. Hoffman-La Roche, Ltd. v. Empagran S.A.*, 542 U.S. 155 (2004) were purchasers of vitamins who challenged an international price-fixing cartel of U.S. and foreign vitamin makers. The plaintiffs were foreign firms that purchased the vitamins for delivery overseas, though they also alleged that, independently, the conspiracy caused prices to increase within the United States. In other words, the plaintiffs challenged foreign conduct—an international conspiracy and contracts for sale of vitamins the price of which was inflated by the conspiracy—that caused both foreign and domestic U.S. injury. However, their own claim was based wholly on foreign injury. The Court held such a claim not actionable under U.S. antitrust.

The second exception to the broad presumptive reach of the Sherman Act under *Hartford Fire* is that U.S. antitrust does not prohibit conduct by U.S. exporters that causes injury abroad.[11] First, FTAIA provides that the Sherman Act does not apply to commerce with foreign nations unless it

11. It helps to remember that our extraterritoriality rules reflect a long-standing political compromise within U.S. foreign trade policy. While U.S. interests obviously desire that foreign firms not be able to harm the U.S. economy, there is little home-grown concern for harm that our firms might cause overseas. So, while the United States frequently reasserts its

causes domestic harms or it harms the export business of a U.S. exporter. Moreover, two separate statutes, the Webb Pomerene Act of 1918 and the Export Trading Company Act of 1982,[12] provide that cartels of U.S. exporters can fix their overseas prices and take some other conduct that might otherwise be illegal, so long as they first disclose their conduct to the federal antitrust agencies and they do not cause domestic injuries.

§20.3.2 The Extraterritorial Reach of the FTC and Clayton Acts

For the most part, the international reach of the FTC and Clayton Acts is the same as that of the Sherman Act. There are two significant exceptions, which are Clayton Act §3 (which applies to some tying and exclusive dealing arrangements) and the Robinson-Patman Act (which appears as Clayton Act §2, and governs price discrimination).

The FTC's primary substantive enforcement provision, FTC Act §5, applies to "unfair methods of competition" that are "in or affecting commerce." The term "commerce" is defined in the FTC Act to include "commerce ... with foreign nations." FTC Act §4, 15 U.S.C. §44. However, FTAIA amended the FTC Act at the same time that it amended the Sherman Act, and its amendments now appear as FTC Act §5(a)(3)(A). That provision gives the FTC authority to enforce §5 against effectively the same conduct as is made illegal under FTAIA. Likewise, Clayton Act §7 applies to acquisitions among persons engaged "in commerce or in any activity affecting commerce," and "commerce" is defined in the Clayton Act to include "commerce ... with foreign nations...." Clayton Act §1(a), 15 U.S.C. §12(a). In effect, acquisitions involving sellers with substantial sales in the United States are subject to §7 even if one or more of the parties to the acquisition is headquartered or has major operations overseas.

The exceptions, again, are Clayton Act §3 and the Robinson-Patman Act. These provisions apply only to transactions in commodities for "use, consumption, or resale within the United States...."[13] While there is less certainty on this point, it appears fairly clear that these statutes require that all sales involved in the challenged conduct take place in this country.

---

commitment to competitive markets, it has for a long time preserved a protectionist stance in favor of American exporters. They have generally been permitted to take anticompetitive actions to increase their profits in foreign countries.

12. The two statutes are, respectively, ch. 50, §1, 40 Stat. 516 (1918), now codified at 15 U.S.C. §§61-65, and Pub. L. No. 97-290, 96 Stat. 1233 (1982), now codified at 15 U.S.C. §§4001-4021.

13. Technically, this limitation only appears in Robinson-Patman Act §2(a), and so it is possible that other provisions of the Robinson-Patman Act can apply to exports. But §2(a) is by far the most important of the statute's substantive provisions.

In effect, they can only apply to domestic conduct or to imports into the United States. *See* 2 Am. Bar Assn., *Antitrust Law Developments (Sixth)* 1186 (6th ed. 2007).

§20.3.3 Extraterritorial Antitrust in Summary

Probably the best way to understand the current law of extraterritorial antitrust is to imagine several classes of possible claims:

1. *Wholly foreign conduct with no U.S. effects* is not subject to U.S. antitrust law under any circumstances.
2. *Wholly foreign conduct with U.S. effects, where the plaintiff's claim is based only on "independent" foreign effects* is also not subject to U.S. antitrust law. These were the facts taken by the *Empagran* Court to be true, and on these facts the Court held that the plaintiff could not sue under U.S. antitrust in U.S. courts.
3. *Wholly foreign conduct with U.S. effects, where the plaintiff's claim is based on the U.S. effects* is subject to the Sherman Act, the FTC Act, and Clayton Act §7 (though probably not Clayton Act §3 or the Robinson-Patman Act).
4. *Wholly foreign conduct that harms only U.S. exporters* is subject to the Sherman Act, the FTC Act, and Clayton Act §7 (though probably not Clayton Act §3 or the Robinson-Patman Act). For example, U.S. exporters might be dependent for sales in Europe on access to distributors there. If their direct competitors in Europe vertically integrate, taking control of most of the distribution facilities on which U.S. firms rely, and deny access to those facilities, U.S. antitrust would apply.
5. *Domestic Conduct affecting exports from the U.S.* is exempt from U.S. antitrust unless it causes some effect within the United States.

§20.4 THE BASIC SCOPE OF ANTITRUST IN SUMMARY

Let us pause also to summarize what we've learned so far about the *general* scope of antitrust law:

- Sherman Act §§1 and 2 and Clayton Act §7 apply to:
  - any exchange of a good or service for money or any other thing of value,
  - regardless of the form of organization of any of the parties,
  - that occurs:
    - Within the United States,

    - Overseas but with the purpose and effect of harming U.S. markets, or
    - Overseas and with the effect of harming U.S. exporters,
- except for professional baseball, and with the exception that the FTC cannot enforce Clayton Act §7 against banks or common carriers.
- Section 5 of the Federal Trade Commission Act applies to effectively everything to which the Sherman Act and Clayton Act §7 apply, except for conduct by nonprofit entities that do not provide economic benefits to their members.
- Clayton Act §3, which creates a special rule for tying and exclusive contracts, and the Robinson-Patman Act, which applies to price discrimination, apply to:
    - transactions in tangible commodities,
    - that directly touch upon two or more U.S. states.

CHAPTER 21

Antitrust and Politics

§21.1 THE INTERFACE OF ANTITRUST AND POLITICS

§21.1.1 Why Political or Government Action Could (Theoretically) Violate Antitrust

It may seem surprising that there is any need for rules to define the relation between antitrust and the political process. Antitrust is law that governs business, whereas actions that take place in the political sphere do not seem all that much like business. People involved in policy making do not typically produce products or services for sale, in the ordinary sense. But recall, as was discussed in Chapter 20, that in the absence of a specific exception, antitrust cuts very broadly. In fact there are many ways that actions in political situations harm competition, and it is fairly easy to come up with ways that at least theoretically they could "restrain[] . . . trade" or help to "monopolize" within the meaning of the Sherman Act. For example, state governments pervasively regulate the professions, such as the practice of law or medicine. State governments require that doctors and lawyers be licensed by public authorities to ply their trades, and the getting of such a license is expensive and difficult. States therefore plainly "restrain[] . . . trade" in these markets very significantly, by impeding entry, and there is little doubt that these rules have increased the price of professional services.

State governments also regulate the doing of business in many other ways, and a fair proportion of their interventions are arguably harmful to competition. States regulate advertising, product safety, employment relations, and many other business activities in ways that might cause price and output levels to differ from the competitive result. Occasionally state governments even directly regulate the prices of goods and services. States have done all of these things for various reasons, and there might be values other than economic efficiency a state might seek to serve through regulation, values that might have to be purchased at the cost of some loss of economic efficiency. But some of them are, on almost anyone's scorecard, unambiguously harmful, well-lobbied-for, and undesirable. Private persons, too, can cause injury to competition in ways that involve their participation in politics. Most obviously, private persons sometimes ask their governments to harm their competitors—by outlawing a competitor's product, for example—and sometimes they very plainly do it for anticompetitive reasons.

Remember, too, that though neither of them explicitly says whether the states are "persons," both the Sherman and Clayton Acts define the "persons" to which they apply very broadly. *See* Sherman Act §7, 15 U.S.C. §7; Clayton Act §1(a), 15 U.S.C. §12(a). And indeed, states *are* persons within the meaning of Clayton Act §4, and this is why they can sue for antitrust injury to their "business or property."[1] In other words, were we writing on a clean slate there are lots of ways we could say that conduct that is in one way or another "political" could violate the plain language of our antitrust laws. But because of the judge-made political immunity doctrines, so long as that conduct is genuinely "political" it normally is not subject to antitrust at all.

The political immunities are commonly thought of as falling into two categories. First is a set of rules that apply to the actions of state governments themselves. State governments can take a variety of actions that might interfere with the workings of markets—as by making statutes, regulations, or judicial decisions that in one way or another affect ordinary competition. For the most part, when they do such things antitrust does not apply to them. This is the so-called "state action" or *Parker* immunity, named for *Parker v. Brown*, 317 U.S. 341 (1943). The only major exception is that when they try to deputize private persons to restrain trade, there is a greater likelihood that their actions will run afoul of antitrust. *See California Retail Liquor Dealers Assn. v. Midcal Aluminum*, 445 U.S. 97 (1980). Second is a set of rules that protect the actions of private persons who participate in the political process. When people ask their governments for government action, they usually

1. Indeed, even in the most fundamental of its political immunity cases, the Court acknowledged as much, having decided the very issue less than a year earlier. *See Parker v. Brown*, 317 U.S. 341, 351 (1943) (citing *Georgia v. Evans*, 316 U.S. 159 (1942)). The Court was careful to explain that this "conclusion[][was] derived not from the literal meaning of the words 'person' and 'corporation,' but from the purpose, the subject matter, the context and the legislative history of the [Sherman Act]." *Id.*

cannot be sued for it, even if the action is anticompetitive and no matter how damaging it might be. This partly reflects a concern for defendants' First Amendment rights, and it also seems to reflect the natural instinct that private persons just should not be held liable for conduct that is compelled or permitted by the government itself. This is the *Noerr-Pennington* rule, so named for *Eastern R.R. Presidents Conf. v. Noerr Motor Freight, Inc.*, 365 U.S. 127 (1961) and *United Mine Workers of Am. v. Pennington*, 381 U.S. 657 (1965).

§21.1.2 The Constitutional Character of Political Immunities Cases

§21.1.2(a) The Immunities Are Not Themselves Constitutional Rules (Apparently)

An important and unresolved problem is the uncertainty whether the immunities doctrines are themselves rules of constitutional law. There are two ways that this question might be answered. On the one hand, it might be the Court has meant to hold in its immunities cases that if antitrust applied to the conduct at issue, the antitrust statutes themselves would be unconstitutional. It is plain that the kinds of cases that give rise to the two political immunities—cases brought to challenge state government policies, which enjoy the *Parker* immunity, and cases brought to challenge private lobbying efforts, which enjoy the *Noerr* immunity—could have been based on the text of the Constitution itself. One might think the *Parker* immunity is required by our rules of federalism, arising from the Tenth Amendment and from the scope of Congress's authority under Article I of the Constitution, and one might think *Noerr* is required by the rights of expression and political participation protected by the First Amendment.

But on the other hand, there is little evidence in the Court's own opinions that it understands these doctrines as themselves required by the Constitution. In the foundational opinions themselves the Court explicitly stated that it was not basing decision on the Constitution itself. Rather, in both *Parker* and *Noerr* the Court made clear that it based decision on the so-called "rule of constitutional avoidance," under which statutes should be construed in such a way as to avoid constitutional questions if a reasonable construction is available to do so.

Moreover, it might lead to certain strange and surprising consequences if the immunities rules were held to be constitutional. For one thing, the rules would apply in cases in which the plaintiff sues to challenge political conduct but asserts claims other than antitrust. The Supreme Court has never applied the immunities rules outside the antitrust context, and apparently once implicitly held that they did not apply outside that context.[2] In any

2. *See McDonald v. Smith*, 472 U.S. 479 (1985). *McDonald* involved a defamation claim against the author of allegedly defamatory letters sent to the President of the United States and other

case, if the immunities so applied, then certain well-recognized common law causes of action might be unconstitutional.[3] Still this question remains an open one, and several lower courts have held that the *Noerr-Pennington* doctrine is a rule of First Amendment law.

§21.1.2(b) State Action Cases Are Definitely Constitutional in Some Sense: They Implicate Sovereign Immunity and Seek Federal "Preemption"

All that said, there is one completely different sense in which one of the political immunities—the state action immunity under *Parker*—indubitably raises an issue of actual, substantive constitutional law. Where the state itself or some local government subdivision is the defendant, the lawsuit is in some sense not an antitrust suit at all, but rather is a claim brought under the Supremacy Clause of the U.S. Constitution. That is, the plaintiff seeks to enjoin enforcement of a state policy that so conflicts with the competition policy embodied in federal antitrust law that it is preempted by antitrust. *See Rice v. Norman Williams Co.*, 458 U.S. 654 (1982) (making this point).[4]

A related problem is that federal antitrust actions can be brought only in federal court,[5] and the Eleventh Amendment to the U.S. Constitution

---

federal officials. The defendant, who wrote those letters, argued unsuccessfully below and in its briefing to the Court that the *Noerr-Pennington* case law should apply to the plaintiff's defamation claim just as it would to an antitrust claim. The Court rather oddly did not address that issue explicitly. However, the Court's holding had the practical effect of rejecting it as a matter of law. The Court held that there was no absolute right to petition government officials under the Petition Clause of the First Amendment, and therefore that the constitutionality of the plaintiff's defamation claim should be judged just like defamation cases that do not involve speech directed toward government. But this could not be the case if the *Noerr-Pennington* cases were actually required by the First Amendment. If they did apply, the effect would be an essentially absolute right to petition that the Court rejected.

3. *See Grip-Pak, Inc. v. Illinois Tool Works, Inc.*, 694 F.2d 466, 471 (7th Cir. 1982), *disapproved of on other grounds*, *Profl. Real Estate Investors, Inc. v. Columbia Pictures Indus., Inc.*, 508 U.S. 49, 55 n.3 (1993) ("If all nonmalicious litigation were immunized from government regulation by the First Amendment, the tort of abuse of process would be unconstitutional—something that, so far as we know, no one believes.").

4. In fact, the entire "state action" doctrine, which is the subject of §21.2, might be thought of as a specialized preemption doctrine that applies only to determine whether a given state policy is preempted by federal antitrust. The Supreme Court has sometimes apparently seen things this way, as indicated in the *Rice* case. But Sullivan and Grimes make the excellent point that if courts applied ordinary constitutional preemption analysis in asking whether the Sherman Act displaces state law, there would be a much more severe intrusion into state regulatory power than is currently the case. As they say, "all state regulatory statutes encouraging or protecting price making or other clear antitrust violations would plainly conflict with antitrust, as might any number of state statutes that draw materially different lines between permitted and forbidden economic cooperation than do the antitrust laws." Lawrence A. Sullivan & Warren S. Grimes, *The Law of Antitrust: An Integrated Handbook* 800 (2d ed. 2008).

5. *See* Chapter 19.

provides that the states are immune from suits brought against them by citizens in the federal courts. *Edelman v. Jordan*, 415 U.S. 651, 663 (1974). It turns out, however, that this rule is subject to a number of broad exceptions, and it is rarely a problem in antitrust cases. First of all, the rule protects only the state itself, as opposed to its subdivisions and municipalities. *Will v. Michigan Dept. of State Police*, 491 U.S. 58, 79 (1989). Those lesser entities can be sued in antitrust actions with no concern for the Eleventh Amendment. Second, even where the suit really is against the state itself, for an act taken in its sovereign capacity—as for example where the challenge is to a state statute—a way around the Eleventh Amendment is usually available in the form of the rule of *Ex Parte Young*, 209 U.S. 123 (1908). There the attorney general of Minnesota was sued in a federal district court injunctive action to prevent him from enforcing a newly adopted statute regulating railroad rates, the basis of the action being that the statute violated constitutional rights of the railroads. The Supreme Court held that the Eleventh Amendment was no bar to the suit because the attorney general was named in his personal capacity, and the state proper was not a party. Where an antitrust plaintiff seeks to enjoin a state statute or some other act of the state itself, there will almost always be some specific official charged with enforcing or applying that state act, and so, under *Young*, the Eleventh Amendment is typically no problem in such cases.

§21.1.2(c) Cases Involving Both Immunities Doctrines Implicate Other Constitutional Issues

The kinds of cases that raise political immunity issues under the antitrust laws tend also to raise all kinds of other constitutional issues, at least potentially. State action cases ordinarily involve efforts of state governments to regulate their internal economies. That ordinarily is their purview, but where they interfere too seriously in markets they often run afoul of various constitutional doctrines. First, they may interfere with the civil rights of individuals, as for example where they take private property without just compensation. They may also raise questions of their own constitutional power to regulate, particularly where their market interferences have incidental effects on commerce in other states or where the commerce they regulate within their own borders is inherently "interstate." In those cases, state government action might implicate the so-called "dormant Commerce Clause" doctrine. State actions might also implicate other federal preemption issues, as, for example, where a state attempts to regulate an industry that is already pervasively regulated by federal law, such as pharmaceuticals or interstate carriage of goods.

Petitioning immunity cases tend to raise a different set of issues. Where an individual is sued for conduct that could be characterized as political, that person may have access to other protections directly under the First Amendment. The Speech Clause provides a general right to engage in consumer boycotts or other public demonstrations, so long as they are not commercially motivated, even though they may cause economic harm or use economic coercion as a tool of persuasion. (*See* §21.4.5.) But the fact that conduct may seem like speech or political conduct does not guarantee that it is constitutionally protected or that antitrust liability for it would be unconstitutional. That same constitutional right of public demonstration is not available for conduct that is commercially motivated, despite what may be a very sincere expressive component. Likewise, freedom of the press has usually done no good for media defendants in antitrust cases.

§21.1.3 The Political Immunities in Summary

Because this issue of political immunity is pretty large and complex, it will be useful to summarize the whole body of law up front:

1. As far as antitrust law is concerned, state governments may fashion their own internal economic policies however they wish, with two exceptions:
   a. Where the state delegates authority to a local government entity or (probably) a state administrative agency, and that entity purports that some restraint of trade was made pursuant to that delegation, the defendant must show that:
      i. the challenged conduct was taken pursuant to a clearly articulated policy of the state that authorized it.
   b. Where the state delegates authority to a private person, and that person purports that some restraint of trade was made pursuant to that delegation, the person must show that:
      i. the challenged conduct was taken pursuant to a clearly articulated policy of the state that authorized it; and
      ii. the conduct is actively supervised by the state government itself.
2. A private person cannot be liable for "petitioning" any entity of federal, state, or local government, even where the person requests government action harmful to competition, unless:
   a. the purported petitioning conduct is a "sham," which is to say that the person did not actually care about the government action requested, and rather meant only to use the petitioning *process* as a way to injure a rival;
   b. the purported petitioning conduct in and of itself constitutes an antitrust violation; or

c. the purported petitioning conduct occurred in some context that was too far removed from the traditional venues of political communication, such as a behind-closed-doors meeting of a private standard setting organization.

§21.2 THE STATE ITSELF AS DEFENDANT: *PARKER* OR "STATE ACTION" IMMUNITY

§21.2.1 The Basic Rule; Genuine State Action Is "Ipso Facto" Immune

Generally speaking, the state action immunity applies in its purest form where the "state" itself acts, in some way that is unequivocally "state" action. So if the uppermost body of a branch of state government—the state legislature, the state supreme court, or (possibly—the case law is less certain on this point) the governor—takes formal action with the force of law, that action cannot be the basis for any sort of antitrust relief (against anyone). This rule is often called the *Parker* rule, after the first case in which it was recognized, *Parker v. Brown*, 317 U.S. 341 (1943). It is also often known as the "state action" immunity. The courts sometimes say that, under this doctrine, "*any* action that qualifies as state action is '*ipso facto* . . . exempt from the operation of the antitrust laws. . . .'" *City of Columbia v. Omni Outdoor Advert., Inc.*, 499 U.S. 365, 379 (1991) (quoting *Hoover v. Ronwin*, 466 U.S. 558, 568 (1984)) (emphasis in original).

This broad statement is actually rather misleading, in one respect. State governments are *not* immune from antitrust challenge in at least one important category of cases, and in those cases the states may in effect be challenged as real party in interest, and their conduct can be enjoined. Specifically, state governments are not ipso facto immune when they attempt to authorize private persons to restrain trade without government oversight. Cases of that nature are governed by the so-called *Midcal* doctrine, which is discussed in §21.3. So, for example, imagine that a state legislature, acting qua legislature and with due regard for all formalities, adopts a statute that says "drug stores within this state are hereinafter permitted to agree among themselves at what price they will sell aspirin." There is no question that this statute is genuine action of the state itself, but also no question that the courts would enjoin it under the *Midcal* rule.

So what can be said, with more accuracy, is that actions *of the state qua state* are ipso facto immune from antitrust. Actions of state administrative agencies are not the actions of the state, except where some official can be said to merely enforce some purely state action, as was the case in *Parker* itself. (There, named defendant Parker was a state official charged with implementing a state statute that regulated the pricing of farm products.) Thus, broad delegations of authority to make regulations to a state agency, which is then used to promulgate trade-restraining rules, likely will be held not to be actions of the state itself. *See Town of Hallie v. City of Eau Claire*, 471 U.S. 34, 46 n.10 (1985) (so suggesting in dicta). Actions of municipalities are not the actions of the state. *Id.* at 38-39.

Example

Joe Dunsmore, J.D., is a recent law school graduate in Indiana who unfortunately has just learned of his failure on his state's bar examination. He wasn't the only one. It seems the Indiana bar authorities made some sort of conscious decision to grade the exam more rigorously this year, and the pass rate fell appreciably from prior years. Joe also has been hearing a lot of rumors lately of funny business among the panel of lawyer volunteers who grade the test every year. They are all lawyers licensed to practice in Indiana, and rumor has it that they used their position to deliberately shrink the pool of new applicants. The volunteers are appointed each year by the Indiana Supreme Court, pursuant to the "Rules for the Governance of the Bar of the State of Indiana." They grade the exam answers and then formally recommend to the nine-member Court those applicants whose exams received a passing score. This year they graded more than 3,000 exams, and none of their recommendations were rejected by the Court.

Does Joe have an antitrust cause of action to challenge his failure on the test?

Explanation

No. These were essentially the facts of *Hoover v. Ronwin*, 466 U.S. 588 (1984). There the Arizona Supreme Court administered admissions to the bar through a bar examination, and did so through a panel of practicing lawyers like the one here. A disappointed applicant sued to challenge his failure on the bar, alleging that the attorneys that graded his exam engaged in a horizontal concerted refusal to deal against him. The Supreme Court said that because the ultimate decision as to all admissions to the bar were formally reserved to the Arizona Supreme Court, even though its review of the test results may have been pro forma, the decision was an action of the state itself. The plaintiff's denial of admission to the bar was therefore "ipso facto" immune from antitrust.

Example

Bob, a plumber based in New Jersey, wants to move to Connecticut. By Connecticut state statute, all plumbers must receive a license from the state Department of Commerce. Among other things, the Department requires all would-be plumbers to pass a written test, which, as required by statute, is administered by the Secretary of Commerce acting through the Department. Rather than sit for the examination, Bob sues the Connecticut Secretary of Commerce, alleging that his licensing authority is a restraint of trade insofar as it operates as a group boycott by Connecticut plumbers of all out-of-state plumbers.

What's the result?

Explanation

At least on his antitrust theory, Bob will lose. The licensing requirement does restrain trade in the literal sense. However, since it follows from a state statute, it is "ipso facto" immune from antitrust. (Bob might have better luck on a theory of constitutional law—that he was denied his constitutionally protected "privileges and immunities.")

§21.2.2 The Several Failed, Would-Be Exceptions and the Lingering Uncertainty of the Market Participant Exception

Over the years the state action doctrine was rumored to contain several exceptions, most of them based on snippets of dicta in the early Supreme Court case law. With one exception—the remaining possibility that there is some "market participant" exception for cases in which a state government restrained trade while also buying or selling something—they have all so far been rejected.

First, there long persisted the suspicion that there might be some sort of "conspiracy" exception, to govern cases where a state government might just have connived with private malefactors in some evil scheme. *Parker* itself recognized this possibility in dicta, writing that the case involved "no question of the state or its municipality becoming a participant in a private agreement or combination by others for restraint of trade," and that

> [t]he state in adopting and enforcing the . . . program made no contract or agreement and entered into no conspiracy in restraint of trade or to establish monopoly but, as sovereign, imposed the restraint as an act of government which the Sherman Act did not undertake to prohibit.

317 U.S. at 351-352. *City of Columbia*, however, laid the possibility completely to rest, holding that there is no such exception. The Court's views were purely practical:

> Since it is both inevitable and desirable that public officials often agree to do what one or another group of private citizens urges upon them, such an exception would virtually swallow up the *Parker* rule: All anticompetitive regulation would be vulnerable to a "conspiracy" charge.

In a similar vein, the Court also rejected any exception that would be based on whether the government action was evilly motivated or somehow criminally tainted—for example, if it were procured through bribery. The Court wrote that, while liability for officials in such cases might "vindicate[] (in a rather blunt way) principles of good government[,] . . . the statute we are construing is not directed to that end. Congress has passed other laws aimed at combating corruption in state and local governments." The Court quoted *Noerr* for the idea that "[i]nsofar as [antitrust] sets up a code of ethics at all, it is a code that condemns trade restraints, not political activity." *Id.* (quoting *Noerr*, 365 U.S. at 140).

Finally, however, one exception might still exist from state action immunity: the "market participant" exception, covering situations in which a state or local government entity acts as a buyer or seller, rather than as a sovereign. Again, *City of Columbia* is important on this point. In the course of rejecting the "conspiracy" exception, the Court distinguished the separate possibility of an exception "where the State acts not in a regulatory capacity but as a commercial participant in a given market." *City of Columbia*, 499 U.S. at 374-375. The Court's discussion there suggested pretty strongly that there is some such exception, but it remains dicta, and the Court has not considered the issue since then. Moreover, those few lower courts to even consider the question have cast doubt on it, and no court appears ever to have held the exception applicable in a case. Whether the exception exists remains subject to doubt.

§21.3 THE PROBLEM OF PRIVATE PERSONS AS TRADE-RESTRAINING DEPUTIES OF STATE GOVERNMENT: *MIDCAL* IMMUNITY

Sometimes state governments will in effect deputize a nonstate actor to undertake some sort of conduct that might in some way or another harm competition. *Parker* itself contemplated this possibility, and seemed to acknowledge that the case before it could be characterized as such a deputization scenario. In *Parker*, boards of raisin growers proposed output quotas that were then put into effect by state officials. The Court implied that it might have been a different case if there were not so much direct involvement by actual state officials in putting the program into effect. The Court observed in dicta that "a state does not give immunity to those who violate the Sherman Act by authorizing them to violate it, or by declaring that their action is lawful. . . ." 317 U.S. at 351.

Still, the Court has always made room for state programs that do rely on the policy-making activities of private actors, and more so than was the case in *Parker*, so long as the state itself retains enough oversight. The set of rules that govern such cases is now known as the *Midcal* doctrine, so named for *California Retail Liquor Dealers Assn. v. Midcal Aluminum*, 445 U.S. 97 (1980). *Midcal* really is just an extension of the *Parker* doctrine. It is simply a reflection of the basic idea in *Parker* that the state governments, acting as states, should be empowered to regulate their own economies, without interference from federal antitrust. But the problem is to ensure that in a given case, it really is the *state* that is doing the restraint. As the Court has explained, the basic policy problem in such a case is that

> where a private party is engaging in the anticompetitive activity, there is a real danger that he is acting to further his own interests, rather than the governmental interests of the State. . . . [*Midcal*] is designed to ensure that the state-action doctrine will shelter only the particular anticompetitive acts of private parties that, in the judgment of the State, actually further state regulatory policies. . . . [T]he State[,][therefore, must] exercise ultimate control over the challenged anticompetitive conduct[,][and][t]he mere presence of some state involvement or monitoring does not suffice. . . . Absent such a program of supervision, there is no realistic assurance that a private party's anticompetitive conduct promotes state policy, rather than merely the party's individual interests.

Patrick v. Burget, 486 U.S. 94, 100-101 (1988). Put slightly differently,

> the purpose of [*Midcal*] . . . is not to determine whether the State has met some normative standard, such as efficiency, in its regulatory practices. Its purpose is to determine whether the State has exercised sufficient independent judgment and control so that the details of the rates or prices have been established as a product of deliberate state intervention. . . . [T]he analysis asks whether the State has played a substantial role in determining the specifics of the economic policy. The question is not how well state regulation works but whether the anticompetitive scheme is the State's own.

FTC v. Ticor Title Ins. Co., 504 U.S. 621, 634-635 (1992). In other words, there is *policy* being made where a state transfers its trade-restraining power to a private person. That is perfectly fine so far as antitrust is concerned, *but only where the policy can be said to be made by the state itself.* Moreover, while as we shall see the *Midcal* doctrine has two separate elements, "[b]oth [of them] are directed at ensuring that particular anticompetitive mechanisms operate because of a deliberate and intended state policy." *Id.* at 636.

The Court actually spent the better part of 20 years working out how it would address this special policy problem, through the 1960s and 1970s. Its thoughts finally culminated in the now famous two-prong test in *Midcal* in 1980. In that case, the state of California adopted a statutory program under which wholesalers of wine would agree to wholesale prices, which they would post, and then no wholesaler could sell at less. While state officials *enforced* the prices, by bringing criminal actions after the fact against wholesalers that undercut the prices, state officials were not involved in setting the prices themselves. The Court ruled that in such a case the private participants in the program and the state itself would enjoy antitrust immunity if two requirements were met:

1. "[T]he challenged restraint must be one clearly articulated and affirmatively expressed as state policy," and
2. "the policy must be actively supervised by the State itself."

445 U.S. at 105. As we shall see in the subsequent sections, both the "clear articulation" (§21.3.1) and "active supervision" (§21.3.2) elements have been the subject of much case-law elaboration. As we shall also see, a bit of a special rule is applied where a state delegates trade restraining authority to its own state agencies or political subdivisions, rather than to private persons. In those cases, a local government defendant need only show "clear articulation." (*See* §21.3.3.)

Anyway, it is critical to work out the differences between *Midcal* and the original *Parker* decision, because the two cases came out differently despite their seemingly similar facts. Both cases involved California state statutory programs that authorized private sellers of a given product—horizontal competitors—to agree on price or output, and both involved some participation by state officials. The difference is the degree of state actor involvement. If a case is like *Parker*—if a court decides that a particular state action is the action of the state itself, and not the deputization of private parties—then the inquiry does not even reach the two *Midcal* factors. In such a case, as the Court has said, the state's actions are "ipso facto . . . exempt" from antitrust.

So let us consider how different the state actors' roles were in the two cases. The simpler of the two cases was *Midcal*, because the state's role was so limited. Critically, state actors had no role at all in making the substantive policy choice. They had no role in choosing the prices to be charged or considering any consequences that might follow. In *Parker*, by contrast, the raisin output quota program was ultimately administered by an "Agricultural

Prorate Advisory Commission" of nine members, one of whom was the state director of agriculture and the other eight of whom were appointed by the governor and confirmed by the state senate. On the petition of ten raisin growers, that Commission could if it chose approve the creation of a "zone" in which raisin output would be limited. If the Commission approved, the director of agriculture would then appoint a local "program committee" composed of raisin growers and some other market participants. The program committee could then propose a "marketing program" to the Commission (which is to say, a raisin output quota), which the Commission could approve only after public hearing and the Commission's formal finding that "the program is reasonably calculated to carry out the objectives of this act." The Commission was authorized by statute to modify the marketing program as necessary. Violations of the quota were then punishable as state crimes. 317 U.S. at 346-347.

The courts occasionally make reference to "hybrid" restraints in state action cases, but this is just a reference to the distinction just described. Hybrid cases are simply those in which "private actors are . . . granted a degree of private regulatory power," *Fisher v. City of Berkeley*, 475 U.S. 260, 268 (1986). In such cases the legality of the restraint is judged under *Midcal*. Accordingly, the term "hybrid restraint" simply describes an arrangement to which *Midcal* applies.

§21.3.1 Clear Articulation

Where a restraint is subject to *Midcal* analysis, the first question is whether it was implemented pursuant to a "clearly articulated" state policy decision to restrain trade. A state can articulate this intent in a variety of ways, as for example in a state constitution or a state statute, or a duly authorized regulation adopted by a state supreme court. However, it is critical that the articulation be made by a state itself—for example, a city government could not "clearly articulate" a state policy to restrain trade, because it does not act as the state itself. *Cf. Cmty. Commcns. Co., Inc. v. City of Boulder*, 445 U.S. 40, 50 (1982) (holding that, for purposes of *Parker* immunity, city governments are not the "state").

The major issue in most cases that consider the clear articulation requirement is whether the purported articulation of state policy was sufficiently "clear." On the one hand, the defendant "need not be able to point to a specific, detailed legislative authorization" for its restraint, *Town of Hallie v. City of Eau Claire*, 471 U.S. 34, 39 (1985), and in particular, "[i]t is not necessary . . . for the state legislature to have stated explicitly that it expected [the defendant] to engage in conduct that would have anticompetitive effects," *id.* at 42. This flexibility serves two policy goals. First, it "preserv[es] to the States their freedom . . . to administer state regulatory policies free of the inhibitions of the federal antitrust laws without at the same time permitting purely parochial interests to disrupt the Nation's free-market goals." *Id.* (citations omitted). Second, the Court has stressed that in applying the *Midcal* immunity, the federal courts should not get caught up in questions of procedural or substantive correctness:

> We should not lightly assume that the [*Midcal*] authorization requirement dictates transformation of state administrative review into a federal antitrust job. Yet that would be the consequence of making antitrust liability depend on an undiscriminating and mechanical demand for "authority" in the full administrative law sense.

City of Columbia, 499 U.S. at 372 (quoting Philip I. Areeda & Herbert Hovenkamp, *Antitrust Law* ¶212.3b, p. 145 (Supp. 1989)). Accordingly, the Court has not required that the trade-restraining authorization must explicitly authorize trade restraints, and has indicated that the state law at issue need be neither specifically "economic" in nature nor related to any specific industry. *Id.* at 372-373 & n.4. Rather, it is enough that suppression of competition is a "foreseeable result" of what the state law authorizes. *See Town of Hallie*, 471 U.S. at 41-42.

On the other hand, this "foreseeable result" requirement is not satisfied by just any general grant of authority. In *Cmty. Commcns. Co., Inc. v. City of Boulder*, 455 U.S. 40 (1982), the constitution of the state of Colorado contained a "home rule" provision giving cities "the full right of self-government in both local and municipal matters," and provided that as to such matters, the cities had "every power theretofore possessed by the legislature. . . ." *Id.* at 43-44, 52. The City of Boulder used this power to impose a temporary moratorium on the expansion of cable television businesses within its territory, while it was formulating a new ordinance to govern that business. A would-be cable provider sued under the Sherman Act and won an injunction against the ordinance. The Supreme Court rejected the city's *Midcal* defense, finding that the home rule provision could not constitute "clear articulation" of a policy for cities to restrain trade in cable television.

> [T]he requirement of "clear articulation and affirmative expression" is not satisfied when the State's position is one of mere *neutrality*. . . . A State that allows its municipalities to do as they please can hardly be said to have "contemplated" the specific anticompetitive actions for which municipal liability is sought.

Id. at 55. Likewise, in *FTC v. Phoebe Putney Health Sys., Inc.*, 568 U.S. 216 (2013), the Court rejected "clear articulation" where a local government entity was given no more than the ordinary corporate powers to enter contracts and buy or sell property. The government entity was a municipally owned "hospital authority," which had powers to own and administer hospitals, and defendants argued that its power to acquire them (especially in the small, sparsely populated territory in which it operated) reflected the state legislature's anticipation that it might acquire enough hospitals in its territory to restrain competition. The Court rejected that argument, writing that mere "state-law authority to act is insufficient to establish state-action immunity; the substate governmental entity must also show that it has been delegated authority *to act or regulate anticompetitively*." Id. at 228 (emphasis added). The Court elaborated further, offering what will likely be taken as an important gloss on the "foreseeability" criterion announced in *Hallie*:

> Thus, we have concluded that a state policy to displace federal antitrust law was sufficiently expressed where the displacement of competition was the *inherent, logical, or ordinary result* of the exercise of authority delegated by the state legislature. In that scenario, the State must have foreseen and implicitly endorsed the anticompetitive effects as consistent with its policy goals.

Id. at 229 (emphasis added).

This test may or may not add more clarity to the clear articulation requirement, but for the time being at least it seems to indicate less tolerance for immunity on the basis of broad delegations, and a demand for evidence of some actual, affirmative consideration within the legislature of anticompetitive effects. The requirement "necessarily implies an affirmative addressing of the subject by the State." *City of Columbia*, 455 U.S. at 55. The state government itself, acting through an appropriate organ of state sovereignty such as the legislature or supreme court, must weigh the substantive merits of making the specific anticompetitive restraint at issue.

§21.3.2 Active Supervision

Where the defendant is a private entity, as opposed to a state agency or local government, there must not only be a "clear articulation" of state government policy to restrain trade, but also "active supervision" by the state itself of the conduct in issue. The Supreme Court has said that "[t]he mere presence of some state involvement or monitoring does not suffice. . . . The active supervision prong of the *Midcal* test requires that state officials have and exercise power to review particular anticompetitive acts of private parties and disapprove those that fail to accord with state policy." *Patrick v. Burget*, 486 U.S. 94, 100-101 (1988). The Court has also explicitly rejected a standard that some courts had applied, under which active supervision could be shown by the mere "existence of a state regulatory program, if staffed, funded, and empowered by law. . . ." *FTC v. Ticor Title Ins. Co.*, 504 U.S. 621 (1992).

In *Ticor*, for example, the Court considered a state regulatory scheme for the business of title insurance that was in force in several states.[6] These state regimes allowed "rate bureaus" composed of title insurer members to fix the rates at which the members would sell. In each state the rate bureau was nominally overseen by the state insurance regulator, and each state had incorporated into its insurance regulatory scheme a so-called "negative option." That is, once the rate bureau filed its rates the insurance regulator retained some power to disapprove the rate if it saw fit, but if it took no action the rate would automatically go into effect. None of the states had ever exercised its negative option. Each of the states also retained some power to hold hearings or take other procedural steps to review a rate, though none of them ever did so. *Id.* at 629-631. The Court found this inadequate.

Example

Under pressure from producer groups, the state of Maine has adopted a statute prohibiting sale within the state of certain seafood products at less than prices fixed by the state Secretary of Agriculture.

1. Is this law enforceable, insofar as federal antitrust is concerned?
2. Assume the same facts, except that the law requires the Secretary to impose a schedule of prices adopted by a council of producers, consumers and representatives from other constituency groups, the members of which are appointed by the Secretary in consultation with the Governor of the state. What facts are relevant to whether this statute is enforceable?

Explanation

1. Very likely yes. Under these facts the prices imposed would likely be held to be actions of the state itself, and therefore "ipso facto" immune from antitrust liability (including from preemption by the Sherman Act). The answer is "likely" yes because the Supreme Court has never explained whether and when actions of a state administrative agency are acts of the state itself, but in this case an apparently very high-ranking official exercises authority delegated directly by the state legislature, and so presumably there is as good a case as could be made that this executive branch action is action of the state itself.

6. Though the industry in question was denominated title "insurance," the antitrust exemption that ordinarily protects the "business of insurance" from antitrust, under the McCarran-Ferguson Act, was held inapplicable for reasons not relevant to the *Midcal* immunity issues.

2. Under these modified circumstances, the relevant facts would be the details under which the council is appointed, under which it does its work, and the degree of oversight imposed by the Secretary and other government officials. If the prices imposed are simply whatever the council determines, then under *Midcal* there would be a lack of "active supervision" and the statute is unenforceable. But if the Secretary has and exercises substantial oversight, then there is "active supervision" and the statute is enforceable notwithstanding the Sherman Act.

§21.3.3 State Agencies and Local Government Subdivisions: The *Town of Hallie* Rule

§21.3.3(a) Municipalities

The Supreme Court has made clear that where an antitrust defendant is a local government entity, state action immunity requires only that there be some "clear articulation" of state policy that the municipality restrain trade. *Town of Hallie v. City of Eau Claire*, 471 U.S. 34, 46-47 (1985). As the Court explained in that case,

> We may presume, absent a showing to the contrary, that the municipality acts in the public interest. A private party, on the other hand, may be presumed to be acting primarily on his or its own behalf.

Id. at 45. That finding justified dispensing with the "active supervision" element.

§21.3.3(b) State Administrative Agencies

The Supreme Court has never reached the question whether state administrative agencies enjoy antitrust immunity, though it has indicated that *Town of Hallie* applies to them as well. If so, state agencies acting pursuant to authority delegated from the legislature would not be the "state" acting qua state. But they would enjoy antitrust immunity wherever they can demonstrate that their actions are taken pursuant to a "clearly articulated" state policy. *See Town of Hallie*, 471 U.S. at 46 n.10. Some lower courts have indicated, however, that at least high ranking executive officials and departments are actually the "state" and therefore are "ipso facto" immune. *See* 2 Am. Bar Assn., *Antitrust Law Developments* (Ninth) 1409-1410 (9th ed. 2022).

§21.3.3(c) Money Damages Against Local Governments: The Local Government Antitrust Act

In cases where an antitrust defendant is a *local* government—meaning a county, city, or town, or an administrative unit of one of those entities, such as a school system—the defendant will enjoy a special protection even if it cannot show that its actions were immune under *Parker*. The Local Government Antitrust Act, 15 U.S.C. §§34-36, provides that in such cases, neither the local government nor its officials or employees acting in their official capacities can be liable in money damages for antitrust violations or be charged for the plaintiff's costs or attorneys fees. Likewise, no person can be liable in money damages or owe fees or costs "in any claim . . . based on any official action directed by" a local government or an official or employee thereof acting in an official capacity. *Id.* at §36(a). The Act has no effect on injunctive relief against any of these persons.

Example

The city of Minneapolis, like other major cities in Minnesota, enjoys certain regulatory powers under a chapter of the state statutory code entitled "Cities and Towns." The relevant provision says that "each Class I City [as defined elsewhere in the statute, and including Minneapolis] shall have power to adopt and amend local laws not inconsistent with the provisions of this chapter or any general law relating to its property, affairs or government." The city has adopted a municipal ordinance requiring any taxi driver that picks up two different customers on the same trip to charge them a specified minimum fee. The city is sued by a consumer rights organization. Following a bench trial, the district court reached a verdict declaring the regulation invalid under federal antitrust and permanently enjoining it, and assessing costs and damages.

Should the verdict withstand appeal (assuming the city asserted and properly preserved all defenses available to it)?

Explanation

The first question is whether Minneapolis would enjoy immunity under *Town of Hallie*, and it would appear that here there is a failure of "clear articulation." This is a very general grant of power, and it is not a "foreseeable result" that one of Minnesota's cities would use it to restrict pricing by taxi cabs (or any other private business). These were essentially the facts in *Hertz Corp. v. City of New York*, 1 F.3d 121 (2d Cir. 1993), and the language quoted in the Example is taken from the New York state constitution's "home rule" provision that was at issue in that case.

So, assuming the restraint is illegal, the declaration and injunction should stand. The award of costs and fees, however, should be reversed. Minneapolis acted in its official capacity and is protected by the Local Government Antitrust Act from any damages liability or any award of fees or costs.

§21.4 *NOERR-PENNINGTON* OR "PETITIONING" IMMUNITY

We now turn to the second major political immunity doctrine, which protects private political conduct from antitrust—the *Noerr-Pennington* or "petitioning" immunity. This fairly complex body of law emanates from a small handful of Supreme Court opinions decided over a long period, mostly a long time ago—a mere five opinions, beginning with *Eastern R.R. Presidents Conf. v. Noerr Motor Freight, Inc.*, 365 U.S. 127 (1961), and spreading out over the next 30 years, but the last of them handed down nearly 20 years ago.[7] Some commentators believe that this law was modified significantly by a pair of cases that came late in the period, *Allied Tube & Conduit Corp. v. Indian Head, Inc.*, 486 U.S. 492 (1988), and *FTC v. Superior Court Trial Lawyers Assn.*, 493 U.S. 411 (1990), in that both cases clarified and perhaps narrowed the definition of "petitioning." But whether or not that is true, the older case law plainly remains relevant. We shall examine all the relevant twists and turns in due course. (*Allied Tube* is discussed further in §21.4.2 and *Superior Court Trial Lawyers* is discussed in §21.4.3.)

The facts in *Noerr* in many ways made for the paradigm "petitioning" case. A group of railroads lobbied the governor and legislature of Pennsylvania for laws limiting the transportation of cargo by truck. In other words, they asked for laws that would directly restrain their horizontal competitors. The Court had no trouble finding that "where a restraint upon trade or monopolization is the result of valid governmental action, as opposed to private action, no violation of the [Sherman] Act can be made out." 365 U.S. at 136. Accordingly, "the Sherman Act does not apply to . . . mere solicitation of governmental action with respect to the passage and enforcement of laws." *Id.* at 138.

Many lower courts and commentators have considered it important that the *Noerr* opinion contained a several page digression on its reasoning, and

7. The cases following *Noerr* were *United Mine Workers of Am. v. Pennington*, 381 U.S. 657 (1965), *California Motor Transp. Co. v. Trucking Unlimited*, 404 U.S. 508 (1972), *Allied Tube & Conduit Corp. v. Indian Head, Inc.*, 486 U.S. 492 (1988), *FTC v. Superior Court Trial Lawyers Assn.*, 493 U.S. 411 (1990), *City of Columbia v. Omni Outdoor Advert., Inc.*, 499 U.S. 365 (1991), and *Profl. Real Estate Investors, Inc. v. Columbia Pictures Indus., Inc.*, 508 U.S. 49 (1993).

in that discussion it identified a few distinct reasons for finding the conduct there immune. It is thought that these rationales should be useful in identifying immune petitioning conduct in other cases. First, the Court focused on the "essential dissimilarity" between political and business conduct. The lobbying coalition before the Court in *Noerr*, for example, bore

> very little if any resemblance to the combinations normally held violative of the Sherman Act, combinations ordinarily characterized by an express or implied agreement or understanding that the participants will give up their trade freedom, or help one another to take away the freedom through the use of such devices as price-fixing agreements, boycotts, market-division agreements, and other similar agreements.

365 U.S. at 136.

Second, the Court expressed concern that antitrust liability for political conduct would interfere with the proper working of democratic processes. In particular, the Court thought that both the executive and the legislature are dependent on the flow of information from private persons, but that the risk of antitrust liability for petitioning would dry up that flow. For all these reasons, the Court held that "[t]he proscriptions of the [Sherman] Act, tailored as they are for the business world, are not at all appropriate for application in the political arena." 365 U.S. at 141.

Finally, *Noerr* introduced two other ideas of lasting importance. First, the Court introduced the crucial notion of "sham" petitioning, which at present remains the only exception from the *Noerr* immunity. The Court thought there might be cases where "a publicity campaign, ostensibly directed toward influencing government action, is a mere sham to cover what is actually nothing more than an attempt to interfere directly with the business relationships of a competitor. . . ." *Id.* at 144. Second, *Noerr* made clear that some communications could be immune even if not made directly to government officials. In addition to their lobbying toward government officials, the *Noerr* defendants also hired a public relations firm to create a public marketing campaign to support their legislation, which the plaintiffs alleged was misleading and anticompetitive. In other words, the defendants also communicated to third parties who had no direct involvement in any policy making, but those communications were held immune as well, as part of an effort to persuade government. Finally, *Noerr* explicitly rejected the possibility that the defendant's evil motivation or conniving tactics could be relevant to antitrust immunity. As will be discussed below (§21.4.1), it is now clear that no question of the defendant's anticompetitive purposes, the methods of the petition, or the competitive consequences of it have any relevance to the immunity. The only questions are whether the defendant's conduct constituted "petitioning" within the meaning of the *Noerr-Pennington* case law and, if so, whether the petitioning was a "sham."

Only a few years later, in *Pennington*, the Court considered a collective bargaining agreement (CBA) that governed a major portion of the coal mining industry. A part of the agreement was held immune under *Noerr*, because it concerned agreements that the union and the major employers — the parties to the CBA — had made with the U.S. Department of Labor. The opinion thus made clear that petitions to executive officials were immune, just as are those to a legislature. The Court also amplified an important theme from *Noerr*, observing that "[n]othing could be clearer from the Court's opinion than that anticompetitive purpose did not illegalize the conduct [in *Noerr*]." 381 U.S. at 669.

§21.4.1 Basic Rule: "Petitioning" That Is Not a "Sham" Is Immune from Antitrust

§21.4.1(a) General Rule

As the law has now developed, the basic rule of the *Noerr-Pennington* immunity can be stated simply enough: Where conduct challenged in an antitrust suit constitutes "petitioning" within the meaning of the immunity, it cannot violate antitrust unless the petitioning is merely a "sham."

The Supreme Court has never explicitly defined the term "petitioning" for purposes of the *Noerr-Pennington* doctrine, and the best one can do to know when conduct constitutes "petitioning" is to synthesize from the facts of the cases. On the most general level, it is clear that the Court intends the petitioning concept to be a very broad one. With only the few limitations to be discussed shortly, it seems to mean roughly any conduct or communication by any private entity directed toward government so long as it asks for something.

Examples of conduct that plainly *do* constitute petitioning include communications made directly to government representatives, such as speaking with or writing to members of the federal, state, or local legislature or to federal, state, or local executive officials. Filing a lawsuit or bringing other essentially adjudicatory actions against someone is also petitioning, but the courts have fashioned somewhat special rules to govern that conduct (as further discussed in §21.4.1(c)). Finally, communications not made directly to government officials, but made in some way meant more or less directly to influence them, can be immune. The chief example would be the publicity campaign at issue in *Noerr*, which included letters to the editor in newspapers and other efforts to sway the public in support of desired legislation.

Examples that plainly do *not* constitute petitioning are harder to come by, but at least two things can be said fairly clearly. First, *FTC v. Superior Court Trial Lawyers Assn.*, 493 U.S. 411 (1990), made clear that if the alleged petitioning conduct is itself a violation of the antitrust laws, it does not constitute "petitioning." Second, in the conceptually more challenging decision in *Allied Tube & Conduit Corp. v. Indian Head, Inc.*, 486 U.S. 493 (1988), the Court set out some rules to govern those cases in which the allegedly immune communications are not made directly to government officials. Specifically, the Court said that the scope of the immunity depends on the "context and nature of the activity." *Id.* at 499. (*Superior Court Trial Lawyers* is considered more fully in §21.4.3. *Allied Tube* is considered in §21.4.2.)

§21.4.1(b) What Is a "Sham"? And Is Sham Petitioning in Itself an Antitrust Violation?

The Court has explained that a "sham" is petitioning conduct

> in which persons use the governmental *process*—as opposed to the *outcome* of that process—as an anticompetitive weapon. . . . A "sham" situation involves a defendant whose activities are "not genuinely aimed at procuring favorable government action" at all, not one "who 'genuinely seeks to achieve his governmental result, but does so *through improper means*. . . .' "

City of Columbia, 499 U.S. at 380 (emphasis in original; internal citations omitted). The sham petitioner, in other words, does not actually care whether the requested government action is ever taken. Instead, it uses the petitioning conduct itself as a way to defame or injure a competitor, or otherwise to frustrate that competitor's ability to compete. The concept was identified in *Noerr* itself, where the Court wrote in dicta that

> [t]here may be situations in which a publicity campaign, ostensibly directed toward influencing government action, is a mere sham to cover what is actually nothing more than an attempt to interfere directly with the business relationships of a competitor and the application of the Sherman Act would be justified.

365 U.S. at 144. Still, the Court did not explicitly find there to have been a sham in any case until more than a decade later, in *California Motor Transp. Co. v. Trucking Unlimited*, 404 U.S. 508 (1972). In that case, the defendants were a group of trucking companies operating in California that filed repeated and allegedly frivolous oppositions to the trucking-license applications of a rival group of trucking companies that wanted to expand business in that state. The Court found that the defendants had no real substantive legal basis for the administrative challenges they had filed. Rather, they just sought to delay the proceedings as long as possible, thereby delaying the competitor's entry. This, said the Court, was a "sham."

Importantly, it is now very clear that petitioning is not a sham just because it seems *bad* in some way. It is not a sham merely because the petitioner makes claims that are false, defamatory, deceptive, or otherwise seemingly wrong or unethical. The Court's most extended rumination on this point is in *City of Columbia*, which began by observing that the fact "[t]hat a private party's political motives are selfish is irrelevant. . . ." 499 U.S. at 380. The Court wrote that "deny[ing] . . . meaningful access to the appropriate city administrative and legislative fora . . . may render the manner of lobbying improper or even unlawful, but does not necessarily render it a 'sham.'" *Id.* at 381. Thus, while the Court has never directly reached the question, there is reason to believe that petitioning is not a sham even if it is otherwise *criminal*. This follows further from Justice Scalia's repeated observation throughout the opinion that antitrust is not needed in the political arena, because wrongdoing there is subject to oversight and sometimes criminal prosecution under other laws. As he wrote, quoting *Noerr*, the antitrust laws, "tailored as they are for the business world, are not at all appropriate for application in the political arena." *Id.* at 380.

Sham petitioning is not in and of itself an antitrust violation. *See Profl. Real Estate Investors, Inc. v. Columbia Pictures Indus., Inc.*, 508 U.S. 49, 61 (1993) ("Proof of a sham merely deprives the defendant of immunity; it does not relieve the plaintiff of the obligation to establish all other elements of his claim."). Accordingly, even after proving that the defendant's conduct was a sham and therefore not immune from antitrust, a plaintiff must then prove that the non-immune conduct was an antitrust violation.

§21.4.1(c) The Special Case of Petitioning in the Adjudicatory Context and the Lingering Uncertainty over Adjudicatory "Frauds"

Though it may seem surprising at first, the filing of a lawsuit can have consequences harmful to competition, and in principle can violate the antitrust laws. For example, a party might claim that it holds intellectual property in a good or process that the defendant desires to use as part of its competitive effort. Filing lawsuits to protect that intellectual property can therefore restrain trade, and if the lawsuits are in one way or another improper, they might themselves violate antitrust. Or a party might use lawsuits or filings before regulatory tribunals to keep a competitor from acquiring license rights or property or some other thing the competitor needs to compete. Parties might be tempted to bring claims like these even when they have no real basis for them, because the mere pendency of those challenges might delay or frustrate the rival's ability to compete. That might be so even if the challenge itself lacks substantive merit.

However, it has been clear since Justice Douglas's opinion in *California Motor Transp. Co. v. Trucking Unlimited*, 404 U.S. 508 (1972), that filing a lawsuit or seeking a determination by a government administrative tribunal is "petitioning" conduct.[8] Lawsuits, after all, are merely requests for redress of grievances addressed to the judicial branch, which is no less a part of government. Likewise, when a government agency contains within it some adjudicatory tribunal whose purpose is to resolve case-by-case issues, participation there too is merely a plea for government relief.

Interestingly, *California Motor Transport* is the only case in which the Supreme Court has ever found there to have been a "sham," and that sham occurred in an adjudicatory context. Moreover, in that case, which in some ways is theoretically odd and seemingly fairly confused, the Court seemed to imply that a sham should be more easily found in the adjudicatory context. As Justice Douglas wrote, "unethical conduct in the setting of the adjudicatory process often results in sanctions. Perjury of witnesses is one example." Accordingly, "[m]isrepresentations, condoned in the political arena, are not immunized when used in the adjudicatory process." *Id.* at 512-513.

That impression, however, turned out to be quite incorrect. When the Court finally gave further guidance as to the adjudicatory sham, in *Profl. Real Estate Investors, Inc. v. Columbia Pictures Indus., Inc.*, 508 U.S. 49 (1993), more than 20 years later, the Court made it *very* difficult to demonstrate that a lawsuit is a sham. An antitrust plaintiff can challenge most lawsuits as antitrust violations only if it can prove two things:

1. that the lawsuit is "objectively baseless in the sense that no reasonable litigant could realistically expect success on the merits," and
2. that "the baseless lawsuit conceals an attempt to interfere *directly* with the business relationships of a competitor, through the use [of] the governmental *process*—as opposed to the *outcome* of that process—as an anticompetitive weapon. . . ."

508 U.S. at 60-61 (internal citations and quotation marks omitted). The Court was at pains to stress that the first requirement had to be satisfied before a court is even permitted to consider the second. That is, a lawsuit must be so bad on the merits that no reasonable party could believe it might succeed before a court is even allowed to consider whether the litigant brought the suit only to harm a competitor. Accordingly, "an objectively reasonable effort to litigate cannot be sham regardless of subjective intent." *Id.* at 57. In an effort to give more content to the "objective baselessness" inquiry of the first element, the Court analogized to the common law tort of "malicious prosecution," under which a party that sues without "probable cause" and malicious intent can be sued for doing so. As *Professional Real Estate*

8. The Court also addressed the issue obliquely in a 1973 opinion, also written by Justice Douglas, *Otter Tail Power Co. v. United States*, 410 U.S. 366 (1973). However, the Court there merely reversed and remanded a lower court ruling that *Noerr* did not apply at all to judicial petitions, noting that that decision was made before the Court had decided *California Motor Transport*.

Investors pointed out, "probable cause" in the common law case law "requires no more than a reasonabl[e] belie[f] that there is a chance that [a] claim may be held valid upon adjudication." 508 U.S. at 62-63 (internal quotation marks omitted).

§21.4.2 *Allied Tube* and the "Source, Context and Nature" of the Restraint

One problem in the petitioning immunity is that not all communications genuinely intended to secure government action are addressed directly or unequivocally to traditional "government" entities. Recall that even *Noerr* had considered the immunity status of communications directed to the public—which were "incidental" to a government petition—and found those communications immune. Specifically, in that case, the defendants had published letters to the editor in various newspapers, which were said to be misleading and anticompetitive. They were not petitions made directly to government decision makers, but they plainly were part of the defendants' effort to influence the governor and legislature of Pennsylvania. They were therefore immune.

Over time, though, courts came to have some qualms about extending immunity to just any sort of anticompetitive conduct that in some way might be directed at government. They also grew more aware just how many different venues there might be in which a person might be said ultimately to be trying to influence government, and that in some of those venues immunizing the would-be "petitioning" could pose some serious risks. *Allied Tube & Conduit Corp. v. Indian Head, Inc.*, 486 U.S. 492 (1988) is the Court's most important statement on point. In that case, the defendant was a maker of a particular kind of conduit pipe used to string electrical wiring throughout buildings. Because electrical wiring poses safety hazards, it is pervasively regulated. Much of the regulation is based on a model code that is produced by a private organization known as the National Fire Protection Association (NFPA). The NFPA's codes are routinely adopted more or less verbatim directly into state and local government regulations, as actual law. The NFPA included voting members from government, academia, and the private sector, but one of them—the defendant—abused the group's standard-setting process to fraudulently procure passage of a model code that prohibited the use of its competitor's product. (The competitor injured by this conduct was the plaintiff in the case.)

Importantly, the plaintiff's theory of harm was based entirely on injury suffered because of the model code's independent market effect—the injury it caused simply by virtue of the NFPA's reputation—rather than on its adoption by government entities. But the defendant nevertheless raised a *Noerr* defense. Its theory was that communications made to an influential standard setting body were analogous to the letters to the editor in *Noerr* itself. Its argument was that because the NFPA's code was so influential, and was often incorporated directly into law, lobbying the NFPA was tantamount to lobbying state and local governments themselves. While the Court expressed sympathy for that view, it ultimately disagreed. "The scope of [*Noerr* immunity]," wrote the Court, "depends . . . on the source, context, and nature of the anticompetitive restraint at issue." 486 U.S. at 499. In this case the Court found the "context and nature" too similar to private marketplace decisionmaking, and too dissimilar from the political process, to support the *Noerr* immunity. The Court stressed that immunizing conduct among competitors in private, closed-door contexts, would pose too significant a competitive risk.

§21.4.3 Conduct That in Itself Violates Antitrust Is Not "Petitioning"

The second limitation on "petitioning" is conceptually simpler: The conduct that is said to be "petitioning," even if it is directed toward government, cannot be immune if that conduct itself is an antitrust violation.

The key case is *FTC v. Superior Court Trial Lawyers Assn.*, 493 U.S. 411 (1990). That case involved a group of criminal defense lawyers, who earned most of their income from court-appointed indigent defense. They sought to protest the long-term failure of their local government (the District of Columbia) to increase the rate at which their work was compensated. In addition to publicizing their cause and communicating directly with the government—conduct that indubitably would be immune from antitrust under *Noerr*—they also took more forceful action: They went on strike. The economic effect was substantial. Though only about 90 lawyers joined in the strike, those 90 carried the large bulk of the District's indigent defense work, and most of the rest of the District's legal community had no interest in taking up the slack. The District's criminal justice system effectively ground to a halt, and the strike was ultimately successful in securing an increase in the rates paid by the DC government. The Federal Trade Commission sued the lawyers for conspiracy in restraint of trade.

Among other defenses,[9] the lawyers argued that their strike was merely a petition protected by *Noerr*. Plainly, had they merely asked government to

9. Importantly, the defendants raised a pure First Amendment defense that was independent of their *Noerr* argument. The First Amendment theory, which is discussed in §21.4.5, was unsuccessful. One might also wonder why this "strike" was not permitted under antitrust in the same way that other labor strikes are permitted. The answer is that the so-called "labor exemption" from antitrust is available only for persons who are "employees." Attorneys and other professionals who sell services to clients, like the lawyers in *Superior Court Trial Lawyers*,

fix their rates at a higher level, there could be no antitrust liability. There also could be no question in the case whether the petitioning was sham. There was no doubt that the lawyers genuinely desired the government relief that they sought. But the Court rejected their *Noerr* argument on the grounds that the purported petitioning conduct *in itself* was illegal under the antitrust laws. The Court explained:

> [I]n the *Noerr* case the alleged restraint of trade was the intended *consequence* of public action; in this case the boycott was the *means* by which respondents sought to obtain favorable legislation. The restraint of trade that was implemented while the boycott lasted would have had precisely the same anticompetitive consequences during that period even if no legislation had been enacted. In *Noerr*, the desired legislation would have created the restraint on the truckers' competition; in this case the emergency legislative response to the boycott put an end to the restraint.

Id. at 424-425 (emphasis in original). Thus, if it can be shown that the purported "petitioning" would itself be illegal if it were not directed at government, it is not immune.

Example

Imagine that a group of retail chain stores get together and decide that they are fed up with Walmart, since it is a very successful price cutter. Answer these questions:

1. Would it be illegal if they collectively visited the major manufacturers whose products they sell, to tell them that they will no longer carry those products unless the manufacturers stop selling to Walmart?
2. Would it be different if, instead, they formed a group and argued to the federal Congress that unless it passed legislation that would make it more difficult for Walmart to compete, they would simply stop selling products that were also retailed by Walmart?
3. Would it be different yet if, instead of threatening Congress in this way, the group paid bribes to Congressman to pass their legislation?

---

generally organize themselves independently of any employer. Therefore, they are treated by both antitrust and labor law as merely independent entrepreneurs, and they are not permitted to collectively fix their rates or go on strike in the way that employees can. The labor exemption is discussed fully in Chapter 23.

Explanation

1. Yes. This is a horizontal boycott aimed at a horizontal competitor; it is therefore a naked, horizontal restraint on price. It is very likely illegal, and probably per se illegal. (*See* §6.2.3.)

2. It is a bit of a hard question, but the result is arguably no different. Although the retailers aim their effort at government, and though their effort is plainly not a sham, the would-be petitioning here is *itself* an illegal boycott. So it would seem to enjoy no *Noerr* protection, a result that would follow from *Superior Court Trial Lawyers.*

3. This, by contrast, probably is protected by *Noerr-Pennington*. There is no doubt that the retailers do in fact desire the government action they request, so it is not a "sham." Moreover, the Supreme Court has indicated in strong dicta that wrongful conduct, even if it is otherwise illegal, can still enjoy *Noerr-Pennington* so long as it is not a "sham."

§21.4.4 Purported Exceptions

As with the state action doctrine, *Noerr* has long been suspected to contain exceptions for specific kinds of conduct. Efforts to find them have been more successful than has been the case with the *Parker* doctrine. On the one hand, one long-sought exemption has failed. It was thought there might be some sort of "conspiracy" exception—that a private petitioner could be liable for petitioning conduct if that conduct was part of entering into an illegal conspiracy with government officials. As with the purported conspiracy exception to the state action immunity (§21.2.2), *City of Columbia* laid this possibility completely to rest.

On the other hand, at least two other exceptions might exist. First, many lower courts believe that *Noerr* contains a "market participant" exception, which would allow an action where persons conspire with a government entity in the purchase or sale of things. (By contrast, the lower courts that have considered whether there is a "market participant" exception to the state action immunity have been more skeptical.) *City of Columbia*, though it considered and laid to rest other exceptions, did not address this one because in that case the government entity had no personal pecuniary interest in the regulations that it had adopted. Some courts doubt it, and, for what it might be worth, a market participant exception to *Noerr* immunity seems at odds with the *Pennington* case. The Court in that decision immunized entreaties to the Secretary of Labor concerning coal that it would purchase for the government-owned Tennessee Valley Authority. The case therefore involved petitioning to a federal agency when the agency itself was arguably the buyer of the defendants' goods.

More important, there may be a "misrepresentation" exception in "adjudicatory" contexts. While quite a number of lower courts have recognized this exception,[10] the most elaborate consideration remains the Federal Trade Commission's opinion in *In re Union Oil Co. of California*, 138 F.T.C. 1 (2004). In that case, defendant Unocal participated in a rule-making process undertaken by a California state agency, which was charged by the California legislature with setting environmental standards for gasoline. Unocal misled the agency into adopting standards that would require all sellers of gasoline in California to use technology covered by patents owned by Unocal, and the Commission brought a monopolization action.

The Commission first noted several strong indications in Supreme Court dicta that there is a misrepresentation exception in the adjudicatory and administrative contexts. *California Motor Transport* observed that "[m]isrepresentations, condoned in the political arena, are not immunized when used in the adjudicatory process." *Id.* at 23 (quoting 404 U.S. at 513). *Allied Tube*, more generally, wrote that, while deceptions are permitted in legislative lobbying, "in less political arenas, unethical and deceptive practices can constitute abuses of administrative or judicial processes that may result in antitrust violations." *Id.* (quoting 486 U.S. at 499). Finally, the Commission noted a passage in dicta at the end of *Professional Real Estate Investors*, mentioned above, giving some support for a misrepresentation exception. The Supreme Court, relying on the *Walker Process* case (*see* §15.2.4) and *California Motor Transport* (*see* §21.4.1(b)), wrote:

> In surveying the "forms of illegal and reprehensible practice which may corrupt the administrative or judicial processes and which may result in antitrust violations," we have noted that "unethical conduct in the setting of the adjudicatory process often results in sanctions" and that "[m]isrepresentations, condoned in the political arena, are not immunized when used in the adjudicatory process." We need not decide here whether and, if so, to what extent *Noerr* permits the imposition of antitrust liability for a litigant's fraud or other misrepresentations.

508 U.S. at 61 n.6 (internal citations and quotation marks omitted). Maybe the most important contribution in *Unocal* is the Commission's explanation of when it would hold a particular case to arise in a "less political arena," in which misrepresentations might constitute antitrust violations. The Commission set out a multifactor inquiry, which effectively asked whether the circumstances indicate that truthfulness would be expected by the government and would be important to the legitimacy of the particular function that it performed. *Id.* at 51-58. Under that test, the Commission found

---

10. *See* 2 Am. Bar Assn., *Antitrust Law Developments* (Ninth) 1438-1440 (9th ed. 2022) (collecting cases).

Unocal's misrepresentations to the California state agency not immune under *Noerr*.

§21.4.5 The Distinct Constitutional Protection of the First Amendment: The Rule of *Claiborne Hardware*

It was mentioned above that the *Noerr* doctrine appears not itself to be a doctrine of substantive First Amendment law. However, the First Amendment independently protects some publicly expressive conduct, even if it happens to cause economic injuries or employ economic coercion as a persuasive tool.

NAACP v. Claiborne Hardware Co., 458 U.S. 886 (1982), recognized a general First Amendment immunity for consumer boycotts and public demonstrations of a noncommercial character, even though they might cause economic harm and might use economic coercion as a tool of persuasion. However, the fact that particular conduct might seem like speech or political conduct does not necessarily immunize it under the First Amendment. For example, the *Claiborne Hardware* right was not available to the defendants in *FTC v. Superior Court Trial Lawyers Assn.*, 493 US. 411 (1990). Though the concerted refusal to deal in that case had a strong expressive component, the sincerity of which the Court did not doubt, the Court found that the defendants' boycott was also "commercially" motivated, and that denied it any First Amendment protection. (It was commercially motivated because, whatever other motivations they might have had, the boycotters sought to increase their own rates.)

§21.5 A NOTE ON ANTITRUST AND *FEDERAL* ACTION: THE DOCTRINE OF IMPLIED REPEAL

One matter that can be a bit confusing is how these political immunity rules work when the government actor involved is the *federal* government. The *Noerr-Pennington* doctrine does not distinguish between petitioning the federal, state, or local governments. The doctrine works the same way in each case. But the analysis is different when there is some clear articulation of *federal* policy to restrain trade. Sometimes federal statutes interfere with competition, and explicitly provide that the conduct to which they apply is therefore exempt from antitrust. This is true to some extent, for example, of labor unions, the business of insurance, ocean shipping, and railroads (all of which are discussed in Chapter 22). But there are also many cases in which a federal statute will require or authorize private conduct that might seem risky under the antitrust laws. To deal with this problem the federal courts have devised a whole separate set of rules, explained in §22.3, known as the doctrine of "implied repeal." While the details are different, in some broad sense the implied repeal analysis is the same as the *Midcal* inquiry. The question is whether the federal government has indicated an intent, acting in its sovereign capacity, to displace competition in a particular context.

Example

The federal Department of Transportation administers a system for licensing the transport of hazardous materials ("hazmat") by truck. DOT enforces that system in part by bringing enforcement actions against any federally licensed hazmat carrier that engages in conduct that is "unreasonably unsafe."

A group of hazmat carriers encourages the Secretary of Transportation to establish an advisory panel to formulate new safety policies meant to lower the risk of terrorist sabotage. Acting under statutory authority to "establish, by rule after hearing, such procedures as it deems necessary for the formulation of safety protocols for the transportation of [hazmat] by truck," the Secretary creates a panel composed of currently licensed hazmat carriers, manufacturers of trucking equipment and other industry representatives, and a few representatives from DOT and other agencies. The panel's recommendations are not themselves federal law, but the Secretary's order creating it states that in disciplinary actions brought by DOT under its "unreasonably unsafe" standard, failure to abide by the panel's safety recommendations would be "prima facie evidence" of a violation. Among its first actions, the panel formulates a protocol for the design of hazmat trailers, and the design mandates the use of certain technology manufactured by one of the panel members. That member's competitor sues the member, the panel, and the Secretary of Transportation, alleging antitrust violations.

What are the immunity issues?

Explanation

There are at least two. First, assuming the defendant was one of the private persons that asked the Secretary of Transportation to create the panel, its participation in that request would be plainly immune under *Noerr*. Second, however, the defendant's participation in formulation of the standard, which was not itself federal law and would only be "adopted" by the Secretary in the most attenuated and after-the-fact way, very well may not be immune. Theoretically, the defendant's participation could be characterized as a petition to the Secretary, which might enjoy *Noerr* immunity, though this situation would seem rather like that in *Allied Tube*. The fact that the federal government ultimately gives the panel's recommendations force may not matter. That was true, for example, in *Walker Process* (discussed in §15.2.4). The defendant might also argue that by granting the Secretary the power to "establish . . . procedures . . . for the formulation of safety protocols," Congress meant to imply its intent to repeal antitrust law as to private parties that participate in such procedures. That is, the defendant might assert an "implied repeal" defense. As discussed in §22.3, that seems awfully unlikely here.

CHAPTER 22

Antitrust and the Regulated Industries

As we are all quite aware, much of the U.S. economy is "regulated" in one way or another by the federal and state governments. Sometimes the fact that a business is subject to both antitrust and some other regulation could put that business in a fairly awkward position. Some conduct that is explicitly encouraged or mandated by regulation, such as collaboration or information sharing, might seem to put businesses at risk of antitrust liability. Defendants have often argued that in such a case they should be exempt from antitrust, and the courts and Congress have had some sympathy. After some brief background, this chapter covers the three closely related antitrust doctrines that make up the law's effort to accommodate the goals of antitrust and regulation:

1. The treatment of explicit statutory exemptions from antitrust
2. The doctrine of "implied repeal"
3. Two related rules that limit or modify antitrust claims against regulated firms, the *Keogh* or "filed-rate" doctrine and the doctrine of primary jurisdiction

§22.1 THE RANGE OF REGULATED INDUSTRIES AND THEIR RELATION TO ANTITRUST

§22.1.1 Introduction

Since the beginning of federal antitrust, defendants have tried to argue that they should be excused from it because they are also subject to some other state or federal regulation. This was true of the railroads, for example, who were among the earliest major antitrust defendants, but who also happened to be regulated by a federal agency known as the Interstate Commerce Commission.[1] Until quite recently the courts were openly hostile to these arguments and they did not often succeed. The courts long observed the "cardinal principle" that "repeals by implication"—that is, a finding that by adopting some other federal regulatory system applicable to a given defendant, Congress meant for antitrust to be limited or inapplicable to that defendant—are "strongly disfavored. . . ."[2] Thus, "[w]hen there are two acts upon the same subject, the rule is to give effect to both if possible."[3] Even where Congress explicitly calls for them—even when some federal statute explicitly says that antitrust is limited or repealed altogether as to some party or conduct—limitations on antitrust are at least nominally disfavored by the courts.[4] In fact, this area is one of the few in antitrust as to which there is much consensus. It is widely held, across the political spectrum, that limitations on antitrust are rarely justified and should be read narrowly.[5]

And yet, various statutory limitations have been with us almost as long as there has been antitrust, and even in those cases where there is no explicit statutory language addressing the scope of antitrust, the Supreme Court has occasionally found antitrust limitations to be implicit in other federal laws. For better or worse, both the courts and Congress believe that sometimes it is better that some regulatory regime other than antitrust apply to some conduct, even though the conduct is just commercial behavior that typically would be subject to antitrust.

Our policy has come to handle this problem in basically three different ways. (1) Over the years, Congress has created several explicit statutory exemptions from antitrust for specific industries and specific kinds

1. *See, e.g., United States v. Trans-Missouri Freight Assn.*, 166 U.S. 290 (1897).
2. *Silver v. New York Stock Exchange*, 373 U.S. 341, 357 (1963) (quoting *United States v. Borden*, 308 U.S. 188, 198 (1939)); *United States v. Philadelphia Natl. Bank*, 374 U.S. 321, 350 (1963).
3. *United States v. Borden Co.*, 308 U.S. 188, 198 (1939).
4. *See, e.g., Chicago Profl. Sports Ltd. Partnership v. NBA*, 961 F.2d 667, 671-672 (7th Cir. 1992) (because "special interest legislation enshrines results rather than principles," the "courts read exceptions to the antitrust laws narrowly, with beady eyes and green eyeshades").
5. *See generally* Am. Bar Assn., Section of Antitrust Law, *Federal Statutory Exemptions From Antitrust Law* (2007); *Antitrust Modernization Commission, Report and Recommendations* 333-337 (2007).

of conduct. The explicit exemptions and the judicial approach to them are briefly discussed later in this section. (2) Next, the courts have devised a judge-made rule of statutory construction to deal with cases in which antitrust seriously conflicts with another federal law, but in which Congress has not explicitly said how the conflict should be resolved. The approach they have devised, known as the doctrine of "implied repeal" of antitrust, totally exempts some conduct from antitrust when application of both antitrust and the other law or regulation would be too much in conflict. This doctrine is discussed in §22.3. (3) Finally, the courts have devised two other rules that do not fully exempt regulated conduct, but sometimes require antitrust courts to give some deference to regulatory agencies having jurisdiction. First, in the special case in which regulation requires a "filed rate"—which means that before the regulated firms can set a price or change an existing price, they must make a filing with the relevant regulatory agency, and may need the agency's approval—there can be no private antitrust suit for money damages to challenge the rate that has been filed. Second, there are some antitrust cases in which some particular issue is raised that is either in the exclusive jurisdiction of a regulatory agency or one that the court feels could better be handled by some agency that has jurisdiction over it. In those cases, the rule of "primary jurisdiction" might call for the court to stay the antitrust action until the agency has had time to resolve the issue. These two doctrines are discussed in §22.4.

But it is well to remember that these seemingly separate doctrines are really just attempts to answer the same question. As the Supreme Court has said, each of these doctrines

> arises when conduct seemingly within the reach of the antitrust laws is also at least arguably protected or prohibited by another regulatory statute enacted by Congress. Often, but not always, the other regime includes an administrative agency with authority to enforce the major provisions of the statute in accordance with that statute's distinctive standards, which may or may not include concern for competitive considerations.

Ricci v. Chicago Mercantile Exch., 409 U.S. 289, 299 (1973). And in every case fitting that description, the problem for the court is the same: to find the intent of Congress as to the applicability of antitrust and the applicability of the other law. Thus, each of these doctrines in effect raises that same narrow question of statutory interpretation.

So in the typical case, an antitrust action will be brought against a defendant that happens to be subject to the oversight of some regulatory agency. A first question will be whether the statute that gives the agency its authority contains an explicit exemption that covers the challenged conduct. Often, even if there is some such exemption, the parties will litigate fiercely over whether it applies to the particular conduct challenged. Anyway, if there is no such exemption, then the question still remains whether some intent to limit antitrust is implicit in the other law that applies. Most typically, the agency will have no very direct control over prices, entry, or other actual business operations, but merely some power to require informational disclosures or compliance with some particular rules. In those cases courts must decide whether those powers of the agency would somehow be seriously frustrated if the regulated businesses could also be sued for antitrust violations. If so, then the doctrine of implied repeal simply holds that the particular conduct challenged in the lawsuit is exempt from antitrust. Finally, even if there is no implied repeal, antitrust suits might still be subject to the special qualifications of the filed rate and primary jurisdiction doctrines. In some special cases the other law actually governs the prices charged by the defendant. If so, and if the law requires that rates to be charged be filed with the agency, then under the filed-rate doctrine antitrust challenge to the rates themselves cannot be brought for money damages. Finally, courts retain some freedom in particular cases to decide that some issue in an antitrust matter would be better resolved in the first instance by an agency, and in those cases they can put the antitrust case on hold until the agency can resolve that issue.

§22.1.2 A History of Economic Regulation: Changing Faith in Competition

Since the late nineteenth century both the federal and state governments have regulated business in various ways, sometimes very extensively. One fact of this history is really critical for our purposes: Regulation in this country has basically come in one or the other of two fundamental forms, and they have different consequences for competition policy.

§22.1.2(a) The Rate-and-Entry Regulation of the "Destructive Competition" Era

First, during the late nineteenth century, economists began to develop the idea that some industries just could not perform properly under pure competition, and needed protection from competition through government oversight. In large part their thinking reflected the rapid changes going on around them. As discussed in Chapter 1, the period following the Civil War was a time of technological change and hugely expanding industrial production, as well as changes in the organization of industry, including a ten-year period of such massive industrial consolidation that it is still known as the "Great Merger Wave." There also occurred severe, calamitous economic downturns in 1873, 1893, and 1907, and throughout the period concerns grew over urban poverty, wealth inequality, and labor unrest. By various arguments that came to be known as the theory of "destructive competition," it was widely feared that in many sectors competition itself was to blame. The central claim was that in those sectors the doing of business had become so expensive that, under competition, no firm could earn enough money to stay in business.

Accordingly, the first of the two major waves of American regulation sought mainly to address destructive competition problems. The idea was that if unfettered competition would force every firm to fail in a given market, the government would step in to keep competition from becoming too fierce. The new body of laws that came to be adopted employed a style of very invasive economic control that actually regulated the price and output decisions to be made by otherwise private firms. Usually, these regulatory schemes also protected the incumbent firms—as part of the effort to ensure they could earn enough of a return to cover their purportedly prohibitive costs—by setting up regulatory barriers for new firms seeking to enter. They ordinarily required new entrants to secure some license or special permission prior to entry, and often required would-be entrants to prove that there was some public need for new entry in the market.

Three major themes running throughout the history of rate-and-entry regulation are especially relevant for us, and each of them nowadays seems fairly foreign. First, an important customer-protection theme was the "common carrier" duty. Most entities regulated under the early twentieth century regimes were required to operate as common carriers, meaning that they performed as truly public utilities. The idea has very old origins,[6] but it spread widely under the early regulatory regimes, to industries never before subject to it. Common carrier firms were obliged to publicly declare rates at which they would provide their services, in documents known as "tariffs"; they were forbidden to deviate from tariff rates; and they were required to provide their services at tariff rates to whomever might wish to buy them.

A second and related consumer-protection theme was the predominant desire to prevent *price discrimination*. In part this reflected the public outcry over alleged abuses by the turn-of-the-century monopolists. It was said that they discriminated in price against those consumers that were most helpless. Accordingly a major motivation of antidiscrimination rules was simple fairness. A related concern was that because of a practice known as "cream skimming," some marginal customers would lose access to the service all

6. Even before the colonization of the New World, English law imposed some common carrier duties, mainly on providers of transportation and lodging. The duty required them to serve all customers, to charge reasonable rates, and to observe a higher standard of care than ordinarily imposed by tort law. *See generally* William K. Jones, *Origins of the Certificate of Public Convenience and Necessity: Developments in the States, 1870-1920*, 79 Colum. L. Rev. 426, 428-431 (1979).

together.[7] In any case, for what it may be worth, theoretical perspectives on price discrimination have changed a lot. Contemporary theory considers it not only not inherently bad, but that sometimes it may enhance efficiency. If some regulated firm happens to be able to sell a good or service more cheaply to a particular buyer because, say, that buyer can buy in bulk, then it is probably allocationally efficient to let it do so. That point of view, however, was absent from early debate over price-and-entry regulation.

The final major theme under rate-and-entry regulation was its goal to ensure that regulated industries remained profitable. Because the regulation largely removed their freedom over both price and output, and because the very underlying rationale of the rules was that these industries were not suited to real competition, it was felt that regulators should ensure them some profitability. Regulators did this by limiting entry, setting rates at remunerative levels, and by preventing cream skimming.

§22.1.2(b) The Health-and-Safety Regulation of the Contemporary Era

Second, a newer sort of regulation emerged after the New Deal and blossomed particularly in the 1960s and 1970s. As an approach to government oversight of private markets it has almost completely replaced rate-and-entry regulation. These more recent regimes tend not to focus on specific markets or specific kinds of firms, but rather on particular kinds of conduct that are thought to be harmful, and apply to any firms or markets in which those problems appear. They include protections for the environment, human safety, labor standards, and other such social concerns. Importantly, contemporary regulatory regimes ordinarily do not incorporate any direct concern for competitiveness or the financial well-being of regulated entities, at least not as particularly central goals. In short, rate-and-entry regulation was regulation of competition, because competition itself was thought to be the problem. The more recent health and safety regulation much more narrowly controls specific conduct that is thought to be harmful. Price, output, and larger organizational decisions are left to private decisionmaking, subject only to antitrust. Contemporary regulation implicitly demonstrates much greater confidence in competition itself.

---

7. The problem is that some customers are more profitable to serve, because it is cheaper to serve them—for example, it is cheaper to sell electricity to a high-volume user in an urban area than to transmit it to residential users in sparsely populated rural areas. Serving those rural customers at the government-approved rate might even be *unprofitable*. So, if one firm could try to win away only the higher-value business—if it could skim off the cream—while a regulated firm was required to serve even the lower-value customers at the approved rate, the regulated firm might falter or be unable to attract the needed capital. If so it might exit the business and there would be no one left to serve the lower-value customers. *See* Jones, *supra* note 6, at 428.

§22.1.2(c) The Ambiguous Term "Deregulation"

Finally, a word should be said about a term of which we have heard a great deal in the past 30 to 40 years—"deregulation." In effect, deregulation is a name for a political movement that first gained significant support in the 1960s. It was driven by great disappointment in the rate-and-entry system. Deregulatory agonists argued that the theoretical grounds on which Congress founded rate-and-entry regulation were false—in fact, competition was rarely "destructive," and even in those industries where it might have been unsustainable in the early twentieth century, technological advancements had made competition quite feasible. Rate-and-entry regulation also produced much higher prices, inefficient investment planning in regulated industries, and a history of protectionist favoritism in Congress and the agencies. These arguments, which came to be supported by substantive empirical and theoretical evidence and are now widely accepted, began to bear fruit in the 1970s. During the Carter administration, Congress and a few agencies took major steps to remove rate-and-entry oversight of the airlines, surface transport, and power utilities. Congress and the executive branch have been working to dismantle the rest of the rate-and-entry regulatory edifice, bit by bit, ever since.

Still, while it is true in some sense that the U.S. economy has been "deregulated," that term can be quite misleading. First of all, it bears repeating that even now some rate-and-entry regulation remains, particularly in insurance (which is mostly state regulated, and in some states is subject to extensive rate-and-entry oversight), the financial sector (especially banking, but even in securities and elsewhere, where federal licensing is often required), telecommunications (overseen by the Federal Communications Commission), energy (subject to much regulation at the state level and to some extent at the federal level), and elsewhere. But more generally, if "regulation" means that government has taken away some choices to be made in the sale of goods and services, then all U.S. firms remain subject to extensive regulation at the federal, state and local levels and they seem likely to stay that way for the foreseeable future. That includes not only contemporary health and safety regulation, but also the law of contract, tort, property, and all the other rules that limit private freedom to some extent. And of more direct relevance for us, all of these government intrusions have some competitive consequences. Regulation tends to affect the costs of decisions that business might make, and so it alters the prices, output, and patterns of investment that would otherwise prevail under genuinely "free" competition.

§22.1.3 A Few Useful Ideas from Administrative Law

Those regulatory regimes that are administered by government agencies—which is to say, most of them—are subject to a body of law known as "administrative law." Administrative law is a set of constitutional and statutory rules that governs the agencies' operation and their relationships with private persons. It sets up procedures they must follow in order to make regulations, adjudicate administrative claims that are brought before them, and do the other things that agencies do. Knowing a few of the basics of this law is helpful in understanding the regulated industries doctrines in antitrust.

Administrative law begins with the "organic statute"—the statute that creates the agency and gives it its basic powers. Almost all agencies are governed by such a statute, and generally speaking an agency cannot take any action that is not authorized in its organic statute or some other federal law. For example, the Federal Trade Commission is created by the Federal Trade Commission Act, and that Act gives the FTC power to bring enforcement actions under its §5. Many agencies are given additional powers under other statutes. For example, the FTC can bring actions to enforce the loan disclosure rules of the Truth in Lending Act.

Agencies can take various different kinds of action. Among their most fundamental roles is to make regulations—rules that have the force of law. Agencies can only make regulations when they are given that power explicitly in their organic statute or some other statute. Many agencies can also adjudicate things. They hold evidentiary trials or hearings following which they make decisions to resolve disputes. Again, an FTC enforcement action under §5 often takes the form of an internal agency adjudication. FTC staff attorneys will have investigated some person or firm for a §5 violation, and they then file a complaint before an agency official whose job is to hold a hearing and decide the case in a fashion that for the most part looks like a regular trial before a court. (In the federal system, most agency hearing officers are known as "administrative law judges" or "ALJs.") One special form of agency adjudication that has some relevance here is the licensing proceeding. Some agencies grant licenses for the performance of particular functions, such as the operation of a broadcast television or radio station, or the building of a new nuclear power plant. Often, especially when the function to be licensed is significant or controversial, the licensing proceeding itself will be an elaborate and trial-like affair, which may be before an ALJ and may include live witnesses and adversarial presentation of evidence. Finally, many agencies also have enforcement powers that require them to take action in the courts. The Justice Department, for example, enforces the antitrust laws by filing criminal or civil suits against defendants in the federal courts.

Administrative law not only sets up procedures to govern agency action, it also provides a mechanism to ensure that agencies follow them: "judicial review." Generally speaking, a person that is aggrieved by some agency action can look to the courts for relief by filing a cause of action for judicial review. That cause of action looks basically just like any other civil lawsuit, in which the aggrieved person argues that the agency violated the law in one way or another that caused that person injury. The violations of law the person may allege in such a case are that the agency took some action that violated the Constitution, that it violated the agency's own organic statute or some other statute, or that its actions were not in compliance with the procedures agencies are required to follow under administrative law. For example, if the FTC enforcement staff brings an action under §5 before an agency ALJ, and is ultimately successful against the defendant before the full Commission, the defendant may seek review in the federal courts. It might argue that the agency failed to make out a case for violation of §5 itself, or that the adjudication was in some way procedurally improper. To take another example, an agency with rule-making power might make a rule that harms some private interest. For example, the Food and Drug Administration might adopt a rule requiring pharmaceutical companies to put new safety information on the labels of their products. A company unhappy with the new rule could sue the FDA in federal court, alleging that the agency somehow misapplied the underlying statute, or that, again, the rule making was in some way procedurally improper or unconstitutional. And finally, consider a license application proceeding—say, the application for a radio broadcast license before the Federal Communications Commission. The application may be the forum for some substantial disagreement. The applicant will have to convince the Commission that the license is appropriate, and the application may be opposed by other would-be applicants or third-party groups who think the license would be inappropriate. If the application is denied, the applicant might seek judicial review, and if the application is granted, the opponents might do so. On judicial review the arguments would be the same—that the Commission's decision was not appropriate under its organic statute, or that the decision was procedurally improper or unconstitutional.

§22.2 THE ONCE-AND-CONTINUING PREVALENCE OF STATUTORY EXEMPTIONS

As one consequence of the theory of destructive competition and the regulatory revolution of the early twentieth century, Congress was persuaded that many industries were just ill-suited for competition. And since it exempted them from competition, Congress largely exempted them from antitrust as well. Antitrust law is in effect a mandate that there *must* be competition in industries to which it applies, and so for those industries that Congress had effectively exempted from competition it would be awkward also to try to comply with antitrust. There have been at any given time since the early twentieth century a few dozen explicit statutory exemptions, though as time passed, a few would be repealed or changed here, a few more added there. There remain even now around 30 of them still in force.[8]

Still, as with the nature of economic regulation itself, the nature of statutory exemptions has changed over time. When they were first widely introduced in the early twentieth century, the exemptions tended to be essentially total. The exemption first adopted in 1916 for the ocean shipping industry was originally very broad—ocean carriers were permitted to form price-fixing cartels that were totally exempt from antitrust. But since then, the breadth of statutory exemptions has been limited in two major ways.

First, more recently adopted statutory exemptions have almost always been much more limited in scope. They tend to be transaction specific. Rather than exempt a whole industry, they exempt only one specific kind of conduct. Often enough things have happened that way because an exemption is adopted in response to some adverse judicial ruling. For example, in the early 1970s Congress carved out a special immunity for production joint ventures among newspaper publishers, in response to the Supreme Court's decision in *Citizen Publg. Co. v. United States*, 394 131 (1969). The resulting statute, the Newspaper Preservation Act, 15 U.S.C. §§1801-1804, exempts the formation of the specific kind of joint venture at issue in *Citizen Publishing*, but it does not exempt anything else that newspapers do. This sort of thing has continued with some frequency, as in the recent exemptions for local governments,[9] college financial aid programs,[10] and the graduate medical resident "matching" program.[11]

---

8. *See* Section of Antitrust Law, Am. Bar Assn., *Federal Statutory Exemptions from Antitrust Law* (2007).

9. In *Cmty. Commcns. Co. v. City of Boulder*, 455 U.S. 40 (1982), and in a few earlier cases, the Supreme Court held that municipal governments and their officials could be liable in antitrust even for official actions, unless they were protected by the "state action" antitrust immunity (which is discussed in Chapter 21). In reply, Congress adopted the Local Government Antitrust Act to exempt local government action from money damages, attorney's fees or costs. *See* 15 U.S.C. §34-36; Jim Rossi, *Antitrust Process and Vertical Deference: Judicial Review of State Regulatory Inaction*, 93 Iowa L. Rev. 185, 195-196 & n.43 (2007) (noting that LGAA was adopted in reply to *City of Boulder*).

10. In *United States v. Brown Univ.*, 5 F.3d 658 (3d Cir. 1993), the court held that an agreement among a number of elite universities to eliminate merit-based scholarships and regulate need-based scholarships was subject to antitrust under a "quick-look" standard. Congress responded with the Need-Based Education Aid Antitrust Protection Act, now codified at 15 U.S.C. §1 (note), to reverse that result.

11. In *Jung v. Assn. of Am. Med. Coll.*, 300 F. Supp. 2d 119 (D.D.C. 2004), a class of medical school graduates participating in the medical residency "matching" program sued the organizations involved in administering that program under Sherman Act §1. The matching program is a system for placing medical school graduates in residency programs on the basis of the applicants' and the programs' stated preferences. The plaintiffs alleged it was a restraint on what would otherwise have been a competitive labor market for medical residents. After the trial court refused to dismiss the case, and at the defendants' behest, Congress ended the suit by providing that matching programs do not violate §1. *See* 15 U.S.C. §37b; *Jung v. Assn. of Am. Med. Coll.*, 399 F. Supp. 2d 26, 40 (D.D.C. 2004) (noting the peculiar circumstances of the statute's passage but dismissing the plaintiff's case nonetheless).

Second, the courts have come to be (or at least purport to be) highly skeptical of statutory exemptions, and often say that they will interpret them narrowly. The enforcement agencies have long opposed them, and they have been criticized by each of the many blue-ribbon panels of policy experts set up over the years to study antitrust, such as the Antitrust Modernization Commission of 2005-2007. Other nations that have antitrust laws have mostly come to hold similar views. The European Commission, for example, has narrowed or repealed a number of its "block exemptions" of various industries.

§22.3 THE DOCTRINE OF "IMPLIED REPEAL"

As originally envisioned, implied repeal was to be reserved for cases of "plain repugnancy between . . . antitrust and [other] regulatory provisions. . . ."[12] It was to be found "only if necessary to make [some other statute] work, and even then only to the minimum extent necessary."[13] Prior to the 1970s, the courts rejected almost all such pleas, except where some agency was given explicit power to oversee conduct plainly in violation of antitrust, and there was apparently some requirement that the agency actually used its oversight power.[14]

However, in recent times the Supreme Court has shown a greater willingness to find implied repeal, and seems less insistent that there be explicit and irreconcilable conflict between antitrust and some other statute. The trend began in the mid-1970s, with decisions concerning the financial sector.[15] But the change became much more dramatic in a recent decision, *Credit Suisse Sec., LLC v. Billing*, 551 U.S. 264 (2007). At least with respect to questions involving securities regulation, the Court explicitly changed its traditional inquiry from a search for "plain repugnancy" between antitrust

12. *United States v. Philadelphia Natl. Bank*, 374 U.S. 321, 350-351 (1963).

13. *Silver*, 373 U.S. at 357.

14. *Borden*, 308 U.S. at 198 (holding that mere regulatory authority vested in a federal official, even if "plenary," does not in itself grant antitrust immunity); *cf. Gordon*, 422 U.S. at 692-693 (Stewart, J., concurring) (noting that, in the concurring Justices' view, the Court did not and never had held that immunity could be found merely on the basis of an unexercised power in some federal official).

15. *See Gordon v. New York Stock Exchange*, 422 U.S. 659 (1975) (finding immunity for securities exchange rules fixing brokerage commission rates, but only where Securities Exchange Act of 1934 explicitly empowered SEC to regulate such rates and SEC actively did so); *United States v. Natl. Assn. of Sec. Dealers*, 422 U.S. 694 (1975) (finding immunity for vertical restraints on distribution of mutual fund shares in secondary markets, but only where Investment Company Act of 1940 explicitly empowered SEC to oversee such restraints).

and some other statute, to a search for no more than a "clear incompatibility." Id. at 275. Clear incompatibility exists where:

1. the antitrust challenge is to "an area of conduct squarely within the heartland of [the other area of law]";
2. there is "clear and adequate [agency] authority to regulate";
3. there has been "active and ongoing agency regulation"; and
4. there is some "serious conflict between the antitrust and regulatory regimes."

Id. at 285. The Court added that implied repeal is more appropriate where the responsible regulatory authority is empowered to consider competition values, and other opinions have stressed this fact as well.[16]

The potential consequences of the new formulation seem fairly dramatic. At least in the financial sector, given the breadth of jurisdiction of the Securities and Exchange Commission (SEC), elements 1 through 3 should be fairly easy for most defendants to meet.[17] Moreover, the Court implied that "conflict," under element 4, requires only that the pendency of an antitrust suit—taking into consideration the costs and risks of false positives that the Court claimed would exist—would "prove practically incompatible with the SEC's administration of the Nation's securities laws. . . ."[18] This practical incompatibility can result from any number of factors that would make it unduly difficult for regulated persons to comply with both antitrust and the other regulatory regime. Among other things, *Credit Suisse* stressed that the same evidence would be relevant in actions against the challenged conduct under both the antitrust and securities laws, and that it might produce different results in the two contexts, even as against the same defendant. Practical incompatibility might occur even as to merely potential conflicts. For example, even if no current agency regulation permits or encourages anticompetitive conduct, the courts can hold that that conduct is exempt from antitrust if the agency *might* adopt such a regulation *someday*. Fundamentally, the "practical incompatibility" element seemed to boil down to whether making defendants subject to both antitrust and some other regulation would be merely burdensome, in the sense that the likelihood of liability is made too complex or uncertain. The Court also added the novel

---

16. *Credit Suisse*, 551 U.S. at 283; *see also Verizon Commcns. v. Law Offices of Curtis V. Trinko, LLP*, 540 U.S. 398, 412 (2004).

17. Importantly, the Court seemed to hold that conduct is in the "heartland," and therefore satisfies element number 1, merely where it is useful to securities markets. The Court held that syndicated underwriting—including collusively anticompetitive restraints—was important in this sense because certain efficiencies arise when an issuance is underwritten jointly. *See* 551 U.S. at 276. But the efficiencies the Court identified were no different than in any other, garden-variety joint venture arrangement.

18. 551 U.S. at 277. The Court's discussion of the costs of antitrust and their relevance to "clear incompatibility" appears at *id.* at 282-285.

observation that the availability of private relief under the securities laws should be relevant to whether antitrust applies to the challenged conduct. 551 U.S. at 277. That seemed rather a large change, since it will frequently be the case that anticompetitive conduct could be the gravamen for more than one cause of action. Over Justice Stevens's objection,[19] the Court held that the difficulties imposed on market participants in complying with both antitrust and securities regulation would constitute the requisite "conflict."

Example

The Centers for Medicare and Medicaid Services (CMMS), an agency within the federal Department of Health and Human Services, has been given a new statutory duty by Congress. In response to widely publicized misconduct in nursing homes, Congress amended the Medicare statute to increase CMMS oversight of homes that serve Medicare patients. Among other things, CMMS was given new authority to prohibit kickback schemes, in which homes make illegal side payments to doctors for referring patients to them. Now, Congress believed that some good had been accomplished as to this sort of conduct by ethical rules developed by private professional organizations, but Congress remained concerned about the risks of collusion or other misconduct by those organizations. Accordingly, the amendment empowered CMMS, "in its discretion," to promulgate rules to govern "procedures and arrangements for discussion or collaboration among nursing home administrators as to admissions and referral practices." In making those rules the agency was directed to "consider harm to competition that might arise from such discussion or collaboration," and to "prohibit undue anticompetitive effects." Finally, the statute makes clear that new rules can be enforced by CMMS through the agency's regular internal administrative enforcement proceedings, and violations can be punished by money penalties. CMMS has not yet promulgated rules as to "discussion or collaboration," and it has never brought enforcement action against such arrangements.

A group of doctors has brought Sherman Act §1 challenge to an alleged conspiracy among members of the National Association of Nursing Home Administrators (NANHA), a trade group of nursing homes. While they do not yet have explicit proof of a conspiracy, the plaintiffs allege that NANHA members have used their meetings at the organization as the opportunity collectively to put limits on how much they will bill Medicare for "visiting physicians"—third-party doctors who treat patients in the home on an as-needed basis. Visiting physician payments are perfectly legal under the Medicare statute, though occasionally circumstances can raise difficult

19. 551 U.S. at 288 (Stevens, J., concurring) ("Surely I would not suggest . . . that either the burdens of antitrust litigation or the risk 'that antitrust courts are likely to make unusually serious mistakes' . . . should play any role in the analysis.").

questions whether a given payment was a legitimate visiting physician fee or was a disguised, illegal kickback.

Will the plaintiffs succeed?

Explanation

It is not an easy question, but several factors under *Credit Suisse* suggest that this conduct might be exempt from antitrust under the doctrine of implied repeal. The problem is that the same collaborative conduct might be illegal under antitrust (at least in cases in which it relates to otherwise legal payments), but encouraged or permitted under rules to be promulgated by CMMS. Here, as in *Credit Suisse*, there is a risk that the same evidence will lead to different results in the two contexts—a finding of no antitrust liability but violation of CMMS regulations, or vice versa. It does not matter that CMMS has not yet made its rules or brought any enforcement actions, since *Credit Suisse* indicated that even the risk of future regulatory changes that might create conflict in the future can be enough for implicit repeal.

Importantly, despite what might appear to be a Congressional intent in favor of competition values, the language in the Medicare amendment requiring CMMS to "consider harm to competition" and "prohibit undue anticompetitive effects" will actually cut in favor of implied repeal. *Credit Suisse* pointed out that implied repeal is more appropriate where some agency has authority to consider competition values.

Still, the plaintiffs might be able to distinguish *Credit Suisse*. Perhaps, depending on the details of the Medicare amendment, they could show that CMMS would not be permitted or would be very unlikely ever to permit or encourage collaborative conduct that could violate antitrust. The plaintiffs also might be able to show that the line-drawing problems that would arise in this context, unlike those in the securities law context in *Credit Suisse*, will not be especially complex or require special expertise. *See In re Western States Wholesale Natural Gas Antitrust Litig.*, 661 F. Supp. 2d 1172, 1180 (D. Nev. 2009) ("Intent and the existence and scope of a conspiracy are matters which judges and juries resolve every day. Antitrust courts are not likely to make 'unusually serious mistakes' regarding intent, knowledge, purpose, or agreement, such that permissible or encouraged conduct under the [underlying regulatory statute, which also applied to defendants' conduct] would be deterred.")

§22.4 RULES OF JUDICIAL DEFERENCE: THE FILED RATE AND PRIMARY JURISDICTION DOCTRINES

The courts have established two doctrines under which the existence of a state or federal regulatory agency with jurisdiction over a given defendant may limit or delay the applicability of antitrust to that defendant—not preclude antitrust, but merely require deference to the regulator. Neither of these doctrines—the filed rate rule nor the rule of primary jurisdiction—is technically a rule of antitrust law. They are both rules of administrative law that apply to *any* cause of action that either challenges a filed rate or raises factual issues better answered in the first instance by a firm's regulatory overseer.

§22.4.1 The *Keogh* or Filed Rate Doctrine

Recall that at one time the U.S. economy was subject to fairly pervasive rate-and-entry regulation. Large swaths of the economy were more or less removed from competition, and operated in markets carefully managed and protected by government. Some of that regime lingers on, almost exclusively in the state governments. Many states still require some form or pre-use filing or even regulatory preapproval for insurance premiums, for example, and rate regulation can also be found in energy, transportation, communications, and other areas. Rate regulation typically requires the filing of a "tariff," which is a statement of the rate that the regulated firm proposes to charge for a particular service. In most cases, once the tariff is filed and approved (if it is subject to government preapproval), the firm *must* charge the tariff price, and cannot deviate from it unless permitted by law. This rule reflects the long-standing commitment within the tradition of rate-and-entry regulation that regulated firms should not be allowed to discriminate as among their customers.

To be clear, the filed rate doctrine is more than just an antitrust immunity. It is really two rules. First, it provides that a filed rate—a rate required to be filed with any federal or state agency—cannot be challenged in court on *any* grounds, not just antitrust. Second, it provides that once a rate is properly filed, the regulated firm *must* charge that rate, and cannot deviate from it for particular customers. Although the very idea of prefiled rates and the emphasis on nondiscrimination is rather out of step with current politics and economic thinking, the Court has reaffirmed its commitment to the enforcement of filed rates quite recently.[20]

Under this rule, private plaintiffs may not sue in antitrust for money damages to challenge a rate that is subject to filing with a state or federal regulatory agency. This aspect of the doctrine originated in *Keogh v. Chicago & Nw. Ry. Co.*, 260 U.S. 156 (1922), where the plaintiff brought antitrust

20. *See Maislin Indus., U.S., Inc. v. Primary Steel, Inc.*, 497 U.S. 116, 126-128 (1990) (canvassing history of the doctrine and observing that "Despite the harsh effects of the . . . doctrine, we have consistently adhered to it.").

challenge to rates fixed by a cartel of railroads, and filed with the federal Interstate Commerce Commission (ICC). The Supreme Court acknowledged that even ICC-approved rates might be lower if they are not the product of collusion, and therefore that Keogh might theoretically have suffered injury of the kind the antitrust laws remedy. The opinion acknowledged that the Court itself had previously held that a *government* suit is permissible to challenge the collusive fixing of rates even if those rates are "fair and reasonable" and are subject to oversight of the ICC. *See id.* at 161-162 (citing *United States v. Joint Traffic Assn.*, 171 U.S. 505 (1898), and *United States v. Trans-Missouri Freight Assn.*, 166 U.S. 290 (1897)). But the Court explicitly rejected an alternative solution proposed by the plaintiff, that his antitrust action could merely be stayed while the ICC conducted hearings to determine whether his proposed rate would be legally permitted under the ICC's statute. *Id.* at 164. Though *Keogh* has been much criticized, it is still the law.[21]

Other case law in the Supreme Court and lower courts have faced a number of issues surrounding the filed rate doctrine. First, a case decided about 20 years later, *Georgia v. Pennsylvania R.R. Co.*, 324 U.S. 439 (1945), held that *Keogh* does not bar private injunctive relief. However, it has since become clear that this injunctive relief is not available to challenge the rate itself—only to conduct surrounding the formulation of the rate.

Next, there remains uncertainty whether the agency must first "approve" or even review the substance of the tariff for the filed rate doctrine to apply. Usually, a party frustrated by some filed rate can seek relief before the agency itself. If disappointed by that result the party may be able to seek judicial review in the courts as a matter of administrative law. That sort of relief might in many ways be fairly disappointing to the party,[22] but many courts have held that as long as there is some such remedy, the party may not bring any other sort of cause of action against the regulated entity to challenge the rate itself.

Thus, *Keogh* only bars private money damages actions by rate payers that seek recovery for harms caused by filed rates themselves. It does not affect any other sort of antitrust action. Thus, it does not affect government antitrust actions at all, it does not bar money damages actions for harms caused by conduct other than the rates themselves, and most courts hold that it does not bar suits by the regulated entity's *competitors*. The rationale for

---

21. Notably, in *Square D Co. v. Niagara Frontier Tariff Bureau*, 760 F.2d 1347 (1986), the esteemed Judge Henry Friendly issued a long and scholarly opinion raising substantial doubts about the doctrine's vitality, which more or less explicitly invited the Supreme Court to overturn *Keogh*. Before the Court itself the U.S. Solicitor General agreed. The Court refused, however, and broadly reaffirmed *Keogh*, mainly on grounds of *stare decisis*. 476 U.S. 409 (1986).

22. It may be disappointing because the standard of review applied by courts is usually deferential to the agency, and because the best remedy that can be hoped for is merely remand to the agency for further proceedings. Ordinarily the party would have no hope of recovery of any money, and would have no rights at all as against the entity that filed the rate.

permitting competitor suits is that, unlike suits by customers, competitor challenge to the propriety of a filed rate is not likely to be at odds with the nondiscrimination policy of rate regulation.

§22.4.2 The Rule of Primary Jurisdiction

There are also cases in which, even though there is no "filed rate" and therefore no bar to private damages actions, the courts will delay an antitrust suit to wait for some action by a federal regulatory agency. The stated rationale is usually that some issues within the case, which are necessary for resolution of the antitrust suit, would be best left to the judgment of the agency. The courts often describe the agency as having more expertise in the particular industry. Courts also often state a concern for the risk of inconsistent judgments. If an antitrust suit finds some conduct to be illegal, but an agency with concurrent jurisdiction finds it to be legal, regulated parties will be subject to conflicting rules.

As Judge Posner explained in a leading opinion, this "doctrine of primary jurisdiction," as it is called, has come to be "really two doctrines. . . ." One of them is mandatory and one of them is within the discretion of a court considering an antitrust suit. *Arsberry v. Illinois*, 244 F.3d 558, 563 (7th Cir. 2001). First, the mandatory rule recognizes that some issues might arise in the course of an antitrust lawsuit that are within the exclusive jurisdiction of a federal agency. In such a case, the federal court must postpone the antitrust action and await final resolution of the agency's issue. Second, the courts, even though they were not required to do so, have also recognized in many cases that some issue *might* be resolved by an agency with regulatory oversight over a party, and they assert some discretion in these cases to postpone a pending federal antitrust case until the agency has had a chance to resolve it. In other words, there are cases in which the courts and an agency have concurrent jurisdiction, as opposed to the agency's exclusive jurisdiction over some matter.

A leading example of the second (and, as we will see, much more complicated) concept is *Ricci v. Chicago Mercantile Exch.*, 409 U.S. 289 (1973). There the Court considered an antitrust challenge by Ricci, a commodities trader, who had been a member of the Chicago Mercantile Exchange. Ricci was effectively expelled when that Exchange transferred his membership to another trader without notice or hearing. The Exchange purported to make that transfer according to membership rules that it was required to adopt as a commodities exchange regulated by the Commodity Futures Trading Commission (CFTC). An important fact in the case was that the CFTC had the power to investigate conduct by the Exchange and to determine whether its actions were made pursuant to rules that were "valid" under the CFTC's organic statute, the Commodities Exchange Act. A private trader like Ricci was entitled under the statute to sue the Exchange before the CFTC, and could have brought such a case to challenge the transfer that was at issue in his antitrust suit.

The *Ricci* Court stayed the antitrust claim until the CFTC could rule on whether the Exchange's membership rule was valid or not. The Court thought there was a significant possibility that the challenged conduct would in fact trigger the "implied repeal" doctrine and be immune from antitrust (*see* §22.3), but only if it turned out that the rule was valid. The Court also emphasized that "prior agency adjudication" of the rule-validity issue "[would] be a material aid in ultimately deciding whether the Commodity Exchange Act forecloses [the plaintiff's] antitrust suit" because of the particular fact issues the case presented. Those fact issues and "questions about the scope, meaning and significance" of various rules of the Exchange "are matters that should be dealt with in the first instance by those especially familiar with the customs and practices of the industry and of the unique marketplace involved in this case." *Id.* at 305.

Importantly, *Ricci* observed the similarity of the case to *Silver v. New York Stock Exchange*, 373 U.S. 341 (1963). Over the defendant's objection that the implied repeal doctrine should apply, *Silver* had held antitrust fully applicable to the conduct of the New York Stock Exchange. The Court so held even though the Exchange was pervasively regulated by the Securities and Exchange Commission, and even though the specific Exchange rules at issue in the case were subject to approval by the Commission. The *Ricci* Court distinguished *Silver* on one specific basis—that, unlike the SEC in the *Silver* case, the CFTC was empowered to hear complaints in individual cases like Ricci's. The Court considered it significant as well that the CFTC's statute did not call on it to consider antitrust law or competition values in adjudicating a challenge to the Exchange's rules. 409 U.S. at 302 n.13.

Ricci noted explicitly that it did not find conduct within CFTC jurisdiction to be exempt from antitrust, 409 U.S. at 302 n.13, and that the purpose of referring the matter to the CFTC was not so that the CFTC could rule on the issue of antitrust immunity. That issue would be for the court. *Id.* at 306. The only issue for the CFTC was whether the Exchange had acted pursuant to a valid rule. If not, then the antitrust suit would be viable, if so, then a federal court would have to determine whether that conduct would be immune from antitrust.

One remaining uncertainty in this area is just how much discretion a district court has to decide whether or not to stay a case to await agency proceedings. The doctrine is plainly discretionary in the sense that it is not absolutely mandatory. In *Arsberry* Judge Posner wrote:

> Cases in which a court refers an issue to an agency because of the agency's superior expertise . . . rather than because of the agency's jurisdiction, are not felicitously described as cases of primary *jurisdiction*. They are akin to those . . .

> abstention cases [in which courts seek agency input because they] concern arcane regulatory issues; or cases in which the court solicits an amicus curiae brief from an interested agency; or cases in which the court has in effect appointed the agency to be a special master. . . . In such cases, either court and agency have concurrent jurisdiction to decide an issue, or only the court has the power to decide it, and seeks merely the agency's advice.

244 F.3d at 563-564. In another leading opinion, Judge Calabresi wrote:

> The concept does not mean that the district court lacks *jurisdiction* over the dispute or that the litigant must bring the relevant claims to the administrative authorityfirst. . . . [P]rimary jurisdiction is neither jurisdictional nor primary. While the court of appeals [in the *Ricci* case] invoked primary jurisdiction to stop the suit from immediately proceeding further in the district court, by instructing the district court to stay the action pending agency review, it implicitly recognized both that the district court had *jurisdiction* and that bringing the suit *originally* in that court was perfectly proper.

MFS Sec. Corp. v. New York Stock Exchange, Inc., 277 F.3d 613, 621-622 (2d Cir. 2002). But on the other hand, MFS itself described the referral to the agency as "what *should* be done in cases of this sort," 277 F.3d at 622 (emphasis added), and reversed the district court for failure to make a referral. Both the Supreme Court and courts of appeals have reversed district courts both for referring and for failing to refer, and there is some authority holding that the doctrine is not discretionary at all.[23]

23. *See, e.g.*, *United States v. Gen. Dynamics Corp.*, 828 F.2d 1356, 1364 n.15 (9th Cir. 1987) ("As we read the cases . . . an issue either is within an agency's primary jurisdiction or it is not, and, if it is, a court may not act until the agency has made its the initial determination. Failure to defer when the doctrine so mandates is reversible error, . . . as is deferral in inappropriate situations").

CHAPTER 23

The Labor Exemption

§23.1 THE PROBLEM OF LABOR IN ANTITRUST

§23.1.1 Introduction

§23.1.1(a) Background

While it may not seem so obvious today, antitrust and labor law are in natural tension. The policy of antitrust is price competition—that sellers of goods and services must fight with one another for sales, and that the only weapons permitted in that fight are to make better goods or sell them more cheaply. Labor policy is essentially the opposite. Sellers of this particular service—human labor—are permitted by law to increase their profits by collectively coercing their buyers. And there is no serious question that successful union activities have consequences of the kind antitrust normally aims to prevent. Where workers succeed in raising their wages or improving benefits or employment terms, they succeed in using market power to increase the cost to producers of an input. The result in at least some cases is likely increased price for consumers.

While there is reason to believe the Congress of 1890 did not intend to outlaw organized labor,[1] if the contemporary law of Sherman Act §1 were

1. *See* Douglas L. Leslie, *Principles of Labor Antitrust*, 66 Va. L. Rev. 1183, 1192 & n.27 (1980) (noting this point and criticizing early antitrust opinions for misunderstanding it); Theodore J. St. Antoine, Connell: *Antitrust Law at the Expense of Labor Law*, 62 Va. L. Rev. 603, 604 & n.7 (1976) (so arguing). Importantly, it is universally acknowledged that the drafters of the Sherman Act

the only applicable law, then collective efforts by labor groups to improve employment terms would probably be "conspiracies in restraint of trade," and serious ones at that. Within the Sherman Act's great generality, workers are like other providers of goods or services engaged in "trade or commerce," and are obliged to provide their services in competition with one another. So if they go on strike—if they refuse to work except in exchange for an increase in their wages—they are engaged in a naked horizontal price-fixing conspiracy, and they are attempting to enforce it through a concerted horizontal boycott. A collective bargaining agreement with an employer, too, would constitute a naked, horizontal price-fixing agreement with a vertical component. Most collective action by workers, in other words, would be plainly illegal under the terms of Sherman Act §1.

But obviously all such things are permitted under current law. Under most circumstances what we think of as ordinary union activity is perfectly legal. In this respect labor is simply one of those many compromises within our economic policy of which antitrust is also a part. While it is true that we ordinarily espouse a strong commitment to price-competitive markets, there are times when other public values—in this case, the hope is to preserve human dignity and living wages—are purchased at the expense of some allocational efficiency.

But saying that much is the easy part. Reaching that accommodation took many years and much give-and-take between Congress and the judiciary. The resulting law is complex and hard to predict, and understanding this so-called "labor exemption" poses certain distinct challenges. First, labor law itself is quite complicated. It is composed of a half-dozen fairly detailed statutes, a body of administrative regulations, and decades of case law from the courts and a federal agency known as the National Labor Relations Board. Second, the nature of the problem does not lend itself to simple solutions. It is an attempt to reconcile two directly opposed policies, and the cases that raise the conflict tend to come up in varying and unpredictable factual scenarios. Finally, a real problem in understanding labor scenarios is that union motives can sometimes be ambiguous. National labor policy obviously contemplates that unions can use coercive force to raise wages or improve terms and conditions of employment. But they might seek to serve those goals in a lot of different ways. They might undertake peaceful, good faith negotiation backed up only by the threat of collective refusal to work. Everyone agrees that that is permitted at current

---

intended the phrase "restraint of trade" merely to incorporate what they believed to be the common-law term of art that went by that name. While there is in fact less certainty what the term meant than the drafters apparently believed, *see* William Letwin, *Law and Economic Policy in America* 15-17, 51-52 (1965), prior to 1890 labor groups were rarely if ever challenged by way of the doctrine of restraints of trade, *see Apex Hosiery Co. v. Leader*, 310 U.S. 469, 502-503 (1940) (surveying common law history); Hans B. Thorelli, *The Federal Antitrust Policy* 40-41 (1955).

law. But they might also engage in violence or, more to the point, they might use their influence to create marketplace mischief. At the extreme, no one believes the labor exemption permits the unions to take part in severe restraints that occur outside the labor market itself, even though that sort of action might help them to achieve their own central goals of better wages and working conditions. As the Supreme Court once wrote,

> [I]f [a group of] unions had made . . . a demand [to establish a schedule of retail prices at which a group of employers could sell their products], we seriously doubt that either the unions or [employers] could claim immunity by reason of the labor exemption, whatever substantive questions of violation there might be.

Amalgamated Meat Cutters v. Jewel Tea Co., 381 U.S. 676, 689 (1965). Accordingly, even in those moments of its greatest sympathy to labor, the Court has always believed that antitrust "embrace[s] to some extent and in some circumstances labor unions and their activities. . . ." *Apex Hosiery Co. v. Leader*, 310 U.S. 469, 487 (1940). The problem remains to say where the line falls between the permitted and the prohibited, and that has proved controversial.

§23.1.1(b) Summary of the Law

It might help to try summarizing this body of law in a few different ways. First, the modern doctrine of the labor exemption can be thought of as, in effect, three separate rules:

1. *The statutory exemption: unilateral union conduct is exempt.* Collective action taken by a group of people who are employees,[2] which the group takes unilaterally in support of its members' personal interests, is exempt from antitrust. Strikes and picketing of the employer are examples. Some such conduct can violate *labor* law, but it does not violate antitrust.

---

2. As opposed to those who act as independent entrepreneurs. Entrepreneurs or independent contractors, who do not enjoy any antitrust exemption for "labor," are those who do not work in exchange for wages and under the supervision of an employer. For example, a group of fishermen who each own their own boats, and individually sell their catch to a fish processing company, cannot form a union to increase the pay they receive for their fish. This is so even though there may be an imbalance of bargaining power between them, even if the fish processor is a monopsonist that abuses its power against them. In the contemplation of antitrust and labor policy, these fishermen are really just independent business people who have conspired to fix their prices. *Columbia River Packers Assn. v. Hinton*, 315 U.S. 143 (1942). *See also Am. Med. Assn. v. United States*, 317 U.S. 519 (1943) (treating doctor members of association as independent contractors where they collectively boycotted parties attempting to develop competing model of health care delivery).

2. *The nonstatutory exemption: collaboration with nonunion parties.* Collective bargaining agreements, other agreements with employers, and agreements with third parties are exempt if they are "intimately related to wages, hours and working conditions. . . ."
3. *The bar against union-employer collusion: the* Allen Bradley *Rule.* One thing a union cannot do is conspire with employers or third parties in those other parties' own antitrust violations. This is the rule of *Allen Bradley Co. v. IBEW Loc.* 3, 325 U.S. 797 (1945).

Second, a different way we can summarize this same body of law is to consider just exactly what sort of conduct unions and employers can engage in. In general, persons engaged in work as employees may:

- Organize for the purpose of improving their wages and terms of employment,
- Use nonviolent means of economic coercion against their employers to secure their desired improvements,
- Enter into agreements with those employers as to wages and terms of employment, and
- To a lesser extent, make agreements with third parties (like agents who find them work) who are especially important to the preservation of their employment terms.

Likewise, employers can:

- Negotiate with labor groups and enter into contracts with them as to terms and conditions of employment,
- Negotiate collectively with other employers, in "multiemployer collective bargaining units," and
- Enter into agreements with one another that do not involve any labor parties, where the agreements concern terms and conditions of employment and are offered to labor before an impasse in negotiations.

Example

The Yankee Clipper Medical Coalition, Inc., is a newly formed nonprofit entity whose members are physicians practicing in the tristate region at the meeting place of Maine, New Hampshire, and Massachusetts. They have begun to struggle financially, and they believe it is because of the rising power of large insurance companies. They have agreed to abide by a set of rules, including among them minimum fees they will charge for certain services. They have incorporated their rules into a document they have entitled the "Yankee Clipper Medical Manifesto." They decide to mail a copy of the Manifesto to each of the insurers with whom they deal. Their cover letter, on the advice of counsel, describes their actions as a "strike" and identifies the Manifesto as a proposed collective bargaining agreement.

They are sued for injunction against their strike by the U.S. Justice Department. What result?

Explanation

The arrangement is illegal and will be enjoined. Physicians and other professionals have traditionally been held to be independent "entrepreneurs" rather than "employees," and therefore they are neither subject to federal labor legislation nor do they enjoy any labor exemption from antitrust law. *See supra* note 2. This particular conspiracy is also a minimum price-fixing conspiracy that is not obviously ancillary to any procompetitive arrangement, and therefore it is probably per se illegal.

§23.1.2 A (Very) Brief History: The Early Judicial Hostility and the Rise of the Modern Statutory Regime

American labor policy is old. The first agitation to organize workers lies somewhere early in the country's history. There are known to have been clashes as early as the late eighteenth and early nineteenth centuries, associated with the disintegration of the traditional, household-based apprenticeship organization of most production, and its replacement by larger-scale manufacturing and broader distribution. Already by the early nineteenth century there were attempts by employers and governments to use doctrines of criminal conspiracy and the common law of restraints of trade to prevent organized efforts by disaffected workers. That approach was successful early in the nineteenth century but, perhaps because of the growing public tolerance of organized labor, legal action against unions had largely waned by mid-century. However, it began to return again with a vengeance after the Civil War. The rapid industrialization of that period, and the much larger, landless and low-paid workforce it engendered, led to more aggressive union agitation and renewed legal attacks against the unions. By the early twentieth century employers and the government retaliated by using Sherman Act §1 as a tool to enjoin labor organization. *See Loewe v. Lawlor*, 208 U.S. 274 (1908).

Congress responded in 1914 with two provisions in the Clayton Act, designed to exempt labor from federal antitrust law. First, Clayton Act §6, 15 U.S.C. §17, provides in relevant part that "[t]he labor of a human being is not a commodity or article of commerce. Nothing contained in the antitrust laws shall be construed to forbid the existence and operation of labor . . . organizations" that do no more than "lawfully carry[] out the legitimate objects thereof. . . ." Further, Clayton Act §20 (which now appears in the labor-relations title of the U.S. Code, at 29 U.S.C. §52), prohibits federal courts from restraining "dispute[s] concerning the terms or conditions of employment," and provides that a specific list of "peaceful [and] lawful" means used in the conduct of such a dispute cannot violate federal law. These two rules turned out to be pretty easy to evade by a recalcitrant judiciary, however, which simply ruled that these statutes, by their language, still left it to the courts to determine what were the "legitimate objects" of labor organizations, and that even those specific actions explicitly protected in §20 were protected only where they occurred exclusively between an employee and his employer. *Duplex Printing Press Co. v. Deering*, 254 U.S. 443, 468-470 (1921).

Congressional frustration with judicial intransigence led to another burst of legislation, between 1926 and 1935. First, the Norris-LaGuardia Act of 1932, 29 U.S.C. §§101-110, 113-115, part of the initial New Deal economic package, amplified the prohibition on labor injunctions that Congress had intended to adopt in Clayton Act §20. Then, in 1935, Congress finally adopted a comprehensive scheme of federal labor regulation, the National Labor Relations Act (NLRA). With adoption of the NLRA, Congress moved beyond mere tolerance to active encouragement of labor organization, and began an effort to readjust the balance of power more in labor's favor. Specifically, the NLRA sets out a procedural framework for the creation of unions and the recognition of particular unions as bargaining representatives in a given industry. That framework imposes a mandatory duty of both employer and employees to negotiate in good faith as to wages, hours and terms and conditions of employment when a union has been formally recognized. The NLRA also regulates the process of collective bargaining itself, by making some practices illegal, and by setting up an administrative agency to enforce and oversee administration of the labor laws, known as the National Labor Relations Board (NLRB).

Two aspects of this labor law regime have special relevance to antitrust. First, the NLRA provides that where employees of a given employer have properly unionized, the union and its employer *must* come together to bargain "in good faith" as to certain subjects. These "mandatory subjects of bargaining" are defined by the NLRA to include "wages, hours and other terms and conditions of employment. . . ." 29 U.S.C. §158(d). To be clear, neither employers nor labor is ever obligated to actually agree to anything, and if they reach "impasse" after good-faith attempts to resolve differences, either of them may take coercive action (the union may strike and the employer may lock workers out of the workplace). But they must make good faith efforts to negotiate, and refusal of a party to do so can result in NLRB order that the parties negotiate (and occasionally in some other penalties). "[W]ages" and "hours" are straightforward enough, but the meaning of "other terms and conditions of employment" has had to be worked out before the NLRB and the courts. Generally speaking, the term entails policies with direct bearing on the worker's experience of working for the employer, such as work assignments and safety rules.

Second, among the "unfair labor practices" prohibited in the NLRA as amended were so-called "secondary" practices, which are actions that parties to a dispute take against neutral third parties. Most common among these are two. A union might try to pressure a firm that does business with an employer to stop dealing with the employer. This is known as a "secondary boycott." Similarly, the union might try to pressure its employer not to deal in the goods of some third-party firm that the union is attempting to organize. This is known as a "hot cargo agreement." Both are illegal as a matter of labor law, and this has consequences for antitrust treatment.

The only explicit statutory exemptions of labor activity from antitrust—which were contained in the Clayton and Norris-LaGuardia Acts—protect the activities of labor *unions*, and not even all actions undertaken by them. A problem the judiciary sooner or later would have to face was that in order for unions to bargain collectively with their employers, they must reach agreements with employers that might constitute "contract[s], combination[s], . . . or conspirac[ies]" under Sherman Act §1. Importantly, the statutory exemptions have been held not to cover a union's agreements with "non-labor parties," including employers and multiemployer groups. The statutory exemptions do not in themselves exempt even the basic "collective bargaining agreement" that a union makes with employers, which is the very purpose for a union's existence. Accordingly, as will be discussed below, the courts have developed what has come to be known as the "nonstatutory labor exemption" to cover those important areas of conduct.

§23.2 THE MODERN DOCTRINAL FRAMEWORK: THE "STATUTORY" EXEMPTION, THE "NONSTATUTORY" EXEMPTION, AND THE *ALLEN BRADLEY* RULE

As mentioned, the modern law of the labor antitrust exemption can be thought of as two separate, complementary rules: a "statutory" exemption that protects the unilateral conduct of employee groups themselves, and a "nonstatutory" exemption that protects their relationships with nonlabor third parties. There also appears to remain one special rule, that no labor-management agreement is legal in which a union conspires with employers to restrain trade outside the labor market (the so-called *Allen Bradley* rule).

The law of the labor exemptions, as we now know it, essentially began its existence only in 1941, and developed in three distinct steps:

- Creation of the "statutory" exemption in 1941 in *United States v. Hutcheson*, 312 U.S. 419 (1941),
- Creation of the *Allen Bradley* rule against union-employer conspiracy in 1945 in *Allen Bradley Co. v. IBEW Loc.* 3, 325 U.S. 797 (1945), and
- Creation of the nonstatutory exemption in 1965 in two companion cases, *United Mine Workers v. Pennington*, 381 U.S. 657 (1965), and *Amalgamated Meat Cutters v. Jewel Tea Co.*, 381 U.S. 676 (1965).

§23.2.1 The Statutory Exemption

The "statutory" exemption is by far the simplest of these rules. The idea originates in *United States v. Hutcheson*, 312 U.S. 419 (1941), where the Court recognized exemption for a union that, displeased with the Anheuser-Busch outfit, struck at one of its locations and orchestrated a nationwide consumer boycott of its beer. *Hutcheson* set out the following, now defining criterion: "So long as a union acts in its self-interest and does not combine with non-labor groups," then the courts will not make "any judgment regarding the wisdom or unwisdom, the rightness or wrongness, the selfishness or unselfishness of the end of which the particular union activities are the means." *Id.* at 232. In other words, as long as two criteria are met—that the union acts only in its own self-interest and does not combine with a nonlabor group—then the effect of Clayton Act §20 and the Norris-LaGuardia Act is to make that conduct fully exempt from antitrust.

The statutory exemption rule of *Hutcheson* has come to be subject to a latter-day nuance. Although strictly speaking the statutory exemption applies only where the union acts unilaterally—where it acts in its own self-interest and does not combine with nonlabor groups—the Supreme Court has occasionally broadened it a bit to cover agreements with groups that are nominally nonlabor but that are essential to the union's pursuit of its central objectives. The Court has explained this nuance in two cases. *Am. Fedn. of Musicians v. Carroll*, 391 U.S. 99 (1968), involved a musicians union that included both ordinary players ("sidemen") and band leaders. The leaders were just players themselves, except that when they acted as leaders, they also took on the role of arranging one-time performances. The union's rules set minimum fees that were to be charged both for leaders and sidemen, and required that a minimum number of sidemen be used for performances. A member acting as leader, strictly speaking, stood in the shoes of an independent contractor and an employer, except that, as players, they also were members of the union and were bound by its rules. The Court held that the band leaders should be considered part of the "labor group" for purposes of the exemption, because failure to do so would erode the wages the union had secured for its members through price competition among leaders. The court wrote that an outside person or group can be within a "labor group" so long as there is some "job or wage competition or some other economic relationship affecting legitimate union interests between the union members and the [outside group]." For similar reasons, *H.A. Artists & Assocs., Inc. v. Actors' Equity Assn.*, 451 U.S. 704 (1981) held exempt a rule of an actors union prohibiting members from using theatrical agents not licensed by the union.

Example

The National Academy of Phlebotomy Arts & Sciences, or NAPAS, is a nonprofit organization whose members are all professional phlebotomists — that is, they are the people who stick a needle in your arm and draw your blood, at the hospital or in a medical lab, or when you donate blood to organizations like the Red Cross. The group does not sell any product or service and depends on its members' annual dues to cover its operating costs.

In all states phlebotomists are required to undergo some minimum training and testing in order to work as phlebotomists. However, membership in the NAPAS is not required in any state. Still, about 65 percent of the working phlebotomists in the United States are NAPAS members, in large part because they receive certain benefits from membership. In particular, they receive free continuing education services that they need in most states to keep their licenses current. They can also purchase cheap insurance through NAPAS and receive certain other promotional benefits.

NAPAS maintains a short list of membership rules, and not infrequently expels members for failure to comply with them. Among other things, the rules require that no member phlebotomist may work more than 40 hours per week. NAPAS defends this rule by pointing out that, in the organization's view, overly tired phlebotomists are at a greater risk of injuring patients and committing malpractice.

Does the NAPAS rule violate federal antitrust?

Explanation

A necessary first question is whether antitrust applies. NAPAS should have a fairly good case here for the statutory labor exemption. The organization is a "labor group" in that it consists of "employees" (or so it would clearly seem — phlebotomists seem likely to be employed by hospitals or organizations). The rule, as far as we can tell from these facts, is unilaterally imposed by NAPAS, and because it relates to a core labor policy concern — hours of work — it would appear to be an action in the employees' own self-interest. If so, the rule would be immune under the statutory exemption under *Hutcheson*. The labor exemption might not apply if the phlebotomists could be shown not to be employees.

If the labor exemption did not apply, then this rule presumably would be illegal. It is a naked restraint on output, so it is either per se illegal or, given the purportedly professional nature of the organization, subject to quick-look review. Presumably the quick look would be a quick one indeed, given cases such as *Indiana Federation of Dentists*, discussed in Chapter 8.

§23.2.2 The Nonstatutory Exemption

A more difficult concept is the "nonstatutory" labor exemption. The courts recognized early that if the only exemption were the statutory exemption of *Hutcheson*, which only protects the unilateral acts of labor groups, then much ordinary conduct necessary for organized labor to work would violate antitrust (e.g., a collective bargaining agreement with an employer—a "nonlabor" party). The need for a judicially created "nonstatutory" exemption to complement *Hutcheson*, now a cornerstone of labor exemption jurisprudence, originates in the thinking of Justice Byron White. His thoughts appeared in two companion decisions, by a badly fractured Court, issued on the same day in 1965, *United Mine Workers v. Pennington*, 381 U.S. 657 (1965), and *Amalgamated Meat Cutters v. Jewel Tea Co.*, 381 U.S. 676 (1965). Neither case produced an opinion for a majority of Justices. They both resulted in three separate opinions joined by three Justices each. However, in each case Justice White wrote an opinion that has been most influential.

Where agreement with a nonlabor group is challenged, Justice White's opinions in *Pennington* and *Jewel Tea* explicitly state that the proper inquiry is a raw balancing of the two conflicting federal policies. Neither those nor the Court's handful of subsequent opinions on point gives much clear guidance on how this balancing is to be done. As Justice White wrote in *Pennington*:

> [W]e are concerned here with harmonizing the Sherman Act with the national policy expressed in the National Labor Relations Act of promoting "the peaceful settlement of industrial disputes by subjecting labor-management controversies to the mediatory influence of negotiation."

Pennington, 381 U.S. at 665. Accordingly, the ultimate question in nonstatutory exemption cases is whether any agreement with a nonlabor group is so

> intimately related to wages, hours and working conditions that the union's successful attempt to obtain [it] through bona fide, arm's-length bargaining in pursuit of their own labor union policies . . . falls within the protection of the national labor policy.

Jewel Tea, 381 U.S. at 689-690. It is hard to make too much more from the language of these opinions than can be gotten in these broad abstractions, but for what it may be worth the question seems broadly to be whether the particular challenged agreement with a nonlabor group has effects too far outside the core concerns of national labor policy (i.e., concerns beyond the wages, hours, and working conditions of the employees at issue).

In *Pennington* itself, a union was alleged to have agreed with a multiemployer bargaining unit that the union would impose the wages agreed to on all other employers, knowing that some of the employers in question would be unable to survive at that wage level. The Court found the agreement unprotected by the labor exemption. It was not determinative that this agreement related to a mandatory topic of bargaining, and the most central of them no less—the union members' wages. *Pennington*, 381 U.S. at 664-665. The Court's chief reason seems to have been that, in its view, the agreement was contrary to the union members' own interests, and therefore not consistent even with labor policy. "The union's [own] obligation to its members," said the Court, "would seem best served" if the union were not "strait-jacketed" by the prior wage agreement in its subsequent negotiations with other employers. *Id.* at 666. Because labor policy would not favor union agreements contrary to union members' own interests, the balancing between labor policy and antitrust policy would be resolved in favor of antitrust.

But Justice White held that the exemption did apply in *Jewel Tea*. There, a union of butchers negotiated a collective bargaining agreement with grocery stores that set not only their own wages and working conditions, but also fixed the hours during which their employers could keep their meat departments open. This had the effect of constraining "self-service" meat counters, which were only then becoming feasible through better packaging and refrigeration. In other words, it was a restraint on competition in the product market, as well as in the market for the butchers' own labor. Nevertheless, the agreement might have had consequences for the butchers' interests, because preparing foods for the self-service counters might have resulted in more work or longer hours for them. Justice White found the agreement exempt from antitrust because it was "intimately related to wages, hours and working conditions. . . ."

By contrast, in *Connell Constr. Co. v. Plumbers & Steamfitters, Loc. Union No. 100*, 421 U.S. 616 (1975), the Court held the consequences of a union agreement to be too far afield from the central concern with wages, hours and working conditions. In this case, the defendant plumbers union, whose members worked for plumbing subcontractor firms, pressured general contractor firms to deal only with unionized subcontractors.[3] The Court found

3. Though this particular sort of secondary boycott seemed to be explicitly permitted by the NLRA, the Court held otherwise.

this to constitute an improper influence by the union with competition among subcontractors.

The nonstatutory labor exemption can be of benefit to employers. In *Brown v. Pro Football, Inc.*, 518 U.S. 231 (1996), professional football players entered negotiations with the multiemployer bargaining unit, the NFL. The parties bargained to impasse, and thereafter the NFL simply imposed a wage agreement on a particular class of players. That collectively imposed wage might otherwise have been an illegal price-fixing arrangement, but it had also been the team owners' last, best offer during negotiations. The Court held that this agreement—even though only employers, and no employees, were parties to it—was within the exemption because multi-employer bargaining was such a fixed feature of the national labor policy. Moreover, the Court felt that if employers could not impose terms and conditions that had been offered at the point of impasse by a multiemployer bargaining unit, they would be in an unfair bind. If some of them stuck with those terms, but others reverted to less favorable terms, said the Court, those imposing less favorable terms could be challenged for an "unfair labor practice."

Example

A group of broadcast and cable television networks recently settled a dispute with the union representing their staff writers by executing a collective bargaining agreement (CBA), governing the writers' wages and terms of employment. However, one of the networks that signed the CBA did so only under protest, and after it was executed that network filed antitrust suit against both the union and the other networks. The plaintiff challenges the following specific terms of the CBA:

1. A requirement that no employers party to the CBA can refuse to deal with a prospective employee writer solely because that person is represented by an agent. Virtually all of the union writers are represented by an agent, and the agents ordinarily negotiate the writers' employment deals with the networks. It so happens that the union also has adopted an internal rule, which is not referenced in the CBA, providing that union writers should only hire agents who are preapproved by the union. The plaintiff challenges this rule as well.
2. A requirement that network-produced television programs run no more than 30 episodes per season.

Will the plaintiff succeed?

Explanation

From what we can tell from these facts, all relevant conduct is at least arguably exempt under either the statutory or nonstatutory labor exemption. First, note that there is no antitrust violation merely in the fact that the employers have each agreed to the CBA. They are horizontal competitors with one another, and they themselves are not protected by the statutory labor exemption because they are not "employees." However, the nonstatutory labor exemption protects multiemployer bargaining, because, even though it is not explicitly exempted from antitrust, it is contemplated by federal labor law.

Both of the arrangements relating to agency representation are also very likely exempt. First, the CBA provision against refusal to deal with represented writers seems to be "intimately related to wages, hours and working conditions," as were the CBA terms in *Jewel Tea*. Second, the union's own internal policy of agent preapproval, perhaps somewhat surprisingly, is likely protected by the statutory exemption. Even though the agents are not employees of the same employers as the writers, and therefore might seem like they are part of a nonlabor group, there probably is an "economic relationship affecting legitimate union interests between the union members and [their agents]" sufficient to bring the policy within the rule of *Am. Fedn. of Musicians v. Carroll* and *H.A. Artists & Assocs., Inc. v. Actors' Equity Assn.*

Finally, the CBA limitation on the length of program seasons seems a much harder case, but it is still arguably exempt. First of all, to be clear, it is not within the statutory exemption, because it is not unilaterally imposed by the union—the term appears in an agreement with employers. Moreover, it is an output restraint on a nonlabor market. However, like the hours-of-operation rule in *Jewel Tea*, this rule is arguably related closely enough to the union members terms of employment—how much they will be required to work—that it falls within the nonstatutory exemption.

§23.2.3 The *Allen Bradley* Rule: Union-Employer Conspiracy

Finally, one last and fairly simple rule is that a union cannot conspire with employers to cause anticompetitive harm outside the labor market. (It is not clear that this should even really be thought of as a separate rule distinct from the nonstatutory exemption; perhaps it is just the result that applies in one special, extreme circumstance under the nonstatutory exemption doctrine.) The rule derives from *Allen Bradley Co. v. IBEW Loc. 3*, 325 U.S. 797 (1945), where an electrical workers union was shown to have conspired with several nonlabor groups in a scheme covering New York City, to make entry into either electrical contracting or electrical equipment manufacturing in New York very difficult. The Court did not find specifically what the union's motive may have been for largely instigating the scheme and then acting as its enforcer, but it seems likely it was to share in the monopoly profits. In any event, the Court had no trouble finding there to be no antitrust exemption. The Court admitted that the union acting on its own might have been free to boycott the goods of an electrical equipment manufacturer that refused to organize. But where a union "aid[s] non-labor groups to create business monopolies and control the marketing of goods and services," *id.* at 808, there is no exemption from antitrust. Thus, later opinions have indicated that any conspiracy with an employer to impose a "direct and immediate" restraint on the product market is not exempt. *See, e.g., Pennington*, 381 U.S. at 663 (dicta; a union that "present[s] a set of prices at which [employers] would be required to sell . . . , the union and the employers who happened to agree" would not enjoy exemption).

APPENDIX

Further Topics in Antitrust Economics

The Problem of Industrial Organization

This appendix covers a few more advanced topics in a branch of economics ordinarily called "industrial organization" theory (IO). IO is concerned with the organization of markets. It asks questions such as how many firms there will be in a given market, how big they will be, how they will relate to each other, and how they will behave when the conditions are less than perfectly competitive.

Two IO topics are covered here. First, §App.1 will discuss a relationship that is pervasive throughout antitrust law, the "vertical" relationship. A relationship is vertical where it is part of the chain of distribution of some given product—for example, the relationship between the Sony electronics firm and the consumer electronics retailer Best Buy is a vertical relationship. The economics of vertical relationships are fairly complex and uncertain, and the antitrust treatment of them has been in a lot of flux.

Second, we will ask what happens when we relax the basic assumption of price theory, that the firms in the market are "price takers" that can only charge the competitive price or go out of business; that is, we will ask what happens when one or more of the firms has market power, but no firm is a perfect monopolist. We will consider a few different scenarios that might characterize such a market. Section App.2 will consider how a market behaves when there are only a few firms, and each of them has some market power. Such markets are "oligopolies," and economists think they usually behave differently than competitive markets. We will also consider a few variations on small-numbers competition, including the concepts of "contestable markets" and "limit pricing."

§APP.1 THE ECONOMICS OF DISTRIBUTION: VERTICAL RELATIONSHIPS AND THEIR ANTITRUST SIGNIFICANCE

§App.1.1 The Horizontal-Vertical Distinction

A question that recurs throughout antitrust, and one that has important legal consequences, is: What is the relationship between two or more firms *in the chain of distribution* of some product? In almost all antitrust cases, the conduct that the plaintiff challenges will involve a relationship between two or more businesses that is either a *horizontal* relationship or a *vertical* one.

A maker of any good or provider of any service must find some way to get the good or service to the consumers who will buy it; that is, they must *distribute* the thing that they make in some way. In simple businesses distribution is very straightforward. An auto mechanic "distributes" his service to people who bring their cars to his shop, and a restaurateur distributes her goods and service directly to customers who walk in the door. But in many businesses distribution is a much more significant, complicated, and often expensive matter, and indeed whole industries are devoted to distributing the goods and services of other businesses. This is true obviously enough of transportation companies (such as railroads and ocean-shipping concerns) and of couriers (such as FedEx), but it is also true that retail stores are "distributors" of goods produced by other businesses. Indeed, distribution is now such a large sector, and the distribution of goods now takes place on such a massive scale, that many transport-sector firms have begun to refashion themselves not just as transportation firms but as providers of "logistics"—a holistic batch of services that include planning the pickup and delivery of cargo, the actual carriage, and compliance with regulatory and planning requirements, designed to handle all the otherwise costly and cumbersome practical problems that might confront a large seller in getting its goods to market.

This problem of product distribution gives rise to a distinction that turns out to be important throughout antitrust—that between horizontal relationships and vertical ones. Antitrust issues can be raised by either, but antitrust normally treats them very differently. In most cases, horizontal arrangements are treated with much more suspicion than are vertical arrangements. First, both vertical and horizontal arrangements can be challenged as "contract[s], combination[s] . . ., or conspirac[ies]" under Sherman Act §1. But courts will look with more concern on an agreement between, say, Sony and Samsung than on an agreement between Sony and Best Buy. The reason is easy enough to see. Head-to-head competitors ordinarily have little reason to cooperate or agree with one another about much of anything. Their normal relation is an adversarial one, and their basic task is to make better, cheaper products to gain at one another's expense. So unless horizontal competitors can show that some agreement between them will result in some new product or some new, better way of doing things that neither of them could accomplish individually, they are at serious risk of antitrust liability (*see* Chapter 6). By contrast, sellers of goods and services *always* have a reason to contract with firms that distribute their goods; it is a fundamental necessity. Accordingly, vertical agreements do not often violate §1. (*See* Chapter 12.) Likewise, mergers and acquisitions can be challenged under Clayton Act §7, whether they are horizontal or vertical. But under current law challenges to vertical merger are rare and very rarely successful. Challenge to horizontal merger tends to face substantially better odds. (*See* Chapter 17.) The distinction is also relevant in the law of monopolization under Sherman Act §2. Unilateral firm conduct is only likely to be illegal if in some way it harms the monopolist's own horizontal competitors or would-be horizontal entrants into its own market. (*See* Chapter 13.)

§App.1.2 Some Basic Features: The Fundamental Problem of Product Distribution and the Goal of Product Differentiation

In understanding why antitrust treats horizontal and vertical relations so differently, it will be useful to give some thought to why firms enter into vertical relations and the pros and cons they consider when deciding how to structure those relationships.

§App.1.2(a) The Problem of Distribution

Generally speaking, distribution can be accomplished in one of two ways. On the one hand, a maker of some good might *integrate* vertically—that is, it might simply own both the manufacturing operation and the distribution operation through which its goods reach consumers. On the other hand, it might sell its goods through independent distributors (sometimes thought of as "integration by contract"). These two options might look like the charts in Figure A.1.

We might ask ourselves why a particular business would choose one form of distribution over another. Standard economic theory suggests that, all other things being equal, a rational firm will choose that form of organization that minimizes its own costs. So a first question to ask about any particular distribution scheme is what costs are involved. It turns out that these cost issues will vary from industry to industry. There may be significant scale economies in distribution of a given sort of product, which would counsel against the manufacturer of that product vertically integrating. It would be better, if there were such economies, for one transportation/distribution firm to carry the products of many sellers rather than just the one manufacturer's

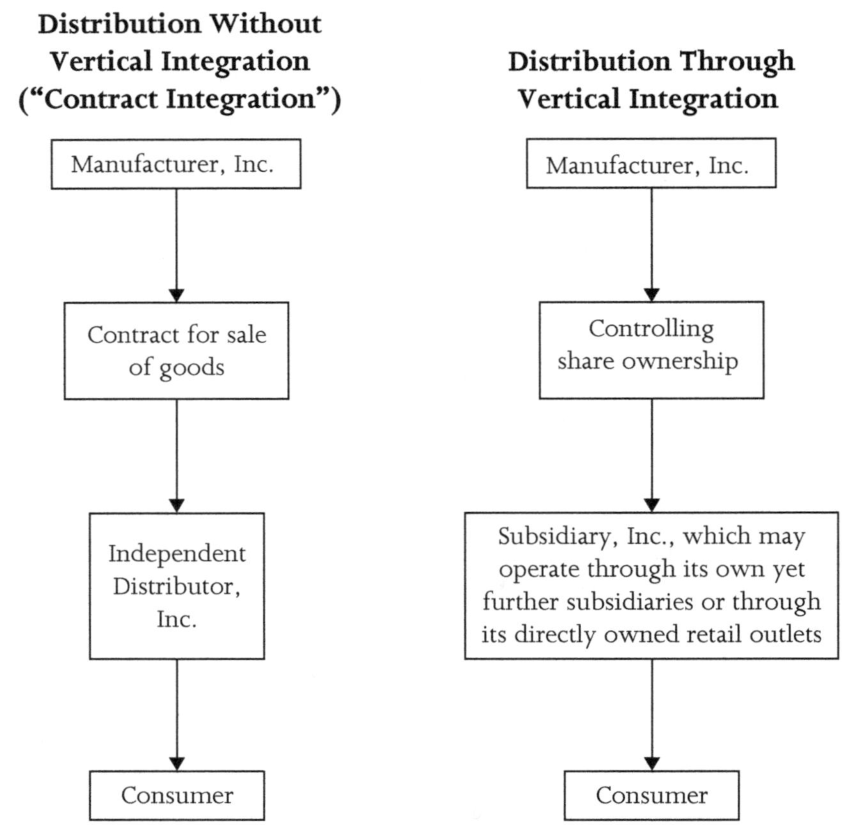

Figure A.1. Two Distribution Models

goods. That higher volume of carriage would allow it to exploit scale economies. Likewise, one basic trade-off in the choice between vertical integration and contract integration is between greater centralized control, on the one hand, and greater risk and cost, on the other. The vertically integrated manufacturer will normally retain much greater control over all aspects of the distribution of its product. That might have a lot of value in itself, by giving the firm some control over operating efficiencies and agency cost. However, the vertically integrated firm also takes all the risks associated with performing the distribution. The products could be damaged in transit, and that is a risk the manufacturer could pass on to another party if it actually sells the goods outright to its distributor. There also are all the legal liability risks involved in any business that can be avoided through contract integration.[1]

1. A large literature discusses these cost trade-offs of the organization of distribution. A leading work on point is Oliver E. Williamson, *Assessing Vertical Market Restrictions: Antitrust Ramifications of the Transaction Cost Approach*, 127 U. Pa. L. Rev. 953 (1979).

§App.1.2(b) Branding or Product Differentiation

There is one wholly different reason that most makers of goods care about their form of distribution: the way that a product is distributed is important to its *branding*. To "brand" a product is a process that economists ordinarily call "product differentiation." It is the process of convincing consumers that one's own product differs from competitors' substitute products, in ways that should make consumers value it more highly. The value of differentiation to a producer is that, by distinguishing the product from what would otherwise have been closer substitutes, it shelters the product from some price competition; that is, it creates some price inelasticity and gives the producer some market power. As a normative matter, differentiation is a bit complex. On the one hand, the market power associated with branding represents a departure from perfect competition, and may cause price to be higher than is socially optimal. It is also thought to encourage excess variety under many circumstances. The profits of existing branded goods may encourage the entry of too many other new brands, each differing in some possibly insubstantial ways. Moreover, differentiation can be misleading. It is empirically well documented that physically identical products can be differentiated through advertising and packaging. Consumers pay more, but the apparent quality differences are only illusory. But on the other hand, brand communicates information about quality, which may be useful to consumers in making decisions that serve them best. For the latter reason, there is no question that at least during the past few decades, branding and differentiation have been considered legitimate and procompetitive activities. Moreover, to whatever extent differentiation imposes costs or causes other harm, such undesirable differentiation could be hard to distinguish from conduct that is unambiguously good: innovation that leads to new and higher quality products.[2]

This has relevance to antitrust because the desire to create a differentiated brand will lead producers to impose some vertical restraints in some cases. In order to build a strong brand, it is believed, some expenditures must be made that are over and above the bare costs of making the product and getting it to consumers. This may include innovations in the design or packaging of the product, which requires research investments, as well as advertising and possibly in-person marketing. Except where all of the work of differentiating the brand could be accomplished by national advertising paid for by the manufacturer, some of that work will be done by distributors and retailers. The problem is that the downstream partners may or may not

2. Differentiation and branding are very nicely explored in Dennis W. Carlton & Jeffrey M. Perloff, *Modern Industrial Organization* 194-215 (3d ed. 2000); Lawrence A. Sullivan & Warren S. Grimes, *The Law of Antitrust: An Integrated Handbook* 316-369 (2d ed. 2006); and Nicholas S. Economides, *The Economics of Trademarks*, 78 Trademark Rep. 523 (1988).

have efficient incentives to provide those services.[3] So, the manufacturer must either pay for them directly in some way or must figure out how to restrain distribution contractually to get the downstream players to pay for them.

§App.1.3 Traditional Theories of Vertical Harm and the Neoclassical Criticism

Traditionally, antitrust treated vertical restraints very harshly. Even now, any of the restraints described in Chapters 10 or 11 (vertical conspiracies, tying, and exclusive contracts) or §13.3.5 (exclusionary distribution arrangements by a monopolist) can be challenged under Sherman Act §1 or §2 or FTC Act §5, and where they involve tying or exclusivity they can be challenged under Clayton Act §3. Also, where a proposed plan of vertical integration might pose effects similar to those achieved through a contractual vertical restraint, it could be challenged as an illegal acquisition under Clayton Act §7. In the heyday of more active enforcement, many of these arrangements were quite easy to challenge, and competitive impacts that now seem small could support illegality. True to form, antitrust dealt with vertical price restraints most harshly. Vertical minimum price fixing—often known as "resale price maintenance" or RPM—was made per se illegal in 1912 and so remained until 2007. Tying arrangements were also viewed with especial harshness, and in the early cases were all but totally outlawed. Other nonprice restraints were also not well tolerated, and for a brief period in the 1960s and 1970s were mostly per se illegal. Finally, vertical integration through merger and acquisition raises similar issues and was also dealt with rather harshly.

The earliest case law on vertical restraints was basically noneconomic, conceiving the harm they caused as a limit on personal liberty. Such an economic theory of harm as the traditional case law developed was the so-called "foreclosure" theory. A seller that can secure exclusivity arrangements covering enough of the market for distribution of its good might impede new entrants who, after all, need access to distribution as well. In the extreme, so much of distribution might be foreclosed that an entrant would have to enter two markets at once—both as to the product both

3. *See* Benjamin Klein, *Competitive Resale Price Maintenance in the Absence of Free-Riding*, 76 Antitrust L.J. 431 (2009) (arguing that manufacturers will often desire more promotion by downstream players than the latter will desire to provide, because the downstream players will earn less reward from doing so). It has also long been argued that even where a distributor or retailer has sufficient incentive to provide promotional services, that incentive will be eroded if other downstream players are able to sell the same branded products without providing those services (therefore enjoying lower costs and an ability to undercut the full-service seller). This problem of "free riding" is discussed in §App.1.3.

firms produce and distribution of it. Likewise, a powerful buyer might lock up sources of supply by entering output contracts with a large proportion of its suppliers, which require the suppliers to deliver their entire output to the buyer.

But the case law has always recognized that vertical restraints might have benefits. They might give the buyer and seller both predictability and stability, or they might give them protection from price fluctuations. They might be part of a seller's interbrand competition plan—it is thought that they might be used to incentivize dealers to market the seller's product more aggressively. For buyers, they might be a way to save on storage or other inventory costs.

The foreclosure theory was long attacked by academic critics. A chief criticism was based on the so-called "one monopoly profit" argument. The argument was that the total amount of supracompetitive profit that could be gotten from any product or service is determined at the point of final sale to the ultimate consumer. In the case of retail products, for example, there is some maximum retail price beyond which so many sales are lost by further price increases that it is no longer profitable to increase that price. This is so whether additional increases are imposed by the manufacturer on its distributors, by the distributors on the retailers, or by the retailers on the consumer. Which of them is able to impose the price increase will depend on which of them has the most market power (i.e., the one of them that faces the least horizontal competition at its level in the chain of distribution).

For example, consider the problem of the "tying" contract (covered in Chapter 11). Imagine the IBM corporation of the 1930s and 1940s. It was a dominant seller at that time of very large, stationary computers. Instead of receiving information through a keyboard, and displaying it on a screen or printout, those computers used stacks of paper punch cards. IBM also produced the punch cards and required its customers to use IBM punch cards in their machines. The "one monopoly profit" claim says that the punch-card requirement could not logically harm consumers any more than they are already harmed by IBM's market power over computers. If IBM already enjoyed some significant market power over its stationary computers, then it already had power to raise prices for them and therefore to earn supracompetitive profits. If it was behaving as a rational profit maximizer, it would already be charging the highest prices that would remain profitable to it. If it also tried to force consumers to take its punch cards, and it tried to charge them a supracompetitive price for those cards, then consumers would simply count that additional price as part of the price of the underlying computer product, and that would by definition drive away some sales for the computers and rob IBM of some of its maximized profits. This argument has taken sway with a number of courts and leading commentators. *See generally* Richard A. Posner, *Antitrust Law* 197-207 (2d ed. 2001). But as we shall see, there may be reasons to expect that at least sometimes tying may be a profitable strategy even where the monopolist is earning significant supracompetitive profits in the "tying" market.

Critics also adduced several reasons that vertical mergers might have procompetitive virtues that would be stifled by undue antitrust enforcement. The obvious procompetitive motivations would be to reduce whatever costs may be associated with distribution in a given market. At least some of those costs may be reduced if the acquiring company can get control of the target company. One cost saving recognized early on was reduction of "double marginalization." The idea is that where firms in both the upstream and downstream markets have some market power, sellers at both levels will charge a markup. The manufacturer has a strong incentive to limit the double mark-up, because its only real interest with respect to retail sales is to maximize volume. For this reason, critics of vertical restraints law often said that the interests of the manufacturer with respect to vertical relationships were aligned with the interests of the consumer. Likewise, opportunism or "agency cost" that might otherwise complicate supply relationships between independent firms might be reduced.

More recently, quite a different argument has developed in defense of vertical arrangements. In the case law, this appeared first in the foundational *Continental T.V., Inc. v. GTE Sylvania, Inc*, 433 U.S. 36 (1977). The Court there began by stating for the first time that "[i]nterbrand competition . . . is the primary concern of antitrust law." *Id.* at 51 n.19. The Court continued by introducing the new argument that consumers at least sometimes benefit from *more expensive promotion*; that is, they can get something good out of it if distributors invest money into promoting particular brands, to inform consumers of the quality advantages of those brands. Consumers benefit if that information causes them to spend a bit more for a product that actually serves them better than a lower-priced good, given its higher quality. But distributors won't invest in those promotional services—which might be expensive—if all the benefits of doing so will just be competed away by other, no-frills distributors selling the same brands. Therefore, vertical restraints might enable manufacturers in effect to bribe distributors to work with them or to work better for them, which might allow the manufacturers to enter new markets or to compete better in those they already serve:

> [N]ew manufacturers and manufacturers entering new markets can use the restrictions in order to induce competent and aggressive retailers to make the kind of investment of capital and labor that is often required in the distribution of products unknown to the consumer. Established manufacturers can use them to induce retailers to engage in promotional activities or to provide service and repair facilities necessary to the efficient marketing of their products. Service and repair are vital for many products, such as automobiles and major household appliances. The availability and quality of such services affect

> a manufacturer's goodwill and the competitiveness of his product. Because of market imperfections such as the so-called "free rider" effect, these services might not be provided by retailers in a purely competitive situation, despite the fact that each retailer's benefit would be greater if all provided the services than if none did.

Id. at 55.

§App.1.4 Recent Reexamination of the Neoclassical Critique

In recent years substantial questions have been raised about the neoclassical view, and some serious concern may be returning about the anticompetitive risks posed by vertical restraints. First, doubts have been cast on the "one monopoly profit" argument. In a widely read article, Harvard Law professor Einer Elhauge has shown that the one-monopoly-profit result may hold in its full form under only highly restrictive conditions.[4] In the case of tying or bundling, the argument assumes that the tying market is perfectly monopolized, that the tied market is perfectly competitive, and that the two products are perfect complements (meaning that a consumer *must* consume both of them in fixed quantities, to get the good out of either of them; a common example is a right shoe and a left shoe). Elhauge argues that if *any* of these assumptions is not met, scenarios might be common in which sellers might find tying or bundling profitable with no benefit to consumers. If either the tied or the tying market is somewhere in between perfect monopoly and perfect competition, then the seller might in fact be able to accomplish some foreclosure or acquire some excess profits that would be unavailable if it merely monopolized the tying market. Likewise, if the products are not close complements, or if different consumers differ in the amount of one of the products that they desire to use, then a seller with power over the tying product can engage in special price discrimination that extracts consumer surplus—and therefore is more profitable than simply monopolizing the tying product—and may also decrease overall efficiency.

Second, it no longer seems so clear that intrabrand restraints are normally harmless. First, even strong defenders of vertical restraints acknowledge that the traditional free-riding rationale probably cannot explain much of the vertically restrictive marketing actually observed in the world.[5] As a former FTC Chair pointed out, the kinds of products as to which the

4. *See* Einer Elhauge, *Tying, Bundled Discounts, and the Death of the Single Monopoly Profit Theory*, 123 Harv. L. Rev. 397 (2009).

5. *See* Benjamin Klein, *Competitive Resale Price Maintenance in the Absence of Free-Riding*, 76 Antitrust L.J. 431, 431-435 (2009).

enforcement agencies have frequently seen RPM agreements are products that seem unlikely to be marketed with promotional services that discount sellers could free-ride upon. They have included things such as pet food, vitamins, shampoo, ammunition, blue jeans, and men's underwear.[6]

Likewise, critics have increasingly marshaled theory and evidence that specific kinds of vertical restraints can lack the procompetitive force they are said to have, and to cause some anticompetitive harm.[7] Intrabrand competition, which is so often said to be comparatively harmless and likely to improve the more important interbrand competition, might not be so harmless in many cases. Competition among distributors and retailers of any individual brand becomes more important as the strength of that brand increases. Where a product is highly differentiated, and therefore has no close substitutes, intrabrand competition among retailers might be the only price competition there is. And indeed, there is emerging empirical evidence that RPM does cause consumer harm through increased prices.[8]

Finally, some doubt has been cast on the benefits that vertical restraints are supposed to produce. For example, while RPM might provide some margin of profit to encourage a retailer to engage in promotions, there will be times when it won't provide much encouragement at all. For one thing, it may be difficult for the manufacturer to ensure that its downstream partners are actually providing the services that are hoped for. They might just sit back and enjoy their small margin of profitability. Also, if the distributor or retailer carries many different brands—as for example with a grocery store—then it will have an incentive for added promotion only if the manufacturer's competing brands are not also imposing RPM requirements. If they are, then the consequence may be just higher retail prices for all brands. It has also been argued that whatever consumer benefits might ensue from vertical restraints, they might be captured nearly as well through means that are less competitively risky. For example, manufacturers could simply pay cash promotional allowances or give discounted wholesale prices in exchange for contractually promised promotional services.

It is too soon to predict the practical consequences of these evolving perspectives. If courts come to digest this more recent critique of the neoclassical perspective, and reconsider the strictness of the vertical rules that evolved under it, there should be basically one major consequence: In

6. Robert Pitofsky, *Are Retailers Who Offer Discounts Really "Knaves"?: The Coming Challenge to the* Dr. Miles *Rule*, Antitrust, Spring 2007, at 61, 63.
7. *See* Warren S. Grimes, *A Dynamic Analysis of Resale Price Maintenance: Inefficient Brand Promotion, Higher Margins, Distorted Choices, and Retarded Retail Innovation*, 55 Antitrust Bull. 101 (2010); Warren S. Grimes, *The Path Forward After* Leegin*: Seeking Consensus Reform of the Antitrust Law of Vertical Restraints*, 75 Antitrust L.J. 467 (2008).
8. *See* Alexander MacKay & David Aron Smith, *The Empirical Effects of Minimum Resale Price Maintenance on Prices and Output* (2013), *available at* http://home.uchicago.edu/~davidsmith/research/Leegin_and_MRPM.pdf.

rule-of-reason challenge to vertical arrangements, be they contractual distribution restraints, tying, or vertical merger,[9] plaintiffs will be afforded new theoretical tools, which should be taken more seriously, to argue that specified conduct is anticompetitive.

As a preview of the directions the developing law might take, courts and commentators have already suggested some theoretical elaboration. Some of the most general points were suggested by the *Leegin* Court itself, and they are discussed in §10.2.3. But commentators have suggested more detail yet. First, vertical *price* restraints are likely to be of more concern where they are imposed in an "open" distribution system. An open system is one in which the manufacturer imposes no territorial or competitor restraints on its dealers. Dealers are left free to compete with one another in whatever locations they choose. This will be of more concern because there is less reason to believe in any procompetitive motive. There would be no protection from free-riding and no obvious incentive for dealers to invest in the aggressive marketing a manufacturer might desire. There also will be some risk where minimum RPM is used as to products sold in multibrand stores (like a grocery store or a hardware store) that other manufacturers will be induced to follow suit. Protection from intrabrand competition is an incentive for retailers to carry a brand, at least where the brand is strong, and competing manufacturers will feel pressure to meet their competition and offer minimum RPM programs of their own.[10]

Vertical restraints of any kind are more suspect where they are pervasive in an industry. The benefits that are thought to flow from some intrabrand restraints occur only if the restraints make it worthwhile to dealers to take on a manufacturer that they otherwise would not, or to make promotional investments that they otherwise would not make. But if every manufacturer offers the same incentives, they will cancel each other out, and the only likely consequence of widespread use of the restraint will be higher retail prices.[11]

Finally, there is also some consensus that one sort of vertical restraint is *not* likely to cause harm. Section 1 challenges to such restraints therefore will likely not fare especially well, absent special circumstances. It is thought that where the restraint is a non-price restraint *limiting* distribution—that is, where it uses territorial or customer restrictions to keep its distributors from competing with each other in sales of its brand—procompetitive benefits

9. All vertical contract restraints are now judged under the rule of reason. *See* Chapters 10 and 11. Tying is nominally judged under a special rule still referred to as a per se rule, but it has come to be subject to so many evidentiary burdens on the plaintiff that it is better thought of as a rule of reason under which the plaintiff enjoys merely a small, rebuttable presumption of anticompetitive effect. *See* Chapter 11. Vertical mergers, like other transactions subject to Clayton Act §7, are subject to what is in effect a rule of reason. *See* Chapter 17.

10. *See* Grimes, *supra* note 2, at 482-483.

11. *See id.* at 483-484.

are fairly likely and harms are relatively unlikely. First, distribution-limiting non-price restraints are useful to help new entrants or small or declining firms secure distribution to expand their output. This is so because this type of agreement in and of itself gives the dealer no benefit unless it actually invests in promotion, and it also limits free-riding. And second, this type of agreement would likely not be imposed by a manufacturer with market power; where there is market power upstream, the seller will ordinarily prefer intrabrand competition. So distribution-limiting restraints are unlikely to be illegal unless there is substantial downstream market power or if they are pervasive in the industry.[12]

§APP.2 MODELING IMPERFECT COMPETITION: THEORIES OF OLIGOPOLY

As the authors put it in one leading textbook on the subject:

> [T]there is only one model of competition and one model of monopoly, [but] there are many models of noncooperative oligopoly: a small number of firms acting independently but aware of one another's existence. Unlike monopolistic and competitive firms, noncooperative oligopolists cannot blithely ignore other firms' actions.

Dennis W. Carlton & Jeffrey M. Perloff, *Modern Industrial Organization* 153 (3d ed. 2000).

We will consider here two ideas about a particular kind of less-than-perfect market — oligopolies, as they are often known — that have been significant in antitrust.

§App.2.1 Oligopoly Interdependence

An oligopoly is simply a market in which there are only a few sellers. Most observers think that oligopoly markets pose competitive problems for two reasons. First, the maintenance of an anticompetitive secret cartel is thought to be easier where there are fewer members. Second, a real problem for antitrust plaintiffs is that oligopolists might be able to achieve anticompetitive results without any agreement at all. They might be able to harm competition in a way that otherwise would be actionable under antitrust law, but there is

12. *See id.* at 481-482.

no "conspiracy" as required by Sherman Act §1 or individual producer with enough market power to be challenged as a monopolist under §2.

The reason for this second problem, according to many economists, is that some oligopoly markets can achieve a long-run "non-cooperative equilibrium" in which prices are supracompetitive but will neither attract new entry nor encourage "cheating" by existing producers. This is because (1) there may be some entry barriers, and (2) existing producers will be able to forecast that short-run profits earned by lowering prices will be more than offset by long-run losses incurred when all other sellers become aware of the price cut and then match it. Thus, even though the theory of perfect competition would suggest that oligopolists should always just compete their prices down to the point of zero economic profits, there may be times when they can all foresee that every sellers' profits will be maximized if they all maintain prices a certain amount above the competitive price. The smaller the number of sellers, the standard argument goes, the more likely it will be for them to be able to predict this. This supracompetitive equilibrium is not healthy, by the way, on any standard economic argument about healthy markets; it just happens to be a situation for which antitrust provides no remedy.[13]

Anyway, the basic problem for antitrust is that under oligopoly conditions, the behavior of the individual sellers will often look as if they have entered a price-fixing conspiracy. Thus, as explained in Chapter 12, the same evidence that plaintiffs often adduce as circumstantial proof of illegal conspiracy—some period of parallel pricing behavior—is as consistent with oligopoly interdependence as it is with collusion. The courts have therefore had to come up with rules to deal with when and how this evidence can be part of a proof of conspiracy; their solution has been the so-called "plus-factors" test explained in Chapter 12.

A separate problem associated with oligopoly and proof of conspiracy is understanding how price-fixing cartels work and in which sorts of markets they are more likely to be present. This also has a bearing on how the courts have handled the problem of proof of conspiracy and the proof requirements they put on plaintiffs. Thinking on these matters is still dominated by one seminal journal article, George Stigler, *A Theory of Oligopoly*, 72 J. Pol. Econ. 44 (1964). Among Stigler's basic contributions was to think about how conspirators can deal with the basic problem of "cheating." For example, in a simple horizontal price-fixing conspiracy each of the members will stand to earn some increased profit through increased prices. However,

13. Indeed, that this situation is not captured by the Sherman Act may just have been a regrettable oversight by the statute's draftsmen, who lacked the economic theory to perceive it as a problem. The issue is frequently enough observed that it is known by some observers as the "oligopoly gap." *See* Jonathan B. Baker, *Two Sherman Act Section 1 Dilemmas: Parallel Pricing, the Oligopoly Problem, and Contemporary Economic Theory*, 38 Antitrust Bull. 143 (1993).

increased price means that every cartel member will also lose some sales. It will occur to every member that if it can secretly reduce its prices just a bit, it should be able to steal business away from its fellow conspirators, but still be able to charge those customers supracompetitive prices. In this way, the cheater could earn even more profits than if it just complied with the terms of the cartel agreement. For this reason, cartels are thought to be inherently unstable, at least as a theoretical matter. But Stigler then observed that two basic traits of certain markets might make cartels in those markets more robust: the ease with which cartel members can detect cheating and the effectiveness with which they can punish cheating.[14] He then discussed a number of factors in some markets that could make both of these basic tasks easier. First, the fewer sellers there are, the easier both detection and punishment will be, for obvious reasons. Likewise, where the product in question is fungible, cheating is much easier to detect. This is so because if the products at issue are differentiated among the different cartel members, an accused cheater can plausibly argue that any price differences or rebates it offers are cost justified and are not evidence of cheating. Also, frequent sales transactions to numerous small buyers make cheating harder to conceal because it is more likely that buyers will demand similar lower prices from other sellers.

Another important market trait that can encourage either collusion or noncollusive interdependence is price inelasticity of demand. If a product is price inelastic, then buyers will tend to buy about the same amount of it even if prices go up. Common examples of very price inelastic goods are staple foods such as milk and bread, health care, or intermediate inputs in a manufacturing process that represent only a small part of the ultimate retail price (such as, sometimes, packaging). The value of inelasticity to cartels and oligopolies is that it will be easier to convince potential cartel members that they can collusively raise prices without driving customers to substitute products.

§App.2.2 Further Variations on Small-Numbers Competition: Limit Pricing and Contestable Markets

One possible limitation on an otherwise oligopolistic market is that it may be *contestable*. The argument is that even though there are only a few firms in

14. Cartels have resorted to a variety of methods of punishment. Typically the conspirators will agree that if a cheater is discovered the other members will retaliate with price competition against the cheater for some period, which may be predatory and the losses of predation funded through some common treasury contributed to by the conspirators. Often in more formal arrangements the conspirators will assess fines against cheaters; though the fine would not be enforceable at law, it could be backed up by the threat of predation if the cheater does not comply.

the market, and they hold very large shares of that market's sales, they may not have any power over price if it is relatively easy for new competitors to enter. In other words, even very small-number markets may in effect behave more like competitive ones if the threat of *potential* competition—the promise that even small supracompetitive price increases will invite quick entry—constrains the pricing discretion of incumbent firms.

Moreover, even where entry is not easy—where there are some entry barriers, such that entry imposes costs over and above the initial entry costs faced by incumbent firms—the possibility of new entry can exert some constraint on incumbent firms' pricing discretion. Under those conditions, the incumbents will have some pricing power, but they will not raise their prices so high that it would make it profitable for entrants to incur the non-trivial entry costs. This phenomenon is known as *limit pricing*, and it has the effect of imposing at least some competitive discipline even where incumbent firms enjoy some market power resulting from the entry barriers that protect them.[15]

15. The idea was introduced in Darius W. Gaskins, Jr., *Dynamic Limit Pricing: Optimal Pricing Under Threat of Entry*, 3 J. Econ. Theory 306 (1971).

Glossary

Accounting Profit: *See* PROFIT.

Allocational Efficiency: *See* EFFICIENCY.

Ancillary: Part of some larger arrangement or institution. In the law of Sherman Act §1, an ancillary agreement is one that is part of some other arrangement. For example, a contract for the sale of a factory might include an agreement that the seller of the factor will not compete with the buyer for some period of time. If that agreement were not ancillary—which is to say, if it were "naked"—it would be per se illegal. But since it is ancillary to a procompetitive arrangement—sales of goods in healthy markets are presumed to be procompetitive, since if they were not mutually advantageous they would not occur—it will be judged differently. *See* §7.2.

Arbitrage: To buy a thing at one price and then sell it for a higher price. Usually, the term implies that the *arbitrageur* hopes to exploit a market imperfection—he has discovered a good that is mispriced in one market and can resell it at a profit in another. In antitrust, arbitrage is mainly important in the law of price discrimination, discussed in Chapter 16. The term is sometimes given very precise or idiosyncratic definitions, especially in the field of finance economics, but those definitions are rarely if ever relevant in antitrust.

Asymmetry of Information: A situation in which one party to a transaction has better information concerning matters relevant to the transaction than does the other party.

Cartel: A group of (usually horizontally competing) market actors who collectively agree to take some action to self-regulate their markets. The term has negative connotations and usually implies a conspiracy of head-to-head competitors who agree to fix prices, allocate markets, or otherwise harm competition.

Competition: Rivalry between persons to sell the same things to the same trading partners. As used in contemporary economics and antitrust, the term has a precise meaning, and it is the meaning used in this book. Competition is the effort to secure a deal by offering a better quality-adjusted price for a good than some other person offers for the same good. Competition exists between both buyers and sellers of goods. For example, a seller of a good will try to win sales by selling it at a lower price or higher quality than sellers of substitute goods. Buyers also must compete for purchases and will offer higher prices or accept lower quality to take sales from competing buyers. In this technical sense, a market is competitive if participants have no power to offer less desirable quality-adjusted prices than their competitors offer.

The term has several vernacular meanings and has been used in different ways in antitrust history. For example, in common discussion a market is often said to be competitive if it contains many firms or if the firms in it spend a lot on advertising or research-and-development. Those facts do not in themselves make a market more competitive in the technical sense, however.

Competitive Price or Competitive Equilibrium: The price that all sellers must charge in perfect competition. This price will exactly equal the prevailing cost of production, which will be the lowest technologically feasible cost at the given time. Any seller unable to produce at that cost will be forced to exit the market.

Complement: A product that is used in combination with another. For example, a toner cartridge is a complement to a computer printer. One important economic relationship between complements is that they will exhibit positive cross-price elasticity. That is so because when consumers buy more of one of them, they will need more of the other. This distinguishes complements from substitutes. Substitutes have negative cross-price elasticity, because when consumers buy more of one of them, they need less of the other. *See* ELASTICITY; SUBSTITUTE.

Conglomerate: A combination of different businesses into one firm, where the individual businesses do not compete and are not related. For example, a firm that manufactures electronics, sporting goods, and office supplies is a conglomerate.

Cost:

Accounting Cost: The cost of producing a good or service, not including any return on the investors' investment in the firm. Accounting cost is the concept closest to "cost" as it is commonly used in the vernacular.

Average Cost: The economic cost of producing a good or service divided by the quantity produced.

Average Total Cost: This term is synonymous with "average cost."

Average Variable Cost: Variable cost divided by the quantity produced.

Avoidable Cost: A cost that will no longer be incurred if the business ceases operations. Such a cost could be either fixed or variable. Fixed costs are avoidable, for example, when leases can be subleased or equipment can be resold at fair value. Variable costs are always avoidable, since all variable costs are zero on exit.

Economic Cost: The cost of producing a good *including* a market rate of return on the investors' investment in the firm.

Fixed Cost: Costs of producing a good or service that do not vary with the quantity produced. The same fixed costs must be incurred no matter how many units are made, even if none are actually made.

Marginal Cost: The cost of producing the *next* unit of a good or service. If a firm has produced 100 units at a total cost of $10, but it would cost a total of $10.05 to produce 101 units, then marginal cost at a quantity of 101 is $0.05.

Sunk Cost: A cost that is not only unavoidable, but that *has already been made.*

Total Cost: The sum total of the cost of producing all units at a given quantity of output.

Variable Cost: A cost of production that varies with output. For example, after the firm has purchased an expensive, installed machine, it might also have to buy some raw material that is fed into the machine to make the good, but only so much of it needs to be used for every unit of the good that is produced. So producing more of the good requires more of the raw material; the expense of the raw material is then a variable cost.

Deadweight Loss: The loss of utility that occurs when a producer or producers with market power raise price or reduce output. In such a case, there will be some sellers who would have purchased the good at lower prices, who will no longer get the good. Some of those purchasers would likely have enjoyed some consumer surplus, because some of them would have been willing to pay at least a little bit more than the competitive market price. Likewise, some producers might have earned some producer surplus at the competitive price, because they would have sold some units that they will no longer sell, and they might have been willing to make some of those sales at less than the competitive price. However, because those sales no longer occur—quantity has been reduced—all consumer and producer surplus that would have arisen from those sales is lost.

[1]**Distribution:** The business of delivering goods from upstream producers to downstream consumers. Examples of distributors include wholesalers, retailers, and logistics firms like trucking companies.

[2]**Distribution:** The degree to which wealth is shared. Distribution poses a problem for the economic theory studied in this book because the theory cannot predict or explain how distribution will occur and cannot make judgments about its desirability. Perfect competition, while it maximizes allocational efficiency, is unable to take account of distributional consequences. This is so because resource allocation is said to be maximized when the most people have the most of what they want, but "wants" in this calculation are measured exclusively in terms of "willingness to pay."

Economics:

Macroeconomics: The study of overall economies at large. For example, the effect of government-imposed interest rates, overall unemployment, and inflation are macroeconomic issues.

Microeconomics: The study of individual markets. For example, the relationship of supply and demand in the market for green beans is a microeconomic issue.

Economic Profit: *See* PROFIT.

Economy of Scale: Any savings in the cost of producing a good or service that arises from producing it in larger volume.

Efficiency:

Productive Efficiency: The degree to which a particular firm can reduce the cost of production (this is the most common vernacular sense of "efficiency").

Allocational Efficiency: The degree to which a particular market is able to allocate all resources to those who value them most highly.

Dynamic Efficiency: The degree to which a particular market achieves technological progress, at lowest cost, over time.

Elasticity:

Cross-Price Elasticity: The sensitivity of consumer demand for one product to price changes that occur in some substitute product. Generally, the relationship between two products will be more cross-price elastic (i.e., more sensitive) if they are close "substitutes" (see below for definition). Thus, the relationship of cable TV to satellite TV is probably fairly elastic (i.e., demand will increase for satellite TV if the price of cable goes up, and vice versa), whereas the relationship of white bread and toothpaste is probably not very elastic because they are not very close substitutes for one another.

Price Elasticity: The sensitivity of consumer demand to price increases in a particular product. For all or almost all goods, demand will fall if price goes up, but for some items (those as to which demand is more "elastic"), demand will fall more quickly. Thus, consumer demand for luxury items tends to be highly price elastic, whereas demand for staple food items is highly inelastic. Technically, "price elasticity of demand" is the percentage change in the quantity demanded in response to a one percent change in price. Generally, a good is said to be "price *inelastic*" if the price-elasticity of demand is less than one. A good is said to be "price *elastic*" if the price-elasticity of demand is more than one.

$$\frac{\text{\% change in Quantity Demanded } \Delta Qd/Qd}{\text{\% change in Price}} = \Delta P/P$$

The reason that an elasticity of 1 is chosen as the important dividing line between "elastic" and "inelastic" is that a value less than 1 implies that price increases are profitable—by definition, when demand is inelastic, a seller can raise price and earn more through the price increase than it loses from lost sales.

Entry: The offer of a good in a market that had not been available before. Entry can include new entry by a firm that had not participated in the market before (often called "de novo entry"), and it may either be by a firm that had sold other goods or sold them elsewhere geographically, or it may be by a newly created firm. Entry is also sometimes used to describe expanded production by a firm already selling the good in question in the market in question. The effects of expanded output and other kinds of entry are generally economically the same.

Entry Barrier: Some cost or impediment that makes it difficult for new producers to enter a particular market.

Equilibrium: A state in a market that will remain stable, because no change could be made that would make any market participant better off.

Long-Run: A period of time during which participants in a market can change their behavior costlessly because no ongoing obligations are legally binding. *See* SHORT-RUN.

Short-Run: A period of time during which participants in a market cannot change their behavior costlessly, because some ongoing obligation is legally binding. For example, if a manufacturer has leased factory space under terms that obligate it to pay rent on the space for one year, then use of the factory cannot be changed without cost for that period.

Externality: Some value that may be important to society but that is not "internalized" by buyers and sellers in a particular market. That is, an externality is a cost or benefit to society at large that those particular buyers and sellers do not consider when they decide how much they are willing to pay or at what price they are willing to sell. For example, harms to the environment are external to the market for a particular good, even though those harms may be caused by the very manufacturing process that produced the good. In a world in which environmental harms are not forcibly internalized to the market participants (by way of environmental law), buyers and sellers of that good will not voluntarily choose to trade at the higher price that would be necessary to reduce production to some more environmentally tolerable level. Accordingly, in the absence of such regulation the product will be overproduced.

Negative Externality: An effect of some market transaction that harms third parties to the transaction, who themselves have no way to influence the frequency of the transaction. The cost to them is a social harm because everyone would be better off if parties to the transaction could be made to engage in less of it. In principle, the third parties would pay the participants to engage in less of the conduct, to reduce the harm to themselves, but generally transaction costs and collective action problems will prevent it. Common examples are pollution and noise nuisances.

Positive Externality: An effect of some market transaction that benefits third parties to the transaction, who themselves have no way to influence the frequency of the transaction. The benefit to them represents a social harm because everyone would be better off if parties to the transaction could be made to engage in more of it. In principle, the third parties would pay the participants to engage in more of the conduct, to increase the benefit to themselves, but generally transaction costs and collective action problems will prevent it. Common examples are the production of art or the provision of police protection, public parks, or infrastructure.

Free-Riding: Taking advantage of a good or service produced by some other person, without paying for it. For example, imagine that a retail store makes substantial investments in in-store displays, luxury showroom space, and well educated sales staff who spend substantial amounts of time with individual customers. If other retailers sell the same products nearby, consumers might visit the full-service store to learn about the products and receive demonstrations, but then buy the products at no-frills competing retailers. The reason antitrust and economics care about free-riding is that will discourage the provision of a good or service that is free-ridden upon. The full-service retailer won't provide full service if consumers just buy the goods at lower-priced competitors, and this is a loss to consumers if in fact they value the full-service sales operation. For this reason, free-riding is a specific example of an "externality" (in this case it is a positive externality—it is a valued good for which the provider of the good is unable to secure full payment).

Function: A mathematical relationship in which one variable causes changes in another variable. For example, if changes in the amount of a good supplied affect the price that sellers can command in the market for that good, then we might say that price is a function of supply.

Inframarginal: Literally, "to the left of the margin"; the term refers to those consumers and producers who would fall to the left of the competitive equilibrium price and quantity on a simple market diagram, like those that appear in Figure 2.1, which appears in §2.3.1. Inframarginal consumers are those who would have been willing to pay more than the market price. Inframarginal producers are those who would have been willing to sell at less than the market price.

Joint Venture: A collaboration between two otherwise distinct firms. The term is not a term of art in either law or economics. Joint ventures typically exist to produce some good or perform some function that the member firms do not otherwise perform on their own, and are generally justified as producing cost savings or other synergies. A joint venture can be organized in different ways. Two firms might agree to create a new corporation and grant themselves the stock in it, for example. Or they might simply cooperate without creating a third firm, in which case their relationship is in effect a common law partnership.

Long Term: In economics, the long term is the period in which fixed costs become variable. For example, if producing a given product requires acquisition of a minimum amount of technology and labor contracts that cannot be varied in less than a year, the long term is one year after the beginning of production.

Marginal Cost: The additional cost incurred from producing one additional unit of a good. For example, if the total cost of producing five units of a good is $5 but the total cost of producing six units if $5.75, then the marginal cost of producing the sixth unit is $0.75.

Marginal: The change in some value that occurs from making a small increase or decrease in some behavior. For example, the marginal cost of producing a good is the increase in cost that a firm incurs by making each additional unit of the good.

Marginal Revenue: The additional revenue earned from selling one additional unit. *See also* REVENUE.

Market: The universe of buyers and sellers for a particular good or service, including all substitutes, within the geographical area in which sellers for that good or service compete with one another.1 *E.g.*, persons offering auto repair services in Juneau, Alaska, are probably not in the same "market" as those who offer such services in Tallahassee, Florida, even though they are producers of the same product, because they likely would not compete with one another for the same customers.1. Another useful definition sometimes used in antitrust caselaw is that a "market" is an "area of effective competition." *Tampa Elec. Co. v. Nashville Coal Co.*, 365 U.S. 320, 327 (1961).

Market Power: The ability to raise prices or restrict output within a particular market.

Maximization: The attempt to achieve the largest amount of something. Oftentimes the benefit of some behavior does not increase indefinitely; the amount of added benefit may begin to decrease after some level of the behavior. As one important example, as the volume of production of a good increase there will come a point beyond which it is less profitable to keep expanding output. The point at which profit is maximize is that point. "Maximization" is used synonymously with "optimization."

Merger: Technically, in the law of business organizations a merger is a specific form of legal transaction in which two previously separate firms are joined into one legal entity. However, in antitrust the term is often used more loosely, to mean any acquisition by one firm of the assets or equity stock of another, which is then subject to antitrust review under Clayton Act §7 and the Hart-Scott-Rodino Act. These matters are discussed in §17.1.

Monopoly: (1) *As Used By Economists:* A market in which there is only one seller. (2) *As Used in Antitrust Law:* A market in which one producer (the "monopolist") holds some market power, and in which no other producer holds any market power. In a monopoly there might still be many small "fringe" producers (referred to as the "competitive fringe"), none of which has any large share of market power.

Monopoly Price: The price at which there is the greatest distance between price and per-unit cost of production, and therefore the greatest possible profit. This price can be charged only by a monopolist that faces no present or potential competition, because any other seller that attempted to sell at that price would be undersold.

Monopsony: A market in which there is only one buyer of the good, or, more loosely, a market in which one buyer holds substantial market power over purchases.

Naked: Unrelated to any other arrangement or institution. The term is used in the law of Sherman Act §1 to refer to agreements that are not part of any larger arrangement among the parties that could be procompetitive. For example, if two retail stores agree that they will not sell the same products, and there is no more to the agreement than that, the agreement is a naked horizontal market allocation and it is per se illegal. But if it is only one clause in a contract between them to set up a jointly owned shopping mall, it is "ancillary" to that larger agreement ("ancillary" being the opposite of "naked"), and it is judged differently. *See* §7.2.

Network Effect: The increase in value associated with a product that is more valuable when more people use it. *E.g.*, VHS videocassette recorders have more value than Beta machines not because they are inherently better or more valuable, but because VHS-compatible tapes are common whereas Beta-compatible tapes are rare. Likewise, a fax machine would have no value unless many consumers have purchased compatible fax machines, and it becomes more valuable as more people buy machines with which it can communicate. Also often known as a "network externality."

Oligopoly: A market in which a number of producers (the "oligopolists") each hold some market power. In an oligopoly there normally will be a small number of oligopolist producers, though there may be many small "fringe" producers (referred to as the "competitive fringe," none of which has market power.

Optimization: *See* MAXIMIZATION.

Perfect Competition: *See* COMPETITION.

Predatory Pricing: Sales made at prices that sacrifice some profits, for the purpose of injuring a rival. Strictly speaking, prices could be "predatory," in the sense of being anticompetitive, even if they are above the predator's costs. They would be anticompetitive if the reduced prices are part of a strategy to destroy or intimidate rivals, with the ultimate goal of preserving higher long-run prices. But in antitrust the term is defined as a matter of law to mean prices below the predator's own costs. *See* §13.3.3.

Price Discrimination: Sales to different buyers at different prices. Strictly speaking, prices are not "discriminatory" just because they are different as between two buyers, because the costs of serving different customers can vary. In any event, price discrimination can sometimes be illegal under antitrust law, as discussed in Chapter 16.

Price Predation: *See* PREDATORY PRICING.

Product Differentiation: The effort to make one's product differ from those of competitors, and more importantly to convince consumers of the difference.

Productive Efficiency: *See* EFFICIENCY.

Profit:

- **Accounting Profit:** Revenue in excess of the cost of production of a particular product or service, not including distributions to owners.
- **Economic Profit:** Revenue in excess of *all* costs of production, including a reasonable return on investment.

Revenue: The total proceeds earned from the sale of a good. Revenue is to be distinguished from profit, which is the amount of revenue received minus the costs of producing the good. *See* PROFIT.

Rationality: Behavior that maximizes self-interest.

Short Term: In economics, the short term is the period in which fixed costs cannot yet be varied. For example, if producing a given product requires acquisition of a minimum amount of technology and labor contracts that cannot be varied in less than a year, the short term is the period of one year after the beginning of production.

Substitute: A good or service that is not identical to some other good or service, but that consumers will substitute for the latter if the price of the latter increases. *E.g.*, butter and margarine are likely substitutes for most consumers.

[1]**Surplus:** Surplus is the amount of extra benefit that a particular consumer or producer gets from a transaction, because the consumer or producer would have been willing to do the deal at some other price.

- **Consumer Surplus:** If a consumer would have been willing to pay more for a good than the market price, that consumer enjoys a surplus. For example, if one would have paid $20 for a computer game, but it only cost $15, then that consumer has a surplus of $5. The consumer has the video game, but has an additional $5 to spend on other goods that he would have been willing to spend on the game.
- **Producer Surplus:** If a producer would have been willing to sell a good at less than the market price, that producer enjoys a surplus.

For example, if the market price is \$20, but a given producer enjoys some technological advantage that allows it to produce at an economic cost of \$15, then it enjoys a \$5 surplus on each unit.

[2]**Surplus:** An oversupply of some good.

Sunk Cost: *See* Cost.

Transaction cost: All costs incurred in the completion of a transaction in addition to the economic costs of producing the good or service being exchanged (i.e., in addition to the costs of labor, material inputs, and a market rate of return on capital).

"Vertical" and "Horizontal" Relationships:

"Vertical": The relationship amongst firms at different levels of the chain of distribution of a particular product or service; *e.g.*, a manufacturer of salt, the trucking company that delivers the salt, and the grocery stores that ultimately sell it are all in a vertical relationship.

"Horizontal": The relationship amongst buyers or sellers of the same product or service and at the same level of distribution; *e.g.*, two manufacturers of salt are in a horizontal relationship.

Utility: The benefit that one enjoys from having a good. Importantly, in economics this value is always measured only according to an individual's willingness to pay for a good. If one is willing to pay \$1 for a hot dog, but no more than that, economics assumes that that individual enjoys exactly the same utility from having a hot dog that he or she enjoys from having a \$1 bill.

Welfare: *See* Utility.

Table of Cases

Index

www.ingramcontent.com/pod-product-compliance
Lightning Source LLC
LaVergne TN
LVHW082018200926
848481LV00010B/2884
* 9 7 9 8 8 8 9 0 6 8 0 9 9 *